Resiliency

An Integrated Approach to Practice, Policy, and Research

2nd Edition

Roberta R. Greene, Editor

NASW PRESS
National Association of Social Workers
Washington, DC

Cheryl Y. Bradley, *Publisher*
John Cassels, *Project Manager and Staff Editor*
Dac Nelson, *Copyeditor*
Lori J. Holtzinger, *Proofreader and Indexer*

Cover by Eye to Eye Design Studio
Interior design and composition by Electronic Quill
Printed and bound by Victor Graphics

CD written and programmed by *Michael Wright*

First impression: April 2012

Library of Congress Cataloging-in-Publication Data

Resiliency: an integrated approach to practice, policy, and research / edited by Roberta R. Greene. — 2nd ed.

p. cm.

Includes bibliographical references and index.

ISBN 978-0-87101-426-9

1. Social service—Psychological aspects. 2. Resilience (Personality trait). I. Greene, Roberta R. (Roberta Rubin), 1940–

HV41.R 46 2012

361.3'1—dc23

2012009897

Printed in the United States of America

Contents

About the Editor v

About the Contributors vii

September 11, 2001 xv

Preface xvii

1 Human Behavior Theory: A Resilience Orientation 1
ROBERTA R. GREENE

2 Resilience: Basic Assumptions and Terms 29
ROBERTA R. GREENE and ANN P. CONRAD

3 Resilience: A Social Construct 63
ROBERTA R. GREENE and NANCY C. LIVINGSTON

4 Resilience Research: Methodological Square Pegs and Theoretical Black Holes 95
WILLIAM H. BARTON

5 Resilience and Physical Health 117
JOYCE GRAHL RILEY

6 Resilience and Mental Health: A Shift in Perspective 139
ROBERT BLUNDO

7 Surviving Violence and Trauma: Resilience in Action at the Micro Level 159
NANCY J. ROTHENBERG

8 Resilience and Violence at the Macro Level 183
IRENE QUEIRO-TAJALLI and CRAIG CAMPBELL

9 Raising Children in an Oppressive Environment: Voices of Resilient Adults 203
ROBERTA R. GREENE, NORMA J. TAYLOR, MARGARET EVANS, and LINDA ANDERSON SMITH

10 Toward a Resilience-based Model of School Social Work: A Turnaround Mentor 239
GERALD T. POWERS

11 Educational Resilience 261
JEAN E. BROOKS

12 Listening to Girls: A Study in Resilience 289
MARIE L. WATKINS

13 Promoting Resilience among Returning Veterans 307
ROBERT BLUNDO, ROBERTA R. GREENE, and JOYCE GRAHL RILEY

14 Resilience and the Older Adult 335
JUDITH S. LEWIS and EVELYN B. HARRELL

15 Applying a Risk and Resilience Perspective to People with Intellectual Disabilities 353
NANCY P. KROPF and ROBERTA R. GREENE

16 Resilience and Social Work Policy 383
CAROL TULLY

Index 397

About the Editor

ROBERTA R. GREENE, PHD, MSW, is a chair in gerontology at the School of Social Work, University of Texas at Austin, and a clinical social worker with a PhD in human development. She has worked for NASW as a staff member and was instrumental in passing the 1987 Nursing Home Reform Act. She has also worked for the Council on Social Work Education as a curriculum development specialist.

Dr. Greene has written a classic text used in schools of social work around the country: *Human Behavior and Social Work Practice,* now in its third edition. That text is complemented by *Human Behavior Theory: A Diversity Framework,* which is in its second edition. Dr. Greene is also known for her expertise on Erik Erikson and has written a chapter for the *Comprehensive Handbook of Social Work and Social Welfare.* Her article on resilience appears in the *Encyclopedia of Social Work.*

The author of 12 books and numerous research articles, Dr. Greene is currently continuing her scholarship through filmmaking and Web site design. In addition, she serves on a number of editorial review boards and was a recipient of the 2004 NASW Pioneer Award and the AGE-SW 2005 Career Achievement Award.

About the Contributors

WILLIAM H. BARTON, PhD, professor, School of Social Work, Indiana University–Purdue University, Indianapolis. Dr. Barton has taught courses in juvenile justice policy, program evaluation research methods, leadership practice, and the philosophy of science. His research interests include juvenile justice, delinquency prevention, youth development, and community collaboration. For more than 30 years, he has conducted evaluations of juvenile justice programs and policies throughout the United States. He has published numerous journal articles and book chapters, coauthored two books, and been a frequent presenter at local, state, and national conferences.

ROBERT BLUNDO, PhD, MSW, LCSW, professor, School of Social Work, University of North Carolina at Wilmington. Dr. Blundo is founder and participant in the Strengths Collaborative established for training, practice and research on strengths- and resiliency-based models of practice. He teaches strengths-based courses and conducts training in military social work, combat stress, child protective services, mental health, and positive psychology.

JEAN E. BROOKS, PhD, MSW, assistant professor, coordinator, bachelor of social work program, Jackson State University, Jackson, Mississippi. Dr. Brooks has contributed to the development of the School of Social Work at Jackson State University and to the initiation of its programs—the bachelor of social work program, the master of social work program, and the PhD program in social work. She has provided leadership in social work accreditation for both the BSW and MSW programs. Her research interests include positive youth development and educational resilience.

CRAIG CAMPBELL, MSW, student services coordinator, School of Social Work, Indiana University. Mr. Campbell worked in the area of youth services for several years before joining the School of Social Work. His areas of interest include macro practice, resiliency, and online teaching.

ANN P. CONRAD, DSW, MSW, L-ICSW, National Catholic School of Social Service, Catholic University of America. Dr. Conrad has served on the faculty in many roles including dean of the school, chair of the master of social work program, director of admissions, and the assistant to the director of field instruction.

MARGARET EVANS, ACSW, program director, Northwestern Technical College, Rock Spring, Georgia. Ms. Evans has had more than 20 years of professional experience in higher education as well as serving as the director of state NASW chapters.

EVELYN B. HARRELL, LCSW-BACS, LAC, associate professor, director, substance abuse counseling program, Southern University at New Orleans. Ms. Harrell's teaching experiences include graduate courses on theories of human behavior, direct practice with individuals, cross-cultural issues in practice, social work history, and policy. She has taught an extensive number of undergraduate courses in the field of addiction.

NANCY P. KROPF, PHD, professor and director, School of Social Work, Georgia State University. Dr. Kropf's area of research and scholarship is late-life caregiving relationships, with the focus on older adults as care providers. Dr. Kropf has over 60 peer reviewed articles and book chapters in the social work and gerontology literature and is editor or author of seven books.

JUDITH S. LEWIS, PHD, MSW, LCSW-BACS, associate professor, director, student affairs, Tulane School of Social Work, Tulane University. Dr. Lewis received her PhD in social work from the University of Maryland in 1993 and MSW from Syracuse University in 1965. She is director of student affairs at Tulane School of Social Work and was director of field education there for the past 13 years. She was project director and principal investigator of the Leanne Knot Violence Prevention Project (1999–2003), a four-year campus education and training project funded by the U.S. Department of Justice in consortium with Southern University of New Orleans and the University of New Orleans. Her publications reflect her research interests in resilience in older adults, advocacy and organizing, natural helping networks, and social work field education as it relates to cultural diversity learning. She is a licensed clinician in the state of Louisiana and has provided pro bono service in the community as a group work specialist.

NANCY C. LIVINGSTON, MSSW, Department of Psychiatry (ret.), Southwestern Medical School, University of Texas, Dallas. Ms. Livingston provided employee assistance counseling to staff, researchers, and faculty.

GERALD T. POWERS, PhD, professor emeritus, School of Social Work, Indiana University. Dr. Powers taught human behavior content at the baccalaureate, masters, and doctoral levels for more than 30 years.

IRENE QUEIRO-TAJALLI, PhD, professor and interim executive director of labor studies, School of Social Work, Indiana University. Dr. Queiro-Tajalli's most recent presentations and writings focus on technology; older adults in the diaspora; community organizing and resilience; globalization; women, with a focus on Latino and Muslim women; Muslims post-September 11, 2001; cultural competency; labor studies and social work; and Latin America.

JOYCE GRAHL RILEY, MA, BSN, associate director, health administration and policy program, University of Maryland, Baltimore County. Ms. Riley previously worked with the Baltimore City Health Department as a senior community nurse.

NANCY J. ROTHENBERG, PhD, MSW, associate professor, School of Social Work, University of Georgia. Dr. Rothenberg (Williams) brings over 30 years of practice experience as a clinician dealing with trauma and families. Her scholarship has spanned the areas of resiliency, spirituality, and the role of experiential learning and community engagement in social work education with a current emphasis on restorative justice and international social work. She is the 2010 recipient of the UGA Scholarship of Engagement Award for her leadership in research, teaching, and service in the creation of sustained service-learning projects both domestically and internationally.

LINDA ANDERSON SMITH, DSW, professor, School of Social Work, Springfield College. As a product of a South Bronx neighborhood, Dr. Smith learned many firsthand lessons about resiliency. She has over 30 years of mental health and family practice with African American and Latino families in urban settings. Her research and practice and teaching interests are evidenced-based practice in mental health and substance abuse, cultural competence, and social policy.

NORMA J. TAYLOR, PhD, MSW, born in Cincinnati, Ohio. Dr. Taylor began her academic pursuits concentrating on natural science and she admits that social science was nowhere on her radar screen. She had a change of heart after serving for two years in Morocco as a Peace Corps Volunteer. At that point, her primary focus became service to others. After completing her MSW, she spent several years working with children in residential care in New York and then as faculty at a graduate school of social work in Knoxville, Tennessee. Being in an academic setting sparked a desire for further study, so she returned to Massachusetts and completed her doctorate in social policy.

Dr. Taylor worked for over 13 years in the national office of the National Association of Social Workers performing a variety of tasks including standards development, conference planning, and grants management. Child Welfare, specifically in the area of training, was her next focal point. As training coordinator, Dr. Taylor was able to enhance the knowledge and skill development of social work staff at Child and Family Services Agency (CFSA) and affiliate agencies in Washington, DC.

Ordained as an Interfaith Ministry in 2003 at New Seminary in New York City, Dr. Taylor works with the counseling ministry in her church in Washington, DC. She is a certified life coach and has a private practice in the District of Columbia. See her Web site, http://www.creatinganew.com, for details.

CAROL TULLY, PhD, LCSW, professor emerita, University of Louisville. Dr. Tully lives in New Orleans, where she remains active as a mental health volunteer with the American Red Cross.

MARIE L. WATKINS, PhD, MSW, professor, Department of Social Work; director, Center for Service Learning; director, Minor in Community Youth Development; Nazareth College, Rochester, New York. Dr. Watkins has over 30 years of youth development experience as a youth worker, a group worker, as an agency administrator, and as a youth development advocate. In 1969, she began her youth work career with the Department of Parks and Recreation for the city of Niagara Falls, New York. For over 25 years, Dr. Watkins was a full-time professional youth worker in Boys and Girls Clubs in Niagara Falls, Syracuse, Albany, and in Indianapolis, Indiana. She continues her involvement and passion for youth development service for youth in her role as a workshop presenter, as a consultant, and an author. She has received local, regional, and national recognition for her youth development expertise and commitment.

Since 2001, Dr. Watkins has served as Nazareth College's Director for the Center of Service Learning. In 2005, she coauthored the book *Service-Learning: From Community to Classroom to Career:* (Jist Works) with Linda Braun. In addition to her scholarship, Dr. Watkins consults with higher education institutions and agencies related to the process of institutionalizing service learning on college campuses, K–12 school settings, and nonprofit organizations.

Dr. Watkins's primary practice expertise is in the areas of strengthening organizational capacity within youth development agencies, building youth–adult partnerships with youth who reside in urban settings, the creation of culturally competent youth services with a special emphasis on gender equity, and establishing and sustaining service-learning partnerships between institutions of higher education and community-based agencies.

Dr. Watkins earned a MSW, a master's degree in marriage and family therapy, and a PhD in child and family studies from Syracuse University, New York.

MICHAEL WRIGHT, PhD, MSW, associate professor, Tennessee State University, Nashville, TN. Dr. Wright leads the research sequence in the social work program, and chairs its committee charged with curriculum renewal and program assessment. A former MSW program director, he has taught a diverse population of students at both the baccalaureate and master degree levels.

Over the past year, Dr. Wright has been working on the Lifespan Project, an initiative to facilitate campus–community collaboration on behavioral health. His other research interests include trauma and resilience, complex adaptive systems, and entrepreneurship. Wright has also been a macro practice consultant more than 12 years for public and private entities seeking capacity development, social research, leadership training, and educational media creation.

This book is dedicated to the

many survivors and helping professionals

who live their lives with strength and hope.

With special regard for T. H.

And with 53 years of memories with DGG.

—RRG

September 11, 2001

When the first edition of the book was written, following the terrorist attacks on the World Trade Center and Pentagon on September 11, 2001, it was not uncommon to hear people say, "The world has changed forever." I know I was shocked by the realization that what my colleagues and I had written for this book took on a startling reality. This remains true a decade later as we added chapters on resilience among returning veterans and schools.

When I began creating this book more than a decade ago, I had no idea of the journey I had undertaken. As the process of learning about resiliency unfolded, I learned that it meant different things to different people. A review of the literature revealed that there were many quantitative studies using large-scale databases that documented the epidemiological nature of risk and resilience. Qualitative studies revealed how people were able to survive unthinkable risks and become successful adults. The review also uncovered the work of many clinicians who believed that a resiliency approach had transformed their own mental health practice. Also, I was not surprised to find resiliency discussed in the popular media including newspapers, magazines, and self-help books.

I experienced powerful learning about resiliency during the 35 interviews conducted for the first edition. Over a hundred more were conducted for this second edition. The stories of survivors and professionals gave credence to the idea that people can be successful despite serious negative life events. Their courageous stories also underscored that although we must acknowledge our clients' troubles and pain, we as social workers cannot afford to overlook their resources and potential.

I could never imagine that the courageous stories I heard during these interviews would be magnified to the degree they have been by the heroic stories following the attacks on the Pentagon and World Trade Center. The heroism of "everyday people" and all professionals at the scene document the stuff of human resiliency.

Preface

Key aspects of resiliency theory and research are synthesized in this volume, and these concepts are then applied to social work practice. The text is intended to provide an integrated foundation framework that addresses human behavior in the social environment, policy, research, social work practice, ethics and values, diversity, and social and economic justice. The contributors are particularly concerned with understanding factors that contribute to people being at risk and learning successful means to redress these difficulties.

Although social workers have long sought a framework that focuses on client strength, the profession has yet to adopt a multisystemic, empirically based theory that can be applied in assessment and intervention across people's life course. Resiliency theory is such an emerging paradigm.

Social work practice demands the ability to understand, critique, and apply a number of human behavior theories. Resiliency theory is best understood in conjunction with ecological and systems thinking that characterizes the profession's person-in-environment approach. To that end, these chapters afford students and practitioners a new, forward-thinking vocabulary and body of knowledge and skills. It is hoped that this will build on social work tradition and provide a context and a belief system that underscores the heroic nature of human endurance and fortitude.

ROBERTA R. GREENE

Human Behavior Theory: A Resilience Orientation

ROBERTA R. GREENE

On finishing this chapter, students will be able to further:

Identify as a professional social worker and conduct oneself accordingly (Educational Policy 2.1.1) by

- Advocating for client access to the services of social work.
- Practicing personal reflection and self-correction to ensure continual professional development (practice behaviors).

Apply social work ethical principles to guide professional practice (Educational Policy 2.1.2) by

- Tolerating ambiguity in resolving ethical conflicts (practice behavior).

Apply knowledge of human behavior and the social environment (Educational Policy 2.1.7(by

- Using conceptual frameworks to guide the processes of assessment, intervention, and evaluation (practice behavior).

The repeated documentation of this "resiliency"—the ability to bounce back successfully despite exposure to severe risk—has clearly established the self-righting nature of human development.

—BENARD, 1993, P. 444

As our clients often underestimate their own resources and potential, do helpers fall victim to the same phenomena?

—BARNARD, 1994, P. 135

Social work practice began with a commitment to help the most economically deprived and vulnerable populations through individual and social change (Gitterman, 1991; Khinduka, 1987). However, social work professionals of the 21st century face dramatic and as yet unforeseen changes in their practice. Unfortunately, some professionals expect that these changes will make the task of helping the most vulnerable populations increasingly difficult (Gitterman, 1991). Concerns such as family and community violence, poverty, and oppression already demand an understanding of how people struggle to surmount difficult or perilous life circumstances. In addition, widespread attention has been given to the status of children—their development, safety, and economic and psychological well-being (Garmezy, 1993; Laursen & Birmingham, 2003; Masten & Coatsworth, 1998).

The literature increasingly reflects the challenges involved in serving clients who face such difficulties. For example, Burman and Allen-Meares (1994) have called on social workers to assist children who have witnessed parental homicide; Carter (1999) has urged social workers to respond to church burnings in ways that will mobilize community strengths; and Garmezy (1993) has challenged mental health professionals to take up the political agenda of children and families "whose danger is accentuated by the threatening ecologies in which they reside" (p. 134). Social work professionals also will need to address the increasing effect of violence and the accompanying sense of fear and powerlessness among urban children and youths (Astor, Behre, Wallace, & Fravil, 1998; DuRant, Cadenhead, Pendergrast, Slavens, & Linder, 1994; Early-Adams, Wallinga, Skeen, & Paguio, 1990; Pierce & Singleton, 1995; Rey, 1996). In addition, military social workers have the challenge of preventing suicides of returning soldiers from Afghanistan and Iraq. Furthermore, the capacity to be culturally competent, the ability to value differences, and the ability to guard against measuring every client by a single standard will become increasingly essential (Greene, 1994). Political, social, and technological developments continue to sharpen cultural awareness (Hoff, Hallisey, & Hoff, 2009). Overall, practitioners will increasingly need strategies to "to promote the full humanity of all voices which have been marginalized in our society" (Hooyman, 1996, p. 20).

Clearly, future social work practice will require the use of human behavior frameworks that better address the complexity of life concerns (Begun, 1993). Social workers will need to understand how people respond positively to adverse situations and how to use this knowledge to foster client strengths, adaptation, healing, and self-efficacy. Theories that examine health-promoting behaviors across the life course and focus on environments that promote personal, family, and community well-being will therefore be increasingly in demand. Social work practice of the 21st century requires theories that allow social workers to build on clients' ability to persist in the face of obstacles and to proceed positively with life events—or what Saleebey (1996) has called "a practice based on the ideas of resilience, rebound, possibility, and transformation" (p. 297).

Social workers have long been committed to a strengths-based practice that mobilizes "people's push toward growth, self-healing, health, and other natural life forces" (Germain, 1990, p. 138). However, a theoretical advance is under way. Social workers and other mental health professionals are increasingly applying the concept of resilience in their work with clients (Benard, 1993; Bogenschneider, 1996; Fraser, 1997; Nash & Fraser, 1998; Tolan, Guerra, & Kendall, 1995; Weick & Saleebey, 1995). The notion of *resilience*—the "manifested competence in the context of significant challenges to adaptation"—builds on the strengths perspective (Masten & Coatsworth, 1998, p. 206) and, when integrated with ecological and developmental theory, can deepen social workers' understanding of adaptive behavior (Kaminsky, McCabe, Langlieb, & Everly, 2007). In fact, a review of the literature has revealed that "the growing salience of the risk and resilience perspective"—the study of the factors that contribute to successful outcomes in the face of adversity—already provides ideas for highly useful intervention strategies (Fraser, Richman, & Galinsky, 1999, p. 131).

In addition, the body of theoretical and research information about resilience is so great that it can be conceptualized as forming a resilience-based human behavior framework for social work practice (Begun, 1993; Fraser & Galinsky, 1997; Gitterman, 1991, 1998; Greene, 2008; Saleebey, 1997a). This conceptual movement stems from several converging sources, including longitudinal research, renewed theoretical perspectives, the experience of survivors, and the wisdom of master practitioners. This book synthesizes the increasingly accepted view of human behavior and applies resiliency theory and research to various populations and issues. The purpose is to understand better how people successfully meet life challenges in the face of stress and or trauma. It focuses on characteristics that foster health-promoting behaviors and competence and examines the environments that further resilience. Furthermore, the book explores concepts that can assist social workers in understanding how people respond positively to adverse situations. Such concepts include client strengths, adaptation, healing and wellness, self-efficacy, and competence.

The book also reviews various theoretical explanations of personal, family, community, and other environmental factors that foster human resilience across the life course. Using an ecological–developmental framework as a conceptual guidepost, the book discusses how social workers select theoretical constructs for resilience-based practice for application at each systems level. There are also quotes from interviews with helping professionals and laypersons who reflect on the topic. Questions explored in the text include the following:

- What are the conditions that facilitate health and wellness?
- How do people navigate threats or overcome adversity?
- How do people handle traumatic events or difficult life transitions?
- What contributes to people's ability to regenerate or bounce back?
- How do humans cope with everyday events and generate problem-solving strategies and solutions?
- What is successful coping?
- What aspects of human behavior in the social environment contribute to survival and growth?
- What types of help do people need or want when events tax or exceed their adaptive resources?
- How can helping professionals best provide this help?

Historical Context: Resilience Theory

These pioneers [investigators of resilience] recognized that such [successful] children could teach us better ways to reduce risk, promote competence, and shift the course of development in more positive directions.

—Masten & Coatsworth, 1998, p. 205

The study of risk and resilience emulated epidemiological public health studies of heart and lung disease in which people were informed about the risks of inactivity, smoking, and a high-fat diet (see chapter 5). It was understood that many but not *all* smokers would develop heart disease. The question was why? Mental health professionals have long wondered why some people withstand adversity or high levels of stress better. To understand this phenomenon, social scientists have conducted numerous studies to explore risk and resilience. In addition, practitioners have shared their observations about client resilience. This chapter provides a historical overview of theorists' and practitioners' contributions to the development of the risk and resilience perspective and outlines the major theoretical concepts converging to form this approach to human behavior.

Studies of Children at Risk

The theoretical understanding of what constitutes resilience emerged, in large measure, from research on "children at risk" (Bogenschneider, 1996; Hawkins, Catalano, & Miller, 1992; Krovetz, 1999; Werner & Smith, 1982). Long interested in understanding what factors contribute to or prevent problem behaviors, developmental theorists conducted longitudinal studies to examine how children face high-risk situations, such as abuse, poverty, substance abuse, and teenage pregnancy. For example, the St. Louis Risk Research Project was intended to help researchers understand resilience among children in St. Louis, Missouri, "who seemed at risk within a disadvantageous milieu [and nonetheless] climbed to success and health through intense affiliations [in this situation] with religious groups" (Worland, Weeks, Weiner, & Schectman, 1982, p. 138).

Research projects were undertaken in numerous U.S. cities, including Minneapolis, Pittsburgh, and Rochester, over more than three decades. International research projects, such as those sponsored by the University of Alabama Civitan International Research Center, explored child well-being in Brazil, Canada, Costa Rica, the Czech Republic, Hungary, Japan, Lithuania, Namibia, Russia, South Africa, Sudan, Taiwan, Thailand, and Vietnam (Grotberg, 1995). These studies attempted to identify the percentage of a child population at risk who might experience future problems. The studies identified potential causative agents, the distribution of problems, and possible preventive treatment measures (Nash & Fraser, 1998). Researchers examined *risk factors*—conditions that increase the likelihood that a child will develop a problem—and *protective factors*—conditions that buffer, interrupt, or prevent problems. The researchers' intent was to "identify the damage done to children and to provide services to help them develop as well as possible" despite the risk (Grotberg, 1995, p. 1).

Studies of children at risk have taught educational and mental health professionals that, although some children may have adverse reactions to negative or traumatic experiences—and should receive the proper help—adverse events in childhood do not inevitably lead to adult pathology. Between one half and two thirds of children growing up in adverse situations "do overcome the odds and turn a life trajectory of risk into one that manifests resilience" (Benard, 1993, p. 444). This finding has led researchers to investigate what distinguishes children who are beating the odds from those who are overwhelmed. How do many children at risk become confident, competent, caring adults (Werner & Smith, 1992)? A summary of study outcomes suggests that resilient children have a strong capacity to form relationships, to solve problems, to develop a sense of identity, and to plan and hope (Benard, 1993). Achievement orientation, school success, sociability, responsible behavior, and active involvement at school are also associated with resilience in children (Reed-Victor & Pelco, 1999; see chapter 2 for a full discussion). The ultimate benefit of these findings is that they provide guidelines for designing services that foster children's innate capacity for resilience (Benard, 1993; Gordon & Song, 1994).

Studies of Children Living with Community Violence

Researchers have examined particular issues of children at risk (for example, how children cope with the consequences of community violence; Coles, 1986;

Garbarino, Dubrow, Kostelny, & Pardo, 1992). Ideally, childhood is a time when children form meaningful attachments, explore their environment, and begin to develop competence. Safe, nurturing social neighborhoods are needed to further children's ability to trust and master their environment. Unfortunately, a safe environment is often not a reality for some children. Many children in U.S. cities grow up in communities where "danger replaces safety as a condition of life" (Garbarino et al., 1992, p. 1). These children must struggle for survival in an environment in which their basic necessities are barely met. Families may isolate themselves from the rest of the community out of fear of violence against them. Communities that have had an exodus of the working-class population may feel defeated by prolonged joblessness and oppression (Wilson, 1987). Children who are exposed to such chronic dangers may live in anxiety and fear, see themselves as having limited futures, feel they have little control over their lives, and develop learning difficulties (Wallach, 1994). Furthermore, children who experience living in chronic danger may have difficulty concentrating, suffer memory impairments, display aggressive play, act tough, show uncaring behaviors, and restrict their activities. Loss is a common theme. In essence, "what has been destroyed for children traumatized by community violence is the idea of home, school, and community as a safe place" (Garbarino et al., 1992, p. 83).

The lack of a safe environment is not experienced exclusively by U.S. children. Robert Coles (1986), a noted researcher of children who have survived adversity, observed Cambodian refugee children and their parents. Many survivors of the 30-year Cambodian civil war and concentration camps suffered posttraumatic stress, experiencing symptoms that included avoidance, hyperactive startle reactions, emotional numbness, intrusive thoughts, and nightmares (Boehnlein, 1987; Carlson & Rosser-Hogan, 1993; Eisenbruch, 1984; Kinzie, Fredrickson, Ben, Fleck, & Karls, 1984; Lee & Lu, 1989). Nonetheless, Coles concluded that despite the horrific political violence under the Khmer Rouge, "I have never seen a group of children, in all the years of my work, who are more resilient and perceptive" (p. 266). He attributed their successful adaptation to caring mothers and fathers. Masten and Coatsworth (1998) also commented on these young people's success, saying "they are absolute, living testimony to the human capacity for resilience" (p. 206). These findings can give further impetus to the design of intervention programs and help convince policy makers that strength not only is inherent, but also can be taught (Blum, 1998).

Studies of children who live with community violence have provided significant knowledge about resilient behavior. Research suggests that children who are cognitively competent, experience self-confidence, are goal oriented, and have active coping styles can be more resilient (Rutter, 1989). Garbarino et al. (1992), who have witnessed children in danger around the world, deduced that children can maintain resilience under adversity if they have sufficient psychological and social resources, are attached to significant adults, develop cultural and spiritual resources, and have an ideology guiding their activism. These findings remind professionals that, to foster resilience, it is wise to think beyond traditional interventions. Garbarino and colleagues are among several researchers (see Wang & Gordon, 1994) who have urged schools to take up the banner of promoting resilience through interventions that are individualized and therapeutic and that mobilize communities into "peacekeeping and prevention zones" (p. 229).

Studies of Adult Survivors

The knowledge that people have a powerful ability to adapt to crises has prompted researchers to shift from thinking that stressful situations inevitability produce negative outcomes to exploring how to foster people's positive adaptation following a high degree of adversity (Fraser, 1997; Reed-Victor & Pelco, 1999). Substantial research on adult survivors provides ideas about resilience and how to promote a return to adaptive functioning. For example, in a 30-year quest to understand coping strategies and resiliency among adult survivors of such horrifying events as the bombing of Hiroshima and the Nazi Holocaust, Lifton (1993) delineated a number of patterns that affect people who have lived through such disasters. Lifton learned that survivors do not escape pain, "as they have observed death—witnessed it—while remaining alive" (p. 231). Rather, survivors may feel a sense of loss and divested of human connectedness. They may go through a lasting *death imprint,* that is, an anxiety about death. In addition, they may experience feelings of *death guilt,* a sense that they have no right to survive or guilt that others were not also rescued. Survivors may undergo *psychic numbing,* a lessened capacity to feel emotions; be *suspicious of counterfeit nurturance,* that is, have a general distrust of help offered; and experience a *struggle for meaning* in that they may attempt to give significance to why they survived.

On the positive side, Lifton (1993) pointed out that as he listened to survivor's stories, he learned that they displayed resilient behavior patterns throughout their life course. He also observed that they were capable of creating and recreating meaning under stressful events and had a commitment to life enhancement. These observations led Lifton to ask, How did these transformations occur? He concluded that if traumatized people are able "to speak, and to be heard," they possess an amazing capacity to overcome pain and to transform themselves. He called this ability, which can be fostered through therapeutic intervention, the "protean self."

The protean nature of survivors' stories has also been confirmed through interviews with people who have lived through genocide, such as the Nazi Holocaust.

For example, Moskovitz (1983) interviewed 23 adult survivors of Nazi concentration camps. As children, these survivors had been airlifted to England following World War II and placed in a therapeutic group home called Lingfield House. On arrival, the children were found to be withdrawn, apathetic, and fearful. However, as they experienced the warm and nurturing care of the therapists who acted as house parents, they gradually became less apprehensive. When Moskovitz (1983) interviewed them as adults, she found that they continued to experience the burden of loss, were still searching for their parents, felt like outsiders, and sometimes experienced a sense of uncertainty about their self-worth. Yet they exhibited "an affirmation of life—a stubborn durability" (p. 199). They also had a high degree of ethical and spiritual involvement, social responsibility, and a strong desire to establish families and homes. Moskovitz (1983) concluded that mental health workers need to rethink the idea that adversity or early deprivation inevitably leads to a negative outcome,

> for despite the persistence of problems and the ashes of the past, what we note in the Lingfield lives are endurance, resilience, and great individual adaptability. . . . Contrary to previously accepted notions, we learn powerfully from these lives that lifelong emotional disability does not automatically follow early trauma, even such devastating, pervasive trauma as experienced here. Apparently, what happens later matters enormously. Whether it is the confidence of a teacher, the excitement of new sexual urges, new vocational interests, or a changed social milieu, the interaction can trigger fresh growth. (p. 201)

This idea was underscored many years later in a nationwide study of 133 Holocaust survivors who were found to be resilient. As a result, survivorship is now better understood as a composite of personal characteristics as well as developmental, sociocultural, historical, and political factors that, when taken together, result in a capacity to overcome even severe adverse events (Greene, 2002). This survivorship centers around resilience, a natural healing process involving the effective use of coping skills (Greene, 2010a; Greene & Graham, 2008)

On the basis of their observations of survivors, practitioners are increasingly recognizing the benefits of interventions that foster a person's strengths and "self-righting" capacities. That is, they are redirecting their interventions to a resilience-based practice approach (Benard, 1993). For example, Wolin and Wolin (1993), psychoanalytically trained master practitioners who have helped survivors of childhood abuse, described the transformation of their clinical practice from what they termed a *damage* model, or a model focused on victimization, harm, and pathologies, to a *challenge* model, which emphasizes self-protective behaviors, strength, and resilience. Borden (1992), a social worker who has used a narrative approach, has assisted people who have had adverse life events reflect on and reconstruct their stories from dysfunction to a strengths-oriented, resilience perspective. In addition, Walsh (1999) has advocated a resilience-based approach to clinical practice with older adults and their families, arguing that it would encourage client–practitioner collaboration, use a strengths perspective, support optimal functioning among family members, and promote community support networks (see chapter 14 for a full discussion).

Resilience: An Emerging Human Behavior Theory

As one examines the history of science, one can see . . . ideas at work in different minds from the same era. . . . They are not theories, but rudiments of potential theories; yet they raise crucial questions that coalesce the activities of a field. Such ideas might be termed generative. . . . The generative ideas presented here are those concerned with risk, vulnerability, and resilience.

—Anthony & Cohler, 1987, p. 3

An increasing number of social work theorists are now interested in the resilience-based approach to human behavior theory (Begun, 1993; Fraser, 1997; Gilgun, 1996a, 1996b; Saleebey, 1997a). In *The Life Model of Social Work,* Germain and Gitterman (1996) presented the idea that social workers should use real-life experiences to mobilize a client's natural forces of health and continued growth. Recognizing that adversity may encompass everyday life as well as disasters, they suggested that social work practice is about problems in living. Therefore, human behavior theory should prepare social workers to model their practice after life itself.

Germain and Gitterman (1996) proposed that, at any time over the life course, people may have to confront the stress associated with *difficult life transitions,* which involve developmental or social changes; *traumatic life events,* which include grave losses or illness; and *environmental pressures,* which encompass poverty and violence. Germain (1990) also suggested that a study of human development should address an understanding of "emotions, spirituality, resilience, relatedness and caring, self-esteem and self-concept, as well as effectiveness and competence, self-direction, the capacity to attribute meaning to life experience, self-help, and mutual aid" (p. 139). In their life model, Germain and Gitterman (1996) based their interventions for meeting life stressors on the ecological principle that the purpose of social work is to elevate the goodness of fit between people and their environments, particularly by securing basic resources.

Theorists have continued to urge social work educators to base human behavior content on a resilience approach to increase the emphasis on client strengths and resources (Bendor, Davidson, & Skolnik, 1997; Greene, 2010b). For example, Saleebey (1997a), a leader in the strengths-based practice movement, has propounded the idea that students receive human behavior content for understanding resilience-based practice because

> the resilience literature satisfies many of the tests of a strengths-based HBSE [human behavior and the social environment] curriculum: it provides ways of thinking about individual and collective assets; it situates the focus of concern in the larger social context; and it traverses the range of experience and response from biological to psychological to social. (p. 33)

Similarly, Gilgun (1996a, 1996b) has argued that resilience content—how people positively respond to adversity—"introduces social work to a language replete with generative concepts and theory that can greatly advance knowledge to inform research, program development, direct practice, and policy" (1996a, p. 400; see chapter 2). Another reason for using a resilience-based model of social work practice is that it has the potential to provide practitioners with an empirically based approach to understanding human behavior. Fraser and Galinsky (1997) argued that practice decisions are best made using empirically supported human behavior theories. This position, which is receiving increased attention in the literature, came out of concern about the growing "chasm" between practitioners and researchers (Fraser, Jenson, & Lewis, 1993; Gambrill, 1999; Howard & Jenson, 1999; Thyer, 1996; Witkin & Nurius, 1997).

Resilience: Neighboring Concepts

One of the surprises constantly encountered in psychiatric research . . . is the way in which language determines the shape of investigation. . . . As a result, parallel processes of inquiry are established, each with its own lexicon, and the language differences give rise to the illusion that one is dealing with quite different study areas. Eventually some inquisitive researcher calls attention to the overlapping concepts and the basic similarities of the research fields.

—Anthony, 1987, p. 6

Researchers interested in stress and resilience have come from various theoretical backgrounds. Because their ideas stem from a number of streams of thought and, hence, they define terms differently, it may appear (erroneously) that they are examining different topics. However, there is considerable overlapping of neighboring concepts that should be considered parallel to resilience (Anthony & Cohler, 1987). This section reviews major concepts that can inform the current understanding of resilience theory and research and spells out how they form a conceptual foundation for resilience-based social work practice.

Medical Anthropology

Medical anthropologists have discovered that all human societies develop culturally specific approaches to healing (Frank, 1975; Kleinman, 1980). According to Frank (1975), healing

> attempts to combat suffering and disability, and is usually labeled treatment. Every society trains some of its members to apply this form of influence. Treatment always involves a personal relationship between healer and sufferer. Certain types of therapy rely primarily on the healer's ability to mobilize healing forces in the sufferer by psychological means. (p. 1)

Helman (1984) provided an example in health care, pointing out that citizens using the British health care system have a choice of popular, folk, and professional healing, including doctors, midwives, social workers, diviners, self-help groups, and ethnic minority healers. However, the concepts of healing and wellness are often addressed solely from a Western orientation. This orientation is *egocentric*—it centers expressly on the individual and a professional helper. However, many social work clients come from a *sociocentric* orientation, or a "worldview that values group cohesiveness and interdependence" (Sullivan, 1998, p. 223). Therefore, a strictly individualistic view of healing may not be suitable. Instead, clients may prefer family, community groups, or ethnic healers. To overcome this impasse, Comas-Díaz (1994) has suggested that practitioners conduct a cultural assessment to determine a client's beliefs about healing and what techniques may create a mutual client–social worker relationship. How a particular client feels about the healing process—specifically, who the client believes is suitable to offer advice and care—is a central ingredient in culturally sensitive social work and essential to a resilience-based approach (Comas-Díaz, 1994; Falicov, 1995; Ogbu, 1992).

Humanistic Tradition

Social workers have historically been drawn to humanistic theories of human behavior, as exemplified by Maslow's (1968) concept of self-actualization and Carl Rogers's (1951) person-centered practice approach. These perspectives on human behavior, which are incorporated into a resilience-based approach, generally suggest that social workers value subjective experience, strive to achieve client–social worker mutuality, and offer a growth-inducing orientation.

FIGURE 1.1 Maslow's Hierarchy of Needs

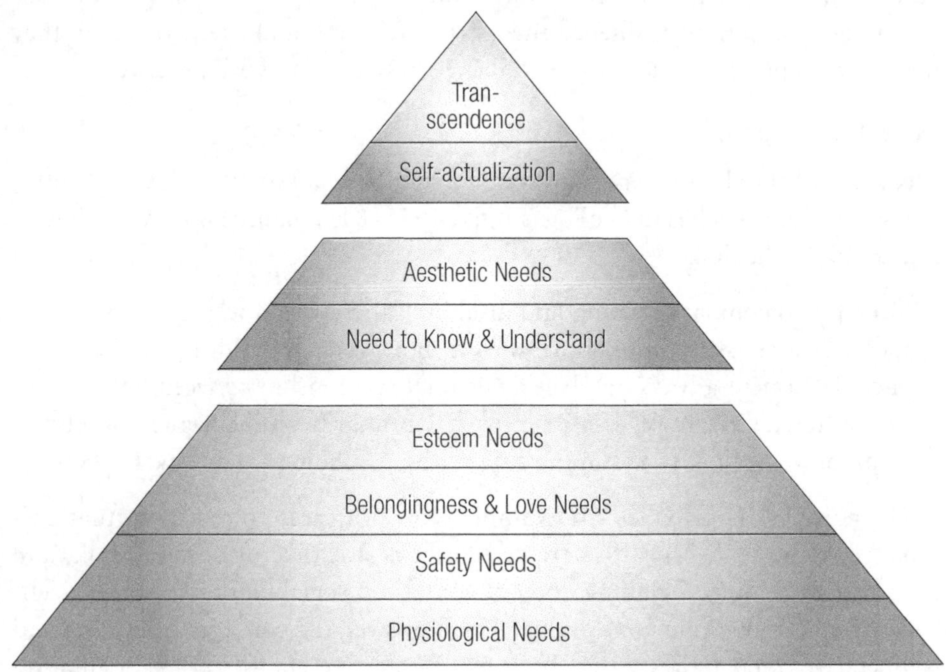

Specifically, the Rogerian approach proposes that if a practitioner is empathetic and genuine and provides a client with unconditional regard, positive change will occur, whereas the Maslow viewpoint argues that people must first receive help with basic needs such as shelter and safety before they can strive for self-actualization (see Figure 1.1). As in Maslow's hierarchy, Richman and Bowen (1997) have suggested that for social workers to understand resilience, they must explore the fit between a person's needs and resources and then evaluate how environmental demands match the person's competencies. The need for human compassion and the immediate provision of basic resources are increasingly seen as the bedrock of disaster relief and the restoration of adaptive functioning (N. Livingston, employee assistance coordinator, University of Texas, Southwestern Medical Center, personal communication, December 15, 1999).

Psychodynamic Theories

Social workers who use psychodynamic theories examine the intrapsychic workings of the personality to ameliorate conflicts in human relationships (Greene, 1999). Although a resilience-based approach is only implicit in the works of psychodynamic theorists, Freud and Erikson addressed some growth-producing concepts

(Anthony & Cohler, 1987). For example, Freud's early work examined the notion of trauma and how people can protect themselves from being overwhelmed by adverse events, particularly anxiety, and he explored what psychic mechanisms prevent people from reaching so-called "breaking points" (Freud, 1949).

Freud called people's ability to establish or reestablish self-control and withstand and manage a stressful environment *ego mastery*. Freud and his followers (Freud, 1949; Hartmann, 1958; Vaillant, 1971) came to see that the appropriate use of *defense mechanisms,* the unconscious mental processes that distort reality to ward off anxiety, could contribute to an individual's ability to achieve ego mastery, and they argued for the enhancement of this adaptive capacity in treatment (see Anthony & Cohler, 1987). During the 1950s and 1960s, this positive view of people's coping mechanisms was prevalent in social work texts (Perlman, 1957). For example, Perlman (1957) pointed out that a client's use of ego defenses was not a personality malfunction. Rather, the well-adapted person made appropriate use of defenses to regain psychological balance and withstand change. Some social workers continue to use a form of ego psychology as their treatment approach. More recently, the term *ego resiliency* has been used to address an individual's resourceful adaptation under stress or recovery from traumatic experiences (Klohnen, 1996).

Erikson (1950) was another psychodynamic theorist concerned with adaptive functioning, originating the idea that ego development occurs in eight stages across the life cycle. Erikson thought that "the ego plays a major role in development as it strives for competence and mastery of the environment" (Greene, 1999, p. 111). He suggested that *competence,* or the ability and skill to complete tasks successfully, is an outgrowth of the fourth stage of ego development—Industry versus Inferiority. Erikson—and other theorists, including Bettelheim (1987) and Piaget and Inhelder (1969)—observed that during this stage, which occurs from age 6 to 12 years, children often work together to make things and, in this way, develop a relative sense of competence. The view that competence is an effective adaptation to the environment and can be cultivated by parents, teachers, social workers, and other mental health practitioners is a major theme in the resiliency literature (Fraser, 1997; Masten & Coatsworth, 1998; Vaillant & Milofsky, 1980).

White (1959, 1963) was another theorist interested in the concept of *ego competence* as people's innate capacity to interact positively with the environment. White argued that competence is the most distinctive attribute of interpersonal behavior and can be observed through everyday interaction. He suggested that as children develop, they naturally engage with and strive to master their environment. This growing sense of mastery is accompanied by a sense of pleasure in their own accomplishments, including such achievements as singing a song or riding a bike. When caretakers nurture such accomplishments, children perceive themselves as successful and are inclined to continue this pattern of behavior. Interest in the development of competence across the life course remains a central tenet in the resilience literature (Masten & Coatsworth, 1998; see chapter 2).

Object Relations

Object relations theorists have suggested that the therapeutic process should focus on the quality of a client's attachments and the nature of his or her relationships. *Attachment,* or the initial mother–child bonding, is often addressed in the resiliency literature. Attachment is thought to be inherent and to have "a survival advantage, in this case through increasing the chances of an infant being protected by those to whom he or she keeps in proximity" (Ainsworth, 1989, p. 709). A strong pattern of attachment is considered necessary for competent functioning and is a model for all future relations or affectional bonds throughout a person's life cycle (Bowlby, 1969, 1973a, 1973b, 1980).

Social Learning Theory

Social learning theorist Albert Bandura (1982a, 1982b) shifted the focus of the study of human behavior from internal stimuli to an examination of behavioral and external environmental factors. Bandura was interested in people's use of proactive coping mechanisms and why people persist in the face of obstacles or adverse events (Bandura, 1977a, 1977b; Bandura & Adams, 1977; Bandura & Schunk, 1981; see chapter 2). As a social learning theorist, Bandura believed that people enlist their cognitive capacities to overcome the physical arousal of fear and that this process of cognitive control is central to remaining adaptive. His views were based on the idea that people are inherently goal setting, are self-motivated, and can "be the principal agents of their own change" (Bandura, 1977b, p. vii). He called this natural ability *self-efficacy.*

A Resilience Perspective: Companion Concepts

A risk and resilience perspective uses epidemiological methods and builds on ecological–developmental theory to identify factors at multiple systems levels (for example, individual, family, neighborhood, or community) that are associated with the occurrence of certain outcomes.

—Nash & Bowen, 1999, p. 172

The study of resilience has its origins in developmental theory and is an emerging theory in its own right. The study of resilience is also grounded in an ecological context and builds on the strengths perspective. These multifaceted ideas and concepts allow for a multisystemic view of resilient behavior across the life course. This section discusses the strengths perspective and defines the developmental and ecological companion concepts associated with the process of resilience.

The Strengths Perspective

Since the beginning of the 20th century, social workers have turned to various theoretical approaches to assess a client's situation and delineate the helping process. These client descriptions and social work strategies, which are dependent on a theorist's language and belief systems, may reflect a strength or deficit perspective with respective implications for practice (Goldstein, 1990, 1998; Longres, 1997; Saleebey, 1996; Schriver, 2001; Weick, Rapp, Sullivan, & Kisthardt, 1989; see Table 1.1). Theories, such as those derived from the psychodynamic school, have been criticized for placing too great an emphasis on client weaknesses, such as a client's problems or abnormality. In such approaches, practitioners take on the role of expert and base their practice on diagnosing clients and ameliorating "problem situations."

Theories that stem from a strengths perspective, such as social construction theory or feminist theory, generally assume that when people are given positive support, they have the inherent power to interpret and transform their own lives (Borden, 1992; Hwang & Cowger, 1998; McQuaide & Ehrenreich, 1997; Saleebey, 1993, 1997b). This is an oversimplification, and the question of what constitutes best social work practices continues to be debated (Longres, 1997; Saleebey, 1997a).

On one side of the debate, theorists have suggested that a strengths perspective involves practitioners redefining the client–social worker relationship (Weick, 1993). That is, for a practitioner to use a strengths perspective effectively, "all [clients] must be understood and assessed in the light of their capabilities, competencies, knowledge, survival skills, visions, possibilities, and hopes" (Saleebey, 1997b, p. 17). To accomplish this, practitioners are asked to make a conscious decision to pay attention solely to those factors of people's lives that can contribute to their growth and well-being. This, in turn, requires that practitioners believe that all clients have untapped potential and have already shown resilience in the face of adversity (Weick et al., 1989). On the other side of the controversy, theorists have contended that social workers must assess both client weaknesses and strengths. For example, Longres (1997) asserted that "life is about strengths and weaknesses, and much of the time these are so intertwined as to be inseparable" (p. 23).

The debate about whether practitioners should focus on strengths or weaknesses extends to the resilience research that discusses the necessary primary targets of preventive interventions. Preventive interventions may follow several

TABLE 1.1. Comparison of Pathology and Strengths

Pathology	Strengths
Person is defined as a "case"; symptoms add up to a diagnosis	Person is defined as unique: traits, talents, resources that add up to strengths
Therapy is problem focused	Therapy is solution focused
Client accounts aid in the evocation of a diagnosis through interpretation by an expert	Personal accounts are the necessary route to knowing and appreciating the client
Practitioner is skeptical of client stories	Practitioner knows the person and his or her environment
Childhood trauma is the precursor or predictor of adult pathology	Childhood trauma is not predictive; it may weaken or strengthen the individual
Centerpiece of the therapeutic work is the treatment plan devised by the practitioner	Centerpiece of the work is the hopes and aspirations of family, individual, or community
Practitioner is the expert on clients' lives	Individuals, family, or community are the experts
Possibilities for choice, control, commitment, and personal development are limited by pathology	Possibilities for choice, control, commitment, and personal development are open
Resources for work are the knowledge and skills of the professional	Resources for work are the strengths capacities and adaptive skills of the individual, family, or community
Help is centered on reducing the effects of symptoms and the negative personal and social consequences of actions, emotions, thoughts, or relationships	Help is centered on getting on with life-affirming activities, developing values and commitments, and making and finding membership in or as a community

Source: Adapted from "The Strengths Perspective in Social Work Practice: Extensions and Cautions," by D. Saleebey, 1996, ***Social Work, 41,*** p. 298. Copyright © by the NASW Press. Used with permission.

directions: They may focus on reducing risk, enhancing protective factors, promoting resilience, or a combination of all three (Pollard, Hawkins, & Arthur, 1999; see chapter 2). Benard (1993), who stated "we must move beyond a focus on the 'risk factors' in order to create the conditions that facilitate children's healthy development" (p. 444), represents one side of the controversy. On the other side, Fraser et al. (1999) cautioned against practitioners using "interventions that are based exclusively on a protection or a strengths orientation" (p. 140). Rather, to understand social problems and devise interventions, social workers need to examine *both* risk and protective factors.

Although it is critical for social workers to be keenly aware that every theoretical perspective has a value base that affects its practice, to some degree it may prove futile to engage in an either–or debate about strengths versus weaknesses (Goldstein, 1990). Chapter 2 explores how a resilience-based perspective on risk and protection can provide the theoretical understanding for helping clients reach their human potential.

Ecological Perspective

Because the phenomenon of resilience occurs in the context of person–environment interaction, and because the circumstances that influence resilience are embedded in family, school, neighborhood, and the larger community, resilience can be understood from an ecological perspective. The ecological perspective offers "a multifaceted conceptual base that addresses the complex transactions between people and environments" and promotes a positive outlook on developmental processes (Greene, 1999, p. 259). The ecological perspective also presents a *nondeterministic* view of human behavior—that is, behavior is not considered the outcome of a single cause but the result of multiple, complex person–environment exchanges over time (Bogenschneider, 1996; Nash & Fraser, 1998). Because this point of view affords a holistic picture of life processes, ecological concepts are often used in conjunction with a resilience approach.

Stress and Goodness of Fit. Although stress is a frequently used and familiar concept, there appears to be widespread disagreement about the definition, often necessitating clarification (Rutter, 1981). For example, Smith and Carlson (1997) have argued that it is important for resilience research to distinguish between stress and risk. Risk involves a cluster of factors associated with negative outcomes, including personal characteristics, such as birth weight, and familial or neighborhood circumstances, such as poverty. Stress can arise from a number of causes, but the outcome depends on how those causes are perceived and dealt with. For example, Kobasa (1979) proposed that stressful life events do not always produce debilitating results, because some people are hardy in that they have a greater commitment to self, have a stronger sense of personal control, and can better face challenges or change. In a similar vein, Pearlin, Aneshensel, Mullan, and Whitlatch (1996) indicated that, although an initial stressful event can bring about distress, people experience stress because there is a need for them to alter or intensify some aspect of a long-standing role.

Resilience research increasingly reflects the view that life events or stressors, such as divorce or natural calamities, place an extra burden on peoples' adaptive capacity (Masten, 1994; Smith & Carlson, 1997; see chapter 2). *Stress* is defined as "an imbalance between the demands impinging on a person and actual or perceived resources available to meet these challenges" (Masten, 1994, p. 5). This definition can be likened to the ecological concept of *goodness of fit*—the match between a person's adaptive needs and the quality of his or her environment (Germain & Gitterman, 1995).

Transaction. Transaction, another concept important to the ecological view, refers to the idea that person and environment are mutually dependent or form a reciprocal single unit. Over time, this mutual influence has a cumulative effect, bringing about change in the total person–environment configuration (Greene, 1999; Kaminsky et al., 2007)). From this perspective, the social worker is interested in not only how people adjust to their environments, but also how people influence the environments in which they live (Greene, 1999; Sullivan, 1992).

Multiple Systems of Influence. Ecological approaches emphasize the multiple systems of influence in which people live. Bronfenbrenner's (1979) description of the ecological metaphor has frequently served as a multilevel visualization of the connections among individuals at various systems levels (Greene & Watkins, 1998). The visualization is like "a set of nested structures, each inside the next, like a set of Russian dolls" (Bronfenbrenner, 1979, p. 22). It describes a person's environment in terms of *microsystems,* including the immediate, personal, day-to-day activities and roles, such as those in the family; *mesosystems,* which encompass the linkages between two or more settings involving the developing individual, such as family and school; *exosystems,* which include the linkages between two or more systems that do not involve the developing individual, such as parents and the workplace; and *macrosystems,* which encompass overarching societal systems, such as cultural and societal attitudes. How families, schools, communities, and so forth influence resilience and are resilient in their own right is discussed in chapter 3.

Relatedness. Because contemporary societal conditions require attention to children, school, family, and community partnership to promote an individual's social competence, the maintenance of social connections is an important element in resilience-based practice (Herrenkohl, Herrenkohl, & Egolf, 1994; Winters & Maluccio, 1988). People's capacity to maintain connections to various social systems is associated with their sense of relatedness or their capacity to retain emotional and social ties (Laursen & Birmingham, 2003).

Life Course. Several ecological theorists have urged social workers to incorporate content into their practice that focuses on natural growth and development across the life course. Germain (1990, 1997) indicated that the life course considers the larger context in which people live and thereby addresses the diversity of life paths. In a similar vein, Saleebey (1993) declared that the life-course concept provides an understanding that life transitions are "both expected and unexpected" and have a sense of "variety and evanescence through time and culture" (p. 204; see chapter 2 for a further discussion).

Diversity practice. Because social work practice requires the knowledge and ability to serve diverse constituencies—including people of differing religions, racial or ethnic groups, abilities, or sexual orientations—concepts that stem from the diversity literature are also critical to a resilience orientation. That is, culturally competent social work practice—practice that is congruent "with a variety of communities and ways of life" (Green, 1995, p. 10)—is essential. Culturally competent social work practice requires that practitioners be self-aware and understand a client's culture—his or her values, belief systems, traditions, and worldview (Lum, 1999; Weaver, 2000; see chapter 2). In addition, culturally appropriate services that reflect a resilience-based orientation require that practitioners open up client opportunities (Croninger & Lee, 2001; Rutter, 1987; Winfield, 1991) and seek to ensure that a client has an equitable distribution of community and societal resources (Gamble & Weil, 1995; Pinderhughes, 1989; Solomon, 1976).

Developmental Theory

Developmental theory is used to examine people's behavior across the lifespan. It encompasses an understanding of biopsychosocial factors as well as the spiritual realm (Conrad, 1999). Social workers traditionally referred to linear approaches to development that focused on age-related stages and tasks. Although these approaches offered an optimistic view of development, according to Schriver (2001) the stage approach did not address the complexities, diversities, or ambiguities of human development. Furthermore, according to Gilligan (1982), such theories were often based only on observations of white male subjects.

The specific area of study that addresses resilience is called *developmental psychopathology,* which involves an examination of developmental differences in people's responses to stress and adversity. Developmental psychopathology is the study of the probability that severe life stress will result in later psychological difficulties (Benson, Galbraith, & Espeland, 1995; Cicchetti & Toth, 1995). The discipline also examines what factors serve as buffers, or those personal characteristics or environmental events that prevent or moderate adverse reactions to stress.

Major terms used in the study of developmental psychopathology include *risk,* or the increased probability that an individual will experience the onset of a serious state or problem condition (Fraser, 1997); *invulnerability,* or a person's capacity not to be wounded or severely hurt by severe stress (Garmezy, 1993); *protective factors,* or those factors that compensate for risks (Rutter, 1989); and *resilience,* or stress resistance (Garmezy, 1993). These concepts are discussed in greater depth in chapter 2.

As discussed earlier in this chapter, the major focus of developmental studies has been on how childhood factors, such as personal characteristics, family or community violence, or economic deprivation, may lead to adaptive or maladaptive adult behavior or outcomes (Fonagy & Target, 1997; Garmezy, 1993; Rutter, 1989). Researchers have found that, despite the overwhelming environmental stress, a large majority of people remain adaptive. Garmezy (1993), one of the early contributors to the study of resilience, concluded that the body of resiliency research indicates that "the central element in the study of resilience lies in the power of recovery and in the ability to return once again to those patterns of adaptation and competence that characterized the individual prior to the pre-stress period" (p. 129). Subsequently, developmental psychopathologists have become increasingly concerned with how people negotiate life transitions with competence (Greene & Kropf, 2011; Rutter, 1989). Fonagy, Steele, Steele, Moran, and Target (1994) are among the theorists who have argued that development is really concerned with children's *assets,* namely, do children "work well, love well and expect well notwithstanding profound life adversity" (Werner & Smith, 1982, p. 8). The chapters that follow support this theme.

Use the CD by Michael Wright to explore the history of resilience. Articulate resilience as theory. Identify neighboring concepts and companion concepts of resilience.

You will find a case study on your CD: *Tracing Concepts: Figuring Out HBSE for Practice*

References

Ainsworth, M. D. (1989). Attachments beyond infancy. *American Psychologist, 44,* 709–716.

Anthony, E. J. (1987). Risk, vulnerability, and resilience: An overview. In E. J. Anthony & B. J. Cohler (Eds.), *The invulnerable child* (pp. 3–38). New York: Guilford Press.

Anthony, E. J., & Cohler, B. J. (Eds.). (1987). *The invulnerable child.* New York: Guilford Press.

Astor, R. A., Behre, W. J., Wallace, J. M., & Fravil, K. A. (1998). School social workers and school violence: Personal safety, training, and violence programs. *Social Work, 23,* 223–232.

Bandura, A. (1977a). Self-efficacy: Toward a unifying theory of behavior change. *Psychological Review, 84,* 191–215.

Bandura, A. (1977b). *Social learning theory*. Englewood Cliffs, NJ: Prentice Hall.

Bandura, A. (1982a). The self and mechanisms of agency. In J. Suis (Ed.), *Psychological perspectives on the self* (pp. 122–147). Hillsdale, NJ: Erlbaum.

Bandura, A. (1982b). Self-efficacy mechanism in human agency. *American Psychologist, 37,* 122–147.

Bandura, A., & Adams, N. E. (1977). Analysis of self-efficacy theory and behavioral change. *Therapy and Research, 1,* 287–310.

Bandura, A., & Schunk, D. H. (1981). Cultivating competence, self-efficacy, and intrinsic interest through proximal self-motivation. *Journal of Personality and Social Psychology, 41,* 356–398.

Barnard, C. P. (1994). Resiliency: A shift in our perception? *American Journal of Family Therapy, 22,* 135–144.

Begun, A. L. (1993). Human behavior and the social environment: The vulnerability, risk, and resilience model. *Journal of Social Work Education, 29,* 26–36.

Benard, B. (1993). Fostering resilience in kids. *Educational Leadership, 51,* 444–498.

Bendor, S., Davidson, K., & Skolnik, L. (1997). Strengths-pathology dissonance in the social work curriculum. *Journal of Teaching in Social Work, 15,* 3–16.

Benson, P. L., Galbraith, J., & Espeland, P. (1995). *What kids need to succeed.* Minneapolis: Free Spirit.

Bettelheim, B. (1987, March). The importance of play. *Atlantic Monthly,* pp. 35–46.

Blum, D. (1998, May). Finding strength: How to overcome anything. *Psychology Today, 31,* 32–45.

Boehnlein, J. K. (1987). Clinical evidence of grief and mourning among Cambodian refugees. *Social Science & Medicine, 25,* 765–772.

Bogenschneider, K. (1996). Family related prevention programs: An ecological risk/preventive theory for building prevention programs, policies, and community capacity to support youth. *Family Relations, 45,* 127–138.

Borden, W. (1992). Narrative perspectives in psychosocial intervention following adverse life events. *Social Work, 37,* 125–141.

Bowlby, J. (1969). *Attachment and loss*. New York: Basic Books.

Bowlby, J. (1973a). Affectional bonds: Their nature and origin. In R. S. Weiss (Ed.), *Loneliness: The experience of emotional and social isolation* (pp. 38–52). Cambridge, MA: MIT Press.

Bowlby, J. (1973b). *Attachment and loss*. New York: Basic Books.

Bowlby, J. (1980). *Attachment and loss* (3rd ed.). New York: Basic Books.

Bronfenbrenner, U. (1979). *The ecology of human development*. Cambridge, MA: Harvard University Press.

Burman, S., & Allen-Meares, P. (1994). Neglected victims of murder: Children's witness to parental homicide. *Social Work, 39*, 28–34.

Carlson, E., & Rosser-Hogan, E. (1993). Mental health status of Cambodian refugees ten years after leaving their homes. *American Journal of Orthopsychiatry, 63*, 223–231.

Carter, C. S. (1999). Church burning in African American communities: Implications for empowerment practice. *Social Work, 44*, 62–68.

Cicchetti, D., & Toth, S. L. (1995). Developmental psychopathology perspective on child abuse and neglect. *Journal of the American Academy of Child and Adolescent Psychiatry, 34*, 541–565.

Coles, R. (1986). *The political life of children*. Boston: Houghton Mifflin.

Comas-Díaz, L. (1994). An integrative approach. In L. Comas-Díaz & B. Greene (Eds.), *Women of color: Integrating ethnic and gender identities in psychotherapy* (pp. 287–318). New York: Guilford Press.

Conrad, A. (1999). Professional tools for religiously and spiritually sensitive social work practice. In R. R. Greene (Ed.), *Human behavior theory and social work practice* (pp. 63–72). Hawthorne, NY: Aldine de Gruyter.

Croninger, R. G., & Lee, V. E. (2001). Social capital and dropping out of high school: Benefits to at-risk students of teachers' support and guidance. *Teachers College Record, 103*, 548–581.

DuRant, R. H., Cadenhead, C., Pendergrast, R. A., Slavens, G., & Linder, C. W. (1994). Factors associated with the use of violence among urban black adolescents. *Journal of Public Health, 84*, 612–617.

Early-Adams, P., Wallinga, C., Skeen, P., & Paguio, L. P. (1990). Coping in the nuclear age: The practitioner's role. *Families in Society, 71*, 558–562.

Eisenbruch, M. (1984). From post-traumatic stress disorder to cultural bereavement: Diagnosis of Southeast Asian refugees. *Social Science & Medicine, 33*, 673–680.

Erikson, E. H. (1950). *Childhood and society*. New York: W. W. Norton.

Falicov, C. J. (1995). Training to think culturally: A multidimensional comparative framework. *Family Process, 34*, 373–388.

Fonagy, P., Steele, M., Steele, H., Moran, G. S., & Target, M. (1994). The Emmanuel Miller Memorial Lecture 1992: The theory and practice of resilience. *Journal of Child Psychology and Psychiatry, 35*, 231–257.

Fonagy, P., & Target, M. (1997). Attachment and reflective function: Their role in self-organization. *Development and Psychopathology, 9*, 677–699.

Frank, J. D. (1975). *Persuasion and healing*. New York: Schocken Books.

Fraser, M. W. (Ed.). (1997). *Risk and resilience in childhood*. Washington, DC: NASW Press.

Fraser, M. W., & Galinsky, M. J. (1997). Toward a resilience-based model of practice. In M. W. Fraser (Ed.), *Risk and resilience in childhood* (pp. 265–276). Washington, DC: NASW Press.

Fraser, M. W., Jenson, J. M., & Lewis, R. E. (1993). Research training in social work: The continuum is not a continuum. *Journal of Social Work Education, 29*, 46–62.

Fraser, M. W., Richman, J. M., & Galinsky, M. J. (1999). Risk, protection, and resilience: Toward a conceptual framework for social work practice. *Social Work Research, 23,* 129–208.

Freud, A. (1949). Certain types and stages of maladjustment. In A. Freud (Ed.), *Writings of Anna Freud: Indications for child analysis and other papers* (Vol. 4, pp. 75–94). New York: International Universities Press.

Gamble, D. N., & Weil, M. O. (1995). Citizen participation. In R. L. Edwards (Ed.-in-Chief), *Encyclopedia of social work* (19th ed., Vol. 1, pp. 483–494). Washington, DC: NASW Press.

Gambrill, E. (1999). Evidence-based clinical behavior analysis, evidence-based medicine, and the Cochrane collaboration. *Journal of Behavioral Therapy and Experimental Psychiatry, 30,* 1–14.

Garbarino, J., Dubrow, N., Kostelny, K., & Pardo, C. (1992). *Children in danger: Coping with community violence.* San Francisco, CA: Jossey-Bass.

Garmezy, N. (1993). Children in poverty: Resilience despite risk. *Psychiatry, 56,* 127–136.

Germain, C. B. (1990). Life forces and the anatomy of practice. *Smith College Studies in Social Work, 60,* 138–152.

Germain, C. B. (1997). Should HBSE be taught from a stage perspective? In M. Bloom & W. C. Klein (Eds.), *Controversial issues in human behavior in the social environment* (pp. 33–48). Boston: Allyn & Bacon.

Germain, C. B., & Gitterman, A. (1995). Ecological perspective. In R. L. Richards (Ed.-in-Chief), *Encyclopedia of social work* (19th ed., Vol. 1, pp. 816–824). Washington, DC: NASW Press.

Germain, C. B., & Gitterman, A. (1996). *The life model of social work: Advances in theory and practice.* New York: Columbia University Press.

Gilgun, J. F. (1996a). Human development and adversity in ecological perspective, Part 1: A conceptual framework. *Families in Society, 77,* 395–402.

Gilgun, J. F. (1996b). Human development and adversity in ecological perspective, Part 2: Three patterns. *Families in Society, 77,* 459–476.

Gilligan, C. (1982). *In a different voice.* Cambridge, MA: Harvard University Press.

Gitterman, A. (1991). Social work practice with vulnerable populations. In A. Gitterman (Ed.), *Handbook of social work practice with vulnerable populations* (pp. 1–32). New York: Columbia University Press.

Gitterman, A. (1998, April). *Vulnerability, resilience, and social work practice.* The Fourth Annual Dr. Ephriam L. Linsansky Lecture, University of Maryland, Baltimore.

Goldstein, H. (1990). Strength or pathology: Ethical and rhetorical contrasts in approaches to practice. *Families in Society, 71,* 267–275.

Goldstein, H. (1998). What is social work, really? *Families in Society, 79,* 343–345.

Gordon, E. W., & Song, L. D. (1994). Variations in the experience of resilience. In M. C. Wang & E. W. Gordon (Eds.), *Educational resilience in inner-city America: Challenges and prospects* (pp. 27–44). Hillsdale, NJ: Erlbaum.

Green, J. (1995). *Cultural awareness in the human services.* Englewood Cliffs, NJ: Prentice Hall.

Greene, R. R. (1994). *Human behavior theory: A diversity framework.* New York: Aldine de Gruyter.

Greene, R. R. (Ed.). (1999). *Human behavior theory and social work practice*. Hawthorne: Aldine de Gruyter.

Greene, R. R. (2002). Holocaust survivors: A study in resilience. *Journal of Gerontological Social Work* 37(1), 3–18.

Greene, R. R. (2008). Resilience. In T. Mizrahi & L. E. Davis (Eds.-in-Chief), *Encyclopedia of social work* (20th ed., Vol. 3, pp. 526–531). Washington, DC: NASW Press & Oxford University Press.

Greene, R. R. (2010a). A Holocaust survivorship model: Survivors' reflections. *Journal of Human Behavior and the Social Environment, 20,* 569–579.

Greene, R. R. (2010b). A study of Holocaust survivors: Implications for curriculum. *Journal of Social Work Education, 46,* 293–304.

Greene, R. R., & Graham, S. (2008). Role of resilience among Nazi Holocaust survivors: A strength-based paradigm for understanding survivorship. *Family and Community Health, 32,* S75–S82.

Greene, R. R., & Kropf, N. P. (2011). *Competence theoretical frameworks*. New Brunswick, NJ: Transaction Press.

Greene, R. R., & Watkins, M. (Eds.). (1998). *Serving diverse constituencies: Applying the ecological perspective*. New York: Aldine de Gruyter.

Grotberg, E. H. (1995, September). *The international resilience project: Research, application, and policy*. Paper presented at the Symposio Internacional Stress e Violencia, Lisbon, Portugal.

Hartmann, H. (1958). *Ego psychology and the problem of adaptation*. New York: International Universities Press.

Hawkins, J. D., Catalano, R. F., & Miller, J. Y. (1992). Risk and protective factors for alcohol and other drug problems in adolescence and early adulthood: Implications for substance abuse prevention. *Psychological Bulletin, 112,* 64–105.

Helman, C. (1984). *Culture, health and illness*. Bristol, England: Wright.

Herrenkohl, E. C., Herrenkohl, R. C., & Egolf, B. (1994). Resilient early school-age children from maltreating homes: Outcomes in late adolescence. *American Journal of Orthopsychiatry, 64,* 301–309.

Hoff, L. A., Hallisey, B. J., & Hoff, M. (2009). *People in crisis: Clinical and diversity perspectives*. New York: Taylor & Francis.

Hooyman, N. R. (1996). Curriculum and teaching: Today and tomorrow. In *White paper on social work education—Today and tomorrow* (pp. 11–24). Cleveland: Case Western University Press.

Howard, M. O., & Jenson, J. M. (1999). Clinical practice guidelines: Should social work develop them? *Research on Social Work Practice, 9,* 283–301.

Huitt, W. (2007). *Maslow's hierarchy of needs*. Educational Psychology Interactive, Valdosta, GA: Valdosta State University. Retrieved from http://www.edpsycinteractive.org/topics/regsys/maslow.html

Hwang, S. C., & Cowger, C. D. (1998). Utilizing strengths in assessment. *Families in Society, 79,* 25–31.

Kaminsky, M., McCabe, O. L., Langlieb, A. M., & Everly, G. S. (2007). An evidence informed model of human resistance, resilience, and recovery: The Johns Hopkins outcome-driven paradigm for disaster mental health services. *Brief Treatment and Crisis Intervention,* 7(1), 1–11.

Khinduka, S. (1987). Social work and the human services. In A. Minahan (Ed.-in-Chief), *Encyclopedia of social work* (18th ed., Vol. 2, pp. 681–695). Silver Spring, MD: NASW Press.

Kinzie, J. D., Fredrickson, R. H., Ben, R., Fleck, J., & Karls, W. (1984). Posttraumatic stress disorder among survivors of Cambodian concentration camps. *American Journal of Psychiatry, 141,* 645–650.

Kleinman, A. (1980). *Patients and healers in the context of culture.* Berkeley: University of California Press.

Klohnen, E. (1996). Conceptual analysis and measurement of the construct of ego-resiliency. *Journal of Personality and Social Psychology, 70,* 1067–1079.

Kobasa, S. (1979). Stressful life events, personality, and health: An inquiry into hardiness. *Journal of Personality and Social Psychology, 37,* 1–11.

Krovetz, M. L. (1999). Resiliency: A key element for supporting youth at-risk. *Clearing House, 73*(20), 121–123.

Laursen, E. K., & Birmingham, S. M. (2003). Caring relationships as a protective factor for at-risk youth: An ethnographic study. *Families in Society, 84,* 240–246.

Lee, E., & Lu, F. (1989). Assessment and treatment of Asian American survivors of mass violence. *Journal of Traumatic Stress, 2,* 93–120.

Lifton, R. J. (1993). *The protean self: Human resilience in an age of fragmentation.* Chicago: University of Chicago Press.

Longres, J. (1997). Is it feasible to teach HBSE from a strengths perspective, in contrast to one emphasizing limitations and weaknesses? In M. Bloom (Ed.), *Controversial issues in human behavior in the social environment* (pp. 16–33). Boston: Allyn & Bacon.

Lum, D. (1999). *Culturally competent practice.* Pacific Grove, CA: Brooks/Cole.

Maslow, A. H. (1968). *Toward a psychology of being.* Princeton, NJ: van Nostrand.

Masten, A. (1994). Resilience in individual development: Successful adaptation despite risk and adversity. In M. C. Wang & E. W. Gordon (Eds.), *Educational resilience in inner-city America: Challenges and prospects* (pp. 3–25). Hillsdale, NJ: Erlbaum.

Masten, A. S., & Coatsworth, J. D. (1998). The development of competence in favorable and unfavorable environments. *American Psychologist, 53,* 205–220.

McQuaide, S., & Ehrenreich, J. H. (1997). Assessing client strengths. *Families in Society, 78,* 201–212.

Moskovitz, S. (1983). *Love despite hate.* New York: W. W. Norton.

Nash, J. K., & Bowen, G. L. (1999). Perceived crime and informal social control in the neighborhood as a context for adolescent behavior: A risk and resilience perspective. *Social Work Research, 23,* 171–186.

Nash, J., & Fraser, M. W. (1998). After-school care for children: A resilience-based approach. *Families in Society, 79,* 370–382.

Ogbu, J. U. (1992). Understanding cultural diversity and learning. *Educational Researcher, 21*(8), 5–14.

Pearlin, L. I., Aneshensel, C. S., Mullan, J. T., & Whitlatch, C. J. (1996). Caregiving and its social support. In R. H. Binstock & L. George (Eds.), *Handbook of aging and the social sciences* (pp. 283–302). San Diego: Academic Press.

Perlman, H. H. (1957). *Social casework: A problem-solving process.* Chicago: University of Chicago Press.

Piaget, J., & Inhelder, B. (1969). *The psychology of the child.* New York: Basic Books.

Pierce, W. J., & Singleton, S. M. (1995). Improvisation as a concept for understanding and treating violent behavior among African American youth. *Families in Society, 76,* 444–450.

Pinderhughes, E. (1989). Understanding race, ethnicity, and power: The key to efficacy in clinical practice. New York: Free Press.

Pollard, J. A., Hawkins, J. D., & Arthur, M. W. (1999). Risk and protection: Are both necessary to understand diverse behavioral outcomes in adolescence? *Social Work Research, 23,* 145–158.

Reed-Victor, E., & Pelco, L. E. (1999). Helping homeless students build resilience. *Journal for a Just & Caring Education, 5,* 51–72.

Rey, L. D. (1996). What social workers need to know about client violence. *Families in Society, 77,* 33–39.

Richman, J. M., & Bowen, G. L. (1997). School failure: An ecological-interactional-developmental perspective. In M. W. Fraser (Ed.), *Risk and resilience in childhood* (pp. 95–116). Washington, DC: NASW Press.

Rogers, C. (1951). *Client-centered therapy*. Boston: Houghton Mifflin.

Rutter, M. (1981). Stress, coping and development: Some issues and some questions. *Journal of Child Psychology and Psychiatry, 22,* 323–356.

Rutter, M. (1987). Psychological resilience and protective mechanisms. *American Journal of Orthopsychiatry, 57,* 316–331.

Rutter, M. (1989). Pathways from childhood to adult life. *Journal of Psychology and Psychiatry, 30,* 23–51.

Saleebey, D. (1993). Notes on interpreting the human condition: A "constructed" HBSE curriculum. In J. Laird (Ed.), *Revisioning social work education: A social constructionist approach* (pp. 197–217). New York: Haworth Press.

Saleebey, D. (1996). The strengths perspective in social work practice: Extensions and cautions. *Social Work, 4,* 296–305.

Saleebey, D. (1997a). Is it feasible to teach HBSE from a strengths perspective, in contrast to one emphasizing limitations and weakness? Yes. In M. Bloom & W. C. Klein (Eds.), *Controversial issues in human behavior in the social environment* (pp. 33–48). Boston: Allyn & Bacon.

Saleebey, D. (1997b). *The strengths perspective in social work practice.* New York: Longman.

Schriver, J. M. (2001). *Human behavior and the social environment.* Needham Heights, MA: Allyn & Bacon.

Smith, C., & Carlson, B. E. (1997). Stress, coping, and resilience in children and youth. *Social Service Review, 71,* 231–256.

Solomon, B. B. (1976). *Black empowerment: Social work in oppressed communities.* New York: Columbia University Press.

Sullivan, W. P. (1992). Reclaiming the community: The strengths perspective and deinstitutionalization. *Social Work, 37,* 204–209.

Sullivan, W. (1998). Culturally sound mental health services: Ecological interventions. In R. R. Greene & M. Watkins (Eds.), *Serving diverse constituencies: Applying the ecological perspective* (pp. 221–239). Hawthorne: Aldine de Gruyter.

Thyer, B. (1996). Thirty years of progress toward empirical clinical practice? *Social Work Research, 20,* 77–81.

Tolan, P. H., Guerra, N. G., & Kendall, P. C. (1995). A developmental–ecological perspective on antisocial behavior in children and adolescents: Toward a unified risk and intervention framework. *Journal of Consulting and Clinical Psychology, 64,* 570–584.

Vaillant, G. (1971). Theoretical hierarchy of adaptive ego mechanisms. *Archives of General Psychiatry, 24,* 107–118.

Vaillant, G. E., & Milofsky, E. (1980). Natural history of male psychological health: Empirical evidence for Erikson's model of the life cycle. *American Journal of Psychiatry, 137,* 1348–1359.

Wallach, L. B. (1994, June). *Violence and young children's development.* Champaign, IL: ERIC Clearinghouse on Elementary and Early Childhood Education. (ERIC Document Reproduction Service No. ED369578.) Retrieved from http://resilnet.uiuc.edu/library/wallac94.html

Walsh, F. (1999). Families in later life: Challenges and opportunities. In B. Carter & M. McGoldrick (Eds.), *The expanded life cycle: Individual, family, and social perspectives* (pp. 307–324). Boston: Allyn & Bacon.

Wang, M. C., & Gordon, E. W. (Eds.). (1994). *Educational resilience in inner-city America: Challenges and prospects.* Hillsdale, NJ: Erlbaum.

Weaver, H. N. (2000). Culture and professional education: The experience of Native American social workers. *Journal of Social Work Education, 36,* 415–428.

Weick, A. (1993). Reconstructing social work education. In J. Laird (Ed.), *Revisioning social work education: A social constructionist approach* (pp. 11–30). New York: Haworth Press.

Weick, A., Rapp, C., Sullivan, W. P., & Kisthardt, W. (1989). A strengths perspective for social work practice. *Social Work, 3,* 350–354.

Weick, A., & Saleebey, D. (1995). Supporting family strengths: Orienting policy and practice toward the twenty-first century. *Families in Society, 76,* 141–149.

Werner, E., & Smith, R. (1982). *Vulnerable, but invincible: A longitudinal study of resilient children and youth.* New York: McGraw-Hill.

Werner, E., & Smith, R. (1992). *Overcoming the odds: High risk children from birth to adulthood.* Ithaca: Cornell University Press.

White, R. W. (1959). Motivation reconsidered: The concept of competence. *Psychological Review, 66,* 297–331.

White, R. W. (1963). Sense of interpersonal competence. In R. W. White (Ed.), *The study of lives* (pp. 73–93). New York: Atherton Press.

Wilson, W. J. (1987). *The truly disadvantaged: The inner city, the underclass, and public policy.* Chicago: University of Chicago Press.

Winfield, L. (1991). Resilience, schooling, and development in African-American youth. *Education and Urban Society, 24,* 5–14.

Winters, W., & Maluccio, A. (1988). School, family, and community: Working together to promote social competence. *Social Work in Education, 10,* 207–217.

Witkin, S., & Nurius, P. (1997). Should human behavior theories with limited empirical support be included in HBSE classes? In M. Bloom & W. C. Klein (Eds.), *Controversial issues in human behavior in the social environment* (pp. 49–64). Boston: Allyn & Bacon.

Wolin, S. J., & Wolin, S. (1993). *The resilient self.* New York: Willard.

Worland, J., Weeks, D. G., Weiner, S. M., Schechtman, J. (1982). Longitudinal, prospective evaluations of intelligence in children at risk. *Schizophrenia Bulletin, 8,* 135–141.

2

Resilience: Basic Assumptions and Terms

ROBERTA R. GREENE and ANN P. CONRAD

On finishing this chapter, students will be able to further:

Apply knowledge of human behavior and the social environment (Educational Policy 2.1.7) by

- Using conceptual frameworks to guide the processes of assessment, intervention, and evaluation (practice behavior).

The term "resilience" is reserved for unpredicted or markedly successful adaptations to negative life events, trauma, stress, and other forms of risk. If we can understand what helps some people to function well in the context of high adversity, we may be able to incorporate this knowledge into new practice strategies.

—FRASER, RICHMAN, & GALINSKY, 1999, P. 136

Despite the growing popularity of the construct of resilience and considerable scientific work, the concept remains broadly defined (Fraser et al., 1999; Gordon & Song, 1994), and the term is often used interchangeably with *positive coping, adaptation,* and *persistence* (Winfield, 1994). Even with these ambiguities, though, over the past three decades, theorists from several fields have contributed to an expanding knowledge base for comprehending resilience (Greene, 2007, 2008b). Many theorists consider this knowledge base sufficiently advanced to provide guidelines for mental health policy and practice

(Begun, 1993; Fraser et al., 1999; Grotberg, 1995; Masten, 1994; Miller & MacIntosh, 1999). This chapter synthesizes the converging theory and research findings and translates them into human behavior principles and resilience-based social work practice guidelines to augment practitioners' theoretical context for social work practice.

Human Behavior Theory: Structuring Professional Activities

The complexity of human concerns with which social workers deal argues against a "hit or miss" approach to their solutions. Rather, this complexity makes imperative the need for consciously held and purposeful conduct of practice.

—Greene, 2008a, p. 8

Throughout the history of social work, practitioners have turned to a number of theoretical perspectives to better understand the clients with whom they work and to inform their practice skills. Theoretical frameworks are useful to social workers to the extent that they provide a conceptual foundation to guide professional activities or afford a context for action. The issues a theory should address to supply such professional guidance are introduced in the next two chapters and applied throughout the book. The following questions are discussed (based on Greene, 2008a):

- What does the theory offer for understanding development across the life cycle? Life course?
- What does the theory suggest about the interaction among biological, psychological, and sociocultural factors of human development and functioning? Spiritual beliefs?
- What does the theory suggest about healthy/functional and unhealthy/dysfunctional behaviors or wellness?
- What does the theory say is adaptive/maladaptive? How does the theory present stress factors and coping potentials?
- Is the theory universal in its application? How does the theory lend itself to cross-cultural social work practice or various life contexts? Does the theory address social and economic justice?
- What does the theory propose about individuals as members of families, groups, communities, and organizations?
- How does the theory lend itself to understanding individual, family, group, community, or organizational behavior?

- How does the theory serve as a framework for social work practice?
- How does the theory suggest the client and social worker go about defining presenting situations, problems, or concerns? Does the theory suggest a strengths perspective?
- What are the implications of the theory for social work interventions or practice strategies? Do the principles of the theory emphasize a client's capacities and resources?
- What does the theory suggest the social worker do? What does it suggest the client (system) do?
- What role does it propose for the social worker as a change agent? What is the aim of treatment/intervention or meaning creation? What does it suggest enhances functioning or promotes change in the client? In society? In societal institutions? (pp. 2–3)

What Is Resilience?

The healthiest members of our [epidemiological] sample often showed little [adverse] psychological reaction to events and situations which cause profound reactions in other members of the group. The loss of a husband or wife, the separation from one's family, the isolation from one's friends, community, or country, the frustration of apparent important desires, or the failure to obtain apparently important goals produced no profound or lasting reaction.

—Hinkle, 1974, pp. 40–41

Historical Context

To understand the definitions involved in building research and theory in risk and resilience, it is necessary to summarize the historical advancement of the field. According to Doll and Lyon (1998), there have been two generations of risk and resilience studies, and each has refined its approach. The first generation focused on the risks for disadvantaged children. The study of risk went through three iterations: (1) The earliest studies included those by Bowlby (1973a, 1973b) and Spitz (1946), who were concerned primarily with infant attachment; (2) The second iteration of risk studies, which used longitudinal and case study methods, explored how single risk factors affect outcomes. This phase continues today but with more sophisticated statistical methods; and (3) The third iteration of risk studies examined the multiple influences and interactions of risk and protective factors on child and adult adjustment. This also involved a movement away from the indiscriminate use of the word *risk,* often viewed as a pejorative term applied to young people growing up in major urban cities where poverty and unemployment rates were high (Winfield, 1991). The central question of this stage of research is, why do some people persevere with few harmful effects despite adversity, whereas others experience serious stress or difficulties? Researchers of psychosocial risk frequently found that a substantial number of children reared in the most unfavorable circumstances developed into successful adults (Rutter, 1985). Thus, resilience research arose from the study of risk.

The second generation of studies has continued to emphasize successful coping, or the ability to overcome risk and adversity. The major concerns have been how children become competent and productive adults as well as how adults are able to maintain healthy functioning. Studies have been conducted on multiple populations that relate to multiple outcomes. As a result of these studies, it is understood that people may face a constellation of risks and may have multisystemic protective factors such as family, school, and neighborhood. People must therefore be understood within an ecological context. In addition, it has been found that the subjective meanings people attribute to adverse life circumstances—how they feel and think about an event—are critical determinants of success (see chapter 3).

During the past several decades of discussion about children and families at risk and an interest in what keeps people successful, resiliency has become part of the strengths tradition (Saleebey, 1997). However, the term appears to go beyond the idea of strengths. It is increasingly used to understand and promote the capability of people to transform and change despite the challenges they face (Benard, 1997; Lifton, 1993). The view that resilience is an innate "self-righting mechanism," as expressed by Werner and Smith (1992), continues to shape interventions. In addition, theorists have broadened their interest to encompass an exploration of resilience across the lifespan and among families and communities. The terms and basic assumptions related to resilience included in the literature follow.

Terms

Risk. Risk is a statistical concept that originated in epidemiology. *Risks* are "any influences that increase the probability of onset, digression to a more serious state, or maintenance of a problem condition" (Kirby & Fraser, 1997, pp. 10–11). Risk factors are those thought to present a group of people, usually children, with a higher probability of an undesirable outcome, such as dropping out of school (Masten, 1994). Risk factor studies investigate what predisposes or increases the likelihood that children from common backgrounds will develop greater emotional or behavioral difficulties compared to children from the general population. That is, researchers have sought to determine the probability that some at-risk children will develop problematic behaviors (such as drug abuse) or emotional difficulties given a certain set of circumstances. Risk factors are considered markers or correlates of related factors, such as poverty or child abuse (Fraser et al., 1999).

Researchers have approached the study of risk factors in one of two ways: (1) They have examined specific risk factors or a particular antecedent that they have then attempted to link to future outcomes; or (2) they have studied cumulative risk, in that they have tried to define the effects of additive risks. This second approach to understanding the multiple factors that may produce a negative outcome seems to be growing in popularity because researchers are increasingly recognizing that "there is no single path to many social problems" (Fraser et al., 1999, p. 131). *Risk chains* refer to the linkages among risk factors.

Ecological theory continues to influence research study design. As a result, risk factors have been identified in people's immediate and more distant environments. *Proximal risk factors*—those closer to the individual, such as an abusive parent—are thought to be more influential, whereas *distal risk factors*—those situated further away, such as the political climate—are considered less influential (Kirby & Fraser, 1997). However, the view that distant (or macrosystem) influences may be less influential may stem from current shortcomings in research methodology (Bronfenbrenner, Moen, & Garbarino, 1984; see chapter 4).

Although the study of risk factors was originally conceived of as a causal mechanistic model in which *x* causes *y*, the concept of risk is currently understood as a dynamic process (Cowan, Cowan, & Shulz, 1996). Response to risk varies among individuals and according to their life contexts. People who may react positively to risk at one point in their lives may not react positively at another point (Rutter, 1981, 1987). In addition, the concept of risk encompasses the notion of cumulative stress (Garmezy, 1993; Masten, 1994). *Stress* has been differentiated from risk as an individual's subjective reaction to life events that require adaptation. That is, a life event is regarded as stressful when an individual appraises the event as so taxing that it poses a threat (Lazarus & Folkman, 1984). This viewpoint is central to understanding resilience (Smith & Carlson, 1997).

Vulnerability. The term *vulnerability* refers to the idea that some at-risk people are more likely to develop an undesirable outcome or disorder. "A vulnerability factor is a characteristic of an individual that makes that person more susceptible to a particular threat to development" (Masten, 1994, p. 7). For example, genetic factors may be responsible for predispositions to disorder or may amplify the probability that a person at risk will have a negative outcome (Cowan et al., 1996). However, Garmezy (1993) has cautioned against the use of the term *invulnerable* because it implies that people are incapable of being wounded or injured.

Protective Factors. The study of protective factors has involved a conceptual shift and changes in the models of inquiry that direct the researcher's attention from risk factors to the process of how people successfully negotiate risk (Jessor, 1993). For example, Rutter (1987) observed that, during the 1970s, the context for understanding the mechanisms that safeguard against the psychological risks associated with adversity led to an examination of protective factors. Similarly, Garmezy (1991) noted that the "sturdy evidence that many children and adults do overcome life's difficulties" (p. 421) suggests that researchers have attempted to identify protective factors.

The term *protective factor* generally describes circumstances that moderate the effects of risks and enhance adaptation (Masten, 1994). Protective factors may buffer, interrupt, or even prevent risk. A *buffer* is a factor thought to decrease the probability that a person at risk will experience an undesirable outcome (Cowan et al., 1996). Despite the research to date, the term *protective factor* remains broadly defined, and the nature of the interplay between risk and protective factors continues to be debated (Kirby & Fraser, 1997). Masten (1987) has argued that risk and protective factors are polar opposites, such that competence decreases as stress increases. A model in which risk factors increase the probability of a negative outcome is called an *additive model*. In contrast, Rutter (1983) has contended that risk and protective factors interact to produce an outcome; when stress is low, protective factors are of less influence. This approach in which risk and protective factors only work in conjunction with each other is termed an *interactive model*. Kirby and Fraser (1997) have suggested that the debate about the usefulness of additive and interactive models is best resolved by examining the daily interaction among risk and protective factors across multiple system levels that provide children with both challenges and opportunities.

Protective factors, both internal and external, help people resist or ameliorate risk. There appears to be general agreement in the literature about the protective characteristics that modify stress and contribute to resiliency among children (see Table 2.1). Three such characteristics are (1) a personal disposition, such as a positive temperament, social responsiveness, ability, and self-esteem; (2) a supportive family milieu, including warmth and cohesion; and (3) an extrafamilial social environment that rewards competence and reinforces belief systems (Garmezy, 1991; Werner, 1989). As with risk factors, protective factors need to be understood as relative, contextual phenomena (Gordon & Song, 1994). Similarly, Rutter (1987) has concluded that

TABLE 2.1 Summary: Correlates of Resilience

Individuals:
• Perceived as more cuddly and affectionate in infancy and beyond
• No sibling born within 20–24 months of one's birth
• Higher level of intelligence
• Capacity and skills for developing intimate relationships
• Achievement orientation in and outside of school
• Capacity to construct productive meanings for events in their world that enhance their understanding of these events
• Ability to disengage from the home and engage with those outside, and then to reengage with the home
• Internally oriented, with an internal locus of control
• Absence of serious illness during adolescence
Family:
• Extent and nature of the fit or "match" between child and parents
• Possession and maintenance of rituals in the family
• Family's assumption of a proactive posture and confrontation of the problem or stressor in contrast to a passive and reactive posture
• Absence of parent–child role reversals
• Minimal conflict in the home during infancy
• Absence of divorce during adolescence
• Substantial and productive relationship with one's mother
• Selection of a nontroubled person as a mate
Resilient children have certain attributes relative to more vulnerable children:
• Higher socioeconomic status
• Female gender before prepubescence, male gender after prepubescence
• Absence of organic deficits
• Easy temperament
• Younger age at the time of trauma
• Absence of early separations and losses
Resilient children have protective features in their environments:
• Competent parenting
• Good (warm) relationship with at least one primary caregiver
• Availability (in adulthood) of social support from spouse, family, or other figures
• Better network of informal relationships
• Better formal social support through better education and religious affiliation

(*continued*)

TABLE 2.1 Summary: Correlates of Resilience (*continued*)

Resilient children tend to have the following psychological characteristics:
• High IQ and problem solving ability • Superior coping styles • Task-related self-efficacy • Autonomy or internal locus of control • Higher sense of self-worth • Interpersonal awareness and empathy • Willingness and capacity to plan • Sense of humor

Source: From "The Emmanuel Miller Memorial Lecture 1992 The Theory and Practice of Resilience" by P. Fonagy, M. Steele, A. Higgitt, and M. Target, 1994, *Journal of Child Psychology and Psychiatry, 35*(2), 231–252. Copyright 1994 by Cambridge University Press. Reprinted with permission.

> protection does not reside in the psychological chemistry of the moment but in ways in which people deal with life changes and in what they do about their stressful or disadvantageous circumstances. Particular attention needs to be paid to the mechanisms operating at key turning points in people's lives when a risk trajectory may be redirected onto an adaptive path. (p. 329)

In his book *Lost Boys,* Garbarino (1999) captured the interplay of risk, vulnerability, and protective factors. He pointed out that teenage boys who are violent often have been subjected to violence themselves or have encountered severe rejection. Lost boys appear tough on the outside, but their inner lives are characterized by vulnerability and pain. Although lost boys are often incarcerated as criminals, Garbarino has witnessed more than one boy he was interviewing suck his thumb. Garbarino's interviews led him to believe that "the ultimate fate of vulnerable young boys is very much wrapped up in issues of resilience. Can they overcome being rejected and abused, abandoned and terrorized?" (p. 161).

Resilience. The study of resilience, according to Garmezy (1993), has focused on answering two major questions: (1) What are the characteristics—risk factors—of children, families, and environments that predispose children to maladjustment following exposure to adversity? and (2) What are the characteristics—protective factors—that shield them from such adjustment problems? In trying to answer these questions, researchers have examined numerous factors related to individual, family, and community life to determine what is likely to lead to adaptive or maladaptive behavior. Those factors that appear to have certain strengths or assets in individual and environmental circumstances that ameliorate risks are called *resilient* (Fraser, 1997; Masten, 1994).

The term *resilience* stems from the Latin *resiliens* and was originally used to refer to the pliant or elastic quality of a substance. The word resilient has generally been applied to people who overcome the odds. Resilience has also come to describe a person having a good track record of successful adaptation in the face of stress or disruptive change (Werner & Smith, 1992).

Grotberg (1995) has pointed out that although *resilience* remains a familiar word in everyday English parlance, this does not mean that there is consensus about its definition, nor do all languages have an equivalent word. Despite the lack of clarity about the domain covered by the resilience construct, some commonly used definitions guide the chapter discussions in this book. For example, Fraser et al. (1999) have suggested that resilience involves overcoming the odds and being successful despite exposure to high risk; sustaining competence under pressure, that is, adapting successfully to high risk; and recovering from trauma by adjusting successfully to negative life events. In a similar vein, Masten (1994) has contended that resilience refers to (1) people from high-risk groups who have had better than expected outcomes; (2) good adaptation despite stressful (common) experiences (when stressors are extreme, resilience refers to patterns of recovery); and (3) recovery from trauma. Despite differences in terminology, resilience must be understood as a process (Fraser, 1997; Masten, 1994). Stewart, Reid, and Mangham (1997) reviewed the numerous definitions of resilience in the literature and discovered several other common themes:

- Resilience can be viewed as a complex interplay between certain characteristics of individuals and their broader environments.
- Resilience consists of a balance between stress and the ability to cope.
- Risk factors that stem from multiple stressful life events and protective factors that ameliorate or decrease the negative influence of risk contribute to resilience.
- Resilience is dynamic. It depends on life context.
- Resilience is developmental. Being successful strengthens a person's competence.
- Resilience is most important in times of life transitions.

On the basis of these themes, Stewart et al. (1997) have defined *resilience* as "the capability of individuals to cope successfully in the face of significant change, adversity, or risk. This capability changes over time and is enhanced by protective factors in the individual and the environment" (p. 22). Higgins (1994) has proposed that, for the moment, theorists and practitioners define *resilience* as broadly as possible "as the ability to function psychologically at a level far greater than expected given a person's earlier developmental experiences" (p. 17). She has argued that such a broad definition allows for the fullest understanding of the factors promoting resilience.

In a similar vein, Greene, Armour, Hantman, Graham, and Sharabi (2010) found that many survivors of the Nazi Holocaust were able to deal with extreme stress and trauma, making meaning of these events. They created a Holocaust survivorship model that suggests that individuals, families, and communities develop a positive engagement with life after long-term exposure to adverse and even life-threatening events.

The definitions that follow also expand the concept of resilience:

> Resilience is a global concept dealing with how a child copes with stress and trauma. Resilience, like competence and adaptation as outcomes of coping, deals with growth and hope. (Anthony & Cohler, 1987, p. 101)
>
> Resilience is concerned with individual variations in response to risk. Resilience refers to the positive pole of individual differences in people's response to stress and adversity, as well as hope and optimism in the face of adversity. (Rutter, 1987, pp. 316–317)
>
> Resilience is not defined in terms of the absence of pathology or heroics. Rather, it is an ability to cope with adversity, stress, and deprivation. (Begun, 1993, pp. 28–29)
>
> Resilience speaks to a person who regains functioning following adversity. Resilience is in the power of recovery and the ability to return once again to those patterns of adaptation and competence that characterized the individual before extreme stress. (Garmezy, 1993, p. 129)
>
> Resilience is the presence of child, family, or extrafamilial environmental characteristics that allow for the chance of adaptive functioning in the face of severe risk. Protective factors are thought to decrease the negative impact of adversity and increase resilience. (Nash & Fraser, 1998, p. 371)
>
> Resilience is a process in which the development of substantive character is made up of greater or lesser periods of disruption and the development and use of greater or lesser competencies in life management. (Palmer, 1997, p. 201)
>
> Resilience is the ability to maintain continuity of one's personal narrative and a coherent sense of self following traumatic events. (Borden, 1992, p. 125)

> Resilience is normal development under difficult conditions. (Fonagy, Steele, Steele, Higgitt, & Target, 1994, p. 233)
>
> Resilience is usually used to describe individuals who adapt to extraordinary circumstances, achieving positive and unexpected outcomes in the face of adversity. (Fraser et al., 1999, p. 136)

The literature also contains discussion about what prompts resilience. Many theorists have suggested that resilient behaviors are positive outcomes when risks are present. However, resilience has been viewed as a process highly influenced by protective factors that involve competencies in individual, interpersonal, and familial domains (Dyer & McGuinness, 1996). Rutter (1981, 1987) has offered still another conceptualization of resilience: As a person develops, risk and protective factors interact to form resilience. From these vantage points, resilience may be understood as individual variation in the way people respond to risk over time. Theorists explore not only the continuity of behaviors over time—with the assumption that patterns are set early in life—but also discontinuity—the assumption that people will change over the lifespan. Because people may be thought of as relatively resilient depending on their response to risk within their life context, resilience is considered a transactional phenomenon. Transactional approaches consider the person and his or her environment as inseparable or as a unitary system in which humans and environment mutually influence each other (Greene, 2008a).

Another way of thinking about risk and resilience is that they form a continuum, with each dimension representing opposite ends: little coping capacity at one end of the continuum and greater coping capacity at the other (Kirby & Fraser, 1997). On the basis of the notion that risk and resilience form a continuum or may vary in degree, Palmer (1997) has described four types of resilience: (1) *anomic survival,* which refers to people and families who are in a continual state of disruption or chaos; (2) *regenerative resilience,* which encompasses incomplete attempts to develop competence or constructive coping mechanisms; (3) *adaptive resilience,* which refers to relatively sustained periods of use of competence and coping strategies; and (4) *flourishing resilience,* meaning that there is extensive use of effective behavior and coping strategies.

The U.S. military has also developed a resilience continuum to delineate the combat readiness of troops (see chapter 13). It consists of four categories: (1) *mission ineffective,* which encompasses soldiers who suffer from depression, anxiety, and anger and who may be a danger to themselves and others; (2) *persistent distress,* which refers to troops who have loss of appetite, decreased energy, and feelings of guilt; (3) *stress response,* which includes soldiers who are irritable, are overwhelmed, or have difficulty sleeping; and (4) *mission ready,* which refers to soldiers with a sense of purpose and a positive outlook (see http://www.dcoe.health.mil).

The capacity to be resilient is not limited to individuals, however. According to Grotberg (1995), resilience

> is a universal capacity which allows a person, group, or community to prevent, minimize or overcome the damaging effects of adversity [or to anticipate inevitable adversities]. Resilience may transform or make stronger the lives of those who are resilient. The resilient behavior may be in response to adversity in the form of maintenance or normal development despite adversity, or a promoter of growth beyond the present level of functioning. (p. 2)

For example, a national-, family-, and individual-level analysis of responses to the Columbine High School murders revealed that many people were coping differently during the aftermath with grief projects, including artwork, symbols, and Web sites. These mourning strategies meant to deal with unanticipated death have become communal symbols to help people resolve personal and public trauma (Fast, 2003). Similarly, on the second anniversary of the September 11, 2001, attacks on the World Trade Center and the Pentagon, it appeared that the events had hardly been forgotten (Bumiller, 2003). This was reflected in Thomas E. Franklin's photograph of firefighters raising the flag, which has been seen around the world and is an image on U.S. stamps (as discussed in Greene, 2007). Resilience, then, is a multifaceted, global concept associated with numerous individual and multisystemic characteristics (see Table 2.2). Furthermore, resilience is considered a fluid, dynamic, and not fully understood process that allows individuals, families, and communities who have experienced difficulties to go on with life (Dyer & McGuinness, 1996).

However, several theorists have critiqued the concept, pointing out its shortcomings. For example, according to Rigsby (1994), the strong individualistic image of success gives the impression that everyone can get ahead, that there is equal opportunity to do so, that one can always "get it together," and that disadvantages are for the individual to overcome. He has gone on to argue that, because these assumptions about success may underlie how theorists think about resilience, the concept of resilience may lead to linear, more simplistic predictions about risk. Such thinking may also draw attention away from the interaction of people, context, and opportunities.

Some theorists have found the use of the term *resilience* vague. For example, Gordon and Song (1994) have claimed that the term currently refers to a wide

TABLE 2.2 Research Findings on Characteristics of Resilient Children

Psychological/Internal

- Personal strengths, including a sense of being lovable
- Autonomous
- Appealing temperament
- Achievement oriented
- Healthy self-esteem
- Trust
- Empathy and altruism
- Sound locus of control
- Intellectual skills

Spiritual

- Hope
- Faith
- Belief in God
- Morality

Interpersonal/Social Skills

- Creativity
- Persistence
- Humor
- Effective communication
- Good problem-solving skills
- Impulse control
- Seeks trusting relationships

Social/External Supports

- Structure and rules at home
- Parental encouragement of autonomy
- Stable home environment
- External supports and resources, including trusting relationships
- Access to health, education, welfare, and security services
- Emotional support outside the family
- Stable school environment
- Good role models
- Affiliated with religious organization

Source: Reprinted with permission from International Resilience Project, Civitan International Research Center, University of Alabama, Birmingham.

array of "behavioral adaptation, human circumstances, and human achievement that are colloquially included in what is referred to as . . . resilience" (p. 27). Moreover, the cardinal difficulty in defining resilience may well be that it is not a single construct. In addition, people's subjective reaction to seemingly similar life circumstances may vary, as might their levels of awareness and responsiveness to an event (Gordon & Song, 1994). On the positive side, Gordon and Song have concluded that study of stressors and their effects has reoriented the practitioner's attention to resilience. However, a more adequate conceptualization of this human phenomenon is necessary. Such continued theory building about individuals with differing risks and assets can allow for a better understanding of human developmental processes in differing times, places, and social contexts (Rigsby, 1994).

Basic Assumptions. Clearly, the concept of resilience can be variously defined and continues to evolve (Fraser, 1997). Nonetheless, the basic premises of the concept of resilience are far-reaching, and its promise as a human behavior and practice concept has yet to be realized. The remaining chapters attempt to illustrate this potential and discuss how resilience may influence a range of social phenomena. The discussion is guided by the following key theoretical assumptions. Resilience

- is a biopsychosocial and spiritual phenomenon;
- involves a transactional dynamic process of person–environment exchanges;
- encompasses an adaptational process of goodness of fit;
- occurs across the life course with individuals, families, and communities experiencing unique paths of development;
- is linked to life stress and people's unique coping capacity;
- involves competence in daily functioning;
- may be on a continuum—a polar opposite to risk;
- may be interactive, having an effect in combination with risk factors;
- is enhanced through connection or relatedness with others;
- is influenced by diversity, including ethnicity, race, gender, age, sexual orientation, economic status, religious affiliation, and physical and mental ability;
- is expressed and affected by multilevel attachments, both distal and proximal, including family, school, peers, neighborhood, community, and society; consequently, resilience is a function of micro-, exo-, meso-, and macrofactors;
- is affected by the availability of environmental resources; and
- is influenced by power differentials.

Resilience: A Biopsychosocial and Spiritual Phenomenon

An understanding of human behavior serves as the basis for social work assessment and intervention. This section synthesizes resiliency research and the theoretical literature to provide human behavior content that is translated into social work practice strategies. It begins with a discussion of a central element in the study of human behavior—the interplay of biopsychosocial and spiritual functioning.

Biological development usually refers to genetic, health, physical, or vital life-limiting organ systems; *psychological development* encompasses an individual's affective, cognitive, and behavioral dimensions; and *social development* deals with cultural, political, and economic aspects as a member of a group. *Spiritual functioning* is the "human quest for personal meaning and mutually fulfilling relationships among people, and, for some, God" (Canda, 1988, p. 243). These dimensions of human development—biopsychosocial and spiritual—are so intertwined that it is almost impossible to separate them as different functions (see Table 2.3). For example, Bronfenbrenner (1989) coined the term *developmentally instigating characteristics* (p. 227) to describe how children use behaviors, such as a smile or frown, to invite or discourage reactions from their environments, thereby contributing to their own growth. Because this term captures the interrelationship among biopsychosocial and spiritual factors, it is important to the concept of resilience. Are babies born with developmentally instigating characteristics? Are those characteristics part of their personality, or are they learned as a part of the child's socialization process? Are these characteristics enhanced through spiritual belief? At what point do children develop spirituality?

Biological Factors

Some theorists believe that resilience, or successful adaptation, is an innate or "biological imperative for growth and development that exists in the human organism and that unfolds naturally in the presence of certain [and despite] environmental characteristics" (Benard, 1995, p. 1). Characteristics that researchers think are inherent, that is, inborn predispositions for certain behaviors, include the development of social competence, the use of problem-solving skills, the ability to strive for autonomy and a sense of purpose, and the achievement of critical consciousness (Garmezy, 1993).

Temperament is another personality characteristic thought to be inherent and related to resilience. For example, children who are perceived by caregivers to have a cuddly and affectionate ("easy") temperament are more likely to get a

TABLE 2.3 Summary of Individual and Contextual Characteristics of Resilient Children and Youths

Individual	Contextual
Good intellectual ability	Family-related
Language competence	Close, affectionate relationship with at least one parent or caregiver
Positive temperament or easygoing disposition	Effective parenting (characterized by warmth, structure, and high expectations)
Positive social orientation, including relationships and peer friendships	Access to warm guidance from other extended family members
High self-efficacy, self-confidence, and self-esteem	School- or community-related
Achievement orientation with high expectations	Access to relationship with positive adult models in a variety of extrafamilial contexts, including schools
Resilient belief systems, faith	Connections with at least one or a variety of pro-social organizations
Higher rate of engagement in productive activities	Access to responsive, high-quality schools

Source: From "Risk and Resilience: Implications for the Delivery of Educational and Mental Health Services in Schools," by B. Doll and M. Lyon, 1998, *School Psychology Review, 27,* p. 354. Copyright 1998 by the National Association of School Psychologists. Adapted with permission.

positive response from their caregivers. Studies have shown that this interaction between temperament and caregiver response shapes resilience (Rutter, 1989). Another example of a behavioral characteristic thought to be innate and related to resilience is a person's motivational system (Masten & Coatsworth, 1998; White, 1959). Babies appear to be naturally motivated: They delight in cooing, blowing bubbles, and throwing food on the floor. If caregivers receive these behaviors well, a child will continue to develop pleasure from his or her sense of mastery, or the ability to manipulate the environment. Clearly, this phenomenon—thought to be part of the constellation of factors that contribute to resilience—may originally be an innate characteristic but cannot develop without positive interaction with the caregiving environment.

This viewpoint is best expressed by Jean Ellison, who was the first person who graduated from Harvard University despite the challenges of having become a quadriplegic following an accident when she was in the seventh grade. Her mother, who had been able to attend every class with her to serve as an aide, recalled that Jean awoke from the accident saying, "When can I get back to school? Will I be left back?" At her graduation, she was quoted in the *New York Times:* "I've always felt that whatever circumstances I confront, it's just a question of continuing to live and not letting what I can't do define what I can" (Steinberg, 2000, p. 17).

Resilient behaviors, then, can be either hindered or fostered by environmental factors. Although development may be shaped by a person's genetic mechanisms and biological substrate, such factors are mediated by the environment (Rutter, 1989). For example, the natural biological propensity to be resilient may be undermined by factors such as poor prenatal care, low birth weight, domestic violence, and smoking (Bradley et al., 1994; Rowe & Kahn, 1998). On the other side of the equation, the natural tendency toward resilience may be strengthened by environmental factors, such as family support. In addition, biological mechanisms may present risks in some situations and be protective in others. For example, carrying a heterozygote status for sickle-cell disease is a serious risk factor, yet it also provides immunity or protection from malaria (Rutter, 1993). According to the World Health Organization, malaria infects up to 500 million people each year. Furthermore, there is increasing evidence that health care will be revolutionized by regenerative medicine that depends on the body's ability to heal itself (Wade, 2000). Clearly, resilience is an outcome of the interaction between nature and nurture.

Psychological Characteristics

Particular psychological traits, for example self-esteem and self-efficacy (Werner, 1989), hope, personal control, self-understanding (Beardslee, 1989), and learned optimism (Seligman, 1990), are often associated with resilience (see Table 2.3). Rutter (1985) has argued that people with a sense of self-esteem and self-efficacy—those who appreciate their own worth—are more likely to cope successfully. Similarly, Werner (1989) has contended that a core element in the lives of resilient people is the feeling that they can overcome the odds. The person who is resilient, then, has the capability to bounce back from adverse events strengthened and more resourceful. He or she actively responds to crises and challenges without becoming victimized (Walsh, 1998). Survivors often emerge from crises with strengths they might not otherwise have developed. "Love prevails over hate" (Higgins, 1994, p. 100). From the psychological vantage point, resilience is the development of clusters of self-protective behaviors or strengths.

In their summary of 20 years of prevention and early intervention research, Guralnick and Neville (1997) noted that particular psychological phenomena, including attachment, social competence, and self-reflection, are associated with resilience. Masten and Coatsworth (1998) found that resilient children owe much of their success to soothing, caring, and stimulating effects of the attachment system. Attachment to a caregiver, which involves a child's innate ability to bond with a parental figure, is a key element in successful adaptation. For example, a close tie to at least one parent has been found to be protective in situations such as divorce, child maltreatment, and homelessness. In addition, when there is severe trauma, such as war or a natural disaster, being near a primary caregiver is one of the most potent predictors of a child's more positive reaction (Coles, 1972; Duncan & Coles, 1989; Masten & Coatsworth, 1998). Furthermore, attachment to parents and surrogate figures is thought to have an effect throughout the life cycle (Ainsworth, 1989).

Practitioners' understanding of the nature of a caregiving system is critical in the development of an intervention strategy. For example, practitioners should know that kinship bonding, which often encompasses father–son attachment (Belsky, 1996; Greif, Hrabowski, & Maton, 1998), may differ with family interactional style (Marvin & Stewart, 1990). In addition, practitioners may want to explore how a client's attachment relates to academic achievement, peer relationships, and general social skills (Benoit & Parker, 1994; Cassidy, Kirsh, Scolton, & Parke, 1996; Hawkins, Doueck, & Lishner, 1988). Moreover, caregiving systems serve multiple functions over and above the provision of physical care, such as helping an infant learn to self-regulate and explore his or her environment (Masten & Coatsworth, 1998). Because attachment is a lifelong process that can be fostered through intervention, such information is critical to assessment.

Practitioners also need to assess the quality of the caregiver–child bond. Bowlby (1969, 1973a, 1973b, 1980) proposed that children and their mothers have three inherent patterns of bonding: (1) secure attachment, (2) anxious or insecure attachment, and (3) detachment. He hypothesized that the more secure the child's attachment, the better able that child will be at forming adult relationships, being autonomous, and making independent judgments. As Coles (1972) pointed out, if a child can develop secure attachments early in life, he or she will have the necessary resilience to deal with adverse life events as an adult.

Because positive attachments can continue to be fostered by teachers, community role models, and mental health workers, secure attachment is an important element of the resilience-based approach. In addition, understanding how children bond is a central concept for developing prevention and early intervention programs. For example, Bowlby (1984) related violence to how children are taught by family members to deal with anger. He urged mental health workers to understand the dynamics of this phenomenon among high-risk individuals as they plan psychoeducational intervention.

Competence, a pattern of effective adaptation, is another essential factor contributing to resilience. People develop competence through daily interaction with their environments. Although a child's competence may be thwarted by poverty, family violence, or lack of opportunity, it can simultaneously be fostered by caregivers, schools, and peers. As the life context changes, so too can one's sense of competence. Everyday competence remains a concern throughout life (Greene & Kropf, in press). For example, older people's ability to care for themselves, manage their affairs, and live independent, quality lives in their communities is of major significance to successful aging (Tinetti & Powell, 1993; Willis, 1996a, 1996b; see chapter 14). Because everyday competence is related to a person's ability to perform tasks associated with daily living (Lawton, 1982), practitioners need to understand how a person copes within his or her milieu. For example, in the case of an older adult or a person with developmental disabilities, the social worker can explore how well the person functions in his or her home. Can he or she negotiate the stairs, get in and out of the bath, or prepare his or her own meals?

Research has also found that people who demonstrate *self-understanding,* an internal psychological process in which a person makes causal relationships or linkages between experiences in the world and his or her inner feelings, are more resilient (Beardslee, 1989). According to Masten and Coatsworth (1998), being self-regulated is another psychological characteristic that is key to resilient behavior and means that a person gains a set of skills related to increased control over his or her attention, emotions, and behavior. Such prosocial behavior, which begins to emerge in the second year of life, is central to success within the classroom and throughout life.

Another psychological phenomenon important to resilience is self-efficacy (Rutter, 1983). *Self-efficacy* is the mechanism whereby people achieve a greater capacity to control personal events. According to Bandura (1977a), self-efficacy develops as people learn that they can be successful. And as people become convinced that they can successfully perform particular activities or reach specific goals, they are better able to affect their environments (Bandura, 1977b). Practitioners who adopt a resilience orientation should use strategies to foster client self-efficacy (Benard, 1993) and to empower clients by promoting their innate ability to change (Bandura, Reese, & Adams, 1982; Furstenberg & Rounds, 1995; Greene, 2000; Tinetti & Powell, 1993).

Spiritual Characteristics

In large measure, social welfare institutions have their origins in religious communities. Yet ironically there has been a lack of integration between religion and professional social work. In fact, many practitioners who view social work as a secular profession have chosen to treat religion and religious issues as private concerns (Greene, 1994). However, "as part of the global consciousness that has come to characterize the end of the twentieth century, religion and spirituality have taken on a new and expanded meaning" (Conrad, 1999, p. 63). In the desire to address the whole person in environment, religion and spirituality are increasingly recognized as components of the helping process (Canda & Furman, 1999; Saleebey, 1994).

It is important for the sake of clarity to distinguish between the terms *faith, religion,* and *spirituality* (Joseph, 1988). *Faith* may be viewed as a person's inner system of beliefs about the meaning of life and relationship with the transcendent or God. For some, faith is developed over the course of a lifetime; for others, it may be experienced as a conversion event related to a life crisis such as an illness or the loss of a loved one. In contrast, *religion* is the external expression of a person's faith. It includes beliefs, ethical codes, and various forms of worship—all of which unite one to a moral community. *Religion* has also been defined as the outward expression of an individual's faith or inner system of beliefs. *Spirituality* differs from faith and religion and refers to how a "person seeks to transcend the self in order to discover meaning, belonging, and relatedness to the infinite" (Conrad, 1999, p. 64). Regardless of whether persons participate in particular faith traditions, they may be aware of a spiritual consciousness that informs and directs their lives.

Some theorists have made a connection between spirituality or religion and resilience. According to Canda and Furman (1999), religion involves "adaptive and transformational properties" (p. 54). It is these transcendent, adaptive, transformational, and often-religious qualities that are most associated with resilience. Angell, Dennis, and Dumain (1998) have proposed that "spirituality is a fundamental form of resilience [and] serves as a modifiable resource that can be drawn upon during times of personal crisis" (p. 616).

Developmental conceptualizations have been formulated that explicate the phases of faith and spiritual formation and growth (Farris, 2006; Fowler, 1995; Westerhoff, 1983), and some approaches have been tested empirically. For example, Ramsey and Blieszner's (1999) study on the spiritual resiliency of older women in the Lutheran tradition fills a void in the literature. On the basis of their analysis of focus groups held with persons identified as resilient older women, the researchers found that the participants' faith, religion, and spirituality were highly integrated. The women's life stories revealed that participation in their faith communities was important in providing a positive self-image, a sense of identity, and personal affirmation. Spiritual resilience also provided them with social structure and meaning as well as a sense of social justice and peace through living a simple nonmaterialistic lifestyle. These experiences, in turn, motivated them to reach out to others who experienced need or challenge.

Further analysis of the interviews suggested that the women's faith tradition provided a context in which they engaged in constructive spiritual reframing of the suffering and loss in their lives through forgiveness and genuinely loving relationships with others. However, Ramsey and Blieszner (1999) cautioned that their study might be limited because the findings might be specific to a religious denomination, and they concluded that these developmental formulations cannot be readily generalized across religious denominations.

Regardless of these conceptual and empirical limitations, there is a growing body of conceptual and practice-based evidence for the claims that resilience and spirituality are distinct but interrelated dimensions of the human person. Various studies conducted over the past 25 years have found a strong association between religious practices and mental health (Chatters & Taylor, 1999; Weaver, Flannelly, Flannelly, Koening, & Larson, 1998). Psychological and spiritual growth can also influence the creation of meaning, life affirmation, the redefinition of relationships, and reckoning with death, such as people living with HIV (Dunbar, Mueller, Medina, & Wolf, 1998; Getzel, 1991). Moreover, spirituality and resilience can benefit children coping with parental death (Angell et al., 1998).

The importance of religion and spirituality during times of distress has been witnessed as congregants have rebuilt following church burnings in African American communities (C. S. Carter, 1999). Although these church burnings were a shock, the subsequent rebuilding is a symbol of community struggle and a sense of agency—a feeling that people can take hold. Social workers should remember that spirituality is an important aspect of the resilience approach to treatment that involves the practitioner promoting an individual's or family's own healing resources and marshaling community resources to foster healing and growth (Walsh, 1998).

Social Characteristics

Theorists have hypothesized that socialization is key to a child developing resilient adult behaviors (Hawkins & Weis, 1985). The social characteristics related to resilience develop as the child begins to learn the rules of how the larger group or society conducts itself (Schriver, 2001). This process begins at home and is continued through formal education in the schools. Children who are socially competent use socially appropriate conduct in the classroom, do not break rules, get along with their peers, and usually are more likely to be competent adults (Garmezy, 1991). Positive socialization with peers and community is also known to affect behavior favorably. Hawkins and Weis (1985) have attributed this success to conditions that extend attachment to others, "commitment to conforming behavior, and belief in the conventional order" (p. 73).

Adults who are successful into old age generally maintain and benefit from their social ties (Rowe & Kahn, 1998). Adults who are resilient have the ability to gain social competence; the capacity to be flexible, to be empathetic, to communicate effectively, and to use problem-solving skills; the ability to plan, seek help, and think critically and reflectively; and the ability to develop a sense of critical consciousness, or an awareness of oppressive structures and how to combat them. Greene (2002) captured this struggle in an interview with Eva, a Holocaust survivor sent to England as part of the *Kindertransport*. She reflected on her family and gave insight into her self-resolve:

> You have a big job writing about resilience [she tells the author]. Kids today [in inner cities] are living their own personal Holocaust. It is a shame because all children need nurturing. When I speak to children at inner city schools, I tell them about the Holocaust. I tell them they must give up being a victim. They must find out what they want to do and be, and do it. I was lucky because I had a secure home life until I was thirteen when I was sent to England. When I arrived, I had the longest cry, and then decided to rise to the occasion. (Greene, 2002, p. 9)

Resilience as Adaptation

Resilience refers to a pattern over time, characterized by good eventual adaptation despite developmental risks, acute stressors, or chronic adversities.

—Masten, 1994, p. 5

The ecological–interactional developmental perspective assumes that resilience is a consequence of favorable "goodness of fit" over time.

—Richman & Bowen, 1997, p. 104

For more than half a century, theorists from different streams of scientific thought have sought to better understand people's coping capacity or adaptational processes (Smith & Carlson, 1997; see chapter 1). For example, Schriver (2001) has pointed out that families of color develop a number of adaptive strategies that help them overcome environmental barriers (see chapter 9). *Adaptation* has been defined from an ecological goodness-of-fit perspective (Richman & Bowen, 1997; see chapter 1). From this perspective, resilience is a dynamic process that is "a function of the individual's unique strengths, capacities, vulnerabilities, and 'goodness of fit' with the demands and opportunities of the environment" (Felsman & Vaillant, 1987, p. 289). That is, resilience depends on the extent of the match between an individual's personal characteristics and the qualities of that person's environment. The goodness-of-fit concept also involves a delineation of which personal, family, and environmental factors promote resilience or the opportunity for adaptive functioning (Nash & Fraser, 1998).

Lazarus and Folkman (1984) developed another conceptualization of successful adaptation addressing how people cope with stress. They defined *coping* as "constantly changing cognitive and behavioral efforts to manage specific external and or internal demands that are appraised as taxing or exceeding the resources of the person" (p. 10). This process involves four steps: (1) appraising or determining the meaning of an event ("Was the event stressful or not?"); (2) selecting a coping strategy, including an evaluation of one's resources ("I think this is the strategy I should try"); (3) carrying out the coping strategy ("I will attempt to do this"); and (4) evaluating one's coping efforts ("Have I overcome this event effectively?").

From this standpoint, stressful life events or stressors, such as divorce or natural calamities, usually place an extra burden on people's adaptive capacity. Simultaneously, resilience can be enhanced through repeated, successful experiences in coping with stress (Masten & Garmezy, 1984). Therefore, *resilience* is increasingly defined as successful adaptation in the face of adversity (Fraser et al., 1999; Gilgun, 1996; Masten, 1994). According to Masten (1994), "The study of resilience [actually] begins with a 'diagnosis' of good adaptation despite risk or adversity" (p. 5). Masten and Coatsworth (1998) suggested that, to identify resilience, practitioners would have to make two judgments: (1) Is there a significant threat to an individual by virtue of a high-risk status such as poverty or homelessness? (2) Is the quality of that person's adaptation good?

To understand circumstances that threaten the process of resilience, Masten (1994) delineated six interacting ingredients that constitute the process of adaptation: (1) a person's developmental path or competence over time, (2) the nature of the adversity faced by the individual, (3) the individual's personal and social assets and risks, (4) individual characteristics that serve as vulnerabilities or protective factors, (5) environmental challenges or protective factors, and (6) the context of adaptation. It is understood that in communities in which there is a high level of violence and poverty, adaptation or resilience is undermined. In such situations, the social worker's goal is to choose interventions that improve adaptation or the person–environment match (Monkman, 1991). According to Dr. Jesse Harris,

> You have to believe in resilience when you have seen what I have. In the situation of the civil war in Mozambique, children of 12 to 16 years of age where forced to commit atrocities. I was sent there to train local people in how to help them heal. We used what we call psychodrama. The children lived together with the community workers and reenacted

the war. This time, they were the victors. They also learned to be caring people again. (J. Harris, former dean, University of Maryland School of Social Work, Baltimore, personal communication, June 12, 2000)

Variations in Resilience: A Diversity Perspective

Deciding whether a child is competent can be difficult when a child lives in a cultural or community context that differs markedly from the larger society in which the community or cultural group is embedded.

—Masten & Coatsworth, 1998, p. 207

Variations in coping are a function of client context, including such factors as gender, race, ethnicity, sexual orientation, religion, and ability. "Because social workers are serving increasingly diverse constituencies, the expectation that practitioners be culturally competent has never been so great" (Greene, 2000, p. 43). Therefore, the definition of *diversity* has expanded to encompass people from various cultures and varying power positions, or those who may be marginalized in society. Cross-cultural social work guards against using a single standard for human behavior and involves strategies that are effective in working with people and communities other than those of the practitioner.

For example, in their discussion of effective coping strategies among African Americans, Daly, Jennings, Beckett, and Leashore (1995) pointed out that an Africentric orientation to coping recognizes affective as well as rational aspects of personal coping styles. The emphasis in the Africentric view is on the human collective and how to foster coping skills at the family, community, and organizational levels. Thus, successful coping among African American men is attributed to individual, family, and societal factors.

The literature on resiliency in ethnic families frequently refers to the importance of a relational framework in understanding families (McCubbin, McCubbin, Thompson, & Thompson, 1998). For example, Agbayani-Siewert (1988) noted that Filipino American families view depending on one another as a family obligation that must be reciprocated, whereas Trask (1998) pointed out that Native Hawaiians generally place affective ties above money making and career.

Another example of variation in client context as it affects resilience was described in a study of adaptation among minority women. Bachay and Cingel (1999) examined 28 women's sense of self-efficacy, faith, and life obstacles. Through focus group discussions, they found that resilience was associated with multiple factors, such as culture, gender, and relationships. However, the women's ability to reframe their barriers to move ahead was a central factor contributing to their resilience. Because the phenomenon of resilience is so multifaceted, Bachay and Cingel chose Butler's (1997) definition of resilience to capture their meaning and to best focus their work:

> What we call resilience is turning out to be an interactive and systemic phenomenon, the product of complex relationship of inner strengths and outer help throughout a person's life span. Resilience is not only an individual matter. It is the outward and visible sign of a web of relationships and experiences that teach people mastery, doggedness, love, moral courage and hope. (Butler, 1997, p. 26)

Variations in resilience involve goodness of fit. For example, Taylor (1991), in a discussion of social competence and early school transitions for African American children, concluded that as a child makes a transition to school, resilience is related to the relationship between child and teacher—the goodness of fit between the child's entry behavior and the teacher's expectations for that behavior. To the extent that a teacher is prejudiced or does not understand a child's cultural expressions, there can be a lack of fit. However, teachers who use culturally sensitive means to foster a child's learning of school-related tasks can help the child establish social competence.

> Yes. I want to go on record. I have figured out how I am able to operate in two or three different worlds. Why not get angry [about racism] and not shoot everything up. I was not brought up that way. I was taught to fight if necessary. I was taught the song, "Jesus loves the little children. All the children of the world—red, yellow, black, and white. For he loves the little children of the world." This was my baseline belief.
>
> I believe that if you don't have belief in your own possibilities, then you can't do anything. This belief has to be reinforced by people and institutions. For example, my high school teacher encouraged me to enter the cultural Olympics and I won. This renewed my belief in myself and opened opportunities. You must have belief in yourself that others help you use. The same is true for social work treatment that helps you move forward and be regenerated. (M. Battle, former executive director, National Association of Social Workers [NASW], Washington, DC, personal communication, December 12, 2000)

Resilience: A Life-Course Phenomenon

War, pollution, unemployment, natural disasters, divorce, "getting ahead," and illness all make us painfully aware of our daily struggles with adversities.

Whether we master these stresses and prosper or become their victim, there is little question that they provide the scientist (and layman) with vital and abundant material for observation and systematic study of human adaptation.

—MONAT & LAZARUS, 1977, P. 1

Resilience needs to be understood within a temporal context. Namely, what are the particular geopolitical or economic events of the time (Hareven, 1996)? The life-course perspective is a useful way of understanding individuals and families as they develop within a larger societal context during their lifetimes (Schriver, 2001). The life-course perspective suggests that people continue to develop and learn across their lifespan (Atchley, 1999). The perspective also assumes that psychosocial development is not uniform but rather reflects social, cultural, and historical change.

In discussing the life course, a distinction is made among *individual time,* which refers to an individual's life continuity or life story; *historical time,* which deals with how people of a particular cohort are affected by social change; and *social time,* which encompasses transitions and life events in families, groups, and communities. Although much of the resilience research originally focused on children at risk, there is a growing body of knowledge about resilience across diverse populations over the life course (Greene, Cohen, Gonzalez, & Lee, 2009; McCubbin et al., 1998; Miller & MacIntosh, 1999).

Life Events

Resilience needs to be understood as a life-event phenomenon. To clarify that complex concept, several alternative topologies have been developed to classify life experiences. Borden (1992) has proposed that adverse events—those that may threaten a person's basic assumptions about self-resilience—be classified into three categories: (1) normative age-graded events, or those shaped by biological and social norms, such as death or retirement; (2) normative historical events, or those experienced by members of a cohort, such as a depression, war, or political shifts; and (3) nonnormative events, or those that are idiosyncratic or limited to a small number of people, such as illness or disability.

Bell (1995) has offered another classification for understanding traumatic events, or those events that lie so far outside a person's usual life experiences that they may overwhelm that person's coping capacity. She categorized these events as natural catastrophes, such as floods, hurricanes, or earthquakes; accidental catastrophes, such as malfunctioning or fatal airplane incidents; and human-induced catastrophes, such as murder, hostage taking, or assault. These types of events are often ameliorated when the practitioner is called in to conduct crisis debriefing to help reduce excessive stress and anxiety and to accelerate the natural recovery process. For example, following Hurricane Katrina, Louisiana NASW members nationwide joined forces with the North Carolina NASW chapter to help people in need of crisis intervention. These various perspectives for thinking about life events give social work practitioners a common message: Social work practice requires an understanding of the nature of stress in everyday life and of those events that deluge natural coping capacities.

Resilience and the Life Course

Resilience is not a fixed characteristic but varies with how people withstand stress across the life course (Winfield, 1994). The concept of resilience can be elucidated through an examination of how people survive adverse and natural events at various times across the life course. For example, in a discussion of the context of resilient behaviors, Gilgun (1996) suggested that people who are not adapting well at one point in their lives may become more adaptive if they have social, economic, and emotional opportunities such as education and work.

Gerontologists have also contributed to an understanding of how to promote continued competence among older adults by "mobilizing coping skills and resources to deal with crises" (Atchley, 1999, p. 77; see chapter 14). Evidence is also mounting that older adults who maintain an optimistic life view outlive their pessimistic counterparts (see chapter 14). Clearly, research has documented that although stressful events that occur at any time of life may threaten people's sense of worthiness and resilience and overextend adaptive capacity, intervention can foster the natural tendency to bounce back (Armstrong, Lund, McWright, & Tichenor, 1995; Borden, 1992).

Resilience and Developmental Tasks

The judgment of whether a person is adapting well and remaining competent or is resilient at various points in the lifespan is often made in reference to normative developmental tasks (Fraser, 1997; Masten, 1994). That is, in each study of resilience, the researcher uses certain criteria to make a judgment about desirable or undesirable behaviors (Rigsby, 1994). Developmental tasks are evaluations of how a person, child, or adult is adapting based on pooled, generalized knowledge of human development. That is, an individual's behavior is considered to be resilient "on the basis of normal development [or] psychosocial milestones" (Masten, 1994, pp. 3–4). For example, using retrospective data from clinical interviews, Wolin and Wolin (1995) identified seven resiliencies that are developed across the life course and that can be tapped in treatment: (1) *insight*—knowing and accepting that one's family of origin had troubles; (2) *independence*—setting safe boundaries with one's family; (3) *relationships*—connecting with, recruiting, and

TABLE 2.4 Developmental Phases of the Seven Resiliencies

Seven Resiliencies	Child	Adolescent	Adult
Insight	Sensing	Knowing	Understanding
Independence	Straying	Disengaging	Separating
Relationships	Connecting	Recruiting	Attaching
Initiative	Exploring	Working	Generating
Creativity	Playing	Shaping	Composing
Humor	Playing	Shaping	Laughing
Morality	Judging	Valuing	Serving

Source: From "Resilience among Youth Growing Up in Substance-abusing Families," by S. Wolin and S. Wolin, 1995, *Pediatric Clinics of North America, 42,* p. 425. Copyright 1995 by W. B. Saunders. Used with permission.

attaching to others; (4) *initiative*—asserting oneself to master the environment; (5) *creativity*—using one's imagination; (6) *humor*—mixing the absurd and the awful; and (7) *morality*—developing the ability to distinguish good from bad. Table 2.4 outlines how these resiliencies develop over time.

Although people's developmental paths continue to be of interest in understanding resilience, theorists are increasingly discussing how an individual's behavior is an outcome of multiple and complex influences over time. Some developmental tasks, such as language development and bonding, may be universal; however, many of these expectations for behavior or milestones reflect mainstream popular culture (Masten & Coatsworth, 1998). In addressing family developmental tasks, B. Carter and McGoldrick (1999) pointed out, "Although it is statistically accurate to outline the widely experienced stages of the family life cycle, focusing on marriage, the birth and development of children, and aging, no single list is sufficient or inclusive" (p. xv). They have suggested that practitioners not think that developmental stages are inherent and identical for all families but rather that stages and the associated developmental tasks are flexible—shaped by family form, culture, and historical period.

Use the CD by Michael Wright to articulate a historically founded definition of resilience. Articulate resilience as a theory integrating biopsychosocial spiritual assessment, adaptation, and diversity across the life course with individuals and families.

You will find a case study on your CD: *Defining Resiliency Theory*

References

Agbayani-Siewert, P. (1988). *Social service utilization of Filipino Americans in Los Angeles*. Unpublished manuscript, University of California, Los Angeles, School of Social Welfare.

Ainsworth, M. (1989). Attachments beyond infancy. *American Psychologist, 44*, 709–716.

Angell, G. B., Dennis, B. G., & Dumain, L. E. (1998). Spirituality, resilience, and narrative: Coping with parental death. *Families in Society, 79*, 615–630.

Anthony, E. J., & Cohler, B. J. (1987). *The invulnerable child*. New York: Guilford Press.

Armstrong, K. R., Lund, P. E., McWright, L. T., & Tichenor, V. (1995). Multiple stressor debriefing and the American Red Cross: The East Bay Hills fire experience. *Social Work, 40*, 83–90.

Atchley, R. C. (1999). *Continuity and adaptation in aging*. Baltimore, MD: Johns Hopkins University Press.

Bachay, J. B., & Cingel, P. A. (1999). Restructuring resilience: Emerging voices. *Affilia, 14*, 162–175.

Bandura, A. (1977a). Self-efficacy: Toward a unifying theory of behavior change. *Psychological Review, 84*, 191–215.

Bandura, A. (1977b). *Social learning theory*. Englewood Cliffs, NJ: Prentice Hall.

Bandura, A., Reese, L., & Adams, N. E. (1982). Microanalysis of action and fear arousal as a function of differential levels of perceived self-efficacy. *Journal of Personality and Social Psychology, 43*, 5–21.

Beardslee, W. (1989). The role of self-understanding in resilient individuals: The development of a perspective. *American Journal of Orthopsychiatry, 59*, 266–278.

Begun, A. L. (1993). Human behavior and the social environment: The vulnerability, risk, and resilience model. *Journal of Social Work Education, 29*, 26–36.

Bell, J. L. (1995). Traumatic event debriefing: Service delivery designs and the role of social work. *Social Work, 40*, 36–43.

Belsky, J. (1996). Parent, infant, and social-contextual antecedents of father–son attachment security. *Developmental Psychology, 32*, 905–913.

Benard, B. (1993). Fostering resilience in kids. *Educational Leadership, 51*, 444–498.

Benard, B. (1995). *Fostering resilience in children*. New York: ERIC Clearinghouse on Elementary and Early Childhood Education. (ERIC Document Reproduction Service No. ED386327.) Retrieved from http://www.eric.ed.gov/PDFS/ED386327.pdf

Benard, B. (1997). *Turning it around for all youth: From risk to resilience*. New York: ERIC Clearinghouse on Urban Education. (ERIC Document Reproduction Service No. ED412309.) Retrieved from http://www.eric.ed.gov/PDFS/ED412309.pdf

Benoit, D., & Parker, K. C. H. (1994). Stability and transmission of attachment across three generations. *Child Development, 65*, 1444–1456.

Borden, W. (1992). Narrative perspectives in psychosocial intervention following adverse life events. *Social Work, 37*, 125–141.

Bowlby, J. (1969). *Attachment and loss* (1st ed.). New York: Basic Books.

Bowlby, J. (1973a). Affectional bonds: Their nature and origin. In R. S. Weiss (Ed.), *Loneliness: The experience of emotional and social isolation* (pp. 38–52). Cambridge, MA: MIT Press.

Bowlby, J. (1973b). *Attachment and loss* (2nd ed.). New York: Basic Books.

Bowlby, J. (1980). *Attachment and loss* (3rd ed.). New York: Basic Books.

Bowlby, J. (1984). Violence in the family as a disorder of the attachment and caregiving systems. *American Journal of Psychoanalysis, 44,* 9–26.

Bradley, R. H., Whiteside, L., Mundfrom, D. J., Casey, P. H., Kelleher, K. J., & Pope, S. K. (1994). Early indications of resilience and their relation to experiences in the home environments of low birth weight, premature children living in poverty. *Child Development, 65,* 346–360.

Bronfenbrenner, U. (1989). Ecological systems theory. *Annals of Child Development, 6,* 187–249.

Bronfenbrenner, U., Moen, P., & Garbarino, J. (1984). Family and community. In R. Parke (Ed.), *Review of child development research* (Vol. 7, pp. 283–328). Chicago: University of Chicago Press.

Bumiller, E. (2003, September 7). Who won? 9/11/01. *New York Times,* p. 1.

Butler, K. (1997). The anatomy of resilience. *Family Therapy Networker, 3–4,* 22–31.

Canda, E. R. (1988). Spirituality, religious diversity, and social work practice. *Social Casework, 5,* 238–246.

Canda, E. R., & Furman, L. D. (1999). *Spiritual diversity in social work practice.* New York: Free Press.

Carter, B., & McGoldrick, M. (1999). *The expanded family life cycle: Individual, family, and social perspectives.* Boston: Allyn & Bacon.

Carter, C. S. (1999). Church burning in African-American communities: Implications for empowerment practice. *Social Work, 44,* 62–68.

Cassidy, J., Kirsh, S., Scolton, K., & Parke, R. D. (1996). Attachment and representations of peer relationships. *Developmental Psychology, 32,* 892–904.

Chatters, L., & Taylor, R. J. (1999, October). *Contextual factors in religion/spirituality and health.* Unpublished paper presented at the Spirituality, Religion, and Health Workshop sponsored by the Office of Behavioral and Social Sciences Research, National Institute of Health, Bethesda, MD.

Coles, R. (1972). *Farewell to the south.* Boston: Little, Brown.

Conrad, A. P. (1999). Professional tools for religiously and spiritually sensitive social work practice. In R. R. Greene (Ed.), *Human behavior theory and social work practice* (2nd ed., pp. 63–72). New York: Aldine de Gruyter.

Cowan, P. A., Cowan, C. P., & Shulz, M. S. (1996). Thinking about risk and resilience in families. In M. Hetherington & E. A. Blechman (Eds.), *Stress, coping, and resilience in children and families* (pp. 1–38). Mahwah, NJ: Erlbaum.

Daly, A., Jennings, J., Beckett, J. O., & Leashore, B. R. (1995). Effective coping strategies of African-Americans. *Social Work, 40,* 240–248.

Doll, B., & Lyon, M. (1998). Risk and resilience: Implications for the delivery of education and mental health services in schools. *School Psychology Review, 27,* 348–363.

Dunbar, H. T., Mueller, C. W., Medina, C., & Wolf, T. (1998). Psychological and spiritual growth in women living with HIV. *Social Work, 43,* 144–154.

Duncan, T., & Coles, R. (Eds.). (1989). *The children in our times: Studies in the development of resiliency.* New York: Brunner/Mazel.

Dyer, J., & McGuinness, T. (1996). Resilience: Analysis of the concept. *Archives of Psychiatric Nursing, 10,* 276–282.

Farris, K. (2006). The role of the African-American pastors in mental health care. In R. R. Greene (Ed.), *Contemporary issues of care* (pp. 159–182). New York: Haworth Press.

Fast, J. (2003). After Columbine: How people mourn sudden death. *Social Work, 48,* 484–491.

Felsman, J. K., & Vaillant, G. E. (1987). Resilient children as adults: A 40-year study. In E. J. Anthony & B. J. Cohler (Eds.), *The invulnerable child* (pp. 289–314). New York: Guilford Press.

Fonagy, P., Steele, M., Steele, H., Higgitt, A., & Target, M. (1994). The Emmanuel Miller Memorial Lecture 1992: The theory and practice of resilience. *Journal of Child Psychology and Psychiatry, 35,* 231–257.

Fowler, J. (1995). *Stages of faith: The psychology of human development and the quest for meaning.* New York: HarperCollins.

Fraser, M. (Ed.). (1997). *Risk and resilience in childhood.* Washington, DC: NASW Press.

Fraser, M. W., Richman, J. M., & Galinsky, M. J. (1999). Risk, protection, and resilience: Toward a conceptual framework for social work practice. *Social Work Research, 23,* 129–208.

Furstenberg, A. L., & Rounds, K. A. (1995). Self-efficacy as a target for social work intervention. *Families in Society, 76,* 587–595.

Garbarino, J. (1999). *Lost boys: Why our sons turn out violent and how we can save them.* New York: Free Press.

Garmezy, N. (1991). Resiliency and vulnerability to adverse developmental outcomes associated with poverty. *American Behavioral Scientist, 34,* 416–430.

Garmezy, N. (1993). Children in poverty: Resilience despite risk. *Psychiatry, 56,* 127–136.

Getzel, G. S. (1991). Survival modes for people with AIDS in groups. *Social Work, 36,* 7–11.

Gilgun, J. F. (1996). Human development and adversity in ecological perspective, Part 1: A conceptual framework. *Families in Society, 77,* 395–402.

Gordon, E. W., & Song, L. D. (1994). Variations in the experience of resilience. In M. C. Wang & E. W. Gordon (Eds.), *Educational resilience in inner-city America* (pp. 27–44). Hillsdale, NJ: Erlbaum.

Greene, R. R. (1994). *Human behavior theory: A diversity framework.* New York: Aldine de Gruyter.

Greene, R. R. (1999). *Human behavior theory and social work practice.* Hawthorne: Aldine de Gruyter.

Greene, R. R. (2000). *Social work with the aged and their families.* Hawthorne: Aldine de Gruyter.

Greene, R. R. (2002). Holocaust survivors: A study in resilience. *Journal of Gerontological Social Work, 37,* 3–18.

Greene, R. R. (2007). *Social work practice: A risk and resilience perspective.* Monterey, CA: Brooks/Cole.

Greene, R. R. (2008a). *Human behavior theory and social work practice* (3rd ed.). New Brunswick, NJ: Aldine Transaction Press.

Greene, R. R. (2008b). Resilience. In T. Mizrahi & L. E. Davis (Eds.-in-Chief), *Encyclopedia of social work* (20th ed., Vol. 3, pp. 526–531). Washington, DC: NASW Press & Oxford University Press.

Greene, R. R., Armour, M., Hantman, S., Graham, S., & Sharabi, A. (2010). Conceptualizing a Holocaust survivorship model. *Journal of Human Behavior and the Social Environment, 20,* 423–439.

Greene, R. R., Cohen, H., Gonzalez, J., & Lee, Y. (2009). *Narratives of resilience and social and economic justice.* Washington, DC: NASW Press.

Greene, R. R., & Kropf, N. (2011). *Competence theoretical concepts.* New Brunswick, NJ: Transaction Press.

Greif, G. L., Hrabowski, F. A., & Maton, K. I. (1998). African-American fathers of high-achieving sons: Using outstanding members of an at-risk population to guide intervention. *Families in Society, 79,* 45–52.

Grotberg, E. H. (1995, September). *The international resilience project: Research, application, and policy.* Paper presented at the Symposio Internacional Stress e Violencia, Lisbon, Portugal.

Guralnick, M. J., & Neville, B. (1997). Designing early intervention programs to promote children's social competence. In M. J. Guralnick (Ed.), *The effectiveness of early intervention* (pp. 579–610). Baltimore: Brookes.

Hareven, T. K. (1996). *Aging and generational relations over the life course: A historical and cross-cultural perspective.* Hawthorne: Aldine de Gruyter.

Hawkins, J. D., Doueck, H. J., & Lishner, D. M. (1988). Changing teaching practices in mainstream classrooms to improve bonding and behavior of low achievers. *American Educational Research Journal, 25,* 31–50.

Hawkins, J. D., & Weis, J. G. (1985). The social development model: An integrated approach to delinquency prevention. *Journal of Primary Prevention, 6,* 73–97.

Higgins, G. (1994). *Resilient adults: Overcoming a cruel past.* San Francisco, CA: Jossey-Bass.

Hinkle, L. E. (1974). The effect of exposure to cultural change, social change, and changes in interpersonal relationships on health. In S. B. Dohrenwend & B. P. Dohrenwend (Eds.), *Stressful life events* (pp. 4–44). New York: Wiley.

Jessor, R. (1993). Successful adolescent development among youth in high-risk settings. *American Psychologist, 48,* 117–126.

Joseph, M. V. (1988). Religion and social work practice. *Social Casework, 69,* 443–452.

Kirby, L. D., & Fraser, M. W. (1997). Risk and resilience in childhood. In M. Fraser (Ed.), *Risk and resilience in childhood* (pp. 10–33). Washington, DC: NASW Press.

Lawton, M. P. (1982). Competence, environmental press, and the adaptation of older people. In M. P. Lawton, P. G. Windley, & T. O. Byerts (Eds.), *Aging and the environment: Theoretical approaches* (pp. 33–59). New York: Springer.

Lazarus, R., & Folkman, S. (1984). *Stress, appraisal, and coping.* New York: Springer.

Lifton, R. J. (1993). *The protean self: Human resilience in an age of fragmentation.* Chicago: University of Chicago Press.

Marvin, R. S., & Stewart, R. B. (1990). A family systems framework for the study of attachment. In M. T. Greenberg, D. Cicchetti, & E. M. Cummings (Eds.), *Attachment in the pre-school years: Theory, research and innovation* (pp. 51–86). Chicago: University of Chicago Press.

Masten, A. (1987). Resilience in development: Implications of the study of successful adaptation for developmental psychopathology. In D. Ciccheti (Ed.), *The emergence of a discipline: Rochester Symposium on Developmental Psychopathology* (pp. 261–294). Hillsdale, NJ: Erlbaum.

Masten, A. (1994). Resilience in individual development: Successful adaptation despite risk and adversity. In M. C. Wang & E. W. Gordon (Eds.), *Educational resilience in inner-city America: Challenges and prospects* (pp. 3–25). Hillsdale, NJ: Erlbaum.

Masten, A. S., & Coatsworth, J. D. (1998). The development of competence in favorable and unfavorable environments. *American Psychologist, 53,* 205–220.

Masten, A. S., & Garmezy, N. (1984). Risk, vulnerability, and protective factors in developmental psychopathology. In B. B. Lahey & A. E. Kazdin (Eds.), *Advances in clinical child psychology* (Vol. 8, pp. 1–51). New York: Plenum Press.

McCubbin, H. I., McCubbin, M. A., Thompson, A. I., & Thompson, E. A. (1998). Resiliency in ethnic families: A conceptual model for predicting family adjustment and adaptation. In H. I. McCubbin, E. A. Thompson, A. I. Thompson, & J. E. Fromer (Eds.), *Resiliency in Native American and immigrant families* (pp. 3–48). Thousand Oaks, CA: Sage.

Miller, D. B., & MacIntosh, R. (1999). Promoting resilience in urban African American adolescents: Racial socialization and identity as protective factors. *Social Work Research, 23,* 159–170.

Monat, A., & Lazarus, R. S. (Eds.). (1977). *Stress and coping: An anthology.* New York: Columbia University Press.

Monkman, M. M. (1991). Outcome objectives in social work practice: Person and environment. *Social Work, 36,* 253–258.

Nash, J., & Fraser, M. W. (1998). After-school care for children: A resilience-based approach. *Families in Society, 79,* 370–382.

Palmer, N. (1997). Resilience in adult children of alcoholics: A nonpathological approach to social work practice. *Health and Social Work, 22,* 201–209.

Ramsey, J., & Blieszner, R. (1999). *Spiritual resiliency in older women.* London: Sage.

Richman, J. M., & Bowen, G. (1997). School failure: An ecological-interactional-developmental approach. In M. Fraser (Ed.), *Risk and resilience in childhood* (pp. 95–116). Washington, DC: NASW Press.

Rigsby, L. (1994). The Americanization of resilience: Deconstructing research practice. In M. Wang & E. Gordon (Eds.), *Educational resilience in inner-city America* (pp. 85–94). Hillsdale, NJ: Erlbaum.

Rowe, J. W., & Kahn, R. L. (1998). *Successful aging.* New York: Pantheon Books.

Rutter, M. (1981). Stress, coping and development: Some issues and some questions. *Journal of Child Psychology and Psychiatry, 22,* 323–356.

Rutter, M. (1983). School effects on pupil progress: Research findings and policy implications. *Child Development, 54,* 1–29.

Rutter, M. (1985). Resilience in the face of adversity: Protective factors and resistance to psychiatric disorder. *British Journal of Psychiatry, 147,* 589–611.

Rutter, M. (1987). Psychological resilience and protective mechanisms. *American Journal of Orthopsychiatry, 57,* 316–331.

Rutter, M. (1989). Pathways from childhood to adult life. *Journal of Psychology and Psychiatry, 30,* 23–51.

Rutter, M. (1993). Resilience: Some conceptual considerations. *Journal of Adolescent Health, 14,* 626–631.

Saleebey, D. (1994). Culture, theory, and narrative: The interpretation of meaning in practice. *Social Work, 39,* 351–359.

Saleebey, D. (1997). Is it feasible to teach HBSE from a strengths perspective, in contrast to one emphasizing limitations and weakness? Yes. In M. Bloom & W. C. Klein (Eds.), *Controversial issues in human behavior in the social environment* (pp. 33–48). Boston: Allyn & Bacon.

Schriver, J. (2001). *Human behavior and the social environment.* Boston: Allyn & Bacon.

Seligman, M. (1990). *Learned optimism.* New York: Random House.

Smith, C., & Carlson, B. E. (1997). Stress, coping, and resilience in children and youth. *Social Service Review, 71,* 231–256.

Spitz, R. A. (1946). Anaclitic depression. *Psychoanalytic Study of the Child, 2,* 313–342.

Steinberg, J. (2000, May 17). An unrelenting drive, and a Harvard degree. *New York Times,* pp. 1, 20.

Stewart, M., Reid, G., & Mangham, C. (1997). Fostering children's resilience. *Journal of Pediatric Nursing, 12,* 21–31.

Taylor, A. R. (1991). Social competence and the early school transition for African-American children. *Education and Urban Society, 24,* 15–26.

Tinetti, M. E., & Powell, L. (1993). Fear of falling and low self-efficacy: A cause of dependence in elderly persons. *Journal of Gerontology: Medical Sciences, 48,* M35–M38.

Trask, H. (1998). Native sovereignty: A strategy for Hawaiian family survival. In H. I. McCubbin, E. A. Thompson, A. I. Thompson, & J. E. Fromer (Eds.), *Resiliency in Native American and immigrant families* (pp. 133–142). Thousand Oaks, CA: Sage.

Wade, N. (2000, November 7). Teaching the body to heal itself. *New York Times,* pp. D1, D8.

Walsh, F. (1998). *Strengthening family resilience.* New York: Guilford Press.

Weaver, A., Flannelly, L., Flannelly, K., Koenig, H., & Larson, D. (1998). An analysis of research on religious and spiritual variables in three major mental health nursing journals. *Issues in Mental Health Nursing, 19,* 263–276.

Werner, E. E. (1989). High-risk children in young adulthood: A longitudinal study from birth to 32 years. *American Journal of Orthopsychiatry, 59,* 72–81.

Werner, E. E., & Smith, R. (1992). *Overcoming the odds: High risk children from birth to adulthood.* Ithaca: Cornell University Press.

Westerhoff, J. (1983). *Building God's people.* New York: Seabury Press.

White, R. W. (1959). Motivation reconsidered: The concept of competence. *Psychological Review, 66,* 297–331.

Willis, S. L. (1996a). Everyday cognitive competence in elderly persons: Conceptual issues and empirical findings. *The Gerontologist, 36,* 595–601.

Willis, S. L. (1996b). Everyday problem solving. In J. Birren & K. W. Schaie (Eds.), *Handbook of the psychology of aging* (pp. 287–307). San Diego: Academic Press.

Winfield, L. (1991). Resilience, schooling, and development in African-American youth. *Education and Urban Society, 24,* 5–14.

Winfield, L. F. (1994). *Developing resilience in urban youth.* Retrieved from http://ncrel.org/sdrs/areas/issues/educatrs/leadrshp/le0win.htm

Wolin, S., & Wolin, S. (1995). Resilience among youth growing up in substance abusing families. *Pediatric Clinics of North America, 42,* 415–429.

Resilience: A Social Construct

ROBERTA R. GREENE and NANCY C. LIVINGSTON

On finishing this chapter, students should be able to further:

Apply knowledge of human behavior and the social environment (Educational Policy 2.1.7) by

- Critiquing and applying knowledge to understand person and environment (practice behavior).

Membership—or the ability and opportunity to form associations—is a critical aspect of personal and societal well-being.

—Greene, 1999, p. 52

There have been a wealth of studies which have looked at delinquency, psychiatric conditions, mental retardation and disorders of all kind in childhood. As a result we know a lot about the origins of insecurity and incompetence. . . . However, we know much less about the conditions that facilitate normal [healthy] development. . . . If we can increase our understanding of these influences and harness the knowledge already available to our policies and to our patterns of treatment, perhaps something useful can be achieved.

—Rutter, 1979, p. 33

Describing the resilience of larger scale social phenomena, as this chapter does, requires an exploration of their functional capacity and their collective contribution to their members. Resilience is an ecological phenomenon, and the use of the ecological model broadens the view of what constitutes resilient behavior (Bronfenbrenner, 1979; Carter & McGoldrick, 1999). The ecological metaphor helps practitioners understand the network of influences—family, peer group, school, neighborhood, and society—that may affect individual resilience (Brooks, Nomura, & Cohen, 1989). Through this understanding, practitioners may recognize the social context in which individual resilience is embedded—the larger social systems that act "as nested contexts for social competence" (Walsh, 1998, p. 12). In addition, the ecological perspective directs practitioners' attention to how each system promotes growth-producing person–environment congruent outcomes (Moos, 1987). Furthermore, the ecological perspective helps practitioners better comprehend how microsystems, including families, are affected by the macroenvironment that encompasses the economic and political climate (Schriver, 2010). The commonalities between mental health workers' and developmental economists' views of how a risk and resilience approach can be helpful following a disaster are striking. For example, triage may be used to meet individual needs and attend to infrastructure and community building (Greene & Greene, 2010)

An ecological conception of resilience shifts attention to a systemic, relational perspective. A systemic perspective of resilience focuses on social systems, that is, resilience as a feature of the collective identity of individuals who are members of the system. A systems model maintains that to understand collective behavior, one should not view each member in isolation. Rather, it is necessary to examine the relationships among members, focusing on the social system's properties in their own right (Greene, 2008a). The systemic point of view maintains that it is necessary to understand the assumption that the whole is more than the sum of its parts. According to Buckley (1967), a pioneer in the development of systems thinking,

> the "more than" points to the fact of organization, which imparts to the aggregate characteristics that are not only different from, but *not found in* the components alone; and the "sum of the parts" must be taken to mean, not only their numerical addition, but their unorganized aggregation. (p. 42)

For example, to study the systemic properties of a community, and whether they produce community effects, requires that researchers demonstrate that the particular characteristics of families and individuals can be ascribed to effects stemming from the community as a whole (Bronfenbrenner, Moen, & Garbarino, 1984).

In addition, ecological thinking affords a conceptualization of adaptive behavior at various systems levels. In 1997, Carter and McGoldrick developed perhaps one of the most useful schemas representing the vertical and horizontal flow of stress in the family life cycle that can be applied to understanding the multisystemic nature of resilience (see Figure 3.1). They suggested that stressors are a natural part of life, take various forms, and have the propensity to induce distress that can occur across the life cycle. As can be seen in their visual representation, stress occurs along several dimensions. Nested concentric circles represent the idea that stress can come about at any system level, from the individual to the sociocultural, political, or economic level.

The vertical axis represents the various types of stressors that may occur at each system level (for example, as racism or homophobia at the larger societal level or the disappearance of community at the community level). The horizontal axis represents development over the lifespan within a specific historical context. Developmental stressors may include life-cycle transitions and migration; unpredictable events may include untimely death, chronic illness, accidents, or unemployment; and historical events may encompass economic depression, war, political oppression, or natural disasters.

Assessing resilience accurately requires an understanding of the combined influences of the systems in which clients participate: family, school, peer, work, neighborhood, community, and the larger society. At the same time, practitioners must evaluate whether families and communities can be considered resilient in their own right "if they provide collective adaptation strategies for their members to confront risks or adverse circumstances" (Bartelt, 1994, p. 101), such as a community offering summer park programs as a means of enhancing peer relationships and reducing risk. Social systems–level resilience has not received as much attention as individual-level resilience, and social institutions have been vaguely defined as neutral, supportive, or oppressive. The family systems discussed below have been found to be the most critical and supportive (Rutter, 1985, 1987).

Family Resilience

The concept of family resilience is relatively new and builds on the strengths-based therapy movement (Walsh, 1998). The idea of family resilience takes its major theoretical ideas from developmental psychopathology as it applies to individuals; from systems–ecological theory, as that theory applies to systems maintaining their balance; and from the family literature, particularly as this literature focuses on "the adaptive qualities of families as they encounter stress" (Hawley & DeHaan, 1996, p. 284). Theorists interested in family resilience focus

FIGURE 3.1 Flow of Stress Through the Family

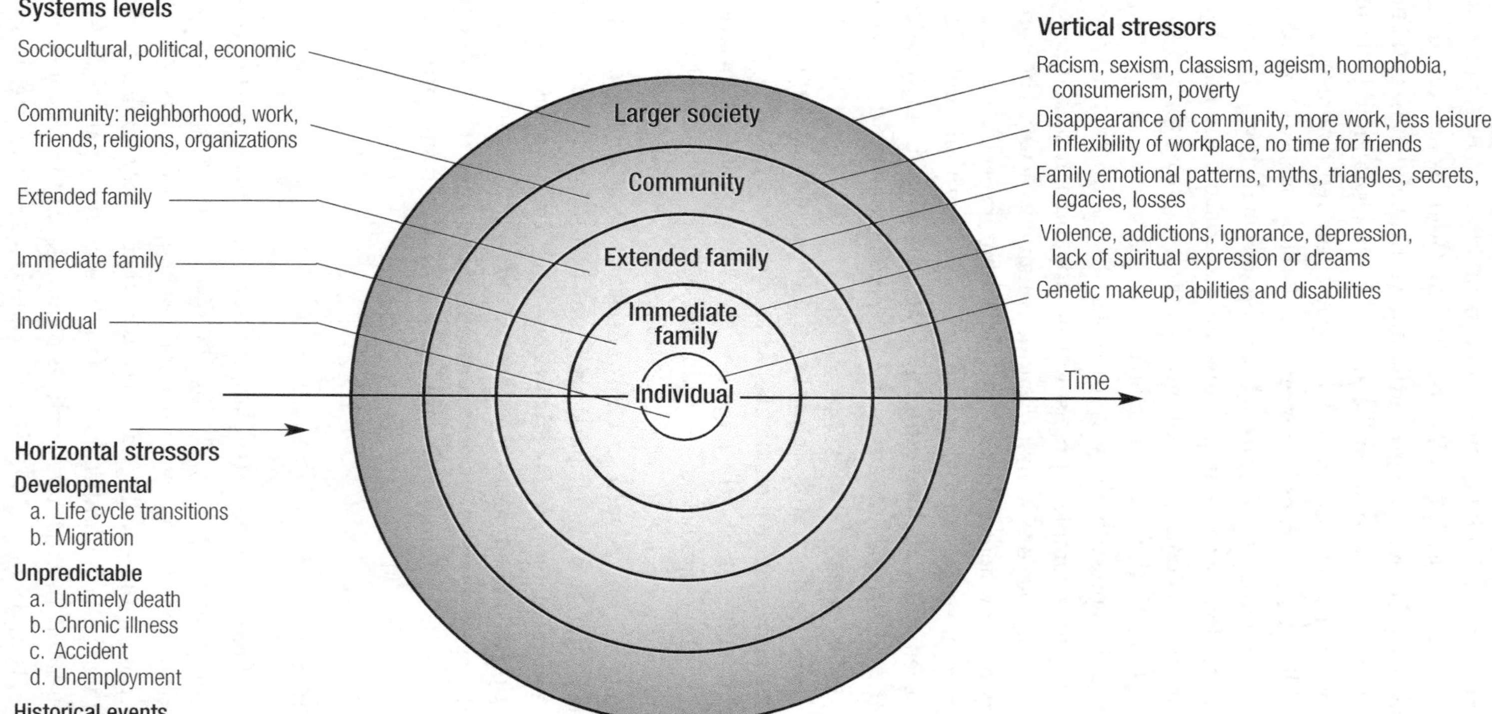

Source: From *The Expanded Family Life Cycle: Individual, Family, and Social Perspectives* (3d ed.), by B. Carter and M. McGoldrick, 2004, p. 6. Copyright 2004 by Allyn & Bacon. Used with permission.

on a family's natural resources, patterns of functioning, and capabilities that enable them to meet and even thrive in the face of crisis. The concept incorporates several theoretical constructs, such as family stress and family coherence, which "fit within the broader rubric of resiliency" (McCubbin, 1998, p. xiii). Various theoretical orientations that emphasize health and well-being contribute to an understanding of how families succeed despite adversity.

Studies that predict the impact of family influence on individual resilience have been important in identifying family risk and protective properties (Benard, 1995; Crosnoe & Elder, 2004; Garmezy, 1993; Hetherington, 1989; Rutter, 1979; Werner, 1993). For example, research conducted by Rutter (1985) and Werner (1993) indicated that resilient children are more likely to grow up in warm, affectionate home environments with clear-cut limits and structure. Longitudinal studies of the prevalence of problem behaviors, such as drug use, have been valuable in establishing prevention programs that address both individual and family well-being (Catalano et al., 1992). For example, Coohey (1996) and Moncher (1995) have urged practitioners to address family social isolation that may contribute to child maltreatment. Brookings, McEvoy, and Reed (1994) have found in their research at rape crisis centers that family and friends play an important role in helping women who have been raped to recover.

Family influences, such as the quality of the parent–child relationship, are known to have predictive power in the understanding of child behavior (O'Keefe, 1994; Rutter, 1979). However, the study of family resilience moves the analysis to a different level. Theorists have suggested that practitioners "conceive of family development as arising from various common and unique life transitions and life events that confront a family over its life course and may set family transformations in motion" (Germain, 1994a, p. 261).

From this viewpoint, the focus is on rules, organizational structures, and belief systems that shape the behavior of the family as a group. Although it is in the early stages of being defined, a key feature of family resilience is the ability to approach life challenges positively. Family resilience is a process that builds on family assets, endurance, and survival skills to avert negative stressors and confront adversity (Germain, 1994b). Resilient families have the capacity to rise above challenges (Wolin & Wolin, 1995). In addition, such families tend to demonstrate commitment, have good communication, are cohesive, appear adaptable, develop a sense of efficacy, are spiritual, experience connectedness, and spend time together (Walsh, 1998).

The family resilience concept draws on a crisis framework to understand family characteristics, dimensions, and properties that allow the unit to overcome crises and adapt to stress. Such family resilience models involve an examination of family risk factors (the pileup of demands), family protective factors (resources and strengths), and family shared worldview (schemas). The approach to family resilience stems from a systemic or relational view that enables practitioners to understand how families succeed (Greene, 2002, 2010). For example, Nazi Holocaust survivors have explained their wartime behaviors accordingly: "I dropped off the work camp line. So if they catch me, so what! I was going to stay with my sister" (Esther L., a survivor, personal communication, Indianapolis, IN, January 2000). "My sister and I were able to hide. As a teenager, you don't know fear. You have a family. Tomorrow will be better" (Eva H., a survivor, personal communication, Indianapolis, IN, February 2000).

Family resilience is a dynamic quality that varies with family context over time. Resilience, according to Hawley and DeHaan (1996), rests on the fit between family strengths and their specific circumstances; that is,

> family resilience describes the path a family follows as it adapts and prospers in the face of stress, both in the present and over time. Resilient families respond positively to these conditions in unique ways, depending on the context, developmental level, the interactive combination of risk and protective factors, and the family's shared outlook. (p. 293)

Practitioners can use the questions on Greene's (2010) Family Resilience Template to assess the family's developmental path (see Table 3.1).

According to Walsh (1998), a family resilience approach "aims to identify and fortify key interactional processes that enable families to withstand and rebound from disruptive life challenges" (p. 3). Family resilience involves "coping and adaptational processes in the family as a unit" (p. 14). Walsh (1996, 1998), who believes that all families facing a crisis have the potential for self-repair and growth, has attributed a family's resilience to its functioning in three domains: belief systems, organizational patterns, and communication processes (see Table 3.2). Family belief systems generally include the values and attitudes that establish a family's ideas about how to act. Family organizational patterns, based on expectations for behavior, involve how the family is structured to carry out its tasks, such as the ability to rally together to deal with stress. Communication processes encompass the exchange of information within the family's relationship.

Family resilience theorists have emphasized how the family system deals with distress and overcomes many different types of crises. A family may be challenged by members returning from war (Hendrix, Jurich, & Schumm, 1995), or by members coping with mental illness (Bentelspacher, Chitran, & Abdul Rahman, 1994), or by members with disabilities (Leyser, Heinze, & Kapperman, 1999). Families may be confronted with parent care or new parents and grandparents (Greene, 2008b). Resettlement, according to Hulewat (1996), is one of the most enormous crises and opportunities a family can face. Numerous

TABLE 3.1 Family Resilience Template Questions

1. What was the economic well-being of the survivor's family of origin?
2. What was the emotional climate in the family of origin?
3. What was the structure of the family of origin? The family of creation? This addresses their level of connectedness, hierarchies, roles, subsystems, and lineage.
4. What are the characteristics of their communication processes? This includes an understanding of family rules (for example, do we talk about the Holocaust?).
5. How does the family—both the family of origin and family of creation—fit into and act upon its environment? This explores how families respond to stress and obtain resources.
6. What are the educational achievements and careers of members of the family of creation?
7. How resilient do the family of origin and the family of creation appear? This examines how families face risk and build on protective factors and assets.
8. What is the family's shared belief system? This includes its values, convictions, attitudes, and norms.
9. How did the family self-repair, rebuild, or reconfigure itself after the Holocaust?
10. Do family members seek justice, want to leave a legacy, or want to create a sense of transcendence? Are they idealistic? Do they strive for a better day?

Source: From "Family Dynamics, the Nazi Holocaust, and Mental Health Treatment," by R. R. Greene, 2010, *Journal of Human Behavior in the Social Environment, 20,* pp. 469–488. Copyright 2010 by Taylor & Francis. Adapted with permission.

theorists (Nicholson, 1997; Petty & Balgopal, 1998) have documented the sense of loss associated with leaving one's country to begin a new life, and the accompanying anxiety and excitement.

Although many families spontaneously transform themselves during a crisis, grave life stressors may require major changes in family structure and meaning, necessitating outside intervention (Germain, 1994a, 1994b; Reiss, 1981; Terkelsen, 1980). In this situation, a resilience approach has implications for practitioners who may help families reconstruct the crisis more positively and change patterns of functioning when needed (Hawley & DeHaan, 1996). An example is the family distress and family outreach model of Cornille, Boroto, Barnes, and Hall (1996), developed for mental health practitioners and teachers (see Figure 3.2). This model focuses on family goals rather than family pathology and is consistent with a strengths-based approach.

The family distress and family outreach model encompasses five phases of family functioning. Phase 1 addresses the family's normal maintenance. Normal

TABLE 3.2 Key Processes in Family Resilience

Belief Systems

Making meaning of adversity
- Affiliative value: resilience as relationally based
- Family life cycle orientation: normalizing, contextualizing adversity and distress
- Sense of coherence: crisis as meaning, comprehensible, manageable challenge
- Appraisal of crisis, distress, and recovery: facilitative versus constraining beliefs

Positive outlook
- Active initiative and perseverance
- Courage and en-*courage*-ment
- Sustaining hope, optimistic view: confidence in overcoming odds
- Focusing on strengths and potential
- Mastering the possible; accepting what can't be changed

Transcendence and spirituality
- Larger values, purpose
- Spirituality; faith, communion, rituals
- Inspiration: envisioning new possibilities, creativity, heroes
- Transformation: learning and growth from adversity

Organizational Patterns

Flexibility
- Capacity to change: rebounding, reorganizing, adapting to fit challenges over time
- Counterbalancing by stability: continuity, dependability through disruption

Connectedness
- Mutual support, collaboration, and commitment
- Respect for individual needs, differences, and boundaries
- Strong leadership: nurturing, protecting, guiding children and vulnerable members
- Varied family forms: cooperative parenting/caregiving teams
- Couple/coparent relationship: equal partners
- Seeking reconnection, reconciliation of troubled relationships

Social and economic resources
- Mobilizing extended kin and social support; community networks
- Building financial security; balancing work and family strains

TABLE 3.2 Key Processes in Family Resilience (*continued*)

Communication Processes
Clarity • Clear, consistent messages (words and actions) • Clarification of ambiguous situation; truth-seeking/truth-speaking
Open emotional expression • Sharing range of feelings (joy and pain; hopes and fears) • Mutual empathy; tolerance for differences • Responsibility for own feelings, behavior: avoid blaming • Pleasurable interactions: humor
Collaborative problem solving • Creative brainstorming; resourcefulness • Shared decision making: negotiation, fairness, reciprocity • Conflict resolution • Focusing on goals: taking concrete steps, building on success, learning from failure • Proactive stance: reinventing problems, crises; preparing for future challenges

Source: From *Strengthening Family Resilience* (p. 133), by F. Walsh, 1998. Copyright 1998 by Guilford Press. Reprinted with permission.

maintenance encompasses the family's patterns—routines, roles, rules, rituals, and relationships—that serve the purpose of stability no matter how these patterns are perceived by outsiders. Normal maintenance involves the family's sense of identity, values, and goals.

Phase 2 involves the event that disrupts the family's stable patterns. Family responses to stressor events may vary, but the activities of this stage aim to reestablish family stability through old or new patterns of functioning. Phase 3 is a crisis that occurs when the family has exhausted its coping strategies. Phase 4 is organized around the crisis. A crisis often creates a sense of urgency that may or may not precipitate a search for help. In times of crisis it may be useful for a school or other community agency to reach out and offer help. Phase 5 involves the family receiving support to resolve the crisis. This support might involve the provision of resources (goods and services), association (a sense of belonging), or affection (caring). The helping person or agency's purpose is to help the family reconnect with its values and goals.

FIGURE 3.2 Family Distress and Family Outreach Model

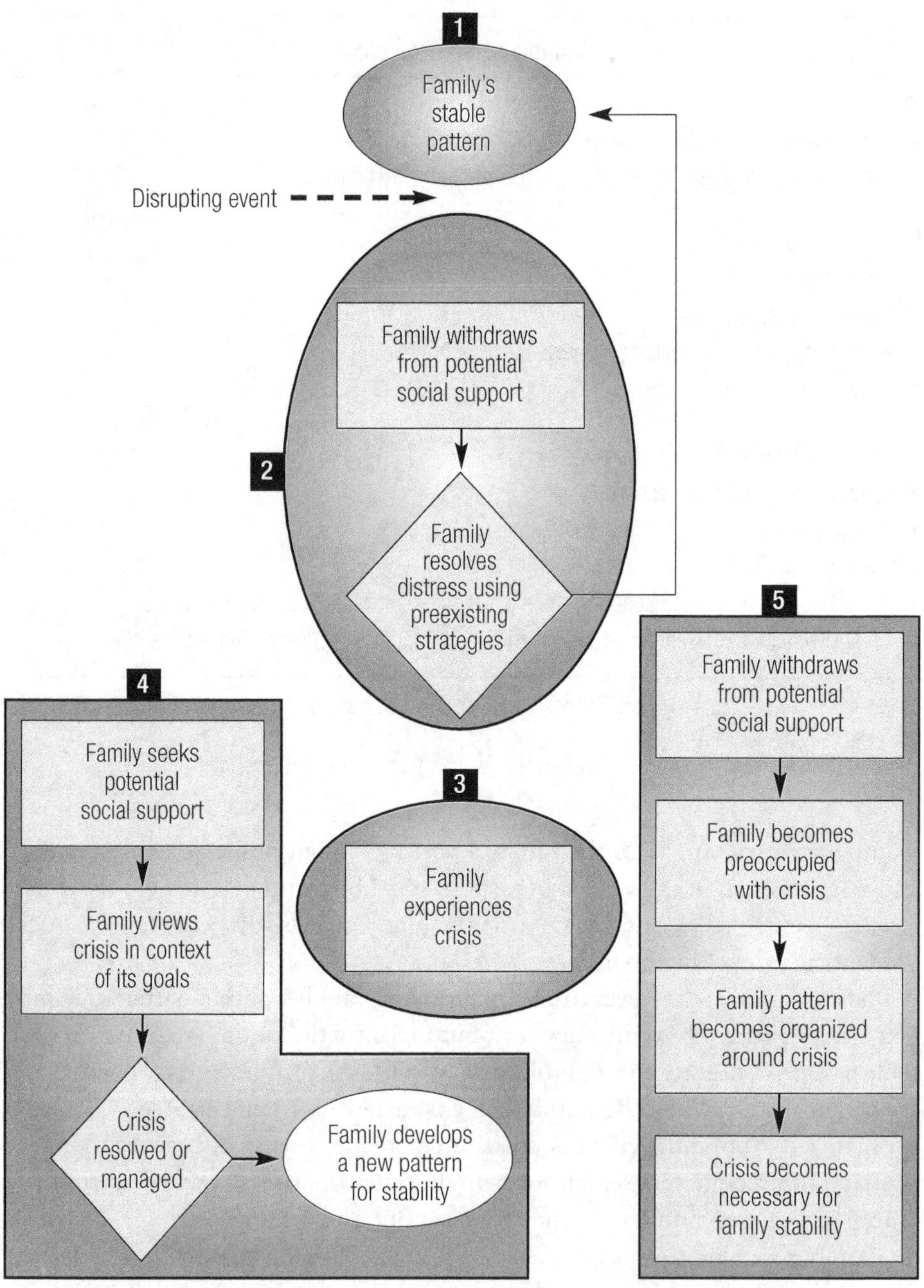

Source: From "Dealing with Family Distress in Schools," by T. A. Cornille, D. R. Boroto, M. F. Barnes, and P. K. Hall, 1996, *Families in Society, 97,* p. 438. Copyright 1996 by the Alliance for Children and Families. Reprinted with permission.

A discussion of family resilience would be incomplete without pointing out the influence of ethnicity and culture (McCubbin, McCubbin, Thompson, & Thompson, 1998). Family stress models originated with the study of Caucasian families. However, more recent frameworks focus on how ethnic background affects a family's response to stress and why cultural patterns may foster adaptive patterns of functioning. In resolving problems, a family's schemas—convictions, values, and worldview—influence the process of adaptation. For example, most Native Hawaiians preserve the philosophy of *Lokahi* or harmony with the land as they seek to achieve balance in all aspects of life (E. A. Thompson, McCubbin, Thompson, & Elver, 1998).

Social workers need to be aware that the family is the major social unit that mediates cultural beliefs and manages stressful life events, and thus culturally competent practice is required. Yet there remain complicated questions involving whether resilience is a culturally specific or universal concept. Furthermore, to understand resilience among minority families, one cannot ignore the impact of racism as well as the fact that "some families live in neighborhoods that are literally in a state of siege" (Genero, 1998, p. 31). More needs to be understood about survival under such circumstances.

It is also important to point out that the structure and functioning of the U.S. family has seen far-reaching changes (Greene, 1999). Since the 19th century, there has been a decline in family size. Moreover, the nature of the family has changed significantly since the predominance of the traditional nuclear family form peaked in the 1950s (Walsh, 1998). Families now encompass single-parent households, families that have remarried, two-career families, commuter families, and stepfamilies (Billingsley, 1987). Furthermore, families may vary by marriage form, choice of mates, postmarital residence, the family kinship system, household and family structures, the nature of family obligations, family–community interaction, and alternative family forms (Tseng & Hsu, 1991). An increasing number of individuals are choosing not to marry or, like gay and lesbian partners, are not afforded the legal opportunity to do so (Carter & McGoldrick, 1999).

As Carter and McGoldrick noted, a discussion of family needs to include all members of society and must address family strengths. For example, practitioners need to be aware that there are resilient single mothers (Brodsky, 1999; Olson & Haynes, 1993). Exploring the processes of resilience among those who are successful can enhance practitioner understanding and choice of interventions. That is, practitioner attention to family resilience comes into play during most social work encounters but is particularly important during stressful events such as domestic and community violence (O'Keefe, 1994). Homelessness is another event that requires that practitioners foster healthy development. In this situation, practitioners should tap family skills to help the family reconnect to basic internal and environmental resources, enabling it to find and maintain permanent housing (Ziefert & Brown, 1991).

Support Systems

Social supports are those interpersonal transactions involving mutual aid and affirmation (Gitterman & Shulman, 1986). Being a part of a social support network has a stress-buffering effect on individual well-being (Tracy, 1990; Tracy & Whittaker, 1990). Social support network characteristics may vary by size and composition, frequency of contact, length of relationships, and perceived availability (Tracy, 1990). The four largest sources of social support are households, relatives, friends, and formal service providers. Social workers often use a form of the social network map shown in Figure 3.3 to assess a client's social network viability.

A widely studied social phenomenon, social supports have been found to contribute to adaptive behaviors across cultures and across the life course. For example, behaviors that have been perceived as supportive by adolescents and that affect their sense of resilience include *listening support,* or the perception that an individual is listening without being judgmental; *emotional support,* or the perception that someone is providing comfort and caring; *emotional challenge,* or the perception that another person is challenging one to evaluate his or her values and attitudes; *reality confirmation support,* or the perception that someone similar to the person sees things the same way as that person; *task appreciation support,* or the perception that another person appreciates one's work; *task challenge support,* or the perception that one is being challenged to stretch his or her creativity or involvement; *tangible assistance support,* or the perception that another person has given a gift or financial help; and *personal assistance support,* or the perception that another person is providing services (Richman, Rosenfield, & Bowen, 1998).

Peer relationships, or interactions with individuals of a similar age who provide a sense of belonging and companionship, are a special type of support system. For young people, peer groups not only offer support, but also afford the opportunity for engaging in joint activities and influence the development of social skills, fashion, attitudes, and behaviors (Safyer, 1994). Nathan McCall (1994), who studied journalism and became a journalist at the *Washington Post* after serving three years in prison, recalled,

> By the time I reached the seventh grade, I'd learned that a dude's life had no meaning unless he hung with someone. You had no identity if you didn't belong to a group. . . . Now, at age twelve, I was trying my

FIGURE 3.3 Social Network Composition ($N = 45$)

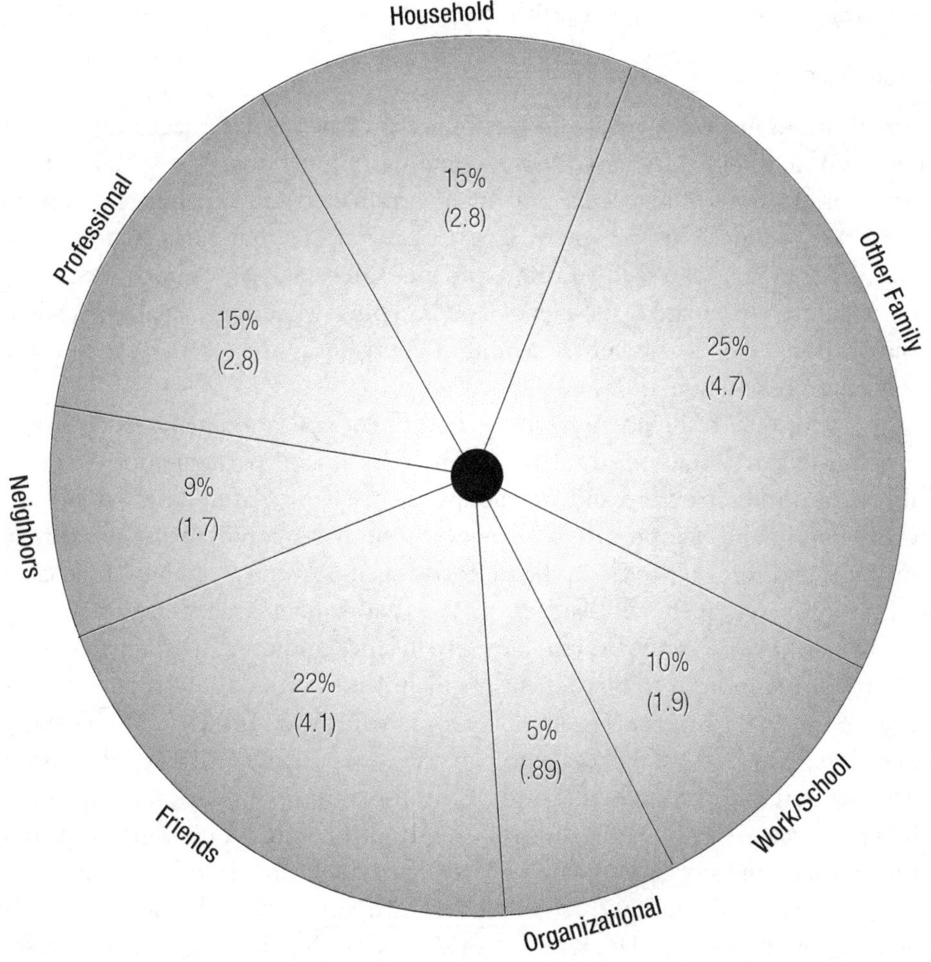

Source: From "Identifying Social Support Resources of At-Risk Families," by E. M. Tracy, 1990, *Social Work, 35,* p. 254. Copyright 1990 by NASW Press. Reprinted with permission.

> damnedest to hang loose with a group and get with those styles. I'd pick up a few decent rags from my brothers to shed that nerdy look and finally got my first pair of All Stars . . . I also got waves on my head. (p. 31)

Looking back at how his peer group affected his life, McCall reflected that even though he participated in peer activities resulting in trouble, he also saw that he had choices and that his possibilities were abundant.

The literature has documented the positive effects of informal social systems or "network embeddedness" in the black community (M. S. Thompson

& Peebles-Wilkins, 1992, p. 322). In addition, social supports, particularly the family, can also be of great importance to older adults and are instrumental in preventing depression (Greene, 2008b).

Organizations

Organizations are a form of social system in which people interact to carry out a number of different roles in work and community functions. As a social system, organizations both influence an individual's resilience and experience a pattern of relative resilience in their own right. Organizations that can promote resilience, such as schools, tend to offer students safety and an opportunity to be heard and to participate (Cole-Henderson & Thurlow, 2000; Katz, 1997). Work organizations may also be instrumental in contributing to competence and life satisfaction (Chatman, 1989).

Organizational resilience necessitates that the organization make a deliberate, conscious effort to demonstrate consistently successful performance. Successful organizations structure and restructure themselves to attain a mission, support the optimal development of shared decision making, build trust, encourage openness, and remain tireless in their efforts to support the growth of individual and collective competence (Anderson, 1991). Resilient organizations display feedback behaviors, set goals, and have intelligence-gathering mechanisms.

For an organization to be resilient, its members must adapt to their environments. Resilient organizations employ people who react quickly and efficiently to change. They have employees who perceive experiences constructively, ensure adequate external resources, expand decision-making boundaries, develop the ability to create solutions on the spot, develop tolerance for uncertainty, and build virtual role systems. Virtual role systems are teams in which individual members know one another's roles so they can ensure that the organization's overarching mission will be carried out (Mallak, 1998). This approach suggests that organizations and their members must have a stake in how people and their abilities fit the job (Caplan, 1987).

Schools

Perhaps one of the most important organizations affecting resilience is the school. At a time when school violence is of increasing concern, it is important to remember that schools are the primary social system—after families—affecting the lives of children. In a *New York Times* report about youths who graduated high school after overcoming difficult circumstances, Brown (2000) indicated that what seems like individual achievement is actually a combination of social support provided by family members, teachers, and the community who believed in the child. She quoted a student who realized his potential: "I've had a lot of people in my family take the wrong path. I've seen what drugs, alcohol and violence did to family members. I said: 'That's not me. That's not my life'" (p. A24).

Similarly, Garbarino and Asp (1981) have argued that as developmental threats accelerate in the home, children need even more support from schools. Other theorists have suggested that schools can act as agents of adaptation (Benard, 1995, 1997; Garmezy, 1991; Perry, Liu, & Pabian, 2010; Rutter, 1979). Schools differ in the way in which they affect children's lives. The question, then, is, what types of schools exercise a positive influence on students (Garmezy, 1991; Katz, 1997; see chapter 11)?

A frequently encountered finding in resilience research is "the power of teachers, often unbeknownst, to tip the scale from risk to resilience" (Benard, 1997, p. 2). Although home academic culture is important, teacher supports, such as giving more classroom attention, may have important results (N. Bowen & Bowen, 1998). Teachers are often instrumental in helping students understand that adversity should not be taken personally, that adversity is not necessarily permanent, and that setbacks are not all encompassing (Seligman, 1991). Teachers accomplish this by expressing support, kindness, compassion, and respect (Higgins, 1994).

Teachers, who provide students with a sense of "safety, love and belonging, respect, power, accomplishment and learning, and, ultimately meaning," are often the important role models who foster a child's resilience (Benard, 1997, p. 2). At the same time, schools should strive to increase family–school partnerships (Cox & Powers, 1998; Wang, Haertel, & Walberg, 1994). The process involved in the home and school working together is often facilitated by school personnel such as the school social worker or psychologist.

Another reason schools are often viewed as being in a position to promote resilience is that they offer many school-based programs, such as parent training, that are committed to children at risk (Wang et al., 1994). According to Miller, Brehm, and Whitehouse (1998), the critical resiliency resources targeted in these programs include maximally supportive behavior management systems; increased opportunities for bonding between adults and peers; and mastery-oriented, highly motivating learning environments. Because schools are an arena of social interaction, they provide an excellent venue for early identification of behavior that, if left unchecked, may lead to further difficulty (Miller et al., 1998). That is, schools are among the most suitable places "to implement resiliency enhancement programs" (Zunz, Turner, & Norman, 1993, p. 171). School personnel, including bus drivers and office staff, are in a position to nurture and stimulate children who might not otherwise receive such attention (Reed-Victor & Pelco, 1999). Mentors may be available to establish close personal bonds (Katz, 1997).

In addition to teacher actions in the classroom and school-based prevention programs, the ethos of the school and classroom has a critical effect. Benard (1997) has suggested that schools take a comprehensive organizational approach to fostering resilience. This approach would include providing teacher support, staff development, and school–community collaboration. She has gone on to say that teachers should use classroom procedures that teach students to find their strengths or their innate resilience. In a similar vein, Winfield (1994) identified four major processes that can foster resilience at the school level: (1) reducing negative outcomes by altering a child's exposure to risk, such as combating an atmosphere of violence by modeling discipline and calm; (2) reducing negative chain reactions following exposure to risk, such as by encouraging pregnant teenagers to receive additional education; (3) establishing and maintaining self-esteem and self-efficacy through the accomplishment of small tasks and the receipt of positive feedback; and (4) opening up opportunities through specific programs that allow students to acquire skills.

Work with inner-city children may also involve changing institutional belief systems, such as school policy and culture (Ogbu, 1992; Winfield, 1994). School programs and structure must be coupled with an understanding of student "relationships, beliefs, expectations and a willingness to share power" (Benard, 1997, p. 2). Such understanding is achieved when teachers encourage self-expression and student involvement in learning and extracurricular activities. Involving students in curriculum planning and helping them create governing structures offer opportunities for student involvement that foster resilience (Benard, 2003).

Community/Neighborhood

Resilience is also a function of the ecological context of neighborhoods (Duncan, Brooks-Gunn, & Klebanov, 1994). Theorists have suggested that people who live in communities that are characterized by social disorganization are at higher risk for "problem" behaviors than those who live in communities with a stronger social fabric (Garbarino, 1995; Garbarino & Kostelny, 1992). Unfortunately, many U.S. citizens live in neighborhoods that have been likened to war zones (Dubrow & Garbarino, 1989). Risk factors at the community level may include low socioeconomic status or poverty (Lyons-Ruth, Connell, & Gruenbaum, 1990) and violence (Bronfenbrenner, McClelland, Wethington, Moen, & Ceci, 1996).

However, a major positive influence on human behavior is the opportunity to live in a socially cohesive community or neighborhood (Sampson, Raudenbush, & Earls, 1997). Communities are territorial social systems comprising interlocking functional subsystems, including economic, political, religious, ethical, educational, legal, social, and reproductive systems. Neighborhoods are smaller versions of the community (Bronfenbrenner et al., 1984). Communities vary in their capacity to cultivate individual resilience and in their collective ability to respond on behalf of the common good. Researchers have documented that a resilient group can establish and maintain community well-being (Greene & Kropf, in press).

Benard (1991) has related three characteristics of communities that promote resilience: (1) the availability of social organizations that provide an array of resources, (2) consistent expression of community norms for members to understand what is "proper" behavior, and (3) opportunities for children and youths to participate constructively in the community. Such opportunities may be more important to individual resilience than the danger or poverty level of a community (G. L. Bowen & Chapman, 1996; Coulton & Pandey, 1992). Community resilience or collective efficacy is based on residents' mutual trust and their readiness to intervene on behalf of the general well-being.

A community's ability to be resilient also depends on macrosystems conditions, particularly on the effects of "racial and economic exclusion on perceived powerlessness . . . that stymies collective efficacy" (Sampson et al., 1997, p. 919). Communities in which people feel powerless may be impeded in meeting the needs of their members and in organizing themselves to garner more support. Such cycles of powerlessness require community development and efforts at structural change (Pinderhughes, 1983). Effective communities can be developed even under the most severe situations—such as in concentration camps. Survivors of Cambodian and World War II concentration camps have reflected on their craving to return to some semblance of a normal life. To achieve this goal, they set up governmental structure and schools, performed concerts, or wrote poetry (Eva H., a survivor, personal communication, Indianapolis, IN, January 2000). These activities clearly contributed to their survival and to their becoming resilient adults. Social workers need to be increasingly involved in community building (Schriver, 2010). In this way, they engage in a process that fosters the interconnectedness of people, reinforces a community's assets, and augments community institutions (Ewalt, 1998; Naparastek & Dooley, 1998). Their major goals are to promote a sense of community and improve health and human services.

Society/Government

Resilience is a macrosystems phenomenon with philosophical, political, and policy connotations. Macrosystems include the overarching social, political, legal, economic, and value patterns of a particular society (Greene & Watkins, 1998). Macrosystems analyses generally deal with those acts of power that impede adaptation and mobility or are a direct threat to survival, also termed *macroaggressions* (Pierce, 1969). Studies of resilience at the macrosystems level address whether societal conditions—unemployment, homelessness, poverty, and discrimination—act as debilitating sources of stress (Conger et al., 1992; Elder, Nguyen, & Caspi, 1985; Greene & Greene, 2010).

For example, Elder (1979) studied the effects of economic hardship during the Great Depression. He found that although families faced severe financial hardships, often ones resulting in discord, they mediated these risks by shifting to more labor-intensive modes. Similarly, Vosler (1990) explored how family economic stressors stem from a structured lack of access to basic resources, whereas Chadiha (1992) explored how black husbands' economic difficulties—structural unemployment or holding vulnerable positions in the labor market—affected resiliency during their transition to marriage.

Some researchers have suggested that such political difficulties require political solutions. In their book *Within Our Reach,* Schorr and Schorr (1988) argued that, given the evaluation of social programs such as the Special Supplemental Nutrition Program for Women, Infants, and Children and Head Start, the knowledge and means now exist in the form of social interventions to improve the lives of high-risk children. They urged that society invest in sustainable services and that policy makers seek the means for resolving basic societal inequities. Garmezy (1993) has captured the challenge before us:

> Two tasks now challenge us. One is scientific, the other political. First, to the scientific agenda. Confirmatory studies are needed to invigorate the reality that in America's city ghettos and rural farm communities, wherever poverty is manifestly evident, a substantial core of poor children, likely a majority, possess a potential for achievement that must be nurtured and expanded. We must learn more about the patterning of functions in these children and the factors housed in person, family, and community that are precursors to survivorship. . . . The focus on resilience amidst disadvantage also carries a political component, for the problem of poverty is a vital aspect of the political agenda of the nation. . . . We need financial support for interventions that shore up the manifest talents of children and families who do not present the problem of cumulative risk, but whose danger is accentuated by the threatening ecologies in which they reside. (pp. 133–134)

In addition, macrosystems issues may encompass historical change and historical dislocations prompted by a breakdown in social and institutional arrangements that ordinarily anchor people's lives (Lifton, 1993). The world is increasingly aware of societies that have undergone civil or tribal wars, such as the Rwandan or Sierra Leone atrocities (Crossette, 2000; Hranjski, 2000).

Healing and reconciliation when there are such atrocities has afforded a serious challenge. According to Lifton (1993), resilience at the societal level generally requires governmental, if not global, efforts. He asserted, "While historical fragmentation of this kind can result in dangerous forms of fragmentation of the self, it can also lead to impulses toward renewal . . . [or the initiation of] searches for new 'places' . . . a quest to overcome spiritual homelessness" (pp. 14–15).

Resilience: Practice Guidelines

The rationale for examining resilience phenomena rests on the fundamental assumption that understanding how individuals overcome challenges to development and recover from trauma will reveal processes of adaptation that can guide intervention efforts with others at risk. . . . When adversity is relieved and basic human needs are restored, then resilience has a chance to emerge. Rekindling hope may be an important spark for resilience processes to begin their restorative work.

—MASTEN, 1994, P. 8

In building resilience, we strive to integrate the fullness of a crisis experience into the fabric of our individual and collective identity, influencing how we go on to live our lives.

—WALSH, 1998, P. 6

Certain assessment and intervention strategies are suggested based on research and clinical findings on how resilience occurs. Practitioners need to evaluate a client's coping capacity and explore internal and external resources to assess resilience. Internal or individual characteristics may include self-esteem, trust, autonomy, strength, and hope, and interpersonal abilities such as social skills, communication, humor, problem solving, and impulse control. External factors explored may involve environmental supports and resources, such as trusting relationships and role models; access to health, education, welfare, and safety services; stable family and school environments; and religious affiliation.

In addition, if practitioners understand the factors that foster resilience, they can develop programs to provide them (Greene & Armenta, 2007; Wang et al., 1994). Resilience-based practice approaches are cognizant of the fact that people's lives involve naturally occurring stressors and day-to-day challenges. Resilience-based practice also builds on earlier theories that focused on client strengths—competence, coping strategies, or adaptation. There is, however, an important difference in emphasis. Resilience-based practice seeks to minimize the effects of adversity, with more attention being given to competence under pressure, successful coping with adverse life events, and effective adaptation following high risk.

To promote resilience, practitioners must consider multisystemic strategies appropriate to a client's life context and position across the life course. These interventions involve a range of competencies and roles. Based on an assessment of client needs and opportunity, practitioners may use interventions that

- provide for basic needs, such as safety, food, water, and electricity;
- help clients access their own resources;
- stabilize and normalize the situation;
- identify the possible;
- tap intrinsic worth;
- illuminate opportunities;
- attend to diversity and respect ethnicity, gender, race, and so forth;
- challenge oppressive situations, seek equity, and combat negative environmental messages;
- motivate and engage clients by focusing on strengths;
- build personal capacity;
- enhance client self-awareness;
- work to clarify the meaning and purpose of events;
- tap innate individual abilities;
- facilitate problem-solving abilities;
- offer group support;
- tap into wellness programs;
- deal with institutional belief systems;
- work with social supports, mentors, peers, clergy, and teachers;
- identify community stakeholders;
- build on community assets;
- engage in community action and renewal strategies; and
- enhance community power.

The need for practitioners to assist clients in self-repair following adverse life events is discussed by numerous theorists. For example, Greene and Armenta (2007) presented a clinical model for use with clients in the aftermath of traumatic events that included

- acknowledging client loss, vulnerability, and future;
- identifying the source of and reaction to stress;
- stabilizing or normalizing the situation;
- helping clients take control;
- providing resources for change;

- promoting self-efficacy;
- collaborating in self-change;
- strengthening problem-solving abilities;
- addressing positive emotions;
- achieving creative expressions;
- listening to client stories;
- making meaning of events;
- finding the benefits of adverse events;
- attending to client spirituality; and
- transcending the immediate situation.

Neimeyer and Stewart (1996) proposed that for clients to feel that their lives are meaningful and manageable following adverse events, practitioners should help them to integrate the event and restore a positive sense of self. Similarly, Borden (1992) contended that following adverse life events, social workers form a therapeutic alliance to help clients reappraise events and use interventions to reorganize client meaning. This reframing of the difficulty can help the client maintain a sense of continuity and coherence, self-esteem, morale, self-satisfaction, and effective social functioning. Practitioners should also focus on problem solving, educational strategies, and the provision of resources. The view that practitioners should concentrate on positive therapeutic outcomes is consistent with the work of Benard (1995). She emphasized the need to move beyond the construction of resilience in terms of protective and risk factors to a study of resilience as a dynamic process that comes into play as individuals maintain health and wellness in the face of naturally occurring challenges over time.

The idea that clinicians should spend less time on how people become maladaptive and more time on fostering mechanisms that lead to resilience is the major theme in the risk and resilience intervention literature (Cowan, Cowan, & Schulz, 1996; Walsh, 1998). Resilience-based approaches to helping are optimistic and rest on the assumption that "development can right itself or is fostered by 'natural' or professional intervention" (Masten, 1994, p. 20). Because resilience is an innate human characteristic, resiliency skills can be fostered by positive interventions over time (Winfield, 1994).

Promoting resilience centers on activating a person's "self-righting mechanism" (Werner & Smith, 1992, p. 202). In this regard, it is regenerative. The central idea of resilience-based approaches is to rekindle hope. According to Higgins (1994), facilitating resilience is a matter of philosophy, rather than technique. She proposed that fostering resilience requires a practitioner mindset that assumes that clients are motivated to overcome hardship: "It requires a firm refusal to join the ranks of the sour and dispirited" (Higgins, 1994, p. 319). Her view is hopeful in that it assumes that practitioners support clients' convictions that, with help, they can choose their own path.

The literature encompasses intervention strategies, many familiar to social workers, that fall under the general rubric of resilience-based approaches. For example, *empowerment practice* helps a person realize his or her own ability to overcome personal or environmental obstacles (Solomon, 1976). The idea that people's resilience or psychological healing from traumatic experiences can be heightened through ideological motivation involving political and economic motivation has been affirmed through such activities as the Civil Rights movement (Proctor, 1995). Such movements carry out collective action to reconstruct conditions such as poverty, racism, and bigotry.

As a result of empowerment practices, clients can develop a more positive sense of self, gain more knowledge about their social and political environments, and obtain more resources and strategies that promote competence (Lee, 1994). Thus, a client who receives rightful resources (such as shelter, education, and health care) and achieves a sense of self-esteem (an internalization of successful performance in social situations) is empowered. Furthermore, empowerment practice involves the transformation of institutional belief systems, such as school policy and culture (Winfield, 1994).

Other eclectic choices included under the umbrella of resiliency include violence prevention programs, such as parent education or school safety programs (Astor, Behre, Wallace, & Fravil, 1998; Burman & Allen-Meares, 1994; Dittrich-McInnis, 1996; see chapter 11); competency-building approaches; and social skills training with maltreated children (Denham & Burton, 1996; Fraser, 1997; Gager & Elias, 1997). Crisis intervention programs, including serial crisis interventions for people with HIV, are not uncommon (Poindexter, 1997). Furthermore, programs may use a psychoeducational format (Franklin & Streeter, 1992). Interventions may take place at schools (Benard, 1995), in houses of worship (Carter, 1999; Haight, 1998), or at health maintenance organizations (Lorries, 2000).

Prevention Strategies

Several authors have proposed global risk and resilience intervention strategies to design what Thomlison (1997) has called "capacity-building services" (p. 50). These strategies generally include "identifying the common factors that produce risk and resilience . . . [by] conducting an ecologically based assessment and [by] designing ecologically focused services" (Kirby & Fraser, 1997, p. 10). Much of the resilience literature has generally suggested what Masten and Coatsworth (1998) have termed "a prevention–intervention design: (a) risk-focused, (b) resource-focused, and (c) process-focused" (p. 214).

Preventive science, or "the study of how to prevent or moderate major human dysfunction[,] has become a conceptual framework guiding national research programs" (Coie et al., 1993, p. 1013). Prevention efforts generally aim to reduce risk, such as by removing lead paint; reduce stressors and stress pileup, such as through programs to decrease bullying in schools; increase available resources, such as public transportation and housing access; and mobilize protective factors, such as parent education (see Begun, 1993; Cox & Powers, 1998; Rutter, 1987).

Study findings on naturally occurring resilience following traumatic events involving children at risk have suggested that efforts are needed to purposely change the course of competence through early childhood education and preventive interventions (Masten, 1994). According to Fonagy, Steele, Steele, Higgitt, and Target (1994), the development of competence should be of great concern to parents and society alike, and it is both an economic necessity as well as inherent in people's desire for social justice.

Other Existing Models

Resilience-based intervention strategies have been developed by combining what is known about resilience with other human behavior theories, including developmental and ecological theory and theories of crisis, stress, and coping (Fraser, 1997; Nash & Fraser, 1998). Models may include family treatment that represents a change in the focus of family therapists. Such family treatment may foster a family's ability to grow and collaborate on solving common problems (see chapter 15). For example, Walsh (1998) proposed that resilience-based therapy be based on healing—a process of transformation that comes from within—and inspire people to believe in themselves.

Some practitioners are using narrative approaches to help people who have faced trauma adjust to loss and to heal (Neimeyer & Stewart, 1996). A *narrative orientation* can help a client cope by listening to his or her story and enable the client to understand and react adaptively to difficult life events. Another tool that fosters resilience was developed in workshop format by the International Resilience Project (Grotberg, 1995). In the workshop, participants are asked to reflect on "what I have (for example, people whom I can trust)," "what I am (for example, willingness to be responsible for what I do)," and "what I can (for example, find ways to solve problems that I face)."

Debriefing models are another mode of intervention intended to process a difficult experience within a short time following a disaster to hopefully prevent posttraumatic stress disorder (Armstrong, Lund, McWright, & Tichenor, 1995; Bell, 1995). Critical incident debriefing may help people overcome the stress associated with traumatic events such as hurricanes, tornados, explosions, mass shooting, fire, or accident (Armstrong et al., 1995; Bell, 1995). Such disasters can cause a ripple effect across the family and into the workplace. Responses to disasters and debriefings may help restore a sense of normalcy, thus meeting people's basic needs. Practitioners explore what people have done to pull through so far. Practitioners help people deal with shock, accept their vulnerability to death, and accept the fact that they have survived.

> Being on call for the federal Employee Assistance Program in Dallas, I was asked to drive at once to Oklahoma City. I went immediately to the site command center that was established to assure the necessary communication and coordination among agencies, including churches. One purpose was to determine who was dead, alive, or missing. As one of the social workers first on the scene, I was asked to talk with people from the bombed building who were in the most distress as well as rescue workers who needed support.
>
> The first thing a practitioner must understand as they begin their work is that, "What is normal has disappeared. People are in a state of terror and shock." In Oklahoma City, people were afraid another bomb might explode. Therefore, the social worker must set a calm tone and meet with people in a secure area. "Establishing a sense of safety is a prerequisite to anything else." The social worker should meet with people in charge to get as much information as possible and share this information with people in distress. Information combats rumors and negative actions being taken. Simultaneously, the social worker recognizes that this is a very difficult time.
>
> I have learned that debriefing is best done in a group. All people at the site are asked to attend a meeting, be introduced to the social worker, and to learn the purpose of the meeting. I believe most people will stay at the meeting, but should not be forced to do so. The group begins with its framework and purpose, that is, to try to understand what has happened and to learn skills to cope with the event. I start the group by teaching the members about what they may feel immediately after a disaster such as being numb, angry, sad, or even guilty that they survived. All of these feelings are "alright," and each person will have different recovery thresholds. The power of the group is as I explain that they are there to support each other—to be compassionate. Group members may want to talk about where they were or who they lost during the disaster or nothing at all. ("I thought my computer exploded, ducked under my desk, and found myself on one small piece of the building completely alone—everyone else was gone.")

> The therapeutic purpose of the group is to promote healing. Healing occurs when there is a resolution of guilt: people must find meaning in the event to carry on. They must find personal ways of establishing a memorial to the lost person, such as planting a tree, creating a scrapbook of pictures, or naming a hiking trail after the deceased. (The Oklahoma bombing memorial is made up of a series of empty chairs reflected in light.)
>
> Healing is not linear or a straight path. Your clients may "go up and down" as they try to resolve their loss. They may experience (and should be advised that this is usual) nightmares, loss of sleep, or aches and pains. The social worker's major task is to say, "Don't let your grief scare you." (personal communication, Nancy Livingston, May 2000)

The Oklahoma City bombing and the terrorist attacks on the Pentagon and the World Trade Center demonstrate that to help people who have experienced a traumatic event, social workers need a knowledge base and a range of skills that can assist their clients in solving a variety of problems. At the outset, this may involve empathetic listening and community renewal (Kirst-Ashman & Hull, 1999).

Use the CD by Michael Wright to articulate resilience as a theory integrating belief systems, organizational patterns, and communication to identify systems of support in response to stress. Identify the goals of resiliency-based interventions in groups, organizations, and communities.

You will find a case study on your CD: *The Resilient Family in the Community: Provision and Prevention*

References

Anderson, T. (1991). *The reflecting team: Dialogues and dialogues about the dialogues.* New York: Norton.

Armstrong, K. R., Lund, P. E., McWright, L. T., & Tichenor, V. (1995). Multiple stressor debriefing and the American Red Cross: The East Bay Hills Fire experience. *Social Work, 40,* 83–90.

Astor, R. A., Behre, W. J., Wallace, J. M., & Fravil, K. A. (1998). School social workers and school violence: Personal safety, training, and violence programs. *Social Work, 23,* 223–232.

Bartelt, D. (1994). On resilience: Questions of validity. In M. Wang & E. Gordon (Eds.), *Educational resilience in inner-city America* (pp. 97–108). Hillsdale, NJ: Erlbaum.

Begun, A. L. (1993). Human behavior and the social environment: The vulnerability, risk, and resilience model. *Journal of Social Work Education, 29,* 26–36.

Bell, J. L. (1995). Traumatic event debriefing: Service delivery designs and the role of social work. *Social Work, 40,* 36–43.

Benard, B. (1991). *Fostering resilience in kids: Protective factors in the family, school and community.* Portland, OR: Northwest Regional Educational Library.

Benard, B. (1995). *Fostering resilience in children.* New York: ERIC Clearinghouse on Elementary and Early Childhood Education. (ERIC Document Reproduction Service No. ED386327.) Retrieved from http://www.eric.ed.gov/PDFS/ED386327.pdf

Benard, B. (1997). *Turning it around for all youth: From risk to resilience.* New York: ERIC Clearinghouse on Urban Education. (ERIC Document Reproduction Service No. ED412309.) Retrieved from http://www.eric.ed.gov/PDFS/ED412309.pdf

Benard, B. (2003). Turnaround teachers and schools. In B. Williams (Ed.), *Closing the achievement gap: A vision for changing beliefs and practices* (2nd ed., pp. 115–247). Alexandria, VA: Association for Supervision and Curriculum Development.

Bentelspacher, C. E., Chitran, S., & Abdul Rahman, M. B. (1994). Coping and adaptation pattern among Chinese, Indian, and Malay families caring for a mentally ill relative. *Families in Society, 75,* 287–294.

Billingsley, A. (1987). Family: Contemporary patterns. In A. Minahan (Ed.), *Encyclopedia of social work* (18th ed., Vol. 1, pp. 520–529). Silver Spring, MD: National Association of Social Workers.

Borden, W. (1992). Narrative perspectives in psychosocial intervention following adverse life events. *Social Work, 37,* 135–141.

Bowen, G. L., & Chapman, M. V. (1996). Poverty, neighborhood danger, social support, and the individual adaptation among at-risk youth in urban areas. *Journal of Family Issues, 17,* 641–666.

Bowen, N., & Bowen, G. L. (1998). The effects of home microsystem risk factors and school microsystem protective factors on student academic performance and affective investment in schooling. *Social Work in Education, 20,* 219–231.

Brodsky, A. E. (1999). Making it: The components and process of resilience among urban, African-American, single mothers. *American Journal of Orthopsychiatry, 69,* 148–160.

Bronfenbrenner, U. (1979). *The ecology of human development.* Cambridge, MA: Harvard University Press.

Bronfenbrenner, U., McClelland, P., Wethington, E., Moen, P., & Ceci, S. J. (1996). *The state of Americans.* New York: Free Press.

Bronfenbrenner, U., Moen, P., & Garbarino, J. (1984). Family and community. In R. Parke (Ed.), *Review of child development research* (Vol. 7, pp. 283–328). Chicago: University of Chicago Press.

Brookings, J. B., McEvoy, A. W., & Reed, M. (1994). Sexual assault recovery and male significant others. *Families in Society, 75,* 295–299.

Brooks, J. S., Nomura, C., & Cohen, P. (1989). A network of influences on adolescent drug involvement: Neighborhood, school, peer, and family. *Genetic, Social, and General Psychology Monographs, 115,* 125–145.

Brown, P. L. (2000, June 14). The pomp of graduation after overcoming difficult circumstances. *New York Times,* p. A24.

Buckley, W. (1967). Systems and entities. In W. Buckley (Ed.), *Sociology and modern systems theory* (pp. 42–66). Englewood Cliffs, NJ: Prentice Hall.

Burman, S., & Allen-Meares, P. (1994). Neglected victims of murder: Children's witness to parental homicide. *Social Work, 39,* 28–34.

Caplan, R. D. (1987). Person–environment fit theory and organizations: Commensurate dimensions, time perspectives, and mechanisms. *Journal of Vocational Behavior, 31,* 248–267.

Carter, B., & McGoldrick, M. (Eds.). (1999). *The expanded family life cycle: Individual, family, and social perspectives* (3rd ed.). Boston: Allyn & Bacon.

Carter, C. S. (1999). Church burning in African American communities: Implications for empowerment practice. *Social Work, 44,* 62–68.

Catalano, R. F., Morrison, D. M., Wells, E. A., Gillmore, M. R., Iritani, B., & Hawkins, J. D. (1992). Ethnic differences in family factors related to early drug initiation. *Journal of Studies on Alcohol, 53,* 208–217.

Chadiha, L. A. (1992). Black husbands' economic problems and resiliency during the transition to marriage. *Families in Society, 73,* 542–552.

Chatman, J. A. (1989). Improving interactional organizational research: A model of person–organization fit. *Academy of Management Review, 14,* 333–349.

Coie, J., Watt, N. F., West, S. G., Hawkins, J. D., Asarnow, J. R., Markman, H. J., et al. (1993). The science of prevention: A conceptual framework and some directions for a national research program. *American Psychologist, 48,* 1013–1022.

Cole-Henderson, S. L., & Thurlow, M. L. (2000). Organizational characteristics of schools that successfully serve low-income urban African American students. *Journal of Education for Students Placed at Risk, 51*(1–2), 77–91.

Conger, R. D., Conger, K. J., Elder, G. H., Lorenz, R. O., Simons, R. L., & Whitbeck, L. B. (1992). A family process model of economic hardship and adjustment of early adolescent boys. *Child Development, 63,* 526–541.

Coohey, C. (1996). Child maltreatment: Testing the social isolation hypothesis. *Child Abuse and Neglect, 20,* 241–254.

Cornille, T. A., Boroto, D. R., Barnes, M. F., & Hall, P. K. (1996). Dealing with family distress in schools. *Families in Society, 77,* 435–445.

Coulton, C., & Pandey, S. (1992). Geographic concentration of poverty and risk to children in urban neighborhoods. *American Behavioral Scientist, 35,* 238–257.

Cowan, P. A., Cowan, C. P., & Schulz, M. S. (1996). Thinking about risk and resilience in families. In M. Hetherington & E. A. Blechman (Eds.), *Stress, coping, and resilience in children and families* (pp. 1–38). Mahwah, NJ: Erlbaum.

Cox, G., & Powers, G. T. (1998). Against all odds: An ecological approach to developing resilience. In R. R. Greene & M. Watkins (Eds.), *Serving diverse constituencies: Applying the ecological perspective* (pp. 135–167). Hawthorne, NY: Aldine de Gruyter.

Crosnoe, R., & Elder, G. H. (2004). Family dynamics, supportive relationships, and educational resilience during adolescence. *Journal of Family Issues, 25,* 571–602.

Crossette, B. (2000, August 15). U.N. to establish a war crimes panel to hear Sierra Leone atrocity case. *New York Times,* p. A6.

Denham, S. A., & Burton, R. (1996). A social–emotional intervention for at-risk 4-year-olds. *Journal of School Psychology, 34,* 225–245.

Dittrich-McInnis, K. (1996). Violence prevention: An ecological adaptation of systematic training for effective parenting. *Families in Society, 77,* 414–422.

Dubrow, N. F., & Garbarino, J. (1989). Living in the war zone: Mothers and young children in a public housing development. *Child Welfare, 68,* 3–20.

Duncan, G. J., Brooks-Gunn, J., & Klebanov, P. K. (1994). Economic deprivation and early childhood development. *Child Development, 65,* 296–318.

Elder, G., Jr. (1979). Historical change in life patterns and personality. *Life-Span Development and Behavior, 2,* 117–157.

Elder, G., Jr., Nguyen, T. V., & Caspi, A. (1985). Linking family hardships to children's lives. *Child Development, 56,* 361–375.

Ewalt, P. (1998). The revitalization of impoverished communities. In P. Ewalt, E. Freeman, & D. Poole (Eds.), *Community building: Renewal, well-being, and shared responsibility* (pp. 3–5). Washington, DC: NASW Press.

Fonagy, P., Steele, M., Steele, H., Higgitt, A., & Target, M. (1994). The Emmanuel Miller Memorial Lecture 1992: The theory and practice of resilience. *Journal of Child Psychology and Psychiatry, 35,* 231–257.

Franklin, C., & Streeter, C. L. (1992). Social support and psychoeducational interventions with middle class dropout youth. *Child Adolescent Social Work Journal, 9,* 131–153.

Fraser, M. (Ed.). (1997). *Risk and resilience in childhood.* Washington, DC: NASW Press.

Gager, P. J., & Elias, M. J. (1997). Implementing prevention programs in high-risk environments: Application of the resiliency paradigm. *American Journal of Orthopsychiatry, 67,* 363–373.

Garbarino, J. (1995). *Raising children in a socially toxic environment.* San Francisco, CA: Jossey-Bass.

Garbarino, J., & Asp, E. (1981). *Successful schools and competent students.* Lexington, MA: Lexington Books.

Garbarino, J., & Kostelny, K. (1992). Child maltreatment as a community problem. *Child Abuse and Neglect, 16,* 455–464.

Garmezy, N. (1991). Resilience in children's adaptation to negative life events and stressed environments. *Pediatric Annals, 20,* 459–466.

Garmezy, N. (1993). Children in poverty: Resilience despite risk. *Psychiatry, 56,* 127–136.

Genero, N. P. (1998). Culture, resiliency, and mutual psychological development. In H. I. McCubbin, E. A. Thompson, A. I. Thompson, & J. A. Futrell (Eds.), *Resiliency in African-American families* (pp. 31–48). Thousand Oaks, CA: Sage.

Germain, C. B. (1994a). Emerging concepts of family development over the life course. *Families in Society, 75,* 259–267.

Germain, C. B. (1994b). Human behavior in the social environment. In F. G. Reamer (Ed.), *The foundations of social work knowledge* (pp. 88–121). New York: Columbia University Press.

Gitterman, A., & Shulman, L. (1986). *Mutual aid groups and the life cycle.* Itasca, IL: Peacock.

Greene, R. R. (1999). *Human behavior theory and social work practice* (2nd ed.). Hawthorne, NY: Aldine de Gruyter.

Greene, R. R. (2002). Holocaust survivors: A study in resilience. *Journal of Gerontological Social Work, 37*(1), 3–18.

Greene, R. R. (2008a). *Human behavior theory and social work practice* (3rd ed.). New Brunswick, NJ: Transaction Press.

Greene, R. R. (2008b). *Social work with the aged and their families* (3rd ed.). New Brunswick, NJ: Transaction Press.

Greene, R. R. (2010). Family dynamics, the Nazi Holocaust, and mental health treatment. *Journal of Human Behavior and the Social Environment, 20,* 469–488.

Greene, R. R., & Armenta, K. (2007). The REM model: Phase II—Practice strategies. In R. R. Greene (Ed.), *Social work practice: A risk and resilience perspective* (pp. 67–90). Monterey, CA: Brooks/Cole.

Greene, R. R., & Greene, D. G. (2010). Resilience in the face of disasters: Bridging micro and macro-perspectives. *Journal of Human Behavior and the Social Environment, 19,* 1010–1024.

Greene, R. R., & Kropf, N. (2011). *Competence theoretical frameworks.* New Brunswick, NJ: Transaction Press.

Greene, R. R., & Watkins, M. (Eds.). (1998). *Serving diverse constituencies: Applying the ecological perspective.* Hawthorne, NY: Aldine de Gruyter.

Grotberg, E. H. (1995, September). *The international resilience project: Research, application, and policy.* Paper presented at the Symposio Internacional Stress e Violencia, Lisbon, Portugal.

Haight, W. L. (1998). Gathering the spirit at First Baptist Church: Spirituality as a protective factor in the lives of African American children. *Social Work, 43,* 213–221.

Hawley, D. R., & DeHaan, L. (1996). Toward a definition of family resilience: Integrating life-span and family perspectives. *Family Process, 35,* 283–298.

Hendrix, C. C., Jurich, A. P., & Schumm, W. R. (1995). Long-term impact of Vietnam war service on family environment and satisfaction. *Families in Society, 76,* 498–506.

Hetherington, E. M. (1989). Coping with family transitions: Winners, losers, and survivors. *Child Development, 60,* 1–15.

Higgins, G. (1994). *Resilient adults: Overcoming a cruel past.* San Francisco, CA: Jossey-Bass.

Hranjski, H. (2000, February 6). Church healing wounds in Rwanda. *Indianapolis Star,* p. 15.

Hulewat, P. (1996). Resettlement: A cultural and psychological crisis. *Social Work, 41,* 129–135.

Katz, M. (1997). Overcoming childhood adversities: Lessons from those who have "beat the odds." *Intervention in School and Clinic, 32,* 205–210.

Kirby, L. D., & Fraser, M. W. (1997). Risk and resilience in childhood. In M. W. Fraser (Ed.), *Risk and resilience in childhood* (pp. 10–33). Washington, DC: NASW Press.

Kirst-Ashman, K. K., & Hull, G. H. (1999). *Understanding generalist practice.* Chicago: Nelson-Hall.

Lee, J. (1994). *The empowerment approach to social work practice.* New York: Columbia University Press.

Leyser, Y., Heinze, A., & Kapperman, G. (1999). Stress and adaptation in families of children with visual disabilities. *Families in Society, 77,* 240–249.

Lifton, R. J. (1993). *The protean self: Human resilience in an age of fragmentation.* Chicago: University of Chicago Press.

Lorries, B. (2000, June). *Fostering resilience in health maintenance organizations: Oxymoron or reality?* Paper presented at the National Association of Social Workers Indiana chapter meeting, Indianapolis, IN.

Lyons-Ruth, K., Connell, D. B., & Gruenbaum, H. U. (1990). Infants at social risk: Maternal depression and family support services as mediators of infant development and security of attachment. *Child Development, 61,* 85–98.

Mallak, L. (1998). Putting organizational resilience to work. *Industrial Management, 40,* 8–14.

Masten, A. (1994). Resilience in individual development: Successful adaptation despite risk and adversity. In M. C. Wang & E. W. Gordon (Eds.), *Educational resilience in inner-city America: Challenges and prospects* (pp. 3–25). Hillsdale, NJ: Erlbaum.

Masten, A. S., & Coatsworth, J. D. (1998). The development of competence in favorable and unfavorable environments. *American Psychologist, 53,* 205–220.

McCall, N. (1994). *Makes me wanna holler.* New York: Vintage Books.

McCubbin, H. I. (1998). Series preface. In H. I. McCubbin, E. A. Thompson, A. I. Thompson, & J. E. Fromer (Eds.), *Stress, coping, and health in families* (pp. xii–xviii). Thousand Oaks, CA: Sage.

McCubbin, H. I., McCubbin, M. A., Thompson, A. I., & Thompson, E. A. (1998). Resiliency in ethnic families: A conceptual model for predicting family adjustment and adaptation. In H. I. McCubbin, E. A. Thompson, A. I. Thompson, & J. E. Fromer (Eds.), *Resiliency in Native American and immigrant families* (pp. 3–48). Thousand Oaks, CA: Sage.

Miller, G. E., Brehm, K., & Whitehouse, S. (1998). Reconceptualizing school-based prevention for antisocial behavior within a resiliency framework. *School Psychology Review, 27,* 364–379.

Moncher, F. J. (1995). Social isolation and child abuse. *Families in Society, 76,* 421–433.

Moos, R. H. (1987). Person–environment congruence in work, school, and health care settings. *Journal of Vocational Behavior, 31,* 231–247.

Naparastek, A., & Dooley, D. (1998). Countering urban disinvestment through community building initiatives. In P. Ewalt, E. Freeman, & D. Poole (Eds.), *Community building: Renewal, well-being, and shared responsibility* (pp. 6–16). Washington, DC: NASW Press.

Nash, J., & Fraser, M. W. (1998). After-school care for children: A resilience-based approach. *Families in Society, 79,* 370–382.

Neimeyer, R. A., & Stewart, A. E. (1996). Trauma, healing, and the narrative employment of loss. *Families in Society, 77,* 360–375.

Nicholson, B. L. (1997). The influence of pre-emigration and postimmigration stressors on mental health: A study of southeast Asian refugees. *Social Work Research, 21,* 19–31.

Ogbu, J. U. (1992). Understanding cultural diversity and learning. *Educational Researcher, 21*(8), 5–14.

O'Keefe, M. (1994). Adjustment of children from maritally violent homes. *Families in Society, 75,* 403–415.

Olson, M. R., & Haynes, J. A. (1993). Successful single parents. *Families in Society, 74,* 259–267.

Perry, J. C., Liu, X., & Pabian, Y. (2010). School engagement as a mediator of academic performance among urban youth: The role of career preparation, parental career support, and teacher support. *Counseling Psychologist, 38,* 269–295.

Petty, G. L., & Balgopal, P. R. (1998). Multigenerational conflicts and new immigrants: An Indo-American experience. *Families in Society, 79,* 410–423.

Pierce, C. (1969). Violence and counter violence: The need for a children's domestic exchange. *American Journal of Orthopsychiatry, 39,* 553–568.

Pinderhughes, E. (1983). Empowerment for our clients and for ourselves. *Social Casework, 64,* 331–338.

Poindexter, C. C. (1997). In the aftermath: Serial crisis intervention for people with HIV. *Health and Social Work, 22,* 125–132.

Proctor, S. D. (1995). *The substance of things hoped for.* New York: Putnam.

Reed-Victor, E., & Pelco, L. E. (1999). Helping homeless students build resilience. *Journal for a Just and Caring Education, 5,* 51–72.

Reiss, D. (1981). *The family's construction of reality.* Cambridge, MA: Harvard University Press.

Richman, J. M., Rosenfield, L. B., & Bowen, G. (1998). Social support for adolescents at risk of school failure. *Social Work, 23,* 309–323.

Rutter, M. (1979). *Fifteen thousand hours.* Cambridge, MA: Harvard University Press.

Rutter, M. (1985). Resilience in the face of adversity: Protective factors and resistance to psychiatric disorder. *British Journal of Psychiatry, 147,* 589–611.

Rutter, M. (1987). Psychological resilience and protective mechanisms. *American Journal of Orthopsychiatry, 57,* 316–331.

Safyer, A. W. (1994). The impact of inner-city life on adolescent development: Implications for social work. *Smith College Studies in Social Work, 64,* 153–167.

Sampson, R. J., Raudenbush, S. W., & Earls, F. (1997, August 15). Neighborhoods and violent crime: A multilevel study of collective efficacy. *Science, 277,* 918–924.

Schorr, L., & Schorr, D. (1988). *Within our reach: Breaking the cycle of disadvantage.* New York: Anchor Books.

Schriver, J. M. (2010). *Human behavior and the social environment.* New York: Prentice Hall.

Seligman, M. (1991). *Learned optimism.* New York: Pocket Books.

Solomon, B. B. (1976). *Black empowerment: Social work in oppressed communities.* New York: Columbia University Press.

Terkelsen, G. (1980). Toward a theory of the family cycle. In E. A. Carter & M. McGoldrick (Eds.), *The family life cycle: A framework for family therapy* (pp. 21–52). New York: Gardner.

Thomlison, B. (1997). Risk and protective factors in child maltreatment. In M. W. Fraser (Ed.), *Risk and resilience in childhood: An ecological perspective* (pp. 50–72). Washington, DC: NASW Press.

Thompson, E. A., McCubbin, H. I., Thompson, A. I., & Elver, K. M. (1998). Vulnerability and resiliency in Native Hawaiian families under stress. In H. I. McCubbin, E. A. Thompson, A. I. Thompson, & J. E. Fromer (Eds.), *Resiliency in Native American and immigrant families* (pp. 115–132). Thousand Oaks, CA: Sage.

Thompson, M. S., & Peebles-Wilkins, W. (1992). The impact of formal, informal, and societal support networks on the psychological well-being of black adolescent mothers. *Social Work, 37,* 322–328.

Tracy, E. M. (1990). Identifying social support resources of at-risk families. *Social Work, 35,* 252–258.

Tracy, E. M., & Whittaker, J. K. (1990). The social network map: Assessing social support in clinical practice. *Families in Society, 71,* 461–470.

Tseng, W. S., & Hsu, J. (1991). *Culture and family: Problems and therapy.* New York: Haworth Press.

Vosler, N. R. (1990). Assessing family access to basic resources: An essential component of social work practice. *Social Work, 35,* 434–441.

Walsh, F. (1996). Strengthening family resilience: Crisis and challenge. *Family Process, 35,* 261–281.

Walsh, F. (1998). *Strengthening family resilience.* New York: Guilford Press.

Wang, M., Haertel, G., & Walberg, H. (1994). Educational resilience in inner cities. In M. C. Wang & E. W. Gordon (Eds.), *Educational resilience in inner-city America: Challenges and prospects* (pp. 45–72). Hillsdale, NJ: Erlbaum.

Werner, E. E. (1993). Risk, resilience, and recovery. Perspectives from the Kauai longitudinal study. *Development and Psychopathology, 5,* 503–515.

Werner, E., & Smith, R. (1992). *Overcoming the odds: High risk children from birth to adulthood.* Ithaca, NY: Cornell University Press.

Winfield, L. F. (1994). *Developing resilience in urban youth.* Retrieved from http://ncrel.org/sdrs/areas/issues/educatrs/leadrshp/le0win.htm

Wolin, S., & Wolin, S. (1995). Resilience among youth growing up in substance abusing families. *Pediatric Clinics of North America, 42,* 415–429.

Ziefert, M., & Brown, K. S. (1991). Skill building for effective intervention with homeless families. *Families in Society, 72,* 212–219.

Zunz, S., Turner, S., & Norman, E. (1993). Accentuating the positive: Stressing resiliency in school-based substance abuse prevention programs. *Social Work in Education, 15,* 169–176.

4

Resilience Research: Methodological Square Pegs and Theoretical Black Holes

WILLIAM H. BARTON

On finishing this chapter, students will be able to further:

Apply critical thinking to inform and communicate professional judgments (Educational Policy 2.1.3) by

- Distinguishing, appraising, and integrating multiple sources of knowledge, including research-based knowledge and practice wisdom.
- Analyzing models of assessment, prevention, intervention, and evaluation (practice behaviors).

Engage in research-informed practice and practice-informed research (Educational Policy 2.1.6) by

- Using practice experience to inform scientific inquiry.
- Using research evidence to inform practice (practice behaviors).

Technically, we are dealing here with a concept that has not yet been empirically specified. Nonetheless, it claims empirical standing by its reference either to an imputed individual characteristic or as a label of a category of events.

—Bartelt, 1994, p. 99

The latter part of the 20th century saw a rich array of research, much of it longitudinal, from several disciplines seeking to delineate the pathways from childhood throughout the life course to adaptation in adulthood. What began as a search for predictors of pathological outcomes, such as serious and persistent mental illness, crime, substance abuse, and family violence, eventually generated interest in the other side of the equation, that is, predictors of positive adaptation, especially those positive outcomes that seemed to defy the odds and that occurred where pathology might well have been expected. This body of research, much of it referenced throughout this book, has used various methodologies and has involved investigators and participants from several cultures and time periods. At the beginning of the 21st century, the results of these studies seem to converge, providing a good general idea of the factors that promote or threaten positive adaptation and under what conditions.

This chapter reviews some of the highlights of this research and examines the status of its claims to knowledge. Following a brief conceptual overview and a summary of selected studies, it looks more closely at core theoretical concepts, their operationalization, and the research designs used to explore their relationships. It is suggested that experts know less than is generally assumed, at least in the manner in which this knowledge is usually described, but, paradoxically, perhaps quite a bit that is useful for social work. The chapter closes with a discussion of the implications of resilience research for social work practice and research.

Conceptual Domain

Resilience, the central focus of this volume, is but one important concept in the theoretical universe of the life course. Risk factors, protective factors, vulnerabilities, and assets are among the other more familiar key terms (see chapter 2). Before critically examining the methods used in resilience research, it is necessary to have some conceptual clarity.

Although outcomes for any individual cannot be predicted with certainty, one can estimate the *risk,* or statistical probability, of a particular outcome for a group of persons sharing some characteristics or experiences that have a demonstrable association with the outcome. Studies have shown, for example, that children exposed to violence in the home are more likely to engage in violent behavior as adults. Thus, exposure to family violence is a risk factor for subsequent violent behavior. Risk factors can be either specific (that is, predictive of a particular outcome, as in the example above) or general (that is, associated with a variety of problematic outcomes). For example, poverty and poor educational achievement, among other problems, have been linked to a variety of negative outcomes (Fraser, Kirby, & Smokowski, 2004). Risk factors may be characteristics of persons, including biological and psychological aspects, and/or their physical or social environments. Risk factors may operate individually, but there is considerable evidence that outcomes worsen in the presence of multiple risks (for example, Newcomb & Felix-Ortiz, 1992; Pollard, Hawkins, & Arthur, 1999; Rutter, 1990, 2001).

It is not always clear whether a risk factor functions as a direct cause or as a *marker* for other more proximal causal processes (Fraser, Richman, & Galinsky, 1999). For example, having a parent with a severe mental illness is a risk factor for a child developing a mental illness in adulthood. The parent's mental illness may provide a direct biological cause (to some extent), and/or its effect on parenting behavior may affect the child's adaptation.

Vulnerabilities are factors that make it more likely that an individual will experience risks or that may amplify the effect of exposure to risk. Individuals may respond differently to the presence of a risk factor depending on their relative vulnerability either to the specific risk or to risks in general. It is not always clear whether a given factor (for example, poverty) should be considered a risk factor or a vulnerability.

Just as the presence of risk factors increases the probability of problematic outcomes, the presence of protective factors increases the probability of positive adaptations by preventing or buffering the effect of risk factors. As with risk factors, protective factors may provide either specific or general protection and may be found in the individual, the family, or the broader environment. Protective factors frequently mentioned in the literature include a child's easygoing temperament, intelligence, a positive relationship with a caregiver or other adult, and economic resources in the environment.

Although Masten (1994) referred to social assets as the counterpart to risks, they may be more accurately contrasted with vulnerabilities. *Social assets* are resources that can potentially promote positive adaptations whether or not one is exposed to risks. As with risks and vulnerabilities, it is often unclear whether a given factor should be considered an asset or a protective factor.

Interest in resilience emerged as developmental researchers puzzled over those empirical outliers who apparently succeeded despite contexts, histories, and stresses that may conspire to condemn many to failure. For example, although many children with mentally ill parents develop such problems themselves, not all do (Anthony, 1987; Worland, Janes, Anthony, McGinnis, & Cass, 1984). Although many who suffer child abuse show persistent effects into adulthood and mirror abuse in their own parenting, not all do (Egeland, Jacobvitz, & Sroufe, 1988). Children growing up in economically poor families in socially disorganized urban neighborhoods tend to have difficulties in school and/or to experience problems with the law, among other things, but not all do

(Furstenberg, Cook, Eccles, Elder, & Sameroff, 1999; Gordon & Song, 1994; Long & Vaillant, 1989; Luthar, 1991). If such factors as parental mental illness, poor parenting behaviors, abuse, poverty, and resource-poor neighborhoods are clear, strong predictors of poor aggregate outcomes across several domains of functioning, why and how do so many individuals escape that grim statistical forecast? Researchers have thus turned their attention to questions about the nature of resilience and how an understanding of it might inform attempts to evoke, nurture, and/or create conditions for such phenomena more widely so that more people can defy the odds.

Quantitative Studies

As outlined by Nash and Randolph (2004), most resilience research has adopted the quantitative methods of epidemiological studies. At the simplest level, broad population surveys can reveal associations between developmental outcomes and characteristics of individuals and their environments, although they cannot address issues of causality. Two common epidemiological approaches are cohort studies and case-control studies. *Cohort studies* begin with two similar groups that differ in their exposure to potential risk and protective factors. These groups are then followed prospectively to track the subsequent incidence of outcomes. The relative risks of the outcomes are then calculated for the two groups. *Case-control studies* begin by identifying a group that already exhibits a problem or adverse outcome (the case group) and then finding a matching control group that does not exhibit that outcome. The relative exposure of the groups to suspected risk (or protective) factors is then measured. The relative exposure rate is expressed as an odds ratio (that is, those who developed the outcome were *x* times more likely than those who did not to have been exposed to the risk factor).

Relative risks and odds ratios are useful for comparing outcomes among groups after some set period of time. Survival analysis, or event history analysis, indicates when such exposures or outcomes occur and whether such timing is different among different groups. Nash and Randolph (2004) provide a more detailed introduction to such methods and examples of their application to the study of the effects of risk and protective factors.

An example of an ambitious cross-sectional survey may be found in a report of early findings from the Add Health national study, a longitudinal study of adolescents in grades 7 through 12 (Resnick et al., 1997). The results support the notion that family and school contexts as well as individual characteristics are associated with healthy and risky behaviors in adolescents. A systematic random sample of 80 high schools was drawn from all high schools in the United States. One component of the study involved in-home interviews with a random sample of the students in the sample schools (N = 12,118). Three fourths of the students also completed an in-school survey. For most (85.6 percent), a parent also completed a half-hour interview. Respondents were randomly partitioned into exploratory and validation samples of approximately equal size. Results were reported for the validation sample. Separate analyses were performed for grades 7 through 8 and 9 through 12. The dependent variables included measures of emotional distress, suicide, violence, substance abuse (cigarettes, alcohol, marijuana), age of sexual debut, and history of pregnancy. Independent variables included measures of stressors and protective factors drawn from the resiliency literature, including several aspects of family context, school context, and individual characteristics. Independent variables were divided into two sets: generic (expected to be associated with every dependent variable, including parent–family connectedness, school connectedness, and self-esteem) and domain specific (applied to specific dependent variables). Stepwise regression analysis strategies were used to estimate the independent contribution of each group of independent variables (family, school, and individual characteristics) to each dependent variable.

Parent–family connectedness and perceived school connectedness were found to be protective against every health risk behavior except a history of pregnancy. Ease of access to guns at home was associated with suicide and violence. Access in the home to substances such as cigarettes, alcohol, and marijuana was associated with their use. High school students who worked 20 hours or more a week experienced more emotional distress and substance use. High school students who appeared older than others their age also had more emotional distress and suicide rates and experimented earlier with substances and sexual experiences. Repeating a grade in school was associated with emotional distress among all students and with tobacco use among junior high school students. In contrast, parental expectations regarding school achievement were associated with lower levels of health risk behaviors; parental disapproval of early sexual debut was associated with a later age of onset of intercourse.

These results are from a cross-sectional study, and there could be questions about the relationships and causal directions among some of the variables. For instance, risky behaviors could jeopardize a youth's school or family relationships rather than the other way around. In short, this ambitious and presumably expensive study seems to have done little more than reaffirm what is already known. The sampling scope does, however, provide some confidence in the generalizability of the associations. Perhaps the Add Health research will produce more valuable findings in its later stages after subsequent waves of data collection.

Among the longitudinal studies that have produced rich insights into resilience, perhaps the best known is the prospective study conducted by Werner and colleagues in Hawaii (Werner, Bierman, & French, 1971; Werner & Smith,

1977, 1982, 1992, 2001). The study examined the 1955 birth cohort on the island of Kauai ($N = 837$) for whom demographic, prenatal, and perinatal data were available. Follow-ups were conducted at ages 2, 10, 18, 31–32, and 40. The majority of the children were of Asian or Polynesian descent, and more than half came from poor families. Data sources included interviews with parents, interviews with cohort members, clinical psychological evaluations, and records from public agencies. The many follow-ups over an extended period of time provide an unusually detailed picture of consistencies and inconsistencies over the life course from birth to adulthood.

Werner and Smith (1982) identified several early predictors of serious coping problems in children and youth. These predictors encompassed biological variables (moderate to severe prenatal stress, congenital defects at birth, moderate to marked physical disability by age 10), the caregiving environment (low level of maternal education, low standard of living, low rating of family stability), and behavioral variables (low infant activity level at age one, low IQ, recognized need for mental health services, placement in a class for students with learning disabilities). Predictions from these variables were stronger for children from poor homes than those from middle-class homes. As Werner and Smith (1982) noted,

> The presence of *four or more* of these predictors in the records of children by age 2 appeared to be a realistic dividing line between children who developed serious learning and/or behavior problems by age 10 or 18, and most of the boys and girls who were able to cope successfully. (p. 47)

However, among those who encountered four or more serious risk factors before age two, about a third managed successful adaptations. These were the focus of Werner and Smith's exploration of resilience. By age 31 or 32, as Werner and Smith (1992) noted,

> Personal competence and determination, support from a spouse or mate, and faith were the shared qualities that characterized the resilient children as adults. With few exceptions they worked well and loved well in contexts far different from the traumatic domestic scenes that had characterized their childhoods. (p. 74)

These individuals had obtained more education and were more likely to be employed than the average person their age, let alone their less successful peers. However, they also experienced more stress-related health problems and exhibited aloofness in interpersonal relationships.

Of particular importance in this study is the subsample of individuals determined to be at high risk from birth and early childhood because of physical complications, poverty, and family dysfunction. The longitudinal design permitted the Kauai researchers to identify early influences that differentiated the resilient children from their equally high-risk but less successful peers. Factors predicting resilience included several personal characteristics (for example, a more easy-going temperament as an infant; more alertness, autonomy, and social orientation as toddlers; more interests and better academic attitudes, effort, and performance; more achievement orientation, assertiveness, and independence) as well as family factors (fewer siblings, fewer prolonged separations from a primary caregiver, a close bond with at least one caregiver) and outside influences (for example, at least one close friend, participation in extracurricular activities).

An additional contribution of the Kauai study is its documentation of the subsequent trajectories of children who had developed serious coping problems by adolescence, including teenage pregnancy, delinquency, or mental health problems. Most showed substantial improvements by age 31 or 32. Most (90 percent) of the teenage mothers were gainfully employed, and the majority (60 percent) had obtained additional schooling. The majority of those with records of juvenile offenses (75 percent of men and 90 percent of women) did not go on to commit crimes as adults, and about half of those in need of mental health services as children or adolescents showed positive adaptations. The factors that seemed to be associated with these positive shifts in life trajectories were education at community colleges, education and vocational skills acquired during military service, and connection to a church or religious community (Werner & Smith, 1992). In the age 40 follow-up, Werner and Smith (2001) developed detailed path models relating protective factors and stressful life events to quality of adaptation and psychological well-being at age 40. These models, although differing slightly for men and women, reflected an ecological interplay between protective factors within the individual (for example, temperament, self-efficacy) and outside sources of support and stress as predictors of developmental outcomes at midlife.

The Seattle Social Development Project (SSDP; see Hawkins, Kosterman, Catalano, Hill, & Abbott, 2008, for an overview of its history and design) is another ambitious longitudinal study that seeks to track the effect of school-based interventions designed to promote protective factors and reduce risk factors on the subsequent incidence of youth problem behaviors. Beginning with a cohort of first-grade students in eight Seattle public schools in 1981, and adding additional students to create a full study cohort of 808 by the fifth grade, the SSDP used a quasi-experimental design to compare outcomes such as alcohol and substance abuse, gang membership, violence, teen pregnancy, educational achievement, civic engagement, and mental health disorders through adolescence to ages 24 and 27 for students assigned to multiple groups (full intervention in grades 1–6, late intervention in grades 5–6 only, and a control group).

SSDP researchers have produced numerous reports of their findings (for example, Hawkins, Catalano, Morrison, et al., 1992; Hawkins, Kosterman, Catalano, Hill, & Abbott, 2005; Hawkins, Kosterman, et al., 2008; Herrenkohl et al., 2003; Hill, Howell, Hawkins, & Battin-Pearson, 1999). Although they do not provide unequivocal support for all of the theoretically based hypotheses, the results have been sufficiently promising such that the SSDP framework has been endorsed as a cost-effective strategy for preventing crime and violence (Aos, Phipps, Barnoski, & Lieb, 2001). As summarized by Hawkins, Kosterman, et al. (2008),

> Our findings indicate that a theory-based intervention that improved parenting practices, children's social competence, and classroom management and instruction during the elementary grades influenced some, though not all, indices of adult functioning in individuals in their mid- to late 20s. The elementary grade intervention was associated with greater accomplishment and engagement in school, work, and community and fewer mental health problems by ages 24 and 27 years. (p. 1139)

Whereas studies such as the Kauai research and the SSDP involved years of prospective data collection, other researchers have turned to the secondary analysis of data collected by others to provide new insights. James and Paul (1993) pointed out several advantages of secondary data analysis: (1) the ability to address new questions without collecting new data, (2) the possibility of extending research questions to larger or differently constructed samples, (3) the ability to conduct follow-up studies of existing cross-sectional or longitudinal studies, and (4) the potential for recoding and reanalyzing qualitative data in light of theoretical advances.

For example, Caspi, Elder, and Herbener (1990) used data from the Berkeley Guidance Study to examine the relationship between early childhood temperament and adult adaptation. The Berkeley Guidance Study was initiated in 1928–1929 and sampled every third birth in the city of Berkeley, California, over 19 months, resulting in a total sample of 214 persons. Caspi and colleagues studied only the males ($N = 102$, of whom 87 were followed into adulthood). Data were obtained from interviews and life records regarding education, work, marriage, and parenthood. The researchers grouped the children into three types: ill tempered (38 percent), shy (28 percent), and dependent (33 percent). Caspi and colleagues documented distinct life-course patterns for the three types, with ill-tempered children showing problems in adulthood such as more limited education and occupational attainments. Ill-tempered children also tended to be earlier in their transitions to adult roles, whereas shy children showed off-time late transitions. The implicit, normative interpretation of these latter findings is somewhat questionable, however, because on-time transitions, attributed to the dependent children and viewed as the norm, were defined as the overall mean for the sample. One could just as easily conclude that the ill-tempered children were on time and everyone else was late, or that the shy children were on time and everyone else was early. Furthermore, one may question the original classification scheme: Were there no children who exhibited neither shyness, dependence, nor ill temperedness?

Qualitative Studies

Several researchers have identified as a limitation of nomothetic, quantitative approaches (those that seek to uncover abstract universal principles) their inattention to the role of the actor's perceptions or constructions of contexts, experiences, and events. Thus, what may appear to many persons, including researchers, as a stressful event may be perceived by others either as neutral or even perhaps as a positive challenge. The subjective construction of meaning may make all the difference in understanding the effects of an event on the individual involved. Gore and Eckenrode (1994), for example, noted that a teenage daughter's pregnancy may precipitate depression in a single mother not because of the pregnancy and its attendant material burdens but because of its meaning as an indicator of failed parenting. Although many resilience theorists mention the active participation of an individual in the resilience process (for example, Egeland, Carlson, & Sroufe, 1993), few quantitative studies include individuals' subjective accounts of their experiences. Qualitative methods are better suited to this task (Ungar & Teram, 2005).

Although the results of many qualitative studies are consistent with those found in quantitative, epidemiological research, the detailed descriptions in the words of the respondents help to bring concepts such as risk pileup, social support, and sense of agency to life. They also highlight the role of subjective meanings that individuals attribute to their contexts and experiences. Gilgun (1999), for example, used interpretive phenomenological methods in her study of the development of violent behaviors and how perpetrators experience their own violent acts. In the course of her interviews with a sample of 66 adults (about two thirds of whom had committed serious violence), she identified seven who provided insights into resilience. These individuals, despite histories of childhood adversities and violent behaviors, had managed by the time of the interviews to develop into adults who met a definitional guideline of resilience as "loving well, working well, and expecting well" (p. 48). From her in-depth interviews, Gilgun identified a general pattern among these individuals:

> experiences of multiple risks over time; using resources within the self and the environment to cope; developing a pro-social sense of agency; coping with, adapting to, and overcoming the risks at the time of their occurrence and well into the future; and adult relationships that were affirming and helpful in terms of dealing with everyday stress. (p. 51)

In another qualitative study, Gordon and Song (1994) used a grounded theory framework to conduct a retrospective life history analysis of 26 African Americans who "made it against the odds." Factors that emerged included effort in conjunction with prosocial goals, support from others (for example, a parent) for development, autonomy (an internal locus of control), a close relationship with a significant other, the subjective meaning of context (for example, "we never thought of ourselves as poor"), and spiritual connections.

Qualitative studies can illuminate how an individual's sense of identity or narrative construction of his or her life can influence life outcomes, even as they shift over time. For example, qualitative studies of adults returning from prisons (Maruna, 2001; O'Brien, 2001) suggest that a key to successful reintegration is found not so much in structured programs offered by professionals but in individuals' abilities to engage their own motivation and strengths, along with social supports from friends and families. Although the professional community has developed reentry programs that involve case management and needs-based services, people released from prisons may not trust such programs, viewing them as extensions of social control. Only qualitative methods can reveal such insights.

Limitations of Resilience Research

All research approaches have their limitations. Purely cross-sectional surveys may identify associations among a host of variables, but they can do little to untangle the nature of any causal relationships among them. Case-control designs, which attempt to identify predictors by comparing a sample that exhibits some outcome (for example, mental illness, crime) with a control group that does not, represent an improvement. However, what about other persons who show similar patterns of predictors but do not exhibit the outcome? The tendency here is to overestimate the importance of an alleged predictor.

The study of resilience requires attention to the life-course perspective, which amounts to a simultaneous consideration of three interactive dimensions: person, environment, and time. The use of longitudinal research, especially prospective, cohort designs such as the Kauai study (Werner & Smith, 2001), is one of the best ways to capture all three dimensions. Yet longitudinal studies can be expensive and logistically challenging, so researchers tend to use relatively narrow samples. Moreover, such studies seldom combine several overlapping cohorts. Thus, prospective, longitudinal cohort designs often have limited generalizability as a result of sampling and cohort effects. In addition, as Coie et al. (1993) noted, "Careful attention must be given in such [prospective] designs to the timing of measurements, both to detect influences that occur only during a limited period of development and to detect lagged effects" (p. 1015).

Variable-centered studies, whether longitudinal or not, are susceptible to the ecological fallacy in aggregate analyses. Variable-centered, multivariate models describe weighted combinations of predictors derived from the aggregation of individuals' values on these predictors. However, no individual need exhibit the weighted combination. In contrast, person-centered approaches (for example, Bergman & Magnusson, 1997; Magnusson & Bergman, 1990) develop typologies of individuals who show distinct patterns of the presence or absence of predictors and then examine the association between types and outcomes as they develop over time (Nash & Randolph, 2004).

All quantitative designs face the issue of model specificity. That is, to what extent is error variance owing to incomplete specification (that is, the omission of important but unknown predictors)? Because resilience is often inferred from the error variance of multivariate risk prediction models, it is impossible to determine whether the error really reflects resilience or whether a better specified model would have explained more of the variance.

To what extent are measured constructs theoretically meaningful versus markers for something else? There is the potential problem of "operationism in reverse," that is, treating what is measured for a reified concept (Bartelt, 1994). As Rigsby (1994) noted,

> For each of the categories of life experiences where resilience has been applied, researchers have made judgments about desirable and undesirable outcomes, about risks and assets (both individual and social), and about assessments of the likelihood of successful adaptations, given the risks and assets. . . . "Resilient" individuals are those whose adaptations represent extreme positive residuals from a prediction equation where adaptations are predicted from a linear combination of risks and assets. (p. 88)

Then there is the question of the role of subjective and intersubjective "meaning," as discussed previously. Meaning could almost be considered a fourth dimension. Qualitative studies are necessary to explore this, but by themselves they cannot yield a complete picture of the complex relationships among risks, protective factors, and outcomes.

The biggest limitations of resilience research may be the result of theoretical problems. First, how can one differentiate between risk factors, vulnerabilities, protective factors, and opportunities or assets? For example, is poverty a risk factor or a contextual vulnerability? Is social support a protective factor or buffer relevant only in the presence of risk, or a direct opportunity factor that enhances outcomes with or without exposure to risk? Seifer and Sameroff (1987), for example, noted that although Werner and Smith (1982) defined risk in terms of perinatal factors, with high socioeconomic status and family support acting as buffers, one could have chosen socioeconomic status as the primary risk indicator with good perinatal status as a protective factor.

Second, is resilience even meaningful, or is it a culturally imposed (prototypically American), artificial, and unnecessary concept? Do theories need to include resilience, or would they do better by elaborating a variety of perhaps complex and bidirectional combinatorial schemes of other developmental concepts? Rigsby (1994), for example, has claimed that resilience, with its emphasis on individualism and mobility striving, is a "quintessentially U.S. concept" (p. 85). He identified several implicit assumptions behind the concept:

1. Everyone can and should strive to "get ahead" . . . (it is left implicit that this will entail surpassing others).
2. The arena of competition for getting ahead is open, fair and accessible to all (no structural impediments for groups defined by race, gender, culture, etc.).
3. The competition for getting ahead is structured like a continuing game, . . . one can always get oneself together and reenter the competition.
4. Disadvantages that affect one's chances of success are individual and can be overcome with individual effort. (p. 87)

At one extreme, some researchers, such as the Search Institute's Peter Benson (1997), advocate focusing exclusively on resilience by promoting assets and protective factors and ignoring risk factors, seeing the latter as emphasizing a person's deficits, rather than strengths. A potential danger in emphasizing resilience, according to those who would share Rigsby's (1994) perspective, is that less attention is then devoted to policies and programs that address the more structural causes of people's differential exposure and susceptibility to risks and, thus, differential probability of developing problematic outcomes. Despite the claims of the more sophisticated scholars that resilience is a process involving the interaction of persons and their environments, there is an inherently individualistic connotation to the concept (Tolan, 1996). Furthermore, to ignore risk factors seems misguided in the face of a wealth of empirical evidence documenting their association with a variety of problematic outcomes. Although it may be true, as stated by Pittman and Cahill (1991), that promoting positive adaptation means more than just avoiding or reducing problematic outcomes, attention should be applied to both reducing risks and promoting assets and protective factors (Fraser & Terzian, 2005; Pollard et al., 1999).

Resilience and the Life Course

Resilience as a concept is embedded in the life-course perspective of human development. A somewhat simplistic outline of the life-course perspective might go roughly as follows:

- Individuals vary among one another in their long-term developmental outcomes (that is, some people exhibit positive internal and external adaptations and others do not).
- Individuals vary within themselves over time and across role/behavioral domains in the quality of their adaptations.
- Several known attributes of persons and their environments, at various levels from the biological to the macrosocietal, tend to be associated with various positive developmental outcomes at various stages.
- Similarly, other attributes of persons and their environments tend to be associated with negative developmental outcomes.
- The relationships among predictors and outcomes are complex. They cannot be fully captured by simple linear, additive models. The relationships include interactions, suppressions, amplifications, and reciprocal causation.
- Outcomes are characterized by both equifinality (that is, there is more than one pathway to a particular outcome) and multifinality (a given set of predictors may produce different outcomes in different individuals or even for the same individual at different times or in different domains).

Consider the life-course perspective and the concept of resilience as applied to the following hypothetical scenario. Justin is 16 years old, nearing the end of his 10th-grade year in a large, urban high school. He has done well in school, earning mostly As and Bs, with regular attendance and participation in some extracurricular activities. He has two younger siblings, and his parents both work and have consistently stressed the importance of education to their children. The family attends a neighborhood church regularly. Justin is generally considered to be a nice guy, even-tempered, clearheaded, and moderately concerned about the feelings and welfare of others. He has a more or less steady girlfriend and a group of other friends among his classmates.

One of these friends is James, whose profile is somewhat different. Although not an outstanding student, James has performed reasonably well in school despite a difficult family situation. His father, an alcoholic, left the family when James was 10, after having physically abused both James and his mother on several occasions. His mother has been unable to maintain steady employment. James has a few friends in school, including Justin, who share his interest in computers.

On one of the first really warm spring days, James suggests to Justin that they skip school, drive out to a suburban park, and get high. Will Justin go? Moreover, what, if anything, would this decision and its sequelae imply for Justin's subsequent adult adaptive outcomes?

Most people would probably respond, "No, Justin doesn't seem to be the kind of boy who would skip school and use illegal drugs." But why? What predictors of conventional conformity are in this scenario? A strong family? Connection to a faith community? Close peer relationships? Good school adjustment, achievement, and involvement? Empathy? Positive self-concept? These are all examples of what much of the research has identified as assets or protective factors predictive of positive, or resilient, outcomes in the face of environmental stress or risk. Which, if any, of these is necessary or sufficient, either singly or in combination, to cause Justin to resist the stress of the peer invitation to engage in deviance? Conversely, would a classmate who appeared to lack all of Justin's assets necessarily be expected to go along with the deviant peer? Moreover, would it matter how Justin perceived the situation, what terms he used to describe himself, the invitation, the potential consequences, and so forth?

To continue with this hypothetical scenario, suppose that, just this once, Justin goes along with his friend and, alas, both boys are arrested for possession of marijuana. Would the effects of this environmental stressor be the same or different on Justin and James? Would Justin, who appears to have a greater array of assets, be the more resilient boy, viewing this experience as an anomaly and quickly returning to his path of successful adaptation?

Alternatively, perhaps James, presumably having had more of an opportunity to develop resilient strategies as a result of greater prior exposure to risk, would be the more resilient one. Current thinking and research in the area of resilience could be used to support either prediction and is thus uninformative.

Therein lies a problem with the concept of resilience. If resilience is defined following Masten (1994) as overcoming unfavorable odds, sustaining competence in the face of risk, or recovering from trauma, the concept can only be applied "after the fact," as it were—after exposure to environmental stress. Thus, does it really provide any additional theoretical clarity beyond the concept of coping?

As difficult as it is to pinpoint the confluence of factors at a given, static point in time, imagine the challenge of trying to elucidate the dynamically evolving tapestry of a life over time. Research tools, and even everyday language, are much better suited to descriptions of static conditions than dynamic processes. The act of measurement freezes time, such that even longitudinal studies can do no better than assemble multiple frames. The time elapsed between frames is too great to permit them to be "animated" like cartoon gels (the individual, static drawings that, when viewed in rapid sequence, produce the illusion of motion). So, one is left with what can be measured and what can be described.

The life-course model begs to be cast in terms of symbolic "interactionism" (Blumer, 1969). Symbolic interactionism posits the centrality of meaning, as constructed by the "actor-in-interaction," for understanding human behavior. An individual approaches an encounter equipped with (1) his or her identity in its current state derived from a history of social interaction; (2) an intention, more or less clearly formed, or desired outcome of the impending encounter; (3) a perception of the other person, derived from some combination of prior experience and/or quasi-stereotypical, learned overgeneralizations; (4) an expectation of what the other person is likely to intend and do; and (5) a resulting plan of initiatory or reactive action. The "other" arrives similarly equipped. As the exchange proceeds, the actions of self and other *as interpreted,* initially in light of expectations, may produce modifications in any or all of the elements. In a smooth interaction, the exchange quickly produces an interpretive consensus and reinforces old learning or instills new interpersonal learning, but this does not always occur.

In the aftermath of this exchange, whatever its outcome, the individual must integrate this experience into the constantly evolving, subjective narrative of his or her life. Through various well-known psychological processes (for example, selective perceptions, attributions, cognitive dissonance reduction), this particular experience and the individual's preexisting constructions accommodate and assimilate to produce some form of narrative consistency.

Now, to apply this perspective to the life course, at any point in time a person inhabits his or her evolving narrative with its multiple plot threads, shaped and informed by prior experience, current motivations, and cognitions. Both the physical and social environments are scanned for their meaning in light of this narrative construction, and actions ensue accordingly. The consequences of the action may or may not be as the individual hopes or predicts, but they are nonetheless incorporated into the dynamically evolving narrative, for better or worse, and become part of the "package" the individual brings to the next encounter. Over time, one can see patterns in one's own and others' lives along with critical "defining moments" or "turning points" in which narratives are clearly reinforced or modified.

This is one way to interpret the longitudinal findings of the Kauai study (Werner & Smith, 2001) as well as Laub and Sampson's (2003) longitudinal study examining desistance of criminal offending over the life course. The life course researcher can study one or more points in a person's life, delineate the risk and protective factors along with assets and vulnerabilities, and either retrospectively interpret a current outcome or prospectively attempt to predict a future one. The retrospective interpretations are overdetermined, that is, it is always possible to construct a coherent retrospective account for any outcome or its opposite. The prospective predictions, in contrast, are greatly underdetermined, primarily because the subjective element of narrative construction cannot be captured with anything less than the lived experience.

Value of Resilience Research for Social Work

If resilience is a vague or empty concept, and if life course research is highly compromised, how can social work benefit from this enterprise? Haggerty and Sherrod (1994) suggested that four important themes have emerged from resilience-related research resulting in implications for intervention or prevention programs. These themes are (1) the interrelatedness of risk factors and problem outcomes, (2) the inter- as well as intraindividual variation that exists in the factors responsible for resilience and susceptibility to stress, (3) the necessity of examining processes and mechanisms that link multiple stressors to multiple outcomes, and (4) the need for intervention and prevention programs to break the link between stress and adverse outcomes that can be designed from a recognition of the previous three themes: interrelatedness and individual variability along with linking mechanisms.

Despite its limitations, the overall body of resilience research from multiple methods has produced a convergence of findings that can usefully inform practice and policy, even in the absence of a definitive theoretical resolution. The concept of resilience, for all its imprecision, serves to orient researchers and practitioners alike to the positive potentials of individuals-in-situations. Whether the positive outcomes are to be attributed to something called "resilience" or to some more complex combination of risk factors, protective factors, vulnerabilities, and assets may not be critical for practice.

It is important to note that research surrounding risk, resilience, and protection has used a wide variety of quantitative and qualitative methods. McGrath (1982) has persuasively advocated for multimethod programs of research. In combination, the strengths of one method may compensate for a weakness of another. A convergence of findings from multiple methods of inquiry thus generates greater confidence than would findings from a body of research consisting largely of replications using a single method. Longitudinal, cross-sectional, quantitative, and qualitative studies in the area of resilience have pointed to similar combinations of personal characteristics, family characteristics, and more macro influences as being associated with positive life outcomes in both the presence and the absence of considerable risk. Masten (1994), for example, listed the following:

> effective parenting; connections to other competent adults; appeal to other people, particularly adults; good intellectual skills; areas of talent or accomplishment valued by self and others; self-efficacy, self-worth and hopefulness; religious faith or affiliations; socioeconomic advantages; good schools and other community assets; and good fortune. (p. 14)

Moreover, these facilitating factors seem to be quite general, that is, they are applicable across cultures and in the face of risks for a variety of unfavorable outcomes. Some of these influences are more malleable than others and can provide targets for policy and program interventions. The targeting of policies and programs toward enhancing positive development can move experts beyond relying solely on categorically addressing the prevention and remediation of multiple, specific problematic outcomes.

At the same time, however, experts must continue to address the very real and powerful risks that differentially beset portions of the population. Those risks are also becoming well understood (Hawkins, Catalano, & Miller, 1992; Jenson & Fraser, 2011; Pollard et al., 1999). The resulting practice implications include support for a range of endeavors from educating community stakeholders about the prevalence of local risk and protective factors, to mobilizing communities to reduce risks and enhance protection, to adopting multisystemic and strengths perspectives when working with individual clients (Fraser & Galinsky, 2004; Fraser & Terzian, 2005).

Communities That Care (CTC; Hawkins, Catalano, & Associates, 1992) is a good example of a community-level strategy to enhance the probability of positive developmental outcomes based on the risk and resilience framework. The social development model (Catalano & Hawkins, 1996), which explicitly incorporates the risk and resilience framework, provides the theoretical foundation for CTC. This model, in turn, has found empirical support in the SSDP's longitudinal research discussed previously. The CTC strategy includes community mobilization, local assessment of risk and protective factors, and a menu of evidence-based programs that can be tailored to meet specific communities' needs. Several communities in Pennsylvania were among the early adopters of CTC, and an evaluation (Greenberg & Feinberg, 2002) showed CTC counties with modestly reduced delinquency rates compared to non-CTC counties, despite somewhat inconsistent implementation of the strategy. More recently, based on an experimental, county-level design in multiple states, Hawkins, Brown, et al. (2008) reported early results showing reductions in targeted risk factors and delayed onset of delinquent behavior among youth in CTC sites.

Research Tasks for the Future

Given what remains unknown, a mix of quantitative and qualitative methods applied across multiple cultures, substantive areas, and historical eras is desirable to further researchers' knowledge of resilience and related concepts. The research should continue to elucidate patterns of life-course trajectories. Some of this research should be person centered rather than variable centered. The suggestions for future research made nearly two decades ago by pioneering resilience scholars remain relevant today. According to Rutter (1994), future research should examine the following:

- What is the overall liability to disorder? Do life events and experiences influence the overall liability to psychopathological disorder? What is the risk mechanism? Can causal mechanisms be determined?
- What are individual differences in vulnerability to stress? Are there genetic factors?
- What are individual differences in exposure to risk? Why do some people go through life with relatively little exposure to risk? Is this the result of temperament, interactions, or context?
- What is the carry forward of stress effects? Are there neural and/or cognitive effects?
- How effective are interventions designed to enhance resilience?

Similarly, Masten (1994) suggested the following:

- Search to identify and specify basic human processes of adaptation that cut across culture and situations (for example, parenting, self-efficacy).
- Focus studies more narrowly on unique protective processes that work in specific situations (for example, the transition to junior high school).
- Evaluate intervention program outcomes.

The top research priority for social workers would seem to be evaluating the effectiveness of interventions at various systems levels: community initiatives, specific organizations (for example, schools), families, and individuals. As suggested in the previous section, enough is enough about factors that promote or threaten positive developmental outcomes to design potentially appropriate interventions. The question remains: How well do these interventions work in their specific sociocultural contexts?

Use the CD by Michael Wright to consider risk and protective factors in assessment. Evaluate interventions at multiple systems levels accounting for sociocultural contexts.

You will find a case study on your CD: *Evaluating Resilience-based Interventions*

References

Anthony, E. J. (1987). Children at high risk for psychosis growing up successfully. In E. J. Anthony & B. J. Cohler (Eds.), *The invulnerable child* (pp. 147–184). New York: Guilford Press.

Aos, S., Phipps, P., Barnoski, R., & Lieb, R. (2001). *The comparative costs and benefits of programs to reduce crime: Version 4.0.* Olympia: Washington State Institute for Public Policy.

Bartelt, D. W. (1994). On resilience: Questions of validity. In M. C. Wang & E. W. Gordon (Eds.), *Educational resilience in inner-city America: Challenges and prospects* (pp. 97–108). Hillsdale, NJ: Erlbaum.

Benson, P. L. (1997). *All kids are our kids: What communities must do to raise caring and responsible children and adolescents.* San Francisco: Jossey-Bass.

Bergman, L. R., & Magnusson, D. (1997). A person-oriented approach in research on developmental psychopathology. *Development and Psychopathology, 9,* 291–319.

Blumer, H. (1969). *Symbolic interactionism: Perspective and method.* Berkeley: University of California Press.

Caspi, A., Elder, G. H., Jr., & Herbener, E. S. (1990). Childhood personality and the prediction of life-course patterns. In L. N. Robins & M. Rutter (Eds.), *Straight and devious pathways from childhood to adulthood* (pp. 13–35). Cambridge, England: Cambridge University Press.

Catalano, R. F., & Hawkins, J. D. (1996). The social development model: A theory of antisocial behavior. In J. D. Hawkins (Ed.), *Delinquency and crime: Current theories* (pp. 149–197). Cambridge, England: Cambridge University Press.

Coie, J. D., Watt, N. F., West, S. G., Hawkins, J. D., Asarnow, J. R., Markman, H. J., et al. (1993). The science of prevention: A conceptual framework and some directions for a national research program. *American Psychologist, 48,* 1013–1022.

Egeland, B., Carlson, E., & Sroufe, L. A. (1993). Resilience as process. *Development and Psychopathology, 5,* 517–528.

Egeland, B., Jacobvitz, D., & Sroufe, L. A. (1988). Breaking the cycle of abuse. *Child Development, 59,* 1080–1088.

Fraser, M. W., & Galinsky, M. J. (2004). Risk and resilience in childhood: Toward an evidence-based model of practice. In M. W. Fraser (Ed.), *Risk and resilience in childhood: An ecological perspective* (2nd ed., pp. 385–402). Washington, DC: NASW Press.

Fraser, M. W., Kirby, L. D., & Smokowski, P. R. (2004). Risk and resilience in childhood. In M. W. Fraser (Ed.), *Risk and resilience in childhood: An ecological perspective* (2nd ed., pp. 13–66). Washington, DC: NASW Press.

Fraser, M. W., Richman, J. M., & Galinsky, M. (1999). Risk, protection, and resilience: Toward a conceptual framework for social work practice. *Social Work Research, 23,* 131–144.

Fraser, M. W., & Terzian, M. A. (2005). Risk and resilience in child development: Principles and strategies of practice. In G. P. Mallon & P. McCartt Hess (Eds.), *Child welfare for the twenty-first century: A handbook of practices, policies, and programs* (pp. 55–71). New York: Columbia University Press.

Furstenberg, F. F., Jr., Cook, T. D., Eccles, J., Elder, G. H., Jr., & Sameroff, A. (1999).

Managing to make it: Urban families and adolescent success. Chicago: University of Chicago Press.

Gilgun, J. F. (1999). Mapping resilience as process among adults with childhood adversities. In H. I. McCubbin, E. A. Thompson, A. I. Thompson, & J. A. Futrell (Eds.), *The dynamics of resilient families* (pp. 41–70). Thousand Oaks, CA: Sage.

Gordon, E. W., & Song, L. D. (1994). Variations in the experience of resilience. In M. C. Wang & E. W. Gordon (Eds.), *Educational resilience in inner-city America: Challenges and prospects* (pp. 27–43). Hillsdale, NJ: Erlbaum.

Gore, S., & Eckenrode, J. (1994). Context and process in research on risk and resilience. In R. J. Haggerty, L. R. Sherrod, N. Garmezy, & M. Rutter (Eds.), *Stress, risk, and resilience in children and adolescents: Processes, mechanisms, and interventions* (pp. 19–63). Cambridge, England: Cambridge University Press.

Greenberg, M., & Feinberg, M. (2002). *An evaluation of PCCD's Communities That Care delinquency prevention initiative: Final report* (NCJ Publication No. 281283). Harrisburg: Pennsylvania State University, College of Human Development.

Haggerty, R. J., & Sherrod, L. R. (1994). Preface. In R. J. Haggerty, L. R. Sherrod, N. Garmezy, & M. Rutter (Eds.), *Stress, risk, and resilience in children and adolescents: Processes, mechanisms, and interventions* (pp. xii–xxiv). Cambridge, England: Cambridge University Press.

Hawkins, J. D., Brown, E. C., Oesterle, S., Arthur, M. W., Abbott, R. D., & Catalano, R. F. (2008). Early effects of Communities That Care on targeted risks and initiation of delinquent behavior and substance use. *Journal of Adolescent Health, 43,* 15–22.

Hawkins, J. D., Catalano, R. F., & Associates. (1992). *Communities That Care: Action for drug abuse prevention.* San Francisco, CA: Jossey-Bass.

Hawkins, J. D., Catalano, R. F., & Miller, J. Y. (1992). Risk and protective factors for alcohol and other drug problems in adolescence and early adulthood: Implications for substance abuse prevention. *Psychological Bulletin, 112,* 64–105.

Hawkins, J. D., Catalano, R. F., Morrison, D. M., O'Donnell, J., Abbott, R. D., & Day, L. E. (1992). The Seattle Social Development Project: Effects of the first four years on protective factors and problem behaviors. In J. McCord & R. E. Tremblay (Eds.), *Preventing antisocial behavior: Interventions from birth through adolescence* (pp. 139–161). New York: Guilford Press.

Hawkins, J. D., Kosterman, R., Catalano, R. F., Hill, K. G., & Abbott, R. D. (2005). Promoting positive adult functioning through social development intervention in childhood: Long-term effects from the Seattle Social Development Project. *Archives of Pediatrics & Adolescent Medicine, 159,* 25–31.

Hawkins, J. D., Kosterman, R., Catalano, R. F., Hill, K. G., & Abbott, R. D. (2008). Effects of social development intervention in childhood 15 years later. *Archives of Pediatrics & Adolescent Medicine, 162,* 1133–1141.

Herrenkohl, T. I., Hill, K. G., Chung, I-J., Guo, J., Abbott, R. D., & Hawkins, J. D. (2003). Protective factors against serious violent behavior in adolescence: A prospective study of aggressive children. *Social Work Research, 27*(3), 179–191.

Hill, K. G., Howell, J. C., Hawkins, J. D., & Battin-Pearson, S. R. (1999). Childhood risk factors for adolescent gang membership: Results from the Seattle Social Development Project. *Journal of Research in Crime and Delinquency, 36,* 300–322.

James, J. B., & Paul, E. L. (1993). The value of archival data for new perspectives on personality. In D. C. Funder, R. D. Parke, C. Tomlinson-Keasey, & K. Widaman (Eds.), *Studying lives through time: Personality and development* (pp. 45–63). Washington, DC: American Psychological Association.

Jenson, J. M., & Fraser, M. W. (2011). *Social policy for children and families: A risk and resilience perspective* (2nd ed.). Thousand Oaks, CA: Sage.

Laub, J. H., & Sampson, R. J. (2003). *Shared beginnings, divergent lives.* Cambridge, MA: Harvard University Press.

Long, J. V. F., & Vaillant, G. E. (1989). Escape from the underclass. In T. F. Dugan & R. Coles (Eds.), *The child in our times: Studies in the development of resiliency* (pp. 200–213). New York: Brunner/Mazel.

Luthar, S. S. (1991). Vulnerability and resilience: A study of high risk adolescents. *Child Development, 62,* 600–616.

Magnusson, D., & Bergman, L. R. (1990). A pattern approach to the study of pathways from childhood to adulthood. In L. N. Robins & M. Rutter (Eds.), *Straight and devious pathways from childhood to adulthood* (pp. 101–115). Cambridge, England: Cambridge University Press.

Maruna, S. (2001). *Making good: How ex-convicts reform and rebuild their lives.* Washington, DC: American Psychological Association.

Masten, A. S. (1994). Resilience in individual development: Successful adaptation despite risk and adversity. In M. C. Wang & E. W. Gordon (Eds.), *Educational resilience in inner-city America: Challenges and prospects* (pp. 3–25). Hillsdale, NJ: Erlbaum.

McGrath, J. (1982). Dilemmatics: The study of research choices and dilemmas. In J. McGrath, J. Martin, & R. Kulka (Eds.), *Judgment calls in research* (pp. 69–102). Beverly Hills, CA: Sage.

Nash, J. K., & Randolph, K. A. (2004). Methods in the analysis of risk and protective factors: Lessons from epidemiology. In M. W. Fraser (Ed.), *Risk and resilience in childhood: An ecological perspective* (2nd ed., pp. 67–87). Washington, DC: NASW Press.

Newcomb, M. D., & Felix-Ortiz, M. (1992). Multiple protective and risk factors for drug use and abuse: Cross-sectional and prospective findings. *Journal of Personality and Social Psychology, 51,* 564–577.

O'Brien, P. (2001). *Making it in the "free world": Women in transition from prison.* Albany: State University of New York Press.

Pittman, K., & Cahill, M. (1991). *A new vision: Promoting youth development* (Commissioned Paper No. 3). Washington, DC: Academy for Educational Development, Center for Youth Development and Policy Research.

Pollard, J. A., Hawkins, J. D., & Arthur, M. W. (1999). Risk and protection: Are both necessary to understand diverse behavioral outcomes in adolescence? *Social Work Research, 23,* 145–158.

Resnick, M. D., Bearman, P. S., Blum, R. W., Bauman, K. E., Harris, K. M., Jones, J., et al. (1997). Protecting adolescents from harm: Findings from the National Longitudinal Study on Adolescent Health. *Journal of the American Medical Association, 278,* 823–832.

Rigsby, L. C. (1994). The Americanization of resilience: Deconstructing research practice. In M. C. Wang & E. W. Gordon (Eds.), *Educational resilience in inner-city*

America: Challenges and prospects (pp. 85–94). Hillsdale, NJ: Erlbaum.

Rutter, M. (1990). Psychosocial resilience and protective mechanisms. In J. Roll, A. S. Masten, D. Cicchetti, K. H. Nuechterlein, & S. Weintraub (Eds.), *Risk and protective factors in the development of psychopathology* (pp. 181–214). Cambridge, England: Cambridge University Press.

Rutter, M. (1994). Stress research: Accomplishments and tasks ahead. In R. J. Haggerty, L. R. Sherrod, N. Garmezy, & M. Rutter (Eds.), *Stress, risk, and resilience in children and adolescents: Processes, mechanisms, and interventions* (pp. 354–385). Cambridge, England: Cambridge University Press.

Rutter, M. (2001). Psychosocial adversity: Risk, resilience and recovery. In J. M. Richman & M. W. Fraser (Eds.), *The context of youth violence: Resilience, risk, and protection* (pp. 13–41). Westport, CT: Praeger.

Seifer, R., & Sameroff, A. J. (1987). Multiple determinants of risk and invulnerability. In E. J. Anthony & B. J. Cohler (Eds.), *The invulnerable child* (pp. 51–69). New York: Guilford Press.

Tolan, P. H. (1996). How resilient is the concept of resilience? *Community Psychologist, 29,* 12–15.

Ungar, M., & Teram, E. (2005). Qualitative resilience research: Contributions and risks. In M. Ungar (Ed.), *Handbook for working with children and youth: Pathways to resilience across cultures and contexts* (pp. 149–163). Thousand Oaks, CA: Sage.

Werner, E. E., Bierman, J. M., & French, F. E. (1971). *The children of Kauai.* Honolulu: University of Hawaii Press.

Werner, E. E., & Smith, R. (1977). *Kauai's children come of age.* Honolulu: University of Hawaii Press.

Werner, E. E., & Smith, R. (1982). Vulnerable, but invincible: A longitudinal study of resilient children and youth. New York: McGraw-Hill.

Werner, E. E., & Smith, R. (1992). *Overcoming the odds: High risk children from birth to adulthood.* Ithaca, NY: Cornell University Press.

Werner, E. E., & Smith, R. S. (2001). *Journeys from childhood to midlife: Risk, resilience, and recovery.* Ithaca, NY: Cornell University Press.

Worland, J., Janes, C. L., Anthony, E. J., McGinnis, M., & Cass, L. (1984). St. Louis Risk Research Project: Comprehensive reports of experimental studies. In N. F. Watt, E. J. Anthony, L. C. Wynne, & J. Rolf (Eds.), *Children at risk for schizophrenia: A longitudinal perspective* (pp. 105–147). Cambridge, England: Cambridge University Press.

5

Resilience and Physical Health

JOYCE GRAHL RILEY

On finishing this chapter, students will be able to further:

Apply critical thinking to inform and communicate professional judgments (Educational Policy 2.1.3) by

- Distinguishing, appraising, and integrating multiple sources of knowledge, including research-based knowledge and practice wisdom.
- Analyzing models of assessment, prevention, intervention, and evaluation (practice behaviors).

Assess individuals, families, groups, organizations, and communities (Educational Policy 2.1.10b) by

- Collecting, organizing, and interpreting client data.
- Assessing client strengths and limitations.
- Developing mutually agreed-on intervention goals and objectives.
- Selecting appropriate intervention strategies (practice behaviors).

What is health? "We know health well in its absence" (Weil, 1995, p. 41). That is, we know when we do not feel well; we know when we feel pain or have some other indication that things are not right with our bodies. The World Health Organization provides a more comprehensive definition of health: Health is not merely the absence of disease or infirmity; health is complete physical, mental, and social well-being. Many would want to add spiritual well-being as well. According to the American Holistic Health Association,

> Rather than focusing on illness or specific parts of the body, [the] ancient [holistic] approach to health considers the whole person and how he or she interacts with his or her environment. It emphasizes the connection of

mind, body, and spirit. (Walter, 1999, para. 1 [for more information, see the association's Web site, http://www.ahha.org])

Optimum health requires balance in all aspects of our existence—maintaining hope, optimism, and a positive attitude. For people to achieve this ideal state, they must cope with constant change. To fully understand health, then, we must conceive of it as "a dynamic and harmonious equilibrium of all the elements and forces making up and surrounding a human being" (Weil, 1995, p. 52). The borders between health and disease are far from clear and are muddied by cultural, social, and psychological considerations (Engel, 1977). Conceptual and analytic models that fail to accommodate and examine psychosocial and biological explanations limit the understanding of health and illness (Fremont & Bird, 1999).

Everyone enters life with a set of risk factors that can affect their physical health, over which they have no control: the genetic material that created them, the life experiences of their mothers as they developed in the womb, and the social and geographical environment into which they were born. Throughout people's lives, the decisions they make and others make for them can increase or decrease their risk for illness, disease, or trauma. Were they adequately nourished as infants and children? Did they receive the appropriate vaccinations? What choices did they make about their diets and other lifestyle issues, such as smoking, that can affect their health? Risk factors may be related to the pathology itself. At what stage was it diagnosed? How much damage has been done to the body? In facing a physical health crisis with what appear to be equally high or low risk factors, some of us will do better than others. This is the essence of resilience; it is the resource practitioners as helping professionals want to understand and to help clients find within themselves. This is also part of the essence of holistic health.

The holistic perspective on health adopted by some clinical practitioners is closely aligned with current thinking about resilience. In fact, various dimensions of resilience are similar to a health and wellness perspective. For example, many resiliency theorists have turned away from a deficit model to explore the factors that help people stay healthy (McCubbin, Thompson, Thompson, & Fromer, 1998). They are also examining the psychosocial resources that buffer the effects of stress and illness (Fiorentino & Pomazal, 1998). There is evidence that the ability to overcome adversity or stress such as an illness is linked to the capacity to cope with change effectively and to maintain hope (Werner & Smith, 1992). In addition, both resilience and health are increasingly understood from an ecological perspective, that is, they are influenced by the interrelatedness of micro- and macrosystems (Engel, 1982). Moreover, health and resilience appear to be enhanced through positive connections or relatedness with others.

This chapter explores the link between resilience and health. Specifically, it examines how people's resilience—maintaining hope, optimism, and positive attitudes and beliefs—can affect their ability to deal with illness or disease. The relationship between social support and recovery from illness is also examined. The chapter also describes how social workers can bring a holistic, biopsychosocial perspective to their client services. Practitioners who use a holistic health model take into account the many factors contributing to health. They also engage the client as a participant in his or her own healing—accessing the internal resource known as resilience to promote well-being. The resilience perspective of social workers in health care—seeing the client as a whole, not just as a condition or disease—can strengthen their ability to promote, support, and develop the client's coping skills (Berkman, 1996). In so doing, practitioners can make a unique contribution to helping clients maintain health and recover from and cope with illness.

Current Health Issues

Many issues related to health and health care have a bearing on social work practice and the social worker's ability to form effective partnerships with clients to improve the quality of their lives and foster resilience. The continuing rise in the proportion of the gross domestic product spent on health care, changes in care settings, how care is reimbursed or paid for, and the availability of insurance coverage are major concerns. According to a recent government fact sheet, health care spending in the United States now exceeds $2 trillion, with continued growth expected (Centers for Medicare & Medicaid Services, n.d.). A variety of factors and economic forces have contributed to increased personal health care spending, particularly the increase in the cost of health services (Sultz & Young, 2011; Thorpe, 1999). One factor influencing spending on personal health care is the change in the use and intensity of health services. The intensity of health services is, in turn, influenced by changes in the population, the introduction and accessibility of new technologies, and the availability and nature of health insurance or reimbursement mechanisms (Barbash & Glied, 2010; Lee & Estes, 1994; Sultz & Young, 2011; Thorpe, 1999).

Because older people use significantly more health care services than expected based on their proportional representation in the population, the increased number of people surviving into old age is a major factor affecting health care costs. The unusually large population increase relates not just to an increased longevity but to the aging of the cohort born following World War II, which is referred to as the "baby boomers" (Takamura, 1999). The prediction is that by the year 2030 this age group will represent 19 percent of all Americans (Administration on Aging, 2010).

Increased life expectancy is certainly an indicator of the improved health of the population. However, aging also increases people's vulnerability to illness. Among those 65 and older, more than half (51.8 percent) have a disability (Brault, 2008). The increase in the number of elderly persons in the population raises concerns about whether society can provide an environment that promotes health, independence, and quality care while managing and containing the costs of health and long-term care services (Takamura, 1999). At the same time, from the mid-1980s to the mid-1990s, disability levels declined among noninstitutionalized older Americans (Kramarow, Lentzner, Rooks, Weeks, & Saydah, 1999). This is an effect of research and development in biotechnology that can have a positive effect on the general economy (Pardes et al., 1999). Persons who remain healthy into old age will remain independent and may stay in the workforce longer. The overall improved health of the workforce means improved productivity, which also benefits nonhealth sectors of the economy.

Whether health care is a right or a privilege, or whether a national program should exist, has been fodder for political and social debate for decades. In 2009, 63.9 percent of U.S. citizens had some health care costs covered by private insurance, and most of this was accessed through their employer (DeNavas-Walt, Proctor, & Smith, 2010). However, there has been and continues to be a growing concern for those who do not have access to health insurance coverage. In 2009, 16.7 percent of the population was without health insurance coverage, representing an increase from the previous year (DeNavas-Walt et al., 2010).

Although still controversial, the Affordable Care Act became law in March 2010. The main premise of this legislation was to extend health insurance coverage to more than 90 percent of Americans by requiring the purchase of private health insurance or coverage through a government-sponsored program. It prevents insurance plans from excluding or dropping those with preexisting conditions and contains details on how insurance plans will operate. The law was written so that different aspects of the legislation will go into effect over a period of time, with mandated health insurance coverage required in 2014. It is still not clear whether this highly debated legislation will remain intact or will be changed dramatically by the U.S. Congress (for more information, see http://www.healthcare.gov).

Social workers must keep informed about changes in the health care system, particularly the provisions of managed care (Carleton, 1998; Greene & Sullivan, 2000). For clients who are coping with health problems, these changes can add to stress by raising concerns about whether the cost of care will be covered or whether they will have access to the services they need. The changes may also have a bearing on when, how, and for how long the social worker will be engaged in working with the client. Being informed can help reduce client stress, foster resilience, and facilitate the effective use of other needed resources.

Health, Resilience, and the Placebo Effect

Scientific medicine has a difficult time dealing with the concept of resilience. The irony of resilience and physical health is that most would agree that resilience makes a tremendous difference in whether a person recovers from a disease or responds optimally to therapy. However, medical personnel are accustomed to basing their treatment of illness on scientific evidence. They tend to recognize the resilience of the individual as a contributing force, but one that has to be distinguished from the "real" effect or cure brought about by the treatment. Yet an examination of the relationship between resilience and physical health reveals some power within us, some internal resource that can affect our physical well-being. This internal resource works in conjunction with and independently of any medical treatment we might receive. It works to prevent disease in our bodies and helps heal us when disease or infirmities occur (Miller, Colloca, & Kaptchuk, 2009). The medical profession has used the term *placebo effect* to distinguish these inexplicable cures.

The placebo effect is an example of resilience as it relates to physical health. Although the placebo effect is an enigma of the human body, mind, and spirit that medical science has yet to unravel, understanding its influences can provide insight into the resilience phenomenon. The placebo effect is a positive response to a treatment or therapy because a person expects such an outcome, not because of any therapeutic effect or beneficial value of the treatment itself. From the Latin "I shall please," the word *placebo* has been associated with the art of healing for many centuries (Straus & Cavanaugh, 1996). It has been proposed that much of the beneficial effect derived from the many therapies used by healers up to the 17th century was a result of the placebo effect (Shapiro, 1960). By the early 1800s, the term *placebo* signified a medicine used to please, rather than benefit, the patient (Straus & Cavanaugh, 1996).

The "sugar pill," which has no medicinal value, is the most commonly recognized placebo. By the 1950s, drug or pharmacological trials consistently used a randomized, double-blind design with a placebo control (Straus & Cavanaugh, 1996). In this arrangement, some subjects receive a placebo or sugar pill, whereas others are given the drug under study. Neither the subjects nor the persons administering the drug know whether they are receiving or giving the real medication or the placebo. This allows investigators a means of controlling for the influence that the beliefs of both the subjects and investigators might have on the outcome of the trials.

As medicine moved from art to science, the placebo effect was seen as a contaminant in research and a detracting factor in clinical care. Those who believed that the biomedical model was the highest standard of care thought that the placebo effect deflated and confused the outcome of biomedical discoveries (Spiegel, 1997). In fact, the placebo effect is so common and powerful that it must be teased out of research data so that the "real" effects of a treatment can be identified and measured. A groundbreaking review of 15 studies in 1955 found that 30 percent of the positive outcomes or treatment benefits were a result of the placebo effect (Lipman, 1996). Later studies found even higher rates of the placebo effect, in some cases approaching 100 percent of the positive outcomes.

One of the components of the placebo effect is the belief or expectation that is produced by the relationship between the practitioner and the client or patient. A study conducted at the Massachusetts General Hospital and reported in the *New England Journal of Medicine* (Egbert, Battit, Welch, & Bartlett, 1964) exemplifies this aspect of the placebo effect. Examining the need for postoperative pain medication, researchers randomly placed patients matched by age, gender, condition, severity, and type of operation into one of two groups. Anesthesiologists visited both groups the night before surgery. One group received only a brief visit and was told in a perfunctory manner not to worry, that everything would be fine. The other group received a warm, friendly visit infused with empathy and a detailed explanation of what to expect from the surgery. Those who provided postoperative care did not know to which group the patients had been assigned. On the day following surgery, both groups were allowed to have any pain medications they required. When the data were analyzed, the researchers found that those who had received the warm, empathetic visits required significantly less pain medication and were released from the hospital an average of 2.5 days sooner than the other group.

When negative rather than positive outcomes are initiated by the attributes of one's belief system, they are usually referred to as *nocebo* effects. This belief system is so powerful that it can destroy or hinder the internal resilience sparked by the placebo effect (Hahn, 1997). Spiegel (1997) identified three ways in which the nocebo effect is triggered: (1) negative messages given by the health care environment or practitioner; (2) a negative message from the person's social or cultural belief system; and (3) secondary gain to the person as a result of a disease or illness, for example if an improved status is attained as a result of having it.

It is important to take into account the powerful forces that both the placebo and nocebo effects have on an individual's response to illness or disease in his or her life. The role of the social work practitioner is especially important in rallying or triggering these forces. In the biomedical–scientific model of illness, these forces are ignored or seen as contaminants that must be weeded out to get to the facts. That model, when inflexible, discourages listening to the person and forces reliance on laboratory results and technical procedures (Engel, 1977; Spiegel, 1997). It "embraces both reductionism, the philosophic view that complex phenomena are ultimately derived from a single principle, and mind–body dualism, the doctrine that separates the mental from the somatic" (Engel, 1977, p. 130). In contrast,

> what the placebo suggests to us is that we may be able to change what takes place in our bodies by changing our state of mind. Therefore, when we experience mind-altering processes—for example, meditation, hypnosis, visualization, psychotherapy, love and peace of mind—we open ourselves to the possibility of change and healing. (Siegel, 1990, p. 21)

Resilience and Health Outcomes

As with the placebo effect, health treatment outcomes can be influenced by people's outlook, disposition, or resilience. A growing body of literature has researched the effect of an individual's attitude or outlook on the leading cause of death in the United States—heart disease. Those interested in the treatment and outcome of coronary disease have linked recovery from heart surgery, recovery from heart attacks, and risk of death and repeat heart attacks to attitude or state of mind. Each year, thousands of people undergo bypass surgery as treatment for coronary artery disease. Dispositional optimism and positive expectations have been related to a lower rate of problems resulting in rehospitalization (Scheier et al., 1999) and a faster and better return to a normal lifestyle (Scheier et al., 1989). In one study, among those receiving heart transplants, presurgical positive expectations were related to a positive effect on health evaluated six months postoperatively and a better level of compliance with the postoperative medical regime (Leedham, Meyerwitz, Muirhead, & Frist, 1995).

From another perspective, some researchers have examined outcomes as they have related to negative attitudes or outlooks. Distress, depression, and low morale were associated with greater risk of death following a heart attack (Bruhn, Chandler, & Wolf, 1969; Garrity & Klein, 1975), increased need for surgery after an attack (Kimball, 1977), increased risk of rehospitalization (Allison, Williams, Patten, Bailey, & Squires, 1995), and poor response to treatment associated with impaired quality of life (Denollet, Vaes, & Brutsaert, 2000). Preoperative fear among women having abdominal surgery was linked to greater use of pain medication and slower recovery following the procedure (Sime, 1976). Hostile emotions were related to reclosure of the coronary artery after a surgical procedure to open it (Goodman, Quigley, Moran, Meilman, & Sherman, 1996). What is perverse is that it is the very clients with whom practitioners would least like to spend time—those with negative affects, those who push away help, and those who are hostile—who appear to need the most attention and intervention for a satisfactory recovery (Scheier et al., 1989). Such studies point for the need for further explanation about resilience as an adaptive mechanism.

Benefit Finding

In a review of their own research and that of others, Affleck and Tennen (1996) examined the adaptive significance of finding benefits, or identifying some positive aspect, for an otherwise negative life experience. They focused on persons experiencing major medical problems. Commonly reported benefits included strengthened family and friendship relations; an improved ability to put things in perspective; and positive changes in the self, such as more patience and empathy. The evidence from study findings indicated that the ability to identify benefits or personal gains in the face of adversity acts as a coping mechanism and helps establish a reality that is more acceptable or comfortable for the individual. This coping process enhances psychological and physical well-being. These study findings correspond to the resilience literature, which suggests that survivors of adverse events cope more effectively when they are able to attribute meaning to a negative life event (Lifton, 1993).

Several of the longitudinal studies reviewed were used to demonstrate the predictive significance of benefit finding on future outcomes. One study examined a cohort of heart attack survivors (Affleck, Tennen, Croog, & Levine, 1987). In this study, seven weeks following an initial heart attack, the participants (all male) were asked about the benefits from the event. More than half (58 percent) cited benefits. In a follow-up eight years later, those who had identified benefits from the experience were significantly less likely to have suffered another heart attack and were in better cardiac health even after age, socioeconomic status, and severity of the initial heart attack were controlled.

Another longitudinal study (Affleck, Tennen, & Rowe, 1991) looked at a group of mothers whose newborns needed intensive care services following delivery. Before the babies were discharged from the intensive care unit, the mothers were asked what, if any, benefits had come from the experience. Three quarters of the participants cited at least one benefit. Mothers who found no benefits in the experience reported more mood disturbances when assessed six and 18 months following the experience. Not only was the mother's emotional well-being related to her ability to find something positive in the experience, but also the child's performance on a developmental test 18 months later was also related. The significance of the positive relationships held true even after the severity of the child's medical problems and characteristics of the mother, such as age, education, and number of children, were controlled.

Affleck and Tennen (1996) pointed out that the coping mechanism is not only the ability to identify the positives or benefits in a threatening or adverse situation, but also the ability to use benefit finding as a tool when faced with the day-to-day stress of the experience. They called the use of this coping strategy *benefit reminding*. A small but intense study examined the effects of benefit reminding on 35 women living with chronic pain. What is interesting is that the ability to identify many benefits was not necessarily related to benefit reminding. Some participants who cited many benefits never reminded themselves, whereas others who cited only a few benefits reported frequent benefit reminding. From their within-person analysis of study subjects, the researchers found that, on the days when the participants more frequently reminded themselves of their identified benefits, they were more likely to record a positive mood regardless of how intensely they rated their pain on that day.

Benefit Finding and Therapeutic Intervention

McMillen (1999) has developed a strategy for introducing and managing benefit content in a therapeutic relationship, which he calls "REEP in the benefits." REEP is an acronym for reflection, encouragement, exploration, and planning.

Reflection

The introduction of threatening content should only be attempted by the social worker when clients demonstrate the ability to recall and discuss the events and what they have meant to their lives. Once a trauma is introduced by clients, it is possible to reflect with clients about how they have coped with it, including the benefit content. These reflections initiate what will become a more in-depth exploration later in the therapeutic relationship.

Encouragement and Exploration

Another way for the social worker to introduce benefit concepts is by encouraging self-assessment by the client. Questions posed by the social worker, such as "When are you happiest? When are you content?" and discussion of what the client most values in life can aid in this process. McMillen (1999) indicated that if client self-assessment does not spontaneously reveal benefit content, it is appropriate for social workers to gently introduce the content themselves.

At some point in the process, they may even want to ask if the client can ever imagine a time when it might be possible to find something positive in having lived through the experience. Helping clients work through the feelings of guilt, shame, and victimization that are associated with traumatic events, and building some positive associations through benefit reminding, can allow clients to reconstitute more optimistic views of life in general and allow memories of the events to be more available for processing in other ways.

Planning

Having done a self-assessment and life review, clients may wish to make changes in their lives. Social workers can play a key role in helping clients plan and implement these positive changes.

> The benefit question does not just highlight client strengths, but a new awareness of these strengths may change profoundly how people view themselves and the world and thus how they see the world. People who re-frame tragic events as benefiting them in some important way have stopped seeing themselves as victims and have begun to construe an image of themselves as capable people. (McMillen, 1999, p. 465)

Resilience, Social Relationships, and Health

Among people with serious health problems, support from family and friends is felt to be very important. Similarly, resilience is enhanced through connection with or relatedness to others and may be strengthened by family supports. In a national survey of people with cancer, participants were asked what was important to them in living with cancer. After "good medical care," 75 percent cited "emotional support within the family" second and "having hope" a close third (73 percent; Clements, 2000). Conversely, persons who were terminally or chronically ill perceived abandonment and isolation to have a negative impact on the ability to hope (Herth, 1990).

A study using longitudinal data from the Veterans Health Study found that perceived social support had a beneficial effect on a variety of health measures, both mental and physical. However, study findings also indicated that poor health might be a barrier to a person's ability to participate in and maintain social relationships (Ren, Skinner, Lee, & Kazis, 1999). The concern about decline and reduced quality of life in old age has made the elderly the focus of such research (see chapter 14). Examining changes in structural social support (contact with family and close friends) and functional social support (belonging, appraisal, and tangible support) at the level of the individual, researchers found that late life is not typically characterized by a decline in important social resources (Martire, Schultz, Mittelmark, & Newsom, 1999).

However, the availability in old age of children, who are often the primary source of social support (Cantor, 1994), appears to have a buffering effect on well-being (Giranda & Atchison, 1999). Longitudinal data from the MacArthur Studies of Successful Aging were used to explore the effects of social support on changes in physical functioning (Unger, McAvay, Bruce, Berkman, & Seeman, 1999). Those with more social ties showed less functional decline over time. This was particularly true for men and for those who had lower levels of physical functioning at the start of the study.

Although the mechanisms by which social relationships affect health and well-being remain unclear, prospective studies controlling for baseline health status have consistently shown an increased risk of death among persons with compromised (low-quantity and/or -quality) social relationships (House, Landis, & Umberson, 1988). Suggested protective effects resulting from social support include facilitation in coping with life stress (Thoits, 1995), encouragement to lead a healthier lifestyle (Mermelstein, Cohen, Lichtenstein, Kanmark, & Baer, 1986), and better use of and access to health care services (Bleeker et al., 1995; Bloom, 1990).

Resilience, Coping, and Hope

Patients' ability to cope effectively with an illness is dependent on their sustaining hope. Coping may involve using an array of strategies to confront a challenge. These strategies may include solving problems or making a decision about a course of action (Willis, Blechman, & McNamara, 1996). Coping strategies are generally intended to help a person gain more control over a situation and experience a greater sense of competence (Masten, 1994). Examining the research on coping between 1970 and 2000, Folkman and Moskowitz (2000) found convergence on the following points:

1. Coping has multiple functions including, but not limited to, the regulation of distress and the management of problems causing the distress.
2. Coping is influenced by the appraised characteristic of the stressful context, including its controllability.
3. Coping is influenced by personality dispositions including optimism, neuroticism, and extroversion.
4. Coping is influenced by social resources. (p. 647)

As indicated, coping can be influenced by personality dispositions such as optimism. Optimism and positive expectations for a future for oneself and others are common elements in various definitions of hope (Herth, 1990; Hinds,

1988). Hope is a multidimensional concept and a dynamic process (Morse & Doberneck, 1995). It is a valued human response, a coping mechanism that affects health, recovery from illness, living with a chronic condition, and facing the end of life (Herth, 1990; Hinds, 1988).

Hope "provides comfort while [one is] enduring life's threats and personal challenges" (Morse & Doberneck, 1995, p. 277). For those living with a terminal illness, hope was found to be "an inner power directed toward a new awareness and enrichment" (Herth, 1990, p. 1257). It has been professed that "the best medicine and best caregivers are powerless to restore health in the absence of hope" (Jevne, 1991, p. 149). The following captures a 12-year-old girl's feelings about the importance of hope as she grapples with cancer:

> Hope is important. If you don't have hope for the future, you can't get well ever. You won't want to get up and get it all done. Emotionally you'll be broken down, and you'll be dead kind of. You still have a body, but it's useless because you're not pushing. You give up on life and the future, and it's harder on you and your family and friends. You are wasting everybody's time, and eventually people around you will lose hope and won't do anything. Others look at you and see, especially the little kids here (at the hospital). We have to have hope for them to see it. If you haven't got hope for yourself you can't help others in the same situation. If you can't go through it hopeful and quickly, you could be in trouble. (Hinds, 1988, p. 87)

The Role of the Social Worker

Because of the interrelatedness between health and social functioning, social workers have a long-established and valued role in the health care system—working with clients and families who are dealing with medical crises, learning to live with chronic health conditions, and coping with terminal illnesses (DuBois & Miley, 1999). The relationship between health and social work is reflected in five basic premises (Bracht, 1978):

1. Illness can negatively affect an individual's ability to cope.
2. In addition to an individual's basic biology, social and psychological factors affect the ability to sustain health and recover from illness.
3. Medical treatment can be enhanced by social support and counseling.
4. Overcoming barriers to accessing health care often requires community action.
5. The psychosocial complexities that frequently accompany medical problems are better resolved by the efforts of a multiprofessional team.

TABLE 5.1 Categories of Hope-fostering Strategies and Practice Application Suggestions

Category	Practice Application
Connectedness/presence of a meaningful relationship with another	Serve as a catalyst, creating conditions that foster caring relationships between the clients and their families or support groups. Provide information as well as physical and emotional comfort.
Lightheartedness/feelings of delight, joy, or playfulness	Where appropriate, use humor and play in the professional relationship.
Personal attributes of determination, courage, and serenity	Support and encourage these personal attributes; when appropriate, use techniques such as values clarification and life-awareness activities to assist clients in recognizing or reinforcing these attributes in themselves.
Attainable aims/realistic goals or purpose	Be an active listener; help clients and families establish realistic goals appropriate to their circumstances.
Spiritual beliefs and practices	Provide an environment and resources that support the expression of spiritual beliefs and practices.
Recalling positive memories	Support and encourage the recall and sharing of positive memories by clients and their families.
Feelings of being valued and accepted	Create an environment and professional relationship in which the client feels valued as an individual notwithstanding physical changes brought about by the illness; support the family in accepting changes in the client and in expressing the client's continued importance to them.

Source: From "Fostering Hope in Terminally-Ill People," by K. Herth, 1990, *Journal of Advanced Nursing, 15,* pp. 1250–1259. Copyright 1990 by Blackwell Science. Adapted with permission.

The holistic health model discussed in this chapter suggests that social workers can play a critical role in helping the client to overcome the challenges associated with illness and disease. Social workers bring an ecological approach to client services, accepting the dynamic interactive relationships of clients with their multileveled environments. They recognize both internal and external factors that influence people's ability to cope (Zastrow, 2009). This approach, with its biopsychosocial perspective, allows the social worker to seek strengths for problem solving not just from within the individual but from within the family and the community. Furthermore, social workers understand the diversity of life paths based on differences in cultural, social, and historical experiences.

Perhaps the central role of social workers in health care is to assess and foster hope (see Tables 5.1 and 5.2). Although the ability to have and maintain hope

TABLE 5.2 Hope Assessment Guide

Stages of Hope (Universal Components)	Professional Assessment	Behavioral Signs	Strategies
1. Recognizing the threat (make a realistic initial assessment of the threat)	Did the impact of the event sink in?	• Reiteration—in speech and thoughts • Connecting—with others to reiterate or release • Stressed—at times overwhelmed by situation • One-way information flow—either reiterates or takes in information with no or few questions	Provide information and monitor level of acknowledgment by 1. Educating • Content: condition/ prognosis/usual outcomes of treatment • Method: repeat the information at different times (repetition)/provide information in small increments/encourage audio-recording, as appropriate/encourage questions • Evaluate: ask the patient to explain the situation to you, assess degree of internalization and comprehension 2. Responding to feelings • Offer sympathy, consolation, or commiseration • Listen attentively for changes in the story • Provide time for rest or healthy releases
2. Making a plan (envision alternatives and set goals/brace for negative outcomes)	Is there a plan? Is the patient prepared for the worst?	• Questioning statistical odds • Seeking direction on "next steps" • May acknowledge reality verbally, weighing options • Seeking others who have had experience • Entering two-way discussions • Physical envisioning • Articulating goals—global or focused • Recognizing the possibility of negative outcomes, then compartmentalizing the possibility that it may eventuate	Assist with the formulation of a plan by 1. Exploring options • Encourage consideration of a full array of available options • Discuss options not considered, including possible negative outcomes • Answer questions realistically, do not "protect" the patient from harsh realities • Provide both statistical and experimental information 2. Making connections • Introduce the patient to others who have managed successfully (successful role models)

		• Conducting personal review of related past experiences/internal resources/external resources (human and material) • Checking the reputation of doctors and others involved in care • Evaluating the ability of friends to "be there"	3. Supporting • Provide emotional support and adequate time for contemplation, rest, and healthy releases 4. Sharing the plan • Encourage the articulation of goals to facilitate mutual objectives in care
3. Taking stock (make a realistic assessment of personal/external resources and conditions)	What resources have been identified?	• Seeking out others who are sympathetic to the mission (new and existing relationships) • May change support persons as goals change	Facilitate full assessment of resources by 1. Supporting realistic self-assessment • Point out personal resources or attributes that may be taken for granted • Engage the patient in discussion regarding healthy releases 2. Orienting to external resources • Explain services that may support the devised plan (including how to access them, eligibility requirements, and expected benefits) 3. Monitoring the support network • Continue to monitor both the internal and external support network throughout the course of treatment • Reinforce the availability of community (external) resources as treatment progresses
4. Reaching out (solicit mutually supportive relationships)	Are there adequate supports?	• Seeking clarification of information—especially the odds of meeting hoped-for goals • May review previous history to determine "what ifs" • Conducting self-examination for signs of recurrence • Comparing self to other survivors • Using techniques that help them get by (for example, how to handle seeing deformed body in mirror) • Focusing energy	Bolster supportive relationships by 1. Setting the scene • Allow liberal visiting time to permit supportive relationships to flourish • Orient to available support groups or networks • Recommend supportive counseling, as appropriate 2. Being there if needed • Know the plan and reinforce it as needed • Listen attentively Do not stereotypically assume supportive relationships

(*continued*)

TABLE 5.2 Hope Assessment Guide (*continued*)

Stages of Hope (Universal Components)	Professional Assessment	Behavioral Signs	Strategies
5. Looking for signs (continuously evaluate signs of reinforcement)	What signs are being received?	• Expressing a new perspective on life	Point out the signs by opening channels of communication by 1. Discussing interpretation of "signs" and perspectives on progress 2. Providing an honest appraisal of progress toward the goal 3. Assisting with the reformulation of the goal or plans as indicated
6. Holding on (determine to persevere)	Does this person have stamina and will?		Provide encouragement by 1. Monitoring energy levels • Provide quiet time as desired by the person • Observe patterns with visitors—who energizes and who drains? • Discuss the energy demands of hope work 2. Supporting endurance • Provide honest praise and encouragement • Give "permission" to attend to personal needs • Teach healthy release

Source: From "Strategies for Assessing and Fostering Hope: The Hope Assessment Guide," by J. Penrod and J. Morse, 1997, *Oncology Nursing Forum, 24,* pp. 1061–1062. Copyright 1997 by the Oncology Nursing Society. Adapted with permission.

during a serious medical crisis often depends on the reciprocal social support relationship experienced with friends and family members (Artinian, 1984), and a personal belief in a higher being or God (Herth, 1990), research has found that professional caregivers (nurses and social workers) have special supportive roles to play in this arena (Artinian, 1984).

Supportive professional relationships can help reduce the stress family members are experiencing. The support provided by the professional can take various forms (Artinian, 1984)—it can mean meeting physiological needs to provide comfort, it can be providing a safe outlet for anger and frustration experienced by family members and the client, or it can be helping family members and the client construct realistic plans for the future. This therapeutic supportive relationship helps the client conserve emotional energy and enhances the probability that the reciprocal supportive relationship between the client and the family will make the circumstances of the illness more endurable and will help the client to sustain hope by planning for the future. Finally, it should be pointed out that the value of a positive attitude sometimes can be distorted, establishing exaggerated expectations for people to cure themselves (Creagan, 1999). That can lead to the notion that if the disease progresses or treatments are ineffective, the individual did not fight hard enough or think positively enough. The failure to get well becomes the individual's fault. It is, however, possible to have a responsible relationship with the client that creates an environment with a belief system that supports possibilities of positive outcomes, reduces anxiety and suffering, and promotes hope for recovery. This does not exclude the biological aspect of the biopsychosocial model and accepts that disease and trauma have consequences that include disability and death.

Social workers must meet the challenge of participating in the ever-changing arena of health care (Keigher, 1997, 1999; Kelly, 1998). Social workers have a place on the health care team addressing the needs of clients for preventive, curative, and rehabilitative services (Berkman, 1996). As a profession that encourages empowerment and seeks out client strengths, social work may sometimes find itself misunderstood in an environment that places a great deal of emphasis on client compliance (Keigher, 1997). Social workers are needed to "create an environment and professional relationship where the client feels valued as an individual notwithstanding physical changes brought about by illness" (Keigher, 1997, p. 248).

Use the CD by Michael Wright to define holistic health, integrating health contributing factors, client as participant, and assessment of the whole client. Explore the impact of expectations, relationship, and relative advantage on health outcomes.

You will find a case study on your CD: *Comparing Two Patients*

References

Administration on Aging. (2010). *Aging statistics.* Retrieved from http://www.aoa.gov/AoARoot/Aging_Statistics/index.aspx

Affleck, G., & Tennen, H. (1996). Construing benefits from adversity: Adaptational significance and dispositional underpinnings. *Journal of Personality, 64,* 899–922.

Affleck, G., Tennen, H., Croog, S., & Levine, S. (1987). Causal attribution, perceived benefits, and morbidity after a heart attack: An 8-year study. *Journal of Consulting and Clinical Psychology, 55,* 29–35.

Affleck, G., Tennen, H., & Rowe, J. (1991). *Infants in crisis: How parents cope with newborn intensive care and its aftermath.* New York: Springer-Verlag.

Allison, T., Williams, D., Patten, C., Bailey, K., & Squires, R. (1995). Medical and economic costs of psychological distress in patients with coronary artery disease. *Mayo Clinic Proceedings, 70,* 734–742.

Artinian, B. (1984). Fostering hope in the bone marrow transplant child. *American Journal of Maternal Child Nursing, 13,* 57–71.

Barbash, G. I., & Glied, S. A. (2010). New technology and health care costs—The case for robot-assisted surgery. *New England Journal of Medicine, 363,* 701–704.

Berkman, B. (1996). The emerging health care world: Implications for social work practice and education. *Social Work, 41,* 541–550.

Bleeker, J., Lamers, L., Leenders, I., Kruyssen, D., Simoons, M., Trijsburg, R., & Erdman, R. (1995). Psychological and knowledge factors related to delay in help-seeking by patients with acute myocardial infarction. *Psychotherapy and Psychosomatics, 63,* 151–158.

Bloom, J. (1990). The relationship of social support and health. *Social Science & Medicine, 30,* 635–637.

Bracht, N. (1978). *Social work in health care: A guide to professional practice.* New York: Haworth Press.

Brault, M. W. (2008). *Americans with disabilities: 2005* (Current Population Reports No. 70–117). Washington, DC: U.S. Census Bureau.

Bruhn, J., Chandler, B., & Wolf, S. (1969). A psychological study of survivors of myocardial infarction. *Psychosomatic Medicine, 31,* 8–19.

Cantor, M. (1994). Family caregiving: Social care. In M. Cantor (Ed.), *Family caregiving: Agenda for the future* (pp. 1–9). San Francisco: American Society on Aging.

Carleton, S. (1998). Does managed care measure up? *Business & Health, 16*(4, Suppl. A), 53–56.

Centers for Medicare & Medicaid Services. (n.d). *NHE fact sheet.* Retrieved from http://www.cms.gov/NationalHealthExpendData/25_NHE_Fact_Sheet.asp#TopOfPage

Clements. M. (2000, February 6). What we can learn from cancer. *Parade Magazine,* p. 12.

Creagan, E. (1999). Attitude and disposition: Do they make a difference in cancer survival? *Journal of Prosthetic Dentistry, 82,* 352–355.

DeNavas-Walt, C., Proctor, B. D., & Smith, J. C. (2010). *Income, poverty and health insurance coverage in the United States: 2009* (Current Population Reports No. 60–285). Washington, DC: U.S. Census Bureau.

Denollet, J., Vaes, J., & Brutsaert, D. (2000). Inadequate response to treatment in coronary heart disease: Adverse effects of type D personality and younger age on 5-year prognosis and quality of life. *Circulation, 102,* 630–635.

DuBois, B., & Miley, K. (1999). Social work in health, rehabilitation, and mental health. In B. DuBois & K. Miley (Eds.), *Social work: An empowering profession* (3rd ed., pp. 328–369). Boston: Allyn & Bacon.

Egbert, L., Battit, G., Welch, C., & Bartlett, M. (1964). Reduction of post-operative pain by encouragement and instruction of the patient. *New England Journal of Medicine, 270,* 825–827.

Engel, G. (1977, April 8). The need for a new medical model: A challenge for biomedicine. *Science, 196,* 129–136.

Engel, G. (1982). Sounding board: The biopsychosocial model and medical education. *New England Journal of Medicine, 306,* 802–805.

Fiorentino, L. M., & Pomazal, R. L. (1998). Sense of coherence and the stress–illness relationship among employees: A prospective study. In H. I. McCubbin, E. A. Thompson, A. I. Thompson, & J. E. Fromer (Eds.), *Stress, coping, and health in families* (pp. 91–106). Thousand Oaks, CA: Sage.

Folkman, S., & Moskowitz, J. (2000). Positive affect and the other side of coping. *American Psychologist, 55,* 647–654.

Fremont, A., & Bird, C. (1999). Integrating sociological and biological models: Editorial. *Journal of Health and Social Behavior, 40,* 126–129.

Garrity, T., & Klein, R. (1975). Emotional response and clinical severity as early determinants of six month mortality after myocardial infarction. *Heart Lung, 4,* 730–737.

Giranda, M., & Atchison, K. (1999). Social networks of elders without children. *Journal of Gerontological Social Work, 31,* 63–84.

Goodman, M., Quigley, J., Moran, G., Meilman, H., & Sherman, M. (1996). Hostility predicts restenosis after percutaneous transluminal coronary angioplasty. *Mayo Clinic Proceedings, 71,* 729–734.

Greene, R. R., & Sullivan, P. W. (2000). Managed care and the ecological perspective: Meeting the needs of older adults in the 21st century. In W. Peebles-Wilkins & N. Veeder (Eds.), *Managed care services: Policy, programs, and research* (pp. 163–186). Oxford, England: Oxford University Press.

Hahn, R. (1997). The nocebo phenomenon: Concept, evidence, and implications for public health. *Preventive Medicine, 26,* 607–611.

Herth, K. (1990). Fostering hope in terminally-ill people. *Journal of Advanced Nursing, 15,* 1250–1259.

Hinds, P. (1988). Adolescent hopefulness in illness and health. *Advances in Nursing Science, 10,* 79–88.

House, I., Landis, K., & Umberson, D. (1988, July 29). Social relationships and health. *Science, 241,* 540–545.

Jevne, R. (1991). *It all begins with hope.* San Diego: LuraMedia.

Keigher, S. (1997). What role for social work in the new health care practice paradigm? *Health & Social Work, 22,* 149–248.

Keigher, S. (1999). Reflections on progress, health, and racism: 1900 to 2000. *Health & Social Work, 24,* 243–248.

Kelly, J. (1998). Social workers and the tradition of charity in the changing health care system. *Health & Social Work, 23,* 236–240.

Kimball, C. (1977). Psychological responses to the experience of open heart surgery. In R. Moos (Ed.), *Coping with physical illness* (pp. 113–133). New York: Plenum Press.

Kramarow, E., Lentzner, H., Rooks, R., Weeks, J., & Saydah, S. (1999). *Health, United States, 1999, with health and aging chart book* (PHS 99–1232–1). Hyattsville, MD: National Center for Health Statistics.

Lee, P., & Estes, C. (1994). Introduction: Chapter 6. In P. Lee & C. Estes (Eds.), *The nation's health* (4th ed., pp. 248–251). Boston: Jonas & Bartlett.

Leedham, B., Meyerwitz, B., Muirhead, J., & Frist, W. (1995). Positive expectations predict health after heart transplant. *Health Psychology, 14,* 74–79.

Lifton, R. J. (1993). *The protean self: Human resilience in an age of fragmentation.* Chicago: University of Chicago Press.

Lipman, M. (1996). Office visit: The power of placebos. *Consumer Reports on Health, 28,* 23.

Martire, L., Schultz, R., Mittelmark, M., & Newsom, J. (1999). Stability and change in older adults' social contact and social support: The Cardiovascular Health Study. *Journal of Gerontology: Social Sciences, 54B,* S302–S311.

Masten, A. (1994). Resilience in individual development: Successful adaptation despite risk and adversity. In M. C. Wang & E. W. Gordon (Eds.), *Educational resilience in inner-city America: Challenges and prospects* (pp. 3–25). Hillsdale, NJ: Erlbaum.

McCubbin, H. I., Thompson, E. A., Thompson, A. I., & Fromer, J. E. (Eds.). (1998). *Stress, coping, and health in families: Sense of coherence and resilience.* Thousand Oaks, CA: Sage.

McMillen, J. (1999). Better for it: How people benefit from adversity. *Social Work, 44,* 455–468.

Mermelstein, R., Cohen, S., Lichtenstein, E., Kanmark, T., & Baer, J. (1986). Social support and smoking cessation and maintenance. *Journal of Consulting and Clinical Psychology, 54,* 447–453.

Miller, F. G., Colloca, L., & Kaptchuk, T. J. (2009). The placebo effect: Illness and interpersonal healing. *Perspectives in Biology and Medicine, 53,* 518–539.

Morse, J., & Doberneck, B. (1995). Delineating the concept of hope. *IMAGE: Journal of Nursing Scholarship, 27,* 277–285.

Pardes, H., Manton, K., Lander, E., Tolley, H., Ullian, A., & Palmer, H. (1999, January 1). Effects of medical research on health care and the economy. *Science, 283,* 36–37.

Penrod, J., & Morse, J. (1997). Strategies for assessing and fostering hope: The hope assessment guide. *Oncology Nursing Forum, 24,* 1055–1063.

Ren, X., Skinner, K., Lee, A., & Kazis, L. (1999). Social support, social selection and self-assessed health status: Results from the Veterans Health Study in the United States. *Social Science & Medicine, 48,* 1712–1734.

Scheier, M., Matthews, K., Owens, J., Magovern, G., Lefebvre, R. R., Abbott, R., & Carver, C. (1989). Dispositional optimism and recovery from coronary artery bypass surgery: The beneficial effects on physical and psychological well-being. *Journal of Personality and Social Psychology, 57,* 1024–1040.

Scheier, M., Matthews, K., Owens, J., Schulz, R., Bridges, M., Magovern, G., & Carver, C. (1999). Optimism and rehospitalization after coronary artery bypass graft surgery. *Achieves of Internal Medicine, 159,* 829–835.

Shapiro, A. (1960). A contribution to a history of the placebo effect. *Behavioral Science, 5,* 398–430.

Siegel, B. (1990). *Peace, love and healing.* New York: Harper Perennial.

Sime, A. (1976). Relationship of preoperative fear, type of coping, and information received about surgery to recovery from surgery. *Journal of Personality and Social Psychology, 34,* 716–724.

Spiegel, H. (1997). Nocebo: The power of suggestibility. *Preventive Medicine, 26,* 616–621.

Straus, S., & Cavanaugh, S. (1996). Placebo effects: Issues for clinical practice in psychiatry and medicine. *Psychosomatics, 37,* 315–326.

Sultz, H., & Young, K. (2011). Financing health care. In *Health care USA: Understanding its organization and delivery* (pp. 221–266). Gaithersburg, MD: Aspen.

Takamura, J. (1999). Getting ready for the 21st century: The aging of America and the Older Americans Act. *Health & Social Work, 24,* 232–238.

Thoits, P. (1995). Stress, coping, and social support processes: Where are we? What next? *Journal of Health and Social Behavior,* (Special Edition), 53–79.

Thorpe, K. (1999). Health care cost containment: Reflections and future directions. In A. Kovner & S. Jonas (Eds.), *Jonas and Kovner's heath care delivery in the United States* (6th ed., pp. 439–473). New York: Springer.

Unger, J., McAvay, G., Bruce, M., Berkman, L., & Seeman, T. (1999). Variation in the impact of social network characteristics on physical functioning in elderly persons: MacArthur Studies of Successful Aging. *Journal of Gerontology: Social Sciences, 54B,* S245–S251.

Walter, S. (1999). *Holistic health.* Retrieved from http://ahha.org/rosen.htm

Weil, A. (1995). *Health and healing.* New York: Houghton Mifflin.

Werner, E. R., & Smith, R. (1992). *Overcoming the odds: High risk children from birth to adulthood.* Ithaca, NY: Cornell University Press.

Willis, T. A., Blechman, E. A., & McNamara, G. (1996). Family support, coping, and competence. In E. Mavis & E. A. Blechman (Eds.), *Stress, coping, and resiliency in children and families* (pp. 107–134). Mahwah, NJ: Erlbaum.

Zastrow, C. (2009). Overview of social work practice. In C. Zastrow (Ed.), *The practice of social work* (3rd ed., pp. 3–28). Chicago: Dorsey Press.

6

Resilience and Mental Health: A Shift in Perspective

ROBERT BLUNDO

On finishing this chapter, students will be able to further:

Apply critical thinking to inform and communicate professional judgments (Educational Policy 2.1.3) by

- Distinguishing, appraising, and integrating multiple sources of knowledge, including research-based knowledge and practice wisdom.
- Analyzing models of assessment, prevention, intervention, and evaluation (practice behaviors).

Intervene with individuals, families, groups, organizations, and communities (Educational Policy 2.1.10c) by

- Helping clients resolve problems.
- Negotiating, mediating, and advocating for clients (practice behaviors).

The two young girls were in bed when the noise of glass breaking startled them awake and into a familiar sense of fear and foreboding. Their father had returned home and the painful ritual had begun once again: I don't know if [Mama] broke it first or he did. But she told him that she would kill him if he hit her again. We heard the table fall down, and we were crying in bed, crying and shaking, and we ran up the hallway and we were peeping around the door, and we saw—we remember we saw—how he grabbed the glass and he pulled it down her arm, a long deep cut in her arm. But that didn't do him no damn good, he beat her for worse, he beat her all in the head, and she was on the floor, there was blood, blood, and we were just too scared . . . to do anything. And Florence was just so frightened, so frightened.

I don't know who called, but she ended up in the hospital. And she didn't live long after that. She died.

—Bolton, 1994, pp. 17–18

What happens to children when they are exposed to such brutality repeatedly? Can they expect anything less than a life of pain and emotional upheaval? Is it inevitable that such trauma results in damage so debilitating that life is forever painful and unfulfilling? Is this life the precursor to what has come to be known as mental illness or its correlate, mental health? How do social workers talk about these two young girls, Ruthie and Florence, and others like them? In what way are they oriented by training and professional language to understand the lives of such individuals and their families?

Social workers are drawn by their training and knowledge base to consider the damage done to these children and to explore how they might repair or treat the "damaged." This conclusion seem obvious, and the idea of questioning plans to treat the children rarely arises. To the social worker, it is obvious that the children are damaged unless he or she intervenes. And social workers sometimes make pessimistic assumptions that the children could never recover. Yet the young girls' story continues. This young girl, Ruthie, grows up not only with hardship and pain, but also with more a more positive story than one might imagine.

So what happens to Ruthie? As she tells her story, she has learned and changed a great deal over the years. She describes her attempts at protecting herself as getting "tough":

> I had to prove that I was [tough]. . . . When Daddy used to beat me, I would pray, Lord, don't let me feel the pain. And it was like I felt it, but then I didn't feel it. . . . I made myself to be hard. Towards men. Towards everybody. I learned how not to feel anything at all. (Bolton, 1994, p. 190)

She then met Ray Bolton, who would later become her husband. Even though she was "tough" and "hard towards men" she got to know and connect with Ray, a man who was at one time a complete stranger, just "a man." She opened herself to a man and his family who were too good to be believed, at least in Ruthie's eyes:

> The Boltons made me feel feelings again. They showed me how to do that. You have to wake up, really. I guess at times you think you've living in a dream, and you really need to wake up. And it happened so fast, just like waking up. You think it might be going to take a long time for someone who has had the life I had, done the things I had done, to

> change inside. Not to completely change the way I was and how I acted, because that took some time, but to change inside. It's like I was waiting for it. Waiting for this family, and when I finally could let myself come in. I couldn't believe these people. To be so nice, and so understanding. (Bolton, 1994, p. 190)

Ruthie then had a positive relationship not only with a man, but with his family as well. More important, Ruthie felt that she had her mother with her all along, even though her mother had died: As Ruthie put it,

> She was in my head. And still is today. I still talk to her. I just did it the other day. I said, "Mama, I am writing this book, if you could only see. . . ." And I said . . . for her . . . "Yeah, I'm watching, baby, I'm watching you. Don't cry, don't worry." (Bolton, 1994, p. 273)

Many children are traumatized and perhaps scarred for life. But research has shown that, in many cases, children who have been abused and moved to foster care actually demonstrate unexpected resiliency (Festinger, 1983). For example, the young child and, later, the mature woman Ruthie wrote her autobiography *Gal: A True Life* (Bolton, 1994). Ruthie Bolton went on to finish her schooling and is now happily married and has three children and a good job. This does not imply that social workers should leave children and others to their own devices. But it says that they can miss strength and resilience when their professional lens see only devastation and brokenness. Thinking in terms of pathology and disability may keep social workers from recognizing human resilience and the ability to find some kind of footing in the world, whatever the challenges.

This chapter considers alternative fundamental assumptions of social work education and practice. These alternatives involve a move away from the focus on the pathology of human development and the social environment and the emphasis on what is wrong or broken. Rather, social workers need to understand self-healing, resilience, and strengths of individuals, families, and communities, aligning themselves with the strengths and resilience of those with whom they may work.

Impact of Traditional Deterministic Theories of Human Behavior

Traditional deterministic models of thinking are focused on categorizing and labeling a set of listed symptoms to describe a special category of mental illness, the diagnosis. This process simplifies the complexity presented by a person and is supposed to make the situation understandable (Wright & Lopez, 2005). The label creates a system that erases the complex differences between members of the diagnostic group, which deindividualizes the person and removes ethnicity and psychosocial and cultural uniqueness. The person becomes a standardized diagnosis. In turn, those so labeled are now seen as different from others not so labeled. The greater the seriousness the label carries with it, the greater the degree of difference between the labeled person and others (Wright & Lopez, 2005). Research conducted by Doise, Deschamps, and Meyer (1978) demonstrated that when people are identified as belonging to a group, such as a diagnostic group, they are judged to be more alike than those not belonging to that group. It is not unusual to hear professionals and trainers use a label such as *borderline* to identify a group of different people, as if they were all the same. The consequences of this simple labeling process leads to biasing what one looks for in the behavior and actions of those so labeled. It leads to assuming things about the people that might be hidden for now because everybody knows that "borderlines" engage in this type of behavior. The focus becomes the symptom picture and this person's skewed perspective on the life in the name of professional diagnostic skills.

Labeling and categorizing only the negative and problematic symptom picture is recognized as legitimate because the pathological focus of traditional practice is fundamentally concerned with this aspect of a person's life. The strengths and resiliency of the individual and his or her social context are relegated to the periphery if ever actually seriously considered. Research on labels has demonstrated that when practitioners are presented with a picture of a client that has negative implications, the practitioner has a more negative perception of the client. The same story is viewed more negatively when it is associated with a person released from a psychiatric ward than an average student (Pierce, 1987). It may be that practitioners are prejudicing themselves unconsciously when they use labels and make assumptions about negative events or settings associated with a client. Negative ideas seem to have a greater strength in U.S. culture and carry more weight than positive ideas. This is a serious distortion in how social workers might see others and proceed with their work. Neglecting possibilities, resiliency, and strengths is a serious threat to working in a respectful way with others, a way that is respectful of diversity in all its forms as well as the particular uniqueness and complexity of those being engaged. Hoyt (1994) stated that the "new direction [in psychotherapy] focuses more on strengths and resources that patients/clients bring to the enterprise than their weaknesses and limitations. Similarly, more emphasis is put on where people want to go than on where they have been" (p. 8).

Generally speaking, social work content in human behavior theory tends to view the world from the perspective of deterministic models. Social workers who have been trained in this perspective tend to identify individual failures and causes of these failures from a normative expectation of growth and development, or the "typical" developmental stages and phases. The deterministic models assume a set series of steps through which all individuals pass as they go through life (Schriver, 2001). Failure to complete a stage or phase, according to these norms, can result in some form of pathology or damaging emotional or psychological impasse, often considered irreversible. Through practice, social workers then address these deficits or failures by attempting to restore the loss, repair the damage, or help rehabilitate developmentally impaired individuals.

The professionalization of social work has been established on the basis of deterministic clinical theories of psychiatry and psychology. These have formed—and may still form—the foundations of many social work theories of human behavior. As a consequence, social workers' focus is shifted away from an understanding of what enables people to survive humiliation and devastation. This traditional perspective may also prevent social work theorists from developing an understanding about the resilience of individuals and families and the sustainability of communities of people who have experienced degradation and oppression, often resulting in their lack of societal influence or exclusion (Schriver, 2001).

Why, then, are traditional theories of human behavior maintained? It is because they appear to provide social workers with a sense of being objective and understanding when tackling the complex lives of clients. Social workers may thus find stable ground given the complexity of human conditions. Take Erikson's (1959) developmental stages, for example: The practitioner finds the answer to a client's problem—a failure to complete a developmental stage—which provides a simple explanation of why a complex, hard-to-understand boy exhibits certain behaviors at school. Theories of human development thus offer "consistent view[s] of the world, [and] a clear set of expectations of what [the social worker] should do" (Lakoff & Johnson, 1980, p. 220). Social workers are then able to listen to the description of a client's life and see that life as manifesting a regressed ego function or, for example, an "enmeshed family." Such conceptualizations act as filters, as organizing systems to create the life social workers think they are viewing, as if what they are seeing is outside of their own conceptual system. Social workers do not question the assumptions but find comfort in being able to understand and know an individual or family. A consequence of this comfortable conceptual system is that the dominant deterministic and pathology-focused theories of the profession do not change easily or often.

The human developmental stages or phases the profession of social work has adopted have been reified to the point that it is nearly impossible to extricate practicing social workers from their presumptions. As the Roman statesman Cicero observed, "The mind becomes accustomed to things by habitual sight of them, and neither wonders nor inquires about the reasons for the things it sees all the time" (see Montaigne, 1958, p. 133). The significance of practitioners' habitual comfort and unquestioned perspectives on how they understand and interact with clients is that they fail to see and understand the resilience and strengths of individuals who show endurance and achieve success.

In the field of mental health, social workers are traditionally trained to look for pathology, deviance, defective development, and premorbid conditions. In fact, the number of behaviors classified as mental illness increased from 59 in 1907 to 292 in 1992 (Goode, 1992). This trend of finding pathology in human life has led some critics of this approach to speculate that "the splendor of human diversity . . . runs the risk of becoming simply a collection of syndromes and disorders" (Goode, 1995, pp. 26–27). Given this, how can social workers understand human behavior mental illness and mental health concepts differently?

Mental Health and Mental Illness

What does it mean when mental health and mental illness are used to describe a person, family, or community? In one sense, *mental health* is a generic term referring to the overall mental state of an individual or community that then subsumes degrees of health and illness. According to the 10th edition of *Merriam Webster's Collegiate Dictionary, mental health* refers to "the total emotional and intellectual response of an individual to external reality" (Mish, 2001). There is a long history of theorizing about what the concepts of mental health or mental illness mean. Because these are socially constructed concepts accounting for something experienced, attempts to define these terms are too numerous to list in this chapter. However, some insight is helpful. For example, Marie Jahoda (1958) described the effort at definition:

> There is hardly a term in current psychological thought as vague, elusive, and ambiguous as the term "mental health." That it means many things to many people is bad enough. That many people use it without even attempting to specify the idiosyncratic meaning the term has for them makes the situation worse, both for those who wish to promote mental health and for those who wish to introduce concern with mental health into systemic psychological theory and research. (p. 3)

Jahoda herself was concerned with the Mental Health Study Act of 1955, which she believed did not go far enough to specify the meaning of mental health. Her comments reflect the ambiguity of observation and the historical context of centuries of attempts to understand the human condition and its variations. Her statement, still relevant today, sums up the present state of knowledge.

Kraepelin (1917) considered mental health as a normality: "The standard we use in recognizing the morbid features of a man's life is his departure from the average in the direction of inefficiency" (p. 295). Freud (1937/1963) considered mental health to be an ideal notion that no person could achieve. He viewed the idea of a normal ego or normality as "an ideal fiction. . . . Every normal person is only approximately normal" (p. 253). This was the thesis of his belief in the psychopathology of everyday life. Menninger (1942) defined mental health in terms of an individual's effectiveness and happiness in relating successfully to the world around him or her. Even in the definition Menninger offered, the domination of pathology and illness is a marker for mental health rather than the study of markers for resilience and strengths that has dominated social work theories and thinking.

Research and speculation derived from studying illness does not necessarily extrapolate to understanding the state of not being ill (see chapter 5). A psychological disorder assumed to exist within an individual does not necessarily lead to an understanding of the complexity of the person beyond the pathology or shed light on the condition of "normal," except in the simplistic sense that health is the absence of pathology.

R. Walsh, Walsh, and Shapiro (1983) posed the possibility that examining people's health should give some insights into not only what clients are like, but how they got there, why the rest of us did not, and how, if we wish, we can begin to move in the directions they reveal to us. In a speech before the American Psychological Association in 1998, Martin Seligman stated, "Social science now finds itself in almost total darkness about the qualities that make life most worth living" (see Monmaney, 2000, p. A1). Seligman reported that more than 46,000 articles had been published on depression in the psychology literature during the past 30-year period. Yet during that same period, only 400 articles had been published on joy. As the newly elected president of the American Psychological Association, Seligman (1999) called for a new mission for the discipline of psychology:

> I look to a new social and behavioral science that seeks to understand and nurture those human strengths that can prevent the tragedy of mental illness. For it is my belief that no medication or technique of therapy holds as much promise for serving as a buffer against mental illness as does human strength. (p. 561)

What is mental health? Or conversely, what is mental illness? These may be the wrong questions, because they insist that social workers think in terms of illness and its opposite, health. That is, they force social workers to look at their understanding from the perspective of the medical model. These two questions allow for no other way of thinking about those with whom social workers work other than through the constructed professional language that leads one to always seeing "pathology lurking behind every door [as if one were] living in a tenuous, dangerous world populated with vulnerable mental constitutions" (Duncan & Miller, 2000, p. 213). A partial response to this dilemma is for social workers to think of others as not so different than themselves in that all are attempting to weather daily "failures, [successes], frustrations, social—interpersonal [involvements as well as] rejections, [gains,] and losses—while maintaining the capacity to continue to meet life as a challenge worth pursuing" (Rowan & O'Hanlon, 1999, p. 164).

Maybe instead of thinking in terms of mental health or mental illness, social workers should ask how they think they are doing in terms of their own sense of self-reflection and how they are doing in relationship to others. This thinking is somewhat similar to Harry Sack Sullivan's theory of mental health as an ongoing process of demonstrating "efficiency as a human being, [his or her] satisfactions, and [his or her] success in living—a tendency which I sometimes loosely call *the drive toward mental health*" (Sullivan, 1953, p. 100, emphasis added). If social workers consider the drive as the process of living day to day with their own ups and downs, then maybe it is this drive, rather than some ultimate goal or achievement, that is mental health. Even if someone is diagnosed as manifesting schizophrenic symptoms, such as hearing voices, that person is often lucid much of the time. Similarly, resilience is a process that works for better or for worse over time throughout one's life.

Concept of Mental Health and Well-Being

Research on the effects of the most severe hazards or stressful events on children's mental health has demonstrated that it is likely that the majority of children will not succumb to the event and manifest psychological problems (Rutter, 1979). Most people do not become depressed (Paykel, 1978), and even in a depressive episode, individuals experience various degrees of depression and functionality. The issue is, what are the protective processes or evidence of resilience being played out in such situations? Understanding these protective factors is one key to social workers understanding resilience. For example, programs that attempt to prepare parents and their children for a hospital stay are effective at reducing emotional disturbances during hospitalization (Rutter, 1977). It is the ameliorative effect in relation to the pending hospital stay that is evidenced, that is, it is the process and not a particular trait or capacity that is seemingly responsible for the resilient behavior. "The promotion of resilience does not lie in an avoidance of stress, but rather in encouraging stress at a time and in a way that allows self-confidence and social competence to increase through mastery and appropriate responsibility" (Rutter, 1985, p. 608).

Resilience is formed as people meet hazards and challenges over time (Rutter, 1979). For example, Sarah Moskovitz's (1983) research has demonstrated that even under the most profound degradation and loss, humans of various ages are capable of going on. She talked with Holocaust survivors and reported that they showed a remarkable "affirmation of life" as well as a "stubborn durability" in facing the challenges of life (p. 233). In none of the survivors she had interviewed was there any evidence of psychiatric disorder. These observations and more recent research suggest that the client needs to be understood on his or her own terms, in all his or her uniqueness and complexity, and within a complex set of relationships. It is the client who is most often the healer.

Resilience and Understanding Emotional Well-Being

Dennis Saleebey (1998b) has stated that the tradition of social work dictates that social workers continue to give "little more than lip service ... [to] centering practice on eliciting and articulating a client's internal and external resources" (p. 3). Rather, within the constraints of this tradition, social workers remain focused on articulating the client's weaknesses, deficits, and pathologies. The outcome of this orientation is that social workers are trained to have a built-in bias toward pathology and rehabilitation rather than individual hopes, possibilities, resources, and resilience. A shift in perspective toward resilience will result in a shift toward promoting strengths and social support in human relationships and within communities. The focus shifts from concentrating on individual deficits to supporting interpersonal and community relationships. In one sense, shifting the focus to strategies for success in helping clients captures the fundamental ideas expressed in the social work concept of person-in-environment. This shift provides an opportunity to build on the interdependent, nested, or mutually reciprocal social processes in which humans live out their lives. From this point of view, practitioners cannot understand the individual client outside of the ongoing systemic process of change and transformation. Rather, their efforts are directed toward understanding and enhancing supporting environments and opportunities to capitalize on individual, interpersonal, and community strengths. In this orientation, mental health is supported by interventions that enhance protective factors or "influences that modify, ameliorate, or alter a person's responses to some environmental hazard" (Rutter, 1985, p. 600).

Personal social networks and school, church, day care facilities, and other community organizations are important in the promotion of protective factors and resilience. For example, Pritchard and Rosenzweig (1942) demonstrated the significance of resilience in children during the bombings of England during World War II. Although not downplaying the enormous effects of being caught in burning buildings, buried under fallen buildings, or injured, the authors noted, "There is a consensus of opinion that children show great adaptability and recover quickly from air-raid effects if simple and sensible measures are taken" (p. 331). The most significant factor was to maintain the children in familiar surroundings and not separate them from family and friends, that is, maintain a sense of community or solidarity. Others who studied these children discovered that removing the child to a safer location without the family resulted in greater immediate and long-term harm, such as depression, anxiety, and hysteria (Klein, 1944). Reflecting on these and other findings, Klein suggested that

> mental health can be promoted by stressing not merely the hazards of wishful thinking, personal conflict, and kindred psychiatric concepts, but also our tolerance for disciplined courage in the face of many hazards. It will make for a more balanced evaluation *to appreciate the ruggedness of most people in all strata of society when faced with trouble;* to note how national crises like wars and depressions find us with enough adjustive capacity as a people to come through without any noticeable increases in mental illness. . . . *The resiliency of the human organism is even more amazing than its vulnerability.* Awareness of these facts is a healthy antidote to the morbid apprehension of those whose perspective is distorted by excessive preoccupation with the literature of the abnormal in mental life. (p. 434, emphasis added)

An orientation toward this human "ruggedness" shifts social workers away from thinking about others in terms of dysfunction, disorder, disturbance, and deficit to thinking in terms of strengths and resiliency, and agency and power. In addition, it focuses on the relationships between the individual and others, as well as the social structures and social policies that either support or inhibit opportunities for resiliency to flourish.

The work to be done now is to understand how anyone might be assisted to rebound from adversity at any point in his or her life (Garmezy, 1994; Wolin & Wolin, 1993). Dennis Saleebey (1998a) has made the connections among individual resilience, group empowerment, and community development. He has pointed out that there are "factors, some operating, others imminent, that elicit and sustain resilient behavior, relationships, and institutions" (p. 199).

The circumstances that are assumed to produce pathology or vulnerability do not always do so (Werner & Smith, 1992; Wolin & Wolin, 1993). Research has shown that what most individuals would consider intolerable occurrences do not inevitably produce social and psychological defects that inhibit future functioning. This finding does not mean that social workers should disregard the pain and scars resulting from stress and trauma but recognizes that, despite these ordeals, people survive amazingly well. Resilience, or what Emmy Werner and Ruth Smith (1992) have termed "self-righting" tendencies, is a complex trajectory of factors that are played out over time between an individual's innate disposition and the world he or she must traverse throughout a lifetime. Anthony and Cohler (1987) noted that for children, a combination of factors such as individual characteristics in the context of early life experiences and actual protective factors contributes to resiliency in the face of adversity and challenges.

The majority of research conducted from the early 1950s to the present on issues such as school failure, criminal behavior, and mental health problems has examined the development and backgrounds of children and adults whose lives were already viewed by researchers as problematic. Werner and Smith (1992) have pointed out that this "retrospective approach can create the impression that a poor outcome is inevitable if a child is exposed to poverty, perinatal trauma, or parental psychopathology, because it examines only lives of the casualties, not the survivors" (p. 189). Their research on resiliency, as well as other similar research, has demonstrated clusters of protective factors that separated out those kids who were resilient against the assumed odds throughout a 40-year longitudinal study:

- Average intelligence.
- A disposition that enables youths to elicit positive responses from family members and strangers—what the authors described as robustness, vigor, and an active sociable temperament. These youths are seen as "easy" infants, characterized by freedom from distressing habits.
- Affectional ties with a significant other or parent substitute, a grandparent, older siblings, or mentoring adult figures such as teachers, youth workers, and later close friends, spouses, or mates. The authors found that these relationships foster trust, autonomy, and initiative on the part of children and later maturing adults. These significant others act as role models and counselors.
- The availability of an external support system such as in school, church, or youth groups that supports a sense of competence and provides a sense of coherence.
- Individual dispositions that lead children and later adults to construct environments that in turn reinforce and sustain their active outgoing disposition and reward their competencies.

Werner and Smith (1992) concluded that "from odds successfully overcome springs hope—a gift each of us can share with a child—at home, in the classroom, on the playground, or in the neighborhood" (p. 209).

Resilience as a Process

F. Walsh (1998) has indicated that resilience must be understood as involving systemic, mutually reciprocal processes within the complexity of inevitable individual change that is embedded within larger and increasingly complex relationships, such as within and between families as well as within cultural and socioeconomic communities. F. Walsh described resilience as a process "woven in a web of relationships and experiences over the course of" a life lived from birth through death (p. 12). Therefore, resilience is neither a trait nor a capacity that is present or not at any given time, nor is it a developmental stage. Resilience is a process that can occur at any age and under any circumstances. Longitudinal studies not only have demonstrated the variability in the process of resilience over the lifespan, but also have shown that change and the ability to bounce back from adversity can happen at any age and can occur repeatedly, but in different ways (Falicov, 1998; Werner & Smith, 1982). Werner and Smith (1982) found that no one short-term or long-term consequence is cast in stone as the result of early life events. For example, response to parental abandonment does not predict future responses to relationship loss (Werner & Smith, 1982, 1992). The confluence of numerous biopsychosocial variables occurring at the same time can have an ameliorative outcome that might not be predicted based on past reactions or responses. The findings of Werner and Smith have been supported by the work of Masten, Best, and Garmezy (1990); Wyman, Cowen, Work, and Parker (1991); and others. All of these efforts at understanding have demonstrated the fluidity of human resilience or human potential expressed within the "web of relationships formed by extended family, friends, and neighbors [that] have a constant, mutually reinforcing effect, in positive life trajectories" (F. Walsh, 1998, p. 14).

Client as Self-Healer

Commenting on studies of outcomes of psychotherapy, Bergin and Garfield (1994) noted that "with some exceptions . . . there is massive evidence that psychotherapeutic techniques do not have specific effects"; that is, the intervention techniques in and of themselves are not what creates the change in psychotherapy sessions (p. 822). After a lengthy review of a complex array of research on common factors for change in psychotherapy, Bohart and Tallman (1999) concluded that treatment or "therapy is a prosthetic provision of contexts, experiences, and events which prompt, support, or facilitate client's self-healing" (p. 114). Basically, clients "figure out what is going on, consider alternatives, review experience, generate possible solutions, imagine alternative outcomes," and experiment by imagining and taking small actions in the environment (Tallman & Bohart,

1999, p. 112). There is evidence that most individuals and families work out solutions without assistance from professionals. Lambert, Shapiro, and Bergin (1986) have estimated that the "spontaneous recovery rate" from mental illness is about 40 percent. For the most part, people recover because they use their own resources, such as personal relationships. Gurin, Veroff, and Feld (1960) concurred—most people facing issues contact those they know rather than a mental health professional. Weiner-Davis, de Shazer, and Gingerich (1987) and Lawson (1994) also found that more than 60 percent of clients had achieved some resolution to their problems after their phone call to set up an appointment with a mental health professional. Rosenbaum (1994) showed that many people improved after just one session. Bergin and Garfield (1994) found that "as therapists have depended upon client's resources, more change seems to occur" (p. 826). These studies support the idea that "human psychological development is highly buffered and self-righting" (Masten et al., 1990, p. 438).

Furthermore, the research and writings of Tallman and Bohart (1999), Prochaska (1999), Rennie (1994), and White and Epston (1990) have converged on particular points that enhance the possibility of change in therapeutic relationships. The following suggests the positioning social workers could take to facilitate the resilience and strengths of their clients within the context of a mental health setting:

- Facilitate generative thinking in contrast to ruminative thinking.
- Facilitate new perspectives.
- Facilitate externalizing conversations or distancing the "problem."
- Facilitate a collaborative, coexploration opportunity.
- Facilitate hope and confidence.
- Facilitate the generation of possible solutions and hopes for outcomes.
- Facilitate a safe holding space with time to consider and talk.
- Facilitate the experience of being heard, respected, and viewed as an expert on one's own understandings and feelings.
- Facilitate a supportive social and community network.

Implications for the Social Work Curriculum

Human behavior and the social environment must expose students to the complexity of human life in all its diversity and uniqueness. Thus, a focus on the contextual nature of human endeavors as expressed by the person-in-environment tradition would form the basis of the course content. Fundamentally, the content needs to reflect a deep respect and belief in the fact that, given the traumas faced in life, humans do remarkably well, not without pain and scars but often with growth and strengths they might not otherwise have had (Saleebey, 1998a). The research of Felsman and Vaillant (1987) has demonstrated that the "events that go wrong in our lives do not forever damn us" (p. 298).

Children living in the midst of poverty, war, discrimination, crime, drug abuse, and mental illness show an ability to take charge of their lives and to live successfully, despite what social workers would predict given theories of human development (Coles, 1964). Social workers seldom consider the complexity of human life, instead often looking only at the broken part—the conditions under which someone lives—assuming the worst possible outcomes. Practitioners need to recognize that human beings are remarkable in their potential to do more than just survive.

For example, noted child psychiatrist and Medal of Freedom winner Robert Coles's small friend, Ruby Bridges, who integrated the schools of New Orleans, was able to reach beyond the cruelty shown her and respond with caring and concern for those who would kill her. Ruby Bridges was the first and only black child to enter the newly court-ordered desegregated elementary school in New Orleans. White parents boycotted the school by keeping their children home. Many of these parents stood outside the school to taunt and harass Ruby as federal marshals brought her to school each morning and returned her home each afternoon. Ruby would stop just before arriving at the school to pray for those very people who threatened her with harm. Ruby remained a healthy and happy person throughout Robert Coles's lifelong contact with her. Such an example underscores that the human potential is to emerge from such an experience wounded yet strengthened. No one would subject anyone to this or any other form of wounding and pain to build courage, but it is becoming quite evident that human potential in the face of adversity is remarkable and almost always a surprise.

Research and practice experience from the strengths perspective, solution-focused family work, and efforts to understand the effectiveness of psychotherapeutic interventions have all yielded similar conclusions: It is the strengths, resilience, social support, and self-determination that appears to powerfully influence how an individual comes to terms with stress and life's hazards. This research and practice experience on resilience points to numerous shifts in perspective that must be considered when thinking of human development in the social environment and practice. The following list reflects the work of F. Walsh (1998), Werner and Smith (1992), Wolin and Wolin (1993), Garmezy (1991), Bronfenbrenner (1979), Higgins (1994), and others as they have begun to draw a more complete picture of the thinking coming out of resilience research. This list reveals a way of thinking about people in the context of their environment that would form the basis of the content in human behavior and social environmental learning and thinking as well as the basis for practice principles:

- Change lenses to view distressed individuals and families as challenged with potential for success and growth rather than as damaged goods.
- Understand human development within the confluence of contextual relationships (interpersonal, familial, social, community, and institutional).
- Recognize that resilience is not a trait but an interactional process that occurs within a social context; it is both nature and nurture.
- Be aware of the necessity to identify and strengthen interactional processes that permit individuals and families to withstand and rebound from disruptive life challenges.
- Maintain a belief in the potential of all individuals and families to rebound from life's challenges.
- Maintain a belief in the ability of individuals and families not only to rebound, but also to be strengthened by the challenges that they face.
- Recognize that resilience is not an impenetrable armor but a process that can be understood as "struggling well" in the midst of both courage and suffering (Higgins, 1994).
- Recognize that resilience is often forged in the midst of adversity; only in the context of challenges can the opportunity arise to bounce back stronger than before.
- Recognize the systemic nature of human lives and how relationships can be reinforced to support people's efforts to grow and live.

The social worker must not mistake resilience for the cultural mentality of individual ruggedness. Research has not demonstrated resilience to be an individualistic capacity or a simple matter of willpower. Instead, it is a complex process and needs to be understood as such. In terms of mental illness, the myth of personal responsibility is still maintained today by many people. Mechanic (1999) noted that, for the most part, people view individuals identified as having a mental illness as responsible for their own condition and, thus, responsible for eliminating the condition. The same holds true for conditions that are not necessarily classified as mental illness according to the *Diagnostic and Statistical Manual of Mental Disorders* (4th ed.; American Psychiatric Association, 1994).

Resilience does not support the "buck-up and take responsibility because others have overcome much worse" attitude directed toward individuals and families who are experiencing difficulties. It is a matter of complex relationships. Research shows that when children "make it," they make it within the context of a community of other caring individuals and changing circumstances. For example, Aseltine, Gore, and Colten (1994) found that, when adolescents reported high levels of family-related stress, they shifted away from the family and turned toward peers, mitigating the consequences of family stress. The children were not escaping or denying the family but finding an alternative—being resilient. Looking toward the solutions generated by clients as possibilities rather than imposing a set of best professional judgments opens up the opportunity to help build resilience.

Conclusion

The complexity of human beings, with all [their] manifested talents, dreams and fears, is obscured as the therapists persevere at "scientific" efforts to describe and comprehend a person in terms of limited sets of variables measuring pathology.

—FARBER, 1993, P. 8

Cultural and professional preoccupations with "what is wrong" and "what made it happen" can keep social workers from seeing that neither are all situations viewed as risks by everyone exposed to any particular situation, nor are the consequences of risk factors the same for all who are exposed to the risk. The world is full of hazards and vulnerability to things both within and outside of one's own personal control. However, the fact is that these realizations have played a very small part in the theories used as explanations in most courses on human behavior and the social environment, as well as in practice.

When social workers start to think from the perspective of client strengths and resilience, they tend to alter their basic assumptions of what human behavior and practice curriculum content might contain. The curriculum content needs to reflect a way of thinking about humans in terms of possibilities. Norlin and Chess (1997) noted that this curriculum and practice content needs to move from looking at "problems and deficits in human social functioning to the strengths and capacities possessed by" individual, family, community, and organizational systems (p. 11). They suggested that this shift be in the direction of "how [these systems] stay healthy, how they grow and develop" (p. 11). Practice should move in the direction of strength and solution-focused efforts that build onto people's capacities and provide an opportunity for individuals, families, and communities to engage in resilient behaviors that will alter their possibilities and enable them to build robustness so that they may meet life's challenges.

How this would look in practice is exemplified by an approach that asks very different questions of a client. It assumes a "not knowing" position or a position of genuine curiosity about a life we as social workers really do not know about (Anderson & Goolishian, 1992). We do not know all of the aspects of a client's life. If we are focused on the pathology or what is going wrong, we miss what is going well and what is right about a client's life. We can never fully understand the confluence of the client's past and present situations or desires for a better life, or even what has been done to make life better. Not knowing refers to social workers not making assumptions about clients but asking them about their life situations.

Working from a resilience and strengths perspective adds a focus that encompasses what is going well. A family worker might enter the conversation with what might be considered a multiproblem family with the question, "What is going well that you would like to continue?" even before asking what the problem is. This question and the others that follow convey a sense that the social worker is taking them seriously and understanding them. This contrasts with questioning clients about what is wrong and why something is happening, which often leads to defensiveness, accusations, and not feeling affirmed and understood. Remaining focused on the process of resilience and strengths enables the social worker to focus on the future and what is working well. This will help to build trust and empowerment (Berg & Kelly, 2000; DeJong & Berg, 1998).

This perspective is an alternative to traditional perspectives based on the theories of mental illness and mental health. This alternative vision builds on people's ability to right themselves, rather than look at what has gone wrong or is damaged. It does not assume that the social worker has the best answer. Thinking in terms of resilience and strengths creates a different place from which to start building a knowledge base for social workers' understanding of human behavior in the social environment and, in turn, their approach to how social work is practiced.

Use the CD by Michael Wright to map resilience as a process of embedded individual change in relationships. Define self-healing.

You will find a case study on your CD: *Comparing Two Points of View on Mental Health*

References

American Psychiatric Association. (1994). *Diagnostic and statistical manual of mental disorders* (4th ed.). Washington, DC: Author.

Anderson, H., & Goolishian, H. (1992). The client is the expert: A not knowing approach to therapy. In S. McNamee & K. J. Gergen (Eds.), *Therapy as social construction* (pp. 25–39). London: Sage.

Anthony, E., & Cohler, B. (Eds.). (1987). *The invulnerable child.* New York: Guilford Press.

Aseltine, R. H., Jr., Gore, S., & Colten, M. E. (1994). Depression and the social developmental context of adolescence. *Journal of Personality and Social Psychology, 67,* 252–264.

Berg, I. K., & Kelly, S. (2000). *Building solutions in child protective services.* New York: Norton.

Bergin, A. E., & Garfield, S. L. (1994). *Handbook of psychotherapy and behavior change* (4th ed.). New York: Wiley.

Bohart, A., & Tallman, K. (1999). *How clients make therapy work: The process of active healing.* Washington, DC: American Psychological Association.

Bolton, R. (1994). *Gal: A true life.* New York: Harcourt Brace.

Bronfenbrenner, U. (1979). *The ecology of human development.* Cambridge, MA: Harvard University Press.

Coles, R. (1964). *Children of crisis: A study of courage and fear.* New York: Dell.

DeJong, P. E., & Berg, I. K. (1998). *Interviewing for solutions.* Pacific Grove, CA: Brooks/Cole.

Doise, W., Deschamps, J. C., & Meyer, G. (1978). The accentuation of intra category similarities. In H. Tajfel (Ed.), *Differentiation between social groups: Studies in the social psychology of intergroup relations* (pp. 159–168). London: Academic Press.

Duncan, B. L., & Miller, S. D. (2000). *The heroic client: Doing client-directed, outcome informed therapy.* San Francisco: Jossey-Bass.

Erikson, E. (1959). *Identity and the life cycle.* New York: Norton.

Falicov, C. J. (1998). *Latino families in therapy: A guide to multicultural practice.* New York: Guilford Press.

Farber, S. (1993). *Madness, heresy, and the rumor of angels: The revolt against the mental health system.* Chicago: Open Court.

Felsman, J. K., & Vaillant, G. (1987). Resilient children as adults: A 40-year study. In E. J. Anthony & B. Cohler (Eds.), *The invulnerable child* (pp. 289–314). New York: Guilford Press.

Festinger, T. (1983). *No one ever asked us.* New York: Columbia University Press.

Freud, S. (1963). Analysis terminable and interminable. In P. Rieff (Ed.), *Therapy and technique* (pp. 233–271). New York: Collier. (Original work published 1937)

Garmezy, N. (1991). Resiliency and vulnerability to adverse developmental outcomes associated with poverty. *American Journal of Orthopsychiatry, 57,* 159–174.

Garmezy, N. (1994). Reflections and commentary on risk, resilience, and development. In R. J. Haggerty, L. R. Sherrod, N. Garmezy, & M. Rutter (Eds.), *Stress, risk, and resilience in children and adolescents: Processes, mechanisms, and interventions* (pp. 1–18). New York: Cambridge University Press.

Goode, E. E. (1992, February 10). Sick, or just quirky? *U.S. News & World Report, 112,* p. 49.

Goode, E. E. (1995). Broad definitions of mental illness may be harmful. In W. Barbour (Ed.), *Mental illness: Opposing viewpoints* (pp. 24–28). San Diego: Greenhaven Press.

Gurin, G., Veroff, J., & Feld, S. (1960). *Americans view their mental health.* New York: Basic Books.

Higgins, G. O. (1994). *Resilient adults: Overcoming a cruel past.* San Francisco: Jossey-Bass.

Hoyt, M. F. (1994). Introduction: Competency-based future oriented therapy. In M. F. Hoyt (Ed.), *Constructive therapies* (pp. 1–10). New York: Guilford Press.

Jahoda, M. (1958). *Current concepts of positive mental health.* New York: Basic Books.

Klein, D. B. (1944). *Mental hygiene: The psychology of personal adjustment.* New York: Holt.

Kraepelin, E. (1917). *Lectures on clinical psychiatry* (3rd ed.). New York: Wood.

Lakoff, G., & Johnson, M. (1980). *Metaphors we live by.* Chicago: University of Chicago Press.

Lambert, M. J., Shapiro, D. A., & Bergin, A. E. (1986). The effectiveness of psychotherapy. In S. L. Garfield & A. E. Bergin (Eds.), *Handbook of psychotherapy and behavior change* (3rd ed., pp. 157–212). New York: Wiley.

Lawson, D. (1994). Identifying pretreatment change. *Journal of Counseling and Development, 72,* 244–248.

Masten, A. S., Best, K. M., & Garmezy, N. (1990). Resilience and development: Contributions from the study of children who overcome adversity. *Developmental Psychopathology, 2,* 425–444.

Mechanic, D. (1999). *Mental health and social policy: The emergence of managed care* (4th ed.). Boston: Allyn & Bacon.

Menninger, K. (1942). *The human mind* (2nd ed.). New York: Knopf.

Mish, F. (Ed.-in-Chief). (2001). *Merriam Webster's Collegiate Dictionary* (10th edition). Springfield, MA: Encyclopedia Britannica Company.

Monmaney, T. (2000, January 8). Optimist may have the last laugh. *Los Angeles Times.* Retrieved from http://www.postgazette.com/healthscience/20000108optimism2.asp

Montaigne. (1958). *Complete essays of Montaigne* (D. M. Frame, Trans.). Stanford, CA: Stanford University Press.

Moskovitz, S. (1983). *Love despite hate.* New York: Norton.

Norlin, J. M., & Chess, W. A. (1997). *Human behavior and the social environment: Social systems theory* (3rd ed.). Boston: Allyn & Bacon.

Paykel, E. S. (1978). Contribution of life events to causation of psychiatric illness. *Psychological Medicine, 8,* 245–253.

Pierce, D. L. (1987). Negative bias and situation: Perception of helping agency on information seeking and evaluation of clients. Unpublished master's thesis, University of Kansas, Lawrence.

Pritchard, R., & Rosenzweig, S. (1942). The effects of war stress upon childhood and youth. *Journal of Abnormal and Social Psychology, 37,* 329–344.

Prochaska, J. O. (1999). How do people change, and how can we change to help more people? In M. A. Hubble, B. L. Duncan, & S. D. Miller (Eds.), *The heart and soul of change* (pp. 227–258). Washington, DC: American Psychological Association.

Rennie, D. (1994). Storytelling in psychotherapy: The client's subjective experience. *Psychotherapy, 3,* 234–243.

Rosenbaum, R. (1994). Single-session therapies: Intrinsic integration. *Journal of Psychotherapy Integration, 4,* 229–252.

Rowan, T., & O'Hanlon, B. (1999). *Solution-oriented therapy for chronic and severe mental illness.* New York: Wiley.

Rutter, M. (1977). Separation, loss and family relationships. In M. Rutter & L. Hersov (Eds.), *Child psychiatry: Modern approaches* (pp. 3–21). Oxford, England: Blackwell Scientific.

Rutter, M. (1979). Protective factors in children's response to stress and disadvantage. In M. W. Kent & J. E. Rolf (Eds.), *Primary prevention of psychopathology: Vol. 3. Social competency in children* (pp. 49–74). Hanover, NH: University Press of New England.

Rutter, M. (1985). Resilience in the face of adversity: Protective factors and resistance to psychiatric disorder. *British Journal of Psychiatry, 147,* 598–611.

Saleebey, D. (1998a). Community development, group empowerment, and individual resilience. In D. Saleebey (Ed.), *The strengths perspective in social work practice* (2nd ed., pp. 199–216). New York: Longman.

Saleebey, D. (1998b). Introduction: Power to the people. In D. Saleebey (Ed.), *The strengths perspective in social work practice* (2nd ed., pp. 3–21). New York: Longman.

Schriver, J. M. (2001). *Human behavior and the social environment* (3rd ed.). Needham Heights, MA: Allyn & Bacon.

Seligman, M. E. P. (1999). The president's address (annual report). *American Psychologist, 54,* 559–562.

Sullivan, H. S. (1953). *The psychiatric interview.* New York: Norton.

Tallman, K., & Bohart, A. C. (1999). The client as a common factor: Clients as self-healers. In A. H. Hubble, B. L. Duncan, & S. D. Miller (Eds.), *The heart and soul of change: What works in psychotherapy* (pp. 91–121). Washington, DC: American Psychological Association.

Walsh, F. (1998). *Strengthening family resilience.* New York: Guilford Press.

Walsh, R., Walsh, F., & Shapiro, D. H. (1983). *Beyond health and normality: Explorations of exceptional psychological well-being.* New York: Van Nostrand Reinhold.

Weiner-Davis, M., de Shazer, S., & Gingerich, W. (1987). Building on pretreatment change to construct the therapeutic solution: An exploratory study. *Journal of Marital and Family Therapy, 13,* 359–346.

Werner, E., & Smith, R. (1982). *Vulnerable, but invincible: A longitudinal study of resilient children and youth.* New York: McGraw-Hill.

Werner, E., & Smith, R. (1992). *Overcoming the odds: High risk children from birth to adulthood.* Ithaca, NY: Cornell University Press.

White, M., & Epston, D. (1990). *Narrative means to therapeutic ends.* New York: Norton.

Wolin, S. J., & Wolin, S. (1993). *The resilient self: How survivors of troubled families rise above adversity.* New York: Villard.

Wright, B. A., & Lopez, S. J. (2005). Widening the diagnostic focus: A case for human strengths and environmental resources. In C. R. Snyder & S. J. Lopez (Eds.), *Handbook of positive psychology* (pp. 26–44). New York: Oxford University Press.

Wyman, L., Cowen, W., Work, W., & Parker, G. (1991). Developmental and milieu correlates of resilience in urban children who have experienced major life stress. *American Journal of Community Psychology, 19,* 405–426.

7

Surviving Violence and Trauma: Resilience in Action at the Micro Level

NANCY J. ROTHENBERG

On finishing this chapter, students will be able to further:

Intervene with individuals, families, groups, organizations, and communities (Educational Policy 2.1.10c) by

- Helping clients resolve problems.
- Negotiating, mediating, and advocating for clients (practice behaviors).

The world breaks everyone and afterward many are strong at the broken places.

—*A Farewell to Arms*, Hemingway, 1929

In the decade since the first version of this chapter was written, violence and traumatic events in people's lives have not only continued, but expanded in ways previously unimaginable. When this chapter was initially written, the life- and society-changing events of September 11, 2001, had not yet occurred. Neither had Hurricane Katrina, the Asian tsunami, or the earthquakes in Haiti and Chile, all of which played out on television for days in horrifying detail. Law-abiding citizens were not subjected to routine pat-downs every time they flew on a commercial airplane, and Internet-linked murder was unheard of.

The international community has become smaller and more intimate. Through global development and the marvels of the Internet, populations around the globe share common experiences as they sit transfixed in front of computers and televisions watching wars, natural disasters, and the effects of human dissent in real time. People are reminded time and again of their vulnerability as well as their connection to one another. Although stories of survival, recovery, and resilience in the wake of these traumas are far less publicized, human beings worldwide demonstrate time and again individuals' capacity to pick themselves up and move forward no matter how seemingly enormous the obstacle.

Research on helping people cope with traumatic events and discover their inner strengths has expanded to include a wide range of healing practices that have incorporated a strengths-based, resiliency focus. Helping professionals have looked to indigenous spiritual practices, meditation, and the emerging field of neurobiology (van der Kolk, 2006) for answers and assistance. For many U.S. families, the notion of trauma now includes the reality of living with the impact of devastating wars that for many have become a way of life. Since 2003, new waves of soldiers have returned home from multiple tours of duty in crisis-ridden and dangerous areas of the world, facing huge challenges physically, emotionally, and economically (see chapter 13). Helping families cope with the effects of posttraumatic stress disorder (PTSD) has become an important focus in this new era of wars, terror attacks, and devastating natural disasters. Indeed, life in the new millennium does not appear to be kinder or gentler. For social workers who are charged with helping people survive traumatic events even while confronted with their own susceptibility in the aftermath of trauma, there is much to learn from the survivors who have found their capacity for inner strength and are able to live their lives with joy and gratitude despite their pain.

This chapter focuses on the common elements that allow survivors to forge resilient comebacks when confronted with extreme adversity. Drawing from research with individuals and groups who have experienced life-shattering events, this chapter reports ways in which professional helpers such as social workers can use their relational skills to assist people in navigating trauma. Borrowing from the title of the classic *When Bad Things Happen to Good People* (Kushner, 1983), I argue that yes, bad things really *do* happen—over and over. Social workers take on the sacred journey of helping people pick up the broken pieces while recognizing that there are riches beneath the surface just waiting to be mined.

Violence, Trauma, and Resilience: A Theoretical Environmental Lens

An ecological perspective, adopted by many social work practitioners, is helpful in conceptualizing the complex relationship between people and their environment because it provides an understanding of the contextual implications of violent events. It also enables practitioners to recognize the capacity of survivors to overcome the effects of adversity. Given the social work profession's multitiered systemic orientation, with its emphasis on strengths-based approaches to practice, self-determination, and community empowerment, social workers are seemingly the ideal helping professionals to negotiate the complex terrain for people directly and indirectly affected by trauma. This creates a strong linkage between the impact of violence in its myriad forms and the inspirational feats of resiliency demonstrated in its aftermath. Helping professionals are an important resource for assisting survivors in navigating through the grief, pain, fear, and disorientation that inevitably emerge following trauma. Assessing survivors' needs within an ecosystemic framework helps to link survivors to social and community supports. Understanding the normative processes of grief, both developmentally as well as behaviorally, allows survivors to heal in their own way and in their own time.

PTSD

Violence has been defined as an action or circumstance in which one individual injures another; it includes both direct physical or psychological attacks as well as destructive actions that do not necessarily involve a direct relationship between the victim and the perpetrator (Bulhan, 1985; Salmi, 1993). The latter part of this definition has special relevance for social workers who may be working with individuals or families who are coping with the legacy of violence. This legacy often includes the lingering aftermath of PTSD, first included in the fourth edition of the *Diagnostic and Statistical Manual of Mental Disorders* (American Psychiatric Association, 1994). PTSD is a cluster of emotional and psychological symptoms and experiences following exposure to a traumatic event that can be summarized as an experience of persistent reexperiencing of the event(s) that may include flashbacks, nightmares, intense physiological response to external triggers, persistent emotional numbing and avoidance, persistent symptoms of increased arousal not present previous to the trauma, or symptoms lasting for at least one month leading to significant impairment in social and occupational functioning (Yehuda, 2002).

A sense of hopelessness is often characteristic of PTSD (Blume, Resor, Villanueva, & Braddy, 2009; Michado, de Azevedo, Facuri, Vieira, & Fernandes, 2011; Scher & Resick, 2005). One of the antidotes to hopelessness is to assist survivors in reclaiming their balance by finding a sense of meaning in their experience. Peres, Moreira-Almeida, Nasello, and Koenig (2007) commented,

> Studies suggest that an increase in hope and decrease in despair and hopelessness may be critically important factors for better health and longevity. When people become traumatized they often look for a new sense of meaning and purpose in their life. (p. 344)

Although the phrase "posttraumatic stress disorder" was initially coined to describe the ordeal facing many returning Vietnam veterans in the 1960s and 1970s, the term has long since been applied more generally to other populations who have experienced trauma through accidents, violence perpetrated on them, and/or witness to traumatic events. Consider the devastation of the events of September 11, 2001, on the people who were physically close to the attack:

> The terrorist attacks on the World Trade Center and the Pentagon on September 11, 2001, represented an amalgam of interpersonal violence, loss, and disaster. Tens of thousands of people ran for their lives in fear, were exposed to graphic scenes of death, or lost loved ones. It is estimated that well over 100,000 people directly witnessed the events, and many people around the world were also exposed to these horrifying scenes through the media. (Yehuda, 2002, p. 108)

Bessel van der Kolk, a leading researcher and clinical psychiatrist in the area of trauma, PTSD, and brain research, focuses his work with trauma survivors on the integration of the mind, body, brain, and socioenvironmental factors. He postulates that context and personal development influence the relationship of the individual to the trauma experience:

> What is most traumatic to the individual—what the individual is least able to process—is not necessarily what is most scary, or most normatively horrible, or what threatens human life the most. Often, what is most traumatic involves some extraordinary betrayal, assault or betrayal of who we know ourselves to be. What is often most traumatic—and also, what ends up containing the map to healing within it—is a detail of self experience. A patient who was raped as she was coming out of the shower said that what bothered her the most was "that I was skinny and naked and he was dressed and big." (van der Kolk, 2006, p. 278)

Van der Kolk's research has expanded to include alternative practices that incorporate biofeedback and yoga practice in treating PTSD as well as the use of improvisational theater to prevent youth violence (van der Kolk, 2007). He also advocates play therapy for children who have been traumatized (van der Kolk, 2010). Other treatment approaches for PTSD and its symptoms that have been the subject of much evidence-based research include eye-movement desensitization and reprocessing (Shapiro, 2004), cognitive behavioral therapies (Seidler, 2006), and yoga (Gerberg & Brown, 2005) and meditation (Folette, Palm, & Pearson, 2006; Kimbrough, Magyari, Langenberg, Cheaney, & Berman, 2010; Lee & Zaharlick, 2009). There are several benefits to using meditation and guided imagery to assist survivors of trauma reestablish safety and control, healing and integration, and clean-up and renewal (Naparstek, 2005).

Secondary Trauma: A Work-related Risk for Social Workers

Researchers have explored the impact of the events of September 11, 2001, on not just the survivors and their families but helping professionals and first responders. One of the many outcomes of that crisis was the profound recognition of the widespread emotional impact on bystanders, relatives of victims, helping professionals such as police officers and firefighters, and the general populace many miles away. Terms such as *vicarious traumatization, secondary trauma,* and *compassion fatigue* have been used to describe the impact on helping professionals of working with victims of trauma by illness, accident, or violent crime (Bride, 2007; Cunningham, 2004; Figley, 2002; Figley & Bride, 1997; Lerias & Byrne, 2003; Thomas & Wilson, 2004). Figley (2002) defined *compassion fatigue* as a process that emphasizes the costs of caring, empathy, and emotional investment in helping the suffering. Bride (2007) postulated that "social workers may be especially vulnerable to compassion fatigue ... Secondary traumatic stress (STS) is becoming viewed as an occupational hazard of providing direct services to traumatized populations" (p. 63). Secondary trauma is a serious consequence for helping professionals who do not attend to self-care. Researchers emphasize the importance of self-care to avoid burnout and the serious side effects caused by the intensity of their work (Bride, 2007; Killian, 2008; Meadors & Lamson, 2008). Practices such as meditation and yoga have been found to be helpful for all populations, including helping professionals (Hesse, 2002). Additional tools include journaling, engaging in peer supervision, taking nature walks, exercising, maintaining a spiritual connection, establishing clear work boundaries, engaging in recreational activities, and using other rituals to release internalized stress.

Vulnerable Populations: From Risk to Resiliency

Violent crime has long been associated with racism and poverty and can be viewed as an outgrowth of a culture of oppression (Van Soest & Bryant, 1995). However, the current societal experience of violence cuts across all cultural, ethnic, class, and gender lines. In recent years, violence has been manifested domestically and visibly on college campuses and in public schools. The horrific shooting of Congresswoman Gabrielle Giffords and the murder of her legislative aids as well as innocent bystanders in January 2011 once again increased the visibility of violence in U.S. society, shattering the denial of the majority culture that "it could never happen here" or that anyone is truly "safe." Although social workers have historically worked with populations that are seemingly more at risk, it is clear that the entire population can be considered at risk and that the aftermath of violent behaviors affects the entire community.

Physical aggression can be experienced as a physical violation and/or as a threat—an expression of power, control, and intimidation. Vulnerable groups who have experienced the fear, degradation, and dire implications of violence directed against them include people of color, children, women, older adults, the homeless, mentally ill and mentally disabled individuals, and persons who identify as gay, bisexual, lesbian, or transgender. Bullying behaviors among children have been the subject of research (Espelage & Swearer, 2003; Juvonen, Graham, & Schuster, 2003; Rigby, 2007). An emerging form of bullying, cyberbullying, has had tragic consequences, resulting in at least two publicized teen suicides (Raskauskas & Stoltz, 2007).

Socioeconomic status also influences a person's vulnerability to crime and violent actions. According to U.S. Bureau of Justice Statistics (Rand & Truman, 2009), people in households with annual incomes less than $7,500 experience the highest rate of violent crime, whereas those in households that earn more than $75,000 experience the lowest rates. Victimization ranges from the devastating subtlety of institutional racism and group ostracism to the sheer terror of a direct physical or sexual assault.

Partner violence includes patterns of intimidation and misuse of power. A child is particularly vulnerable to the intimidation of others, including other children, especially if he or she is physically smaller or weaker. Children may witness violence in the home over time; experience violence as an assault on their person from family, other adults, peers, other children, or strangers; or witness random violence in their communities or homes (Richters & Martinez, 1993). Researchers have indicated, however, that a quality parent–child relationship can function as a protective buffer for children who are the victims of violence, particularly boys (Aceves & Cookston, 2007).

Resilience Research with Traumatized Populations

Resiliency research, first introduced in the 1970s, represented a significant shift away from pathology models as researchers began to view risk through a broad social lens, rather than assigning blame to individuals and families (Benard, 1999). Much of the focus of the early studies was on child development and protective factors that could ameliorate the effects of risks. The main focus of resiliency research was on competence—the presence of good outcomes based on life tasks that could be measured—as well as the development of qualities that serve as protection against future adversity. This research was intertwined with studies examining developmental processes in individuals and families across the life cycle as well as on a socioenvironmental level. Conclusions from Werner and Smith's (1992) landmark study indicated that resiliency can be developed at any point in the life cycle. Other researchers have concurred with this view of resiliency by challenging the notions of some child development researchers that earlier traumas cannot be overcome. Froma Walsh (2006), a leading social work family researcher, summed it up succinctly when she stated, "The qualities of resilience enable people to heal from painful wounds, take charge of their lives, and go on to live fully and love well" (p. 4). Child development theorists suggest that a biological imperative for growth and development exists in the human species (Zautra, 2009). Ann Masten (2001), a leading developmental researcher, argued,

> The study of resilience in development has overturned many negative assumptions and deficit-focused models about children growing up under the threat of disadvantage and adversity. The most surprising conclusion emerging from studies of these children is the ordinariness of resilience. An examination of converging findings from variable-focused and person-focused investigations of these phenomena suggests that resilience is common and that it usually arises from the normative functions of human adaptational systems. (p. 227)

Over the past decade, there has been a focus on resiliency among traumatized populations such as battered women and those impacted by family violence (Cairns-Descoteaux, 2005; Humphreys, 2003; Young, 2007); returning veterans (Pietrzak, Johnson, Goldstein, Malley, & Southwick, 2009); Holocaust survivors (Cohen, Meek, & Lieberman, 2010; Corley, 2010; Liat, 2005); older adults (Cohen, Greene, Lee, Gonzalez, & Evans, 2006); burn survivors (Askay & Magyar-Russell, 2009; N. R. Williams, Davey, & Klock, 2003); survivors of political violence (Hernandez, Gangsei, & Engstrom, 2007); survivors of major disasters (Bonanno, 2004; Walsh, 2007); African Americans exposed to severe trauma (Alim et al., 2008); at-risk youth (N. R. Williams & Lindsey, 2010); survivors of workplace violence (Bishop, McCullough, Thompson, & Nakiya, 2006); gay, lesbian, bisexual, and transgender populations (Kulkin, 2006; Munroe, 2008); street prostitutes (Prince, 2008); people with depression (Edward, 2005); people facing trauma and addiction (Cunningham, 2004); people with mental illness (Edward, Welch, & Chater, 2009); parents of children with disabilities (Heiman, 2002); survivors of Hurricane Katrina (Goodman & West-Olatunji, 2008); and international youth at risk (Hodges, Jagdev, Chandra, & Cunniff, 2008; Levine, Laufer, Stein, Hamama-Raz, & Solomon, 2009; Zahradnik et al., 2010). This is only a partial list of studies that have emerged over many helping disciplines with a large range of vulnerable populations.

In the face of enormous challenges, a paradigm shift seems to have taken place in the area of resiliency to counter the helplessness and suffering that is associated with the experience of victimization. Helping professionals have been challenged to move beyond what they think they know about risk and pathology, as resiliency research promotes optimism and hope. Applying these ideas is especially useful in working in a multicultural context and in evaluating family forms, attitudes toward violence and trauma, and definitions of mental health (see chapter 6). This perspective has great relevance to the social work profession because it lends support and justification to a strengths-based approach to practice in which the individual's unique coping process is viewed in context (Bachay & Cingel, 1999).

As mentioned earlier, direct practitioners can find themselves at risk when working with survivors of trauma, especially if they have had similar experiences in their own lives (Carbonell & Figley, 1996). These professionals need an arsenal of tools, support, and methods of release, both physical and emotional. The capacity to *reframe* obstacles—or the ability to make lemonade when life hands you lemons—permeates survival stories and appears to be a crucial aspect of resiliency (Bachay & Cingel, 1999). Social workers can use this as a powerful intervention tool to help guide people through the trauma recovery process as well as to enable themselves to move beyond their clients' tragedies. This attitude, in turn, can enable clients to embrace the changes that have been thrust on them, empowering them to shed their identification as victims. Finding meaning in experience can become a deep well of inspiration for both client and practitioner and an antidote for some of the pain. Viktor Frankl's (1959) classic *Man's Search for Meaning* describes his journey against the odds to face his own trauma. He postulated that helping professionals must be willing to tap their own basic beliefs about healing, optimism, and the meaning of life and adversity.

Risk and Resilience in Adolescence

Youth are vulnerable to both violence and trauma. *Youth violence* is defined as an act—intentional, actual, or implied—against oneself or another person, group, or community that leads to injury, death, or psychological harm, in which the individuals—perpetrator or victim—are 10 to 24 years old (World Health Organization, 2002). Although youth homicide rates have declined in recent years, it remains the second leading cause of death among people in this age group. Another alarming statistic is that nearly 48 percent of homicides in the United States in 2000 were committed by individuals younger than age 24. Homicide is the leading cause of death for African American youth; second-leading cause for Hispanic American youth; and third-leading cause for Native American, Alaska Native, and Asian and Pacific Islander youth. Of the 5,486 youth homicides reported in 2001, 85 percent involved boys and 15 percent involved girls (Centers for Disease Control and Prevention, 2011).

An especially vulnerable group of adolescents who have long been a focus of concern is runaway and/or homeless youth, sometimes referred to as *unaccompanied* youth. According to the National Coalition for the Homeless (2007), there are approximately 1.7 million homeless and runaway youth in the United States, defined as "individuals under the age of 18 who lack parental, foster, or institutional care" (Molino, 2007, p. 1). Unaccompanied youth account for 3 percent of the urban homeless population (U.S. Conference of Mayors, 2005). About 6 percent of these youths have been identified as gay, lesbian, bisexual, or transgender (Molino, 2007). The number of homeless youth is estimated by the Office of Juvenile Justice and Delinquency Prevention in the U.S. Department of Justice. In 2002, their most recent study reported an estimated 1,682,900 homeless and runaway youth. This number was equally divided between boys and girls, and the majority were between the ages of 15 and 17 (Molino, 2007).

Suicide is one of the leading causes of death among adolescents. Although teenage girls are more likely than boys to attempt suicide, boys use more lethal methods and thus are more likely to die in the attempt. Boys struggling with sexual identity issues are at particular risk. Cultural influences also suggest risk and protective factors. In a cross-cultural study, researchers found that ethnic groups differed in rates of suicidal behaviors, vulnerability and protective factors, and patterns of help-seeking behaviors among youths. Implications for suicide prevention and treatment, including the roles of religion, spirituality, and the family in culturally sensitive interventions, were discussed, with the researchers calling for culturally sensitive community-based interventions (Goldston et al., 2008).

Self-esteem is a prominent protective resource that youths may use against daily negative life events. Problem-solving and coping strategies are also instrumental in helping adolescents deal with stress and depression (Dumont & Provost, 1999). The importance of young people having access to experiences that allow them to develop a sense of self-esteem and self-efficacy has been borne out in research (Rutter, 1985; Werner & Smith, 1992). To a certain extent, the process of becoming more resilient is self-reinforcing. As people begin to exert their determination to turn their lives around, take care of themselves, assert their independence in positive ways, and accept help from others, they experience successes that reinforce their efforts.

There has been a shift since the 1990s in work with youth violence to focus more on the notion of community mobilization, in which comprehensive community-based engagement is cultivated to address social issues (Kim-Ju, Mark, Cohen, Garcia-Santiago, & Nguyen, 2008). The researchers defined *community mobilization* as individuals taking action organized around specific community issues. This concept is based on social empowerment models and attempts to better explain the interplay of individual characteristics, health conditions, and environmental factors in relationship to the family and neighborhood. This approach is collaborative at its base, building on the inherent strengths in grassroots organizing in conjunction with researchers engaged in participatory action research. These approaches are based on the notion that an engaged, participatory community will lead to greater efficacy in addressing problems.

Resiliency among Adolescents

In exploring resiliency among adolescents, it is useful to remember that adolescence is a stage of human development when youths face many critical decisions and have a greater capacity to influence their own developmental pathways than they had when they were younger (Crockett & Crouter, 1995). Developmental psychologists have emphasized two primary forces that influence development: personal characteristics and contextual factors (social environment). Contextual influences include the nature of the environment within which adolescents are developing (family, school, peers, and neighborhood), as well as the normative and nonnormative events that they experience. According to Crockett and Crouter (1995), the effects of nonnormative events are believed to be especially "pronounced in adolescence because they co-occur with other developmental and contextual transitions experienced during that period" (p. 7). They concurred with other researchers in citing several personal characteristics that affect individuals' responses to challenges, including "temperament, biological predisposition to specific types of stressors, intelligence, coping style, and social skills" (p. 5). In many cultures, adolescents experience some measure of personal and familial difficulties as they attempt to navigate the transition from adolescence to young adulthood. Although adolescence can be fraught with challenges for adolescents and their families, most adolescents are able to weather these storms with relative success, maintaining the integrity of the family and family support as they move into adulthood. The use of humor has been cited as a stress reliever and can indicate good coping skills. Erickson and Feldstein (2007) commented, "Humor has often been conceptualized as a form of coping in that it involves a multidimensional, transactional process concerning how people handle stress" (p. 257).

Engaging youth in community-based service activities is beneficial to the community as well as aids in the development of self-esteem and self-efficacy among the youth involved (N. R. Williams & Lindsey, 2005, 2010; N. R. Williams, Lindsey, Kurtz, & Jarvis, 2001). A sense of optimism is frequently associated with the experience of helping others. This quality has been cited as an important factor that promotes positive adjustment in youths exposed to violence in their homes and in the community, even though exposure, particularly to uncontrollable events, creates great challenges (Egger, 1998). Interventions that attempt to increase optimistic beliefs by encouraging mastery of challenging situations may provide a means of improving adjustment and self-esteem among adolescents.

In addition to internal resources such as self-esteem, social support is an important protective factor that buffers the effects of stress to which adolescents are vulnerable. The mitigating impact of social support on adolescents has been investigated among teens exposed to community violence (Brookmeyer, Henrich, Cohen, & Shahar, 2010), adolescents with cancer (Corey, Haase, Azzouz, & Monahan, 2008), adolescents suffering from depression (Ellis, Nixon, & Williamson, 2009), and sexual minority youth (T. Williams, Connolly, Pepler, & Craig, 2005). There is an indication that social support reduces adolescents' perceptions of stress and contributes to greater physical health and psychological well-being. Conversely, there are indications that dissatisfaction with social support is often associated with depressive or psychosomatic symptoms and anxiety that may result in impulsive, self-destructive behaviors such as suicide or externalized aggression toward others.

Role of Spirituality in Resiliency

Spirituality, once seemingly in conflict with the social work profession's ethical commitment to self-determination and religious neutrality, has emerged as a substantive focus of research on healing and resiliency. In fact, social work scholarship has moved to include conceptualizing spirituality as a dimension of practice (Smith, 1995). Several studies exploring the relationship between spiritual or religious affiliation and good mental health in adolescents corroborate earlier findings (Knight et al., 2007; N. R. Williams & Lindsey, 2005; Wilson, 2005). In addition, spiritual practices reinforce community values by providing a structure for ritual, creating an atmosphere of compassion and forgiveness and a sense of group belonging that may fill a void for disenfranchised adolescents (DiBlasio & Benda, 1991).

Spirituality has been defined as a "human quest for personal meaning, mutually fulfilling relationships among people, the nonhuman environment, and, for some, God" (Canda, 1988, p. 243). Although spirituality and religiosity are often intertwined, there are also substantive differences: The former can be considered any beliefs or practices that facilitate wholeness and connection beyond the individual, and the latter can be considered a specific set of beliefs and/or practices that promote an adherence to an established faith (N. R. Williams &

Lindsey, 2010). Spirituality can be a significant ingredient in the healing process for survivors of violence or trauma, providing a sense of connectedness to self and others and an ability to see a larger meaning or purpose in life events (Dyer, 2006; Shuler, Gelberg, & Brown, 1994). Researchers also report that spirituality imparts emotional protection and provides ways to cope with the trials of everyday life as it expands a person's values and perspectives, allowing for the possibility of viewing adversity as an opportunity for personal growth and development (Feinstein, 1997; N. R. Williams & Lindsey, 2005, 2010). Spirituality allows humans to accept their foibles and lays the foundation for self-acceptance and tolerance of others, as it provides a context for understanding the unfathomable. Most important, the development of resiliency is reportedly tied to the ability to have hope and find reassurance in the face of distress. For many people, this support and nurturance can be found within an organized spiritual community or within a personal relationship with a higher power.

The notion of forgiveness in healing from the lingering remnants of inflicted trauma, particularly for adults who experienced abuse in their childhood, has been a subject of interest. Spirituality places an emphasis on belonging to a greater whole, creating a sense of meaning and purpose, as well as generating a feeling of acceptance of self and others that often involves the act of forgiveness. In fact, Knight et al. (2007) have linked the act of forgiveness with effective substance use prevention and treatment approaches, particularly with adolescents. Incorporating spiritual processes allows an individual to make respectful choices because of a stronger individual and collective sense of self. These processes can be a particularly amenable treatment tool in working with adolescents who are seeking to create their identity.

The healing powers of forgiveness have been evidenced as a byproduct of victim–offender mediation within the restorative justice movement (Umbreit, 2001). This experience allows for victims to confront offenders. Although forgiveness is never a goal, when it occurs, there is often discharge and relief for both the offender and the victim (or family member of the victim in the case of homicide; Armour & Umbreit, 2006). Restorative justice is an approach to recovering to crime in which the focus of the process is on creating an opportunity for emotional reparation for the victim. Howard Zehr (2002), a pioneer in the field of restorative justice, wrote the following:

> Restorative justice expands the circle of those with a stake in the criminal justice case beyond just the government and the offender to include victims and community members. . . . In the traditional criminal justice system, offenders are discouraged from acknowledging their responsibility and are given little opportunity to act on their responsibility. Real

accountability means encouraging offenders to understand the impact of their behavior and urging them to take steps to put things right.

Within this approach, a crime is considered a crime against a person rather than the state, as it is often considered in the traditional justice system. Thus, the focus of this process is on accountability and personal responsibility, and the offender and victim actively participate in the presence of a trained mediator. After conducting a rigorous comparative study, Poulson (2003) reported that restorative justice models outperformed court models on every variable (fairness, personal responsibility, reduction of fear, and increased respect, and so forth) for both the victim as well as the offender. In addition, he found a reduction in youth offender suicide under this model. Restorative justice models such as truth and reconciliation forums are being implemented on an international level as well, particularly in countries torn apart by civil war and/or apartheid, such as South Africa and Liberia.

Assessment and Intervention

The important role of helping professionals—to provide comfort, support, and restabilization to victims of trauma—cannot be overstated. Social workers can offer significant leadership, from accessing concrete resources to mobilizing natural support networks and disseminating vital information. They can also play a key role in facilitating the deep healing work of survivors of violence by using the therapeutic relationship to create corrective attachment experiences. This phenomenon is particularly effective in working with adult survivors of childhood trauma who seek more satisfying, less maladaptive relationships as adults. This section introduces several general treatment approaches, including grief work and critical incident debriefing, that address the healing work necessary to deal with the recovery process. Also addressed in this section is a key prevention tool—conflict resolution training—for facilitating improved communication in families and preparing children for adulthood, which is an essential skill for competent and prepared practitioners.

Grief Work

Grief is a natural emotional, physical, and cognitive expression in reaction to a loss or trauma. Dealing with the grief that comes in the aftermath of violence is crucial. The act of bearing witness to another's pain is as potent as it is natural but can be overlooked in a practitioner's zeal to help a survivor move forward. When children experience loss or survive violence, the trauma can interrupt the developmental process if the grief is not addressed. Often, it is difficult for children to identify what, specifically, has been lost as a result of a traumatic event because the loss may have been a loved one, a sense of security, a body part, or something less tangible. The concept of resilience is a dynamic process that spans an individual's life, so the concept of development is crucial in considering how children and adolescents deal with violence and loss (Masten, 2001).

A significant body of research in developmental psychology suggests that children interpret the world and communicate about their feelings differently from adults (Howard, Dryden, & Johnson, 1999). Thus, it is imperative that intervention strategies reflect that children may express their grief differently than adults and that children's response to grief and loss will vary depending on their stage of development, their past experiences with grief and loss, and the influence of the family's handling of loss. Because each child is unique, the way a child deals with violence and death may vary with his or her understanding of the concept of death.

One of the first models to conceptualize how children process trauma and death was developed by Marie Nagy (1948). Her model illustrated how a changing perception of the concept of death might influence the behavior and coping ability of a child who has been the victim of violence or loss. During the first stage, the child views death as reversible. Because he or she may not understand that death is permanent, the child may wish to visit the deceased person or may be unable to separate fact from fantasy. During the second stage, the loss is personalized. A child in the second stage may think that the death or trauma was his or her fault because the child was "bad" and may feel guilt or shame when he or she is reminded of the traumatic event. The child may also act as if the event did not occur and may attempt to deny it. Speece and Brent (1987) indicated that the average age when children understand death in an adult-like manner is seven years. At that point, in the third and final stage, the child views death as permanent. The child may express concerns about death as a result of natural causes and may understand that death is irreversible and inevitable. The concept of death, the idea of permanence, and the perception of loss as real are relevant to any traumatic event. Awareness of a child's ability to conceive of death is directly related to the choice of intervention used with that child.

The stages of grief work with adults are moderated by whether the traumatic event was expected or unexpected. If an event was expected or anticipated, then the effects of the event are reduced because adults are able to mobilize their internal, endogenous resources to defend against the shock of the incident. If an event is unanticipated, such as being the object of violent behavior or facing someone's violent death, the effects of the trauma may be exaggerated or complicated by the legal aftermath (Sprang, McNeil, & Wright, 1989). The grief process may be prolonged and resolution elusive. Individuals manifest grief differently based on circumstances, background, and history. The realization that a traumatic event has occurred and that something must be done is often the point at which people seek the assistance of a helping professional. This opportunity to intervene is available because an individual may have exhausted his or her resources or is unable to perceive options and feels unbearably vulnerable. Helping professionals must be able to understand the unique dynamics involved in traumatic grief and respect the power of listening to each story to enable the individual to find comfort and heal from these deep wounds.

Critical Incident Stress Debriefing

A high school student is murdered, and a community of friends, neighbors, and family members absorb the shock and horror of this event. A man is critically wounded in a hunting accident with a group of his friends. A young woman takes her life after a relationship breaks up. A tornado tears up a section of a small town, leaving many people homeless, injured, or dead. A nation and a world is left immobilized when airplanes crash into the World Trade Center and the Pentagon, leaving many thousands dead and families shattered. The list of sudden traumas that throw individuals, families, and communities into crisis is endless and ongoing.

Critical or unusual stress occurs as a result of events that threaten life, body, or a person's normal and expectable experience of life. People experience psychological and spiritual trauma as a result of critical incidents that, if left unexpressed, can result in a multiplicity of physical and psychological disturbances, including suicide or chronic illness. Structured approaches to helping victims of trauma minimize the long-term impact of such events have long been institutionalized into practice since first responders were introduced in the late 1970s and early 1980s. In recent years, however, structured, often manadatory approaches have received criticism, debunking its effectiveness in preventing PTSD.

Critical incident stress debriefing is one such approach that has been offered to survivors of trauma. It provides survivors an opportunity to describe the event; offer their interpretation; and receive education about the normal physical, cognitive, emotional, and spiritual signs and symptoms that many people experience as a result of such trauma (Everly & Mitchell, 1999; Mitchell, 1983). Research and clinical evidence suggests that this process is most effective if facilitated within three days of the critical incident, and it can occur with an individual or in a group setting with family members or coworkers or among friends and colleagues. The debriefing process can last from one to three hours and typically takes place in one or two sessions. The purpose of this process is to prevent long-term damage of critical stress by normalizing people's responses, providing cognitive awareness, and validating feelings. Helping people make sense out of the unthinkable can sometimes provide a platform for building coherence. This sense of coherence is an orientation that life is ultimately comprehensible, manageable, and meaningful. This belief system is gravely challenged in a crisis situation but is vital to developing resiliency in relation to the traumas that life presents. However, some researchers have suggested that instead of preventing PTSD, this practice can in fact worsen the symptoms (Mansdorf, 2008; McNally, Bryant, & Ehlers, 2003). They argue that in the case of witnessing a traumatic event (such as the events related to September 11, 2001), intervention it not necessarily advised for all who may show some symptoms, because arbitrarily revisiting the trauma may have retraumatizing effects. Despite this viewpoint, critical incident stress debriefing continues as a popular intervention, particularly with first responders such as firefighters and emergency personnel.

Conflict Resolution as a Pathway to Prevention

As previously mentioned, trauma and violence can happen anywhere, at anytime, to anyone. However, the likelihood of violence being committed between people who know each other is dramatically high, especially within a family setting. The anger and conflict that trigger the violence are often forgotten, and when weapons are involved, the results are often tragic. All too often, the original conflict goes unresolved. Social workers are trained to deal with the results of violent behavior—whether it is to comfort a direct victim, find foster placement for a displaced child, or provide advocacy for a battered spouse. However, their preparation for preventing violence through the development of conflict negotiation skills seems at times to be woefully inadequate. In most generalist texts, conflict—if mentioned at all—is regarded as a problem to get rid of rather than an opportunity to clarify differences. As a profession, social work would seem to be ideally suited to promoting prevention strategies such as providing educational opportunities to learn healthy ways to navigate through differences. Practitioners at all levels, however, must first learn how and when to use these tools themselves. As promoters of social justice and community empowerment, it is critical that social workers learn techniques for helping people respect and negotiate differences. Methods of conflict resolution should be included in the curricula of both bachelor's and master's of social work degree programs, and schools of social work have a responsibility to help students to identify and challenge old, unproductive patterns of dealing with conflict.

Many individuals approach conflict from a place of fear, mistrust, and anger, yet it has been demonstrated that conflict can have positive end results that change or transform the individuals involved. The profession would be well-served to borrow from the marriage and family therapy and family mediation fields to reframe the notion of conflict to one of opportunities to deepen an understanding of self and others. Evidence-based models of practice such as emotionally focused therapy (Johnson, 2002) use conflict as the potentially healing ingredient in helping clients confront their inevitable "power struggle." Evidence-based models may also provide an opportunity to heal early attachment wounds, and achieve a more conscious and deeper bond between the individuals involved. Conflict is seen as a rich opportunity to promote healthy growth through heightened awareness that accompanies differentiation of self and others.

Family mediation theorists such as Robert Bush and Joseph Folger (2005) focus on the transformative potential in conflict based on an assessment of the larger underlying values people bring to conflict. They suggest that there is a moral imperative in working through conflict that transforms human relationships, thereby facilitating healing relationships. Tenets of this approach emphasize the creation of a safe environment for dialogue, as well as acceptance and respect of all viewpoints. The combination of safety, empathy, nonjudgmental thinking, and confidentiality enables the parties to explore all options for resolution. Parties are empowered in this process, which helps them to continue their relationships in a new mode of respect and understanding. When applied on multiple levels, this approach is quite applicable to social work's focus on valuing diversity.

Conclusion: Lessons for Social Workers

Violence is a part of culture and is embedded in art, entertainment, lifestyles, and behaviors. Children cannot be completely shielded from its effects, even by the most vigilant of parents. Some children, however, grow up more directly impacted because of family violence, because of a community milieu associated with poverty, or because they are victims of random crime. Resiliency researchers have been grappling not just with the effects of violence on children but with how children develop resilient behaviors in the face of adversity and what allows some to do so when others facing the same challenges falter. This chapter has examined some of these issues, the impact of violence on different populations, and the acquisition of resilient functioning in the wake of violence. Traditionally oppressed groups have much to teach social workers about the nature of resiliency and healing from a long experience coping with violence, victimization, and its aftermath. In addition, social workers are urged to implement the values of their profession to address the implications of poverty and oppression by proactively fighting against the social injustices that underscore violence in today's society.

The clinical skills involved in working with survivors of violence, especially adolescents, present many challenges for new social workers. Survivors of childhood trauma develop coping skills that are self-protective in nature. These coping mechanisms can include being distrustful, being self-destructive, using testing and manipulative behaviors, and/or expressing rage. It behooves helping professionals to have faith in their clients' quest toward wholeness even as they struggle with all of the distracting behaviors and scar tissue that have resulted from victimization. It is an important issue for social workers to address because working with survivors, especially adolescents, can be daunting.

Maintaining an understanding of the developmental processes at work and the context and meaning of self-destructive behaviors enables social workers to adopt a strengths-based perspective when working with survivors of violence and traumatic experiences, even when their clients' potential seems hidden. Recovery is an ongoing process, and survivors of trauma have attained their learning through firsthand experience over time. There is no timetable, and there is no magical cure. Each person must be empowered to search within and draw out his or her own unique strengths and inner sense of resiliency when he or she is ready. When that time comes, someone, whether a professional social worker or a kind friend, must be able to tolerate the pain of listening to that person's suffering and losses and enter into the sacred healing ground of what Frank (1997) labeled "bearing witness," the deeply attentive listening that this work requires. A helping professional's role takes on significant meaning when helping people deal with wrenching losses, fear, pain, violation, rage, and disorientation associated with the impact of violence and other traumas. Social workers must be able to look into their hearts, identify their spiritual grounding, and work on their own losses and deepest fears to be able to walk with their clients on their clients' timetable.

> The patient needs to process the experience of healing. In its every aspect, it is a triumph in the face of trauma. The experience of healing is an act of reclaiming of the self, an act of trust, an act of acknowledging deep impact upon the self, though this time, benevolent impact, a moment of vulnerability and trust rewarded. (van der Kolk, 2001, p. 9)

Use the CD by Michael Wright to explore a theoretical environmental lens for assessing resilience in the context of violence. Explore grief work, critical incident, and conflict resolution interventions.

You will find a case study on your CD: *Watching "If Kameka Kept a Diary: A Dramatization"*

References

Aceves, M. J., & Cookston, J. T. (2007). Violent victimization, aggression, and parent-adolescent relations: Quality parenting as a buffer for violently victimized youth. *Journal of Youth and Adolescence, 36,* 635–647.

Alim, T., Feder, A., Graves, R. E., Wang, Y., Weaver, J., Westphal, M., Ö Charney, D. S. (2008). Trauma, resilience and recovery in a high-risk African-American population. *American Journal of Psychiatry, 165,* 1566–1575.

American Psychiatric Association. (1994). *Diagnostic and statistical manual of mental disorders* (4th ed.). Washington, DC: Author.

Armour, M. P., & Umbreit, M. S. (2006). Victim forgiveness in restorative justice dialogue. *Victims & Offenders, 1*(2), 123–140.

Askay, S. W., & Magyar-Russell, G. (2009). Post-traumatic growth and spirituality in burn recovery. *International Review of Psychiatry, 21,* 570–579.

Bachay, J., & Cingel, P. S. (1999). Restructuring resilience: Emerging voices. *Affilia, 14,* 162–175.

Benard, B. (1999). Applications of resilience: Possibilities and promise. In M. D. Glantz & J. L. Johnson (Eds.), *Longitudinal research in the social and behavioral sciences* (pp. 269–277). New York: Kluwer Academic/Plenum.

Bishop, S., McCullough, B., Thompson, C., & Nakiya, V. (2006). Resiliency in the aftermath of repetitious violence in the workplace. *Journal of Workplace Behavioral Health, 21,* 101–118.

Blume, A. W., Resor, M. R., Villanueva, M. R., & Braddy, L. D. (2009). Alcoholic use and co-morbid anxiety, traumatic stress, and hopelessness among Hispanics. *Addictive Behaviors, 34,* 709–713.

Bonanno, G. A. (2004). Loss, trauma, and human resilience: Have we underestimated the human capacity to thrive after extremely aversive events? *American Psychologist, 59,* 20–28.

Bride, B. (2007). Prevalence of secondary traumatic stress among social workers. *Social Work, 52*(1), 63–70.

Brookmeyer, K. A., Henrich, C. C., Cohen, G., & Shahar, G. (2010). Israeli adolescents exposed to community and terror violence: The protective role of social support. *Journal of Early Adolescence.* Advance online publication: doi:10.1177/0272431610366247

Bulhan, H. A. (1985). *Frantz Fanon and the psychology of oppression.* New York: Plenum Press.

Bush, R. A., & Folger, J. P. (2005). *The promise of mediation: The transformative approach to conflict* (2nd ed.). New York: Jossey-Bass.

Cairns-Descoteaux, B. (2005). The journey to resiliency: An integrative framework for treatment for victims and survivors of family violence. *Social Work & Christianity, 32,* 305–320.

Canda, E. (1988). Spirituality, religious diversity, and social work practice. *Social Casework, 69*(4), 238–247.

Carbonell, J., & Figley, C. (1996). When trauma hits home. *Journal of Marital and Family Therapy, 22*(1), 53–58.

Centers for Disease Control and Prevention. (2011). *Web-based injury statistics query and reporting system (WISQARS)*. Retrieved from http://www.cdc.gov/ncipc/wisqars/Index.html

Cohen, H., Greene, R. R., Lee, Y., Gonzalez, J., & Evans, M. (2006). Older adults who overcame oppression. *Families in Society, 87*(1), 1–8.

Cohen, H., Meek, K., & Lieberman, M. (2010). Memory and resilience. *Journal of Human Behavior in the Social Environment, 20*, 525–541.

Corey, A. L., Haase, F. E., Azzouz, A., & Monahan, P. O. (2008). Social support and symptom distress in adolescents/young adults with cancer. *Journal of Pediatric Oncology Nursing, 25*(5), 275–284.

Corley, C. (2010). A tale of three women: Holocaust experience and transformation through creative expression and engagement. *Journal of Aging, Humanities, and the Arts, 4*(4), 262–275.

Crockett, L. J., & Crouter, A. C. (1995). *Pathways through adolescence*. Mahwah, NJ: Erlbaum.

Cunningham, M. (2004). Teaching social workers about trauma: Reducing the risks of vicarious traumatization in the classroom. *Journal of Social Work Education, 40*, 305–317.

DiBlasio, F. A., & Benda, B. B. (1991). Practitioners, religion and the use of forgiveness in the clinical setting. *Journal of Psychology & Christianity, 10*(2), 166–172.

Dumont, M., & Provost, M. (1999). Resilience in adolescents: Protective role of social support, coping strategies, self-esteem, and social activities on experience of stress and depression. *Journal of Youth and Adolescence, 28*, 343–363.

Dyer, F. (2006). *The spiritual journey for youth: Spiritual themes can take on real-world focus for adolescents*. Retrieved from http://findarticles.com/p/articles/mi_m0QTQ/is_3_4/ai_n24988127

Edward, K. (2005). Resilience: A protector from depression. *Journal of the American Psychiatric Nurses Association, 11*(4), 241–243.

Edward, K., Welch, A., & Chater, K. (2009). The phenomenon of resilience as described by adults who have experienced mental illness. *Journal of Advanced Nursing, 65*, 587–595.

Egger, S. (1998). Optimism as a factor that promotes resilience in inner-city middle-school students exposed to high levels of community violence. *ProQuest Digital Dissertations*, AAT 9906743.

Ellis, A. A., Nixon, R. D., & Williamson, P. (2009). The effects of social support and negative appraisals on acute stress symptoms and depression in children and adolescents. *British Journal of Clinical Psychology, 48*, 347–361.

Erickson, S. J., & Feldstein, S. W. (2007). Adolescent humor and its relationship to coping, defense strategies, psychological distress, and well-being. *Child Psychiatry & Human Development, 37*, 255–271.

Espelage, D. L., & Swearer, S. M. (2003). Research on school bullying and victimization: What have we learned and where do we go from here? *School Psychology Review, 32*, 365–383.

Everly, G. S., Jr., & Mitchell, J. T. (1999). *Critical incident stress management (CISM): A new era and standard of care in crisis intervention* (2nd ed.). Ellicott City, MD: Chevron.

Feinstein, D. (1997). Personal mythology and psychotherapy: Myth-making in psychological and spiritual development. *American Journal of Orthopsychiatry, 67,* 508–521.

Figley, C. R. (2002). Compassion fatigue: Psychotherapists' chronic lack of self-care. *Journal of Clinical Psychology, 58,* 1433–1441.

Figley, C. R., & Bride, B. E. (1997). *Death and trauma: The traumatology of grieving.* Washington, DC: Taylor & Francis.

Folette, V., Palm, K. N., & Pearson, A. N. (2006). Mindfulness and trauma: Implications for treatment. *Journal of Rational-Emotive & Cognitive Therapy, 24*(1), 24–61.

Frank, A. E. (1997). *The wounded storyteller: Body, illness, and ethics.* Chicago: University of Chicago Press.

Frankl, V. (1959). *Man's search for meaning.* New York: Washington Square Press.

Gerberg, P. L., & Brown, R. B. (2005). Yoga: A breath of relief for Hurricane Katrina refugees. *Current Psychiatry, 4*(10), 55–67.

Goldston, D. B., Molock, S. D., Whitbeck, L. B., Murakami, J. L., Zayas, L. H., & Hall, G. C. (2008). Cultural considerations in adolescent suicide prevention and psychosocial treatment. *American Psychologist, 63,* 14–31.

Goodman, R. D., & West-Olatunji, C. A. (2008). Transgenerational trauma and resilience: Improving mental health counseling for survivors of Katrina. *Journal of Mental Health Counseling, 30*(2), 121–136.

Heiman, T. (2002). Parents of children with disabilities: Resilience, coping and future expectations. *Journal of Developmental and Physical Disabilities, 14,* 159–171.

Hemingway, E. (1929). *A farewell to arms.* New York: Scribner.

Hernandez, P., Gangsei, D., & Engstrom, D. (2007). Vicarious resilience: A new concept in work with those who survive trauma. *Family Process, 46,* 229–241.

Hesse, A. R. (2002). Secondary trauma: How working with trauma survivors affects therapists. *Journal of Clinical Social Work, 30,* 293–309.

Hodges, M., Jagdev, D., Chandra, N., & Cunniff, A. (2008). Risk and resilience for psychological distress amongst unaccompanied asylum seeking adolescents. *Journal of Child Psychology & Psychiatry, 49,* 723–732.

Howard, S., Dryden, J., & Johnson, B. (1999). Childhood resilience: Review and critique of literature. *Oxford Review of Education, 25,* 307–323.

Humphreys, J. (2003). Resilience in sheltered battered women. *Issues in Mental Health Nursing, 24*(2), 137–153.

Johnson, S. M. (2002). *Emotionally focused couple therapy with trauma survivors: Strengthening attachment bonds.* New York: Guilford Press.

Juvonen, J., Graham, S., & Schuster, M. A. (2003). Bullying among young adolescents: The strong, the weak, and the troubled. *Pediatrics, 112,* 1231–1237.

Killian, K. D. (2008). Helping till it hurts? A multimethod study of compassion fatigue, burnout, and self-care in clinicians working with trauma survivors. *Traumatology, 14*(2), 32–44.

Kim-Ju, G., Mark, G. Y., Cohen, R., Garcia-Santiago, O., & Nguyen, P. (2008). Community mobilization and its application to youth violence. *American Journal of Preventative Medicine, 34*(3), S5–S12.

Kimbrough, E., Magyari, T., Langenberg, P., Cheaney, M., & Berman, B. (2010). Mindfulness intervention for child abuse survivors. *Journal of Clinical Psychology, 66,* 17–33.

Knight, J., Sherritt, L., Sion, K. H., Holder, D. W., Kulig, J., Shrier, L. A., Ö Chang, G. (2007). Alcohol use and religiousness/spirituality among adolescents. *Southern Medical Journal, 100,* 349–355.

Kulkin, H. S. (2006). Factors enhancing adaptive coping and mental health in lesbian youth: A review of the literature. *Journal of Homosexuality, 50*(4), 97–111.

Kushner, H. (1983). *When bad things happen to good people.* New York: HarperCollins.

Lee, M. Y., & Zaharlick, A. M. (2009). Treatment of trauma survivors: Effects of meditation practice on clients' mental health outcomes. *New Research in Mental Health, 18,* 155–161.

Lerias, D., & Byrne, M. K. (2003). Vicarious traumatization: Symptoms and predictors. *Stress and Health, 19*(3), 129–138.

Levine, S. Z., Laufer, A., Stein, E., Hamama-Raz, Y., & Solomon, Z. (2009). Examining the relationship between resilience and posttraumatic growth. *Journal of Traumatic Stress, 22*(4), 282–286.

Liat, A. (2005). Challenges associated with the study of resilience to trauma in Holocaust survivors. *Journal of Loss & Trauma, 10,* 347–358.

Mansdorf, I. (2008). Psychological interventions following terrorist attacks. *British Medical Review, 88,* 7–22.

Masten, A. S. (2001). Ordinary magic: Resiliency processes in development. *American Psychologist, 56,* 227–238.

McNally, R. J., Bryant, R. A., & Ehlers, A. (2003). Does early psychological intervention promote recovery from posttraumatic stress? *Psychological Science in the Public Interest, 4*(2), 45–79.

Meadors, P., & Lamson, A. (2008). Compassion fatigue and secondary traumatization: Providing self care on intensive care units for children. *Journal of Pediatric Health Care, 22*(1), 22–34.

Michado, C. L., de Azevedo, R. C., Facuri, C. O., Vieira, M. J., & Fernandes, A. M. (2011). Posttraumatic stress disorder, depression, and hopelessness in women who are victims of sexual violence. *International Journal of Gynaecology and Obstetrics.* Advance online publication. PMID:21255779

Mitchell, J. T. (1983). When disaster strikes: The critical incident stress de-briefing process. *Journal of Emergency Services, 13,* 47–52.

Molino, A. C. (2007). *Characteristics of help-seeking street youth and non-street youth.* Retrieved from http://aspe.hhs.gov/hsp/homelessness/symposium07/molino/index.htm

Munroe, I. (2008). The lived experience of gay men caring for others with HIV/AIDS: Resilient coping skills. *International Journal of Nursing, 14*(2), 122–128.

Nagy, M. (1948). The child's theories concerning death. *Journal of Genetic Psychology, 73,* 3–27.

Naparstek, B. (2005). *Invisible heroes: Survivors of trauma and how they heal.* New York: Random House.

National Coalition for the Homeless. (2007). *NCH Fact Sheet #11: Homeless youth.* Retrieved from http://www.nationalhomeless.org/youth.html

Peres, J. F. P., Moreira-Almeida, A., Nasello, A. G., & Koenig, H. G. (2007). Spirituality and resilience in trauma victims. *Journal of Religion & Health, 46,* 343–350.

Pietrzak, R. H., Johnson, D. C., Goldstein, M. B., Malley, J. C., & Southwick, S. M. (2009). Psychological resilience and post-deployment social support protect against traumatic stress and depressive symptoms in soldiers returning from Operations Enduring Freedom and Iraqi Freedom. *Depression & Anxiety, 26,* 745–751.

Poulson, B. (2003). A third voice: A review of empirical research on the psychological outcomes of restorative justice. *Utah Law Review,* 167–203.

Prince, L. M. (2008). Resilience in African American women formerly involved in street prostitution. *ABNF Journal, 19*(1), 31–36.

Rand, M., & Truman, J. (2009). *Criminal victimization, 2009.* Retrieved from http://bjs.ojp.usdoj.gov/index.cfm?ty=pbdetail&iid=2217

Raskauskas, J., & Stoltz, A. D. (2007). Involvement in traditional and electronic bullying among adolescents. *Developmental Psychology, 43,* 564–575.

Richters, J. E., & Martinez, P. (1993). The NIM community violence project: I. Children as victims of and witnesses to violence. *Psychiatry, 56,* 7–21.

Rigby, K. (2007). *Bullying in schools and what to do about it.* Camerwell, Australia: Acer Press.

Rutter, M. (1985). Resilience in the face of adversity: Protective factors and resistance to psychiatric disorder. *British Journal of Psychiatry, 147,* 598–611.

Salmi, J. (1993). *Violence and democratic society.* London: Zed Books.

Scher, C., & Resick, P. (2005). Hopelessness as a risk factor for post-traumatic stress disorder symptoms among interpersonal violence survivors. *Cognitive Behavior Therapy, 34,* 99–107.

Seidler, G. H. (2006). Comparing the efficacy of EMDR and trauma-focused cognitive behavioral therapy in the treatment of PTSD: A meta-analytic study. *Psychological Medicine, 36,* 1515–1522.

Shapiro, F. (2004). EMDR: The breakthrough therapy for overcoming anxiety, stress, and trauma. New York: Basic Books.

Shuler, P., Gelberg, L., & Brown, M. (1994). The effects of spiritual/religious practices on psychological well-being among inner city homeless women. *Nurse Practitioner Forum, 5,* 106–113.

Smith, E. (1995). Addressing the psychospiritual distress of death as reality: A transpersonal approach. *Social Work, 40,* 402–413.

Speece, M., & Brent, A. (1987). Irreversibility, nonfunctionality and universality: Children's understanding of three components of a death concept. In J. Schowalter, P. Buschman, P. Patterson, A. Kutscher, M. Tallmer, R. Stevenson, & J. Cole (Eds.), *Children and death* (pp. 19–29). New York: Praeger.

Sprang, V., McNeil, J. S., & Wright, R., Jr. (1989). Psychological changes after the murder of a significant other. *Social Casework, 70,* 159–164.

Thomas, R. B., & Wilson, J. P. (2004). Issues and controversies in understanding and diagnosis of compassion fatigue, vicarious traumatization, and secondary traumatic stress disorder. *International Journal of Emergency Mental Health, 61*(2), 81–92.

Umbreit, M. (2001). *The handbook of victim-offender mediation (VOM).* San Francisco: Jossey-Bass.

U.S. Conference of Mayors. (2005). A status report on hunger and homelessness in America's cities. Washington, DC: Author.

van der Kolk, B. (2001). Beyond the talking cure: Somatic experience, subcortical imprints and the treatment of trauma. In F. Shapiro (Ed.). *EMDR: Toward a paradigm shift* (pp. 47–53). Washington, DC: American Psychological Association Press.

van der Kolk, B. (2006). Clinical implications of neuroscience research in PTSD. *Annals of the New York Academy of Sciences, 1071,* 277–293.

van der Kolk, B. (2007). *Trauma center at justice resource institute.* Retrieved from http://www.traumacenter.org/research/research_overview.php

van der Kolk, B. (2010). *Working with children to heal interpersonal trauma: The power of play.* New York: Guilford Press.

Van Soest, D., & Bryant, S. (1995). Violence re-conceptualized for social work: The urban dilemma. *Social Work, 40,* 549–557.

Walsh, F. (2006). *Strengthening family resilience.* New York: Guilford Press.

Walsh, F. (2007). Traumatic loss and major disasters: Strengthening family and community resilience. *Family Process, 46,* 207–227.

Werner, E. E., & Smith, R. S. (1992). *Overcoming the odds.* Ithaca, NY: Cornell University.

Williams, N. R., Davey, M., & Klock, K. (2003). Rising from the ashes: Stories of recovery & resiliency in burn survivors. *Social Work in Health Care, 36*(4), 53–77.

Williams, N. R., & Lindsey, E. W. (2005). Spirituality and religion in the lives of runaway and homeless youth: Coping with adversity. *Journal of Religion & Spirituality in Social Work, 23*(4), 19–38.

Williams, N. R., & Lindsey, E. W. (2010). Finding their way home: Utilizing spiritual practices to bolster resiliency in youth at risk. *Currents, 9*(1), 1–16.

Williams, N. R., Lindsey, E. W., Kurtz, P. D., & Jarvis, S. (2001). From trauma to resilience: Lessons from formerly runaway and homeless youth. *Journal of Youth Studies, 4,* 233–253.

Williams, T., Connolly, J., Pepler, D., & Craig, W. (2005). Peer victimization, social support and psychosocial adjustment of sexual minority youth. *Journal of Youth & Adolescence, 34,* 471–482.

Wilson, M. (2005). *From adolescent heart and soul: Achieving spiritual competence in youth serving agencies.* Unpublished manuscript, New England Network for Youth and Family Services, Charlotte, Vermont.

World Health Organization. (2002). *Youth violence facts.* Retrieved from http://www.who.int/violence_injury_prevention/violence/world_report/factsheets/en/youthviolencefacts.pdf

Yehuda, R. (2002). New post-traumatic stress disorder. *New England Journal of Medicine, 346,* 108–114.

Young, M. D. (2007). Finding meaning in the aftermath of trauma: Resilience and posttraumatic growth in female survivors of intimate partner violence. *Dissertation Abstracts International: Section B. Sciences and Engineering, 68*(3), 1951.

Zahradnik, M., Stewart, S. H., O'Connor, R. M., Stevens, D., Ungar, M., & Wekerle, C. (2010). Resilience moderates the relationship between exposure to violence and posttraumatic reexperiencing in Mi'kmaq youth. *International Journal of Mental Health and Addiction, 8,* 408–420.

Zautra, A. (2009). Resilience: One part recovery, two parts sustainability. *Journal of Personality, 77,* 1935–1943.

Zehr, H. (2002). *The little book of restorative justice.* Retrieved from http://www.ncjrs.gov/App/Publications/abstract.aspx?ID=198100

8

Resilience and Violence at the Macro Level

IRENE QUEIRO-TAJALLI and CRAIG CAMPBELL

On finishing this chapter, students will be able to further:

Intervene with individuals, families, groups, organizations, and communities (Educational Policy 2.1.10c) by

- Initiating actions to achieve organizational goals (practice behavior).

Advance human rights and social and economic justice (Educational Policy 2.1.5) by

- Understanding the forms and mechanisms of oppression and discrimination (practice behavior).

It was the break of dawn; the silhouettes of the city buildings were just beginning to emerge from under heavy, dark clouds of fog. Icy patches in the streets bore witness to a cold, wet night. An unmarked car stopped in front of an apartment building. Two men stepped out, while another stayed at the steering wheel with the engine running. The two men moved swiftly up the stairs to the third floor. The silence was broken by two hard knocks on the door. Someone opened the door, and the men pushed their way into the apartment. Sounds of a struggle were heard from inside the apartment. Then silence; then a female voice pleaded, "Leave him alone," "He is my son," and "He is just a teen!" The door opened, with the two men carrying a tall man wearing pajamas, a heavy coat, slippers, and a hooded ski mask on his head. They dragged the man down the stairs, entered the car, and disappeared into thin air.

This is just an example of how abductions by the Military Junta occurred in Argentina during 1976–1983, when the country went through one of the darkest periods in its history. In fact, the 20th century was plagued with worldwide attacks to ethnic, political, and religious groups as well as the general public. There is evidence of such events as Nazi annihilation during World War II, oppressive government regimes in Latin America and Eastern Europe, and terrorist acts throughout Western Europe and the Middle East. The United States also endured its share of assaults. For example, the crashing of airliners into the World Trade Center and the Pentagon on September 11, 2001, and the 1995 bombing of the Alfred P. Murrah Federal Building in Oklahoma City carry memories, images, and repercussions for loved ones who mourn the loss of a spouse, parent, or child long after attacks like these have occurred. These acts of terror drove some individuals inward, leery of returning to public buildings, unable to cope with crowded areas and strangers, some still dealing with physical injuries sustained in the blasts. Most still do not understand how and why such calamitous events could have happened.

As one observes human rights violations at the national and international levels, the question is always how and why such horrible events happen. There may be many answers, yet the philosophical question of why society attacks its most precious members—its fellow humans—has not been satisfactorily answered. Perhaps it is because no answer exists. Resistance to and survival from such atrocities demonstrates the potential power within groups, communities, and societies to rise up against such aggression and emerge from the process not only transformed, but also ready for social change.

This chapter discusses resilience at the societal or macro level and how communities overcome large-scale calamities such as attacks from repressive governments, terrorist acts, or natural disasters. It presents a schema that depicts the steps that communities may go through as they experience catastrophic events and explores some of the approaches used to reconstitute these communities. Although there remains a void in the social work literature as it relates to macro-level resilience, the works cited in this chapter provide some direction, particularly in terms of the community capacity enhancement and strengths-based literature (Breton, 2001; Delgado, 2000; Poole, 1997; Saleebey, 1996, 2002). By assessing traumatic events at the community level—such as disappearances in Argentina, the bombing in Oklahoma City, the Columbine High School shootings, numerous incidents of church burnings, and the terrorist attacks of September 11, 2001—we hope to move the discussion of resilience from the micro to the macro level. Some of the questions that guide the discussion include the following:

- How do communities navigate threats or overcome adversity?
- What contributes to people's ability to regenerate or bounce back?
- What is successful coping at the macro level?

Resilience: A Schema at the Societal Level

A useful way of dissecting the intricacies of resilience at the macro level is by means of a schema, or a diagram that models a series of steps illustrating the resilience process. The schema presented in this chapter is based on the literature, media sources, personal interviews, and field observations. It delineates six steps that a community may take to overcome a catastrophic event and how the path to resilience is manifested in each (see Table 8.1 and Figure 8.1). Step 1 occurs at the time of the assault on humanity, when people are in a stage of shock and crisis. In step 2, there are incipient signs of resistance when citizens must establish mutual trust, find some meaning in the adverse event, and begin to rebuild their communities. During step 3, citizens begin to organize and identify collective strategies for mutual support. In step 4, people formally organize, seek out support from other constituencies, and set up communication networks. During step 5, people seek to keep the memory of the adverse event alive. If these memories build sufficient community capacity, step 6 may bring about organizational change and a transformation of community life.

Examples and select theoretical concepts related to each of these steps are provided. Processes and protective factors that nurture resilience are also identified; such a discussion provides an understanding of the differences among macro-level catastrophic events. For example, in the isolated terrorist attack on

TABLE 8.1 Steps in Reestablishing a Resilient Community

1. Recognizing that there has been an assault on humanity
2. Identifying signs of resistance and defiance
3. Promoting the organization of citizens
4. Helping citizens develop a sense of community identity
5. Supporting a continuous struggle by the citizenry
6. Anticipating and actualizing changes in societal structures

FIGURE 8.1 Resilience Schema

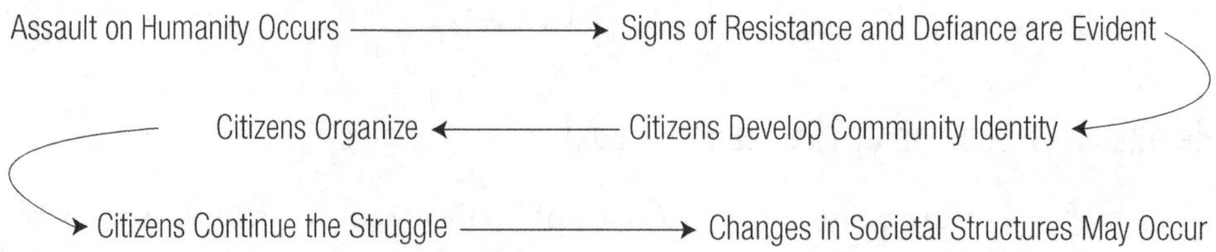

the Murrah Federal Building in Oklahoma City, after people experienced fear, anger, and mourning, they then felt the need to stay connected; thus, they created the Murrah Building Survivors Association. On the whole, the survivors of this terrorist event concentrated on the positive aspects of the event, and as a result, many have developed a new appreciation for the meaning of life. However, in government-sponsored terrorist acts, like the ones committed by the Military Junta in Argentina, there may be different reactions. In this case, personal and community resistance have emerged. There have been acts of defiance to denounce and try to stop the ongoing atrocities. One example is Madres de Plaza de Mayo (Mothers of Plaza de Mayo), a group of anti–Military Junta activist mothers of "detained or disappeared" daughters and sons. The Mothers have been struggling for the return of their children since 1977, when they came out into the open and started meeting in the Plaza de Mayo, a central location in Buenos Aires. Since then, they have walked or marched every Thursday for 30 minutes around the Pyramid of the Plaza de Mayo. They wear white head scarves embroidered with the names of their loved ones that were abducted by the military regime.

In addition, community organizing may take on a different meaning depending on the nature of the traumatic event. That is, in isolated attacks, community members may organize to support one another, work to keep the memory in the public eye, or build memorials to the victims. In contrast, with government-sponsored terrorism, the community may often organize secretly with the purpose of creating an organized resistance and ultimately bringing about structural change. The following discussion explores these various paths to establishing a resilient community.

Step 1: Assault on Humanity Occurs

In the aftermath of catastrophic events, community members are consumed with a broad range of feelings—dismay, disbelief, fear, and anger. Because the event is so overwhelming, community members may be in such a deep state of shock that they deny the event. Individuals as well as the community are painfully reminded of their vulnerability and may be seized by a feeling of powerlessness. Depending on the catastrophic event, the situation may be kept secret from the outside world, hidden within families and among friends. This was the case with many of the Argentinean abductions. For example, consider Maria Gutman, who had been an active member of Madres de Plaza de Mayo since 1977 because of the abduction of her 19-year-old son in 1976 by the military regime. She talked about her sense of dismay that such an act could be committed against another human being (M. Gutman, personal communication, Buenos Aires, July 10, 2000). In the beginning, she did not realize what was happening and knocked on all government doors to get answers about the whereabouts of her son. She met other mothers in the various government and military offices who were involved in the same search. Officials typically gave the Mothers the same answers: "Don't worry, your son probably ran away with his girlfriend" or "We do not know where he is." Listening to these answers, Ms. Gutman and other mothers were besieged with the fear that they might not see their loved ones again. They also feared that something might happen to their families if their inquiries continued. Clearly, feelings of fear (loss of a loved one) were mixed with feelings of anger (no satisfactory response from public officials).

This phenomenon of simultaneously experiencing fear and anger after catastrophic situations can be explained by several theoretical concepts taken from the literature on crisis theory (Frederick, 1985; Watson, David, & Suls, 1999). An assumption about a crisis is that the cognitive understanding of the event is closely related to the individual's perception of the event (Rapoport, 1965). At the macro level, it is important to analyze what the event means to the community. These personal and community meanings contribute to the natural process of disorganization that follows a crisis. According to crisis theory, because humans cannot tolerate long periods of disorganization, the instability following a crisis is time limited (Slaikeu, 1990). However, the effects of the crisis event may last for many years, and adverse consequences may linger long after the traumatic event (Bernstein Carlson & Rosser-Hogan, 1994; Foner, 2005).

For example, examining the aftermath of the events at Columbine High School, Gordon and Doka (2000) advanced the concept of *resonating trauma,* which "occurs when an initial traumatic event creates such fear and anxiety that rumors of future similar events affect many communities, even communities far away and with far different conditions" (p. 292). Likewise, given the secret nature of abductions in Argentina during the military regime, rumors of such acts were a painful reminder to parents that their children were in danger should they be involved in political activities against the government. In fact, these rumors served as mechanisms of social control and covert oppression.

Another dimension of crisis is that a traumatic event produces a state of reduced defensiveness when an individual's traditional coping patterns are less effective (Halpern, 1973). In cases of state-sponsored terrorism, those individuals affected by the event may try to use previously established coping strategies, such as seeking legal advice or reporting the event to the police. Because the legal and political systems no longer operate as expected and do not fulfill their assigned functions, these acts often lead to more confusion and feelings of powerlessness.

Many people may feel a sense of disbelief. In the case of the 1970s abductions in Argentina, the parents received no answers from government officials as to the whereabouts of their children. Yet between 340 and 365 detention centers were in place throughout the country where those who were abducted were jailed, tortured, raped, and murdered, so, clearly, there was a complicity of silence among government officials (Abuelas de Plaza de Mayo, n.d.; Guzman Bouvard, 1994).

Under such circumstances, how does a community regain its just functions, let alone become resilient? According to social theorists such as Parsons (1971), a community consists of individual actors who interact with one another and are guided by "a system of culturally structured and shared symbols" (p. 5). When communities or societal systems no longer share established symbols, such as freedom, and do not function as expected, community members may have to find other ways of coping.

From an ecological perspective, stress may occur when environmental processes remain unresponsive. However, people's determination to transform their environment can bring about a change in how their society functions (Germain & Gitterman, 1996). For individuals and communities to survive catastrophic events and regain a state of trust, members of society have to work together to foster protective factors, or processes that moderate stress and risk and enhance competence (Masten, Best, & Garmezy, 1991). Protective factors that can provide the necessary supports may be found among family, neighbors, and friends. The local community may also have sociocultural, political, and economic systems that historically have been critical to the reestablishment of necessary protective factors.

What protective factors help a community pull together after devastating events? As in the case of the Oklahoma City bombing, how do people move from "This is America; things like this just don't happen here" to "I like sunny days, I like rainy days, I like cool breezes at night" or "I don't worry about what others want me to do anymore; I take stock of what I have"? One of the protective factors against isolated terrorist acts seems to be the promptness with which the community can pull together and show support for its members. Another factor may be the presence of community members, professionals, and organizations that attend to the survivors' immediate physical and emotional needs. In the attacks on the Pentagon and the World Trade Center, many community resources were quickly mobilized to meet basic needs.

In cases of state-sponsored attacks, such as abductions, protective factors may also rest within the person, his or her spiritual beliefs, and the type of support he or she receives from close family members and friends. In those situations, before the individual goes public with information about the terrorism, there is a sense of secrecy to avoid attracting the attention of government agents. However, anger against the perpetrators and the desire to retaliate give the individual the strength to start thinking in a more public way about his or her tragedy and to move to the resistance and defiance step.

Step 2: Signs of Resistance and Defiance Are Evident

Although resistance or defiance is marked by mixed feelings of hurt and mistrust, there is an ongoing effort to make sense of the senseless. As those affected by the event talk to one another, there is a realization that a collective effort is needed to face those responsible for the attack. People affected by an event of this nature may not know who to trust. As the community works through these feelings, a sense of recovery starts to emerge, and community members search for ways to fight back. According to Guzman Bouvard (1994),

> At the end of their first year, the [Argentinean] Mothers experienced a profound inner transformation in response to the tragedy of their loss, were redefining their sense of self, analyzing their own situation as part of a broader pattern of repression, and discovering their own inviolable dignity and worth. (p. 79)

It is in resistance and defiance that people start meeting with those in like circumstances and expressing their defiance toward their oppressive system. For example, Margarita Peralta de Gropper reflected on the abduction of her 19-year-old son in 1977. She reported that, after the initial shock, she started meeting with other mothers in the Plaza de Mayo and had no fear. Although she had a husband and two daughters, her pain was so great that she felt she "had nothing to lose" (M. P. de Gropper, personal communication, Buenos Aires, July 14, 2000).

Koetze (1986–1987) indicated that communities start organizing when they perceive that they have reached a certain level of safety. Although this may hold true in certain circumstances, it was not the case with the Mothers, who took a defiant position against the military government without much protection. Numerous examples of people taking action despite dangerous circumstances can be found in cases of church burnings. Communities touched by these events continued their resistance despite of the possibility of further retaliation from the perpetrators. Instead of terrorizing local African American communities, the church burnings created strong bonds that led to further solidification of community identity and unity.

Practitioners can turn to two theoretical orientations to better understand the resistance and defiance step: the social constructionist approach and the strengths perspective. Although a wide range of orientations exist within the social constructionist line of thinking (Berger & Luckmann, 1967; Gilligan, 1982; Wittgenstein, 1963), one of the common denominators is that reality is socially or psychologically constructed (Green, Jensen, & Harper Jones, 1996; Queiro-Tajalli, 1999). Practice based on this approach relies on language, cultural assumptions, and historical events to understand clients' worldviews. Personal and communal narratives are essential to the construction and definition of reality as experienced by the community, rather than as defined by those in power. In interviews, the Mothers repeatedly mentioned that to relive the events of the abductions among themselves and to feel that they understood one another had positive effects. This mutual support came at a critical time when their denunciations of the abductions were discounted and members of the government referred to them as "those crazy women," hoping to destroy their credibility.

Equally effective in understanding the Mothers' movement is the strengths perspective, which builds on people's assets, talents, vision, values, hopes, and competencies (Saleebey, 1996, 2002). Working with clients' strengths at the macro level involves the community as an "oasis of resources" (Kisthardt & Rapp, 1992, p. 113). From this perspective, it is clear that community members and practitioners can pull together to begin the long and often draining process of rebuilding. Rediscovering and mobilizing community resources is imperative at a time when the community is trying to establish meaning and is struggling with issues of doubt and lack of trust. Practitioners well versed in the strengths perspective see an opportunity to engage the community in tangible helping efforts and build on community capacity to positively respond to a tragedy.

The body of literature on community capacity can be applied here (Bowen, Martin, Mancini, & Nelson, 2000; Delgado, 2000). In his writing on community capacity building and resilience, Saleebey (2002) described the importance of the connectedness of individuals and communities:

> The research on resilience challenges us to build this connectedness, this sense of belonging by helping to transform families, schools, and communities to become "psychological homes" where people can find caring and support, respect, and opportunities for meaningful involvement. Everyone has the potential for self-righting, the self-correction of life course, but it doesn't happen in a vacuum; it operates when environments challenge and support, provide protection and generative factors. (p. 203)

In the resistance and defiance step, the community begins to mobilize its resources and build on its natural desire for resilience. Resilience is fostered by the continuing interplay between capacities and competencies gained in the process of facing challenges and mobilizing protective factors (Luthar, 2003; Rutter, 1985; Saleebey, 1996; Wolin & Wolin, 1993). One of the Mothers' protective factors was the support and information they gave one another and their development of mechanisms to share possible leads as to the whereabouts of their children (M. P. de Gropper, personal communication, Buenos Aires, July 14, 2000).

Step 3: Citizens Develop Community Identity

In this step, a community transforms itself in response to a given tragedy. There is movement away from a sense of individuality—"my tragedy"—to a sense of the collective—"our tragedy." To develop identity, the community strengthens relationships and builds trust and group cohesion. As the community begins to develop an identity, people realize that they not only share similar traumatic events, but also want to denounce the offenses. The community members need to trust one another, yet they are conscious that "outsiders" who are undercover or in disguise may be around; these outsiders can compromise the outcome of the community's organizing efforts and place the organizers' lives in danger. This was the case in the early days of the organization of Madres de Plaza de Mayo, when people from the military government infiltrated the community and reported the community's activities to the authorities, with tragic consequences for some community members.

A strong sense of mutual support and the building of strong empathic relationships are some of the protective factors that allow community members to face adversity with a unified front. Although the community begins to create a public presence, the full realization or crystallization of this process does not happen until the next step. Essential to this step is the realization by community members that they should not dwell on their personal pain, because doing so would drain their energies to fight the aggressor.

At this point in the schema, it is also essential for practitioners to understand various conceptualizations of community and community functions. The term *community* is one of the most difficult to define, and there is little agreement about it as a universal concept. Community members share common ends, a common life, or a common consciousness. Furthermore, communities can be classified as geographical units or functional communities. The school shootings at Columbine High School occurred in a geographical community, whereas Madres de Plaza de Mayo organized to form a functional community. Geographical or urban landmarks demarcate a geographical community, whereas common interests or bonds define a functional community, although its members may live in different locales. In a similar vein, communities may be identified as place and nonplace (Anderson, Carter, & Lowe, 1999). Place communities are associated with a common residence, whereas nonplace communities are linked to how people identify themselves.

Some important definitions that relate to group cohesiveness include the idea that a community

- is a "structure of relationships through which a localized population provides its daily requirements" (Hawley, 1950, p. 180);
- "springs from powerful human needs [and] breeds a clear sense of cultural purpose, membership, status, and continuity" (Nisbet, 1971, p. 73);
- is "a place where a group of people live and conduct various activities of daily living: earn a living, buy goods and services they are unable to produce for themselves, school their children, transact their civic and governmental affairs, etc." (Cox, 1987, p. 233);
- "includes groups of people who share some common interest or function, such as welfare, agriculture, education, or religion" (Ross, 1967, pp. 41–42); and
- "is an entity with its own character, ability, and power to accomplish results" (Bowen et al., 2000, p. 1).

Communities also need to be understood by the functions they perform. According to Warren (1977), there are five functions of communities: (1) production, distribution, and consumption; (2) social control; (3) mutual support; (4) socialization; and (5) social participation. In the case of functional communities, mutual support and social participation are key to keeping members engaged. In addition, communities are brought together by people's common quest for meaning (Cnaan & Rothman, 2001; Nisbet, 1971; Rothman, 1995; Warren, 1963). As emphasized in this chapter, the community is an important social unit that is capable of dealing with economic restraints, social inequalities, and political power abuses. Whether geographical or functional, the community is the cornerstone of macro-level resilience. It is the interactions of the community that produce the protective factors that help people survive community crises.

As the community understands the power in unity and joint participation and develops a commitment to search for justice, community identity begins to crystallize. According to Guzman Bouvard (1994),

> After two years of work [the Mothers] realized that they had acquired a stature and an identity. They were now faced with the questions of whether to continue being a gathering of tireless Mothers or to give more definition to their struggle. (p. 93)

Fortunately, the Mothers decided to formalize their search for human rights.

Step 4: Citizens Organize

The literature on organizing provides a solid foundation for understanding this step of the process (Cnaan & Rothman, 2001; Delgado, 2000; Dobbie, 2009; Gutierrez, 2001; Pyles, 2009; Weil & Gamble, 1995). In this organizing step, community members refuse to be victimized by their aggressor and are more systematic in their defense tactics. In interviews, some of the Mothers recalled beginning their organizing efforts as a natural rather than a planned process. It was humbling to listen to them say, "We did not plan our activities; we just did it" and "It was a reaction to the irrational silence and an unwillingness to help on the part of the police and the military."

Another important characteristic of the organizing step is the development of principles that help the community endure adversities such as harassment and threats. In the case of the Mothers, the members developed principles based on people's rights to human dignity. This effort helped them to create a vision to guide their organizational strategies and their goals for a better society. In implementing the vision, community members believed that they spoke for those who no longer could represent themselves or no longer had a voice. Their denouncements were intended to reveal unpleasant truths that, quite often, the rest of society did not want to hear. In the case of Madres de Plaza de Mayo, the abductions were a painful reality that many citizens refused to believe. To counteract such avoidance, the Mothers pledged that they would not rest until "the disappeared" were returned alive.

Community members may request public support for their demands to engage a larger constituency to achieve far-reaching changes in societal structures. Support from other organizations sympathetic to the organizing effort is important in the organizing process (Zullo & Pratt, 2009). Early in the struggle, the Mothers understood the importance of cultivating the participation of other groups, including student groups, human rights organizations, labor organizations, exiles, and international organizations, to assist them in the return of the disappeared. This type of "outside" support was invaluable to the Mothers because it provided them with strength, hope, an enhanced sense of well-being and protection, and the Mothers soon recognized that they would not have survived without the help of these groups.

In this step, the community develops structures to divide the tasks among its members, and it is more systematic in the implementation of community goals. In addition, the community develops covert and overt means of communication to protect its members and to denounce atrocities. The community members also become more knowledgeable about the target system they want to change. In the case of the Mothers, community members studied the laws and regulations that would support their causes, and by doing so they discovered flaws in the target system that enabled them to attack its vulnerable points.

This step may take a different shape depending on the type of crisis event experienced by the community. In 1995, the students in Chisholm Elementary School, seven miles away from the Murrah Federal Building, not only felt the impact of the bomb, but also lost 20 community members in the incident. This community of children and teachers grieved and coped with the event through a number of tangible and spiritual activities. From the beginning, they organized themselves to write letters of support to the rescue workers. They collected food and supplies for the victims and workers. Later on, they had a tree-planting ceremony. They organized a reunion in honor of Chisholm parents who were part of the rescue teams. At the end of the year, they tied ribbons around the trees they had planted (Aspy & Aspy, 1996).

Although these activities may sound simple compared with other projects, they reflect many of the principles of organizing. According to Ross (1967), one of the principles of organizing is the presence of a pervasive and widely shared sense of discontent that must be channeled into organization, planning, and action. There should be an attempt to involve formal and informal leaders. The community must formulate a common purpose and goals. In addition, the community should include activities with emotional content to reach people at the feeling level. Some more specific principles include the need to develop active and effective lines of communication; to support and strengthen member groups; and to foster strength, stability, and prestige. Implicit in these principles is that community members remain dedicated and actively involved in the resolution of their circumstances.

These principles are clearly reflected in the work of the Mothers and others who have made considerable sacrifices to achieve a common purpose. The Mothers understood the importance of dramatizing their cause to gain support. They accomplished this by establishing a ritual of marching for 30 minutes hand in hand around Plaza de Mayo once a week. They have maintained their solidarity in carrying out this activity for more than 30 years. Also, in 1981 the Mothers started the Marches of Resistance, a 24-hour march in the Plaza de Mayo. This annual convocation lasted until 2003 and represented a unique way of occupying a public space to make their demands known to those in power. Each march had specific demands based on the sociopolitical context of that year. The theme of the first march was the Mothers' original demand: the return of the disappeared (Vazquez et al., 2004).

Step 5: Citizens Continue the Struggle

In this step of the process, the community is resilient enough to continue its struggle regardless of verbal attacks or harassment. The community continues working on the initial goals of the organizing efforts and on revised or new goals. A distinctive characteristic is the strong will to keep the memory of the initial events alive. The community solidifies many of its alliances with other groups and asserts revised action principles.

Given that the initial catastrophic event(s) may seem a distant reality, this step may be marked by tension among community members reflecting the long and draining process of trying to bring about social change. In 1986, after facing the most dangerous times in its advocacy endeavors, Madres de Plaza de Mayo divided into two groups: Asociacion Madres de Plaza de Mayo and Madres de Plaza de Mayo–Linea Fundadora. The split resulted from a disagreement about the goals and tactics to be used under a democratic government. However, both groups still keep marching every Thursday in the Plaza de Mayo and proclaim that they will not forget the atrocities of the military regime. Both groups continue their struggle to achieve truth and justice and the full implementation of human rights.

Interviews with Mothers and an examination of their printed material revealed that one of their major objectives is to preserve the collective memory of the abductions so that they will not be repeated. They have struggled to promote their cause and to advance other principles, such as

- denouncing the forced disappearance of people;
- demanding truth and justice concerning crimes against humanity;
- stopping societal and historical negation of assaults to humanity;
- urging that impunity not be granted to those responsible for the abductions;
- implementing national and international legislation to eradicate crimes against humanity;
- providing unconditional support to a democratic government that protects freedom and security;
- promoting social education about the need to defend fundamental human rights;
- working for the future of new generations, preserving principles of solidarity, freedom, and democracy;
- joining with others in the struggle for human rights; and
- courting trials for ex-military leaders of the *Dirty War*.

During this step, the Mothers also began social education projects. Currently, the Asociacion Madres de Plaza de Mayo issues a monthly newspaper, prints position papers, writes open letters to the public, and maintains a presence on the Internet; moreover, in 2000 they founded a university and a bookstore. Perhaps this can be summarized best with Si Kahn's (1997) recommendation that during times of assault, community organizing becomes a call, a cry, or a demand for fundamental change. It is a means of confronting the existing economic and political establishments.

Step 6: Changes in Societal Structures May Occur

The final step is related to change in societal structure. This step involves community members embracing a cause and reinventing the community with protective factors. At this time, the creation of community consciences can enhance community capacity as well as accelerate social change. Just as in the previous steps, the practitioner's intervention may be guided by the literature on social change. According to Sorokin (1967), regardless of the nature or makeup of a system, "it bears within itself the seeds of incessant change, which mark every action and reaction even in a fixed environment" (p. 69). Intrinsic in Sorokin's statement is the concept that this type of change is based on a community's unique "inherent potentialities. Only from an acorn can spring an oak" (p. 69).

Sorokin (1967) theorized that all systems have some measure of self-determination, but the autonomy of the system and its unique environments are regulated differently. Sorokin concluded that once a system has changed, it cannot return to its original state. This conclusion applies to the ongoing organizing of the Mothers; the communities of Columbine, Oklahoma City, Ground Zero in New York, and locations where churches have been burned; and so many other communities that are prepared to risk themselves in the quest for human justice. Once they set in motion the mechanisms of change, they are on the way to bringing transformation to societal structures.

Roland Warren (1977) has provided a classic model of social change that includes six dimensions. The first dimension is the identification of the *change objective,* or the determination of what change is needed and at what system level. In the case of the Mothers, the change objective adopted was the return of their abducted children. In adopting this objective, the Mothers sought to change the behavior of Argentinean government agents from spreading terror to respecting human life.

The second dimension is the identification of the *target system,* or the selection of the system in which change needs to occur, whether it is the individual, community, or organization. A key issue in the identification of a target system is the target system's readiness for change. The Mothers, for example, clearly met a great deal of resistance from the military government (their target system). The Mothers were verbally and physically attacked and ridiculed, and the "detained disappeared" were labeled "subversive," "communist," and "enemies of the nation."

The third dimension specifies the *change-inducing system,* which involves deciding which groups should plan to come together to achieve a common goal. This step involves collaboration between various change agents. Madres de Plaza de Mayo became the nucleus of a functional community that has enjoyed the support of human rights organizations at both the national and international levels.

In the fourth dimension, the community members select *strategies* that will work best to bring about change, such as cooperation, media campaigns, or physical and verbal contests. For example, because the Argentinean military power structure was not ready to give up its vested interest—control and privileges—without a contest, the Mothers had no choice but to meet them on their terms. One of the Mothers' slogans says "The only struggle that is lost is the one that we abandon."

The fifth dimension, *resistance,* involves analyzing the possible reasons for the target system to resist change. In the case of the Mothers, the military government had much to lose if it acknowledged the abductions, so it was not willing to stop its human rights violations and become more open to change. Therefore, resistance by the Mothers needed to persist.

The sixth dimension is the *stabilization of change,* or the development of mechanisms to ensure that change will remain stable. The process of stabilization involves the institutionalization of community protective factors. Protective factors can assist community members in establishing a sense of organizational control and bringing change to societal structures. These changes are in line with current thinking on empowerment, which includes a belief that power is not a scarce commodity but, rather, one that can be generated in the process of empowerment (Gutierrez, 2001, p. 210).

Communities become more resilient as a result of community empowerment and start a process of reconstruction and, in some instances, reconciliation. Similarly, on April 6, 2000, the Asociacion Madres de Plaza de Mayo founded the Universidad Popular de Madres de Plaza de Mayo (Popular University of Mothers of Plaza de Mayo), a local university designed for the education and promotion of social transformation. The main objective is to promote critical thinking and organize group opportunities for creative reflection. Hebe de Bonafini, president of the Asociacion Madres de Plaza de Mayo and chancellor of the university, wrote the following:

> On April 6 the Asociacion Madres de Plaza de Mayo will start a new chapter by being the bridge that links the aspirations of our children with that of the new generations that love life, that know that blood is not negotiable, and who know that for each drop of blood that once covered the soil of our beloved country, today flourishes hope of freedom and solidarity. (Universidad Popular Madres de Plaza de Mayo, 2000, p. 3)

Communities navigate threats with a great deal of courage and to such an extent that community members are prepared to place themselves at risk. They organize and become a unified front. Bonding, mutual support, understanding, a sense of togetherness, mobilization of community assets, and support from external groups and communities are some of the factors that contribute to a community's ability to bounce back. Successful coping at the macro level takes shape when community members realize that their change efforts and their continued search for human rights have produced social change.

Implications for Practice

This chapter has illustrated how communities may move from a state of chaos and uncertainty to one of clear goals and commitment. The discussion suggests that practitioners adopt a philosophical and political orientation that leads them to critically analyze all elements of society, particularly those related to the power structure. Practitioners also need to respect and mobilize community strengths, resources, and assets. Perhaps the most valuable lesson learned is that a community has the capacity to turn the long-lasting effects of atrocities into a process that builds more responsive structures that may prevent the recurrence of similar assaults.

The discussion on resilience at the macro level in situations of assault raises a number of implications for social work practice. More than anything, it calls for practitioners to be well versed in micro- and macro-level theories, to be politically astute, to be savvy in terms of coalition building, and to have a firm belief that they can be agents of change and have the ethical responsibility to work with communities to challenge social injustice (NASW, 2008). We recommend that practitioners who work with communities that have suffered traumatic events follow these six practice principles:

1. Denounce oppressive acts aimed at silencing communities.
2. Recognize that the power of change lies within the community.
3. Advocate for community members who are willing to risk their well-being to make a difference in the community.
4. Recognize that resilience manifests itself in numerous ways during the change process, which in turn leads to the accomplishment of community goals.
5. Identify and nurture those assets, talents, and protective factors that will assist the community in accomplishing its goals.
6. Celebrate communities that successfully emerge from the organizing process as a new and transformed, with no tolerance for human injustice.

Use the CD by Michael Wright to identify six practice principles in applying resilience schemas at the macro level. Explore the use of both real and virtual social networks for community organizing.

You will find a case study on your CD: *Learning About Tyranny, Community, and Facebook*

References

Abuelas de Plaza de Mayo. (n.d.). *Memoria.* Argentina: Author.

Anderson, R. E., Carter, I., & Lowe, G. (1999). *Human behavior and the social environment: A social systems approach.* New York: Aldine de Gruyter.

Aspy, D. N., & Aspy, C. B. (1996). How a school coped with the Oklahoma City bombing. *Educational Leadership, 54*(2), 82–84.

Berger, P., & Luckmann, T. (1967). *The social construction of reality: A treatise in the sociology of knowledge.* London: Penguin.

Bernstein Carlson, E., & Rosser-Hogan, R. (1994). Cross-cultural response to trauma: A study of traumatic experience and posttraumatic symptoms in Cambodian refugees. *Journal of Traumatic Stress, 7,* 43–58.

Bowen, G. L., Martin, J. A., Mancini, J. A., & Nelson, J. P. (2000). Community capacity: Antecedents and consequences. *Journal of Community Practice, 8*(2), 1–21.

Breton, M. (2001). Neighborhood resilience. *Journal of Community Practice, 9*(1), 21–36.

Cnaan, R. A., & Rothman, J. (2001). Locality development and the building of community. In J. Rothman, J. L. Erlich, & J. E. Tropman (Eds.), *Strategies of community intervention* (6th ed., pp. 251–267). Itasca, IL: F. E. Peacock.

Cox, F. M. (1987). Communities: Alternative conceptions of community. Implications for community organization practice. In F. M. Cox, J. L. Erlich, J. Rothman, & J. E. Tropman (Eds.), *Strategies of community organization: Macro practice* (4th ed., pp. 232–243). Itasca, IL: F. E. Peacock.

Delgado, M. (2000). *Community social work practice in an urban context: The potential of a capacity-enhancement perspective.* New York: Oxford University Press.

Dobbie, D. (2009). Evolving strategies of labor-community coalition-building. *Journal of Community Practice, 17,* 107–119.

Foner, N. (Ed.). (2005). *Wounded city: The social impact of 9/11.* New York: Russell Sage Foundation.

Frederick, C. (1985). Children traumatized by catastrophic situations. In J. Laube & S. A. Murphy (Eds.), *Perspectives on disaster recovery* (pp. 110–130). Stamford, CT: Appleton-Century-Crofts.

Germain, C., & Gitterman, A. (1996). *The life model of social work practice* (2nd ed.). New York: Columbia University Press.

Gilligan, C. (1982). *In a different voice.* Cambridge, MA: Harvard University Press.

Gordon, J. D., & Doka, K. J. (2000). Resonating trauma: A theoretical note. In K. J. Doka (Ed.), *Living with grief: Children, adolescents, and loss* (pp. 291–292). Washington, DC: Hospice Foundation of America.

Green, G. J., Jensen, C., & Harper Jones, D. (1996). Constructivist perspective on clinical social work practice with ethnically diverse clients. *Social Work, 1,* 172–180.

Gutierrez, L. M. (2001). Working with women of color: An empowerment perspective. In J. Rothman, J. L. Erlich, & J. E. Tropman (Eds.), *Strategies of community intervention* (6th ed., pp. 209–217). Itasca, IL: F. E. Peacock.

Guzman Bouvard, M. (1994). *Revolutionizing motherhood: The mothers of the Plaza de Mayo.* Wilmington, DE: SR Books.

Halpern, H. A. (1973). Crisis theory: A definitional study. *Community Mental Health Journal, 9,* 342–349.

Hawley, A. (1950). *Human ecology: A theory of community structure.* New York: Roland Press.

Kahn, S. (1997). Leadership: Realizing concepts through creative process. In M. Weil (Ed.), *Community practice: Model in action* (pp. 109–136). Binghamton, NY: Haworth Press.

Kisthardt, W. E., & Rapp, C. A. (1992). Bridging the gap between principles and practice: Implementing a strengths perspective in case management. In S. M. Rose (Ed.), *Case management and social work practice* (pp. 112–125). New York: Longman.

Koetze, D. A. (1986–1987). Contradictions and assumptions in community development. *Community Development Journal, 22,* 31–35.

Luthar, S. S. (Ed.). (2003). *Resilience and vulnerability. Adaptation in the context of childhood adversities.* New York: Cambridge University Press.

Masten, A. S., Best, K. M., & Garmezy, N. (1991). Resilience and development: Contributions from the study of children who overcome adversity. *Development and Psychopathology, 2,* 425–444.

NASW. (2008). *NASW Code of Ethics.* Washington, DC: NASW Press. Retrieved May 14, 2011, from http://www.socialworkers.org/pubs/code/code.asp

Nisbet, R. A. (1971). *The quest for community.* New York: Oxford University Press.

Parsons, T. (1971). *The system of modern societies.* Englewood Cliffs, NJ: Prentice Hall.

Poole, D. L. (1997). Building community capacity to promote social and public health: Challenges for universities. *Health & Social Work, 22,* 163–170.

Pyles, L. (2009). *Progressive community organizing: A critical approach for a globalizing world.* New York: Routledge.

Queiro-Tajalli, I. (1999). How useful is the social constructionist approach? In R. R. Greene (Ed.), *Human behavior and social work practice* (2nd ed., pp. 341–349). New York: Aldine de Gruyter.

Rapoport, L. (1965). The state of crisis: Some theoretical considerations. In H. J. Parad (Ed.), *Crisis intervention: Selected readings* (pp. 22–31). New York: Family Services Association of America.

Ross, M. G. (1967). *Community organization: Theory, principles, and practice* (2nd ed.). New York: Harper & Row.

Rothman, J. (1995). Introduction. In J. Rothman, J. L. Erlich, & J. E. Tropman (Eds.), *Strategies of community intervention* (5th ed., pp. 3–25). Itasca, IL: F. E. Peacock.

Rutter, M. (1985). Resilience in the face of adversity: Protective factors and resistance to psychiatric disorder. *British Journal of Psychiatry, 147,* 598–611.

Saleebey, D. (1996). The strengths perspective in social work practice: Extensions and cautions. *Social Work, 4,* 296–305.

Saleebey, D. (Ed.). (2002). *The strengths perspective in social work practice* (3rd ed.). Boston: Allyn & Bacon.

Slaikeu, K. A. (1990). *Crisis intervention: A handbook for practice and research* (2nd ed.). Boston: Allyn & Bacon.

Sorokin, P. A. (1967). Reasons for sociocultural change and variably recurrent processes. In W. E. Moore & R. M. Cook (Eds.), *Readings on social change* (pp. 68–80). Englewood Cliffs, NJ: Prentice Hall.

Universidad Popular Madres de Plaza de Mayo. (2000). *Inauguracion de la Universidad Popular Madres de Plaza de Mayo.* Buenos Aires: Author.

Vazquez, I., Gorini, U., Gallegos, M., Nielsen, G., Epstein, E., & Rodriguez, C. (2004). *Luchar siempre. Las Marchas de la Resistencia 1981–2003*. Buenos Aires: Ediciones Madres de Plaza de Mayo.

Warren, R. (1963). *The community in America*. Chicago: Rand McNally.

Warren, R. (1977). *Social change and human purpose: Toward understanding and action*. Chicago: Rand McNally.

Watson, D., David, J. P., & Suls, J. (1999). Personality, affectivity, and coping. In C. R. Snyder (Ed.), *Coping: The psychology of what works* (pp. 119–140). New York: Oxford University Press.

Weil, M., & Gamble, D. N. (1995). Community practice models. In R. L. Edwards (Ed.-in-Chief), *Encyclopedia of social work* (19th ed., Vol. 1, pp. 577–594). Washington, DC: NASW Press.

Wittgenstein, L. (1963). *Philosophical investigations*. Oxford, England: Blackwell.

Wolin, S. J., & Wolin, S. (1993). *The resilient self: How survivors of troubled families rise above adversity*. New York: Villard.

Zullo, R., & Pratt, G. (2009). Critical pedagogy as a tool for labor-community coalition building. *Journal of Community Practice, 17*, 140–153.

9

Raising Children in an Oppressive Environment: Voices of Resilient Adults

ROBERTA R. GREENE, NORMA J. TAYLOR,
MARGARET EVANS, and LINDA ANDERSON SMITH

On finishing this chapter, students will be able to further:

Engage diversity and difference in practice (Educational Policy 2.1.4) by

- Recognizing the extent to which a culture's structures and values may oppress, marginalize, alienate, or create or enhance privilege and power.
- Recognizing and communicating their understanding of the importance of difference in shaping life experiences.
- Gaining sufficient self-awareness to eliminate the influence of personal biases and values in working with diverse groups (practice behaviors).

Advance human rights and social and economic justice (Educational Policy 2.1.5) by

- Understanding the forms and mechanisms of oppression and discrimination (practice behavior).

The socialization of children remains, perhaps, the most exclusive domain of the family. . . . For the Negro family, socialization is doubly challenging for the family must teach its young members not only how to be human, but also how to be black in a white society.

—Billingsley, 1968, pp. 27–28

Although resilience research is burgeoning, there must be additional attention given to vulnerable children and those ethnic minority adolescents living in poverty and the manner in which resilience develops.

—D. B. Miller & MacIntosh, 1999, p. 167

Theorists who study resilience continue to grapple with why, despite the increased risk of racism and discrimination, many children do not surrender to the effects of oppression and the attendant inordinate environmental stress (Garmezy, 1991; D. B. Miller & MacIntosh, 1999). How do children raised in an oppressive society become competent adults? What factors contribute to the family's ability to cope with such stress and to promote resilience in their children? Because social workers can use such information about how families foster success despite the high risk of discrimination to help others who are wrestling with these difficulties, there is still a need for more research (Cohen & Greene, 2005; Greif, Hrabowski, & Maton, 1998).

The literature increasingly supports the idea that a supportive family and a positive relationship with at least one parent or adult outside the family circle can favorably affect and promote resilience (Denby, 1996). In addition, a growing body of literature suggests that resilience is enhanced by an ethnic family's cultural values and provision of mutual psychological support (Genero, 1998; McCubbin, Thompson, Thompson, & Futrell, 1998). There is also increasing evidence that by socializing children to have a positive racial or ethnic as well as personal identity and by providing them with strategies to resist discrimination, families can raise children effectively in an oppressive society. For example, in examining what promotes resilience and academic achievement among urban African American adolescents, D. B. Miller and MacIntosh (1999) have suggested that the capacity to transcend the risk of oppressive environments can be attributed to a family's "culturally unique protective factors" (p. 159). In their discussion of racial socialization and identity, they pointed out that parental messages given to black children—whether direct or indirect—can prepare them to function in an environment of inequality. They concluded that racial socialization, although not the same in all African American families, should be thought of as providing children with a suit of armor worn to protect them against discrimination and the daily hassles of their environment. Although parents may be challenged by what can be the debilitating effects of bigotry and prejudice, they can successfully socialize their children by transmitting values and teaching adaptive strategies that make it possible for them to succeed. Social workers can also enhance this process through culturally sensitive practices that use the dual perspective and build on a family's coping strategies.

This chapter discusses the theoretical frameworks that contribute to an understanding of family socialization processes among oppressed groups. The discussion assumes that culturally specific adaptive strategies learned in the family can protect children from the adverse effects of oppression, enabling them to transcend discrimination and become resilient adults (Chestang, 1972). That is, the chapter describes specific family cultural forms that contribute to a child's capacity to overcome the risks associated with discrimination and to withstand stress (Genero, 1998; Solomon, 1976). Although the literature primarily reflects the views of African American theorists, the framework should not be limited to any particular group; rather, it can be applied to clients from any population group that has been oppressed. A strengths-based orientation to social work practice and the dual perspective serve as a foundation for relevant practice strategies.

Socialization and the Dual Perspective

The paradigms and concepts developed by social scientists to describe human behavior have traditionally been "inordinately influenced by . . . white persons of European descent" (Schriver, 2001, p. 66). Socialization from the dual perspective was first described by DuBois (1903), a freed slave, who said, "One ever feels his twoness—an American; a Negro; two souls, two thoughts, two unreconciled strivings; two warring ideals in one dark body, whose dogged strength alone keeps it from being torn asunder" (p. 17). Chestang (1972) and S. Miller (1980) further defined the dual perspective as a process of consciously and systematically understanding the values, attitudes, and behaviors of both the minority and mainstream cultures. These theorists proposed that individuals first learn about their immediate culture in the nurturing family system. People later encounter the majority, sustaining cultural system as they interact with the institutions that control the provision of goods and services, such as schools and health and human services agencies.

The perspective assumes, then, that every individual is part of two systems: the smaller system of his or her immediate environment and the larger societal system. For example, Boykin and Toms (1985) found that African American children first develop an understanding of many African cultural forms that are passed on to each generation, and as they go through this development, they also engage with the mainstream ethos. The social worker's understanding of the client's view of his or her immediate and sustaining culture can provide a picture of the client's sociocultural context and can prevent stereotyping, misinterpretations, and inappropriate interventions (Norton, 1978). In addition, although the various elements of the client's two systems exist side by side, the two systems may or may not be congruent. Because from the dual perspective

FIGURE 9.1 Dual System of All Individuals

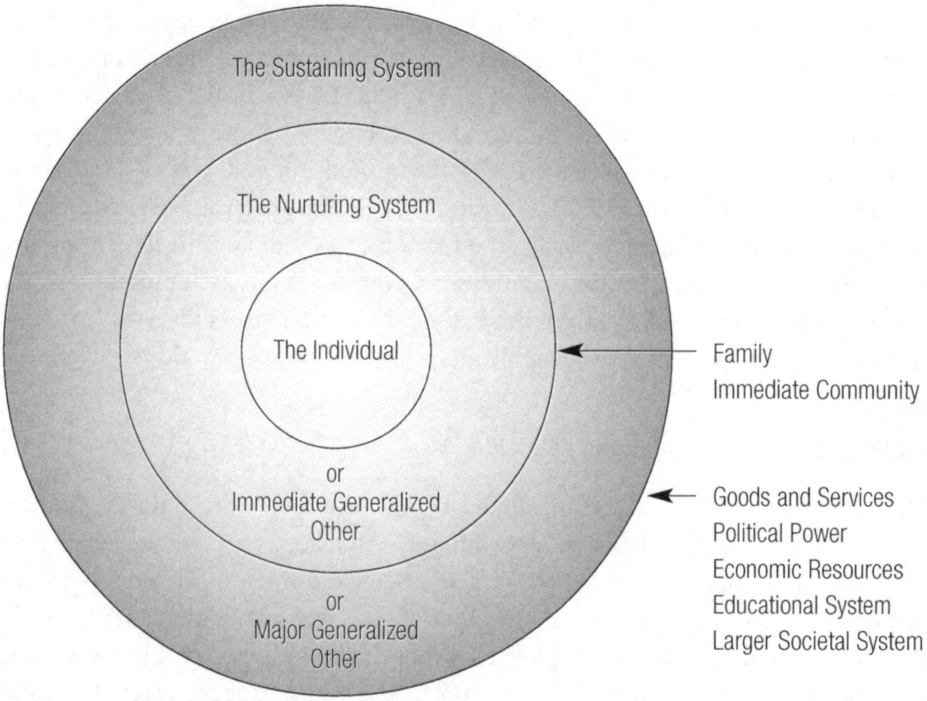

The Sustaining System

The Nurturing System

The Individual

or
Immediate Generalized
Other

or
Major Generalized
Other

Family
Immediate Community

Goods and Services
Political Power
Economic Resources
Educational System
Larger Societal System

Source: From "The Dual Perspective of Ethnic Minority Content in the Social Work Curriculum," by D. G. Norton, 1978, p. 5. Copyright 1978 by the Council on Social Work Education. Reprinted with permission.

an evaluation involves reconciling "these disparate systems and [determining] where the major stress lies" (Norton, 1978, p. 7), the degree of incongruence is an important element in social work assessment (see Figure 9.1). In this manner, the social worker can arrive at a mutually based decision about how to intervene to enhance family resilience.

Green (1999) cautioned that social workers should be aware that there might also be "dualistic opposition between the stocks of knowledge between clients and [human services] professionals" (p. 57). He outlined four types of knowledge that coexist in clinical settings that may present differences or even polarity between the interpretations and expectations of the client and the professional: (1) what the client knows from daily experiences, (2) what the practitioner knows from formal education and training, (3) what the practitioner knows as a private citizen, and (4) what the agency allows given the institutional history and policy directives. Thus, the social worker's conscious use of the dual perspective can assist in bridging these possible misunderstandings in the clinical encounter.

Closely tied to the notion of the dual perspective is bicultural competence. When socialization is culturally specific, children can learn modes or styles of behavior appropriate for each group. *Bicultural competence* is the ability to alternate and integrate cultural forms. According to McAdoo (1992), black parents must prepare their children to function in both black and white societies. Moreover, immigrant children may struggle with how to become new Americans. Irving Howe (1982), the son of Russian immigrants who grew up to become a social critic and professor of English at Hunter College in New York, explained:

> Home meant snugness and deprivation, a place and a feeling I kept to myself. It could not be part of one's new life. The thought of bringing my friends home was inconceivable, for I would have been ashamed to show them to my parents as to show my parents to them. I had enough imagination to suppose that each could see through the sham of the other, but not enough courage to defend one against the other. Besides, where would people sit in those cramped apartments? (p. 5)

Biculturalism allows a child to learn about and take advantage of mainstream culture without compromising ethnic pride. For the child to develop knowledge of and a positive attitude toward both cultures, the family needs to validate that it is acceptable to live in two communities (Genero, 1998). A child who is bicultural can communicate effectively across cultures and feels effective and well grounded in both the ethnic and mainstream cultures. This grounding can contribute to the development of resilience (La Fromboise, Coleman, & Gerton, 1993). For example, urban Native American children, who may be members of one of the 505 federally recognized tribal groups, may learn the tools of mainstream culture while making a commitment to tribal traditions (Attneave, 1982). Latino children whose parents teach them *respeto,* or respect for authority within the home, are better prepared to interact with appropriate authority figures (Hill, Soriano, Chen, & La Fromboise, 1994).

Because the concept of biculturalism is dynamic and subjective, it has been used to mean more than moving between one ethnic culture and another. The concept can enable social workers to better understand the structural and political differences of how oppressed people may be rejected by the larger society (R. R. Greene & Watkins, 1998). For example, Lukes and Land (1990) have suggested, "Even if sexual minorities do not have a culture in the traditional sense, there are several reasons for examining sexual minorities from a cultural context" (p. 155). That is, it provides an understanding of how people who are different from the normative group may be denied institutional and economic power (Van Voorhis, 1998).

Defining Terms: *Culture, Race, Ethnicity, Minority, and Racism*

The idea that children must learn to function in two cultural systems applies to children who may experience unequal treatment. Because the composition of U.S. society has become increasingly multicultural, social workers need to prepare to serve increasingly diverse families. Knowledge of how culture can further resilience can help social workers meet the growing demand for services within a culturally diverse system (Ewalt, Freeman, Kirk, & Poole, 1996; Germain, 1992; R. R. Greene & Watkins, 1998; Tully, 1994).

Culture

In his book *Cultural Awareness in the Human Services,* Green (1998) recommended that social workers take a broad view of culture and the constituencies that they serve. He indicated that social workers should consider culture as a community of interest encompassing communities that are not explicitly racial or ethnic, such as a school for the deaf, street people, or a drug house. Green went on to state that culture is not a specific value, physical appearance, or something that people have. Rather, culture should be understood as people's shared cognitive map, their discourse, and how they go about their lives—their life perspective.

A family's culture is the sum total of its way of life that relates to how it meets basic psychosocial needs (Pinderhughes, 1989). *Culture* encompasses the values, norms, beliefs, attitudes, and folkways of a specific family and community group, as well as their behavior styles and traditions. Furthermore, culture includes customs that, as with other cultural forms, are passed along to future generations through socialization, thus ensuring the continuation of community values (Hill et al., 1994; Hines, Preto, McGoldrick, Almeida, & Weltman, 1999). Because culture may act as a protective mechanism and may contribute to resilience, often binding a group together and offering a set of norms and values that assist people in facing stress, culture is an important component in the discussion of how to raise resilient children in an oppressive society. For social workers to understand this process of transcendence in a particular family, it is necessary that they take a positive learning stance (Green, 1998; Pinderhughes, 1989).

Race

An individual's sense of resilience is also influenced by racial identity. Because theorists have defined race differently and the term has been often used in a pejorative manner, it is meaningful to first clarify its usage (Devore & Schlesinger, 1996; Green, 1999; Pinderhughes, 1989). According to Pinderhughes (1989), *race* is a biological term to classify people who have similar physical characteristics, and it has come to mean differences between people based on color. However, Green (1998) has argued that, because there are as many physical differences within a "race" as there are between races, the concept has no scientific merit. He suggested that the groups that people tend to think of as racial groups are really populations or gene pools that have evolved over the years with people living in the same geographical area. Because of the widespread misconceptions about the term *race,* other theorists reserve the term *people of color* for those groups of people who have faced oppression and racism because of their skin color (Hoops, 1982). The autobiographical accounts at the end of this chapter poignantly illustrate how important it is to ascertain clients' personal sense of how race has affected their lives.

Ethnicity

Theorists tend to agree that a family's ability to be resilient is best understood by examining its ethnicity and culture (Devore & Schlesinger, 1996; Green, 1999). Ethnicity pertains to the connections and commonalities among people, such as religion, nationality, or country of origin. The sharing of cultural patterns over time and a common sense of social history are also factors associated with ethnicity (Pinderhughes, 1989). Furthermore, *ethnicity* "refers to the sense of peoplehood experienced by members of the same group" (Devore & Schlesinger, 1996, p. 45). *Ethnic group members* have a sense that they are like others in the group. The expression ethnic minority encompasses people who share a common story of their beginnings, sense of history, and worldview (Green, 1999). *Ethnic minority* generally refers to African Americans, Asians, Latinos, and Native Americans as groups that have historically been oppressed (Bush, Norton, Sanders, & Solomon, 1983).

In taking social histories, social workers need to explore the meaning a client attributes to being a member of an ethnic group (Helton & Jackson, 1997). Does the client view his or her ethnicity as something to be celebrated, a political process, something associated with social class or economic situation, or a token identity? Members of ethnic groups may be more or less *assimilated;* that is, the extent to which they have given up their ethnic uniqueness in favor of generalized cultural forms may vary (Green, 1998). There are costs and benefits to each position. Some African American families socialize their children to have a more mainstream identity. The cost can be a loss of preparation for racism and the loss of support of the African American community. The benefit is the appearance of "sameness"—shared values and customs and so forth with the white world.

This may make whites more comfortable and more accepting of them (W. E. Cross, 1991).

Minority

In socializing their children, parents often contemplate how their children will cope with the "minority experience" (Thorton, 1998, p. 57). The term *minority* does not necessarily refer to a quantifiable minority or to cultural differences. Rather, the term applies to people who experience a lack of societal power or limited economic and social circumstances—for example, women who have historically been given differential treatment based on gender roles and power issues (Greene, 2008). According to Devore and Schlesinger (1996), minority groups are those that are underprivileged in a system of ethnic stratification. Minority group members, then, may be thought of as "singled out by society for differential and unequal treatment" (Bush et al., 1983, p. 105). Client assessment should encompass an understanding of the client's worldview, as well as how he or she has specifically experienced or been affected by minority group status, as can be seen in the personal reflections at the end of the chapter.

Racism

Theorists have focused on the way in which racism affects child raising. Racism, according to Pinderhughes (1989), is more than a prejudice. Rather, *racism*—the belief that one race is superior to another—is embedded in social structures and is sanctioned by society through policies and institutional arrangements. Institutional racism consists of the social policies and societal structures that limit people's opportunity and availability of resources. Just as with other forms of discrimination, institutional racism may interfere with or limit any child's capacity to fulfill a developmental task (Hill et al., 1994). However, parents can deliver both specific and subtle messages that help children develop resistance strategies that lead to resilience. Thorton (1998) has called this "process of explicit racial socialization a distinctive childrearing activity that black parents engage in to prepare their children for life in America" (p. 56).

Oppression

What does it mean to be raised in an oppressive society? *Oppression* is a process in which the dominant group(s) in a society imposes a negative view about a minority group's value or place in the world. According to R. R. Greene (2008), oppressed populations who face discrimination and limited political power may include

- minority groups, which are defined by limited political power;
- ethnic groups, which are characterized by a shared peoplehood;
- women, in terms of gender roles and power issues;
- the aged population, which is affected by devalued status;
- members of certain social classes, in terms of their economic and educational advantage or disadvantage;
- developmentally disabled persons, who are perceived as challenged by mental or physical ability;
- people of varying sexual orientations, who are affected by misconceptions and discrimination about their affectional ties; and
- religious groups, which are defined by their spiritual needs, religious beliefs, and practices.

According to hooks (1984), a feminist thinker, the oppressor group may be thought of as the center or the seat of political, economic, and social power. The oppressor group also has control of resources and dominates the choice of cultural and linguistic forms used in the social structure. As a result of this domination, the group lacking power and resources is at the *margin,* or outside the main body of society. Such inequities may take the form of racism, sexism, heterosexism, ageism, classism, and so forth. People at the margin may develop a sense of futility or feel hopeless, helpless, or estranged. As a consequence of this insidious process, a person's sense of self-worth can be undermined (Van Voorhis, 1998).

R. R. Greene (2002, 2010) provided an example from the Holocaust, in which over the course of Hitler's reign in Germany and other occupied countries, Jews were demoralized; removed from positions in government, education, business, newspapers, or media; barred from the military; and prohibited from owning land. By August 2, 1935, all German armed forces had to swear allegiance to Hitler, and on September 15, the Nuremburg Race Laws were enacted, making Jews second-class citizens. An 80-year-old survivor recalled such discrimination many years after it occurred: Her German teachers and school principal let her know that, as a Jewish child, somebody had "recognized her" and did not want her to participate in a school play.

Ethnosystems

Oppressive societies are characterized by power differentials. Solomon (1976) conceptualized the ethnosystem approach to describe the organizing power principle guiding interrelationships among groups in U.S. society. She defined an *ethnosystem* "as a collective of interdependent ethnic groups sharing unique historical and/or cultural ties and bound together by a single, political system"

FIGURE 9.2 Framework for Understanding the Behaviors of an Ethnosystem

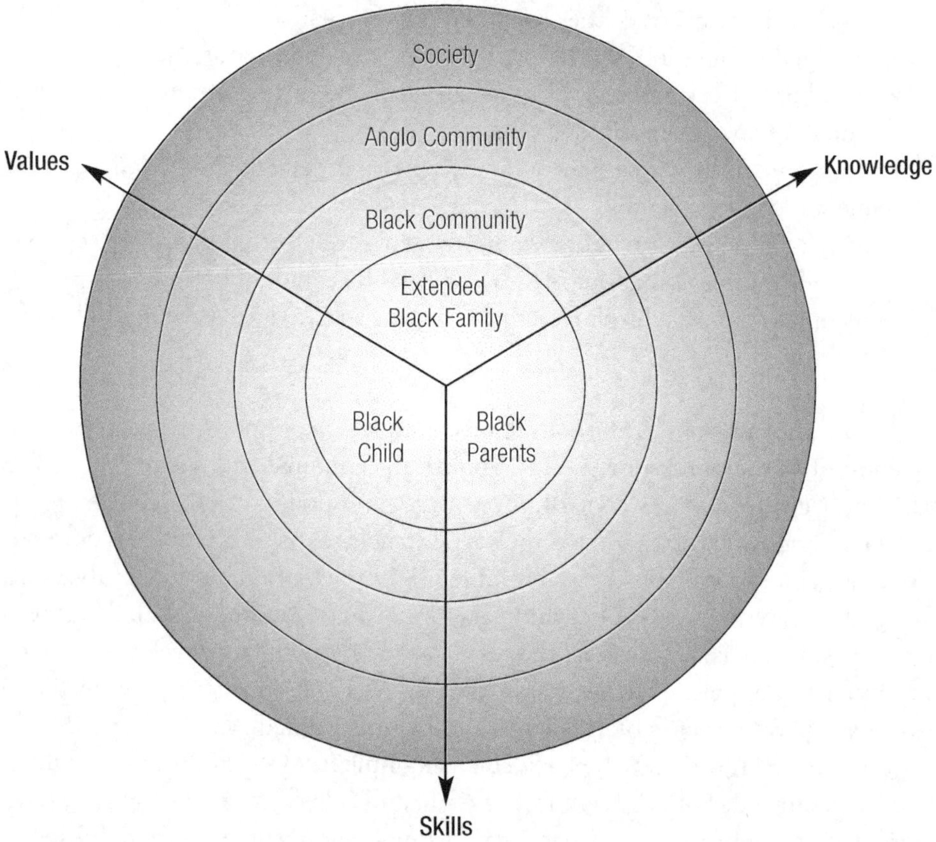

Source: From "An Integrative Approach for the Inclusion of Content on Blacks in Social Work Education," by J. A. Bush, D. G. Norton, C. L. Sanders, and B. B. Solomon, 1983, in *Mental Health and People of Color,* p. 112. Copyright 1983 by Howard University Press. Reprinted with permission.

(p. 45; see Figure 9.2). This conceptualization of ethnicity as bound together by a political system provides social workers with an understanding of how various ethnic groups have relative power vis-à-vis other groups as well as mainstream society.

Power Differentials

In large measure, oppression is related to *power,* or "the ability to control or influence, directly or indirectly, the conditions under which one lives" (Goldenberg, 1978, p. 59). Although there are specific power differentials based on factors such as race, gender, and class, Davis, Leijenaar, and Oldersma (1991) have proposed seven common features that can be used to understand client circumstances. The social worker should ask whether the client is experiencing

1. inequality in social resources, social position, or political and cultural influences
2. inequality in opportunities to make use of existing resources
3. inequality in the division of rights and duties
4. inequality in implicit or explicit standards of judgment, often leading to differential treatment (in law, labor market, educational practices, and so forth)
5. inequality in cultural representations: devaluation of the powerless group, stereotyping, references to the "nature" or (biological) essence of the less powerful
6. inequality in psychological consequences: a "psychology of inferiority" (insecurity, "double-bind" experiences, and sometimes identification with the dominant group) versus a "psychology of superiority" (arrogance, inability to abandon the dominant perspective)
7. social and cultural tendency to minimize or deny power inequality: (potential) conflict often represented as consensus, power inequality [seen] as "normal." (p. 52)

Oppressive societies also contribute to a personal and community sense of powerlessness. The belief system of mainstream U.S. society suggests that people who have power and resources are valuable, whereas individuals who are oppressed or marginalized may be socially conditioned to believe that they are failures (Solomon, 1976). The greater the power differential—or the more one group dominates another (subordinate) group—the greater the sense of oppression (Wilson, 1973). Therefore, according to Pinderhughes (1983), the other side of the coin of power is powerlessness:

> A cycle of powerlessness in which the failure of the larger social system to provide needed resources operates in a circular manner. . . . The more powerless a community the more the families within it are hindered from meeting the needs of their members and from organizing the community so that it can provide them with more support. (p. 332)

There can be no more poignant accounts of a people's sense of powerlessness and aspirations as those recounted in the stories of emancipated slaves. Their stories juxtaposed the joys of childbirth and marriage against the fears of a family member's being sold, attempts to run away, and the harshness of whippings if they were caught fleeing. Miraculously, many former slaves expressed a sense of hope and religiosity: "Freedom for us was the best thing ever happened. Prayer is best thing in the world. Everybody ought to pray, 'cause prayer got us out of slavery'" (Backer & Backer, 1996, p. 75).

The question may well be raised, Why go back to a discussion of slavery? Does that historical perspective reinforce misconceptions about current day racism? (L. Smith, associate professor of social work, Springfield College, Springfield, MA, personal communication, November 2000). The socialization of black children hundreds of years later still reflects the lessons of those times. For example, Proctor (1995), an honored educator and theologian who grew up in the South during segregation, attributed his success to his reliance on his rock-bottom foundation of belief. Proctor recounted the faith of his grandparents:

> When I think about my grandparents making the giant step from slavery to freedom, I realize that none of my accomplishments can ever live up to their legacy. . . . The spiritual resilience derived from their faith allowed most enslaved African Americans to come through their degrading experience whole, without losing their humanity. . . . Like millions of other black Americans, I am heir to the faith that was born the day twenty frightened black captives were unloaded at Jamestown in 1619. . . . I believe that enough idealism and faith remain among all of us to generate a soaring national quest for a new kind of human paradigm in which all diverse peoples of America can participate. (p. xxi)

Historical and Economic Differentials

Researchers continue to explore how oppressive historical and economic conditions can ultimately result in a child's either remaining at risk or developing resilience (Hill et al., 1994). In an economic and historical macroanalysis of poverty among African Americans from 1960 to 1980, Wilson (1987) described how the U.S. economy shifted from a manufacturing economy to a service economy. Wilson pointed out that with the closing of manufacturing companies, there was a decline in traditional jobs available to individuals with a high school diploma, leaving many people of color without viable incomes. At the same time that this process was taking place, many middle-class families left the inner city for the suburbs. Wilson coined the term *underclass* to describe the poorest of the poor who were left behind in inner cities without sufficient political power to work for change. Wilson, who argued for structural societal change to redress these inequities, provided a context for understanding the vexing difficulties of unemployment that continue as the nation experiments with welfare reform.

The late anthropologist Ogbu (1985, 1988) offered a similar argument in his examination of the relative success of inner-city youths. He proposed that there is a *status mobility system* in U.S. society, a system through which societal, social, and economic resources are accessed. The ability of a youth to succeed or negotiate the status mobility system is shaped by whether he or she is a member of a minority group that perceives itself as *autonomous,* a group that is small in number but has power; *immigrant,* a group that migrates voluntarily to the United States for social, economic, and possibly political reasons; or *involuntary,* a group that is part of U.S. society as a result of slavery or conquest. Furthermore, movement up the status mobility system is related to skin color: The darker and more ethnically distinct a person is, the less likely he or she will be successful. Similarly, with schooling, the less access, the lower the achievement.

The status mobility system strongly influences a person's sense of personhood. That is, a person is often defined by his or her ability to compete for a good job, a higher income, and the seeming stability of his or her household. Ogbu (1985) argued that four factors can affect a minority youth's movement up the status ladder: (1) the influence of structural inequities on education and power, (2) the presence of a job ceiling for minorities that may limit career choice, (3) the response of parents to these systemic constraints and how they socialize their children, and (4) the extent to which minority individuals develop an oppositional social identity and strong cultural frame of reference. According to Solomon (1988), "The message is clear: The first line of defense in preparing young black males to take advantage of employment opportunities or to fight effectively against systemic employment discrimination is a nurturing family" (p. 312).

Community Well-Being

Community violence consists of acts that cause physical and psychological harm and also characterizes an oppressive society (Dubrow & Garbarino, 1989; Garbarino, 1999; Solomon, 1976). According to Metzenbaum (1994), from 1980 to the mid-1990s, fatal violence from guns alone killed more U.S. children and youths than the total number of U.S. soldiers killed in the Vietnam War. Children growing up under violent conditions may experience a constellation of feelings, including depression, guilt, hopelessness, low self-esteem, a sense of danger, and worries about injury and death.

In a study conducted in a public housing development in Chicago—where fear was heightened because of shootings, gangs, unsafe elevators, and an inability to go out safely at night—Dubrow and Garbarino (1989) found that community violence resulted in parents feeling powerless and fearful about their children's future. Nathan McCall (1994), a journalist with the *Washington Post,* wrote an autobiographical account of violence and the challenges of growing up in his community of origin:

> For those who'd like answers, I have no pithy social formula to end black-on-black violence. But I do know that I see a younger, meaner generation out there now—more lost and alienated than we were, and placing even

> less value on life. We were at least touched by role models; this new bunch is totally estranged from the black mainstream. Crack has taken the drug game to a more lethal level and given young blacks far more economic incentive to opt for the streets.
>
> I've come to fear that of the many things a black man can die from, the first may be rage—his own or someone else's. For that reason, I seldom stick around when I stop on the block. One day not long ago, I spotted a few familiar faces hanging out at the old haunt. . . . I wheeled into the parking lot . . . and high-fived the guys I knew. Within moments, I sensed that I was in danger. . . . I felt hostile stares from those I didn't know. . . . I eased back into the car and left, because I knew this: that if they saw the world as I once did, they believed they had nothing to lose, including life itself. It made me wanna holler and throw up both my hands. (p. 416)

Solomon (1976) has argued that the concept of community needs to encompass the notion of "the defended neighborhood," a neighborhood in which fear is so great that the socialization of children can be adversely affected (p. 57). In a defended neighborhood, there is often a high crime rate and a diminished sense of trust, safety, and intimacy (Garbarino, 1995; Garbarino, Kostelny, & Dubrow, 1991). Defended communities may also be a result of wartime conditions, such as the Holocaust during World War II and the civil war in Mozambique. Children's sense of security and safety may be affected by *microaggressions,* such as daily name calling or snubs; or *macroaggressions,* which are direct actions that can even threaten survival (Pierce, 1969; Seliger, 1996). A unifying theme regarding racial or ethnic socialization is that parents who take into account the fact that their children will face a hostile environment raise their children with this discord in mind.

In addition, Holocaust survivors provide powerful examples of how people can continue to function in a hostile environment, including by stealing food and escaping from a ghetto. One survivor reflected, "We learned to survive by our wits. We learned to scrape and save whatever we could barter with others. We learned to work hard for our supervisors if they were kinder than usual" (R. R. Greene, 2010, p. 295).

> Never shall I forget that night, the first night in camp, which was turned into one long night, seven times cursed and seven times sealed. Never shall I forget that smoke. Never shall I forget the little faces of the children, whose bodies I saw turned into wreaths of smoke beneath a silent blue sky. (Wiesel, 1960, p. ix)

> Ugly racial memories of the past flashed through my mind. Years ago, while driving from New York to teach at Williams College, I was stopped on fake charges of trafficking cocaine. When I told the police officer I was a professor of religion, he replied, "Yeh, and I'm the Flying Nun. Let's go, nigger!" (West, 1993, p. xv)

Violence can also be used to intimidate and increase people's sense of danger and oppression—for example, the destruction of a place of worship or the events of September 11, 2001, in which symbols of U.S. democracy were attacked. Such events test a community's sense of coherence and simultaneously demonstrate peoples' determination:

> On October 12, 1958, the Temple, Atlanta's oldest and most prominent synagogue, was bombed: 3:37 A.M. In the middle of the night fifty sticks of dynamite blew apart the side wall of the Temple. . . . The brick walls flapped upward like sheets on a line. Offices and Sunday school classrooms burst out of the building; the stairwell came unmoored and hung like a rope ladder. Bronze plaques commemorating the war dead from the two world wars spun out like tablecloths shaken after dinner; and all was momentarily red-hot, white-lit, and moving like lava.
>
> "There was a huge shockwave," recalled Richard Wasser, "a loud noise that I could hear. I felt the windows rattle, I heard them rattle. And that was the night the Temple was bombed. The next morning I read in the paper about the explosion and said, 'That's what I felt last night.'"
>
> "I was sheltered from the bombing," said Marcia Rothchild . . . now a specialist in educational computer software. "I had to get up and ask what was going on. It was the day before my eleventh birthday. I remember waking up to a lot of commotion. . . . Their effort was to keep everything as normal as possible for us." (M. Greene, 1996, p. 238)

Similarly, Carter (1999) has attested to the resilience among African American communities that have faced church bombings. She pointed out that, because the church occupies such a vital role in African American communities, social workers should be aware that an epidemic of church fires could be a traumatic event. Nonetheless, most communities have faced these devastations by focusing on rebuilding projects. As recounted in a Web-based account,

> The centrality of the church in African-American life is the primary reason black churches have been targeted in an epidemic of what appears to be racially motivated church-burnings over the last two years from 2000–2002, experts say.

> The black church has been extraordinarily important source of health, education and welfare in the African-American community for several hundred years, explained Halford H. Fairfield, PhD, past president of the Association of Black Psychologists and associate professor of psychology at Pitzer College in Claremont, California.
>
> The burning of these institutions is more than the bombing of buildings; it's more like the burning of the symbol and the actual agency of collective struggle. (Clay, 2000, p. 1)

The determination to prosecute offenders and the rebuilding efforts of African American communities illustrate how neighborhoods can develop personal and collective efficacy despite such negative events (Sampson, Raudenbush, & Earls, 1997). Children receive a strong message from such activities. According to Garbarino (1992), who has interviewed children and families living in violent communities around the world, children who have strong attachments and unconditional love as well as spiritual support can overcome such risks to become resilient adults. In her work with single mothers living below the poverty line in the Clements Park area of Washington, DC, Brodsky (1996, 1999) has found resilience. Despite the ongoing concern about safety and meeting basic needs, the mothers she interviewed described how they made it day by day and created their own success for themselves and their children. The personal accounts at the end of this chapter capture the heroism of people's actions on a daily basis.

Socialization

Socialization involves preparing children through the teaching and learning of traditional beliefs, values, and standards of behavior necessary to assume the adult roles and obligations of society (Boykin & Toms, 1985). Socialization usually begins in a person's family and continues as youngsters interact with the major societal socialization agents, such as schools, the mass media, and the world of work. Socialization and the process of a youth's developing a positive identity are also influenced by role models and mentors who may serve as exemplars of behavior or symbolic values (Taylor, 1989). The purpose of socialization is to ensure that an individual is ready to be a successful or competent adult participant in society.

Socialization and Marginalized Groups

Families that are marginalized by prejudice and discrimination socialize their children under circumstances that are dramatically different from those of U.S. mainstream families and that flagrantly contradict national ideals of equality

(Peters, 1985, 1988). Family crises may be prompted or exacerbated by discrimination experienced in schools, hospitals, the workplace, or other societal institutions. Environmental conditions that may threaten personal and community well-being include poverty (Garmezy, 1991), violence (Garbarino, Dubrow, Kostelny, & Pardo, 1992), and limited access to resources such as health care (Arroyo & Zigler, 1995; Auslander, Thompson, Dreitzer, & Santiago, 1997). The social ecology in which many minority children must grow up is often characterized by substandard housing conditions, high rates of unemployment and underemployment, and disproportionately high rates of substance abuse (Bronfenbrenner, McClelland, Wethington, Moen, & Ceci, 1996). In affluent areas, parents are particularly concerned with the hostile and restrictive environment in which they live and how incidents of discrimination affect their children (D. B. Miller & MacIntosh, 1999).

Socialization in Ethnic Cultures

Ethnic family cultures provide the bedrock of child socialization and comprise several important dimensions. One of the most important dimensions is that socialization is considered a collective activity. A striking feature of socialization among ethnic minorities is the use of extended networks (Bowman & Howard, 1985; M. Thompson, 1986). In many African American communities, parenting is shared through the *kin network*—relatives by blood and marriage and close nonfamily ties who often enhance the family's strength and resilience (Scannapieco & Jackson, 1996; Stack, 1974).

Socialization among ethnic communities often goes beyond the extended kinship network. For example, African Americans have established their own support systems, such as black-owned businesses, funeral homes, churches, and black organizations, including the Urban League and the National Association for the Advancement of Colored People (NAACP; Bagley & Carroll, 1998).

In her autobiography, Public Broadcasting System television journalist and Peabody Award winner Charlayne Hunter-Gault recalled her support network on the day she and Hamilton Holmes, former director of Grady Hospital in Atlanta and now deceased, integrated the University of Georgia in 1961:

> On January 9, 1961, I walked onto the campus at the University of Georgia to begin registering for classes. Ordinarily, there would not have been anything unusual about such a routine exercise, except, in this instance, the officials at the university had been fighting for two years to keep me out. I was not socially, intellectually, or morally desirable. I was Black. And no Black student had ever been admitted to the University of Georgia in its 176-year history. . . . It would take us two and a half years of

> fighting our way through the system and the courts, but finally, with the help of the NAACP Legal Defense and Educational Fund, Inc., and with the support of family and friends, we won the right that should have been ours all along. (Hunter-Gault, 1992, p. 3)

Socialization among ethnic minorities has a strong spiritual component. That is, the teaching of a belief system is a central element in child socialization and is often recognized as a protective factor in children's lives. There is also mounting research corroborating the fact that religion can help people cope with threatening events, thus contributing to their resilience (Ellison, 1993). In a study of the role of Sunday school as it relates to socialization practices, Haight (1998) found that in a society that was "viewed as negligent at best and virulently racist at worst . . . church was described as a haven in which children could learn about their heritage from other African Americans who valued and nurtured them" (p. 216).

Perhaps the central goals of socialization among parents of minority children are to provide a buffer against racism and oppression, offering parents a means of interpreting mainstream culture, racism, and conflicts between groups (Boykin & Toms, 1985; Hill et al., 1994). In his book *Makes Me Wanna Holler,* McCall (1994) described one of his mother's socialization strategies:

> Whenever we were going to restaurants or other public places where a lot of white folks would be around, my mother insisted that we get meticulously groomed and pressed beforehand, and when we got there she reminded us (it was more of a threat) to sit, stiff as a soldier, and be quiet. (p. 12)

The family plays a critical role in socialization in a society that may even cultivate negative conceptions of minority group members through direct action, the media, and institutional barriers. Families may have to act as a buffer filtering and insulating children from negative experiences encountered in the larger society (Jackson, McCullough, & Gurin, 1988). For example, in a study of self-esteem among black children, Clark (1992) found that general self-esteem was linked to physical appearance, particularly skin color. As Roger Wilkins (1982)—former assistant attorney general under President Lyndon B. Johnson, president of the Urban League, and currently endowed professor of history and U.S. culture at George Mason University in Virginia—attested in his autobiography:

> America told us we were inferior, and most of us believed it. . . . Until I lived in Grand Rapids among all those white people I never had been forced to confront the enormity of the inferiority that America had slammed into my soul, and despite the fierce pride as human beings my family had, I couldn't help but accept it.

> I didn't look like my friends, and I didn't have their heritage. Parents didn't tell Negro children in those days of the heroism, intelligence and courage that it took for their slave ancestors to survive during that brutal time. (p. 47)

The socialization of white children and children of color differs because of messages received from the broader society about the value and identity of a child's ethnic group. Generally speaking, white children are encouraged by the images they perceive in the media, whereas black children are often faced with derogatory or ambivalent messages at best (Hawkins & Jones, 1989). The difficulties parents experience as they attempt to achieve racial socialization were best described by Peters (1985):

> The socialization of children in Black families occurs within the mundane extreme [stressful] environment of real or potential racial discrimination and prejudice. The tasks Black parents share with all parents—providing for and raising children—not only are performed within . . . the stress of racism but include the responsibility of raising physically and emotionally healthy children who are Black in a society in which being Black has negative connotation. This is racial socialization. (p. 161)

Socialization of children may also differ among those who immigrate to the United States. As pointed out by Lee (2010), new immigrants are concerned about creating a safe and secure environment for their children:

> We talk about what happened to us in a day and listen to others' stories. Traditionally in Korea, fathers are assumed to talk more than children at a dinner table. I have been changed. My viewpoint has been mixed in the U.S. I had very traditional Korean viewpoints, but I have been changed for the last 10, 20, 30 years. (p. 23)

Proactive Socialization

How does the family socialize a child to face such racist feelings and become a highly successful adult? Adaptive responses have been examined from multiple perspectives. For example, Boykin and Toms (1985) contended that African American families are faced with a triple quandary in raising their children that involves a dynamic interrelationship among three rivaling socialization contexts: (1) socialization in the mainstream U.S. society, (2) socialization informed by oppressed minority status, and (3) socialization connected to a proximal black cultural context that is largely unbalanced with the social dictates of mainstream U.S. life. Other questions asked have included the following: Is an individual taught to take an active or a passive role in confronting racism and oppression? Does the individual fully or marginally participate in mainstream institutions? Does the individual work toward systems maintenance or systems change?

To try to answer these questions, researchers have examined the effects of *proactive socialization* (Hill et al., 1994; Peters, 1985), a process by which minority children consciously learn to understand the multiple demands they must face. It is an active attempt by the family and other socializing agents to strengthen cultural pride and group identity while "integrating select values of the ethnic and mainstream culture" (Hill et al., 1994, p. 77). In a study of how 30 black children were socialized, Peters (1985) found that raising black children in a society that devalues blacks was a difficult task for black families. Parents knew that their children would ultimately experience racism and believed it was their responsibility to both provide care and teach children how to survive prejudice and discrimination. To be able to cope with prejudice, parents thought it was important that children develop self-respect and pride, understand that fair play may not be reciprocal, and give a good education a top priority. The literature suggests that parents who proactively socialize their children and make them aware of the consequences of ethnic and racial barriers are more likely to have competent children (Bowman & Howard, 1985). The parents of successful children also tend to emphasize ethnic pride, motivate their children, and point out the importance of achievement and upward mobility.

For example, Carranza (2007), who studied 32 Salvadoran mothers and daughters who had settled in Canada, provided documentation of how parents can foster resilience and resistance to racism and discrimination. Salvadoran mothers taught their daughters strategies to resist prejudice, focusing on raising consciousness, stressing ethnic pride, and continuing to speak their native tongue of Spanish. The result was the daughters feeling a sense of belonging and pride in their Salvadoran roots. This allowed them "to carry sources of strength and resilience" (p. 398).

The Self

Several theorists have described the development of the self among minority children. They have provided a foundation for understanding how family and community socialization can protect children from the adverse effects of discrimination (Chestang, 1972; T. Cross, 1998; Erikson, 1959; Mead, 1934). For example, Erikson (1963) postulated that people solidify their personal identity—or historical and self-representation with its links to one's past, present, and future—during adolescence, from ages 12 through 22. At this time, young adults are seen as particularly vulnerable to risk, and to achieve competence, they need specific attention from families, schools, and role models (Benard, 1997).

Similarly, Mead (1934) contended that the self is essentially a social construction that arises through social experiences. He organized the self into two dimensions: (1) the "I," or the spontaneous aspects of self; and (2) the "me," or the organized expectations of others. From this perspective, a person develops a self-image as good or bad, attractive or ugly, and so forth as part of his or her social encounters. The process of taking on the attitude of the wider society in regard to oneself is called the *generalized other* (Cooley, 1956). Families and other socializing agents in the community can help their children cope with a negative public image of the self by teaching survival skills and affirming ethnic pride.

Nontraditional Views of the Self

The study of self-development processes has been dominated by an Anglo-Saxon ideal (Boykin & Toms, 1985); many of the traditional views about development have been biased toward a Western orientation that suggests that people develop an autonomous or independent self. However, in the past three decades, theorists have developed conceptual models that originate from specific sociocultural frames of reference. According to Nobles (1973), an African view of the self should be contrasted with a Western view encompassing the concept of "we." The idea of "we" extends the notion of the self and is more inclusive of community or ethnic group behaviors. This expanded conceptualization of the development of the self within the context of ethnicity, race, class, gender, culture, and so forth promotes an understanding of how healthy people develop connections with, and empathy for, others (Chestang, 1972; T. Cross, 1998; McGoldrick & Carter, 1999). Furthermore, according to Boykin and Toms (1985), rather than "using an Anglocentric perspective yardstick by which to judge normalcy, [these new conceptualizations have] provided fresh insights into the resilience, adaptive strength, and integrity attendant to [black] families" (p. 36).

Relational View of the Self

Ethnic groups frequently assume a relational perspective to the development of the self. A relational perspective to human development explores psychological growth as "a process of differentiation and separation *in* relationships rather than disengagement and separation *from* relationships" (Genero, 1998, p. 33). Mutually close relationships are maintained through openness and emotional availability. For example, Daly, Jennings, Beckett, and Leashore (1995) have pointed out that the Africentric paradigm suggests that humanity be viewed as a collective with shared responsibility for the well-being of others.

FIGURE 9.3 Relational Worldview Model

The things listed below are meant to be examples only. All of life and existence is included in the circle. Balance between all four of these parts brings harmony and harmony is the same as health. Nothing in the circle can change without every other thing in the circle changing as well. The circle is in constant change due to the cycles of the days, weeks, and seasons and because of development and changing experience. We are said to be ill if the circle becomes out of balance. Lack of balance causes "dis-ease." In this way of looking at health or mental health, healing may come from any or all of the four parts of the circle.

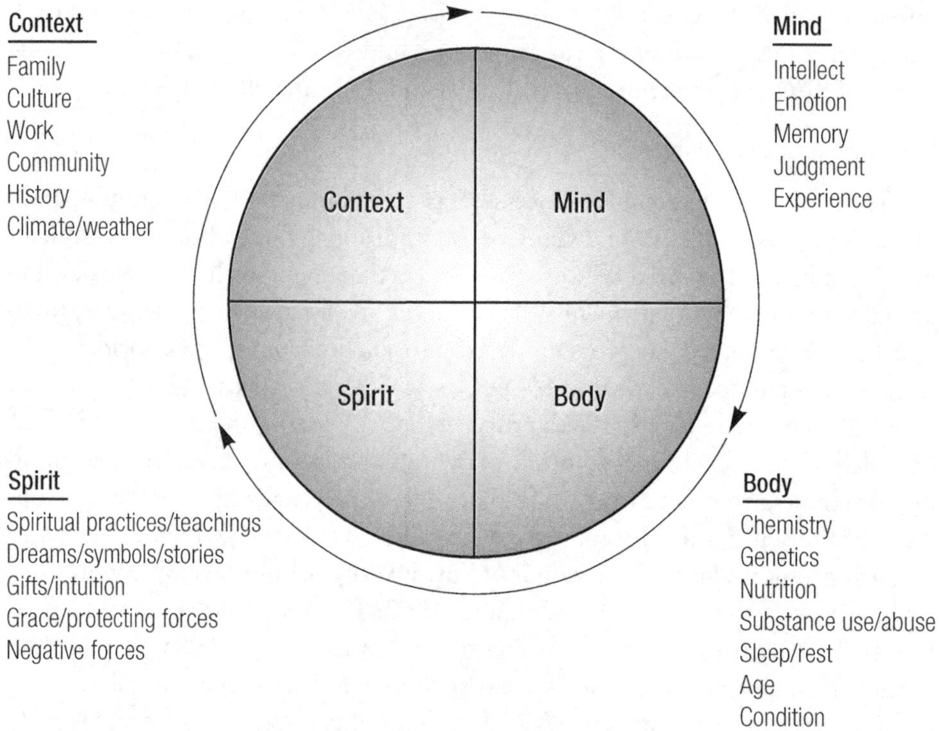

Source: From "Understanding Family Resiliency from a Relational World View," by T. L. Cross, 1998, in *Native American and Immigrant Families*, p. 148. Copyright 1998 by Sage Publications. Reprinted with permission.

Similarly, T. Cross (1998) described the relational worldview based on Native American tribal culture as "the collective thought process of a people or a cultural group" (p. 144). A relational model of the self that stems from tribal cultures encompasses four interacting evolving factors: (1) context, or culture, community, family, and so forth; (3) spirit, or metaphysical or innate forces; (3) mind, or cognitive processes such as thought and emotions; and (4) body, or physical aspects such as sleep and nutrition (see Figure 9.3).

Self and a Hostile Environment

Chestang (1972) was among the earliest theorists to call attention to the way in which the environment can be detrimental to the development of the self. He suggested that *social injustice*, or the denial of legal rights, and *societal inconsistency*, or the double standard for blacks and whites and the disparity between societal ideals and actions, can lead to a feeling of personal impotence or a sense that one is powerless to remove these prejudicial conditions. Chestang argued that children who are not protected from hostile environments could develop a deprecated self characterized by suspicion and mistrust. He recognized that one purpose of the black family was to nurture, protect, and sustain a child so that the child does not develop a negative sense of self. According to Chestang, through the nurturing environment of the family, children can develop a transcendent character—a character with faith, hope, and optimism and a belief in people's essential humanity.

Chestang (1984) researched his theory about the process and dynamics of identity formation among a group of 20 black Americans. He wanted to understand how they were able to establish a transcendent sense of identity despite limited opportunities and obstacles to success. On the basis of accounts of their lives, Chestang attributed their success to forbearance and perseverance as well as to their decision to prove themselves competent. According to Chestang, the analysis of group members' lives led him to believe that the self is defined through racial identification, support, cohesion, and pride. Chestang illustrated this point by quoting Ethel Waters (1952), a Hollywood screen actress who transformed the image of black actresses. She spoke of her own resilience:

> I have the soundest of reasons for being proud of my people. We Negroes have always had such a tough time that our survival in this white world with the dice always loaded against us is the greatest possible testimonial to our strength, our courage, and our immunity to adversity. (p. 92)

Chestang (1972) concluded that people who have overcome adversity "chose a particular path because of their socialization, especially the sense of pride, self-respect, and hope for the future that was laid down for them in the early interactions with their families" (p. 84).

The Social Worker's Role in Intervention

According to Van Voorhis (1998), culturally relevant social work practice synthesizes information about the psychosocial effects of oppression with the skills of listening to clients' stories, evaluating the psychosocial effects of oppression on clients, intervening to promote identity and change oppressive social conditions, and appraising practice strategies. Listening to the stories of clients who have been oppressed is in itself a "revolutionary act, because their lives and experiences have typically been ignored by people at the center" (p. 101). Assessing the effects of oppression involves understanding *violations,* or roadblocks to client freedom and independence; *alienation,* or a lack of synchronicity between a client and the larger society; *identity formation,* or the degree to which a client claims his or her identity; and *patterns of coping with oppression,* or the manner in which the client faces life at the margin.

By providing culturally sensitive services that enhance a family's adaptive mechanisms, social workers can foster resilience among oppressed children and families. Effective cross-cultural social service delivery also embodies programs that foster clients' coping strategies by strengthening their connection with their own ethnic group (Pinderhughes, 1989). For example, social workers who are respectful of cultural differences must understand that, in some communities, the basis of healing may involve *natural helpers*—people who are members of the community. When a Native American is in need of help, he or she first goes to the immediate family. If the problem is not resolved, he or she seeks out members of his or her social network. The next step in help seeking is consulting a spiritual or religious leader and then the tribal council. If all else fails, the person may use a formal agency (Lewis, 1980).

Helping professionals can also foster hope in people's lives by supporting their clients' spirituality. In addition, social workers have been urged to help children form bonds with traditional community socializing institutions, such as schools and houses of worship, whereas Native Hawaiians have established specific social support networks that are available to enhance a child's socialization (E. Thompson, McCubbin, Thompson, & Elver, 1998). Such bonds can serve as protective mechanisms for children exposed to risks such as crime and other community violence (Hawkins, Lishner, & Catalano, 1985).

Researchers are increasingly urging policy makers to create social services that foster resilience. For example, Garbarino (1992) has argued that seven factors are needed to raise resilient children and families: (1) a stable environment, (2) security, (3) emotionally positive time together, (4) a strong belief system, (5) an active and caring community, (6) justice, and (7) access to basic resources. In a similar vein, Schorr and Schorr (1988) have contended that

> successful [social services] programs try to reduce the barriers—of money, time, fragmentation, geographic and psychological remoteness. Rather than to wait passively to serve only those who make it through the daunting maze, these programs persevere to reach the perplexed,

discouraged, and ambivalent, the hardest to reach, who are often the ones to benefit most.

> In successful programs, professionals are able to redefine their roles to respond to severe, but often unarticulated, needs. . . . These professionals have found a way to escape the constraints of a professional value system that confers highest status on those who deal with issues from which all human complexity has been removed. (p. 259)

Researchers are also pressing for interventions that help clients affirm life's meaning, seek to give people control over their own lives, and assist with community structural change (Aponte, 1994; Garbarino, 1992). In his book *Race Matters,* Cornel West (1993), who has taught at Harvard, Princeton, and Yale universities, captured the challenge:

> One essential step is some form of large-scale public intervention to ensure access to basic social goods—housing, food, health care, education, child care, and jobs. We must invigorate the common good with a mixture of government, business, and labor that does not follow any existing blueprint. . . . Let us hope and pray that the vast intelligence, imagination, humor, and courage of Americans will not fail us. Either we learn a new language of empathy and compassion, or the fire this time will consume us all. (p. 13)

Reminiscences, Resilience, and Social Work Practice

MARGARET L. EVANS

As I pondered the content of the chapter "Raising Children in an Oppressive Environment," I reflected on my own childrearing, especially in the South during the segregation era of the 1950s and 1960s. I then began a somewhat cathartic journey. My journey began with a statement about my family, particularly with my father, who was my primary role model into my adulthood until his death in 1995. It is a reflection about resilient socialization.

As I recalled my father's contributions to his family and the African American community in which we lived, I felt a tremendous surge of pride. Notwithstanding his flaws, this pride was not only because of what he gave to me as my father, but also because of what he gave to our community as an African American. He provided our family with a strong, supportive, positive self-image, including an environment of high expectations and a hard work ethic, which was facilitated by his role modeling.

His work ethic as a person without formal education beyond the elementary school level was proof that even in a very oppressive society of segregation and racial tension, one could achieve success as defined by the majority population. His storytelling of his life events included his grandmother, who had been a slave and the family matriarch, and his father, a white musician who was not allowed by law to be in my father's life. That stigma had created within my father, a child born from an unlawful relationship, extraordinary resilience and coping mechanisms. This resilience propelled him to create a life for his family and a place in our community that would foster respect and success according to the standards of both the white and African American communities.

In the days of community segregation, my dad described our town of 10,000 residents as a "one-horse" town, and with amusement and truth called himself "the horse" in our part of town (the segregated black community). My stepmother, from age 10 years, was an elementary schoolteacher and later a principal. My family was very fortunate to have been the first middle-class black family in the community and held that status throughout my childhood.

My father was the person to whom blacks and whites in our community looked for support and resolution when problems occurred. African Americans came to him for employment recommendations, financial assistance, college recommendations, and advice on how to intervene with the legal system and government. He registered blacks to vote, carried them to the polls, and lobbied for politicians who would ensure that policies would benefit our community. He was highly respected by local and state politicians. My first job as a college student was secured from his call to the governor for an employment reference on my behalf. I still have that letter as a reminder of his political advocacy.

Like my father, I was the firstborn in the family, taking on the prescribed role of pathfinder and pioneer for the siblings who followed. In his case there were several siblings. In my case there is one younger sister—17 years younger. My first experience in such a pioneer role was when I was six years old. I was the first African American to take piano lessons and give piano recitals. I was aware that my piano teacher, who was white, closed the drapes across the large picture window where the piano sat when I came for weekly lessons. However, I was not acutely aware of the danger for her safety or mine until much later. I had confidence in my dad's decision making and his constant reminder that I could achieve the way to success and a life wherever I wanted to live only through education and by having a variety of skills to market. In later years I was able to participate in integrated music recitals. Subsequently, during my high school years, I was a member of the traveling school choir, and another family member was a member of the high school band.

Because of the size of our community, cultural events were not offered; consequently, we took many trips to large cities for exposure to those events. I spent my summer vacations in northern cities with relatives and family friends. These trips were designed to broaden my sense of the world outside the segregated South and increase my exposure to life's opportunities for African Americans.

During the 1990s, I returned to live in the South. The reality of being employed and having been appointed to community board positions that had not previously been held by African Americans brought up many memories of the early years of segregation. Each of these situations required me to draw from my survival library a series of coping resources, because my instinct was to pave the rocky road for others who would come after me.

The coping mechanisms and survival strategies I learned from my dad and stepmother were invaluable. Many instances of traumatic and adversarial events threatened my psyche from a social and professional perspective. However, my strength continues to be nurtured by my early socialization and the notion of "keeping my eye on the prize," which was always instilled in my upbringing.

The important and sustaining lessons that were "modeled" came from historical anecdotes, actual events, and life's successes. Perhaps the most important lessons learned were those that taught me how to look for the "rules of the game" and devise a strategy to conform to the rules and not to compromise my own values in the process. This is a delicate balancing act to live in and embrace my world of "blackness" while maintaining my sense of individuality and openness to other cultures. I have been fortunate to live in several states in the North and South and have gained a keener acknowledgment of the socialization of other cultures, which, in part, has helped me value more deeply what I had taken for granted for so many years.

Professional intervention by social workers can be enhanced by their knowledge and by embracing the cultures of other ethnic groups. Practitioners' knowledge base needs to go beyond the external reading of information and get beneath the surface to actually learn about the nuances of different groups. Such nuances may contribute to people's behavioral responses in different situations. Understanding another group's culture requires thinking "outside the box" and, perhaps, outside the social worker's comfort zone. If a social worker is not trained in cultural responses to oppression, he or she may require more supervision or a referral to another practitioner. This approach to intervention requires a new way of thinking and a commitment that exceeds the usual social work curriculum training. One size does not fit all; to generalize oppression, without knowledge of cultural and ethical responses, could impede a client's progress and damage the client–therapist relationship, whether one is working with a case manager or a community organizer.

I have found conclusions in the literature to be "right on" when it comes to resiliency. However, I typically come back to this question: What do we do with the findings? As a profession, social work tends to repeat the same questions in a philosophical way but have a great deal of difficulty applying a proactive action plan for intervention. Is it because the profession asks questions of the majority? Is it because the minority groups have focused their energies on "survival" and consequently may offer insufficient responses? Is it because minority groups are segregated and unable to see commonalties that perhaps could have a greater influence if expressed collectively? Is it because minority groups have maintained their individuality to the extent that they have created irreconcilable differences between themselves and others?

Living in two worlds—one's own culture and the mainstream culture that historically has been oppressive—is not an easy task, but then who said life was meant to be easy? Life's successes are achieved and maintained through the strength and resilience that come from a variety of internal resources. It takes daily vigilance. However, the rewards are great, and one feels a tremendous sense of accomplishment despite of the adversarial roadblocks that arise.

Thoughts on Resilience

NORMA J. TAYLOR

Just a few thoughts on "Raising Children in an Oppressive Environment": I am a product of World War II, born 11 years before schools were integrated in 1954. I was raised in Cincinnati, Ohio, the heart of the Midwest, a city considered by some to be progressive, albeit conservative. My family was slightly above the working poor, according to the economic classifications, with both parents working—my father in the steel mills and my mother in food preparation in a large hospital. The work ethic was very strong in my family, perhaps because of our labor union affiliation.

A major theme throughout my childhood was the importance of a good education—that meant college. Both parents had a high school education. My mother, although smart enough to have attended college, was unable to do so for economic reasons and racial discrimination. So she was going to make certain that her children received higher education regardless of the sacrifices she had to make. She also believed that if you steer the oldest child—me—in the right direction, the other children would follow that lead. Therefore, I was pushed toward college very early in my life. Of course, the fact that I attended predominantly white schools and my peers were college bound also influenced me.

Much of the time during my adolescence, I thought I was fulfilling my mother's unrealized dream of a college education. Interestingly enough, there was a double edge to my mother's prodding. Although encouraged to achieve, on the one hand, I was also cautioned, on the other hand, about the dangers of being too ambitious. She warned me about racism and stressed that I would have to work twice as hard to "get ahead." So I was armed with the belief that education, although not a panacea, would at least help to level the playing field a little.

Although the inequality between the races was a constant theme, you were still expected to be true to your ideals no matter what. So I was given a sense of determination to move ahead despite the seeming obstacles that would confront me because of my racial heritage. What I observed about my parents, some family members, and friends was that they were able to cope with whatever came their way. My parents had come through the Great Depression and two world wars, and they were still intact. They had resilience that was passed on to their children. That does not mean that I or my siblings coped in the exact manner as my parents but that we were taught that striving forward is how one lives in this world.

A critical ingredient in a resilience model for an African American or for any person is perseverance. The ability to stick it out and continue to forge ahead, despite the obstacles that are in your path. My mother is a survivor, and she passed that desire on to everyone she met. It is this sense of believing and knowing that one can overcome a particular situation.

I believe that each of us has the innate qualities of resilience and perseverance; however, not everyone chooses to exercise these abilities. Somewhere along the road of life, an individual has to be shown how to be resilient, usually through an example such as parents, family members, a teacher, a coach, a religious leader, a mentor, or just someone you choose to emulate. In other words, someone has to assist you in understanding that life is a series of ups and downs, bumps and bruises, and the victory goes to the individual who decides to continue running the race without giving up.

Resilience has another component, and I am uncertain what to call it. In my mind, resilience works best, especially for me as a woman of color, when I can approach life without a lot of negative feelings about myself and without bitterness toward those who are in the majority. Otherwise, what is the point of persevering? I think of resilience as almost a peaceful self-empowering spirit that gives one the will to fight. It was this kind of spirit that was evident during the Civil Rights movement in the 1950s and 1960s. You see everyone has the capacity to be resilient. One can say that the thousands of men and women who are in correctional facilities for long periods of time exhibit a degree of resilience. However, the quality of their lives is questionable.

I like the resilience method of practice because it deals with an individual's strengths, rather than weaknesses or pathology. I would love to believe that this approach is appreciated and embraced within the social work foundation courses and the entire curricula. I doubt this is the case. So my question is, Who will teach this approach to practice? This is really a paradigm shift from what is presently taught. Yes, you will teach it in your human behavior class, but who will make the connection between human behavior, practice, research, and the other courses in those other schools of social work? Unless things have changed drastically, most students come with an altruistic desire to assist others whom they believe are in need of some guidance and/or therapy. The resilience model, once applied, really asks the social worker to work herself (or himself) out of a job. Because I believe that this kind of coping mechanism is inherent within each person, it would be a matter of evaluating an individual's strengths and then assisting her (or him) in the acquisition of additional strengths. Of course, this is the simplistic version.

Now that I am connected with the Child and Family Service Agency in Washington, DC, my thoughts are always focused on teaching social workers in a public human services environment. Although I agree totally with a strengths-based model, I find that social workers, at least the ones at my agency, are not familiar with this approach. Once exposed to this approach through training (there is a three-day training course titled "Strengths-Based Interventions in Child Welfare"), few are willing to use it because of a number of factors: the high volume of cases, the fact that the nature of the work often involves the removal of children from the birth parent, the belief that the social worker is saving the child from a mother who should not have her or him, and the pressure of time. In an agency that operates in a crisis mode and has few resources, thoughts of resilience or strengths-based interventions often seem like a luxury. I am not trying to make excuses; I am just trying to find application for resilience theory and approach in my present setting. If I worked as a therapist in the public or private sector, I would be more willing to totally embrace the resilience approach.

The model assumes that social workers want to do good, that is, they want to be helpful to their clients through empowering them and assisting them in achieving a better quality of life. This may be true as long as you do not introduce racial, cultural, or ethnic prejudices. It is extremely difficult, if not impossible, for someone who is Caucasian to understand what it is like to be an African American or any other ethnic minority. There is no way to adequately explain what it is like to be treated "less than" merely because of one's skin color or cultural background. Discrimination is something that is experienced not just for a day or two but for a lifetime, and it is a legacy that is passed on. Racism is so institutionalized that it has become a fundamental part of our society. There must be a minority, that is, someone on the bottom, in order for the majority, those at the top, to look good. Most Caucasians have no reference point to work effectively with African Americans and other groups of color because their basic values and life experiences are so very different. Although the social work profession embraces self-determination, it is hard to actualize this when one is convinced that there is something wrong with your clients because their life experiences do not mirror your own.

So, is there a solution? I do not know. I am clear that until social workers can genuinely respect their clients as people of worth, it will be impossible for them to recognize the strengths of the human spirit. Without this recognition, social workers will engage in activities and in case plans that can serve as an obstacle to the resilience model. I hope I have not sounded too negative. I have spent my life working and walking in two worlds, one African American and one white. At this juncture, I see two parallel paths, and I find it harder and harder to see a true coming together in equality and harmony. Yet I know there must be a working together for the good of the nation and for the good of the universe. I just don't know how we get there in peace and love.

Use the CD by Michael Wright to articulate the dual perspective of the immediate environment and the larger society. Define terms, including *culture, race, ethnicity,* and *minority.*
You will find a case study on your CD: *Watching "Your Children Are So Well Behaved"*

References

Aponte, H. J. (1994). *Bread and spirit: Therapy with the new poor.* New York: Norton.

Arroyo, C. G., & Zigler, E. (1995). Racial identity, academic achievement, and the psychological well-being of economically disadvantaged adolescents. *Journal of Personality and Social Psychology, 69,* 903–914.

Attneave, R. (1982). American Indians and Alaska Native families: Emigrants in their own homeland. In M. McGoldrick, J. K. Pearce, & J. Giordano (Eds.), *Ethnicity and family therapy* (pp. 55–83). New York: Guilford Press.

Auslander, W. F., Thompson, S. J., Dreitzer, D., & Santiago, J. V. (1997). Mothers' satisfaction with medical care: Perceptions of racism, family stress, and medical outcomes in children with diabetes. *Health & Social Work, 22,* 190–199.

Backer, T. L., & Backer, J. P. (1996). *The WPA Oklahoma slave narratives.* Norman: University of Oklahoma Press.

Bagley, C. A., & Carroll, J. (1998). Healing forces in African-American families. In H. I. McCubbin, E. A. Thompson, A. I. Thompson, & J. A. Futrell (Eds.), *Resiliency in African-American families* (pp. 117–142). Thousand Oaks, CA: Sage.

Benard, B. (1997). *Turning it around for all youth: From risk to resilience.* New York: ERIC Clearinghouse on Urban Education. (ERIC Document Reproduction Service No. ED412309.) Retrieved from http://www.eric.ed.gov/PDFS/ED412309.pdf

Billingsley, A. (1968). *Black families in white America.* Englewood Cliffs, NJ: Prentice Hall.

Bowman, P. J., & Howard, C. (1985). Race-related socialization, motivation, and academic achievement: A study of black youths in three-generation families. *Journal of American Academy of Child Psychiatry, 24,* 134–141.

Boykin, A. W., & Toms, F. D. (1985). Black child socialization: A conceptual framework. In H. P. McAdoo & J. L. McAdoo (Eds.), *Black children* (pp. 33–52). Beverly Hills, CA: Sage.

Brodsky, A. (1996). Resilient single mothers in risky neighborhoods: Negative psychological sense of community. *Journal of Community Psychology, 24,* 347–363.

Brodsky, A. (1999). "Making it": Among urban, African-American, single mothers. *American Journal of Orthopsychiatry, 69,* 148–160.

Bronfenbrenner, U., McClelland, P., Wethington, E., Moen, P., & Ceci, S. (1996). *The state of Americans.* New York: Free Press.

Bush, J. A., Norton, D. G., Sanders, C. L., & Solomon, B. B. (1983). An integrative approach for the inclusion of content on blacks in social work education. In J. C. Chun, P. J. Dunston, & F. Ross-Sheriff (Eds.), *Mental health and people of color* (pp. 97–126). Washington, DC: Howard University Press.

Carranza, M. (2007). Building resilience and resistance against racism and discrimination among Salvadorian female youth in Canada. *Child and Family Social Work, 12,* 390–398.

Carter, C. S. (1999). Church burning in African America communities: Implications for empowerment practice. *Social Work, 44,* 62–68.

Chestang, L. W. (1972). *Character development in a hostile society* (Occasional Paper No. 3). Chicago: School of Social Service Administration.

Chestang, L. W. (1984). Racial and personal identity in the black experience. In B. W. White (Ed.), *Color in a white society* (pp. 83–94). Silver Spring, MD: NASW Press.

Clark, M. L. (1992). Racial group concept and self-esteem in black children. In H. Burlew, W. C. Banks, H. P. McAdoo, & D. A. Azibo (Eds.), *African American psychology: Theory, research, and practice* (pp. 159–172). Newbury Park, CA: Sage.

Clay, R. A. (2000). *Monitor.* Retrieved from http://www.apa.org/monitor/aug96/faithd.html

Cohen, H., & Greene, R. R. (2005). Older adults who overcame oppression. *Families in Society, 87*(1), 1–8.

Cooley, C. H. (1956). *Human nature and the social order.* New York: Free Press.

Cross, T. (1998). Understanding family resiliency from a relational world view. In H. I. McCubbin, E. A. Thompson, A. I. Thompson, & J. E. Fromer (Eds.), *Resiliency in Native American and immigrant families* (pp. 143–158). Thousand Oaks, CA: Sage.

Cross, W. E. (1991). *Shades of black: Diversity in African-American identity.* Philadelphia, PA: Temple University Press.

Daly, A., Jennings, J., Beckett, J., & Leashore, B. R. (1995). Effective coping strategies of African Americans. *Social Work, 40,* 240–248.

Davis, K., Leijenaar, M., & Oldersma, J. (Eds.). (1991). *The gender of power.* Newbury Park, CA: Sage.

Denby, R. W. (1996). Resiliency and the African American family: A model of family preservation. In S.L. Logan (Ed.), *The black family strengths, self-help, and positive change* (144–163). Boulder, CO: Westview Press.

Devore, W., & Schlesinger, E. G. (1996). *Ethnic-sensitive social work practice.* Boston: Allyn & Bacon.

DuBois, W. E. B. (1903). *Souls of black folk.* Chicago: McClurg.

Dubrow, N. F., & Garbarino, J. (1989). Living in the war zone: Mothers and young children in a public housing development. *Child Welfare, 58,* 3–20.

Ellison, C. (1993). Religious involvement and self-perception among black Americans. *Social Forces, 71,* 1027–1055.

Erikson, E. H. (1959). *Identity and the life cycle.* New York: Norton.

Erikson, E. H. (1963). *Childhood and society.* New York: Norton.

Ewalt, P., Freeman, E. M., Kirk, S., & Poole, D. L. (Eds.). (1996). *Multicultural issues in social work.* Washington, DC: NASW Press.

Garbarino, J. (1992). The meaning of poverty in the world of children. *American Behavioral Scientist, 35,* 220–237.

Garbarino, J. (1995). *Raising children in a socially toxic environment.* San Francisco: Jossey-Bass.

Garbarino, J. (1999). *Lost boys: Why our sons turn out violent and how we can save them.* New York: Free Press.

Garbarino, J., Dubrow, N., Kostelny, K., & Pardo, C. (1992). *Children in danger: Coping with the consequences of community violence.* San Francisco: Jossey-Bass.

Garbarino, J., Kostelny, K., & Dubrow, N. (1991). What children can tell us about living in danger. *American Psychologist, 46,* 376–383.

Garmezy, N. (1991). Resilience in children's adaptation to negative life events and stressed environments. *Pediatric Annals, 20,* 459–466.

Genero, N. P. (1998). Culture, resiliency, and mutual psychological development. In H. I. McCubbin, E. A. Thompson, A. I. Thompson, & J. A. Futrell (Eds.), *Resiliency in African-American families* (pp. 31–48). Thousand Oaks, CA: Sage.

Germain, C. B. (1992). A conversation with Carel Germain on human development in the ecological context. In M. Bloom (Ed.), *Changing lives: Studies in human development and professional helping* (pp. 406–409). Columbia: University of South Carolina Press.

Goldenberg, I. (1978). *Oppression and social intervention.* Chicago: Nelson-Hall.

Green, J. (1999). *Cultural awareness in the human services.* Boston: Allyn & Bacon.

Greene, M. (1996). *The temple bombing.* Reading, MA: Addison-Wesley.

Greene, R. R. (2002). Holocaust survivors: A study in resilience. *Journal of Gerontological Social Work, 37*(1), 3–18.

Greene, R. R. (2008). *Human behavior theory: A diversity framework.* New Brunswick, NJ: Transaction Press.

Greene, R. R. (2010). A study of Holocaust Survivors: Implications for curriculum. *Journal of Social Work Education, 46,* 293–304.

Greene, R. R., & Watkins, M. (Eds.). (1998). *Serving diverse constituencies: An ecological perspective.* New York: Aldine de Gruyter.

Greif, G., Hrabowski, F., & Maton, K. (1998). African American fathers of high achieving sons: Using outstanding members of an at-risk population to guide intervention. *Families in Society, 79,* 45–52.

Haight, W. (1998). "Gathering the spirit" at First Baptist Church: Spirituality as a protective factor in the lives of African American children. *Social Work, 43,* 213–221.

Hawkins, D., & Jones, N. (1989). Black adolescents and the criminal justice system. In R. L. Jones (Ed.), *Black adolescents* (pp. 403–428). Berkeley, CA: Cobbs & Henry.

Hawkins, D., Lishner, D., & Catalano, R. R., Jr. (1985). Childhood predictors and the prevention of adolescent substance abuse. In C. L. R. Jones & R. J. Battjes (Eds.), *Etiology of drug abuse* (NIDA Drug Research Monograph No. 56, pp. 75–125). Rockville, MD: National Institute of Drug Abuse.

Helton, L. R., & Jackson, M. (1997). *Social work with families: A diversity model.* Boston: Allyn & Bacon.

Hill, H. M., Soriano, F. I., Chen, S. A., & La Fromboise, T. D. (1994). Sociocultural factors in the etiology and prevention of violence among ethnic minority youth. In L. D. Eron, J. H. Gentry, & P. Schlegel (Eds.), *Reason to hope* (pp. 59–100). Washington, DC: American Psychological Association.

Hines, P. M., Preto, N. G., McGoldrick, M., Almeida, R., & Weltman, S. (1999). Culture and the family life cycle. In B. Carter & M. McGoldrick (Eds.), *The expanded family life cycle: Individual, family, and social perspectives* (pp. 69–87). Needham Heights, MA: Allyn & Bacon.

hooks, b. (1984). *Feminist theory: From center to margin.* Boston: South End.

Hoops, J. G. (1982). Oppression based on color. *Social Work, 27,* 3–5.

Howe, I. (1982). *A margin of hope.* San Diego: Harcourt Brace Jovanovich.

Hunter-Gault, C. (1992). *In my place.* New York: Farrar, Straus & Giroux.

Jackson, J. S., McCullough, W. R., & Gurin, G. (1988). Family, socialization environment, and identity development in black children. In H. P. McAdoo (Ed.), *Black families* (2nd ed., pp. 242–256). Beverly Hills, CA: Sage.

La Fromboise, T. D., Coleman, H. L. K., & Gerton, J. (1993). Psychological impact of biculturalism: Evidence and theory. *Psychological Bulletin, 114,* 395–412.

Lee, Y. (2010). Abandoning Hwa-byung. In R. R. Greene, H. Cohen, J. Gonsalez, & Lee, Y. *Narratives of social and economic justice* (pp. 107–120). Washington, DC: NASW Press.

Lewis, R. (1980). Cultural perspective on treatment modalities with Native Americans. In M. Bloom (Ed.), *Life span development* (pp. 434–441). New York: Macmillan.

Lukes, C. A., & Land, H. (1990). Biculturality and homosexuality. *Social Work, 35,* 155–161.

McAdoo, H. P. (1992). Upward mobility and parenting in middle-income black families. In H. Burlew, W. C. Banks, H. P. McAdoo, & D. A. Azibo (Eds.), *African American psychology: Theory, research, and practice* (pp. 63–86). Newbury Park, CA: Sage.

McCall, N. (1994). *Makes me wanna holler.* New York: Vintage Books.

McCubbin, H. I., Thompson, E. A., Thompson, A. I., & Futrell, J. A. (Eds.). (1998). *Resiliency in African-American families.* Thousand Oaks, CA: Sage.

McGoldrick, M., & Carter, B. (1999). Self in context: The individual life cycle in systemic perspective. In B. Carter & M. McGoldrick (Eds.), *The expanded family life cycle: Individual, family, and social perspectives* (pp. 27–44). Needham Heights, MA: Allyn & Bacon.

Mead, G. H. (1934). *Mind, self, and society.* Chicago: University of Chicago Press.

Metzenbaum, H. M. (1994, March 1). Statements on introduced bills and joint resolutions. In *Congressional Record* (Daily ed., pp. S2169–S2183). Washington, DC: U.S. Government Printing Office.

Miller, D. B., & MacIntosh, R. (1999). Promoting resilience in urban African American adolescents: Racial socialization and identity as protective factors. *Social Work Research, 23,* 159–170.

Miller, S. (1980). Reflections on the dual perspective. In E. Mizo & J. Delany (Eds.), *Training for service delivery to minority clients* (pp. 53–61). New York: Family Service Association.

Nobles, W. W. (1973). Psychological research and the black self-concept: A critical review. *Journal of Social Issues, 29,* 11–31.

Norton, D. G. (1978). *The dual perspective: Inclusion of ethnic minority content in the social work curriculum.* New York: Council on Social Work Education.

Ogbu, J. U. (1985). A cultural ecology of competence among inner-city blacks. In M. Spenser, G. K. Brookins, & W. R. Allen (Eds.), *The beginnings: The social and affective development of black children* (pp. 45–66). Hillsdale, NJ: Erlbaum.

Ogbu, J. U. (1988). Cultural diversity and human development. *New Directions for Child Development, 42,* 11–28.

Peters, M. F. (1985). Racial socialization of young black children. In H. P. McAdoo & J. L. McAdoo (Eds.), *Black children* (2nd ed., pp. 159–173). Beverly Hills, CA: Sage.

Peters, M. F. (1988). Parenting in black families with young children: A historical perspective. In H. P. McAdoo (Ed.), *Black families* (2nd ed., pp. 228–241). Beverly Hills, CA: Sage.

Pierce, C. (1969). Violence and counter violence: The need for a children's domestic exchange. *American Journal of Orthopsychiatry, 39,* 553–568.

Pinderhughes, E. B. (1983). Empowerment for our clients and for ourselves. *Social Casework, 64,* 331–338.

Pinderhughes, E. (1989). *Understanding race, ethnicity, and power: The key to efficacy in clinical practice.* New York: Free Press.

Proctor, S. (1995). *The substance of things hoped for: A memoir of African-American faith.* New York: Putnam.

Sampson, R. J., Raudenbush, S. W., & Earls, F. (1997, August 15). Neighborhoods and violent crime: A multilevel study of collective efficacy. *Science, 277,* 918–924.

Scannapieco, M., & Jackson, S. (1996). Kinship care: The African American response to family preservation. *Social Work, 41,* 190–196.

Schorr, L., & Schorr, D. (1988). *Within our reach: Breaking the cycle of the disadvantaged.* New York: Doubleday.

Schriver, J. M. (2001). *Human behavior and the social environment.* Boston: Allyn & Bacon.

Seliger, M. (1996). *When they came to take my father away.* New York: Arcade.

Solomon, B. (1976). *Black empowerment.* New York: Columbia University.

Solomon, B. (1988). The impact of public policy on the status of young black males. In J. T. Gibbs (Ed.), *Young, black, and male in America: An endangered species* (pp. 294–316). Dover, MA: Auburn House.

Stack, C. (1974). *All our kin.* New York: Harper & Row.

Taylor, R. L. (1989). Black youth, role models and the social construction of identity. In R. L. Jones (Ed.), *Black adolescents* (pp. 155–174). Berkeley, CA: Cobbs & Henry.

Thompson, E., McCubbin, H. I., Thompson, A., & Elver, K. M. (1998). Vulnerability and resiliency in Native Hawaiian families under stress. In H. I. McCubbin, E. A. Thompson, A. I. Thompson, & J. E. Fromer (Eds.), *Resiliency in Native American and immigrant families* (pp. 115–139). Thousand Oaks, CA: Sage.

Thompson, M. (1986). The influences of supportive relations on the psychological well-being of teenage mothers. *Social Forces, 64,* 1006–1024.

Thorton, M. (1998). Indigenous resources and strategic resistance: Informal caregiving and racial socialization. In H. I. McCubbin, E. A. Thompson, A. I. Thompson, & J. A. Futrell (Eds.), *Resiliency in African-American families* (pp. 49–66). Thousand Oaks, CA: Sage.

Tully, C. T. (1994). Power and the social work profession. In R. R. Greene (Ed.), *Human behavior theory: A diversity framework* (pp. 235–245). New York: Aldine de Gruyter.

Van Voorhis, R. (1998). Culturally relevant practice: Addressing the psychodynamics of oppression. In R. R. Greene & M. Watkins (Eds.), *Serving diverse constituencies: Applying the ecological perspective* (pp. 97–112). New York: Aldine de Gruyter.

Waters, E. (1952). *His eye is on the sparrow.* New York: Bantam Books.

West, C. (1993). *Race matters.* New York: Vintage Books.

Wiesel, E. (1960). *Night.* New York: Bantam Books.

Wilkins, R. (1982). *A man's life: An autobiography.* New York: Simon & Schuster.

Wilson, W. J. (1973). *Power, racism, and privilege.* New York: Free Press.

Wilson, W. J. (1987). *The truly disadvantaged.* Chicago: University of Chicago Press.

10

Toward a Resilience-based Model of School Social Work: A Turnaround Mentor

GERALD T. POWERS

On finishing this chapter, students will be able to further

Apply critical thinking to inform and communicate professional judgments (Educational Policy 2.1.3) by

- Distinguishing, appraising, and integrating multiple sources of knowledge, including research-based knowledge and practice wisdom (practice behavior).

Our greatest glory is not in never falling, but in rising every time we fall.

—Confucius

Numerous scholars have devoted their professional lives to the study of resilience (see, for example, Anthony, 1987; Garmezy & Rutter, 1983; Smokowski, 1998; Werner & Smith, 1992). Their collective work chronicles the emergence of the resilience construct and the subsequent transition from a deficit- to a strengths-based conception of human behavior. Despite the proliferation of research on how interdependent theories of risk and protective factors help to explain the complex phenomenon of resilience (Fraser, Richman, & Galinsky, 1999; Jenson & Fraser, 2006; Luthar & Zigler, 1991), relatively little has been written about a parallel theory of action. This may in part account for why so many social workers typically endorse a strengths-based perspective but, when pressed to explain it, have so much difficulty articulating exactly how it gets translated into their practice routines. In this chapter, I attempt to overcome the sense of disconnect between professional values related to a strengths-based approach and professional actions. I also explore the meaning of resilience in my own life, and, in so doing, I hope to illustrate basic practice principles.

Background

The resilience construct gained prominence in the professional literature in the 1960 and 1970s in response to a perplexing question: Why is it that so many children seem to have the ability to deal with adversity, despite exposure to severe risk? In the intervening decades, this question has captured the imagination of a growing number of researchers and practitioners in the human services field. The question itself reflects an important conceptual shift in the dominant view of human development. During the 1950s and beyond, the prevailing paradigm was tied to the linear notion that personality evolves over time in response to a series of challenges associated with a set of relatively fixed developmental stages (Erikson, 1950; Kelly, 1955). Given this model, it was assumed that the critical components of personality were for the most part determined during the formative years of psychosexual development. It was believed that once that personality template was in place, it was more or less frozen in time and immutable over the life course.

A number of longitudinal studies based on this notion, such as those of Moss and Susman (1980), attempted to identify patterns of consistency between personality types and the nature of problems encountered at various developmental stages. Although these longitudinal studies failed to sustain the underlying theoretical premise that personality and developmental stages must grow hand in hand, the research itself served to reinforce a deficit view of human behavior, or a view that characterizes individuals as victims of their own epigenetically encoded limitations. Unfortunately, the notion of human development in which one size fits all failed to recognize adequately the combination of idiosyncratic capacities and strengths that speak to individual uniqueness. As Murphy (1962) observed,

> It is something of a paradox that a nation which has exulted in its rapid expansion and its scientific technological achievements should have developed so vast a "problem" literature: a literature often expressing difficulties, social failures, blocked potentialities, and defeat. . . . In applying clinical ways of thinking formulated out of experience with broken adults, we were slow to see how the language of adequacy to meet life's challenges could become the subject matter of psychological science. (p. 17)

Paralleling the development of the deficit model has been a substantial body of epidemiological research indicating that people vary widely in their individual responses to the events of early life, including adversity, depending on the nature and type of subsequent life experiences (Clarke & Clarke, 1984). Many people, including children, simply do not behave the way theorists think they should, given the constellation of toxic conditions in which they live. In fact, Rutter (1989) found that even the most "adverse experiences in infancy carry few risks for later development if the subsequent rearing environment is a good one" (p. 23).

There is an impressive and expanding body of research to support Rutter's (1989) contention. For example, it is well documented that poverty is associated with poor academic achievement (Sherman, 1994). Yet not all poor children fail in school (Duncan, Brooks-Gunn, & Klebanov, 1994). The literature also suggests that adult abusers are more likely to have grown up in abusive families. Yet the vast majority of abused children never become abusers themselves (Farber & Egeland, 1987). Although the children of parents with schizophrenia clearly have a higher risk of also developing the illness (Rende & Plomin, 1993), about 90 percent of these children remain symptom free throughout their lives (Garmezy, 1987). Similar paradoxical findings apply to children of divorce as well as to children who grow up in substance-abusing families (Wolin & Wolin, 1995). A consistent finding across a growing body of both qualitative and quantitative research is that notwithstanding the untoward conditions they experience during their formative years, the overwhelming majority of children grow up to lead rewarding and productive lives (Benard, 2004). As Garmezy noted, these children "upset our prediction tables and in childhood bear the visible indices that are hallmarks of competence—good peer relations, academic achievement, commitment to education and to purposive life goals" (see Masten & Coatsworth, 1998, p. 206).

Rutter (1985) found that "even with the most severe stresses and the most glaring adversities, it is unusual for more than half of children to succumb" (p. 598). How do researchers explain these apparent anomalies, and what can they learn from the lives of those who seem to somehow beat the odds? What are the mitigating or protective factors that seem to not only protect some children from the toxic influence of negative life circumstances, but also somehow empower them to flourish and ultimately thrive? Most important, how can this knowledge be reenvisioned in terms of practice principles that can effectively guide social workers' interventions with children in schools?

The purpose of this chapter is to explore these issues from a personal perspective, from the perspective of what it means to be someone on the receiving end of a strengths-based approach to helping. It is an autobiographical account, the story of how a relationship with a caring adult forever changed the course of my life. It attempts to explain those experiences within the context of a resilience framework, moving back and forth between first-person accounts of personal experiences and a theoretical justification supported by a growing body of empirical research. It concludes with a discussion of how the lessons I learned from this experience can contribute to a resilience model for school-based social work practice consistent with a research foundation.

Problem

It is difficult to pinpoint exactly when I first became aware of the fact that I hated school. It certainly wasn't obvious to me the day I entered the first grade, but it did become increasingly apparent as the year unfolded. At first it was a sort of generalized dislike not clearly associated with anything in particular. As a six-year-old child, I couldn't quite comprehend why I seemed to be so different from my closest friends, all of whom appeared to look forward to the time they spent in school. I can recall the sense of relief I felt each day when the 3 o'clock bell signaled the end of the school day. At 3 o'clock, order was somehow restored to the universe. I could once again compete as an equal with friends whom I was certain had come to view me as a dummy during the previous eight hours.

It was sometime during the second grade that I became aware that my aversion to school was somehow linked to my inability to read. It became increasingly apparent to me that most of the other kids seemed to be enjoying the required reading classes and associated spelling bees. Whereas most of the children competed eagerly for the teacher's attention in their desire to read aloud, I dreaded the public embarrassment and humiliation. The more I struggled to maintain composure, the more anxious I became. I can recall the other students giggling as I stumbled over the simplest of words. Frequent admonishments and the occasional physical punishment served to reinforce the prevailing assumption that I wasn't trying hard enough, a message that elicited both frustration and anger. It took all the bravado I could muster to fight back the tears that accompanied an overwhelming sense of shame.

As is so often the case, what began as a fairly simple and circumscribed problem gradually took on meaning at a much deeper level. Not only was I experiencing difficulties in school, but there was a growing concern among friends and relatives regarding how quiet and shy I had become. By the third grade, it had become obvious to everyone, including my parents, that my inability to read was affecting virtually every aspect of my academic performance. By that time, I was beginning to experience somatic symptoms. Every time I would attempt to read, my eyes would begin to water and I would feel nauseous. I remember being taken to an ophthalmologist in what I suspect was a form of wishful thinking on the part of my parents. Maybe faulty eyesight was the culprit. Maybe a pair of glasses would provide the magical solution to this troubling dilemma. My vision was fine. Because adults were unable to solve "the problem," it became increasingly clear to me that the deficit must reside within me.

As I reflect on this difficult period, I can imagine how this cluster of symptoms might have been viewed within the context of a deficit model had today's managed care environment existed during the 1940s. At the very least, the problem would likely have been classified in the fourth edition of the *Diagnostic and Statistical Manual of Mental Disorders* (*DSM–IV;* American Psychiatric Association, 1994) as a learning disorder coded on Axis II—315.9: "Reading achievement, as measured by individually administered standardized tests of reading accuracy or comprehension, is substantially below that expected given the person's chronological age, measured intelligence, and age-appropriate education" (p. 53). In light of the accompanying excessive anxiety, it would not have been surprising to find a secondary diagnosis on Axis I, such as 300.02—generalized anxiety disorder. Unfortunately, the driving imperative of deficit models such as the *DSM–IV* is essentially one of identifying what is wrong with people. To the extent to which individual liabilities and limitations become the primary locus of the professional's attention, individual strengths tend to get ignored, systemic factors fade into the background, and concern for the transactions between people and their environments becomes largely transparent. As a result, solutions get tied almost exclusively to efforts to remediate personal deficits. Such models not only serve to stigmatize the client, but also tend to divert attention away from any meaningful consideration of the inevitable and remarkable cluster of strengths that seems to reside within every individual as well as the environments they inhabit.

Relationship with a Caring Adult

Over the years, I've come to appreciate some of the simple blessings of having grown up in a small coal-mining town in Pennsylvania more than a half-century ago. Ironically, one of those blessings was the total absence of any formal human services network. At that time, and in that place, when problems emerged, typically one or more members of the extended family handled them informally. In my case, it was my uncle Edgar. It seemed both inevitable and altogether natural to me that he would take me under his wing during this crisis because I had always felt that I held a special place in his life.

The year was 1947, long before the concepts of resilience and strengths-based practice had appeared on the professional horizon. Although he had no formal training in the behavioral sciences, Uncle Edgar seemed to have an intuitive sense of what the concepts of resilience and strength were all about. It has never been clear to me exactly how he had attained these insights. I have always assumed that it was a product of his having experienced both extremes of the human condition—remarkable individual achievements and great personal tragedy. He had initiated several very successful business ventures, only to witness their demise as a result of the stock market crash of 1929. He was later disabled in an auto accident that left him partially paralyzed and hearing impaired. Despite these personal setbacks, he seemed to have an indomitable spirit, a sense of optimism, and self-confidence that was contagious and admired by virtually everyone who knew him, including me.

Uncle Edgar always went out of his way to make me feel special. I became his indispensable little helper, his protégé. Whenever it came to important projects, he would make me feel as though the job could never have been completed without my help. He seemed to want to teach me everything he knew, patiently explaining even the smallest detail of everything we did together.

I mention all of this simply to emphasize the importance of how the helping person is seen in the eyes of the person being helped. Among the protective factors found to correlate most positively with resilience in children is the availability of caring adults (Smokowski, 1998). Social workers have always emphasized the importance of the helping relationship as a necessary if not sufficient condition for meaningful change. Especially during the formative years, children seem to have a natural propensity to follow the lead of role models whose behavior they admire, and this was certainly the case with respect to my uncle Edgar. Although we never spoke of such matters, he was my hero, and somehow I knew that he knew that.

Helping Process

I can recall vividly the excitement I felt as a child in anticipation of my visits to Uncle Edgar's apartment. It was during these biweekly ventures that a whole new world opened up to me. Indeed, in less than a year, my life was transformed. In retrospect, I never really thought of my regular visits with Uncle Edgar as occasions to "work on my problem." As far as I was concerned, they were simply special opportunities for the two of us to share time together, opportunities to engage in all kinds of unique and interesting activities that made me feel good about myself.

During my initial visits, I can remember spending all of our time exploring the wonders of his woodworking shop, a haven that seemed to me to house virtually every tool known to humankind. It was clear that these tools were important to him, a realization that took on added meaning as he taught me how they worked and gradually entrusted me with their use. I can still recall the enormous sense of achievement I felt as we designed and completed our first project together—a birdhouse with a removable roof. He took this occasion to patiently read aloud the directions and safety precautions for every tool, a ritual that I subsequently came to realize was his subtle way of demonstrating how important it was that we knew how to read. I think that he was convinced that I would be more likely to want to learn to read if I first had a compelling reason for doing so. As I look back on the time we spent together, nothing we did seems to have occurred by happenstance. He was planful and intentional every step along the way.

Our evenings together were carefully orchestrated. As we made our way to his den, a slightly disorganized but comfortable office area that guarded the door to his workshop, he would typically begin by asking me how my day had gone. Listening carefully, he would gently encourage me to share any struggles or frustrations I had experienced since our last visit together. As the evening unfolded, he would invariably find numerous opportunities to explore these experiences in greater depth, always uncovering new ways to enable me to see them as interesting challenges rather than defeats. The activities that surrounded our woodworking efforts always seemed to provide useful metaphors for the handling of day-to-day problems. Each project provided not only a tangible monument to our joint efforts, but, more important, a unique opportunity for me to learn important lessons about life itself in an unobtrusive way. It is apparent to me now that, during these encounters, his immediate goal was to build my self-confidence, to convince me that I had special talents that were unlike those of any of my peers. He wanted me to believe that I could accomplish just about anything I put my mind to. That was the beginning.

One of the things that impressed me most about Uncle Edgar was his ability to get me to believe that everything we did together was for his benefit. There was always the pretense that our activities were designed to meet his needs rather than mine. He was the one who needed me, rather than vice versa. I can recall the first time we actually sat down to read together. He asked me whether it would be okay if we spent a little time reading from a short story he had started the day before. He was eager to find out how the story would end before we worked on our next woodworking project.

I can recall sitting on the soft blue velvet sofa that dominated his den. We sat side by side, his right arm around my shoulder and his left hand balancing the book on a pillow that sat on his lap. To this day, I can sense the warmth and safety of his body next to mine as I followed his bony index finger tracing each word across the page. His bifocals sitting precariously at the end of his nose, he pronounced each word slowly and with great affect. It was immediately apparent that this was not the usual Dick and Jane fare to which I had become accustomed at school. It was an intriguing mystery about a young boy stranded on an island inhabited by beings from another planet. In some strange way, the dilemma experienced by this young protagonist seemed to resonate with my personal plight. It captured well the kinds of feelings I was experiencing during the seemingly endless hours I spent in school each day. It was not until many years later that I fully appreciated how clever he really was in his efforts to capture my interest and imagination. He seemed intent on having me follow the words as he carefully and skillfully got me absorbed in the story. At the most compelling point, he tilted his head back, rubbed his eyes, and announced that he had a headache. He wondered whether I would continue reading the story so that we could discover the fate of our hero. As if passing on an important responsibility, he slid the book onto my lap, closed his eyes, and waited for me to continue the story.

At that moment, I was so engrossed in the plot that I was virtually unaware that I had begun to read. It was as if both of us had become an integral part of the story and that now it was my turn to continue the journey. Although I was aware that now it was Uncle Edgar who was following my finger as it made its way across the page, I felt no pressure to "perform." I was moving at my own pace, and he seemed unconcerned whenever I stumbled over words and made what must have seemed like obvious and sometimes humorous mistakes. His prompts were few in number and occurred only when the pronunciation of a word was crucial to the meaning of the story. He consistently acknowledged my efforts to pronounce words correctly and never failed to reassure me that I was doing an excellent job. I remember his reassuring admonition that "the most important thing about reading is that we understand what the author is trying to say." What Uncle Edgar was trying to say in his quiet and unassuming way was that it was okay for me to make mistakes. He was giving me permission to fail, a luxury I had never really experienced before.

That first reading encounter with Uncle Edgar was truly a transforming experience. For the first time in my life I realized that reading could indeed be fun. Uncle Edgar had made it fun. He had enabled me to feel that despite my many mistakes I had accomplished something very special. We celebrated that achievement, as became our custom every Tuesday and Thursday evening thereafter, by working together in his shop on one of our pet "projects."

From that evening on, we devoted a part of our time together to reading a story. At first these sessions lasted about 15 minutes. Gradually they expanded to 30 minutes and sometimes as long as a full hour, always culminating with a rewarding trip to Uncle Edgar's shop and a treat prepared by Aunt Marie.

The more we read together, the more active Uncle Edgar became in teaching basic principles. His emphasis was always on comprehension, but he gradually worked at expanding my vocabulary. As we read, he would stop on certain words that he felt were important for me to be able to sound out phonetically. At the end of each reading session we would spend some time learning to spell the most interesting new words we had encountered in the story. He would carefully dissect each word into syllables from which we would then construct new and increasingly complex words. It became a sort of game in which he challenged me to create new words and new sounds. Each session, although much the same as the one before, always held new surprises and new challenges.

I remember one particularly empowering spelling session in which Uncle Edgar revealed that he was going to share with me a word that no other human being in the known universe knew how to spell. He guaranteed me that no one, other than he and I, would ever be able to spell this special word—including my reading teacher, who by now he knew had become my nemesis! In fact, as if to emphasize the certainty of his claim, he suggested that I challenge her to spell this mysterious word. However, to be fair he suggested that I give her at least three chances to accomplish the feat.

It is impossible for me to explain how excited and filled with anticipation I was at that very moment. Uncle Edgar looked over his shoulder as if to assure himself that no one else was eavesdropping and then in a barely audible voice slowly pronounced and spelled the illusive word: "S-Y-Z-Y-G-Y." The word, he explained, was pronounced "siz-i-gee." As I recall, it has something to do with the axis created by the alignment of celestial bodies. But that wasn't important at that particular moment—what was important was that I now had a word that no one in the world knew how to spell save Uncle Edgar and me. I could hardly contain my enthusiasm as I waited for an opportunity to confront my reading teacher with this newly discovered Gordian knot. As Uncle Edgar had predicted, she was unable to unravel the mystery of that magical word, even after the allotted three attempts. The insight I gained and the sense of personal satisfaction and empowerment I felt at that moment have remained with me to this day. It was a turning point, an epiphany of sorts. I felt that I had gained control of an important part of my life. Knowing that others as important as teachers could also misspell words somehow reassured me that I was not alone in my painful predicament. As my vocabulary grew, these spelling sessions took on added significance. My growing capacity to spell was improving my ability to read and vice versa. I discovered a newfound sense of confidence that was beginning to carry over to virtually every aspect of my academic performance.

Werner and Smith (1992) referred to the convergence of personal and environmental phenomena in ways that empower individuals as *self-righting tendencies*. They argued that the factors or processes that facilitate self-righting capacities "make a more profound impact on the life course of children who grow up under adverse conditions than do specific risk factors or stressful life events"

(p. 202). The notion that all people are born with at least some innate self-righting capacity is consistent with White's (1959) earlier concept of motivation, which he coined *effectance*. *Effectance* refers to that innate urge that presumably resides within each of us to engage with our environment actively in an effort to make our influence felt, and to master tasks in a competent fashion. I felt that sense of competence on that memorable day, even as an eight-year-old child.

Despite the plausibility of innate capacities, there is little evidence to suggest that such capacities can be actualized in the absence of appropriate environmental conditions. Individual capacities flourish to the extent to which opportunities available within the environment both permit and enable the individual to fulfill his or her potential. Although there is little evidence to support Anthony's (1987) characterization of resilient children as being "psychologically invulnerable," a growing body of research suggests that vulnerability to risk can be mitigated substantially if the social ecology of the child's environment contains appropriate protective factors (Luthar & Zigler, 1991; Mrazek & Haggerty, 1994). Coie et al. (1993) found that protective factors can not only serve to buffer the effects of risk, but also facilitate intervention by directly decreasing an existing dysfunction.

Among the protective factors available to me were two that seemed particularly significant—a supportive and committed family atmosphere and a positive adult role model who possessed the interest and skills necessary to tip the scale from risk to resilience. Although it is unlikely that any of the events I have described would have occurred without the strong and consistent support of my parents, for the purposes of the current discussion I shall emphasize the lessons learned within the context of my relationship with Uncle Edgar. It was he who served as the primary catalyst for constructive change. For all practical purposes, he played the role that comes closest to my vision of an enlightened social worker, a role that Benard (1991) referred to as a *turnaround mentor*.

Lessons Learned

My early experiences suggest a number of practice-related principles that speak directly to a strengths-based perspective of practice, all of which are entirely consistent with the existing body of research on resilience as well as traditional social work interventions within the school environment (Galassi & Akos, 2007).

Practice Grounded on Resilience Principles Assumes a Strengths-based Perspective and Is Implemented through Human Relationships

Resilience can be thought of as the human capacity of individuals to transform and change despite the risks. It presumes what Werner and Smith (1992) referred to as an "innate self-righting mechanism" (p. 202) present in all human beings. Exposure to risk increases the probability of difficulties, whereas protective factors buffer against the exposure to risk. The more risk factors that are present, the greater the risk. Although exposure to a single risk factor does not condemn a child to problems later in life, exposure to a greater number of risk factors increases a young person's risk exponentially (Hawkins, Catalano, & Brewer, 1995). That is, the presence of two or more risk factors in combination is likely to have a multiplicative rather than an additive effect (Rutter, 1983).

Some risk factors, such as poverty, racial discrimination, inadequate educational opportunities, and parental conflict, are common to most childhood problems (Coie et al., 1993; Luthar & Zigler, 1991; Mrazek & Haggerty, 1994). Fraser et al. (1999) referred to them as *keystone risks,* that is, "those conditions or processes that make a child most vulnerable to problems and that, if left unattended, will cause problems to remain or worsen. On balance, keystone risks are the markers for intervention" (p. 132). However, the relative impact of any given risk factor may vary widely as a function of various demographic variables (for example, race, ethnicity, gender, and age) and/or individual traits (for example, one's genetic endowment and biological capacity). The probability of a child succeeding in school correlates positively with the adequacy of the school the child attends (Rutter, 1983), and children who experience some degree of success during the early stages of their academic careers are more likely to continue in school (Benard, 1995; Comer, 1984). Despite generalizations of this type, it is difficult to disentangle how variables interact in ways that place some children at greater risk than others. Exposure to similar risk constellations seems to impact children differently depending on where a particular child is relative to his or her developmental process as well as how the surrounding protective mechanisms function to interrupt the risk cycle (Masten, 1994; Rutter, 1987, 1994).

Although it is enormously helpful to understand the factors that place some children at greater risk than others, a cautionary note is in order. It is extremely important to guard against the tendency to develop an at-risk mindset. The danger in developing such a mindset is that it can tend to influence the way practitioners view the children they serve, often leading to a search for problems rather than strengths. It may also incline practitioners to categorize children as victims rather than as competent resources capable of making meaningful changes in their own lives.

Winfield (1994) argued, "We need to change our approach from one that emphasizes risks, deficits, and psychopathology to one that capitalizes on protection, strengths, and assets" (p. 3). This is the essence of what Uncle Edgar did for me. He seemed to intuitively understand the dispositional and contextual conditions that predisposed me toward negative outcomes. Although his approach appears to have taken these factors into consideration, he scrupulously avoided references to any deficits I may have had and went out of his way to build our relationship on the strengths he perceived to exist within me and the immediate surrounding environment—my "problem" was recast as a challenge as well as an opportunity for growth. As early as 1952, French suggested that without the spark of hope individuals are not likely to make the investment necessary to change the conditions of their lives. Uncle Edgar supplied the miracle of hope in the form of a caring relationship grounded on unconditional trust and the steadfast belief that I was capable of more than I had ever imagined.

Schools Are Ideally Positioned to Serve as the Catalyst for the Development of Resilience in Children

The prevailing research on resilience suggests that schools provide ideal environments within which to promote the kinds of academic, personal, and social competencies that correlate most highly with the development of resilience in children, which in turn foreshadows effective adult adaptation. They are, as Doll and Lyon (1998) suggested, "ubiquitous caretaking environments" (p. 356) that persist across numerous developmental periods in the lives of most American children. No other existing social institution, save the family itself, is as well positioned to serve as an effective catalyst for social workers' efforts to translate the emerging body of research on resilience into practice.

Although they should not be viewed as panaceas for all the world's ills, schools that foster resilience in children embody a range of protective factors and opportunity structures frequently cited in the research literature (Luthar, 2006). For example, in her review of research on resilience, Benard (1991) found that schools "that establish high expectations for all kids—and give them the support necessary to achieve them—have incredibly high rates of academic success" (p. 11). Similarly, one of the most reliable predictors of academic success among children is the accompanying level of family involvement. Many parents feel disenfranchised by the very schools to which they are required by law to send their children (Cox & Powers, 1998). It is not surprising, therefore, that many of these same parents are reluctant to become actively involved in the day-to-day life of the school. Nevertheless, studies have consistently demonstrated that parental involvement correlates positively with student achievement, academic attendance, and graduation rates (Chan, 1987; Epstein, 1987; Moles, 1982), a finding that appears to cut across racial, ethnic, and social class differences (Peterson, 1989).

Children typically spend about one third of each day in school, where they are usually exposed to competent caring adults. Most schools—at least those that have been found to be most effective—provide supportive environments in which high performance expectations are valued and children are held in positive regard (Comer, 1980; Freidberg, Prokosch, Treister, & Stein, 1990; Rutter, Maughan, Mortimore, Ouston, & Smith, 1979). There is also compelling evidence to support the contention that school-based family involvement programs have been effective (Graue, Weinstein, & Walberg, 1983; Maughan, 1988). In fact, efforts to involve parents in school activities produce more positive results than programs targeted exclusively at students (Comer, 1986; Walberg, 1984; Weikart, Epstein, Schweinhard, & Bond, 1978). The types of family involvement programs being implemented across the country vary widely and address a range of issues directly or indirectly related to strengthening the resilience of the family unit, including, for example, family involvement in school management, job training, career counseling, health care, mental health, and social support (Wang, Haertel, & Walberg, 1992). All such programs seem to have an empowering influence and reduce the level of stress experienced by at-risk families.

The key to motivating children to learn, therefore, seems to be closely linked to the ability to empower parents in ways that actively involve them in the education of their children. After all, for most children, parents are the caring adults and mentors to which the research refers when it identifies the kinds of protective factors that foster resilience (Masten, Best, & Garmezy, 1990). Masten et al. (1990) noted that parents

> nurture mastery, motivation, and self-esteem as well as physical growth. Parents provide information, learning opportunities, behavior models, and connections to other resources. When these transactional protective processes are absent or are severely limited for prolonged periods, a child may be significantly handicapped in subsequent adaptation by low self-esteem, inadequate information or social know-how, a disinclination to learn or interact with the world, and a distrust of people as resources. (p. 438)

These critical functions can be supported and strengthened to the extent to which schools provide members of each child's extended family with opportunities for meaningful involvement in the daily life of the school. To accomplish this end, resilience models for school social work must be viewed within a larger ecological context based on a child-centered, family-focused, neighborhood-based frame of reference. It is at this most proximal level that school social workers can have an immediate and meaningful influence on the lives of children and their families. By suggesting this, I do not mean to discount the value and importance of their role as advocates for broader social change in the form of enlightened public policy at the macro level. Indeed, the kinds of problems that children experience on a personal level are inextricably tied to the larger public issues that confront society as a whole, including discrimination, inadequate housing, and the lack of universal health care. However, as Masten (1994) noted, the correlates of individual resilience in children that are more or less ubiquitous across diverse situations suggest a set of factors that are most typically played out at the micro level, including

- effective parenting;
- connections to other competent adults;
- appeal to other people, particularly adults;
- areas of talent or accomplishment valued by self and others;
- self-efficacy, self-worth, and hopefulness;
- religious faith or affiliations;
- socioeconomic advantages;
- good schools and other community assets; and
- good fortune.

Opportunities to influence most if not all of these protective factors are readily available within the ecological niche that exists when individual families, schools, and neighborhoods interact in an intentional manner. Although any one of these microsystems can potentially have a positive impact on a child's development, there is, as Epstein (1987) put it, some evidence and strong logic behind the argument that "when the home, the school, peers, and the larger community are working together, the greater impact is in a consistent direction" (p. 122). In addition, recent research corroborates the notion that over time successes in one area of a child's functioning can create "developmental cascade effects" in other areas (Burt, Obradovic, Long, & Masten, 2008).

Resilience Is a Value-laden Concept That Gains Meaning Only Within the Context of Prevailing Societal Norms

As much as one might like to idealize the concept of resilience and treat it as an innate capacity that emerges miraculously in some children in the face of adversity, there is little empirical evidence to support such a notion. Nevertheless, there has sometimes been a tendency to hypostatize the construct of resilience, to treat it solely as an idiosyncratic human characteristic or trait that some children seem to possess and some do not. Such a view presumes a genetic foundation for resilience, the existence of which can be neither created nor fostered (Rigsby, 1994).

There is, of course, a problem with this narrow conception of resilience. It requires a post hoc explanation. As Bartelt (1994) correctly pointed out, "Resilience is never directly observed—it is always imputed" (p. 101). Because the existence of resilience can only be inferred on the basis of an individual's response to some perceived adversity, it is impossible to validate the concept in any scientific sense except in the context of a set of accompanying environmental conditions.

A value judgment is made that an individual has somehow managed to triumph despite a set of circumstances that would reasonably lead one to predict failure. When people defy the odds, they are classified as resilient. When they fail to do so, they are assumed to be nonresilient.

Bartelt (1994) questioned this logic on two fronts: "First it makes resilience an artifact of the investigator's model of achievement, a statistical residual of a specific causal model. Second, it fails to distinguish between adaptation to socially approved goals and to those that may be personally meaningful" (p. 101). When children adapt in ways that correspond to a socially approved set of expectations, observers tend to think of them as being resilient. When they adapt in ways that fulfill some other set of expectations, people are inclined to think of them less favorably.

As Rigsby (1994) cautioned, one of the dangers of viewing resilience solely as a component of the self that enables success in the face of adversity is that it may inadvertently "reinforce the negative consequence of the old Horatio Alger myth: an implicit belief that anyone can make it if he or she tries hard enough" (p. 92). The corollary to this myth, of course, is the equally dangerous tendency to "blame the victim" (Ryan, 1971) whenever efforts to adapt prove unsuccessful.

It is important to keep in mind, therefore, that at its core the concept of resilience is meaningless except as it is viewed within the context of some normative frame of reference that inevitably conveys prevailing social and political biases. Given the contextual nature of resilience, it is important to begin any discussion involving the creation of programs designed to foster resilience with a deliberate consideration of the value issues that inevitably give meaning and substance to the criteria that will be used to define success. These values should inevitably reflect the views of the major stakeholders, including, in the case of school-based programs, students and their families, teachers and school administrators, as well as representatives from the broader community within which the school is located.

Resilience Is the Response to a Complex Set of Interactions Involving the Person, the Environment, and the Available Opportunities

In describing the school community, Oxley (1994) drew on Max Weber's sociological notion of community as a social group bound by personal as well as utilitarian ties. She suggested that "members of a community care about one another on the basis of shared values and experiences and, in addition, perform practical functions for each other. Communities bestow feelings of belonging and identity" (p. 181).

These relational ties go well beyond the walls of the school and the involvement of families. They include the immediate neighborhood and the surrounding social institutions—including, churches, businesses, industries, police departments, community centers, health services, and so on—all of which share a common vision. As these various elements of the school and community begin to come together, there is a synergistic effect that results in reduced risk and increased protective processes. As Rigsby (1994) pointed out, "Resilience grows out of the interaction of personality, social context, and opportunities for, or demands on, the person" (p. 89). At the same time, Wang et al. (1992) cautioned that schools need to mount a concerted effort to "identify school/community connections that serve to mobilize resources, promote positive attitudes and behavior that strengthen the enabling role of families, and ensure student learning success" (p. 66).

This contextual view of the resilience construct is consistent with the findings of an analysis of the research on the subject conducted by the National Institute of Mental Health, Committee on Prevention Research (1996):

> Studies to date suggest that there is no single source of resilience or vulnerability. Rather, many interacting factors come into play. They include not only individual genetic predispositions, which express themselves in enduring aspects of temperament, personality and intelligence, but also qualities such as social skills and self esteem. These, in turn, are shaped by a variety of environmental influences. (p. 25)

In their review of the research, Doll and Lyon (1998) found that virtually all studies on resilience in children have revealed that "resilience to adversity depends as much upon the characteristics of the important contexts in which children develop (for example, family, school, community) as upon the characteristics of the children themselves" (p. 356). Masten and Coatsworth (1998) also argued,

> Resilient children do not appear to possess mysterious or unique qualities; rather they have retained or secured important sources representing basic protective systems in human development. In other words, it appears that competence develops in the midst of adversity when, despite the situation at hand, fundamental systems that generally foster competence are operating to protect the child or counteract the threats to development. (p. 212)

There is a dynamic interplay among these internal and external sets of interactions across the lifespan. Implicit in this framework is the assumption that resilience varies in its nature and intensity over time in relation to a complex set of ever-changing internal and external variables (Masten, 2006).

Although resilience is known to be nurtured by positive developmental experiences, it is reasonable to assume that a person's capacity for resilience can be either enhanced or eroded depending on the complex interplay among risk and protective factors encountered in the environment at any given point in time. If this is true, then school social workers are ideally positioned to help facilitate student access to the kinds of common experiences prevalent among schools found to be the most effective at fostering resilience in children: (1) supportive relationships with adults and peers, (2) cohesive and structured learning experiences, (3) high expectations for achievement and participation, and (4) increased opportunities for self-direction and development (Oxley, 1994).

As I reflect on my early experiences with Uncle Edgar, these four characteristics capture well the essence of his intervention strategy. It was within the context of our relationship that cohesive and structured learning experiences took place. He not only held out high expectations for achievement, but also did so in a manner that both encouraged and reinforced participation. It was through his imaginative use of available environmental resources—especially within the safe environs of his study and the exciting challenges made available through his workshop—that he found ways to nurture and sustain my fledgling efforts toward self-direction and personal growth. In the final analysis, it is probably fair to say that none of the changes that took place within me during that pivotal developmental year would have or could have occurred without his planful intervention. Whatever innate capacities I may have had at the time would likely have gone unrealized in the absence of our relationship and the appropriate set of intervening environmental conditions.

Conclusion

Writing this chapter has allowed me to revisit my childhood in memory. However, as Edelman (1992) cautioned, memory is an active process of recategorization and reconstruction heavily influenced by one's imagination and the values and perspectives one has adopted over the intervening years. It is never a matter of simply recording and reproducing the events of the past. As seen through the eyes of an adult and the lens of the resilience construct, remembering has undoubtedly forced me to reconstruct the events of my childhood in ways that have given those events very personal and idiosyncratic meaning.

Any lessons derived from anecdotal experiences of this type should always be taken with a grain of salt, especially when those experiences are the product of individual constructions of "reality" recorded more than 50 years after the fact. Researchers are quite familiar with the methodological perils associated with any attempt to generalize from an *N* of one. There is certainly no way to validate any of my assumptions regarding the rationale behind my uncle Edgar's actions, nor is it reasonable to assume that someone else observing the same phenomena would have necessarily perceived or experienced those actions in exactly the same way. Despite these limitations, however, such constructions can be useful because they speak to the phenomenological nature of the human condition, including the subjective meanings we impose on the events that define the contours of our lives.

Under usual circumstances, qualitative inquiries of this type typically precede and ultimately lead to the creation and testing of grounded theory. In this instance, however, I have described a series of personal events that I believe are consistent with and lend credence to an extant body of empirical research derived largely by means of quantitative methods. Because the cluster of interventions used by my uncle obviously preceded the onset of resilience research, it cannot be argued that any of the insights derived from that research could possibly have helped inform his actions. The true test of a viable theory, however, is not only its ability to predict and control the future, but also its capacity to explain the past. The fact that Uncle Edgar functioned in ways that in retrospect have been vindicated by subsequent research provides a compelling argument regarding the credibility of an emerging theory of resilience and strengths-based practice.

Use the CD by Michael Wright to identify the correlates to resilient children in school. Reflect on the notion that a dislike of school can be unrelated to ability to perform in school.

You will find a case study on your CD: *Learning About Uncle Edgar, My Favorite "Teacher"*

References

American Psychiatric Association. (1994). *Desk reference to the diagnostic criteria from* DSM–IV. Washington, DC: Author.

Anthony, E. J. (1987). Risk, vulnerability, and resilience: An overview. In E. J. Anthony & B. J. Cohler (Eds.), *The invulnerable child* (pp. 3–48). New York: Guilford Press.

Bartelt, D. (1994). On resilience: Questions of validity. In M. Wang & E. Gordon (Eds.), *Educational resilience in inner-city America* (pp. 97–108). Hillsdale, NJ: Erlbaum.

Benard, B. (1991). *Fostering resilience in kids: Protective factors in the family, school and community.* Portland, OR: Northwest Regional Educational Laboratory.

Benard, B. (1995). *Fostering resilience in children.* Champaign, IL: University of Illinois at Urbana-Champaign. (ERIC Clearinghouse on Urban Education Digest No. EDO-PS-95–9.) Retrieved from http://resilnet.uiuc.edu/library/benard95.html

Benard, B. (2004). *Resiliency: What we have learned.* San Francisco: WestEd.

Burt, K. B., Obradovic, J., Long, J. D., & Masten, A. S. (2008). The interplay of social competence and psychopathology over 20 years: Testing transactional and cascade models. *Child Development, 79,* 359–374.

Chan, Y. (1987, November 16). *Parents: The missing link in educational reform.* Prepared statement presented at the Hearing Before the Select Committee on Children, Youth, and Families, House of Representatives, 100th Cong. (MF01/PC06), Indianapolis, IN.

Clarke, A. D. B., & Clarke, A. M. (1984). Consistency and change in the growth of human characteristics. *Journal of Child Psychology and Psychiatry, 25,* 191–210.

Coie, J. D., Watt, N. F., West, J. D., Hawkins, J. R., Asarnow, H. J., Markman, S. L., et al. (1993). The science of prevention: A conceptual framework and some directions for a national research program. *American Psychologist, 48,* 1013–1022.

Comer, J. P. (1980). *School power.* New York: Free Press.

Comer, J. P. (1984). Home–school relationships as they affect the academic success of children. *Education and Urban Society, 16,* 322–337.

Comer, J. P. (1986). Parent participation in the schools. *Phi Delta Kappan, 67,* 442–446.

Cox, G., & Powers, G. (1998). Against all odds: An ecological approach to developing resilience in elementary school children. In R. Greene (Ed.), *Serving the diverse constituencies of social work: Contributions of the ecological perspective* (pp. 135–166). Hawthorne, NY: Aldine de Gruyter.

Doll, B., & Lyon, M. (1998). Risk and resilience: Implications for the delivery of educational and mental health services in schools. *School Psychology Review, 27,* 348–363.

Duncan, G. J., Brooks-Gunn, J., & Klebanov, P. K. (1994). Economic deprivation and early childhood development. *Child Development, 65,* 296–318.

Edelman, G. M. (1992). *Bright air, brilliant fire: On the matter of the mind.* New York: Basic Books.

Epstein, J. (1987). Toward a theory of family-school connections: Teacher practices and parent involvement. In K. Hurrelmann, F. Kaufmann, & F. Losel (Eds.), *Social intervention: Potential and constraints* (pp. 121–136). New York: Aldine de Gruyter.

Erikson, E. (1950). *Childhood and society.* New York: Norton.

Farber, A., & Egeland, B. (1987). Invulnerability among abused and neglected children. In E. Anthony & B. Cohler (Eds.), *The invulnerable child* (pp. 253–288). New York: Guilford Press.

Fraser, M., Richman, J., & Galinsky, M. (1999). Risk, protection, and resilience: Toward a conceptual framework for social work practice. *Social Work Research, 23,* 131–143.

Freidberg, H., Prokosch, N., Treister, E., & Stein, T. (1990). A study of five at-risk inner city elementary schools. *Journal of School Effectiveness and School Improvement, 1,* 5–25.

French, T. (1952). *The integration of behavior: Basic postulates.* Chicago: University of Chicago Press.

Galassi, J., & Akos, R. (2007). *Strengths-based school counseling: Promoting student development and achievement.* Mahwah, NJ: Erlbaum.

Garmezy, N. (1987). Stress, competence, and development: Continuities in the study of schizophrenic adults, children vulnerable to psychopathology, and the search for stress-resistant children. *American Journal of Orthopsychiatry, 57,* 159–174.

Garmezy, N., & Rutter, M. (Eds.). (1983). *Stress, coping, and development in children.* New York: McGraw-Hill.

Graue, M., Weinstein, T., & Walberg, H. (1983). School-based home instruction and learning: A quantitative synthesis. *Journal of Educational Research, 76,* 351–360.

Hawkins, J. D., Catalano, R. F., & Brewer, D. D. (1995). Preventing serious, violent and chronic juvenile offending. In J. C. Howell, B. Krisberg, J. D. Hawkinns, & J. J. Wilson (Eds.), *Serious, violent, and chronic juvenile offenders: A source book* (pp. 47–60). Thousand Oaks, CA: Sage.

Jenson, J. M., & Fraser, M. W. (Eds.). (2006). *Social policy for children and families: A risk and resilience perspective.* Thousand Oaks, CA: Sage.

Kelly, E. L. (1955). Consistency of the adult personality. *American Psychologist, 10,* 659–681.

Luthar, S. S. (2006). Resilience in development: A synthesis of research across five decades. In D. Cicchetti & D. J. Cohen (Eds.), *Developmental psychopathology: Vol. 3. Risk, disorder, and adaptation* (2nd ed., pp. 739–795). New York: Wiley.

Luthar, S., & Zigler, E. (1991). Vulnerability and competence: A review of research on resilience in children. *American Journal of Orthopsychiatry, 61,* 6–22.

Masten, A. (1994). Resilience in individual development: Stressful adaptation despite risk and adversity. In C. Wang & E. Gordon (Eds.), *Educational resilience in inner-city America: Challenges and prospects* (pp. 3–23). Hillsdale, NJ: Erlbaum.

Masten, A. S. (2006). Promoting resilience in development: A general framework for systems of care. In R. J. Flynn, P. Dudding, & J. G. Barber (Eds.), *Promoting resilience in child welfare* (pp. 3–17). Ottawa: University of Ottawa Press.

Masten, A., Best, K., & Garmezy, N. (1990). Resilience and development: Contributions from the study of children who overcame adversity. *Development and Psychopathology, 2,* 425–444.

Masten, A. S., & Coatsworth, J. D. (1998). The development of competence in favorable and unfavorable environments: Lessons from research on successful children. *American Psychologist, 53,* 205–220.

Maughan, B. (1988). School experiences as risk/protective factors. In M. Rutter (Ed.), *Studies of psychological risk: The power of longitudinal data* (pp. 200–220). Cambridge, England: Cambridge University Press.

Moles, O. (1982). Synthesis of recent research on parental participation in children's education. *Educational Leadership, 40*(2), 44–47.

Moss, H. A., & Susman, E. J. (1980). Longitudinal study of personality development. In O. J. Brim & J. Kagam (Eds.), *Constancy and change in human development* (pp. 530–595). Cambridge, MA: Harvard University Press.
Mrazek, P. J., & Haggerty, R. J. (Eds.). (1994). *Reducing risks for mental disorders: Frontiers for preventive intervention research.* Washington, DC: National Academies Press.
Murphy, L. B. (1962). *The widening world of childhood.* New York: Basic Books.
National Institute of Mental Health, Committee on Prevention Research. (1996). *A plan for prevention research for the National Institute of Mental Health* (Rep. No. 96–4093). Washington, DC: Author.
Oxley, D. (1994). Organizing for responsiveness: The heterogeneous school community. In M. Wang & E. Gordon (Eds.), *Educational resilience in inner-city America: Challenges and prospects* (pp. 179–189). Hillsdale, NJ: Erlbaum.
Peterson, D. (1989). *Parent involvement in the educational process.* Urbana: University of Illinois. (ERIC Clearinghouse on Educational Management No. ED312776)
Rende, R., & Plomin, R. (1993). Families at risk for psychopathology: Who becomes affected and why? *Development and Psychopathology, 5,* 529–540.
Rigsby, L. (1994). The Americanization of resilience: Deconstructing research practice. In M. Wang & E. Gordon (Eds.), *Educational resilience in inner-city America* (pp. 85–94). Hillsdale, NJ: Erlbaum.
Rutter, M. (1983). Stress coping and development: Some issues and some questions. In N. Garmezy & M. Rutter (Eds.), *Stress, coping and development in children* (pp. 1–41). New York: McGraw-Hill.
Rutter, M. (1985). Resilience in the face of adversity: Protective factors and resistance to psychiatric disorder. *British Journal of Psychiatry, 147,* 598–611.
Rutter, M. (1987). Psychosocial resilience and protective mechanisms. *American Journal of Orthopsychiatry, 37,* 317–331.
Rutter, M. (1989). Pathways from childhood to adult life. *Journal of Child Psychology and Psychiatry, 30,* 23–51.
Rutter, M. (1994). Stress research: Accomplishments and tasks ahead. In R. Haggerty, L. Sherrod, N. Garmezy, & M. Rutter (Eds.), *Stress, risk and resilience in children and adolescents: Process, mechanisms, and interventions* (pp. 354–385). Cambridge, England: Cambridge University Press.
Rutter, M., Maughan, B., Mortimore, P., Ouston, J., & Smith, A. (1979). *Fifteen thousand hours: Secondary schools and their effects on children.* Cambridge, MA: Harvard University Press.
Ryan, W. (1971). *Blaming the victim.* New York: Pantheon Press.
Sherman, A. (1994). *Wasting America's future: The Children's Defense Fund report on the costs of child poverty.* Washington, DC: Children's Defense Fund.
Smokowski, P. R. (1998). Prevention and intervention strategies for promoting resilience in disadvantaged children. *Social Service Review, 72*(3), 337–364.
Walberg, H. (1984). Families as partners in educational productivity. *Phi Delta Kappan, 65,* 397–400.
Wang, M., Haertel, G., & Walberg, H. (1992, October). *The effectiveness of collaborative school-linked services.* Paper presented at the CEIC School/Community Connections Conference, Leesburg, VA.

Weikart, D., Epstein, A., Schweinhard, L., & Bond, J. (1978). *The Ypsilanti Preschool Curriculum Demonstration Project: Preschool years and longitudinal results.* Ypsilanti, MI: Monographs of the High/Scope Educational Research Foundation.

Werner, E., & Smith, R. (1992). *Overcoming the odds.* Ithaca, NY: Cornell University Press.

White, R. W. (1959). Motivation reconsidered: The concept of competence. *Psychological Review, 66,* 297–333.

Winfield, L. F. (1994). *Developing resilience in urban youth* (NCREL Urban Education Monograph). Washington, DC: North Central Regional Education Laboratory.

Wolin, S., & Wolin, S. (1995). Resilience among youth growing up in substance abusing families. *Pediatric Clinics of North America, 42,* 415–429.

Educational Resilience

JEAN E. BROOKS

On finishing this chapter, students will be able to:

Respond to contexts that shape practice (Educational Policy 2.1.9).

- Or continuously discover, appraise, and attend to changing locales, populations, scientific and technological developments, and emerging societal trends to provide relevant services (practice behavior).

A key underlying premise is that educational resilience can be fostered through interventions that enhance children's learning, develop their talents and competencies, and protect or buffer them against environmental adversities.

—Wang, Haertel, & Walberg, 1997, p. 1

Successful teachers of poor children refuse to label their students "at risk"; they look at each child and see the gem that is inside and communicate this vision back to the child.

—Benard, 1996, p. 108

As important as education is to future employment and economic success, many children and youth in the United States are performing at less than satisfactory levels of academic achievement and are likely to leave school before earning a high school diploma. High school dropouts fortunate enough to find year-round full-time employment earn only 78 percent of the wages and salaries of those with high school diplomas or general equivalency diplomas and only 51 percent of the salaries of those with baccalaureate degrees (Aud et al., 2010). In addition to the economic consequences of school failure and dropout, other social problems associated with lack of success in school include delinquency and crime, early sexual involvement and pregnancy, higher mortality rates, higher costs for health care and social services, increased admissions for mental health services, and decreased political participation (Richman, Bowen, & Woolley, 2004).

Low-income and ethnic minority youth are disproportionately affected by the problems of school failure and dropout (Aud et al., 2010; Swanson, 2010). Whereas as many as 91 percent of students attending low-poverty schools graduated in 2007–08, only 68 percent of students attending high-poverty schools graduated (Aud et al., 2010). Similarly, Swanson found that only about 55 percent to 60 percent of students graduated in school districts that served large numbers of ethnic minority and/or low-income youth. Whereas more than two thirds of white and Asian students graduated from high school, only about 54 percent of African American students and 56 percent of Hispanic students graduated (Swanson, 2010).

Low-income and ethnic minority youth are also at greater risk of having low test scores. Aud et al. (2010) reported sizable gaps in achievement scores for fourth- and eighth-grade students depending on whether they attended a high-poverty school (in which 76 percent or more of enrolled students were eligible for free or reduced price lunches) or a low-poverty school (in which fewer than 26 percent of students were eligible). The situation was compounded by the link between segregation by class and segregation by ethnicity. Aud and colleagues found that African American and Hispanic students were much more likely to attend high-poverty elementary and secondary schools.

The literature on resilience suggests that interventions to facilitate the development of more favorable classroom and school environments can offset educational risk and enhance academic outcomes for students at risk of falling behind in their educational achievements. Supported by research on educational environments associated with positive student outcomes, Benard's (1991, 2004) theory of resilience provides guidance for developing such interventions. Schools characterized by caring relationships, high expectations, and opportunities for participation and contribution are more likely to have students who persist in school and succeed in their educational endeavors.

Educational Resilience

Educational resilience has been defined as "the heightened likelihood of success in school and in other aspects of life, despite environmental adversities, brought about by early traits, conditions, and experiences" (Wang, Haertel, & Walberg, 1995, p. 5). This construct is based on theories of resilience developed from prevention research and the field of developmental psychopathology. It incorporates research on the characteristics of resilient children as well as the characteristics of the environments with which they interact, including research on schools that work effectively with students at risk for poor academic outcomes.

The concept of resilience is embedded in an ecological context (Greene, 2002; Jozefowicz-Simbeni & Allen-Meares, 2002; Richman & Fraser, 2001). Someone who is at risk cannot develop resilience through sheer willpower; rather, resilience is developed through the interactions of people with their environments—families, schools, neighborhoods, and the larger society. Failure to recognize the role of the environment in developing resilience may result in placing the blame on individuals who have difficulty overcoming the risks in their lives. As Rigsby (1994) stated,

> A danger of employing the concept of resilience as it has heretofore been understood is that we may reinforce the negative consequences of the old Horatio Alger myth: an implicit belief that anyone can make it if he or she tries hard enough. An inevitable result is that we will again "blame the victim" of the complex processes that create and perpetuate poverty and stress in our society. Although we will be talking about resilience, we will be inferring "nonresilience" as well. (pp. 92–93)

Thus, efforts to enhance educational resilience should incorporate family, school, community, and societal supports in recognition of the significance of the environment in promoting healthy development.

Because environmental factors can enhance resilience, they can be modified to increase the likelihood of positive outcomes. Zimmerman and Arunkumar (1994) considered interventions directed at changing the environment to be more efficient and economical than interventions directed at changing individuals. Likewise, Benard (1991) focused on developing positive environmental contexts in families, schools, and communities in recognition of the protection that one of these systems can provide to counteract risks experienced in another system.

When focusing on educational outcomes, it is particularly important to examine the voluminous research on schools. One classic study is Coleman's (1966) *Equality of Educational Opportunity*, in which he found greater variations within rather than between schools, with the greatest proportion of between-school variation related to differences in the family backgrounds of students enrolled in the school. Although this finding led to a "widespread acceptance among academics that schools made little difference" (Rutter, Maughan, Mortimore, Ouston, & Smith, 1979, p. 1), Coleman also found that the achievement of ethnic minority students was more dependent on school characteristics than was the achievement of nonminority students. School characteristics that made a difference in the achievement of ethnic minority students included school facilities, teacher quality, and the educational backgrounds and goals of other students in the school—factors that were not then and that still are not equitably available to low-income and ethnic minority students. Because of the "differential sensitivity to school variations" (Coleman, 1966, p. 297), Coleman found that "it is for the most disadvantaged children that improvements in school quality will make the most difference in achievement" (p. 22).

Rutter et al. (1979) conducted an observational study over three years (when students were ages 11 through 14) of the school processes of 12 secondary schools in an inner borough of London to examine whether schools made a difference in student outcomes. Even after controlling for characteristics of the students enrolled at the schools, he and his colleagues recognized differences in student outcomes that were systematically related to the characteristics of the schools as social institutions. Except for the academic abilities of the students entering the school, the factors that made a difference in this study were under the control of the teachers—"the degree of academic emphasis, teacher actions in lessons, the availability of incentives and rewards, good conditions for pupils, and the extent to which children were able to take responsibility" (p. 178). Rutter et al. (1979) concluded that "the importance of the separate school process measures may lie in their contribution to the ethos or climate of the school as a whole" (p. 183). The schools with the most successful student outcomes were those in which students were actively engaged in classroom activities and assigned specific responsibilities, in which teachers expected and emphasized student success, and in which there were positive relationships between teachers and students.

The extensive body of research examining the ways in which schools influence the achievement of their students, including research identifying the characteristics of high-poverty, high-achieving schools, explores the impact of tangible school inputs (funding, teacher quality, the student–teacher ratio, and facilities) as well as less tangible school characteristics (academic press and sense of community) on student outcomes. The education production studies focused on tangible school inputs have produced mixed findings. After conducting a meta-analysis of 187 such studies, Hanushek (1989) found that there was not a consistent or direct relationship between school inputs and student performance. However, in a reanalysis of these studies, Hedges, Laine, and Greenwald (1994) identified a systematic and positive pattern of relationships between school resources and student achievement.

Among the educational resources associated with improved student outcomes are smaller schools and classes. Bickel, Howley, Williams, and Glascock (2000) found that economically disadvantaged students attending smaller schools have higher levels of academic achievement than do students attending larger schools. Similarly, in Tennessee, children in early elementary classes of 17 or fewer students performed better than their peers enrolled in classes of 22 or more students, which was particularly advantageous for inner-city and ethnic-minority students (Tennessee State Department of Education, 1990).

Teacher quality is another educational resource associated with student outcomes. Rice (2003, p. v) considered it to be "the most important school-related factor influencing student achievement." In her review of numerous empirical studies on teacher quality, she found that the teacher characteristics associated with better student performance included experience, scores on tests of verbal abilities, selectivity or prestige of the college or university the teacher had attended, coursework in academic content and pedagogy, advanced degrees, and certification. In a value-added approach to studying teacher quality in teaching mathematics, Sanders and Rivers (1996) found that highly effective teachers produced substantially more gains in student achievement compared to the least effective teachers. They concluded that the effects of teacher quality are both additive and cumulative, having an effect on student performance as many as two years later regardless of the effectiveness of subsequent teachers.

Edmonds (1979) directed his efforts to identifying the characteristics of schools that were effective in educating low-income inner-city students. He believed that all children could be educated and that the quality of the school was critical in shaping student learning. He was particularly concerned with the findings from many studies and the common belief that family background is the most important factor influencing student achievement, because this belief provided a rationale that minimized the responsibility of teachers and schools to provide effective education for all students regardless of family background. It was his opinion that "a climate in which it is incumbent on all personnel to be instructionally effective for all pupils" (p. 22) was the critical component of effective schools. Other important characteristics included the expectation that all students meet specific achievement goals, an orderly climate, a focus on acquiring academic skills, and the ongoing monitoring of student progress.

The expectation that all students can be successful appears to be a central feature of high-performing, high-poverty schools (Bell, 2001; Cole-Henderson, 2000; Kannapel & Clements, 2005; Picucci, Brownson, Kahlert, & Sobel, 2002). Such schools engage students in a challenging learning environment that supports a vision of school success; emphasize rigorous standards for all students with a focus on high-quality teaching and learning in a safe, orderly environment; and intervene early and frequently to support the academic success of each student (Bell, 2001). They are characterized by relatively low teacher and student turnover, high attendance, competent teachers, and strong agreement about the importance of the school's mission (Cole-Henderon, 2000). They provide a caring atmosphere, assess the needs of individual students, and tailor instruction to meet those needs (Kannapel & Clements, 2005). They provide the support needed to enable teachers and students to reach their goals, extend the school day for academic and nonacademic services to students, and develop structures to ensure that each student is known by at least one adult (Picucci et al., 2002).

School Environments that Promote Educational Resilience

Given the educational risks experienced by ethnic minority and low-income children, educators, researchers, and government officials have an obligation to explore ways in which schools can foster resilience and improve educational outcomes (Borman & Rachuba, 2000; Downey, 2008; Learning First Alliance, 2001; National Governors Association Center for Best Practices, 2000; Nettles & Robinson, 1998; Picucci et al., 2002; Wang, Haertel, & Walberg, 1994, 1998). The role of schools in promoting the cognitive development of children leads to a logical focus on strengthening the positive impact of the school environment on educational outcomes of at-risk students.

Benard's (2004) model of resiliency (Youth Development Process: Resiliency in Action) offers a framework for understanding how schools can promote educational resilience. In her model, protective factors within the family, school, and community (caring relationships, high expectations, and opportunities for participation and contribution) meet the basic developmental needs of youth (safety, love or belonging, respect, autonomy or power, challenge or mastery, and meaning). When these needs are met, youth develop internal resilience strengths (social competence, problem-solving skills, autonomy, sense of purpose and bright future) that lead to improved social, health, and academic behaviors as well as reduced health-risk behaviors (pp. 107–108). It is Benard's (1991) belief that "the development of human resiliency is none other than the process of healthy human development—a dynamic process in which personality and environmental influences interact in a reciprocal, transactional relationship" (p. 20). To the extent to which children and youth are exposed to healthy environments, it is likely that they will develop into healthy adults.

Benard (2003) discussed the "power of one person—often unbeknownst to [the youth]—to tip the scale from risk to resilience" (p. 116). The "turnaround people" she identified provide caring relationships with children and youth, demonstrating an active interest in getting to know them as individuals. Their positive and high expectations reflect their "deep belief in the young person's innate resilience and self-righting capacities" (p. 117). In addition, they create opportunities for participation and contribution that allow each person to exercise his or her own social competence in the community. According to Benard's (1991, 2003, 2004) theory, schools can develop improved academic outcomes if they strengthen the extent to which students experience caring relationships within school, foster an atmosphere of high expectations for all students, and provide multiple opportunities for students to participate and contribute to the school and the surrounding community.

Caring relationships, high expectations, and opportunities for participation and contribution have been part of the focus of many efforts to improve schools. To enhance students' connections with school and their academic outcomes, the Oregon State Department of Education (2000) used resiliency theory as a basis for developing a sense of belonging, a sense of competence derived from meeting expectations, empowerment through meaningful participation, and usefulness through service. Henderson and Milstein (2003) also used Benard's theory in their model for developing resiliency in the schools. Yamauchi (2003) described the use of resiliency-promoting school environments in a Hawaiian Studies program to promote a sense of belonging among students and enhance their retention in school.

Caring Relationships

Caring, supportive relationships with trusted adults who fulfill the need for a sense of belonging and connectedness with others serve as an essential protective factor for developing youth (Benard, 1991, 1996; Pianta & Walsh, 1998; Schorr, 1997). Caring relationships are demonstrated by teachers and other adults who know each student by name, take the time to listen and pay attention to the students, communicate their high expectations, recognize students' strengths and accomplishments, show respect by involving students in making decisions, develop opportunities to build relationships within the classroom, and intervene when students are having problems (Brooks, 2006; Henderson & Milstein, 2003; Laursen & Birmingham, 2003; Wang et al., 1998).

"Sustained, caring, supportive interactions among teachers and students" (Wang et al., 1997, p. 16) are essential in resilience-promoting schools. Students who experience positive social interactions with their peers and with the adults at school are likely to be more attached to the school and more engaged in its activities (Wang et al., 1997, 1998). Such schools foster an atmosphere in which teachers and students feel a sense of involvement and belonging, also known as a *sense of community* (Learning First Alliance, 2001).

> The objective of creating a supportive learning community ought to be that everyone involved—staff, parents, and especially students—feels a

> strong sense of belonging in school, being concerned about one another's welfare, making significant contributions, having opportunities for ongoing learning and growth, and holding important goals and values in common with others. Students must be central in the effort to build the school community because students themselves—their relations with each other and with adults in the school—are key to their motivation, attitudes, and interpersonal behavior, and are the single greatest influence on school climate. Adults should share responsibility with students for creating and maintaining a supportive school environment. (Learning First Alliance, 2001, p. 3)

Connections to school developed through these caring, nurturing relationships are likely to enhance students' academic goals and achievement (Resnick et al., 1997).

High Expectations

High expectations are an essential component of a resilience-promoting school. High academic expectations are conveyed through evidence-based instructional practices, engaging learning activities, challenging curricula, maximizing time spent on academic tasks, and teaching higher order thinking skills (Krovetz, 1999; Wang et al., 1997, 1998). Engaging students in challenging academic content and critical thinking learning activities is one way to let students know that they are capable of solving complex problems (Benard, 1996).

> Students are most motivated to learn, feel the greatest sense of accomplishment, and achieve at the highest levels when they are able to succeed at tasks that spark their interest and stretch their capacities. To be meaningful, learning must effectively connect to students' questions, concerns, and personal experiences, thereby capturing their intrinsic motivation and making the value of what they learn readily apparent to them. . . . When students find purpose in their learning, and when they feel challenged and successful much of the time, they become more involved in their own learning and more invested in, and attached to, the school community. (Learning First Alliance, 2001, pp. 4–5)

Teachers communicate their high expectations by their active interest in the performance of each student, through constructive feedback, and through the message "I know you can do it." They also demonstrate their high expectations when they fairly enforce clear rules about behavioral expectations (Brooks, 2006).

To promote educational resilience for all of their students, it is imperative that teachers believe that children can succeed despite diversity in their family, social, and educational backgrounds. Teachers who believe that their efforts can make a significant contribution to their students' development are more likely to assume a sense of responsibility for their students' academic success (Wang et al., 1997). "Successful teachers of poor children refuse to label their students 'at risk'; they look at each child and see the gem that is inside and communicate this vision back to the child" (Benard, 1996, p. 108). Students internalize the high expectations communicated to them with increased levels of self-esteem and self-efficacy (Benard, 1996).

Opportunities for Participation and Contribution

Resilience-promoting schools provide numerous opportunities for students to participate in activities that are meaningful to them (Benard, 1996; Wang et al., 1997; Zimmerman & Arunkumar, 1994). Such participation lets students see themselves as respected resources in the school (Henderson & Milstein, 2003). Engaging teaching strategies in which students actively participate with others contribute to students' development of the individual characteristics of resilience—a sense of a future, autonomy, problem-solving skills, and social competence (Benard, 1996). Participation in school governance and service learning can also help students see their value within the school and the community.

Participation in extracurricular activities provides additional opportunities through which students can build their competence and strengthen their connections to caring adults and peers (Brooks, 2006). By reflecting and enhancing students' attachment to the school, such participation results in higher levels of academic achievement, attendance, and educational aspirations (Learning First Alliance, 2001). Such activities are particularly important for at-risk students because they provide a positive and voluntary experience that enhances students' experiences within the classroom and extends their connections and relationships within the school (Wang et al., 1998).

Indeed, opportunities for participation and contribution are so significant in promoting educational resilience that these opportunities, including extracurricular activities, should be developed to encourage the maximum participation of all students regardless of skill level (Learning First Alliance, 2001). Those students with the fewest positive connections within the school and who are at the greatest educational risk may benefit even more from such participation than more advantaged students who are more likely to have strong attachments to the school.

Active engagement in school is most likely to be a consequence of a school environment that is rich in caring relationships, high expectations, and opportunities for participation and contribution. Engagement includes behavioral components such as active participation in the classroom and extracurricular activities as well as emotional components such as identification with the school and cognitive components (investment in the effort to participate in school). Engaging schools

> promote students' confidence in their ability to learn and succeed in school by providing challenging instruction and support for meeting high standards, and they clearly convey their own high expectations for their students' success. They provide choices for students and they make the curriculum and instruction relevant to adolescents' experiences, cultures, and long-term goals, so that students see some value in the high school curriculum. . . . Engaging schools promote a sense of belonging by personalizing instruction, showing an interest in students' lives, and creating a supportive, caring social environment. (National Research Council and the Institute of Medicine, 2004, pp. 2–3)

The National Research Council recognizes the importance of engagement, particularly for students attending high-poverty urban schools. Although disengaged students from more advantaged backgrounds may get second chances and graduate, those from disadvantaged backgrounds are more likely to drop out from school. The disadvantages that some students face because of marginalized families and communities may be lessened through participation in an engaging school.

Research Findings in Support of Benard's Theory

Benard's (1991, 2004) theory of resilience has been supported by substantial educational research directed toward the characteristics of effective schools associated with improved educational outcomes for their students. These studies show that schools in which students experience high levels of caring relationships, high expectations, and opportunities for participation and contribution are more likely to have students with better levels of academic achievement and greater high school graduation rates.

Caring Relationships

Caring relationships are one ingredient of a resilience-promoting school, with research evidence supporting the role of such relationships in promoting positive student outcomes. As shown in Table 11.1, caring relationships are identified in the research through student reports of caring relationships with their teachers, student reports of negative interactions with others, teacher reports of talking with individual students outside of class, lower student–teacher ratios, and school practices of prompt notification to parents of student absences.

Several research studies have used some measure describing students' relationships with their teachers as one independent variable. For example, Croninger

TABLE 11.1 School Characteristics That Promote Educational Resilience

Caring Relationships
Absence of negative interactions with others
Caring relationships with teachers
Low student–teacher ratio
School policy of prompt notification to parents of student absences
Teacher reports of talking with students outside of class
High Expectations
Administrators' perception of the school's academic emphasis
Administrators' perception that learning is not hindered by lack of discipline
Clear, high, and consistent academic and behavioral expectations
Enrollment in academic curriculum/college preparatory program in high school
Parents' perceptions of the school's high academic and behavioral expectations
School personnel recommend college after high school graduation
Teacher expectations for how far in school students will go
Opportunities for Participation and Contribution
Hours per week in school-sponsored extracurricular activities
Number of sports activities offered at school
Overall participation in school-sponsored extracurricular activities
Participation in sports
Participation in school-sponsored community service
Student reports of participating in interesting activities and making a difference at school

and Lee (2001), analyzing data from the National Educational Longitudinal Study from 1990 to 1992, found that students' reports of their relationships with their teachers were associated with a reduced risk of high school dropout, particularly for students at risk because of academic difficulties prior to entering high school and for those from socially disadvantaged backgrounds. Similarly, Crosnoe and Elder (2004), using data from the National Longitudinal

Study of Adolescent Health, found that teacher support was associated with on-track academic behavior. Using data from the Prospects Study of elementary students, Borman and Rachuba (2000) found that positive and supportive relationships with teachers in third grade were associated with performing better than expected on a sixth-grade math test. Hanson, Austin, and Lee-Bayha (2003, 2004), using the Resilience Module from the California Healthy Kids Survey, found that school levels of caring relationships with adults at school were positively associated with school levels of the Academic Performance Index as well as the annual changes of schools on the Stanford Achievement Test. Lee and Burkam (2003), using a subsample of 190 urban and suburban schools from the High School Effectiveness Supplement to the National Educational Longitudinal Study of 1988, found that positive student–teacher relationships were associated with lower school dropout rates in Catholic schools as well as small and medium-size public schools. In a study of secondary students in Ireland, Smyth (1999) found that positive student–teacher relationships were associated with better examination scores, lower absenteeism, and lower dropout rates at the individual level.

Brooks (2010) studied the effects of caring relationships on mathematics achievement and the likelihood of timely graduation from high school using data from the Educational Longitudinal Study of 2002. The population she studied included public high school students who had not transferred to another school, which allowed her to focus on the effects of the schools in the 10th grade on student outcomes in the 12th grade. In addition to her focus on public high school students in general, she also studied four groups that were at risk for lower mathematics achievement and a greater likelihood of high school dropout: (1) students from the lowest-socioeconomic quartile; (2) African American students; (3) Hispanic students; and (4) a generic at-risk group that included the first three groups along with students from nontraditional families (without both biological parents), students with disabilities, and students who had been retained a grade in school. In her study, student reports of caring relationships with teachers were associated with higher 12th-grade mathematics achievement scores for the overall population of public high school students as well as for students from the lowest-socioeconomic quartile and those in the generic at-risk group. Student reports of caring relationships with teachers were associated with increased odds of timely graduation for each group in her study.

Brooks (2010) also included negative interactions with others as a measure of the extent to which caring relationships were missing from students' experiences within the schools they attended. This measure was associated with lower mathematics scores for students in the overall, low-socioeconomic status, Hispanic, and generic at-risk samples. Negative interactions with others were associated with reduced odds of timely graduation for students in all samples. Brooks's (2010) study also included school practices on timely notification to parents of student absences as a measure of caring relationships. This variable was associated with higher mathematics scores for the overall and Hispanic samples and with slightly increased odds of timely graduation for the overall sample.

Another measure of caring relationships is reports from teachers of talking with individual students outside of class. This measure was associated with reduced odds of high school dropout in Croninger and Lee's (2001) study and with higher levels of educational expectations and participation in postsecondary education in Wimberly's (2002) study, both of which used data from the National Educational Longitudinal Study. In Brooks's (2010) study, reports of math teachers that they talked with individual students outside of class were associated with higher mathematics achievement in 12th grade and greater odds of timely graduation for the overall and generic at-risk samples. Reports of English teachers that they talked with their individual students outside of class were associated with higher odds of timely graduation for students from the overall, African American, and generic at-risk samples.

One additional measure of caring relationships is the student–teacher ratio, because students are more likely to have personalized relationships with their teachers when there are fewer students per teacher. In an analysis of data from the High School and Beyond Study, McNeal (1997) found that smaller student–teacher ratios were associated with reduced risks of high school dropout. In Brooks's (2010) study, higher student–teacher ratios were associated with reduced odds of timely graduation for students from the overall, low-socioeconomic status, African American, and generic at-risk samples.

High Expectations

High expectations have been examined in various research studies on the educational process. Measures that have been used in such studies include whether the student was enrolled in an academic curriculum or a college preparatory program in high school, teachers' expectations of how far in school the student would go, recommendations by school personnel of what the student should do after graduation from high school, perceptions of students and parents of high academic and behavioral expectations, and administrators' perceptions of the academic emphasis of the school and the extent to which learning at the school is not hindered by lack of discipline.

Enrollment in an academic curriculum in high school was significantly associated with improvement in reading scores in the National Educational Longitudinal Study of 1988 in Cappella and Weinstein's (2001) study. In Brooks's (2010) study, student reports of their enrollment in a college preparatory program were associated with higher mathematics scores for students in the overall, low-socioeconomic status, and generic at-risk samples. Enrollment in a college preparatory program was associated with significantly higher odds of timely graduation for students from the low-socioeconomic status, African American, and generic at-risk samples of students.

Teacher reports of their expectations of how far each student would go in school were associated with more positive educational outcomes. In Schoon, Parsons, and Sacker's (2004) study of 16-year-old students from the National Child Development Study in Great Britain, whether or not the teacher considered the student suited for further education was the most significant protective factor in reducing the impact of social adversity on academic attainment by age 33. Dalton, Glennie, and Ingels (2009), using data from the Educational Longitudinal Study of 2002, found higher dropout rates among students whose teachers expected them to go no further than high school. In Brooks's (2010) study, teacher expectations were associated with significantly higher mathematics scores and significantly increased odds of timely graduation for all groups.

Two studies have also used a measure of what students' counselors, favorite teachers, or coaches thought they should do after graduation from high school as a predictor of academic outcomes. In Wimberly's (2002) study, such perceptions were related to students' educational expectations and participation in postsecondary education. In Brooks's (2010) study, these perceptions were associated with higher mathematics achievement for Hispanic students. Similarly, in Smyth's (1999) study of students in Ireland, student reports of how far in school their teacher expected them to go were associated with school levels of better examination scores, lower absenteeism, and lower dropout.

Students' perceptions of high expectations at school are also associated with improved academic outcomes. Hanson et al. (2003, 2004), using the Resilience Module of the California Healthy Kids Survey, found that school levels of high expectations were associated with the schools' performance on the Academic Performance Index and with annual changes in student performance on the Stanford Achievement Test. Shin, Lee, and Kim's (2009) study of 15-year-old students in Korea, Japan, and the United States, which used 2003 data from the Program for International Assessment, found that students in all three countries had higher mathematics scores if their school mean on the school's disciplinary climate was rated more highly. Student reports of the school's academic and disciplinary climates were integrated into Shouse's (1995) measure of academic press (from the National Educational Longitudinal Study), which was associated with positive mathematics achievement at all schools, with the greatest effect for schools serving larger proportions of economically disadvantaged students. In Brooks's (2010) study, student perceptions of high academic expectations were associated with increased odds of timely graduation for students from the overall and generic at-risk samples.

Brooks's (2010) study also included parents' perceptions of the academic and disciplinary climates of the school. In her study, parents' perceptions of high academic expectations were associated with increased odds of timely graduation for the overall and generic at-risk samples. Parents' perceptions of a positive school disciplinary climate were associated with higher mathematics scores for all samples and with increased odds of timely graduation for the overall sample.

Administrators' reports of the academic emphasis of the school have also been used as a measure of high expectations. Administrators' reports were used as one measure of academic press in Shouse's (1995) study and were associated with positive effects on mathematics test scores. In Brooks's (2010) study, the academic emphasis of the school as reported by school administrators was associated with higher mathematics scores for the overall, African American, and generic at-risk samples. Also in Brooks's (2010) study, administrators' reports that learning at the school was not hindered by a lack of discipline were associated with increased odds of timely graduation for students from the overall and generic at-risk samples.

Opportunities for Participation and Contribution

Opportunities for participation and contribution have also been associated with positive educational outcomes in several studies. Among the variables that have been explored in relation to opportunities for participation and contribution are student reports of participation in interesting activities and making a difference at school; student participation in school-sponsored community service, sports, and non-sports extracurricular activities; the hours per week students spend in extracurricular activities; and the number of sports offered at school.

In the Resilience Module of the California Healthy Kids Survey, meaningful participation was measured by student responses to the items "I do interesting activities at school," "At school, I help decide things like class activities or rules," and "I do things at my school that make a difference" (Hanson et al., 2003, 2004). In these studies, school levels of meaningful participation were associated with increased school levels on the Academic Performance Index and with annual changes at the school in performance on the Stanford Achievement Test. In another study using this measure, meaningful participation was positively associated with school connectedness, school grades, and scores on the California Standardized Test (Hanson & Kim, 2007).

In Brooks's (2010) study, student participation in school-sponsored community service was associated with higher mathematics achievement for students in the overall and Hispanic samples. Community service was associated with increased odds of timely graduation for students in the overall and generic at-risk samples.

Participation in school-sponsored extracurricular activities is perhaps the most widely studied opportunity for participation and contribution in educational research studies. In Camp's (1990) study of a subsample of students from the High School and Beyond Study, the overall level of participation in extracurricular and cocurricular activities was associated with higher grades. In Dumais's (2008) study of students in the Educational Longitudinal Study of 2002, hours per week in school-sponsored extracurricular activities was associated with higher math scores in 12th grade. In Jordan's (1999) study using data from sophomores in the National Educational Longitudinal Study, sports participation was associated with higher self-reported grade point averages and higher achievement scores in 10th grade. Other studies have found that participation in extracurricular activities was associated with an increased likelihood of high school graduation (Mahoney, 2000) and with a substantial reduction in the likelihood of high school dropout (Mahoney & Cairns, 1997; Randolph, Fraser, & Orthner, 2004). In a qualitative study of 35 low-income high school students, Reis, Colbert, and Hebert (2005) found that participation in multiple extracurricular activities was one factor that distinguished students who achieved academically from underachievers. In Wimberly's (2002) analysis of data from the National Educational Longitudinal Study of 1988, participation in extracurricular activities was significantly related to educational expectations and participation in postsecondary education.

Participation in extracurricular activities was also included in Brooks's (2010) study. The hours per week that students spent in extracurricular activities was associated with higher mathematics scores and increased odds of timely graduation for students in all samples. Participation in nonsport extracurricular activities was associated with higher mathematics scores for all samples of students and with increased odds of timely graduation for students from the overall, low-income, African American, and generic at-risk samples. Participation in interscholastic sports was associated with higher mathematics scores for students from the overall, low-socioeconomic status, Hispanic, and generic at-risk samples. Participation in interscholastic sports was associated with increased odds of timely graduation for students from the overall, African American, and generic at-risk samples. One related measure used in Brooks's (2010) study was the number of sports offered at school. This variable was positively associated with senior-year mathematics scores for students from all samples and with slightly increased odds of timely graduation for students from the overall sample.

Implications of Findings for Practice

Overall, these research studies support Benard's (1991, 2004) theory that caring relationships, high expectations, and opportunities for participation and contribution within the school make a difference in student academic outcomes. It is significant to note that these protective factors contributed to two important educational goals—academic achievement scores and high school graduation. It is also noteworthy that improved academic outcomes were experienced by multiple groups of students, including student populations at large as well as those at risk educationally. Thus, efforts to increase levels of caring relationships, high expectations, and opportunities for participation and contribution within the schools are likely to enhance both persistence and achievement for all students even while they serve a protective function for those at risk.

Case Study: The Development of a Resilience-promoting School

Hope High School was an inner-city school in a large city. The majority of its students were African American, and many others were Hispanic. More than 70 percent of the students qualified for a free or reduced price lunch. District officials were concerned about a number of problems. The school had the highest dropout rate in the city, and scores on achievement tests were among the lowest in the city. In addition, there was a general lack of discipline at the school, and there had been several incidents of bullying, recurrent loud confrontations, and frequent fights. Although many inner-city schools across the nation experience similar problems, clearly something had to be done to improve the situation at this school.

The response of the school district was to hire a new principal to bring about some changes. Dr. John Rogers had an impressive background in bringing about changes in similar schools, and the school district was optimistic that he could achieve positive changes at Hope High School. His first step was to find out more about the city and the state in which the school was located. He found out that the city was deeply affected by the nation's economic issues and that in the past two years unemployment had jumped from 7 percent to 12 percent. Loss of tax revenue had had a negative impact on state and city funding for the operation of the schools. As a result of budget cuts, the district made deep cuts in the arts and physical education programs at the schools.

During his first month at the school, Dr. Rogers spent some time getting to know more about Hope High School by meeting with the key stakeholders—the students and their parents, the teachers and other employees at the school, district officials, and some of the leaders in the local community. Most of the people he met were not very optimistic that substantial improvements were possible. Several people expressed the viewpoint that it was unlikely that these students would ever be successful in high school and that, even if they did somehow manage to graduate from high school, it was unlikely that they would be able to find meaningful employment or pursue education beyond high school. A few of the teachers and other employees complained about being assigned to Hope High School when there were better schools in the district serving students who were more like to succeed.

Being a seasoned educator, Dr. Rogers was familiar with the latest research about school improvements. He was concerned about the low expectations that seemed to be pervasive throughout the school community and decided that a more formal assessment of the overall climate at the school would be in order. Because there was no district funding available to support such an assessment, he asked a local businessman who was concerned about the schools to provide the funding. The instruments he chose to use were the California Healthy Kids Survey, the California School Climate Survey, and the California School Parent Survey (WestEd., 2011a, 2011b, 2011c). With the assistance of the school social worker, three teachers, and two parents who were very active in the school's parent–teacher association, Dr. Rogers also conducted an environmental scan to determine available resources within the community (Adelman & Taylor, 2006).

The results from the surveys confirmed Dr. Rogers's informal assessment of the school. Only a minority of the students reported that it was "pretty much true" that adults at the school cared about them and their success, and fewer reported that they did anything interesting or made a difference at their school. About half of the parents responded that the school treated students with respect, promoted their success, and was a safe place. A substantial minority of the school staff who completed the California School Climate Survey disagreed with the statements that the school provided a supportive environment for students and promoted their academic success.

The environmental scan conducted by the school's team showed that there were very few professionals other than teachers assigned to the school. In addition to the social worker, who was assigned there 2.5 days per week, an attendance counselor was assigned there one day a week and a psychologist was available for testing about half a day per week. Relatively few extracurricular activities were offered—a football team, girls' and boys' basketball teams, a cheerleading squad, and an honor society that honored high-achieving students in an induction ceremony once a year. Meetings of the parent–teacher association were infrequent and sparsely attended. The only school–community partnership that had been developed was an adopt-a-school program. The main highlight of that program was an annual schoolwide sports day for which the business adopting the school provided t-shirts and refreshments.

Dr. Rogers's next step was to meet with the school staff to discuss the statistics concerning achievement and dropout rates along with the assessment of the school climate and the results of the environmental scan. He expressed his concern that students are more likely to succeed when they feel connected with the school and when they are actively engaged in school activities. He shared his belief that students are most likely to reach their potential in an environment in which all students are expected to be successful and are provided the support needed to reach academic goals. He tried to mobilize school staff to work with him in an effort to improve student outcomes by building an environment rich in caring relationships, high expectations, and opportunities for participation and contribution, and he encouraged their feedback in the process.

Professional development activities at the school that year were focused on achieving Dr. Rogers's vision for the school. Consultants were brought in to discuss how schools can promote educational resilience. Listening to Students Circles, as developed by Benard and Burgoa (Benard & Slade, 2009), were initiated in which students discussed their experiences within the school and hopes for improvement of the school while staff sat outside the circle and just listened. Additional learning circles were conducted in which school staff listened to the views of parents. Finally, staff met in small groups with some of the students and parents to identify specific objectives and strategies for building caring relationships, high expectations, and opportunities for participation and contribution at the school. Having involved the school stakeholders in the planning, Dr. Rogers was pleased with many of the responses generated in these planning efforts.

In terms of building caring relationships, there was a suggestion to hire more teachers to improve the student–teacher ratio and allow teachers more time to interact informally with their students and to express their concerns for student well-being and academic success. Given the economic challenges, Dr. Rogers knew that neither the state nor the city would provide the additional funding to support this objective. However, with suggestions from participants in the change effort, the school developed other ways to enhance the student–adult ratio. Hope High School actively recruited volunteers from local colleges, members of the local chapter of the AARP, and parents who could be available during the school day. Eventually, as the number of volunteers expanded, there was a volunteer assistant in each classroom.

Once the number of adults at the school had increased, the school social worker suggested that each student in the school be matched with a specific adult at the school, following Benard's (2004) suggestion. Teachers, volunteers, and all school staff (custodians, bus drivers, and clerical and food service staff) were assigned specific students with whom they would talk once a week to find out how they were doing and provide some support. It was hoped that these adults would be the "turnaround people" (Benard, 2003, p. 116) for at-risk students through the provision of a caring relationship with them.

The school social worker and several of the teachers were concerned about the multiple issues (disabilities, family and financial problems, health issues, mental health diagnoses) that hindered the well-being of students at the school. Although the school social worker did her best to provide referrals and assist students as she could, she was unable to find any agencies willing to provide such services at the school, and the school district did not have sufficient funding to provide for more social workers. A grant was written and funded to provide a counseling center at the school staffed by three full-time social workers to address the personal challenges of the students. Social work students from the area colleges served as interns at the counseling center.

Challenged by Dr. Rogers to promote an environment in which academic success was expected for all students, one of the teachers researched the idea of developing a college culture at the school. She found that some schools had developed a college culture in which the mission was that *all* students would be expected to go to college after graduation (Corwin & Tierney, 2007; Farmer-Hinton, 2008; Farmer-Hinton & Adams, 2006; Holland & Farmer-Hinton, 2009; Knight-Diop, 2010; McClafferty, McDonough, & Nunez, 2002; Terrell, 2010). The teachers discussed this idea at several meetings. Some were skeptical because they saw this as unlikely for most of the students they served. Others thought that the idea might work with the help of the additional volunteers at the school. A few thought that the students were deserving of the best the school could offer and that this was worth a try. Five of the skeptical teachers sought and received transfers to another school for the following school year. When interviewing their replacements, Dr. Rogers actively sought teachers who were supportive of the mission to prepare all students for college.

To carry out this mission, the school initiated the following changes:

- Student volunteers from the colleges worked with their respective schools to develop a college fair to which both students and parents were invited. Knowing the importance of financial aid for most of the students at Hope High School, financial aid counselors from the local colleges discussed the process of applying for financial aid. Recognizing the interest of both students and parents in this activity, another college fair was held the following semester.
- Two of the college student volunteers requested and were granted the use of the school's computer lab after school two days a week. They used the

lab to help the high school students explore possible colleges and complete college and financial aid applications.

- Two of the older volunteers were retired teachers. They developed a workshop to help students prepare for the SAT. The workshop was conducted on Saturday mornings at the school.
- Teachers, other school staff, and volunteers were encouraged to discuss college expectations on an ongoing basis in their interactions with their students.
- Each classroom was named after a college or university and decorated with images from that college or university.
- Dr. Rogers met with the principals of the feeder schools (middle and elementary schools) in the area to discuss the revised mission of Hope High School. They discussed the shared problem of student performance at the schools. They developed a program in which students from the high school would provide after-school tutoring for students at the elementary and middle schools.
- Dr. Rogers also met with the teachers to review the curriculum. There was not enough focus at Hope High School on college preparatory courses. The decision was made to enroll all students the following year in college preparatory classes rather than the general educational program.
- To address the concerns that students were underprepared for such courses, the school developed an active tutoring program to help students who were struggling to meet course expectations. Volunteers helped substantially with tutoring sessions that were conducted throughout the school day, including before and after school.
- To foster this culture of high expectations, Dr. Rogers initiated a policy of recognition for the accomplishments of students, teachers, and school volunteers. This was communicated at school assemblies and meetings of the parent–teacher association, during the daily announcements, and through a school newsletter. Everyone appeared to respond well to this recognition and support and put forth more effort in meeting their responsibilities.

Although progress was being made to implement Dr. Rogers's vision of a resilience-promoting school, more needed to be done to provide opportunities for participation and contribution. The listening circles had been a start to let students know that their opinions mattered, but a structure had to be developed for this to continue. One of the school volunteers, a member of the city council, agreed to form a student council. Under her guidance, the student council met on a weekly basis after school and discussed what students could do to make improvements. The student council was recognized for its contributions to the school, and representatives of the council met regularly with Dr. Rogers. As a result of the efforts of the student council, a school beautification project and a peer-helping program were initiated at the school.

There was concern about the deep cuts in the arts program within the city schools. Dr. Rogers and the school social worker worked with the local colleges to recruit students and faculty to develop an extracurricular program in the arts. A drama club, a photography club, a school choir, and after-school art and music classes were developed to increase students' exposure to the arts. The performances and exhibitions produced by the arts activities were well attended by students, parents, school staff, and volunteers.

Recognizing that community service has the potential to enhance student outcomes, the school social worker networked with community agencies to identify service opportunities for students at Hope High School. In addition to tutoring elementary and middle school students, students from the high school began volunteering at a Boys and Girls Club, a nursing home, and a homeless shelter. Student participation in community service and arts activities was recognized on a regular basis in school communications.

Over the next five years, test scores at the school were raised from near failing to the district average. Graduation rates at Hope High School increased substantially. The enrollment of graduates in postsecondary education rose from 20 percent to 55 percent. The school climate became much more welcoming for students, parents, school staff, and volunteers. Energized by working in such a positive atmosphere, all involved continued to actively work to further enhance student outcomes at Hope High School as well as at its feeder schools.

Use the CD by Michael Wright to articulate the environmental and personal supports of resilience in schools.

You will find a case study on your CD: *Aspiring to College From Hope High*

References

Adelman, H. W., & Taylor, L. (2006). Mapping a school's resources to improve their use in preventing and ameliorating problems. In C. Franklin, M. B. Harris, & P. Allen-Meares (Eds.), *The school services sourcebook: A guide for school-based professionals* (pp. 977–990). Oxford, England: Oxford University Press.

Aud, S., Hussar, W., Planty, M., Snyder, T., Bianco, K., Fox, M., . . . Drake, L. (2010). *The condition of education 2010* (NCES Report No. 2010–028). Washington, DC: National Center for Education Statistics.

Bell, J. A. (2001). High-performing, high-poverty schools. *Leadership, 31*(1), 8–11.

Benard, B. (1991). *Fostering resiliency in kids: Protective factors in the family, school, and community.* Minneapolis: National Resilience Resource Center. Retrieved from http://www.cce.umn.edu/pdfs/NRRC/Fostering_Resilience_012804.pdf

Benard, B. (1996). Fostering resiliency in urban schools. In B. Williams (Ed.), *Closing the achievement gap: A vision for changing beliefs and practices* (pp. 96–119). Alexandria, VA: Association for Supervision and Curriculum Development.

Benard, B. (2003). Turnaround teachers and schools. In B. Williams (Ed.), *Closing the achievement gap: A vision for changing beliefs and practices* (2nd ed., pp. 115–137). Alexandria, VA: Association for Supervision and Curriculum Development.

Benard, B. (2004). *Resiliency: What we have learned.* San Francisco: WestEd.

Benard, B., & Slade, S. (2009). Listening to students: Moving from resilience research to youth development practice and school connectedness. In R. Gilman, E. S. Huebner, & M. J. Furlong (Eds.), *Handbook of positive psychology in the schools* (pp. 353–370). New York: Routledge.

Bickel, R., Howley, C., Williams, T., & Glascock, C. (2000). *High school size, achievement equity, and cost: Robust interaction effects and tentative results.* Washington, DC: Rural School and Community Trust.

Borman, G. D., & Rachuba, L. T. (2000, April). *The characteristics of schools and classrooms attended by successful minority students.* Paper presented at the annual meeting of the American Educational Research Association, New Orleans, LA.

Brooks, J. E. (2006). Strengthening resilience in children and youth: Maximizing opportunities through the schools. *Children & Schools, 28*(2), 69–76.

Brooks, J. E. (2010). *School characteristics associated with the educational resilience of low-income and ethnic minority youth.* Unpublished doctoral dissertation, University of Texas, Austin.

Camp, W. G. (1990). Participation in student activities and achievement: A covariance structural analysis. *Journal of Educational Research, 83*(5), 272–278.

Cappella, E., & Weinstein, R. S. (2001). Turning around reading achievement: Predictors of high school students' academic resilience. *Journal of Educational Psychology, 93,* 758–771.

Cole-Henderson, B. (2000). Organizational characteristics of schools that successfully serve low-income urban African American students. *Journal of Education for Students Placed at Risk, 51*(1–2), 77–91.

Coleman, J. S. (1966). *Equality of educational opportunity.* Washington, DC: U.S. Department of Health, Education and Welfare; Office of Education.

Corwin, Z. B., & Tierney, Z. B. (2007). *Getting there—and beyond: Building a culture of college-going in high schools.* Los Angeles: University of Southern California Center for Higher Education Policy Analysis.

Croninger, R. G., & Lee, V. E. (2001). Social capital and dropping out of high school: Benefits to at-risk students of teachers' support and guidance. *Teachers College Record, 103,* 548–581.

Crosnoe, R., & Elder, Jr., G. H. (2004). Family dynamics, supportive relationships, and educational resilience during adolescence. *Journal of Family Issues, 25,* 571–602.

Dalton, B., Glennie, E., & Ingels, S. J. (2009). *Late high school dropouts: Characteristics, experiences, and changes across cohorts* (NCES Report No. 2009–307). Washington, DC: National Center for Education Statistics.

Downey, J. A. (2008). Recommendations for fostering educational resilience in the classroom. *Preventing School Failure, 53*(1), 56–64.

Dumais, S. A. (2008). Adolescents' time use and academic achievement: A test of the reproduction and mobility models. *Social Science Quarterly, 89,* 867–886.

Edmonds, R. (1979). Effective schools for the urban poor. *Educational Leadership, 37*(1), 15–24.

Farmer-Hinton, R. L. (2008). Creating opportunities for college access: Examining a school model designed to prepare students of color for college. *Multicultural Perspectives, 10*(2), 73–81.

Farmer-Hinton, R. L., & Adams, T. L. (2006). Social capital and college preparation: Exploring the role of counselors in a college prep school for black students. *Negro Educational Review, 57*(1–2), 101–116.

Greene, R. R. (2002). Human behavior theory: A resilience orientation. In R. R. Greene (Ed.), *Resiliency: An integrated approach to practice, policy, and research* (pp. 1–27). Washington, DC: NASW Press.

Hanson, T. L., Austin, G., & Lee-Bayha, J. (2003). *Student health risks, resilience, and academic performance: Year 1 report.* Los Alamitos, CA: WestEd.

Hanson, T. L., Austin, G., & Lee-Bayha, J. (2004). *How are student health risks and resilience related to the academic progress of schools?* Los Alamitos, CA: WestEd.

Hanson, T. L., & Kim, J. O. (2007). *Measuring resilience and youth development: The psychometric properties of the Healthy Kids Survey* (Issues & Answers Report, REL 2007-No. 034). Washington, DC: U.S. Department of Education, Institute of Education Sciences, National Center for Education Evaluation and Regional Assistance, Regional Educational Laboratory West.

Hanushek, E. A. (1989). The impact of differential expenditures on school performance. *Educational Researcher, 18*(4), 45–51, 62.

Hedges, L. V., Laine, R. D., & Greenwald, R. (1994). An exchange: Part I: Does money matter? A meta-analysis of studies of the effects of differential school inputs on student outcomes. *Educational Researcher, 23*(3), 5–14.

Henderson, N., & Milstein, M. M. (2003). *Resiliency in schools: Making it happen for students and educators* (Rev. ed.). Thousand Oaks, CA: Corwin Press.

Holland, N. E., & Farmer-Hinton, R. L. (2009). Leave no schools behind: The importance of a college culture in urban public high schools. *High School Journal, 92*(3), 24–43.

Jordan, W. J. (1999). Black high school students' participation in school-sponsored sports activities: Effects on school engagement and achievement. *Journal of Negro Education, 68*(1), 54–71.

Jozefowicz-Simbeni, D. M. H., & Allen-Meares, P. (2002). Poverty and schools: Intervention and resource building through school-linked services. *Children & Schools, 24*(2), 123–136.

Kannapel, P. J., & Clements, S. K. (2005). *Inside the black box of high-performing high-poverty schools.* Lexington, KY: Prichard Committee for Academic Excellence.

Knight-Diop, M. G. (2010). Closing the gap: Enacting care and facilitating black students' educational access in the creation of a high school college-going culture. *Journal of Education for Students Placed at Risk, 15,* 158–172.

Krovetz, M. L. (1999). Resiliency: A key element for supporting youth at-risk. *Clearing House, 73*(2), 121–123.

Laursen, E. K., & Birmingham, S. M. (2003). Caring relationships as a protective factor for at-risk youth: An ethnographic study. *Families in Society, 84*(2), 240–246.

Learning First Alliance. (2001). *Every child learning: Safe and supportive schools.* Washington, DC: Association for Supervision and Curriculum Development. Retrieved from http://www.learningfirst.org

Lee, V. E., & Burkam, D. T. (2003). Dropping out of high school: The role of school organization and structure. *American Educational Research Journal, 40,* 353–393.

Mahoney, J. L. (2000). School extracurricular activity participation as a moderator in the development of antisocial patterns. *Child Development, 71,* 502–516.

Mahoney, J. L., & Cairns, R. B. (1997). Do extracurricular activities protect against early school dropout? *Developmental Psychology, 33,* 241–253.

McClafferty, K. A., McDonough, P. M., & Nunez, A. (2002, January). *What is a college culture? Facilitating college preparation through organizational change.* Paper presented at the annual meeting of the American Educational Research Association, New Orleans, LA.

McNeal, R. B. (1997). High school dropouts: A closer examination of school effects. *Social Science Quarterly, 78,* 209–222.

National Governors Association Center for Best Practices. (2000). *Improving academic performance by meeting student health needs* (NGASI Issue Brief 10/13/2000). Retrieved from http://www.nga.org/cda/files/001013performance.pdf

National Research Council and the Institute of Medicine. (2004). *Engaging schools: Fostering high school students' motivation to learn.* Committee on Increasing High School Students' Engagement and Motivation to Learn. Board on Children, Youth, and Families, Division of Behavioral and Social Sciences and Education. Washington, DC: National Academies Press.

Nettles, S. M., & Robinson, F. P. (1998). *Exploring the dynamics of resilience in an elementary school* (Report No. 26). Baltimore: Center for Research on the Education of Students Placed at Risk.

Oregon State Department of Education. (2000). *Keeping kids connected: How schools and teachers can help all students feel good about school . . . and why that matters.* Salem: Author.

Pianta, R. C., & Walsh, D. J. (1998). Applying the construct of resilience in schools: Cautions from a developmental systems perspective. *School Psychology Review, 27,* 407–417.

Picucci, A. C., Brownson, A., Kahlert, R., & Sobel, A. (2002). *Driven to succeed: High-performing, high-poverty, turnaround middle schools: Vol. I. Cross-case analysis of high-performing, high-poverty, turnaround middle schools.* Austin, TX: Charles A. Dana Center.

Randolph, K. A., Fraser, M. W., & Orthner, D. K. (2004). Educational resilience among youth at risk. *Substance Use & Misuse, 39,* 747–767.

Reis, S. M., Colbert, R. D., & Hebert, T. P. (2005). Understanding resilience in diverse, talented students in an urban high school. *Roeper Review,* 27(2), 110–120.

Resnick, M. D., Bearman, P. S., Blum, R. W., Bauman, K. E., Harris, K. M., Jones, J., et al. (1997). Protecting adolescents from harm: Findings from the National Longitudinal Study on Adolescent Health. *Journal of the American Medical Association, 278,* 823–832.

Rice, J. K. (2003). *Teacher quality: Understanding the effectiveness of teacher attributes.* Washington, DC: Economic Policy Institute.

Richman, J. M., Bowen, G. L., & Woolley, M. E. (2004). School failure: An eco-interactional developmental perspective. In M. W. Fraser (Ed.), *Risk and resilience in childhood: An ecological perspective* (2nd ed., pp. 133–160). Washington, DC: NASW Press.

Richman, J. M., & Fraser, M. W. (2001). Resilience in childhood: The role of risk and protection. In J. M. Richman & M. W. Fraser (Eds.), *The context of youth violence: Resilience, risk, and protection* (pp. 1–12). Westport, CT: Praeger.

Rigsby, L. C. (1994). On Americanization of resilience: Deconstructing research practice. In M. C. Wang & E. W. Gordon (Eds.), *Educational resilience in inner-city America* (pp. 85–94). Hillsdale, NJ: Erlbaum.

Rutter, M., Maughan, B., Mortimore, P., Ouston, J., & Smith, A. (1979). *Fifteen thousand hours: Secondary schools and their effects on children.* Cambridge, MA: Harvard University Press.

Sanders, W. L., & Rivers, J. C. (1996). *Cumulative and residual effects of teachers on future student academic achievement.* Knoxville: University of Tennessee Value-Added Research and Assessment Center. Retrieved from http://www.cgp.upenn.edu/pdf/Sanders_Rivers-TVASS_teacher%20effects.pdf

Schoon, I., Parsons, S., & Sacker, A. (2004). Socioeconomic adversity, educational resilience, and subsequent levels of adult adaptation. *Journal of Adolescent Research, 19,* 383–404.

Schorr, L. B. (1997). *Common purpose: Strengthening families and neighborhoods to rebuild America.* New York: Anchor Books.

Shin, J., Lee, H., & Kim, Y. (2009). Student and school factors affecting mathematics achievement: International comparisons between Korea, Japan, and the USA. *School Psychology International, 30*(5), 520–537.

Shouse, R. C. (1995, February). *Academic press and school sense of community: Sources of friction, prospects for synthesis.* Paper presented at the annual meeting of the American Educational Research Association, San Francisco, CA.

Smyth, E. (1999). Pupil performance, absenteeism and school drop-out: A multi-dimensional analysis. *School Effectiveness and School Improvement, 10,* 480–502.

Swanson, C. B. (2010). Progress postponed: U.S. graduation rate continues decline. *Education Week, 29*(34), 22–30.

Tennessee State Department of Education. (1990). *The state of Tennessee's Student/Teacher Achievement Ratio (STAR) project.* Technical report, 1985–1990. Nashville: Author.

Terrell, K. (2010). The 100 percent promise. *U.S. News & World Report, 147*(8), 34–36.

Wang, M. C., Haertel, G. D., & Walberg, H. J. (1994). Educational resilience in inner cities. In M. C. Wang & E. W. Gordon (Eds.). *Educational resilience in inner-city America* (pp. 45–73). Hillsdale, NJ: Erlbaum.

Wang, M. C., Haertel, G. D., & Walberg, H. J. (1995, April 18). *Educational resilience: An emergent construct.* Paper presented at the Annual Meeting of the American Educational Research Association, San Francisco, CA.

Wang, M. C., Haertel, G. D., & Walberg, H. J. (1997). *Fostering educational resilience in inner-city schools* (Publication Series No. 4). Philadelphia: National Research Center on Education in the Inner Cities.

Wang, M. C., Haertel, G. D., & Walberg, H. J. (1998). *Educational resilience* (Publication Series No. 11). Philadelphia: National Research Center on Education in the Inner Cities.

WestEd. (2011a). *About the California Healthy Kids Survey.* Los Alamitos, CA: Author. Retrieved from http://chks.wested.org/about

WestEd. (2011b). *About the California School Climate Survey.* Los Alamitos, CA: Author. Retrieved from http://cscs.wested.org/about

WestEd. (2011c). *About the California School Parent Survey.* Los Alamitos, CA: Author. Retrieved from http://csps.wested.org/about

Wimberly, G. L. (2002). *School relationships foster success for African American students.* Iowa City, IA: ACT.

Yamauchi, L. A. (2003). Making school relevant for at-risk students: The Wai'anae High School Hawaiian Studies Program. *Journal of Education for Students Placed at Risk, 8,* 379–390.

Zimmerman, M. A., & Arunkumar, R. (1994). Resiliency research: Implications for schools and policy. *Social Policy Report: Society for Research in Child Development, 8*(4), 1–17.

12

Listening to Girls: A Study in Resilience

MARIE L. WATKINS

On finishing this chapter, students will be able to:

Advance human rights and social and economic justice (Educational Policy 2.1.5) by
- Understanding the forms and mechanisms of oppression and discrimination (practice behavior).

Respond to contexts that shape practice (Educational Policy 2.1.9) by
- Providing leadership in promoting sustainable changes in service delivery and practice to improve the quality of social services (practice behavior).

Listening to girls poised at the edge of adolescence, I hear them speak of their confusion and their fight, their struggle for understanding and a great desire to be heard, to be in authentic relationships, and to know what they know with a sense of personal authority.

—GILLIGAN, 1990, P. 65

This quote from Gilligan (1990) captures key resilience strategies developed by adolescent girls as they overcome the odds of growing up in environments that are hostile to young women. The terms "fight" (Robinson & Ward, 1991), "struggle for understanding" (Gilligan, Rogers, & Tolman, 1991) and "be in authentic relationships" (Brown, 1990; Brown & Gilligan, 1992; J. M. Taylor, Gilligan, & Sullivan, 1995; Watkins, 1995) represent resilient attempts to traverse the passageway from girlhood to womanhood. Some of the early works of Gilligan and colleagues that studied adolescent girls from privileged backgrounds (Gilligan, Lyons, & Hanmer, 1990) focused on girls' range of adaptive behaviors for becoming competent adults. The findings suggested that girls' strategies moved beyond the traditionally defined, socially expected female behavior of "nice and kind" to include forms of resistance such as "fight and struggle." The use of these resiliency strategies in the helping process offers practitioners the possibility of a more girl-centered, strengths-based, and relationship-oriented social work practice. Similarly, the findings presented in this chapter of a qualitative study that examined the development of six early adolescent girls will help enable readers to personalize the tenets of risk and resiliency. What separates this group of girls from those in Gilligan's studies is the girls' environmental risk factors—the effects of growing up in poor families, living in unsafe neighborhoods, and attending underresourced schools.

The girls' stories clarify how, despite their experience growing up with the risks of being poor, female, and undereducated, their resilience allowed them to mediate their personal relationships and navigate their social environments successfully. Their stories testify to their resilience as they used buffering behaviors to guard against risk factors present in their families, schools, and communities. Behaviors that are typically identified by social workers as resistance—fighting, school avoidance, and arguing with family and friends—are reframed as resiliency strategies needed to survive hostile community, school, and family environments. The case studies presented in this chapter spell out how these various strategies allowed the girls to sustain themselves and stay safe in relationships and on the streets. The chapter also outlines a girl-centered youth development model to foster resiliency strategies based on an asset-based, relationship-oriented approach to social work practice with girls.

Risk Factors for Early Adolescent Girls

A risk-focused model identifies community, family, school, individual, and peer risk factors that could potentially increase the probability of youth-related problems (Hawkins, Catalano, & Miller, 1992). Risk factors are greater when more risks are present; risk factors also predict diverse behavior problems and have consistent effects across races, cultures, and classes (Hawkins et al., 1992). Moreover, multiple interactive risk factors influence early adolescent female development. Biological, cognitive, emotional, and social changes are intertwined and interconnected with community, family, and school hazards (Garbarino, 1995; Garbarino, Dubrow, Kostelny, & Pardo, 1992). Risk factors in early adolescent girls may be as broad as constitutional risk factors that include the early onset of menstruation or stressful life events such as the transition from elementary to middle school, changing body shape, or sexual molestation (Werner & Johnson, 1999).

The comments of a 13-year-old study participant (Watkins, 1995) suggest that growing up female has its challenges:

> When I was younger, it was fun. And as I started to get older, it's like starting to get real hard. Well you gotta go through different stages, like you gotta get a job, help your mother out and go to school at the same time. And by me being in the seventh grade, it's like sorta hard because as you move up, it'll get harder and harder for you. It's hard cause you gotta go though the stages with boys like "going with" and having sex and all. (p. 241)

Research has indicated that during childhood, boys are more vulnerable than girls to the effects of economic hardship, insufficient caregiving, and physical abuses (Mann, 1997; Werner & Johnson, 1999). However, this reverses during adolescence, when girls become more vulnerable than boys, especially given the possibility of teenage pregnancy. The factors that put young people at risk have a far more negative effect and take a higher toll on adolescent girls' emotional and physical health than boys'.

Poverty, poor parental education, tenuous family structure, geographic mobility, a history of abuse or neglect, and the influence of negative home environments further exacerbate the negative influences on the emotional and physical health of girls (Eckenrode, Laird, & Doris, 1993; Garnier, Stein, Jacobs, & Jennifer, 1997). According to Harris and Associates, Inc. (1997), one out of four girls shows signs of depression, one in five girls states that she has been physically abused or sexually molested (usually by a family member), and one in four girls does not receive adequate health care. Teen pregnancy, consumption of drugs or alcohol, and cigarette smoking remain major health issues for girls (Brooks, Whiteman, Gordon, Nomura, & Brook, 1986; Centers for Disease Control, 1997).

Other challenges include being pushed out of schools because of lack of resources, or difficulties involving school personnel, parents, and other female students (Eckenrode et al., 1993; Fine, 1987; Garnier et al., 1997). Girls who repeat grades or are pushed out of school face serious consequences: They are less likely than their male counterparts to return and complete school. Being pushed out of school or dropping out contributes to a lack of fundamental academic skills and language fluency and an inability to relate to authority figures (del Portillo & Segura, 1996).

Resiliency is the "capacity of those who are exposed to identifiable risk factors to overcome them and avoid long-term negative consequences such as delinquency" (Rak & Patterson, 1996, p. 368). The resiliency approach moves beyond a focus on risk to an examination of conditions or protective factors that facilitate healthy development (Pittman, 1993; Pittman & Fleming, 1991). What are the factors that contribute to a young teenage girl's capacity to prosper regardless of adverse conditions? Landmark studies documenting the resiliency of adolescent girls as they cope, adjust, and persist in the face of adversity and life's difficulties have suggested some such factors.

Classic research (Coles, 1964; Konopka, 1976; Ladner, 1971; Stack, 1974) as well as later works (Gilligan, Brown, & Rogers, 1990; J. M. Taylor et al., 1995; Wolin & Wolin, 1993) have provided evidence of adolescent girls' adaptational skills, particularly among those girls identified as "at risk." Using these seminal works as a foundation, I conducted a qualitative study to examine the daily experiences of six at-risk early adolescent urban girls. A qualitative methodology was chosen as a descriptive, ethnographic, and phenomenological approach to data collection. In-depth interviews were coupled with the participant observation activity of "hanging out" at a place of the girls' choosing. This allowed me to be an active participant. Such a relationship-oriented methodology was thought to create minimal interference or change in the setting in which the girls interacted (Bogdan & Biklen, 1982; Patton, 1990; Strauss & Corbin, 1990; S. Taylor & Bogdan, 1984).

An interview protocol was developed using a set of questions adapted from the Harvard Project on the Psychology of Women and the Development of Girls and feedback from the girls (Graduate School of Education, Harvard University, 1990–1995). The participants lived in Indianapolis, Indiana, and were selected using the following criteria: They needed to be between 11 and 14 years of age, to be from working poor and poor families, and to voluntarily agree to participate in the study. They also needed to fit an at-risk profile. At-risk criteria based on Gilligan and Taylor's (1992) work included that the girl be older than average for her grade, exhibit absenteeism and tardiness, and attend a school resource program.

Six girls participated: three African American girls and three Caucasian girls (see below).

Alice

Alice was a petite 11-year-old African American girl who was about five feet tall. The contours of her body showed through her T-shirt and denim shorts, suggesting that she had matured early. Alice's brown doe eyes were framed by thinly administered black eyeliner, and her full lips were colored with dark red lipstick. She had light brown skin and was adorned with three gold chains and large gold hoop earrings.

At the first meeting, Alice ran into the room screaming at three adolescent boys to "mind your own f—king business and leave me alone." After she introduced herself to me, she apologized for "cussin." She described her attempts to protect herself from the boys' teasing: "They been saying that I'm pregnant, but I just ain't ready for all of that, I'm only eleven." Although she acknowledged that she was not ready for "all of that," she stated that it was fun "to get all of that attention" that the neighborhood boys were giving to her changing body.

Sunny

Another 11-year-old, Sunny was a tall, gangly Caucasian girl with shaggy straight brown hair highlighted by natural blond streaks. Her bangs were strewn across her forehead and a clip held one side of her hair back. With a skip in her gait, Sunny, exhibiting a full smile, hopped down the steps where I was sitting. Sunny's hazel green eyes sparkled as she said, "Hi! I'm ready for my interview!" For the occasion, Sunny had replaced her usual uniform of a baggy, extra large T-shirt, cutoff denim shorts, and high-top sneakers with rolled-down sweat socks with a freshly laundered and ironed shirt and short pants.

Shatika

This 12-year-old African American girl was tall and thin. She described herself as follows: "I'm what you call light-skinned." Adolescent acne (which she called "skin bumps") was noticeable on her forehead, nose, and cheeks. Shatika's brown hair with red highlights was pulled behind her ears with a rubber band. She explained that her hair "needed to be done" but that her mother was unable to afford the cost of a permanent. Shatika was very soft spoken and hesitatingly made eye contact as the interview process was explained.

Cindy

Cindy was a 12-year-old who peered through a veil of straight dark bangs that hid her crystal green eyes. Her cream-colored skin was flawless. She pointed out the freckles on the bridge of her turned-up nose, saying, "I hate my freckles. Kids call me 'dot face.'" She indicated that she wanted to participate in the project because her friends had told her it was fun.

Faith

This tall, thin, 13-year-old African American girl had almond-shaped eyes lined with black eyeliner; her lips were neatly colored with mauve lipstick. Her jet-black hair was expertly wrapped in a red bandana that matched her short outfit. When her friends chided her for "talking with that white lady," Faith encouraged me to "pay them no mind, I'll help you with your project." As dates for interviews were scheduled, Faith informed me that she was having an abortion within the next couple of days but that she still wanted to help.

Daisy

This 13-year-old Caucasian girl was petite with symmetrical fullness of hips and breasts. Her heavily permed dark blond hair was shoulder length, and she wore a ribbon to keep her hair out of her small and closely set gray eyes. Daisy was dressed in "daisy dukes"—short shorts with a matching gingham shirt. As she spoke in soft, hushed tones, Daisy made it clear that she was willing to help with the project only if she could be assured that no one would "find out my secrets." She said, "I ain't never got to talk about me before and it could help me. It's good to talk with someone sometimes to hear yourself."

Findings

The six teenage girls revealed numerous examples of their resilience. They sought out key relationships and experiences that fostered health and promoted competencies in different environments. For example, the study interviews illustrated that the girls sought out and identified with positive role models who helped them enhance their self-esteem. The teenagers also indicated that they participated in youth-serving agencies' after-school skill development programs that often served as a preventive measure against exposure to risk (Heath & McLaughlin, 1993). In addition, the interview findings showed that the girls experienced a sense of self-efficacy as they developed feelings of internal control and were able to delay immediate gratification to achieve long-term goals (Watkins, 1995).

Three major themes emerged as the girls articulated the protective factors that fostered their resilience: (1) the centrality of relationships, (2) the importance of resistance strategies, and (3) the need for physical resistance. These themes paralleled research that has identified the following critical components for resilience development: having one caring adult (Bernard, 1992; Garbarino, 1995), accessing open opportunities (Bernard, 1999; Garbarino et al., 1992), and developing a sense of self-efficacy (Rutter, 1987).

Centrality of Relationships

Researchers have found that an easygoing temperament—which may encourage positive reactions from others—is a predicator of a child developing positive relationships that can result in resilience. Both the presence of someone to relate to and the ability to create a relationship can be linked to such personally attractive qualities (Masten & Coatsworth, 1998; Werner, 1984). The present findings supported this view: The girls' ability to develop and sustain relationships appeared to revolve around temperamental dispositions. For example, Sunny bragged that she was "nice and kind" to others. The girls often commented that being "nice, cheerful, and fun" or "being good" and being "helpful" was appreciated by others.

Theorists have suggested that the ability to form a stable emotional relationship with at least one parent or other reference person and social support from persons outside of the family can serve as important protective factors in the lives of children growing up in "socially toxic environments" (Garbarino, 1995, p. 4). Resiliency researchers have demonstrated that at-risk youth "who are involved with at least one caring adult are more likely to withstand negative influences, including poverty, parental addiction, family mental illness, and family discord, than are their peers who are not involved in a similar relationship" (U.S. Department of Justice, Office of Juvenile Justice and Delinquency Prevention, 1998, p. 12). The present findings substantiate this research. When asked "what is important to you in your world?" the girls cited their mothers, fathers, and favorite "aunties."

Relationships with Mothers and Fathers

A consistent finding from the girls concerned the effect of having a working mother. Four girls' mothers worked two jobs to help the families remain financially solvent. Three of the girls' mothers were the sole income providers for the household, and two girls resided in families in which the father worked but earned a low salary. The girls discussed their mothers' financial constraints and efforts to make ends meet. The girls also discussed their mothers' unavailability to attend school functions or be present when daily challenges arose.

Each girl also stated that having a relationship with her father was important. Although the girls acknowledged the importance of father–daughter relationships, they described limited—and sometimes an absence of—involvement with their fathers. Only Cindy's father lived full time with the family. Nonetheless, the vision of a father figure loomed large in each girl's ideal set of relationships:

> Daisy said, "I just started seeing him in February. My dad was never around and now he says he wants to make up for the lost years for when he was in prison. It makes me feel happy to know that I deserve to have father in my life." (Watkins, 1995, p. 135)

Other Adult Relationships

Resilient children often have at least one significant person who accepts them unconditionally and provides guidance and supervision. These caring adults include youth workers, coaches, clergy, neighbors, teachers, and others who serve in mentoring roles throughout a child's development (Anthony & Cohler, 1987; Brooks et al., 1986; Rhodes, Gingiss, & Smith, 1994). Such relationships can provide young persons with "personal connectedness, supervision and guidance, skills training, career or cultural enrichment opportunities, knowledge of spirituality and values, a sense of self worth and perhaps, most important, goals and hope for the future" (U.S. Department of Justice, 1998, p. 12).

The resourcefulness of the girls to seek relationships with others beyond their parents can be viewed as a resiliency strategy. A meaningful relationship identified by all of the girls was with a significant adult woman referred to as "aunt" or "auntie." The aunt or auntie, who was either a biological relative or someone else, appeared to provide important support for the girls. Providing information and transportation and sharing activities were the primary functions performed by the aunts on behalf of the girls. For example, Daisy felt that her relationship with her Aunt Sally was nice because "she doesn't yell at me like everyone else."

The African American girls described their aunts as "someone I can tell things." Aunts acted as confidants and resources about life skills and streetwise protective strategies. The girls' statements were consistent with the tenets of Afrocentrism that highlight reciprocity, mutuality, and connection with mothers, family, and community (Ladner, 1971; Stack, 1974; Tatum, 1995). These relationships allowed for the development of intimacy, rather than the expectations of separation or autonomy.

In addition to recounting daily interactions with their aunts, the girls reported that teachers informed each of their lives on a regular basis. The girls revealed that the teachers were important figures in their success or failure in school; however, they did not name teachers with whom they had positive relationships. The girls constantly highlighted some of the negatives of the school setting and their teachers' roles. Daisy raised concerns expressed by all of the girls:

> The teachers are all mean to you . . . they yell at you, put you out in the hall. I've been yelled at for not paying attention. . . . I was talking. [The teacher] said to either be quiet or she'd send me to the principal. So I be quiet, you don't want to go nowhere near our principal cause he's got a big paddle. (Watkins, 1995, p. 156)

However, the girls viewed relationships with the staff at the Boys and Girls Clubs (1999) as serving as a source of protection and support as they attempted to mediate the sometimes-conflictual relationships between themselves, their teachers, and their peers. Sunny stated,

> I tell the new kids not to be scared because the people there [at the clubhouse] won't mess with you. All you got to do is go tell Dave and them

> [the other staff]. They just tell us that if anybody is going to mess with you to come tell them [the staff], that they won't let them bother you. It makes me feel good so I don't have to get hurt or anything. Cause Dave helps kids out when they're not feeling well or they're getting into fights. (Watkins, 1995, p. 175)

Peer Relationships

Key peer relationships identified by the girls included their (girl) friends and the boys that they "go with." Friendship activities were identified by each of the girls as important adaptive strategies: sharing activities, hanging out together, keeping secrets, and "keeping me out of trouble." As Cindy stated, "How I know they are my friends is because they try to get me out of trouble." Faith also had a friend who had helped her stay out of trouble by encouraging her to become involved in activities and protecting her: "When I got in trouble, my friend Jody, she got in trouble with me. She ain't let nobody mess with me and when she's around she wouldn't let me get into no kinda trouble" (Watkins, 1995, p. 195).

Boys were another relationship identified by the girls as "important." A boy with whom one "goes with" or "you have a relationship with" was a vehicle to "feel special" and enter into a different set of relational dynamics—talking on the phone, hanging out together, and exploring adult couple roles, including sexual experimentation. However, narrative themes of mistrust and harassment emerged as the girls described their interactions with boys. For example, Daisy stated that she warned others to be "careful around them boys, cause boys can do bad things to girls, like hurt them, punch them and call them virgins" (Watkins, 1995, p. 206).

Resiliency Strategies

The study findings suggested that the girls developed different types of resistance strategies to maintain a sense of competence and self-confidence while in relationships with others. Resistance is a coping mechanism to prevent disassociation from self or others. That is, the girls struggled to remain true to themselves. They may or may not have chosen socially acceptable behaviors to maintain connections with others. These strategies may be identified as psychological resistance, a form of resisting distress, and political resistance, a means of maintaining psychological health (Gilligan, 1991; Gilligan & Taylor, 1992). Psychological resistance is a sign of psychological distress and capitulation. For example, a girl may not openly voice her opinion or expose what she knows. Girls may wish to escape or to be left alone. The pervasive use of such phrases as "I don't know" or "This may sound strange" or "I probably sound weird" are other indications of psychological resistance. An example was found in Daisy's comment that she used her "small voice" when she disagreed with her friends so that they "don't get mad and leave me." This type of secrecy can endanger relationships and may also involve mood changes and increased rates of sleeping or overeating (Gilligan & Taylor, 1992).

In contrast, political resistance, a sign of psychological health, demonstrates an insistence and willingness to speak and acknowledge what one sees and hears. In this instance, girls may exhibit keen observations about their social environment and demonstrate high levels of articulating what they see, think, and feel. Political resistance strategies among the study participants were represented by the conscious speaking out or acting out against "domination, oppression, false relationships or debilitating conventions of female behavior such as self-silence, self-sacrifice or self-negation to fend against acts of capitulation" (Gilligan & Taylor, 1992, p. 103). For example, in this study, girls said they had arguments, disagreements, or fights with their mothers, friends, and boy friends. The girls' fighting may be reframed as political resistance or attempts to sustain and strengthen intimacy. This flies in the face of the traditional implication that fighting is a symptom of the adolescent drive for independence and fear of relationships (Gilligan, Brown, & Rogers, 1990; J. M. Taylor et al., 1995).

Although the girls indicated that they may initially attempt to negotiate relationships or ignore hurtful interactions, they said that, eventually, "we just gonna hafta fight." With the exception of Daisy, the urban girls assumed an "in your face" stance to maintaining their sense of integrity as they resolved their tensions between self-knowledge and external social pressures. The girls' political resistance strategies of "act smart," "smart mouth," "go off," and "get into trouble" kept them active participants within their worlds.

Ironically, the girls' "out there and in your face" stance presented personal gains and social costs. The personal gains included a longer period during which they were able to stay connected to their internal voices or true selves. Because these girls stood at the "figurative edge" of society by virtue of their neighborhood residence, academic status, race, and social class, the expectations that they be perfect girls or nice girls did not carry much weight (Gilligan & Taylor, 1992). Attempts to become the perfect girl—a prominent theme for girls in economically and educationally privileged environments—did not have a dominant place among the girls in the study. The study participants occupied a less visible place in society (Brown, 1990; Brown & Gilligan, 1992; Watkins, 1995). Therefore, they were less inclined to use psychological resistance strategies and more frequently used a "being out in the world" or a political resistance stance.

However, the social and material costs of maintaining their political strategies were dear. The girls may have spoken about what they saw and knew, but the consequences of this expression were social containment and censoring by adults. The girls often felt ostracized and punished. The political resistance behaviors, such as "smart mouth[ing]," "go[ing] off," "say[ing] whatever," rolling of eyes and sucking of teeth, and "getting attitudes," were often met with consternation. Family and peer group members may have "screamed and yelled," "called me out of my name," or "stole me in my face." School authorities may have "suspend[ed]," "expel[ed]," or "ship[ped] me to Juvenile."

The school context poignantly illustrated the complications of political resistance as a resiliency strategy. The girls in the study spoke about how they challenged the lack of accessibility of teachers and the quality of their education. Sunny's statement reflected all of the girls' sense of isolation: "It don't matter about the teacher, I just sit there and do my work by myself" (Watkins, 1995, p. 194). The girls' attempts to "do my work" and "get good grades" were further frustrated by their academic difficulties and lack of consistent remedial assistance.

The desire to get ahead and the lack of support can become a conflict in the formation of self-esteem. The girls struggled with how they could get good grades and feel good about themselves. They worked hard to avoid social conflict in school—"don't get into trouble and just do my work." As the girls' attempts to be heard went unnoticed, they acted out and became a source of condemnation. Each of the girls articulated their experiences with being moved into special classes and later being suspended or expelled from school because of "smart mouthing the teacher."

Need for Physical Resistance

The study findings revealed the girls' feelings about unsafe relationships and urban settings that kept them constantly aware of the potential dangers and the need for physical resistance (Watkins, 1995). The girls would deliberately prearrange travel companions when walking to the corner store. To avoid danger, they would map out the route they would take through the streets. They also developed other physical resistance strategies, such as having personal safety plans or not "hanging on the streets."

The girls described physical resistance strategies that involved skillful observation and action. For example, the girls observed and determined the type of "traffic" on the streets. That is, they consciously identified and avoided persons who used drugs, stalked, or "punked" others. The girls also armed themselves with defensive fighting skills to protect themselves on the streets and in aggressive relationships. In addition, the girls discussed contacts with "safe persons" and "safe places" for protective passageways from one friend's house to another.

As the study findings suggest, psychological resistance provides an underground retreat for girls. Political resistance serves as a vehicle to "stay out there" in relationships. Physical resistance provides basic physical self-protection tools to remain not just emotionally healthy but physically safe. The girls' stories indicated their strengths as they used protective strategies and attempted to emerge from adolescence as resilient adults.

Social Work Practice: A Girl-centered Youth Development Approach

The stories of these six early adolescent girls testify to the importance of daily survival strategies in the face of adverse environmental conditions. The findings have profound implications for the social work profession. The girls' stories suggest that social workers need to expand their understanding of adolescent girls' survival and resiliency strategies. Furthermore, a core component of social work practice with girls requires that social workers reevaluate their personal belief systems and practice strategies.

A social worker's personal beliefs about adolescent girls are central to effective social work practice with girls. The social worker's ability to stay grounded and understand a young adolescent's perspective is at the core of building relationships, making decisions, and sharing power *with* and not *at, for,* or *by* the girls. More specifically, social workers need to do the following:

- Become aware of their gender socialization biases and personal internalization of sexist value systems.
- Become aware of their biases related to the concept of acceptable and unacceptable codes of behavior, dress, language, and other means of expression for girls.
- Become aware of their preconceived notions of the capacity and ability of girls from diverse populations.
- Be in tune with their styles and patterns of verbal and nonverbal communication.
- Assess the parameters of the client–social worker relationship so that it is mutually determined and understood.
- Accept that girls have authority over their personal realities.
- Practice humility and acceptance when girls act on their own sense of power.

The girls' stories also suggest that social workers must modify traditional techniques and skills so that practice strategies honor the needs of girls to remain "relational" and "in connection" (Jordan, Kaplan, Miller, Stiver, & Surrey, 1991; Stern, 1990). Bernard (1999) highlighted the significance of connectedness to resiliency:

> Research on resilience challenges the field to build a connectedness or sense of belonging, by transforming our families, our schools and

> communities to become "psychological homes" where youth can find mutually caring and respectful relationships and opportunities for meaningful involvement. (p. 272)

To foster resilience, social workers need to do more to move beyond "fix a girl" remedial interventions to a "prepare a girl" youth development paradigm. The youth development paradigm is based on a developmental approach that emphasizes asset building, focuses on preparation for adulthood, builds youth capacity through relationships, and fosters skill development and interconnectedness with the girl's environment (Hawkins & Catalano, 1993).

Furthermore, a youth development model focuses on the interconnectedness between risks and protective factors. In this instance, the social worker addresses environmental and personality influences that "interact in a reciprocal, transactional relationship" to form resilience (Bernard, 1999, p. 270). This emphasis provides a holistic perspective that assumes that resiliency cannot be examined in isolation. Rather, a youth development–based, resiliency-oriented model embodies a systems approach that encourages social workers to examine and understand the interrelatedness of biological, psychological, social, and environmental risk and protective factors. This, in turn, may encourage "interventions that both attempt to minimize risk factors and maximize protective or resilience factors" (Lesher, 1999, p. 2).

The youth development model is also congruent with the ecological model that acknowledges the interrelatedness between young people and their environments in the formation of resilience (Watkins & Iverson, 1997). Environments consist of the different contexts and networks in which young people grow and learn and the interactional systems of family, kin, peers, school, youth agencies, and community—all of which are important contributors to healthy development (Bronfenbrenner, 1979). Moreover, the youth development model offers the social worker a planning, analysis, and evaluation framework to foster resiliency, relationships, and positive resistance strategies among girls.

Girl-centered youth development interventions might include opportunities to

- learn how to form close, durable relationships (even if they are short-lived);
- find a valued place in a constructive group;
- feel a sense of worth as a person;
- achieve a reliable basis for making informed choices;
- know how to use available support systems;
- express constructive curiosity and exploratory behaviors;
- find ways of being useful to others; and
- believe in a promising future with real opportunities.

Through the integration of practices such strategies enhance a girl's sense of "belonging, usefulness, power, and competency," and a young teen may become "bold, smart and strong" (Girls, Inc., 1996). "The voices of those who have overcome adversity tell us that ultimately resilience is a process of connectedness—of linking to people, to interests and ultimately to life itself" (Bernard, 1999, p. 272).

Use the CD by Michael Wright to explore the centrality of relationships in the resilience of girls. Articulate the considerations in a girl-centered approach.

You will find a case study on your CD: *Reading "This May Sound Strange, But . . ."*

References

Anthony, E. J., & Cohler, B. J. (Eds.). (1987). *The invulnerable child.* New York: Guilford Press.

Bernard, B. (1992). *Mentoring programs for urban youth: Handle with care.* Portland, OR: Western Regional Center for Drug-Free Schools and Communities, Far West Laboratories.

Bernard, B. (1999). Application of resilience: Possibilities and promise. In M. Glantz & J. Johnson (Eds.), *Resilience and development: Positive life adaptations* (pp. 269–280). New York: Kluwer Academic/Plenum.

Bogdan, R., & Biklen, S. (1982). *Qualitative research for education: An introduction to theory and methods.* Boston: Allyn & Bacon.

Boys and Girls Clubs. (1999). *Annual report.* Atlanta: Author.

Bronfenbrenner, U. (1979). *The ecology of human development.* Cambridge, MA: Harvard University Press.

Brooks, J. S., Whiteman, M., Gordon, A. S., Nomura, C., & Brook, D. W. (1986). Onset of adolescent drinking: A longitudinal study of intrapersonal and interpersonal antecedents. *Advances in Alcohol and Substance Abuse, 5,* 91–110.

Brown, L. (1990). A problem of vision: The development of relational voice in girls ages 7 to 16. *Women's Study Quarterly, 19,* 55–71.

Brown, L., & Gilligan, C. (1992). *Meeting at the crossroads: Women's psychology and girls development.* Cambridge, MA: Harvard University Press.

Centers for Disease Control. (1997). *National youth risk survey.* Atlanta: U.S. Department of Health and Human Services, Public Health Service. Retrieved from http://www.cdc.gov/nccdphp/dash

Coles, R. (1964). *Children of crisis: A study of courage and fear.* New York: Dell.

del Portillo, R., & Segura, M. (1996). Foreword. In J. A. Burciaga (Ed.), *Cada cabeza es mundo/Each mind is a world.* Sausalito: California Latino–Chicano High School Dropout Prevention Project.

Eckenrode, J., Laird, M., & Doris, J. (1993). School performance and disciplinary problems among abused and neglected children. *Developmental Psychology, 29,* 53–62.

Fine, M. (1987). Silencing in public schools. *Language Arts, 64,* 157–174.

Garbarino, J. (1995). *Raising children in a socially toxic environment.* San Francisco: Jossey-Bass.

Garbarino, J., Dubrow, N., Kostelny, K., & Pardo, C. (1992). *Children in danger: Coping with consequences of community violence.* San Francisco: Jossey-Bass.

Garnier, H., Stein, J. A., Jacobs, J. K., & Jennifer, K. (1997). The process of dropping out of high school: A 19-year perspective. *American Educational Research Journal, 34,* 395–419.

Gilligan, C. (1990). Teaching Shakespeare's sister: Notes from the underground of female adolescence. In C. Gilligan, N. Lyons, & T. Hammer (Eds.), *Making connections: The relational worlds of adolescent girls at Emma Willard School* (pp. 65–82). Cambridge, MA: Harvard University Press.

Gilligan, C. (1991). Women's psychological development: Implications for psychotherapy. In C. Gilligan, A. Rogers, & D. Tolman (Eds.), *Women, girls and psychotherapy: Reframing resistance* (pp. 5–33). New York: Haworth Press.

Gilligan, C., Brown, L., & Rogers, A. (1990). Psyche embedded: A place for body, relationships, and culture in personality theory. In A. Rabin, R. Zucker, R. Emmons, & S. Frank (Eds.), *Studying persons and lives* (pp. 86–147). New York: Springer.

Gilligan, C., Lyons, N., & Hanmer, T. (Eds.). (1990). *Making connections: The relational worlds of adolescent girls at Emma Willard School.* Cambridge, MA: Harvard University Press.

Gilligan, C., Rogers, A. G., & Tolman, D. L. (1991). *Women, girls, and psychotherapy: Reframing resistance.* New York: Harrington Park Press.

Gilligan, C., & Taylor, J. (1992). *Final report: A study of urban girls considered to be at-risk.* Indianapolis, IN: Lilly Endowment.

Girls, Inc. (1996). *Becoming strong, smart and bold: Girls Incorporated program directors as change agents.* Indianapolis: Girls Incorporated National Resource Center.

Graduate School of Education, Harvard University. (1990–1995). *Project on the psychology of women and the development of girls.* Cambridge, MA: Author.

Harris, L., & Associates, Inc. (1997, September). *The Commonwealth Fund of the health of adolescent girls.* New York: Commonwealth Fund.

Hawkins, J. D., & Catalano, R. F. (1993). *Communities that care: Risk-focused prevention using the social development model.* Seattle: Developmental Research and Programs.

Hawkins, J. D., Catalano, R. F., & Miller, J. Y. (1992). Risk and protective factors for alcohol and other drug problems in adolescence and early adulthood. *Psychological Bulletin, 112,* 64–105.

Heath, S., & McLaughlin, M. (1993). *Identity and inner-city youth.* New York: Teachers College Press.

Jordan, J., Kaplan, A., Miller, J., Stiver, I., & Surrey, J. (1991). *Women's growth in connection: Writings from the Stone Center.* New York: Guilford Press.

Konopka, G. (1976). *Young girls: A portrait of adolescence.* Englewood Cliffs, NJ: Prentice Hall.

Ladner, J. (1971). *Tomorrow's tomorrow: The black woman.* New York: Doubleday.

Lesher, A. (1999). Introduction. In M. Glantz & J. Johnson (Eds.), *Resilience and development: Positive life adaptations* (pp. 2–25). New York: Kluwer Academic/Plenum.

Mann, J. (1997, October 10). A perilous age for girls. *Washington Post,* p. E3.

Masten, A., & Coatsworth, J. D. (1998). The development of competence in favorable and unfavorable environments. *American Psychologist, 53,* 205–220.

Patton, M. Q. (1990). *Qualitative evaluation and research methods.* London: Sage.

Pittman, K. (1993). *Stronger staff, stronger youth* (Conference Summary Report, October 1992). Washington, DC: Academy for Educational Development, Center for Youth Development and Policy.

Pittman, K., & Fleming, W. (1991). *A new vision: Promoting youth development.* Washington, DC: Academy for Educational Development, Center for Youth Development and Policy.

Rak, C. F., & Patterson, L. E. (1996). Promoting resiliency in at-risk children. *Journal of Counseling and Development, 74,* 368–373.

Rhodes, J. E., Gingiss, P. L., & Smith, P. B. (1994). Risk and protective factors for alcohol use among pregnant African-American, Hispanic, and white adolescents: The influence of peers, sexual partners, family members, and mentors. *Addictive Behaviors, 8,* 555–564.

Robinson, T., & Ward, J. V. (1991). A belief in self far greater than anyone's disbelief: Cultivating resistance among African-American female adolescents. In C. Gilligan, A. Rogers, & D. Tolman (Eds.), *Women, girls and psychotherapy: Reframing resistance* (pp. 87–104). New York: Haworth Press.

Rutter, M. (1987). Psychological resilience and protective mechanisms. *American Journal of Orthopsychiatry, 57,* 316–331.

Stack, C. (1974). *All our kin: Strategies for survival in a black community.* New York: Harper & Row.

Stern, L. (1990). Conceptions of separation and connections in female adolescents. In C. Gilligan, N. Lyons, & T. Hanmer (Eds.), *Making connections: The relational worlds of adolescent girls at Emma Willard School* (pp. 73–87). Cambridge, MA: Harvard University Press.

Strauss, A., & Corbin, J. (1990). *Basics of qualitative research: Grounded theory, procedure and techniques.* Newbury Park, CA: Sage.

Tatum, B. (1995, March). *Racial identity and relational therapy: Black women in white communities.* Paper presented at the 20th Annual Feminist Psychology Conference, Indianapolis, IN.

Taylor, J. M., Gilligan, C., & Sullivan, A. M. (1995). *Between voice and silence: Women and girls, race and relationships.* Cambridge, MA: Harvard University Press.

Taylor, S., & Bogdan, R. (1984). *Introduction to qualitative research: The search for meanings* (2nd ed.). New York: Wiley.

U.S. Department of Justice, Office of Juvenile Justice and Delinquency Prevention. (1998). *Juvenile mentoring program: 1998 report to Congress.* Washington, DC: Author.

Watkins, M. (1995). *Where are the girls? A study of the relational experiences of early adolescent girls considered to be at-risk.* Unpublished doctoral dissertation, Syracuse University, Syracuse, NY.

Watkins, M., & Iverson, E. (1997). Youth development research–teaching–service field units. In R. R. Greene & M. Watkins (Eds.), *Serving diverse constituencies: Applying the ecological perspective* (pp. 167–197). New York: Aldine de Gruyter.

Werner, E. E. (1984). Resilient children. *Young Children, 40,* 68–72.

Werner, E. E., & Johnson, J. (1999). Can we apply resilience? In M. Glantz & J. Johnson (Eds.), *Resilience and development: Positive life adaptations* (pp. 259–268). New York: Kluwer Academic/Plenum.

Wolin, S., & Wolin, S. (1993). *The resilient self: How survivors of troubled families rise above their adversity.* New York: Villard Books.

13

Promoting Resilience among Returning Veterans

ROBERT BLUNDO, ROBERTA R. GREENE,
and JOYCE GRAHL RILEY

On finishing this chapter, students will be able to further:

Respond to contexts that shape practice (Educational Policy 2.1.9) by

- Continuously discovering, appraising, and attending to changing locales, populations, scientific and technological developments, and emerging societal trends to provide relevant services (practice behavior).

Assess individuals, families, groups, organizations, and communities (Educational Policy 2.1.10b) by

- Assessing client strengths and limitations.
- Developing mutually agreed-on intervention goals and objectives.
- Selecting appropriate intervention strategies (practice behaviors).

Intervene with individuals, families, groups, organizations, and communities (Educational Policy 2.1.10c) by

- Helping clients resolve problems (practice behavior).

The worst was picking up body parts, "bagging," standing by helplessly as the Bradley burned after we had tried to get our buddies out but were overcome by the heat. The smell sticks.

—Enlisted soldier in Iraq,
quoted in Hoge, 2010, p. 20

Two days ago I killed an Iraqi for the first time. He was a triggerman and had an IED 500 meters down the road. I shot his ass with 60 rounds of coax 7.62 [machine gun] and then 15 rounds of the 25MM. I have not been so happy since I've been in Iraq. This fuck was going to kill us and I killed him.

—NONCOMMISSIONED OFFICER IN IRAQ, QUOTED IN HOGE, 2010, P. 21

Hearing the men screaming that they were dying and calling for their mothers and I couldn't get to them. Waiting for the next assault.

—VIETNAM VETERAN, 1968, PERSONAL COMMUNICATION

Soldiers returning from Iraq and Afghanistan may face many serious health and psychosocial issues and may return having survived grievous wounds and trauma (Bilmes, 2007). During time in combat, combat stress reactions or posttraumatic stress disorder (PTSD) are not uncommon. Combat stress reactions usually fade over time, but changes in behavior may be brought home or may be triggered by seemingly innocuous events. Estimates of the rate of PTSD among veterans range from 12 percent to 20 percent (Roehr, 2007).

This chapter builds on chapter 6, which introduced the shift in the mental health paradigm from an emphasis on pathology and dysfunction to resilience, hope, and transformation (see chapter 6). The idea that soldiers and veterans who have experienced trauma may still be resilient may be difficult to accept, considering that many may have experienced two or three extremely stressful combat deployments as well as physical injury. This shift in paradigm turns providers' attention to strengths and survival skills that can help people overcome the adverse effects of war, especially the trauma of injury and the difficult transition to civilian life. The chapter explores how soldiers and veterans are able to go on with their lives and find new meaning in lives that have been radically changed. In addition, the chapter discusses the assessment of different responses to combat stress, including the use of interventions designed to promote resilience and posttraumatic growth.

A Shift to Survivorship

People invariably first experience trauma in a negative way. Intensive psychotherapy might be needed when distressing symptoms such as deep depression and loss persist for long periods of time. However, contrary to popular belief, many people exhibit a "collective sense of determination" (Kaniasty & Norris, 1999, p. 29). Growing evidence shows that despite their loss, survivors and their families show remarkable resilience, contributing to an evidence-based survivorship approach to trauma (Greene, 2002; Norris, Friedman, & Watson, 2002; Norris et al., 2002).

Sense of Coherence

One of the most prominent researchers to introduce a survivorship/resilience approach to helping military personnel was Antonovsky. In an effort to explain individual differences between stressors, coping, and health, Antonovsky (1979, 1987) developed the salutogenic model of health. Antonovsky's (1987) model derived from interviews with Israeli women who had been in a World War II concentration camp. He observed that some had managed to maintain good health and lead full lives despite their experiences and remarked that it was a wonder that they had survived at all. He assumed that stress was a part of the natural condition and found a much more interesting question: "How come we survive in spite of this?" (Lindstrom & Eriksson, 2006). Rejecting the traditional pathogenic model, Antonovsky (1998) observed that despite high levels of exposure to stress, *some* individuals remain healthy. This led him to describe a "health–ease/disease continuum."

Antonovsky (1987) was interested in how people develop a *sense of coherence,* or the capacity to perceive life and to manage successfully the infinite number of complex stressors encountered in the discourse of life (Lindstrom & Eriksson, 2006). Antonovsky (1987) defined *sense of coherence* as "a global orientation that expresses the extent to which one has a pervasive, enduring though dynamic feeling of confidence." (p. 5). In addition, he noted that stressors can be *comprehensible,* or structured, predictable, and explicable; *manageable,* or available to meet demands; and *meaningful,* or challenges worthy of investment and engagement.

Antonovsky (1987) developed the Sense of Coherence Scale, a seminal tool that has been used to evaluate the well-being of soldiers. The scale has been used extensively, with many studies affirming its reliability, validity, and cross-cultural potential (Lindstrom & Eriksson, 2006). At the time of Antonovsky's (1993) review of the extant research on the Sense of Coherence Scale, the scale had already been used across many cultures and had been translated into 14 languages, setting the stage for a resilience approach to survivorship.

Resilience

Resilience is the human capacity to adapt in the face of stress, adversity, trauma, or tragedy. Resilience involves overcoming the odds and being successful despite exposure to high risk, sustaining competence under pressure, and recovering from trauma by adjusting to negative life events successfully (Fraser, Richman, & Galinsky, 1999). *Survivorship* refers to the ability to overcome the damaging events of trauma, to rebuild one's life, and to maintain a coherent family life story. It is a complex phenomenon that describes how individuals, families, and communities return to basic functioning. It involves innate and learned abilities (traits or capacities) for taking action (following adaptive or coping strategies) to survive, to deal with feelings of distress and anxiety, and to overcome adversity (Greene & Graham, 2008). Survivorship begins when returning soldiers

- find some sense of safety in recognized routines;
- obtain information and resources useful in their particular situation;
- resolve stressors;
- reestablish a sense of control or self-mastery or the sense that there are choices to be made, no matter how small;
- seek out and provide mutually supportive relationships;
- identify meaning that may be related to spirituality;
- maintain positive emotions and creativity; and
- learn to appreciate newfound strengths and affirmations of life embodied in resilience (Greene, 2002, 2008, 2010).

A survivorship approach recognizes that traumatic events cannot be undone; the event cannot be erased. A veteran will grieve the loss and how his or her life has changed forever. Nevertheless, a survivorship approach helps the veteran and his or her family explore what is feasible and what opportunities and choices can be made (Greene, 2002).

Assessment

Risk and resilience theory provides a process for assessing individual and family assets, endurance, and survival skills to avert negative stressors and confront adversity (Germain, 1994). A central feature is the ability to approach life challenges positively. Continuous exposure to deadly dangers and threats of danger creates a unique traumatic experience over time that becomes the norm when one is living in a war zone. It is important for returning soldiers and veterans and for those training future soldiers to understand resiliency in the face of this ongoing traumatic atmosphere. Likewise, practitioners who will be engaging the men and women who experience posttraumatic challenges need to appreciate the possibilities of resiliency and growth following traumatic events. It is important to begin to understand what is known about resiliency under such circumstances and how the traumatic experiences of soldiers, veterans, and their families might be addressed.

One particular line of research and practice is referred to as *posttraumatic growth* (Tedeschi & Calhoun, 1995). This research asks the following: How do individuals keep going after traumatic events, and specifically when the experience (for example, time in a combat zone) lasts a considerable length of time? How are soldiers and veterans able to go on with their lives and find new meaning in a life that has been radically changed?

Resiliency in the face of such traumatic experiences can be viewed from the perspective of posttraumatic growth. Posttraumatic growth represents not a loss of distress but a means of living with loss and distress in unique and individualistic ways. Calhoun and Tedeschi (2006) described the perspective in broad terms:

> The satisfactory engagement with and, for many persons who have struggled with trauma, the satisfactory response to the major existential questions and to questions about how to live one's life in the fullest way possible, may be more important than the reduction of psychological discomfort. Reducing distress and thinking deeply about how best to live are not mutually exclusive possibilities, but they are not always likely to correlate either. (p. 7)

It is very important to clarify that we do not imply an expectation that growth will always occur. Many who make small steps to recovery still experience considerable distress and may always do so. Wortman (2004) poignantly noted that

> we honor people by acknowledging what they are up against following a trauma, not by holding false hopes that if they have the right personality characteristics, if they process the event the right way, and if they adopt the right coping strategies, they will be able to grow from their experience. If outsiders believe that growth is prevalent, then this can become a new standard that survivors' progress is measured against. Such a standard may lead to negative judgments toward those who do not show personal growth, making them feel like coping failures. (pp. 88–89)

Although there is considerable evidence that surviving traumatic events can lead to seeing one's life in a more meaningful way (Blundo & Greene, 2007), with greater appreciation of many aspects that were previously not fully recognized, such as family, friends, and life itself, there is not always a reduction in distress and pain. Although some individuals consider the crisis or traumatic event as a turning point in their lives that they would not want to change, others would prefer to go back to their lives before the trauma. Judith Viorst (1986) quoted Rabbi Harold Kushner on the loss of his son:

> I am a more sensitive person, a more effective pastor. A more sympathetic counselor because of Aaron's life and death than I would ever have been without it. And I would give up all of those gains in a second if I could have my son back. If I could choose. . . . But I cannot choose. (p. 295)

Posttraumatic growth is the potential when there is no choice to return to a previous condition. Once a trauma has taken place, a person's choices are limited to how he or she will live the rest of his or her life. There is no going back. *How one proceeds is the only question.* Even this is not a mere personal choice but a *voyage* of sorts through feelings of being out of place in what was once home, one's assumptive world of stability and routine. With war veterans, it is a matter of *navigating* one's way back into life at home, a home that will never be the same again (Hoge, 2010).

> When I returned from Vietnam I was alone with other brothers who were in a way alone too. We were curiously silent on the long flight back to the "world." We went as individual replacements and not as cohesive units; we returned the same way. Things went quickly. In a round the clock effort, those of us to be discharged were discharged and on our own in a matter of a couple of days. There I was standing in a commercial airport with my "class A" uniform waiting for a standby flight home; I had been standing on a dusty field in Vietnam three days before. When I arrived home, the plane landed at an airport outside of L.A. and I had to find a pay phone to call my wife and let her know where I was. I remember setting on the curb with my duffle bag in a very strange place with cars and people rushing around while feeling very out of place and anxious and somehow unexcited about being home. (Vietnam veteran, 1968, personal communication)
>
> Being a soldier in wartime is a sick profession. How is it that I hear the word "deployment," I am able to effortlessly flick a switch and shut off my family? Yet when I returned from deployment, there was no such switch to reconnect me to my children and parents? It doesn't equate. I don't get to pick up where I left off. I will have to rebuild. (Master Sergeant Robison, quoted in Holmstedt, 2009, p. 38)

Traumatic growth, which is often referred to as *combat operational stress (COS)* and/or *posttraumatic stress (PS)*, results from the potential consequences for veterans and their family of the veterans having been in a war zone. In the next sections, we focus on the experience of posttraumatic stress among veterans. We describe the context of military training and life that determines how veterans might think about and approach their troubling experiences. Finally, we address ways in which resiliency can be supported in veterans' efforts to navigate the road to growth and thriving.

Posttraumatic Stress

A Brief History

Posttraumatic stress is usually described as a disorder, although some consider it the normal result of exposure to traumatic events. Posttraumatic stress has many historical and political causes. Ben Shepard (2001) traced its history to the Vietnam era, to what was then referred to as "post-Vietnam syndrome" (p. 357). Some psychiatrists found that from within months to three years after returning, the veteran would experience

> growing apathy, cynicism, alienation, depression, mistrust and expectation of betrayal, as well as an inability to concentrate, insomnia, nightmares, restlessness, uprootedness, and impatience with almost any job or course of study. [He saw this as] delayed massive trauma [or] . . . impact grief. (Shatan, 1972, p. 357)

Politics during the Vietnam era affected the choices being made in the field of psychiatry. Some clinicians recognized that many who served in Vietnam could experience posttraumatic symptoms. Others recognized few, if any, consequences of serving in the military. A shift in acceptance of the existence of a condition caused by traumatic events occurred when the *Diagnostic and Statistical Manual of Mental Disorders* (American Psychiatric Association, 1980) included "post-traumatic disorder" in its list of psychiatric disorders (Shepard, 2001). This new posttraumatic condition among veterans and soldiers was distinguished from the traditional idea of "'shell-shock' by [an] emphasis on traumatic memory and by offering a standardized model of how traumatic memory operates across time. Traumatic memory is the glue that holds the diverse symptoms of PTSD together" (Shepard, 2000, p. 389). Although there has been some controversy about the diagnosis, it helped validate for those suffering an array of life disrupting symptoms that the onset of symptoms was attributable to a traumatic life experience and not some individual inherent weakness (Lasiuk & Hegadoren, 2006)

General Symptoms

The current description of PTSD has evolved to include a wide range of symptoms that cover a range of traumatic situations in addition to combat and war zone experiences. Therefore, veterans and soldiers must be understood as experiencing a constellation of symptoms. For example:

- The patient has been exposed to a traumatic event involving intense fear, helplessness, or horror *and* the patient has experienced or witnessed an event or events that involved actual death, threatened death, serious injury, or a threat to the person's physical integrity or to the physical integrity of others.
- The traumatic event is persistently reexperienced through intrusive recollections, distressing dreams, or acting or feeling as if the traumatic event were recurring.
- The patient demonstrates persistent avoidance of stimuli associated with the trauma.
- The patient demonstrates numbing of general responsiveness.
- The patient demonstrates increased arousal not present before the trauma.
- The above noted symptoms have duration of more than a month.
- The patient demonstrates impaired social, occupational, relationships or other areas of functioning that were generally acceptable before the trauma.
- The symptoms can be acute (<3 months) or chronic (>3 months).
- The symptoms may appear after a period of 6 months from the stressor and are noted as delayed onset (Freeman & Freeman, 2009, pp. 166–167).

It is important to take a closer look at these symptoms from the perspective of the veteran or soldier. In the next sections, we look at how PTSD is unique to veterans and soldiers.

Trauma Defined

According to the Center for Disease Control and Prevention (CDC), "traumatic events are characterized by a sense of horror, helplessness, serious injury, or the threat of serious injury or death" (see http://www.emergency.cdc.gov/masscasualties/copingpro.asp). In combat or war zone situations, reactions to traumatic events are seen as "normal" responses to "abnormal events" (Hoge, 2010). Because events vary in terms of how horrifying they can be, and because combat soldiers can have a range of reactions to an event, more research is needed to understand individual responses to trauma among this population.

Trauma can be interpreted in many ways. It may involve engaging in direct hand-to-hand combat, rifle fire, or mortar fire; killing; being shot at; being in a compound providing medical services to combatants under a constant threat of being attacked; and/or working with wounded or dying soldiers every day. Yet the most common definition of a traumatic event is culturally based in part on the ethos of "John Wayne masculinity," rather than known facts of nature. A comprehensive definition of *traumatic exposure* includes being surrounded by uncertainty and experiencing threats of injury and/or death on a constant, day-to-day basis.

It is not necessary to be on the front line or killing alone to experience trauma. Hoge (2010) pointed out that many support troops have less experience and are not as cohesive as combat units, who develop a way of supporting one another and who expect to be engaged by the enemy. Combat team members may be better prepared than support troops to deal with uncertainty. Thus, support troops may feel guilty that they are not on the front line; they may not be inclined to seek help because they may feel that they should not have any posttraumatic reactions or symptoms. Yet trauma can affect anyone serving in a war zone.

> Fundamentally, everyone's experiences are important, and we can't define what a traumatic event is for one warrior compared to another. Anyone deployed to a war zone, whether in line or support roles, has likely experienced some level of trauma exposure. Each person's experience is unique and relative, and only relevant to them. (Hoge, 2010, p. 18)

An important element of trauma for soldiers is that it is an ongoing event rather than a single episode, such as a flood or personal tragedy. The constant presence of potential threat over time (in Vietnam it was referred to as "365 days and a wake up") creates a state of alertness and preparedness that is in itself stressful. Bruce McEwen (2007) writes about the damaging effects of chronic stress on the individual. He introduces the concept of "allostatic load" referring to the wear and tear on the body and brain as they respond to stress and work to maintain stability. "Allostatic load reflects the impact not only of life experiences but also of genetic load; individual habits reflecting items such as diet, exercise, and substance abuse; and developmental experiences that set life-long patterns of behavior and physiological reactivity. All of these factors influence the temporal patterning and efficiency of turning on and turning off the hormonal mediators of stress " (McEwen & Seeman, 1999, p. 41).

Living with a weapon in one's hands or nearby every day for months and years at a time is different than spending a day hunting deer. In direct combat units many events happen; most are expected, but unexpected encounters of severe danger can occur. Being alert to this danger is what soldiers call "situational awareness" or "tactical awareness"; although it is necessary in a war zone, hyper vigilance becomes problematic when one is not in the war zone. Living in this state of heightened awareness and uncertainty day after day is obviously stressful and traumatic. Yet it is important to recognize and acknowledge that each soldier responds differently to this exposure. It is not unusual for some soldiers to seek multiple tours, as they find it difficult not to be on the front line.

Fear and helplessness are part of the reality of war and are not the same for civilians experiencing a particular event. "Warriors don't speak of their wartime experiences in the same way. . . . During combat, warriors report 'locking down' their emotions, falling back on their training, or feeling anger . . . they do not feel like a victim" (Hoge, 2010, pp. 23–24). At the same time, helplessness is evident when soldiers cannot take action because there are civilians in the area or because they have to wait until they themselves are fired on. This can have an impact over time and after one returns home. Fear becomes a signal to "lock and load" (that is, prepare to fire a weapon, round in the chamber and clip inserted) and represents a heightened sense of alertness that becomes a normal response in the war zone. Heightened alertness experienced upon returning home is one of the signs of PTSD (Hoge, 2010).

Biological Reactions

In the 1920s, Walter Cannon was the first to describe the physiological response to stress by the sympathetic nervous system (see http://www.psychologistworld.com/stress/fightflight.php0). He is credited with coining the phrase "fight or flight responses" (Neylan, 1998). The American Psychological Association defines stress as "the pattern of specific and nonspecific responses an organism makes to stimulus events that disturb its equilibrium and tax or exceed its ability to cope" (see http://www.apa.org/research/action/glossary.aspx#s).

According to Cannon, exposure to stress causes the preganglionic, sympathetic nerves to release acetylcholine which in turn triggers the release of adrenaline and norepinephrine from the adrenal glands. The presence of these hormones raises the rate of the heartbeat and breathing, causes constriction of blood vessels and tightening of muscles (see http://www.psychologistworld.com/stress/fightflight.php). This allows the body to prepare to fight or flee.

Hans Selye was influenced by the work of Walter Cannon and went on, himself, to put together an impressive body of research on biological effects of exposure to stressful stimuli. He examined the effect of stress on hormones focusing on corticosteroids on brain function (Neylan, 1998). "The brain is a primary mediator and target of stress resiliency and vulnerability processes because it determines what is threatening and because it regulates the behavioral and physiological responses to a given stress" (McEwen & Gianaros, 2010).

Through his research, Seyle developed the concept of the three-stage General Adaptation Syndrome, including initial reaction to the stress, a period of resistance and finally exhaustion and possible death (Seyle, 1936). With the syndrome there is enlargement of the adrenal gland, atrophy of the thymus, spleen and other lymphoid tissue, and gastric ulcerations. His bench research lead to research by others on the biological functioning of glucocorticoids and a better understanding of the physiological and psychological consequences of exposure to stress. The release of the steroid-like hormones or glucocorticoids during periods of prolonged stress can have harmful effects such as elevated blood pressure and increased risk of infection or cancer because of suppression of the immune system (Thibodeau and Patton, 2010). "As the interpreter of and responder to what is stressful, the adult brain is a malleable organ and adapts structurally and functionally to experiences including those which are stressful and potentially deleterious" (McEwen, 2007, p. 894).

As indicated, exposure to the stress and the traumatic events of a combat zone are not without possible long-term consequences. The Substance Abuse and Mental Health Services Administration (SAMHSA) did a survey covering the period 2004 through 2006 that included military veterans (2007). The survey looked at prevalence of serious psychological distress (SPD) and substance use disorder (SUD). Among the veterans surveyed, there were clear differences by age, gender, and income. Those 18–25 were the age group most likely to experience SPD and/or SUD. Women were more likely to experience SPD but less likely to have SUD as an independent problem. By income, those with low incomes of less than $20,000 were more likely to experience one or both mental health problems.

A frequently occurring consequence of modern military conflict is traumatic brain injury (TBI) as result of exposure to blasts from explosions. It has become a major mechanism of injury accounting for 78 percent of combat injuries between 2001 and 2005 (French, 2010). There were a total 195,547 cases of militarily diagnosed TBI between 2000 and the third quarter of 2010 (see http://www.dvbic.org/TBI-Numbers.aspx). The largest category of diagnoses was in the mild or concussion level of severity. Some research has indicated that TBI is associated with increased risk for PTSD. Increased exposure to this type of injury through multiple deployments to the combat zone increases the likelihood that military personnel will experience TBI and/or PTSD (Jaffee & Meyer, 2009).

Symptoms of PTSD vary by soldier, even though some common symptoms include flashbacks, intrusive thoughts, strong feelings of anger, anxiety, and feelings of dread.

> I was walking across the area between the cafeteria at college and the building I needed to get to for my class. Each time I did this I had a sudden sense of fear and anxiety that lasted for a while after entering the building. Then one day as I looked out the window back over where I had come, I saw the fifty gallon steel drums lined up along where they were working. I suddenly recalled the same 50 gallon drums we used to build bunkers around our base camp. (Vietnam veteran, 1968, personal communication)

> Whenever there are crowds I start feeling like I'm in Iraq and have to get out of there fast. (Junior enlisted soldier, post-Iraq, quoted in Hoge, 2010, p. 29)

These responses originate in the limbic system, part of the instinctive and rapid response system with which the brain processes fight-or-flight responses. This is where primitive instinctual survival mechanisms process events and prepare the body for danger by increasing the amount of adrenaline in the body and increasing the emotional states of fear and anger. This area of the brain is important for survival because it causes a very fast response based on long-term "memories" of potential threatening events. There is now some scientific evidence that indicates that stress hormones are more controlled or shut down in persons who are resilient (Stix, 2011). There are chains of interacting proteins including the presence of neuropeptide Y that lessen the effects of the stress hormones. A study of combat veterans reported on in *Scientific American* (Stix, 2011) found those with elevated levels of neuropeptide Y were at reduced risk for PTSD. This could be important when one is confronting a saber-toothed tiger, a strange tribe, or a war zone. Physical symptoms such as increased heart rate, trembling, and sweating along with a sense of rage and anger occur when one is confronted with the need to survive in a war zone. However, when one leaves the war zone, these types of memories do not shut down or distinguish between actual threats and the stimuli that can set off these responses. A smell, heat, a taste, the sound of a particular engine (Huey helicopters in Vietnam had a distinct engine sound), loud noises, and many more idiosyncratic stimuli can set off the limbic system many years later.

Social Responses

Social relationships are impacted when the soldier withdraws from others, even those closest to him or her, and experiences a kind of emotional detachment within a social setting. The soldier may feel detached from others, even though others may not notice. There is a shutting down of emotions or a shutting down of interest in what were personal interests before the combat experience. Numbing down and shutting down attachments help protect a soldier during combat. Soldiers must focus on performing a task and continuing to do so, even when people are being wounded and killed. Once these emotions are opened up, the sudden release can surprise even the soldier:

> I don't know what happened. I was with colleagues at lunch and someone asked me a question about my experience in Vietnam [some 30 years before], I had not talked about any of this that I can remember. For some reason I started to say something about a situation we had found ourselves in and within fifteen seconds I started to cry so deeply I had to leave. I remember saying I was sorry and leaving. (Vietnam veteran, 1968, personal communication)

The Military Culture and Preparing for the War Zone

Marine Corps basic training is more a matter of cultural indoctrination than teaching soldiering, which comes later, at combat training or, for the real grunts, at infantry school.

—RICKS, 1997, P. 37

D. I. S. C. I. P. L. I. N. E. Discipline, sir. Discipline is the instant willing obedience to all orders, respect for authority, self-reliance, and teamwork, sir. Stop, sir.

—RICKS, 1997, P. 71

The discipline chant is repeated over and over again in unison at the demand of the sergeant during recruit training at Paris Island. Similar training chants are repeated throughout training at other military service facilities. The infamous "I can't hear you!" demands that recruits speak out loudly and quickly at every request of the training cadre. Orders and at times demeaning comments about each soldier's pedigree are yelled out often and swiftly. For those who catch the eye of the instructor by messing up, even breathing becomes an offense.

> No detail of military life—even as minor as a haircut, the pitch of a sailor's white cap, or the chants sung out in basic training—is without significance . . . members of the military distinguish themselves not only by the jobs they do but by the rituals they share, the anecdotes they exchange, even the slang that lards their everyday conversations . . . designed to produce efficient, disciplined soldiers and sailors with transformation of boys into men. (Burke, 2004, p. ix)

All soldiers are trained first and foremost to be prepared for combat situations and war zone duty. This demands immediate obedience to orders and quick responses to ensure a cohesive carrying out of duties without question. The instinct for individual preservation is lessened, and the team or group becomes the primary concern. Selflessness is required to fulfill missions in the face of serious threats to the group or team. Learning to think of oneself as a member of a combat team in a very different way than one would as a member of a team at work or any other group in the community is key to the significance of selflessness and depending upon one's team in combat or in a war zone.

The stress induced by basic training is intentional and is meant to push men and women to their limits and heighten stress. Part of even the most basic initial training has soldiers crawling under barbed wire and through mud as tracer rounds from machine guns are going a few feet overhead. Controlled explosions are going off all around, and debris comes down all around. Sometimes slaughtered animal remains must be crawled over. All of this and the constant pressure to perform quickly and on command creates a level of stress and exhaustion.

The military recognizes *combat stress control* as an important part of military training and military conduct:

> Controlling combat stress is often the deciding factor—the difference between victory and defeat—in all forms of human conflict. Stressors are a fact of combat and soldiers must face them. It is controlled combat stress (when properly focused by training, unit cohesion, and leadership) that gives soldiers the necessary alertness, strength, and endurance to accomplish their mission. (Department of the Army, 2003, p. 1)

In military training, stress is recognized as a part of readiness for combat. It is necessary for effective soldiering. The idea is how to induce it and control it at the same time. Thus, the intense socialization into a system that recognizes not individuality but group membership and discipline is introduced to enable soldiers to sustain the level of combat stress required for the duties they will perform. Leadership, cohesion, and group identity and support are the key elements, and they must be at a very different level than what one normally finds in a business office or even a football team. In the military there is no questioning of orders and, in a sense, no self but the team. The life of every person is dependent on this configuration, which is reinforced in combat situations where it is lived out not only in the sergeant's leadership, but also in the face of deathly force with the soldier next to you. When this occurs from basic training through advanced training and then in war zones, it becomes more than an idea but a way of life much different than anything the soldier has ever experienced as a civilian. In some ways the person is forever transformed in terms of how he or she relates to others and situations.

> It sounds silly, but over the last 40 years, in all types of settings I have never had an experience of being a part of something, a team, unit, in such a deep way as when I was in the military and in Vietnam. Nothing since then has ever come close to the feeling of cohesion and mutual reliance. (Vietnam veteran, 1968, personal communication)

It is important that social workers recognize the feelings in those with whom they might be working. This odd sense of reliability is often used to compare and evaluate the present moment, which does not and can never feel the same. In contrast, the civilian life feels unreliable and undependable.

Another important factor about training and socialization was best expressed by Major General Smedley D. Butler of the U.S. Marine Corps, two-time winner of the Congressional Medal of Honor:

> Boys with normal viewpoints were taken from the fields and offices and factories and classrooms and put into the ranks. There they were remolded; they were made over; they were made to "about face," to regard murder as the order of the day. They were put shoulder to shoulder, and through mass psychology they were entirely changed. We used them for a couple of years and trained them to think nothing at all of killing or of being killed. Then suddenly, we discharged them and told them to make another "about face." This time they had to do their own readjusting without mass psychology, without officer's aid and advice, without nation-wide propaganda. We didn't see them anymore. So we scattered them about without speeches or parades. Many, too many, of these fine young boys are eventually destroyed mentally, because they could not make the final "about face" alone. (Quoted in Cantrell & Dean, 2007, p. xi)

The important factor in all of this is the fact that once the soldier leaves the cohesion and leadership of a unit, he or she is now without the built-in structure required to manage the stress inherent in a combat and war zone unit. Being stationed in the United States is different; the intensity of the immediate dangerous situation changes to one of calm and routine. This can have an impact by requiring a different way of relating that is not as immediate and interdependent. Rules and orders become just that—rules and orders—compared to war zone requirements for mutual respect and dependency. The rules and orders can seem superficial and controlling rather than cohesive and mission-directed. Soldiers who served in Vietnam were not used to saluting in a combat zone and were also accustomed to working very closely with their leadership. The leadership depended on the soldier just as the soldier depended on the sergeant or platoon leader. Discipline as one knew it stateside changed and in a way became functional and not ceremonial. Returning stateside brought ceremonial and ritualized obedience even in a simple salute. Many Vietnam veterans ended up breaking the rules and found themselves in constant trouble in the military stations. Around 1969, the military decided to discharge soldiers who had only a few months left on their enlistments or draft-time requirements when they returned from Vietnam. This prevented a lot of problems for the military and the soldiers. Of course, many of these soldiers were discharged within days of returning from Vietnam without a thought of the adjustment they would have to make in a hostile home environment. Many just shut down emotionally and repressed the experiences. Some turned to drugs and alcohol.

> I had access to medications since I worked in a medical unit. I brought back a lot of Thorazine, an antipsychotic drug. I used about 100 mg [as needed] for months after returning. It was the only thing I could do to control the severe panic and anxiety. (Vietnam veteran, medical corps, 1968, personal communication)

Resiliency: Navigating a Path to Growth and Thriving

Those of us who did make it have an obligation to build again, and to teach others what we know, and to try with what's left of our lives to find goodness and meaning to this life.

—Chris Taylor in *Platoon*

There is no substitute for the experiences of combat and the excitement of a war zone. Combat is an adrenaline-fed, high-speed, whirlwind, tiger-on-the-loose, exhausting daily dose of life and death. To think that you won't react, feel, behave, and think differently than before your tour of combat duty is, of course, incorrect. Your experiences in combat will forever be a part of you. Allow those combat experiences and knowledge to become your strength.

—First Sergeant Mike Schindler, quoted in Hoge, 2010, p. 51

The simple fact is that soldiers return home with a wide range of responses to their experiences, from severe to less severe, and all have some level of adjustment to make over time. Posttraumatic growth is a matter of degree. Tedeschi and Calhoun (2004) described the idea of posttraumatic growth in work with veterans and soldiers as dependent on taking the perspective of a learner and rather than viewing the person as a set of symptoms, and respecting and appreciating the value in the soldier's experiences as potential sources of growth. Posttraumatic growth is not a treatment or intervention method but a perspective conducive to enhancing the potential for resiliency and growth.

Posttraumatic growth was described by Calhoun and Tedeschi (2006), who noted that "the experience of a traumatic set of circumstances usually produces distress, disrupts one's understanding of the world, makes salient one's vulnerabilities and lack of power and control, and may make more salient one's mortality" (p. 7). The process of growth often takes place within a painful experience.

It is the difficult life experiences that somehow confront people with possible insights into themselves and their world in a very new way; they permit them to go on with a previously unrecognized ability to go on. How people accommodate their life perspective to include the traumatic event or events into an awareness of being able to make it or keep going even in the face of difficult experiences and reactions is a key element of resiliency and posttraumatic growth.

What is a "normal" reaction to a stressful situation? Most practitioners assume that following stressful and traumatic events it is normal for individuals to go through stages of grief or loss that include distress that subsides over time with a return to some resolution and equilibrium. Research by Bonanno (2004) revealed different patterns of bereavement, with some individuals demonstrating little grief response or delayed grief. The lesson from this and other studies is that there is not one normal pattern but several individual patterns. The consequence is that practitioners attempt to engage and maybe even force individuals to undergo "debriefing." Suzanna, Jonathan, and Simon (2002) are among the researchers who have found that this assumption of normal patterns of dealing with traumatic events and subjecting people to debriefing treatment can make stress-related symptoms worse.

Resiliency is a factor in play with individuals who navigate through traumatic events and their aftermath. Resiliency is a complex idea. It can refer to a process or an outcome:

> Resilience is not a static property of individuals, nor is it immutable: Individuals may experience good outcomes in the face of adverse events but not others, may experience both good and bad outcomes in response to the same adversity, or may experience a bad outcome in the face of an adverse event at one time but not at another time. (Lepore & Revenson, 2006, p. 29)

Destigmatizing Treatment

Destigmatizing responses to war zone–related stress is a first step in treatment. "Stigma, the shame or disgrace attached to something regarded as socially unacceptable, remains a critical barrier to accessing needed psychological care" (Department of Defense Task Force on Mental Health, 2007, p. 5). An important component of resiliency is supportive systems and communities (O'Leary, Alday, & Ickovics, 1998). Unless the stigma associated with psychological issues is abated, soldiers and their families will likely avoid seeking out support. The issue of the military culture and the threat to one's advancement in the military is a strong factor in why men and women do not seek help or confide in their fellow soldiers. It is important to note that if a person's experience does not fit the cultural expectations for being invulnerable to psychological stress, he or she may consider these symptoms unacceptable. Obviously, when a soldier returns home or is discharged, the cohesion of the unit, the supportive community, is no longer available, creating a greater sense of loss and lack of support. Family members and civilians are not a part of the cohesive unit that has provided support.

Social Support

Social support is also a factor for resiliency and posttraumatic growth (Tedeschi & Calhoun, 2004). This support comes in the form of being able to self-disclose and talk openly about experiences, particularly when they are happening. The cohesion of the unit lets members grieve and share fears in particular ways that are acceptable within the group. If a soldier talks about something being "all fucked up" (the old FUBAR—fucked up beyond all repair), he or she is expressing the anxiety and stress of the situation in an acceptable way, and others will usually confirm the statement. Men and women will at times actually cry, and this is most often accepted by the members of the unit given their experiences and losses. The question is how to make this support possible once a soldier has returned home.

Social Capital

Social capital is an element of the social context that enhances resiliency (Lepore & Revenson, 2006). *Social capital* refers to mutual trust, reciprocity, and membership or participation in a community or combat unit. This cohesion provides a strong bond that supports the individual soldier in managing stressful events. The idea of relying and depending on one gives significance to each member of the unit. When the soldier returns home or to stateside duty, this element is lost. This support is fluid and stems naturally from the shared experiences of the members of the unit. This type of ongoing support is not readily available to veterans and returning soldiers.

Potential Opportunity for Resiliency and Posttraumatic Growth for Veterans

You can't expect a private or specialist to be willing to seek counseling when his or her captain or colonel or general won't do it.

—Admiral Mike Mullen,
Chairman of the Joint Chiefs of Staff
(http://www.rollingthunder/.com/news.htmh)

I can't see how my problems are worth talking about since I am alive and in one piece. I feel stupid talking about what is happening with me when others had it so much worse than I did.

—VIETNAM VETERAN, 1968, PERSONAL COMMUNICATION

Resilience Continuum

The U.S. military currently uses a resilience approach to assess soldiers' readiness for redeployment and reintegration. According to the Department of Defense, the resilience approach represents a shift in emphasis from treatment of illness to prevention and health. The military has embraced a resilience philosophy and has implemented a resilience continuum designed to assist soldiers with issues of stress during and after combat (see Table 13.1). The Defense Centers of Excellence for Psychological Health and Traumatic Brain Injury Resilience Continuum uses four levels of resilience to guide soldiers' reintegration and recovery. Similarly, a social work practitioner should evaluate the level of well-being and level of psychosocial care returnees who have sustained combat injuries perceive that they need. Information about what factors military personnel feel disrupt their daily functioning can then suggest interventions to reestablish or enhance individual and family functioning.

According to the Department of Defense, reintegration involves not just returning soldiers to their unit or home but incorporating experiences into a "new normal." They suggest that this is primarily a nonmedical function that includes outreach, family programs, and close coordination and transition to the community.

TABLE 13.1 U.S. Department of Defense and Defense Centers of Excellence for Psychological Health and Traumatic Brain Injury Resilience Continuum

Optimal	Reacting	Injured	Ill
• Peak performance • Positive outlook • Sense of purpose • Embraces challenges	• Irritable • Feeling overwhelmed • Difficulty sleeping and inability to relax • Problems concentrating	• Feelings of guilt • Decreased energy • Anxiety • Loss of interest • Social isolation	• Depression and anxiety • Anger and aggression • Danger to self or others
Mission Ready	Stress Response	Persistent Distress	Mission Ineffective
Education and Training	Risk Mitigation	Combat Stress Intervention	Treatment and Reintegration

That is, postdeployment and, specifically, posthospitalization efforts should involve family readjustment activities provided by family support programs.

The levels of resilience may be likened to Maslow's (1970) hierarchy of needs: (1) physical and life sustaining needs, such as the need for food, water, and shelter; (2) physical safety, including the need for protection from physical attack, bodily harm, and disease; (3) love, involving the need to be cherished and supported; (4) self-esteem, including the need for family members to have a sense of personal worth; and (5) self-actualization, or the need to be creative and productive (see Figure 1.1 in chapter 1).

Military Efforts at Culture Change

The military is attempting to alter the attitudes and the culture of the system that creates a barrier to personnel who are experiencing emotional or psychological problems. In most cases these individuals are regarded as malingerers and cowards. Promotions, retention in the service, and relationships with fellow soldiers would be seriously jeopardized if they were to acknowledge their emotional problems. Those who drank too much or got into fights were traditionally merely punished and often discharged. A famous incident in which General George S. Patton slapped a soldier who was experiencing "battle fatigue" is an example. The military is attempting to change this culture by training soldiers and commanders in what some refer to as the *Warrior Mind* method. This involves using cognitive and rational emotive procedures to help soldiers develop ways of changing their negative and irrational thoughts with self-awareness and better self-regulation as they build optimistic mindsets.

The military has also initiated a program to instill the potential for resiliency during the training of officers and enlisted men. It is referred to as Army Master Resilience Training (Torres-Cortes, 2010). The military is also developing programs such as the Warriors Combat Stress Reset Program (Army News, 2009), which focuses on helping returning combat units readjust to civilian or stateside duty after serving in a combat zone. The process is "designed to reduce hyperarousal symptoms and inappropriate reactions to every day events . . . [by means of] a variety of relaxation and soul-strengthening activities, [and] . . . process group" discussions of issues faced by each of the soldiers. The program lasts for two weeks, five days a week. No research has yet been published on outcomes.

Potential Areas of Focus for Nonmilitary Programs

The following material is not prescriptive but suggests potential areas of help in working with veterans. Being aware of the culture of soldiering and the combat zone experience is a very important first step. Applying an awareness of the warrior mindset necessary for survival is the base on which positive change (that is, navigating to a new place and possibly gaining perspective and growth in the process) might be possible. One must first remove the idea that the soldier has a disorder. Rather than PTSD, it can be referred to as *posttraumatic stress* or *combat stress*. This involves a normal reaction to a very abnormal set of circumstances over a long period of time. This is a very important statement for the soldier to hear. The potential might be enhanced by group work. It is important that veterans learn to respect and care for one another, as feeling understood and accepted is an important element of resiliency.

Resilience-supporting Personal Characteristics

Whatever success the military has with its "reset" and prevention programs can be useful for engaging veterans and returning soldiers. In addition, and potentially overlapping these efforts, are those things experts understand about resiliency and potential posttraumatic growth. These include resilience factors that might be influential in navigating the shoals or difficulties. Resilience is usually thought of as the capacity to be able to sustain oneself and move on with life, changed but satisfactory. Notice that we are not talking about finding a cure and returning to a previous state. Resilience involves the idea of moving on with life—not without some fears—and possibly succeeding in ways not expected. Resilience thus can be considered both a process and an outcome.

The concept of Battle Mind described by Slone and Friedman (2008) is an important element in understanding the necessity for specific ways of thinking and behaving in the war zone and then adapting them when back in civilian life. This framework alludes to how and to what degree a set of skills that are required for battle and thus must become automatic can be reset for civilian life. The list is as follows in Table 13.2.

Recognizing that some skills are required in the abnormal context of combat is very important. Using these skills successfully promotes a form of resilience in the combat zone. Shifting away from these useful skills is an important step in creating better relationships and functioning successfully in civilian life. *After the War Zone: A Practical Guide for Returning Troops and Their Families* (Slone & Friedman, 2008) provides materials that can be usefully integrated to support resiliency. Again, the issue is for soldiers to recognize that the skills used in combat were strengths that protected them and their buddies and then learn how these strengths might be translated into successful behaviors back home (Cantrell & Dean, 2007).

Staying Present and Future Focused. Robert Schwarz (2002) suggested that the symptoms of combat stress be translated into alternative behaviors in very

TABLE 13.2 Battle Mind

	During Combat	→ transforms into when →	Returning Home
B	Buddies (cohesion)		Withdrawal
A	Accountability		Controlling
T	Targeted		Inappropriate aggression
T	Tactical awareness		Hyper vigilance
L	Lethally armed		Locked and loaded
E	Emotional control		Detachment
M	Mission operational security		Secretiveness
I	Individual responsibility		Guilt
N	Nondefensive driving (combat)		Aggressive driving
D	Discipline/ordering		Conflict

Source: Slone and Friedman (2008), p. 57.

specific ways. That is, in combat one is operationally alert and very aware of everything that is going on around him or her. At home this type of behavior translates into unhelpful defused anxiety. Cantrell and Dean (2007) suggested using this awareness to differentiate which specific events are more likely to set off a reaction from those that are less likely to do so. The next step is to use previous training to redefine one's reaction to the particular event or setting. Recall the veteran described earlier who was able to recognize that the vision of oil drums was setting off a panic attack. When he recognized this and made the connection between past and present situational awareness, the panic attacks became less severe and more manageable.

This is similar to strengths-based, solution-focused work that helps people translate what they do not want or what they fear into what they do want, a future orientation. Rather than trying to undo the past, the idea is to join it with changes that are already going on to lead to a manageable future. Moving from the past to the present and then to a possible future involves a shift in mood. The future holds out possibilities and hope. If a person states, "I do not want to be so depressed," the question becomes, "What would it look like when you are not so depressed?" and "What would your friends or spouse see different about you that they would say, 'Something is different; Joan doesn't seem so depressed'?" This is followed by asking, "When have you had even a small positive event or feeling in the past few weeks?" Most often there have been times when things have been a little better. These *exceptions* can become the foundation for hope and potential growth.

Resilience-supporting Environments

Social cohesion and support that allows for talking together and sharing concerns reduces the intrusion of unwanted thoughts and results in an enhanced quality of life (Lepore & Helgeson, 1998). Having good social support and mutual trust makes it possible to share, accept, and be understood. As Lepore and Revenson (2006) have reported, some support can be restricting and can interfere with the veteran learning to navigate on his or her own. Each individual soldier has his or her own unique characteristics and means of managing life. This must be respected. These factors might help, and they might not. Resilience is a fluid concept, and, according to Lapore and Revenson, has reservations as well:

> We must be cautious not to overly prescribe tonics associated with resilience, such as optimism, disclosure and positive social exchanges. If individuals are not feeling particularly optimistic, talkative, or social, they may feel that they are failing to live up to others' expectations. Inhibiting one's true feelings can create a sense of alienation and may give others the wrong impression that social support or help is needed. (p. 39)

The supportive and nurturing processes associated with resilience in children do not translate into smothering them but respecting them and demonstrating a belief in them and what they do. These processes provide children with opportunities to take on challenges and even fail, but with the knowledge that support is still there. Tedeschi (2011) refers to this relationship as "expert companionship" by which he means listening without trying to solve the situation. Let them share what is important to them, not what you deem necessary. Pay attention to ways that the person has already changed in ways they have managed the situation. Reflect on new ways of rebuilding the assumptive world. For example, building on recognizing that even with all the pain and challenges they are continuing on with life. Remember that post traumatic pain can coexist with growth, survivorship, and thriving. Assist by pointing out what you hear that demonstrates this in the person's life narrative they are sharing with you. It provides them opportunities to take on challenges and even fail, but with the knowledge that your support is still there. A supportive environment is one of being respectful of each veteran's experience.

One possible way in which a support person can do this, if acceptable to the veteran, is to provide information about what is known about posttraumatic events in combat and the consequences of training in managing such situations over time. Knowledge is an important ingredient of resilience. Being aware and being given the opportunity to use information is a form of support without intrusion. Knowledge made available can be used only when the veteran is ready to connect it with his or her own experience. Recognizing normal responses to abnormal events is an important step in navigating one's way back into civilian life. By providing veterans with the opportunity to see the connections between necessary training and ways of adjusting to constant stress and how these survival mechanisms play out in civilian life is a big step in helping them make possible adjustments. By being constructed in a time-limited and focused way, the work becomes similar to a "mission" and has the intention of gaining understanding and normalizing what is still painful.

Use the CD by Michael Wright to recite the resilience continuum used by the U.S. Department of Defense to assist soldiers.

You will find a case study on your CD: *Learning About "Returning Home"*

References

American Psychiatric Association. (1980). *Diagnostic and statistical manual of mental disorders* (3rd ed.). Washington, DC: Author.

Antonovsky, A. (1979). *Health, stress and coping.* San Francisco: Jossey-Bass.

Antonovsky, A. (1987). *Unraveling the mystery of health.* San Francisco: Jossey-Bass.

Antonovsky, A. (1993). The structure and properties of the sense of coherence scale. *Social Science Medicine, 36,* 725–733.

Antonovsky, A. (1998). The sense of coherence: An historical and future perspective. In H. I. McCubbin, E. A. Thompson, A. I. Thompson, & J. E. Fromer (Eds.), *Stress, coping, and health in families* (pp. 3–20). Boston: Allyn & Bacon.

Army News. (2009). *Reset program aims to standardize delivery of excellence for deploying soldiers' families.* Retrieved from http://www.army.mil/news

Bilmes, L. (2007, January). *Soldiers returning from Iraq and Afghanistan: The long-term costs of providing veterans medical care and disability benefits* (Faculty Research Working Paper No. RWPO7–001). Cambridge, MA: Harvard University, John F. Kennedy School of Government.

Blundo, R., & Greene. R. R. (2007). Survivorship in the face of traumatic events and disasters: Implications for social work practice. In R. R. Greene (Ed.), *Social work practice: A risk and resilience perspective* (pp. 160–176). Belmont, CA: Thomson Higher Education.

Bonanno, G.A. (2004). Loss, trauma, and human resilience: Have we underestimated the human capacity to thrive after extremely adverse events? *American Psychologist, 59,* 20–28.

Burke, C. (2004). *Camp all-American, Hanoi Jane, and the high-and-tight.* Boston: Beacon Press.

Calhoun, L. G., & Tedeschi, R. G. (2006). The foundations of posttraumatic growth: An expanded framework. In L. G. Calhoun & R. G. Tedeschi (Eds.), *Handbook of posttraumatic growth: Research and practice* (pp. 1–23). Mahwah, NJ: Erlbaum.

Cantrell, B. C., & Dean, C. (2007). *Once a warrior: Wired for life.* Seattle, WA: Wordsmith Books.

Department of Defense Task Force on Mental Health. (2007). *An achievable vision: Report of the Department of Defense Task Force on Mental Health.* Falls Church, VA: Defense Health Board. Retrieved from http://www.health.mil/dhb/mhtf/MHTF-Report-Final.pdf

Fraser, M. W., Richman, J. M., & Galinsky, M. J. (1999). Risk, protection, and resilience: Toward a conceptual framework for social work practice. *Social Work Research, 23*(3), 129–208.

Freeman, A., & Freeman, S. M. (2009). Assessment and evaluation: Collecting the requisite building blocks for treatment planning. In S. M. Freeman, B. A. Moore, & A. Freeman (Eds.), *Living and surviving in harm's way* (pp. 147–168). New York: Routledge.

French, L.M. (2010) Military traumatic brain injury: an examination of important differences. *Annals of the New York Academy of Sciences, 1208,* 38–45.

Germaine, C. (1994). Human behavior and the social environment. In F.G. Reamer (Ed.), The foundation of social work knowledge (pp. 88–121). New York: Columbia University Press.

Greene, R. R. (2002). Holocaust survivors: A study in resilience. *Journal of Gerontological Social Work 37*(1), 3–18.

Greene, R. R. (2010). A Holocaust Survivorship Model: Survivors' Reflections. *Journal of Human Behavior and the Social Environment, 20*(4), 569–579.

Greene, R. R., & Graham, S. (2008). Role of resilience among Nazi Holocaust survivors: A strength-based paradigm for understanding survivorship. *Family and Community Health, 32,* S75–S82.

Hoge, C. W. (2010). *Once a warrior—Always a warrior.* Guilford, CT: Global Pequot Press.

Holmstedt, K. (2009). *The girls come marching home.* Mechanicsburg, PA: Stackpole Books.

Jaffee, M. S., & Meyer, K. S. (2009) A brief overview of traumatic brain injury (TBI) and post-traumatic stress disorder (PTSD) within the Department of Defense. *Clinical Neuropsychologist, 23,* 1291–1298.

Lasiuk, G. C., & Heagadoren, K.M. (2006) Posttraumatic stress disorder part I: Historical development of the concept. *Perspectives in Psychiatric Care, 42,* 13–20.

Lepore, S. J. & Helgeson, V. S. (1998). Social constraints, intrusive thoughts, and mental health after prostate cancer. *Journal of Social and Clinical Psychology, 17*(1), 89–106.

Lepore, S. J., & Revenson, T. A. (2006). Resilience and posttraumatic growth, recovery, resistance, and reconfiguration. In L. G. Calhoun & R. G. Tedeschi (Eds.), *Handbook of posttraumatic growth: Research and practice* (pp. 24–46). Mahwah, NJ: Erlbaum.

Lindstrom, B. & Eriksson, M. (2006). Contextualizing salutogenesis and Antonovsky in public health development. *Health Promotion International, 21,* 238–244.

Maslow, A. (1970). *Motivation and personality.* New York: Harper & Row.

McEwen, B.S. (2007) Physiology and neurobiology of stress and adaptation: Central role of the brain. *Physiology Review, 87,* 873–904.

McEwen, B. S., & Gianaros, P. J. (2010). Central role of the brain in stress and adaptation: Links to socioeconomic status, health and disease. *Annals of the New York Academy of Sciences, 1186,* 190–222.

McEwen, B. S., & Seeman, T. (1999) Protective and damaging effects of mediators of stress: Elaborating and testing concepts of allostatis and allostatic load. *Annals New York Academy of Sciences, 896,* 30–47.

Neylan, T. C. (1998) Hans Selye and the field of stress research. *Journal of Neuropsychiatry, 10,* 230.

Norris, F. H., Friedman, M. J., & Watson, P. J. (2002). 60,000 disaster victims speak: Part II. Summary and implications of the disaster mental health research. *Psychiatry, 65,* 240–250.

Norris, F. H., Friedman, M. J., Watson, P. J., Byrne, C. M., Diaz, E., & Kaniasty, K. (2002). 60,000 disaster victims speak: Part I. An empirical review of the empirical literature, 1981–2001. *Psychiatry, 65,* 207–239.

O'Leary, V. E., Alday, C. S., & Ickovics, J. R. (1998). Life change and posttraumatic growth. In R. G. Tedeschi, C. R. Park, & L. G. Calhoun (Eds.), *Posttraumatic growth: Positive changes in the aftermath of crisis* (pp. 127–151). Mahwah, NJ: Erlbaum.

Ricks, T. E. (1997). *Making the Corps.* New York: Scribner.
Roehr, B. (2007). *High rate of PTSD in returning Iraq War veterans.* Retrieved from http://www.medscape.com/viewarticle/565407
Schwarz, R. (2002). *Tools for transforming trauma.* New York: Brunner-Routledge.
Selye, H. (1936) A syndrome produced by diverse nocuous agents. *Nature, 138,* 32.
Shatan, C. (1972, May 6). The post-Vietnam syndrome. *New York Times.*
Shepard, B. (2001). *A war of nerves.* Cambridge, MA: Harvard University Press.
Slone, L. B., & Friedman, M. J. (2008). *After the war zone: A practical guide for returning troops and their families.* Philadelphia: Da Capo Press.
Stix, G. (2011) The neuroscience of true grit. *Scientific American, 304,* 28–33.
Substance Abuse and Mental Health Services Administration (SAMHSA), Office of Applied Studies. (2007, November 1). *The NSDUH Report: Serious Psychological Distress and Substance Use Disorder among Veterans.* Rockville, MD: Author.
Suzanna, R. O., Jonathan, B. I., & Simon, W. E. (2002). *Psychological debriefing for preventing post traumatic stress disorder (PTSD).* Cochrane Database of Systematic Reviews (2), CD000560.
Tedischi, R. (2011, March). *Posttraumatic growth: Basic concepts and strategies for facilitation in warriors and their families.* Presentation at conference on Post Traumatic Stess Disorder, University of North Carolina, Wilmimgton.
Tedeschi, R. G., & Calhoun, L. G. (1995). *Trauma and transformation: Growing in the aftermath of suffering.* Thousand Oaks, CA: Sage.
Tedeschi, R. G., & Calhoun, L. G. (2004). Posttraumatic growth: Conceptual foundations and empirical evidence. *Psychological Inquiry, 15,* 1–18.
Thibodeau, G. A., & Patton, K. T. (2010). Chapter 11: The endocrine system. In *The human body and disease* (5th ed., 308–339). Maryland Heights, MO: Mosby Elsevier.
Torres-Cortes, M. (2010). *Army master resilience training course provides valued instruction.* Retrieved from http://www.army.mil/-news/2010/03/29/36520-army-master-resilience-training-course-provides-valued-instruction/
Viorst, J. (1986). *Necessary losses.* New York: Fawcett Gold Medal.
Wortman, C. B. (2004). Posttraumatic growth: Progress and problems. *Psychological Inquiry, 15,* 81–89.

14

Resilience and the Older Adult

JUDITH S. LEWIS and EVELYN B. HARRELL

On finishing this chapter, students will be able to further:

Apply social work ethical principles to guide professional practice (Educational Policy 2.1.2) by

- Recognizing and managing personal values in a way that allows professional values to guide practice (practice behavior).

Engage diversity and difference in practice (Educational Policy 2.1.4) by

- Gaining sufficient self-awareness to eliminate the influence of personal biases and values in working with diverse groups (practice behavior).

This chapter discusses key societal issues facing the social work profession that necessitate a resilience-based approach to social work practice with older adults. Comparative terms and concepts related to resilience are presented in light of their relevance to elders. Selected assumptions from human behavior theory central to a resilience-based perspective are examined with reference to older adults, and suggestions are made for future research. Finally, we present a preliminary model of a resilience-based ecological practice with older adults. The model builds on current strengths-based approaches, using a relational framework that incorporates the concepts of safety and support, affiliation, and altruism (Atkins-Burnett & Allen-Meares, 2000). Guidelines for practitioners and case vignettes are included.

Select Societal Issues and Resilience

Although social workers see a diverse population of older adults, the common popular image is of a frail, if not debilitated, senior. *Resilience* is certainly not a term many people associate with old age (Butler, 1975). However, current societal issues require that social work professionals as well as the general public alter their image of older adults. The United States is in the midst of a historic demographic change. Since 1900, the population older than 65 years of age has increased tenfold, and it is predicted to double to 25 percent of the total population by 2030 (Recer, 2000). People over the age of 75 are the fastest-growing group of older persons. This is in part owing to the aging of baby boomers (those born in the post–World War II years) and to improved health and an increase in life expectancy among minority groups.

Social workers must reexamine their attitudes and the nature of agency programs and policies to meet the predicted service needs of this growing and diverse older adult population. For example, preventive programs designed to support older adults' strengths have the potential to reduce the numbers of elders who may later need intensive health and mental health services (Greene, 2000). Furthermore, rather than being peripheral players, older adults can be important stakeholders in program design and in problem-solving activities. They can build on their own inherent strengths, find their own solutions, and provide agencies with much needed information about service needs. Recent literature on self-directed policy and services provides new directions and ideas about the roles older adults can play in designing and implementing services to meet their particular needs (Centre for Policy on Ageing, 2011; Leung, 2011). In addition, the more social workers and agencies become culturally sophisticated and/or sensitive to the needs of the increasing number and diversity of older adults, the more likely these adults are to become senior partners in meeting their own needs (Gant, 1996; Torres-Gil & Pucinelli, 1995).

Obviously, although not all future older adults will need social services, they may still face other societal demands. For example, age-related workplace issues are a growing phenomenon in this time of dramatic demographic shifts. With increased life expectancy and better health in advanced years, many older adults choose to remain employed. Older adults have a continued need for rewarding work roles, particularly those that allow for part-time work. Those who have technical skills may be asked to remain in the workforce. Many other jobs, such as sales, may be available in the service sector. Because historically service workers have been young, this shift in employment patterns can present a challenge to employers. Fortunately, some large corporations, such as Wal-Mart and grocery store chains, seem to be responding to this challenge by hiring older adults in part-time positions (Gill, 2007; Roth, 2011).

Changes in attitudes related to older workers are occurring. Service industries that have discriminated against older adult workers are coming to appreciate and value older employees, especially for their dependability (Gill, 2007). According to Salthouse (1990), when older adults are evaluated in terms of their work contributions, they are found to compensate for their age and produce as well as their younger counterparts. This underscores the notion that older workers are a resource that can provide economic benefits to their employers. The fact that increasing numbers of employers are willing to hire older adults and view them as a resource is an important dimension in fostering resilience in the next cohort of older Americans (Torres-Gil & Pucinelli, 1995).

Nevertheless, the differential treatment of older women in the workplace is a concern. Older women continue to be disproportionately affected by wage discrimination, low retirement benefits, and responsibilities for family care (especially parenting grandchildren). As more older adults reenter the workplace and/or are retained in the workforce, benefits and compensation packages, including family leave policies, will have to be redesigned to reflect the contributions of older women (Dunke & Norgard, 1995; Torres-Gil & Pucinelli, 1995). This will enable future generations of working women to retire with sufficient benefits and foster their sense of security. In short, the graying of U.S. society can result in a visible, viable, diverse network of older adults.

Defining Resilience

Resilience has a range of meanings both within the professional literature and in the vernacular. Generally speaking, *resilience* is the ability to recover strength, spirits, good humor, and so on, following misfortune or negative life changes. In social work, *resilience* describes the ability to spring back or return to previous circumstances after encountering adverse stress or serious problems (Barker, 1995). The study of resilience has been associated primarily with developmental research dealing with early childhood and adolescence (Ryff, Singer, Love, & Essex, 1998). Some related concepts associated with older adults' ability to counteract stress are autonomy, competence, self-efficacy, and sense of coherence. These various terms address client strengths, falling generally under the rubric of resilience. Is it important to choose the most relevant concept for older adults and use it consistently? Does one term fit the life stage of old age better than others? Why is resilience more commonly associated with the young? The following discussion makes a distinction between these terms and their meanings for the study of old age and for social work practice with older persons.

Autonomy is a human characteristic often considered important to people's ability to combat stress. *Autonomy* is an individual's sense of being capable of independent action, the ability to provide for one's own needs, or independence from the control of others (Barker, 1995). This definition—reflecting the individualistic nature of Western culture—can become problematic: Everyone, whether he or she acknowledges it or not, remains relatively dependent even after childhood, and the likelihood of depending on others increases as one ages. Therefore, use of the term *autonomy* requires that practitioners understand that autonomy and dependence are interrelated. Dependence does not end the need for autonomy. Furthermore, clients may often fear dependency and old age, and they may still want to pursue opportunities in which their autonomy is preserved.

Competence is another term frequently used in the literature on aging to describe client's abilities to overcome distress. A social worker's assessment of everyday competence requires gaining a broad view of a person's ability or potential to perform adequately in biological, psychological, and social activities essential for living on one's own (Willis, 1991). Social workers may also use familiar assessment instruments that measure functional health related to instrumental activities of daily living, such as preparing meals, performing household chores, and so forth (Fillenbaum, 1985).

As one ages, some aspects of former competence (driving, cooking, accomplishing career tasks) may be relinquished to others, but new areas of competence may develop as one adapts to life changes (Antonovsky & Sagy, 1990). For example, although retirement can sometimes result in the loss of status through work, a man in his nineties may refine and develop an early hobby such as painting, a talent in which he may have had an interest in earlier years but for which he had little time because of a demanding career.

In addition, client competence may be assessed by examining the connections between the person and others at various systems levels, addressing "the totality of the client's life experience and contexts as a harmonious whole" (Greene & Watkins, 1998, p. 64). The balance between independence and autonomy naturally shifts throughout the life cycle. In some respects competence has been likened to resilience (Masten, 1994)—competence being the ability to function effectively in one's environment and resilience being the ability to maintain competence despite adversity.

Another term related to a client's ability to resist stress is *efficacy,* that is, the power to produce effects or intended results—effectiveness. Self-efficacy is a central psychological component of competence (Bandura, 1977) describing "a client's expectation and belief in [his or] her ability to accomplish specified tasks that are needed to reach therapeutic goals" (Barker, 1995, p. 340). With a client's ability for self-direction in mind, social workers can enhance the client's sense of achievement by seeking mutual solutions, pointing out strengths, and using available resources.

The term *sense of coherence* is another construct that generally fits under the resilience rubric. It is used to describe the factors that allow people to remain healthy (McCubbin, Thompson, Thompson, & Fromer, 1994). A sense of coherence has three major components: (1) comprehensibility, or the ability to understand a situation; (2) manageability, or the capacity to manage the situational demands; and (3) meaningfulness, or the ability to derive meaning from the situations and demands one encounters (Antonovsky, 1979, 1987). This idea, originated by Antonovsky (1979), a medical sociologist interested in the origins of health, departs from illness-based models and proposes a *salutogenesis orientation*—a philosophical contention that people possess the perceptions and resources to strive for health.

Researchers worldwide have used Antonovsky's (1987) normed instrument to measure people's sense of coherence with all age groups. For example, Lewis (1993) used this concept as a predictor variable in a study of factors that could enhance successful independent living in a sample of elderly women in a community-based housing complex. She concluded that a sense of coherence is a useful construct for social work practitioners and researchers putting into practice a strengths-based resilience perspective (Lewis, 1996).

All of these terms—*autonomy, competence, self-efficacy,* and *sense of coherence*—are relevant to the study of old age. However, *autonomy* and *self-efficacy* are terms that seem to fall short of characterizing the range of experiences in old age. *Sense of coherence* seems most useful as a measurable construct that could further knowledge for a resilience-based ecological practice model with older adults. However, the broader concept of *competence* seems to incorporate self-efficacy and autonomy as aspects of psychological capability or potential. In our view, the term *resilience* best captures the notion that people recover or bounce back in response to life stress and adversity, and it provides an important context for understanding older adults.

Even the healthiest elder can expect to be challenged by the usual stresses of old age, such as loss of loved ones, career, and social activity. Models of successful aging notwithstanding (Rowe & Kahn, 1987, 1998), for adults fortunate enough to live long enough, physical, mental, and social losses are inevitable, and these adults are challenged to confront them (Leder, 1999–2000; Martindale, 2007). A review of the literature suggests that the study of resilience in later life is largely uncharted territory (Ryff et al., 1998), with the social work literature providing little evidence to the contrary. This may be because of the fact that most of the early pioneers who have studied resilience, such as Werner (1993) and Garmezy (1993), have focused on younger people. Another possible reason theorists have not associated resilience with older adults may be the societal tendency to connect old age with characteristics quite the opposite of resilience or a time in life when resilience is especially challenged (Martindale, 2007). *Ageism*, or negative stereotypes about old age, is pervasive even in the helping professions (Butler, 1975).

Nonetheless, with the current emphasis of social work on a strengths perspective (Saleebey, 1992; Tice & Perkins, 1996) and the dramatic increase in the number of older persons, the time seems right to advance the study of resilience to include older adults. Finally, two definitions might guide researchers' efforts to understand resilience in older adults. Ryff et al. (1998) defined *resilience* as "the maintenance, recovery, or improvement in mental or physical health following challenge" (p. 74), whereas we suggest that resilience in old age is continued competence across the lifespan despite adversity and serious stressors.

Human Behavior Theory Applications

The key human behavior assumptions that serve as the theoretical foundation for understanding resilience were introduced in chapters 1, 2, and 3. This section examines selected aspects of that foundation as it applies specifically to a strengths-based philosophy of social work practice with older adults.

Resilience: A Biopsychosocial and Spiritual Phenomenon

Aging, which begins at conception, refers to the behavioral changes that occur as people advance in chronological age. Three types of age-associated changes affect a person's ability to cope effectively with the environment: (1) biological, or changes in the structure and function of bodily organs; (2) psychological, or changes in the capacity to adapt to and modify the environment; and (3) social, or changes in the capacity to carry out roles and maintain social networks (Greene, 2000). As aging is highly variable and proceeds at different rates in different people, it is therefore important to explore the process and its relationship to resilience (Martindale, 2007).

The biological side of understanding resilience is largely underdeveloped because research has generally focused on people's failure to adapt (Kiecolt-Glaser, Malarkey, Cacioppo, & Glaser, 1994; Ryff & Singer, 1998; Ryff et al., 1998). Current research directed toward establishing connections between the biological and psychosocial aspects of resilience can further facilitate the use of the concept in understanding older adults. This view is consistent with the work of Ryff and colleagues, who emphasized the need to move beyond the construction of resilience in terms of protective and risk factors to a study of resilience as a dynamic process that comes into play as individuals maintain health and wellness in the face of naturally occurring challenges over time.

The ability to maintain meaningful social relationships has been identified in the resilience literature as a key protective factor (Werner, 1995). However, more research is needed to track the specific contributions of social connection to resilience in old age. Ironically, the health-enhancing nature of social support and connectedness among older adults is well documented (Antonucci & Akiyama, 1991; Cohen & Syme, 1985), making the connection between health, well-being, and resilience among older adults a challenging agenda for research.

Although spirituality has been identified as contributing to a person's resilience, once again researchers have insufficiently addressed this phenomenon among older adults (Canda, 1988a, 1988b). Enhanced spirituality can serve as a protective factor in the health of older Americans (Blazer, 1991; Koenig, George, Blazer, Pritchett, & Meador, 1993; Wilson-Ford, 1992) and as an important dimension of social support (Chatters & Taylor, 1996). Consequently, the lack of attention to the study of resilience and spirituality is particularly unfortunate, as older adults often give spiritual renewal a priority (Kleyman, 2000; Wilson-Ford, 1992). For example, Lewis (1993) found an 89 percent participation rate in weekly religious activities in a study of 128 elderly residents at an independent living complex.

Resilience across the Life Course

With the aging of longitudinal samples of young people and a growing interest in resilient older adults, researchers are now studying resilience as a dynamic process over the life cycle, rather than an outcome of one's coping abilities during a singular time of stress. As Ryff et al. (1998) have noted, the aging of longitudinal research samples has already led to a shift in the focus of resilience research to early and middle adulthood. Not surprisingly, research has begun to clarify "diverse pathways through adversity to high [levels of] psychological well-being" (Singer, Ryff, & Magee, 1998). Although individual paths to resilience vary, key factors contributing to well-being—including the quality of social relationships, advancement in work activities, and positive resources in early life—reappear consistently in individual stories.

Today more than ever there are examples of resilient communities where older adults reside and thrive. Retirement communities of all kinds have mushroomed because of dramatic demographic shifts in the population of older adults. Many older adults live independently in age-integrated communities, although increasing numbers are opting for residence in continuing care retirement communities (Erickson, 2000). In the larger community older adults play active, productive roles in every sphere of life and have a strong voice in public advocacy for community issues that influence their well-being.

Resilience and Diversity

The literature is beginning to document the fact that the ability to manage life's challenges and stresses is linked to a person's societal context and is influenced in particular by cultural differences (McCubbin et al., 1994). At the personal level, gender or health status may have a significant impact on one's ability to manage life challenges. How one is perceived by others as well as one's perception of self in relation to others influence one's ability to marshal internal and external resources for coping with life tasks. At the same time, societal factors such as relative access to social status or wealth are resources that support resilience (Sokolovsky & Vesperi, 1991).

Researchers have not yet made explicit the links between resilience, diversity, and aging. Nonetheless, it is generally understood that age itself can limit one's visibility and credibility in the larger world, but membership in multiple diverse groups compounds the challenges one must face on the path to resilience. Sokolovsky and others have noted the importance of applying a cultural lens in studying the relationships among aging, personal and social context, and perceptions of well-being (Sokolovsky, 1990). Although more empirical research is needed, a rich body of literature on the lived experiences of diverse elders has expanded researchers' understanding of the many paths to resilience in old age (Dawson & Glaubman, 2000; Delany, Delany, & Hearth, 1993; Peters, 1997; Sarton, 1993).

Power and privilege, whether based on economic, gender, racial, or another social position, are viewed as protective factors that tip the balance in favor of resilience. For example, it is clear that access to social, economic, and political resources and support for one's needs are different for an elderly African American lesbian than for a white male widower. However, the literature contains many examples of resilience among those who had neither power nor privilege, reminding us that there are many paths to resilience. Today's elders experienced the Civil Rights, antiwar, and women's movements, as well as an unprecedented period of prosperity. Given their sheer numbers, cultural diversity, and life experiences, their impact will affect all cohorts of elders as well as those who follow them. Understanding such differences as social class, range of health and autonomy, gender, sexual orientation, ethnicity, and distinctive age cohorts within the older adult population provides social workers with opportunities to embrace diversity and to foster resiliency among older adults (Gant, 1996; Torres-Gil & Pucinelli, 1995).

Facilitating Resilience in Social Work Practice

The social work profession must position itself to meet the needs of an aging society. Learning how to facilitate resilience in old age can help meet this challenge. To that end, this section describes a preliminary model of resilience-based ecological practice with older adults. The model is predicated on the understanding that resilience among older adults is fostered by relationships with others that, in turn, influence older adults' adjustment to life's challenges. The engagement between older adults and their significant relationships are discussed within three constructs that are thought to be important in facilitating resilience in social work practice: (1) safety and support, (2) affiliation, and (3) altruism. That is, the individual needs to move from an understanding of self that looks at the relation of self to self (safety and support), self to others (affiliation), and self to greater good (altruism; see Table 14.1). Each component can be examined from the micro, meso, or macro level, providing an understanding of resiliency from a dynamic perspective.

As is discussed in each of the sections that follow, as older adults seek services, a general model of practice applications for the social worker in the area of safety and support

- is guided by the client's perceptions of personal and interpersonal functioning;
- builds client–social worker trust and allows for accurate assessment and a relationship-based approach to planned interventions;
- guides conversations to explore environmental and cultural dynamics as they relate to the assessment of safety and support; and
- is sensitive to the client's expressions of self-determination that might involve a collective experience of self—as a result, the therapeutic relationship might include extended family and significant others while safeguarding confidentiality.

As with safety and support, practice applications for the social worker in the area of affiliation

- cast a wide net to explore a client's meaningful social relationships and needs for expanded affiliations, particularly with links to indigenous informal groups;
- are sensitive to factors of culture, ethnicity, and sexual orientation;
- recognize the social work profession's historical link to vulnerable populations; and

TABLE 14.1 Resiliency and the Older Adult

Engagement Construct and Practice Level	Resiliency-based Goals/Needs	Resiliency Factor(s)	Worker Guidelines
Safety and Support			
Micro	Individual, sacred space Personal, immediate physical safety	Psychological well-being; outgoing personality	Guided by client's own story
Meso	Trust of family and peers	Pattern of successful relationships	Perception, cultural framework, memberships included in an ecological framework focused on interacting systems; relationship centered
Macro	Safe neighborhood and community Access to services such as health care	Economic stability; adequate housing; interested in others and the world	
Affiliation			
Micro	Family (of origin and procreation) creating a sense of belonging	Attitudes toward the contribution of aging self	Client as expert
Meso	Small group/social establishing a sense of connection	Attitudes toward the contribution of aging elders	Collaboration Consultation, collateral contacts
Macro	Networks/relationships foster generativity and a sense of being needed and helpful	Attitudes toward the contribution of aging community	Coalition building
Altruism			
Micro	Reciprocity, spiritual values	Values and beliefs	Concern for others Family intervention/preservation
Meso	Generational benefit, legacy	Common universal values	
Macro	Betterment of the community/environmental factors	Societal/community sanction of values/environmental factors	Community development Organizational skills Program development Policy practice

- create and maintain an organizational or agency structure responsive to the client's needs, addressing accessibility, availability, affordability, and appropriateness of services.

And finally, in the area of altruism, the social worker

- explores the client's experiences of familial and social relationships;
- focuses on the client's perception of reciprocity in personal and social relationships;
- explores a client's worldview and perception of need for connectedness, including aspects of meaning, reciprocity, respect and self-efficacy, and self-actualization; and
- looks into linkages with extended family and the indigenous groups available in the immediate community, including clubs, self-help groups, churches, and so forth.

Safety and Support

Barker (1995) described basic needs as physiological needs, which include food and rest. Safety needs are described as security, stability, and freedom from fear. *Safety and support* are defined here as a state of being in which the basic physiological and environmental needs of older adults, including food, housing, health, finances, and protection from environmental hazards, are met and stabilized. Safety and support are necessary factors to resilience inasmuch as they create secured space in the older adult's immediate and surrounding environment.

An older adult's secured space includes physical and psychological space and ensures safety and continued growth. Safety and support provide protection and care for such basic needs as nutrition, housing, and health care. When the older adult is able to meet these needs, they should be viewed as strengths in the aging process. Of course, if they are jeopardized, risks can be addressed by the social worker, who is able to link the older adult to available and accessible resources or advocate with the client for the development of new resources. From an ecological perspective, safety and support are also related to trust and acceptance among family, friends, houses of worship, and community.

When older adults seek services from the social work profession, this trust and acceptance must be present in the client–worker relationship. This creates an atmosphere of safety for the older adult that may serve as a protective factor, even as it minimizes risks. This sense of security is important because many older adults feel vulnerable and are concerned about health care providers. As older adults access the health care system, consistency, honoring the time spent in relationships, frequency of contact, and appropriate follow-up can facilitate their sense of resiliency. Follow-up may require coordination with service providers and/or informal helpers, such as family or church members. Increased understanding of how such factors interact with resilience is likely to improve clients' level of satisfaction with social service agencies. The model suggests that safety and security combined with affiliation and altruism strengthen and support resiliency in older adults.

Affiliation

Affiliation may also strengthen resiliency among older adults. Barker (1995) defined *affiliation* as a "coping strategy to deal with emotional conflict or stress by turning to others for help and support and mutual problem solving" (p. 11). As a means of enhancing resiliency, affiliation is a dynamic component that is sometimes taken for granted. Research focused on the older adult has shown that affiliation, through connections with family and houses of worship, is linked to life satisfaction (Coke & Twaite, 1995). It was a motivator for volunteering in a study that viewed older adults as an important resource. Furthermore, the quality of relationships that characterize affiliation is more positively related to life satisfaction than is simply active involvement with others (Salamon, 1985). Affiliation as a predictor of life satisfaction serves as a protective factor in the understanding of resiliency.

Connection to others is important. The family can serve as a source of this buffering, but other groups should be considered, given the likelihood of widowhood and retirement, which typically provide less daily connection to others. Support groups, such as church groups, senior citizen groups, civic groups, and, when appropriate, self-help groups such as Alcoholics Anonymous (AA), should be considered. In the case of affiliation, in a group such as AA, the older adult can be viewed as both resource and benefactor. This dual relationship fosters resiliency through the concept of reciprocity. The fellowship promotes connections, acts as a buttress against illness, and serves the need for companionship. Social workers should encourage participation in such alliances to promote relationship-enhancing behaviors.

Affiliations may also influence an older adult's health status. An African American elder who is a recovering alcoholic recounted her affiliation with AA and how it offered her a source of support:

> They welcomed me. I took the 12 steps and by the grace of God, I BECAME to know that higher power. And I got so, such a long story about it. But I tell you, I been to hell and back. And the grace of God brought me back. I died when I was 21 years old. God resurrected me. I said I was going to write a book, you know, about my life. I've wrecked so many people. Alcoholics Anonymous, alcohol, has no respect of

> person, like God. It will take anybody. I've seen priests, preachers, all, all walks of life came to those AA meetings. (Harrell, 2000)

This testimony suggests that affiliation with support groups and, in this case, reliance on a higher power can facilitate resilience. In addition, social work practice can be enhanced by the use of support groups and clients' spirituality, which can serve as protective factors and complement resiliency.

Altruism

Altruism, or selfless acts, is also a factor that characterizes resiliency in the older adult. Barker (1995) defined *altruism* as the unselfish regard for the well-being of others, accompanied by a motivation to give money, goods, services, or companionship. Midlarsky and Kahana (1994) studied altruism in later life from multiple theoretical perspectives, including philosophy, theology, economics, evolution, and the psychoanalytic and behavioral domains. They concluded that altruism in later life provides an opportunity to view older adults through a positive lens that captures the full human potential empowered by compassion, a sense of competence, and personal meaning to the end of their days.

When acts of altruism are performed by older adults, it may mean the difference between integrity and despair and may contribute to their resilience. Integrity implies that individuals are capable of accepting the life course and are interested in giving back, particularly to the community. The motivation may be tied to leaving a legacy. A socially responsible behavior, it tends to benefit both the individual and the recipient of one's altruism. The older adult reflects altruistic behavior in volunteer experiences, including work with disadvantaged groups, fundraising or gift giving, and caregiving. The following narrative illustrates this point:

> I got the feeling when people are in need and you can help, go on and do it to the extent of your ability to do it. And that is what I've been doing all of my adult life. I got that lesson from there. Plus with education, that is one of my bugbears for education. I retired from teaching. I taught 37 years and I retired in 1972 and I still help the children sometimes. Some of them I tutor to help them along with their lessons . . . and to keep them in school, to try to help them go on through school. I have a cash award program for scholars every year that I sponsor children of my (geographic) area. I'm prejudiced about that. They have to live within my area in order to perform, participate in my program. This is what I've been doing since 1988 and I'm still doing it. I have a fund for that purpose. I'm still helping and love to do it. I help with my church also. I don't belong to the church in the community but I feel that I belong to them because

> I'm always at a church in the community. I belong to [a historically African American Catholic church]. That's where my membership is but it seems like my membership is here also. Because that's how I feel and I'm still helping. I wish my middle name was help. . . . I do believe, I'm the last one living of the nine children. And I know God has blessed me, in unison, Oh yes, for what I've done for my parents and for my community and for my relatives and friends. So I feel that God has blessed me for this, for taking care. (Harrell, 2000)

The act of altruism for this individual, an 87-year-old widow with no children, spanned her entire life, as did a history of wellness. Finally, altruism served as a means of self-actualization. Her life illustrates the fact that when the social worker honors the spirit and contribution of the older adult, this can have buffering effects that may facilitate resilience.

Finally, concepts such as competence, efficacy, and sense of coherence are all related to resilience. Conceptualized as continued competence across the life span despite adverse stressors, resilience is a dynamic phenomenon as clearly relevant for the study and understanding of older adults as for any other age group. Provocative and challenging research and practice agendas in this area of study are evident at the individual, social, and environmental levels. In addition, advances in health care and the increase in the older adult population, particularly among minority groups, present new challenges and opportunities to serve this group as valued stakeholders and active participants in planning and implementing the services that best fit their needs (Leung, 2011). The voices of older adults guided our development of a model of resilience including safety and support, affiliation, and altruism that adds to the knowledge base on resilience and old age and challenges outdated beliefs and practices that stereotype older adults. Factors of demographic diversity and the importance of spirituality for older adults also are included as key concepts vital to the study and understanding of well-being in old age. Given their sheer number and their greater health, education, and experience, older adults will be increasingly active players in shaping programs and policies that affect them (Centre for Policy on Ageing, 2011; Coleman, 2001). For professional practitioners and scholars using an inclusive, participatory model that values the diversity among older adults, a cultural lens can provide a panoramic view of resiliency among older adults that changes problems to possibilities and replaces despair with integrity and hope for the future.

References

Antonovsky, A. (1979). *Health, stress, and coping.* San Francisco: Jossey-Bass.

Antonovsky, A. (1987). *Unraveling the mystery of health.* San Francisco: Jossey-Bass.

Antonovsky, A., & Sagy, S. (1990). Confronting developmental tasks in the retirement transition. *Gerontologist, 30,* 362–368.

Antonucci, T. C., & Akiyama, H. (1991). Social relationships and aging well. *Generations, 15*(1), 39–44.

Atkins-Burnett, S., & Allen-Meares, P. (2000). Infants and toddlers with disabilities: Relationship-based approaches. *Social Work, 45,* 371–379.

Bandura, A. (1977). Self-efficacy: Toward a unifying theory of behavioral change. *Psychological Review, 84,* 191–215.

Barker, R. L. (1995). *The social work dictionary* (3rd ed.). Washington, DC: NASW Press.

Blazer, D. (1991). Spirituality and aging well. *Generations, 15*(1), 61–65.

Butler, R. N. (1975). *Why survive: Being old in America.* New York: Harper & Rowe.

Canda, E. (1988a). Conceptualizing spirituality for social work: Insights from diverse perspectives. *Social Thought, 14,* 30–46.

Canda, E. R. (1988b). Spirituality, religious diversity, and social work practice. *Social Casework, 69,* 238–247.

Centre for Policy on Ageing. (2011). *How can local authorities with less money support better outcomes for older people?* Retrieved from http://www.jrf.org.uk/publications/local-authorities-better-outcomes-older-people

Cohen, S., & Syme, S. L. (Eds.). (1985). *Social support and health.* Orlando, FL: Academic Press.

Coke, M. M., & Twaite, J. (1995). *The black elderly.* New York: Haworth Press.

Coleman, B. (2001). *Consumer-directed services for older people* (Issues Brief No. 53). Washington, DC: AARP Public Policy Institute.

Dawson, G., & Glaubman, R. (2000). *Life is so good.* New York: Random House.

Delany, S., Delany, A. E., & Hearth, A. H. (1993). *Having our say: The Delany sisters first 100 years.* New York: Kodansha International.

Dunke, R., & Norgard, T. (1995). Aging overview. In R. L. Edwards (Ed.-in-Chief), *Encyclopedia of social work* (19th ed., Vol. 1, pp. 142–152). Washington, DC: NASW Press.

Erickson, M. A. (2000). Moving to a CCRC: How elders experience the transition. *Aging Today, 21*(5), 16.

Fillenbaum, G. (1985). Screening the elderly: A brief instrumental activities of daily living measure. *Journal of the American Geriatrics Society, 33,* 698–706.

Gant, L. M. (1996). Are culturally sophisticated agencies better workplaces for social work staff and administrators? *Social Work, 41,* 163–171.

Garmezy, N. (1993). Vulnerability and resistance. In D. C. Funder, R. D. Parke, C. Tamlinson-Keasey, & K. Wideman (Eds.), *Studying lives through time: Personality and development* (pp. 377–398). Washington, DC: American Psychological Association.

Gill, M. G. (2007). *How Starbucks saved my life.* New York: Gotham.

Greene, R. (2000). *Social work with the aged and their families.* New York: Aldine de Gruyter.

Greene, R. R., & Watkins, M. (1998). *Serving diverse constituencies: Applying the ecological perspective.* New York: Aldine de Gruyter.

Harrell, E. B. (2000). [The religious and spiritual values of older African American women that strengthens communities]. Unpublished raw data.

Kiecolt-Glaser, J. K., Malarkey, W. B., Cacioppo, J. T., & Glaser, R. (1994). Stressful personal relationships: Immune and endocrine function. In R. Glaser & J. K. Kiecolt-Glaser (Eds.), *Handbook of human stress and immunity* (pp. 321–340). San Diego: Academic Press.

Kleyman, P. (2000, March–April). The aging spirit: Two studies raise questions on health–religion connection. *Aging Today,* p. 13.

Koenig, H. G., George, L. K., Blazer, D. G., Pritchett, J. T., & Meador, K. G. (1993). The relationship between religion and anxiety in a sample of community dwelling older adults. *Journal of Geriatric Psychiatry, 26,* 65–93.

Leder, D. (1999–2000). Aging into the spirit: From traditional wisdom to innovative programs and communities. *Generations, 23*(4), 36–41.

Leung, T. T. F. (2011). Client participation in managing social work service—An unfinished quest. *Social Work, 56*(1), 43–52.

Lewis, J. S. (1993). Independent living among community based elderly: The impact of social support and sense of coherence. *Dissertation Abstracts International, 54*(3), 1094A.

Lewis, J. S. (1996). Sense of coherence and the strengths perspective with older persons. *Journal of Gerontological Social Work, 26*(3–4), 99–111.

Martindale, B. (2007). Resilience and vulnerability in later life. *British Journal of Psychotherapy, 23*(2), 205–216.

Masten, A. (1994). Resilience in individual development: Successful adaptation despite risk and adversity. In M. C. Wang & E. W. Gordon (Eds.), *Educational resilience in inner city America* (pp. 3–25). Hillsdale, NJ: Erlbaum.

McCubbin, H. I., Thompson, E. A., Thompson, A. I., & Fromer, J. E. (1994). *Sense of coherence and resiliency: Stress, coping, and health.* Madison: University of Wisconsin System.

Midlarsky, E., & Kahana, E. (1994). *Altruism in later life.* Thousand Oaks, CA: Sage.

Peters, M. (1997). *May Sarton: A biography.* New York: Knopf.

Recer, P. (2000, August 10). Seniors living longer, in better health, report says. *Times-Picayune* (New Orleans), p. A-17.

Roth, D. (Ed.). (2011). *Why you should hire older workers.* Retrieved from WalMart-Stores Retired message boards (WMT) AOL.Fortune.com/aol/en 11/27/11

Rowe, J. W., & Kahn, R. L. (1987, July 10). Human aging: Usual and successful. *Science, 237,* 143–149.

Rowe, J. W., & Kahn, R. L. (1998). *Successful aging.* New York: Pantheon.

Ryff, C. D., & Singer, B. H. (1998). The contours of positive human health. *Psychological Inquiry, 8,* 1–28.

Ryff, C. D., Singer, B. H., Love, G. D., & Essex, M. J. (1998). Resilience in adulthood and later life. In J. Lomranz (Ed.), *Handbook of aging and mental health* (pp. 69–96). New York: Plenum.

Salamon, M. J. (1985). Sociological role theories in the elderly: A replication and extension. *Activities, Adaptations and Aging, 7,* 111–122.

Saleebey, D. (Ed.). (1992). *The strengths perspective in social work practice.* New York: Longman.

Salthouse, T. A. (1990). Cognitive competence and expertise in aging. In J. E. Birren & K. W. Schaie (Eds.), *Handbook of psychology of aging* (3rd ed., pp. 310–319). San Diego: Academic Press.

Sarton, M. (1993). *Encore: A journal of the 80th year.* New York: W. W. Norton.

Singer, B. H., Ryff, C. D., & Magee, N. J. (1998). Linking life histories and mental health: A person centered strategy. *Sociological Methodology, 28,* 1–51.

Sokolovsky, J. (Ed.). (1990). *The cultural context of old age: World-wide perspectives.* New York: Bergin & Garvey.

Sokolovsky, J., & Vesperi, M. D. (1991). The cultural context of well-being in old age. *Generations, 15*(1), 21–24.

Tice, C. J., & Perkins, K. (1996). *Mental health issues and aging: Building on the strengths of older persons.* Pacific Grove, CA: Brooks/Cole.

Torres-Gil, F., & Pucinelli, M. (1995). Aging: Public policy issues and trends. In R. L. Edwards (Ed.-in-Chief), *Encyclopedia of social work* (19th ed., Vol. 1, pp. 159–164). Washington, DC: NASW Press.

Werner, E. E. (1993). Risk, resilience, and recovery: Perspectives from the Kauai Longitudinal Study. *Development and Psychopathology, 5,* 503–515.

Werner, E. E. (1995). Resilience in development. *Current Directions in Psychological Science, 4,* 81–85.

Willis, S. L. (1991). Cognitive and everyday competence. *Annual Review of Gerontology and Geriatrics, 11,* 80–109.

Wilson-Ford, V. (1992). Health-protective behaviors of rural black elderly women. *Health & Social Work, 17,* 28–36.

15

Applying a Risk and Resilience Perspective to People with Intellectual Disabilities

NANCY P. KROPF and ROBERTA R. GREENE

On finishing this chapter, students will be able to:

Engage in policy practice to advance social and economic well-being and to deliver effective social work services (Educational Policy 2.1.8) by

- Analyzing, formulating, and advocating for policies that advance social well-being (practice behavior).

Intervene with individuals, families, groups, organizations, and communities (Educational Policy 2.1.10[c]) by

- Helping clients resolve problems.
- Negotiating, mediating, and advocating for clients (practice behaviors).

More people with intellectual disabilities (ID) are living in community settings than ever before, yet the social work profession has been relatively unresponsive to the needs of this client population. For example, social work educators frequently overlook this client population in university curriculums (DePoy & Miller, 1996; DeWeaver & Kropf, 1992; Mackelprang & Salsgiver, 1996). Although people with ID and their families can benefit from working with a social work practitioner, few students of social work have received training in this area or have completed internships with this client population (DeWeaver, 1982, 1994; Hanley & Parkinson, 1994). Many social workers enter the profession unprepared to assess, intervene on behalf of, or evaluate practice issues in the ID field.

This chapter provides an overview of the concepts of risk and resilience as they apply to the population with ID. In the previous edition of this book, persons with cognitive disabilities were described as having a *developmental disability.* This diagnostic category was defined as including disabilities that occurred from the neonatal period up to 22 years of age (U.S. Congress, 1990). However, the term *intellectual disability* is now used with some concomitant changes in the conceptualization of both the disability and the diagnosis. Whereas the previous classification was based upon IQ score, the new classification includes the assumption that an intellectual disability is based on impairments in functioning but that these conditions are strongly influenced by the individual's interaction with the environment (Toth & King, 2010). This new definition and classification system emphasizes the individual's *strengths and adaptations* instead of the conditions that limit his or her functioning.

The concept of resilience is associated with the experience of people with ID and their families. Having a family member with ID can pose unique challenges, yet families are also often able to see the rewards, which include learning new coping skills and enhancing certain aspects of family relationships (Petrowski, Edwards, Isaacs, Baum, & Brown, 2008; Seltzer, Krauss, Choi, & Hong, 1996). Individuals with ID also demonstrate the ability to cope with life transitions and changes. Adults with ID have experienced a tremendous amount of change, as services have evolved from having an institutional- to a community-based focus (Toth & King, 2010). Consequently, many individuals who were previously institutionalized are unprepared to assume the roles and responsibilities of adulthood upon discharge. Social workers who work with people with ID are able to take the concepts of risk and resilience and use them to understand this population's challenges and successes.

Major Social Issues

Social workers face several issues in providing services to people with ID and their families. The population with ID is living longer, similar to the general population. A fairly dramatic example of this demographic shift is illustrated by the change in lifespan for persons with Down syndrome, the most common genetic form of intellectual disability. In 1929, the average lifespan for a child with this type of disability was nine years; today, people with Down syndrome can live into their 60s (Eyman, Call, & White, 1991). However, the aging of the population with ID is more accelerated than that of the general population. In addition, health disparities for the population with ID may be more acute than for the general population, partly because the former population has less access to health care and treatment, and the care they can access is of poorer quality (Sohler, Lubetkin, Levy, Soghomonian, & Rimmerman, 2009; Ward, Nichols, & Freedman, 2010). Therefore, "late life" is defined as occurring earlier than in the general population—the usual demarcation to later life being more than 55 years of age (Seltzer & Krauss, 1987). This situation is relevant because older adults with ID and their aging parents may require additional support as both generations enter into later life simultaneously.

Another critical issue is the change in service delivery to people with ID over the past several decades. Before the deinstitutionalization movement of the 1970s, the predominant form of service for people with ID was institutionalization. Conditions were often deplorable and even inhumane (Blatt & Kaplan, 1966). Over the ensuing decades, the populations in state-run institutions have decreased or the institutions have closed (Lakin, Prouty, Anderson, & Sandlin, 1997), and services have become increasingly community based. The cohort that has experienced this change has had to deal with a tremendous transition, as chronicled in a qualitative study on deinstitutionalized adults conducted by Edgerton and Gaston (1991). That research attested to the degree of resilience these adults demonstrated despite their discharge from state hospitals directly into community settings with minimal or no transition aid. Deinstitutionalization has increased the number of people with ID who live, work, recreate, and socialize in community—not segregated—settings.

Because people with ID are living longer lives in their communities, it is necessary to provide opportunities that allow them to lead as productive and satisfying lives as possible. An important issue is that the population with ID needs to know how to make decisions about pursuing social roles (for example, worker, community member, sexual being). Furthermore, practitioners need to know how to support families as the family member with ID begins to take on additional experiences. Risk is involved in this endeavor, and families are often reluctant to allow their sons or daughters with ID to try out new roles. This often stems from a desire to protect or shield the person with ID from rejection, failure, or hurt. Although many parents struggle with the concept of helping a son or daughter enter into new situations, having a child with a disability may make this task especially difficult for family members.

Current models of service provision for people with ID emphasize that population's participation in service delivery. Families and people with disabilities are considered "service consumers" instead of "patients" or "clients." Although consumers are involved in creating their own service plans and often serve as members of boards and advisory groups, a continuing focus involves changing the social perceptions of persons with ID. Changes in services have promoted the strengths and contributions of persons with ID (Mackelprang & Salsgiver, 1996). Yet too often the stigma of disability continues at the personal level because people with ID are still considered "different," "slow," or "undesirable." In this area, social workers and advocates in the disability movement can continue to prioritize change. Myths and stigma for people with disabilities are still a major barrier to fuller inclusion in the various realms of society.

The following demonstrates the concept of risk in a family with a person with ID:

> Charles is a 24-year-old mentally challenged man who lives at home with his widowed mother. The community mental health agency started a program to provide supported employment for people with severe disabilities. Charles was a candidate for one of the positions in this program because he has a pleasant disposition and, at the time, was not a participant in any day programs for people with ID. In this supported employment model, Charles would work one on one with a job coach who would help him learn skills for competitive employment. Charles would be matched with a job at a food court in a shopping mall, where he would clear the tables and place the trash in the containers located throughout the court.
>
> The social worker who served as the job coach was very enthusiastic about working with Charles. Charles's position would help him reach another goal the family had set, which was to provide his mother with some respite so that she could prioritize her own needs. To the social worker's surprise, the mother was unwilling to have Charles participate in the program. The mother recounted how she had allowed him to participate in a recreation program for people with disabilities several years ago. When the program ran out of funds, Charles was extremely disappointed that he could no longer participate. The mother stated that too much risk was involved with the supported employment options: What if funding ran out again? What if Charles did not have the skills to stay in the job? The potential for failure was too much for the mother to consider, because she had had to cope with the outcomes of her son's disappointment when a previous opportunity did not work out positively.

This example highlights how past experiences (successes, failures, and frustrations) can affect the current assessment of risk for a family. This situation is paramount for individuals with ID and their families, because service options are often very limited. As Kropf and Greene (1993) indicated, the cumulative effects of multiple disappointments for people with ID and their families can result in feelings of despair, mistrust, or isolation. Part of the task of social workers in this field is to assist consumers and their families in moving beyond painful experiences and preparing for new challenges that can enhance individual and family functioning.

Defining Risk and Resilience in ID

The concepts of risk and resilience are used extensively when describing people with ID. The concept of resilience has become an integral part of the literature on disabilities. For example, an entire issue of the *Journal of Intellectual Disability Research* (2009 [Vol. 53, No. 12]) addressed the concept of resilience in this population and their family systems. As stated in the preface to this special issue,

> It is now well known that a child with ID does not inevitably cause stress and depression in parents; individual variations in parent well-being are great and depend on a number of factors. . . . Individual variations in the experience of positive and negative aspects of parenthood are evident as well as individual variation in outcome. (Broberg, Blacher, & Emerson, 2009, p. 955)

This special issue, and much of the other research in the area of resilience, has tried to identify factors associated with more positive and successful functioning in individuals with ID and their families. This knowledge provides practitioners with a foundation for developing intervention strategies to assist individuals and families with tasks and challenges in ways that enhance their functioning and coping.

Part of this line of research is a shift toward identifying the means of coping demonstrated by people with ID and their families (for example, Glidden & Natcher, 2009). Included in this trend is a focus on the social barriers that exclude people with ID from participating fully in society. People with disabilities continue to have lower levels of *self-determination*—that is, the ability to make their own life choices—than people without disabilities (Clark, Olympia, Jensen, Heathfield, & Jenson, 2004). Despite the limited social roles they are "allowed" to pursue, people with ID are becoming more involved in their communities. For example, there is "a rising self-advocacy movement is demanding a fuller participation in society among people with all types of disabilities" (Miller & Keys, 1996).

This idea is reflected in the story of Carl, the son of Kelli Nicks, a bachelor's of social work student at a state university who interviewed her son for a class project:

> Carl, a 12-year-old African American boy, was born in June 1988 to relatively young parents. Carl is an extremely shy boy who appears

withdrawn around strangers. His mother recalled that he was a happy and responsive baby. He recognized faces, cooed, and ate finger foods at 6½ months of age. When Carl was 10 months old, his parents became concerned that he did not stand up or show any signs of walking. This was the first indication that there might be developmental delays. Carl went on to walk at 22 months of age. He played easily with other children and enjoyed watching *Sesame Street.* As Carl entered nursery school, he played well with other children but had difficulty riding a bike.

Carl's kindergarten teacher was the first to raise concerns about Carl's ability to perform the necessary skills for his age. When the family moved to a new city, away from extended family, he appeared to have trouble separating fantasy from reality. He began to increasingly play alone. He did not enjoy school and tested poorly on the Wechsler Achievement Test. The diagnosis appeared to be developmental delay with mild retardation. The family then decided to move back home.

Carl currently enjoys school somewhat, and he has made a few close friends. His cousin Mickey is his best friend. He is repeating sixth grade to gain more time to develop academically and socially. He has the following to say about his mom for her class assignment: "the most, greatest mom I ever had":

Mom: Speak as loud as possible, I want you to be comfortable and I want you to be as open and honest as possible. State your name, clearly.
Carl: Okay, Carl.
Mom: Do you go to school?
Carl: Yeah.
Mom: What's the name of your school?
Carl: Fishback Creek Public Academy.
Mom: All right, and what is your teacher's name?
Carl: Miss Ailes.
Mom: Do you like your teacher?
Carl: Yes.
Mom: Why?
Carl: Because, um, she's so funny and she helps me on the … any hard things that we do in class. She just helps me, she's a great teacher.
Mom: All right, that's a good answer. Do you like school?
Carl: Yes.
Mom: What's your favorite subject?
Carl: Reading.
Mom: And why do you like reading?

Carl: Because, every time I pick up a book and I start reading.

Mom: So, it's your favorite subject because you pick up a book and start reading?

Carl: Um, hmm.

Mom: What else do you like about reading?

Carl: Um, I like to sound out words and I like to see what's happening in the book.

Mom: All right. Do you have friends in school?

Carl: Yeah.

Mom: How many?

Carl: Three.

Mom: Three. Do you get along good with your friends?

Carl: Yeah.

Mom: What do you like best about having friends?

Carl: Um, it's so wonderful; you think you can do anything with your friends. It's wonderful to have friends.

Mom: And what is it about them that makes them friends?

Carl: Um. When they like, when they like say, um, you want to play with us, you say sure. When you play with 'em, and you think that's so great.

Mom: I don't think this is something we've discussed before, but do you understand that sometimes you have a hard time thinking or, not thinking, finding answers to the big math problems or sometimes you might have a hard time sounding out a word? Do you understand sometimes that maybe kids your same age that it's real easy for them to work on big math problems or read big words? It might be harder for you and you might have a little bit harder of a time getting your brain to move as fast as you want it to?

Carl: Um.

Mom: Say yes or no.

Carl: Yes.

Mom: You understand that?

Carl: Um, hum.

Mom: How does that make you feel?

Carl: Um. It doesn't make me feel sad because, um. I don't care if they're like good than me but, but, I'll be good just like them. I'll work hard at it.

Mom: So, you don't feel sad or like, like, it's just that you have a hard time?

Carl: No, I don't feel sad because I don't care about them. I don't care if they say, "I'm better than you Carl," or "You don't know anything," and when they say that to me then, I say, "I can do anything just like you."

Mom: Okay, and my last question is, what do you want to be when you grow up?

Carl: A teacher.

Mom: A teacher. Why do you want to be a teacher?

Carl: So I can teach kids.

Mom: So you can teach kids, okay. Well, thank you for your time Carl and you've done a very good job of answering the questions.

Carl: Okay.

Human Behavior Theory

Human behavior theory provides a lens with which to understand individuals within the context of the physical and social environment. Practitioners need to have the skills to assess the particular areas of risk that can negatively affect the level of functioning of an individual and his or her family. In addition, practitioners need to be able to identify protective factors that enhance resilience. From an ecological perspective, the following sections provide an overview of individuals with ID in the context of family, community, and cultural systems.

Family Factors. Research on families that include a person with ID has identified areas of both resilience and risk. The focus of previous research was on the problems or stresses that these families have experienced. Although researchers continue to study stressors, another line of research has identified areas of strength in these families. For example, findings from a study on Down syndrome suggested that families raising children with and without a disability share some of the same parenting stresses (Cunningham, 1996). Similarly, research on stresses has indicated that families are able to cope with and adjust to caregiving demands quite well (Costigan, Floyd, Harter, & McClintock, 1997; Sanders & Morgan, 1997). Families are able to adjust to the particular situations of caregiving for a child with ID without becoming overwhelmed or ineffective.

On the basis of the assumption that most families are able to function fairly well, a fruitful line of research would be to identify the situations in caring for a son or daughter with ID that are most problematic or stressful. One research study on adjustment to disability compared families who had children with either autism or Down syndrome to families with children without disabilities (Sanders & Morgan, 1997). The families with autistic children reported the greatest amount of stress and difficulty in adjusting to caregiving demands. This may be because of the difficult behaviors that many children with autism demonstrate, such as behavioral outbursts and lack of interpersonal awareness. Other research on family adjustment has indicated that child behavior problems can result in major caregiving demands. Therefore, one of the risk factors for the family of a child who has ID is that the demands of caregiving are intensified when the child exhibits challenging behaviors (Costigan et al., 1997).

Using a life-course perspective, practitioners need to continually assess the goodness of fit in caregiving needs in families. In early life, children with ID encounter a variety of potential problems that can negatively affect their development (Greenbaum & Auerbach, 1998), such as rejection and isolation by peers, a lack of educational and social opportunities, and inadequate supports for the family (for example, in terms of the availability of respite care). These experiences can translate into developmental risks that increase the vulnerability of these children and their families.

Particular risk factors also exist in later life, creating the need for shifts in the family's organization and functions. As a result of increasing lifespans, more families need to provide care for a child with ID into the later years. There is a sizable body of literature on late-life caregiving in these families (for example, see Bigby, Ozanne & Gordon, 2002; Greenberg, Seltzer, & Greenley, 1993; Jokinen, 2006; Kropf, 1997; Llewellyn, Gething, Kendig, & Cant, 2004; Lutzer & Brubaker, 1988; Roberto, 1993; Seltzer et al., 1996; Smith & Tobin, 1993; Smith, Tobin, & Fullmer, 1995). As parents grow older, they may begin to experience age-related changes that decrease their ability to provide care for their son or daughter. Concomitantly, adult children with ID may experience an accelerated aging process as a result of their disability. This creates a situation in which the son or daughter requires additional care at a time when the parent is less able to provide it. Because this process is dynamic across the entire life course, social workers must continually assess family functioning.

Not only do families face changing issues because of extended lifespans, but also family forms have become more diverse over recent decades. Sadly, research on diverse family systems that include persons with ID only focuses on how mainstream families demonstrate aspects of strength and resilience. For example, much of the research has been concentrated on children in two-parent families instead of children with ID who are being raised in single-parent family systems (cf. Gardner & Harmon, 2002). In a qualitative study, Levine (2009) analyzed the various experiences of single mothers raising children with disabilities. Four major resilience-building themes emerged from the narratives of these parents:

- *Transforming the "stigma of single mothers" to "chosen mothers."* These women reported having a sense that they were "chosen" for this role (many stated by God) because they were able to handle the responsibilities of raising a child with a disability. A major part of this narrative was the women's ability to sustain their belief in being adequate parents in light of the negative valuing of single parents that is part of the social construction of raising children.

- *Disability as normal.* These mothers reframed the issue of disability from something that connoted "damage" or "inability" to an attitude of recognition of their child's potential. Their children were viewed beyond the particular diagnosis as developing people who had areas of strength and growth.
- *Family support.* Mothers also developed resilience in their role by drawing on resources for support. In particular, purposeful and strategic relationships were developed within the family to provide resources for the mothers, within the parenting role, and for their children.
- *Authoritative knowledge.* The mothers in this study described moving beyond the position of listening to others to respecting their own voice and knowledge about themselves as parents and their children.

These mothers demonstrate the shift in assumptions associated with parenting children with disabilities. This experience was previously one of grief and the loss of a "normal" child, and being a single parent of a child with a disability was seen as particularly daunting. Although the role is not without challenges, these mothers demonstrated numerous forms of strength and resilience. As Levine stated, these results challenge prevailing views, as "resiliency-building was enhanced when mothers created meanings about their children's disabilities in a way that concurrently acknowledged and resisted the externally applied labels" (p. 412).

Another diverse family form occurs when the primary caregiver of a child with a disability is a grandparent. Grandparents may assume care of grandchildren, including children who have ID or other disabilities, because of the abuse or addiction of their parents(Janicki, McCallion, Grant-Griffin, Kolomer, 2000). Because many of these grandparents assume responsibility informally, they often may lack access to supports and programs that can augment and support their role in caring for their grandchild with a disability. As McCallion, Janicki, Grant-Griffin, and Kolomer (2000) advocated, providing outreach to these grandparents and assisting with long-range planning in their caregiving role can decrease their stress and enhance their competence in raising their grandchildren with disabilities.

Community Factors. Part of the struggle for people with ID involves the social barriers that inhibit their full participation in society. Despite the numerous obstacles they must overcome, many people with disabilities have made relationships and established networks of support. Edgerton and Gaston (1991) carried out a qualitative analysis of the experience of deinstitutionalization for adults with ID, describing the lives of those who left institutions and reintegrated into their communities. Their book chronicles the transitions these adults experienced upon leaving institutions where many had lived their entire lives. Although many of the adults with ID continually struggled to reintegrate into community life, many had stories of success finding places to live, making new friends, and getting jobs. For those without ID, these are the typical roles of adulthood. For people who have lived the majority of their lives in an institutional environment, these achievements are a testament to their ability to negotiate tremendous risk.

Elements of community life can aid individuals with ID in functioning socially. One is the degree to which people with ID integrate into the social network of their neighborhood. Research on social integration indicates that a tension exists in promoting the involvement of people with ID with others without fostering a sense of "overinvolvement" that can lead to neighbors feeling a degree of intrusion (van Alphen, Dijker, van den Borne, & Curfs, 2010).

The church is a community institution that has been found to enhance the functioning of adolescents with ID, especially African Americans who face the stigma of having a disability as well as experience the ill effects of racism (Frison, Wallander, & Browne, 1998; Haight, 1998). Church membership and participation are protective factors for these youths, enhancing social participation and adjustment. The particular effects can be attributed to a positive ethnic identification that results from being part of a church community as well as to intergenerational support and acceptance from members (see chapter 9).

Another social institution that offers support for children and adolescents with ID is the school system. Research on different types of classrooms (for example, integrated and segregated) indicates that students with ID can have successful academic outcomes in various types of settings (Hardiman, Guerin, & Fitzsimons, 2008). In addition, after-school programs provide an atmosphere in which children can be safe, can learn developmentally appropriate skills, and can have experiences that are culturally relevant; such programs offer a sense of stability in the children's lives (Nash & Fraser, 1998). These programs are appropriate for all children but are especially crucial for those who are poor performers or who lack sufficient relationship skills. School-based programs can provide support for children who are performing marginally academically as well as prevent children of all kinds from being at risk because of a lack of supervision and structure.

School-based programs are successful in fostering competence in at-risk youths. One study examined the effect of school-based programs among 1,170 African American adolescents who had multiple risk factors in terms of academic performance (Reynolds, 1998). The teenagers had participated in an early intervention program from preschool to second or third grade. The goal of the program was to increase social resilience—that is, competence in scholastic and social areas—as measured by both academic performance and teacher ratings. Participation in the early intervention program was associated with social resilience among the teenagers. The findings suggest that school systems that target programs to at-risk children have the potential to positively affect behavior and achievement.

Family Stress Theory and Resilience

Social workers who use a resilience model to assess families must include content on family stress and coping. Theory suggests that adaptation within the family is characterized by a striving toward healthy functioning. In work with persons who have ID and their families, the goal is often to foster skills to negotiate changes in levels of functioning or in the environment. Some practice issues in ID include helping individuals and families during times of transition as well as linking them to community resources. At the macro level, working to reduce risk situations is also an important goal because a child can exhibit or acquire an ID even during late adolescence.

An assumption of systems theory that lends itself to understanding family resilience in the face of illness or disability is that systems try to maintain their stability even as they change (Kazak, 1989; McDonald, Couchonnal, & Early, 1996). The concept of stress originated with an examination of individuals' coping capacities. However, since the 1930s and 1940s, theorists have also been concerned with the threats that stress can place on a family. This viewpoint recognizes that the collective must successfully cope with the distress precipitated by stressor events such as chronic illness or disability (Antonovsky, 1998).

Reuben Hill (1949, 1958) developed the earliest family stress model (the ABCX model) to delineate a family's response to separation during war and reengagement. McCubbin and Patterson (1983) expanded on that model (the double ABCX model) to concentrate on a family's level of adaptation after a family member was reported missing in action in the Vietnam War. In the double ABCX model, the *aA* factor is the family's perception of the pileup of general stressors and strains, the *bB* factor is the family's perception of its crisis-meeting resources, and the *cC* factor is the family's perception of the original stressor event—such as a family member missing in action. In the double ABCX model, family resources, perceptions, and behavior interact to explain whether the family experiences a crisis, or the *x* factor (Patterson & Garwick, 1998).

As the double ABCX model evolved, it was renamed the family adjustment and adaptation response (FAAR) model (Patterson, 1988), and other elements were added to accentuate adaptation as the cardinal outcome of the stress process (Patterson & Garwick, 1998; see Figure 15.1). This change primarily reflected Antonovsky's (1998; Antonovsky & Sourani, 1988) work on family coherence, particularly a family's response to stress. A sense of coherence is the family's ability to balance control and trust (Antonovsky, 1979). That is, family coherence is

> a global orientation that expresses the extent to which one [a family] has a pervasive, enduring though dynamic feeling of confidence that (1) the stimuli deriving from one's internal and external environments in the course of living are structured, predictable and explicable; (2) the resources are available to one to meet the demands posed by these stimuli; and (3) these demands are challenges, worthy of investment and engagement. (Antonovsky, 1979, p. 19)

These theoretical discussions were congruent with the studies of resilience and furthered the double ABCX model by incorporating a *salutogenesis orientation*—a philosophical assertion that people possess the perceptions and resources to strive for health (Antonovsky & Sourani, 1988). A salutary orientation—which came to be called *a sense of coherence*—encompasses three natural processes that people use to counter stress: (1) comprehensibility, or the capacity to understand life; (2) manageability, or the competence to manage demands; and (3) meaningfulness, or the aptitude to draw meaning from a situation and its demands.

The FAAR model highlights a family's attempts to exercise its coping behaviors and use its resources to meet the challenges of stress. During the adjustment phase, the family experiences relative stability, and challenges are met with existing capabilities. A crisis develops when challenges become too great and exceed demands, causing a state of disequilibrium. The meaning that families attribute to these demands is a critical factor in their capacity to meet them and ultimately affects their ability to remain in equilibrium or balance. During the adaptation phase, families try to restore their balance by attaining new resources and coping strategies, reducing demands, and changing their perception of their situation. Adapting to a crisis also involves the family's regenerative power (Antonovsky & Sourani, 1988).

Another key to the FAAR model is that families share collective meanings that are distinct from individual meanings. Family meanings are also more than a consensus among family members. Family meanings are collective constructs created through life experiences as family members interact over time (Patterson & Garwick, 1998). The FAAR model suggests two levels of meaning: (1) situational meaning, which involves the individual's and family's perceptions of their

FIGURE 15.1 Family Adjustment and Adaptation Response

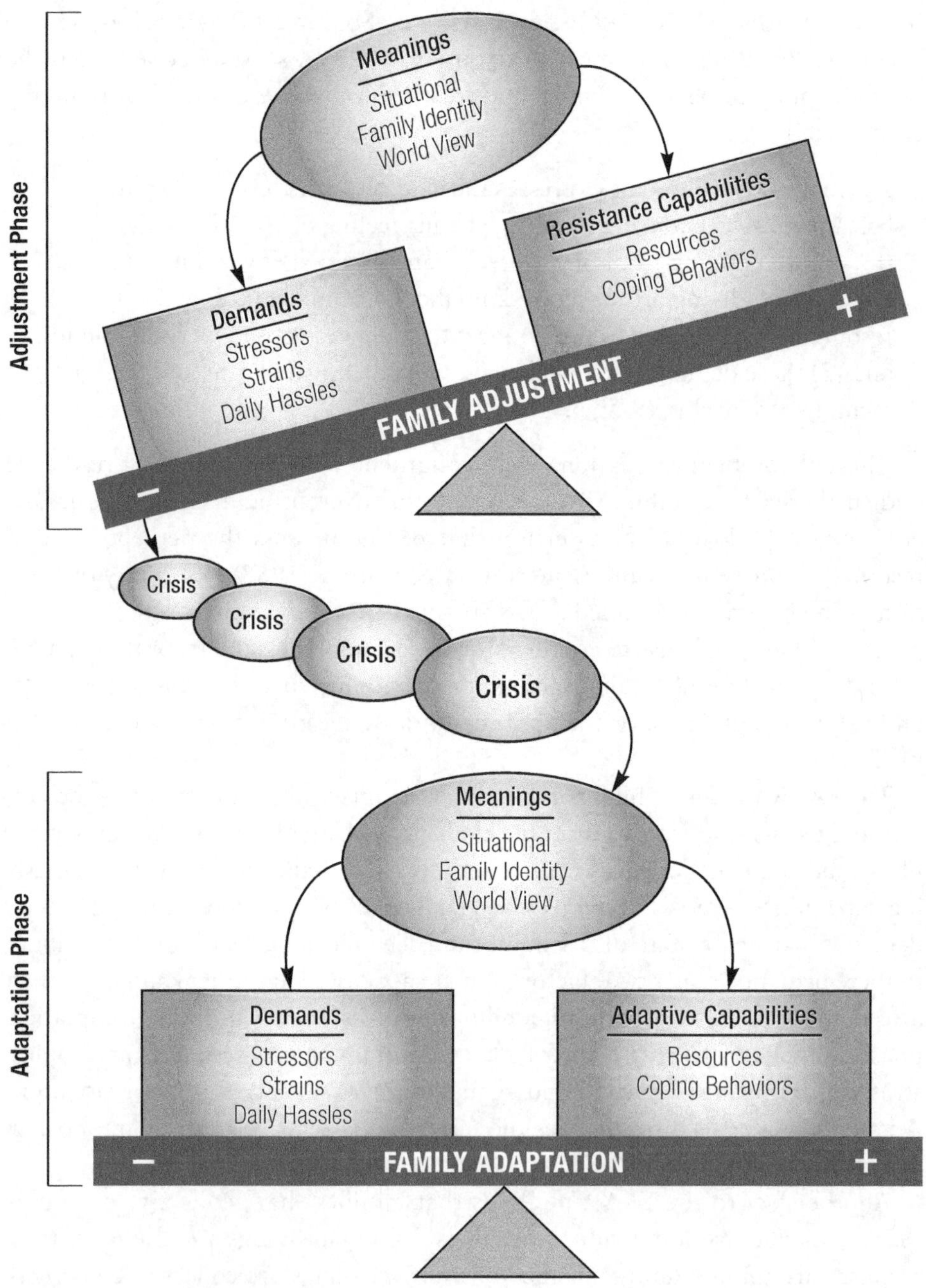

Source: From "Theoretical Linkages: Family Meanings and Sense of Coherence," by J. Patterson and A. W. Garwick, 1998, in *Stress, Coping and Health in Families: Sense of Coherence and Resiliency,* p. 77. Copyright 1998 by Sage Publications. Reprinted with permission.

demands and their capabilities; and (2) global meaning, which encompasses a transcendent set of beliefs about the relationships of family members and the family to the community. To establish a global meaning, families have a shared purpose; recognize that they are a collective; and are able to frame their situation optimistically, view life in a context relative to today's demands, and have shared control and trust.

Because the notion of shared meaning during a crisis is central to the FAAR model, this model is particularly useful as a guide to family interventions. One case in point is social workers' use of narrative therapies with families, in which the focus is reframing or changing meaning. For example, when a child is first diagnosed with an intellectual disability, family members may respond with a sense of disbelief and denial. They may search for a cause or interpretation of the disability. According to the FAAR model, the family will attempt to understand how the situation fits with its worldview and ability to manage (Patterson & Garwick, 1998).

In addition to establishing how a family can manage when a member has a disability, the social worker may find that the family identity is influenced by the disability. Stable patterns may be disrupted as the family shows concern about being a family with a child with ID: How will we keep going? Will we have enough resources? What will others say? The disability may also redefine family goals and purposes, centering most of the family's activities on the member with a disability. These concerns become central to family–social worker discussions.

Social workers must also pay attention to how ethnicity and culture influence the family's resilience. McCubbin, Thompson, Thompson, Elver, and McCubbin (1994) developed the resiliency model of family adjustment and adaptation (see Figure 15.2) to depict how a family's culture influences the appraisal of a crisis situation. They identified five fundamental levels involved in family appraisal processes in times of crisis:

> Level 5. Family schema. A generalized structure of shared values, beliefs, goals, expectations, and priorities, shaped and adopted by the family unit, thus formulating a generalized informational structure against and through which information and experiences are compared, sifted, and processed. A family schema evolves over time and serves as a dispositional worldview and framework to evaluate crisis situations and legitimate adherence to and change in the family's established patterns of functioning. . . .
>
> Level 4. Family coherence. A construct that explains the motivational and cognitive bases for transforming the family's potential resources into actual resources, thereby facilitating coping and promoting the health of family members and the well-being of the family unit. . . .

FIGURE 15.2 Focus on Appraisal Processes in the Resiliency Model of Family Adjustment and Adaptation

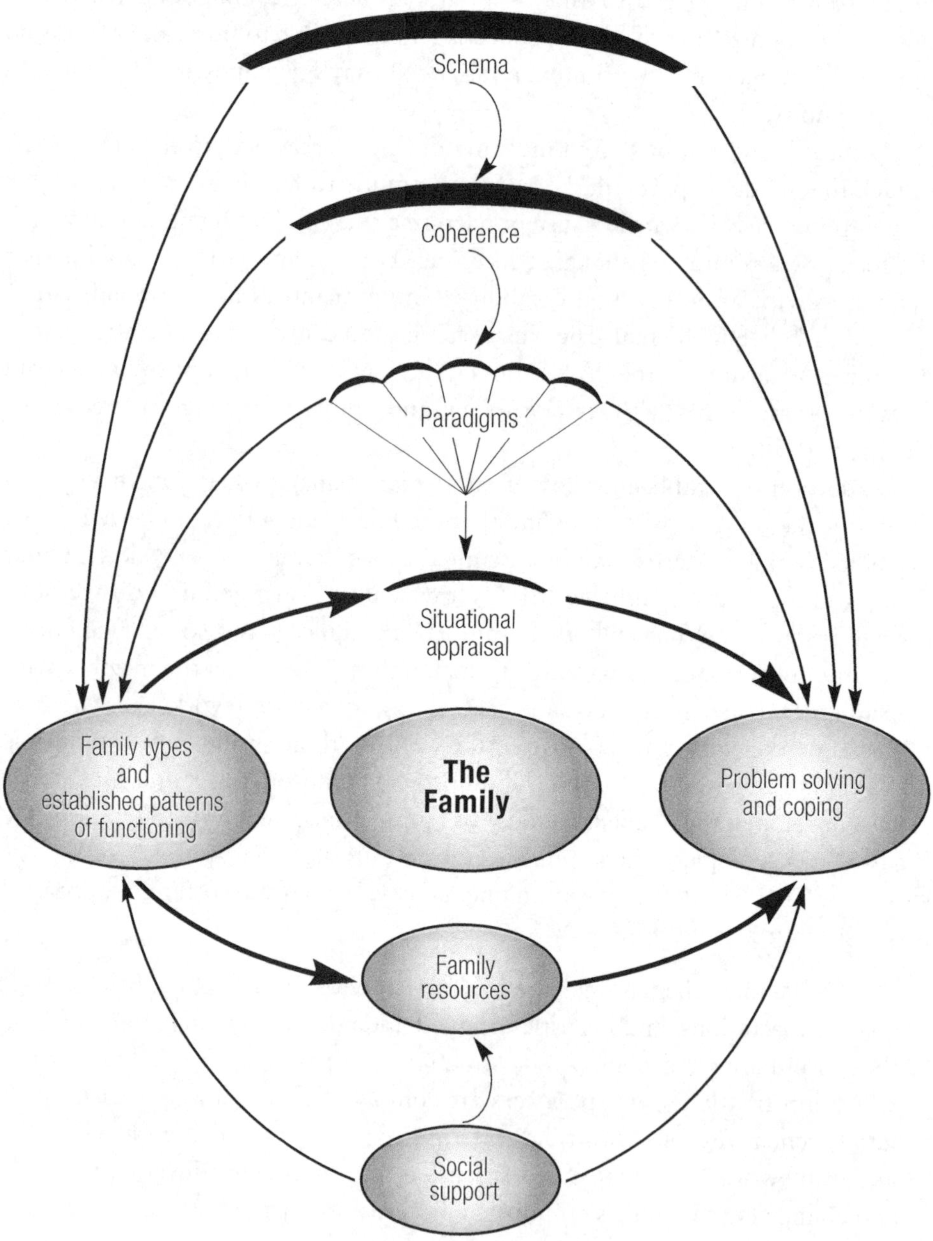

Source: From "Ethnicity, Schema, and Coherence: Appraisal Processes for Families in Crisis," by H. I. McCubbin, E. A. Thompson, A. I. Thompson, K. M. Elver, and M. A. McCubbin, 1994, in *Stress, Coping and Health in Families: Sense of Coherency and Resiliency,* p. 44. Copyright 1998 by Sage Publications. Reprinted with permission.

> Level 3. Family paradigms. A model of shared beliefs and expectations shaped and adopted by the family unit to guide the family's development of *specific* patterns of functioning around *specific* domains or dimensions of family life (for example, work and family, communication, spiritual/religious orientation, child rearing). . . .
>
> Level 2. Situational appraisal. The family's shared assessment of the stressor, the hardship created by the stressor, the demand upon the family system to change some established patterns of functioning. The appraisal occurs in relation to the family's capability for managing the crisis situation. . . .
>
> Level 1. Stressor appraisal. The family's definition of the stressor and its severity is the initial level of family assessment. (pp. 43–46)

In everyday situations, the family may go through the five levels of the resiliency model of family adjustment and adaptation with little explicit concern. However, in the case of a more severe stressor, such as the birth of a child with a physical disability, established patterns of family functioning are challenged (McCubbin, McCubbin, Thompson, & Thompson, 1998). Family routines and role configurations are likely to be changed. Social workers can play a key part in helping families reexamine their expectations of one another, support viable old means of functioning, and establish new patterns when necessary. Because this resiliency model incorporates family beliefs and culture, this process can respect a family's right to self-determination and be congruent with its choices and goals.

Walsh's (1998) proposal for family interventions captures this resilience approach. She suggested that family treatment from a resilience perspective would involve the practitioner

- tracking coping and adaptation over time;
- creating meaning out of crisis situations;
- normalizing family disasters by (a) depathologizing and contextualizing family problems, (b) using respectful language, and (c) reframing and relabeling issues;
- identifying, affirming, and building family strengths by (a) crediting positive intentions, (b) praising efforts and achievements, (c) drawing out hidden resources, (d) finding strengths in the midst of adversity, and (e) building empathetic connections among family members;
- adapting a positive, future-oriented focus by (a) refocusing from complaints to goals; (b) instilling hope and optimism; (c) encouraging shared efforts, concrete steps, and perseverance; and (d) helping families to accept human limitations;

- involving the family in recovery from individual trauma;
- revising services by using (a) collaboration and team work, (b) multi-systemic and community-based interventions, and (c) systems-oriented approaches and prevention; and
- strengthening therapist resilience.

A Consumer Orientation

In clinical practice with people who have ID and their families, practitioners need to promote resilience by identifying and incorporating consumer strengths into practice and service. Unfortunately, previous practice approaches with individuals with ID and their families have emphasized pathology, limitations, and stresses instead of those factors that promote empowerment (McCallion & Toseland, 1994). Social work intervention and policies must refocus on transitions between the person with the disability and the goodness of fit with the physical, social, and political environments.

Transitions can be a time of stress and change for people with ID and their families, because life changes may afford limited options for this population. People with ID may require enhanced support at developmental junctures or transition points that are difficult adjustment periods. The environment can enhance or prohibit adjustments. Jacobson and Kropf (1993) provided an example of an ecological approach to enhancing residential transitions for older people with ID. Residential relocation, such as moving from an independent living situation to a nursing home, can be a risk factor for all older adults. However, older adults with ID may be especially vulnerable to a change in residence because of their limited ability to build skills that will enable them to cope with this change. From an ecological perspective, various levels of preparation can enhance the resilience of the older adult with ID to adjust to the new location. For example, practitioners can prepare the individual for life in the new residence; prepare the new environment to include the older adult; and prepare those who have been "left behind," such as the caregivers, for this change. This ecological approach can promote resilience and minimize the trauma of this major life change for the older adult, his or her new care providers, and family and friends who are transitioning out of their caregiving roles.

Community-level practice approaches are appropriate for reducing risks that may lead to an ID. Interventions may include immunization programs, parenting programs to decrease child abuse and neglect, vehicle safety and restraint programs, and possibly programs that increase awareness of fetal alcohol syndrome (Adams & Hollowell, 1992). The practitioner who works with a consumer who has ID and his or her family can assess particular areas of risk and vulnerability. The practitioner may need to help some consumers assume greater levels of functioning by taking on additional risks, such as applying for a job or a more independent living arrangement. Using an ecological perspective to practice, the practitioner should structure multiple levels of intervention. The case example of Charles provided earlier in this chapter illustrates an ecological approach to practice. On the individual level, the social worker functioned as a job coach in making the best possible match between Charles's skill level and job opportunities. In his situation, Charles was sociable and enjoyed being around people; therefore, a job in a mall was ideal, because he would be socially interactive. The job coach's role was to teach Charles the skills needed to master the tasks of the job as well as modify the environment when necessary. For example, Charles was unable to use the twist ties to close the garbage bags because of his poor fine motor skills. The job coach, who finally overcame Charles's mom fear of the sheltered workshop, was able to order different types of bags so that Charles could tie the bag by using two ends, similar to tying his shoes. This environmental change enhanced his ability to be successful in his job responsibilities.

Several other interventions were involved in the supported employment process. On a macro level, the placement agency spent considerable time advertising the supported employment program and advocating hiring workers with disabilities. In addition, the placement agency provided training to coworkers (most of whom had no disabilities) on how to help integrate a worker with an intellectual disability. This process included deconstructing some of the myths about people with disabilities. In addition, the social worker helped the family to support Charles in his new job. Because of Charles's mother's hesitations, the social worker spent considerable time discussing the program with her and dealing with her fears about Charles's chances for success in his position. Although the goal was to help the consumer secure and maintain a job in a nonsegregated work environment, several different interventions were involved in administering this supported employment program.

In work with people with ID, the basic questions of practice involve the goodness of fit between the person, the family, and the social and physical environments. The following assessment questions can guide the practitioner in determining goodness-of-fit issues:

- What stress or condition is currently facing this consumer or family? How have they previously coped with this or similar situations?
- What changes or transitions have the person and family faced that have affected/stressed their ability to maintain their level of functioning? Is this a temporary situation, such as a parent's loss of a job? Or is it a permanent

situation, such as death or incapacitation of a parent that places the family at risk?

- How do the past experiences of these families influence their perceptions of the current situation? Do these perceptions enhance or inhibit their ability to cope with the situation?
- What community resources are available to support the individual with ID and the family? Are the consumer and family using resources to their fullest? What barriers exist to using available resources?
- What cultural factors are involved in this issue? How does the social worker practice with the individual and family so that his or her perceptions about caregiving, disability, and formal service provision are culturally congruent with those of the consumer?
- How can the situation experienced today help prepare the individual with ID and the family for future related issues? Can this experience build resilience and coping abilities?

These questions provide practitioners with information about the individual, the family, the community, and cultural areas. Within this ecological model, a practitioner evaluates the developmental issues of the individual and family, including historical aspects, current functioning, and expectations. A thorough assessment process using a combined ecological and developmental approach provides the most comprehensive method for understanding the person with a disability, the person's family system, and other sources of support.

Conducting Practitioner and Client Interviews: One Case Example

The following life history illustrates the various concepts outlined in this chapter and throughout the book. The family, the Hamiltons, is a middle-aged African American family that includes an adult son with an intellectual disability. The set of questions presented in the previous section is discussed in relation to the Hamiltons' situation. In addition, this example highlights the practice implications that preserve current family strengths. The example also identifies particular stressful aspects of the situation that the practitioner targeted for intervention to decrease additional areas of vulnerability and risk.

Issues the Family Is Facing

The Hamiltons live in a medium-size city in the southeastern part of the United States. Members of the family who live together are Arthur Sr. age 63, who suffers from complications from diabetes, including visual impairment and circulation problems; his wife Audrey, age 58; and their son Elton, age 22, who has Down syndrome. Because of Arthur's health impairments, Audrey has had primary responsibility for taking care of Elton and has had increased responsibility for taking care of Arthur because his health has worsened over the past few years. Two other sons, Arthur Jr. and Trevor, live in other states. Arthur Jr. has a military career, and Trevor works as an accountant for a large hospital corporation. Arthur, Jr., is divorced and currently single; Trevor has a wife and three young children. Neither son has much contact with his parents, and neither is close to their youngest brother Elton.

The issues facing the Hamiltons at this point in their family life cycle revolve around managing the care of two family members with disabilities. Until Arthur Sr.'s functional level declined, both parents were able to share responsibility for assisting and supervising Elton. However, Arthur Sr. is almost totally blind, and all caregiving tasks fall on Audrey. In addition to shouldering these responsibilities, Audrey is employed as a grade school teacher; it is critical that she receive this income to maintain the family's financial status. Because of his disability, Arthur Sr. opted for an early retirement and receives a modest pension from his previous employment as a physical plant manager.

Elton has moderate functional ability and is in fairly good physical health. He has some level of independence: For example, he can feed himself if someone cuts up food for him, and he can dress with minimal assistance (for example, if a zipper is already connected, he can zip a coat). However, he has limited language skills and cannot be left unsupervised for any length of time. Elton is very friendly, is social, and enjoys being around people. He finished his special education courses and currently is in a special vocational placement for persons with disabilities. He enjoys his work and gets along well with the staff and his coworkers.

Although Elton's parents have coped fairly well with providing care for him, the added stress of the increased caregiving demands has created difficulties. Elton has been known to developmental disability services for several years, and the agency has been providing his parents with respite care. Because of their difficulties, the Hamiltons have requested additional assistance through the agency and are considering residential options for Elton. They have approached a social worker about potential placements and residential possibilities.

Assessment and Intervention

At this point in the Hamiltons' family life cycle, a major aspect in assessment was to determine the degree of risk that had resulted from the existing caregiving demands. However, the family had functioned well together over the course of raising a son with an intellectual disability. Thus, the practitioner needed to identify particular ways of coping and maintaining functioning to deal with the current issues facing the family system. In addition, the social worker needed to structure the assessment around the following questions, highlighting particular areas for intervention:

> *Question:* What stress or condition is currently facing this consumer or family? How have they previously coped with this or similar situations?
>
> *Area of intervention:* The Hamiltons were experiencing stress as a result of the degree of caregiving required within the family. Audrey was solely responsible for the provision of assistance to both her son and her husband, who was becoming increasingly more dependent. In addition, she needed to maintain her full-time job as a schoolteacher. Although the family was able to manage the responsibilities of raising a son with a disability effectively, the family functioning was more at risk. The Hamiltons identified one way to manage the current situation—to decrease caregiving demands by moving Elton into a residential facility.
>
> *Question:* What changes or transitions have the person and family faced that have affected/stressed their ability to maintain their level of functioning?
>
> *Area of intervention:* The issues facing the Hamiltons were permanent ones and were not associated with a temporary or acute stressor. Several factors were involved: the continuing need to provide support for Elton; the increased need for support for Arthur Sr.; competing demands on Audrey's time and energy; and financial pressures resulting from a decrease in wages. The service request by the family was to explore residential placements for Elton. Although this was one possible outcome, several other options were available to the family as intermediate steps or as possible resolutions to the family's current situation.

Because the identified issue was caregiving demands, the social worker and family could explore several options to relieve the stresses within the family. One option would be support for both the care of Elton and Arthur Sr. For example, the family might consider in-home services that involve light meal preparation and chores (for example, light cleaning or laundering). Another possibility would be to provide opportunities for Arthur and Elton to enhance their level of functioning by learning additional skills. Elton was able to handle certain responsibilities at his vocational program. Perhaps some of these responsibilities could be translated into household skills such as light cleaning, unloading the dishwasher, or folding laundry. Although Arthur Sr. had limited vision, vocational trainers could assist him with regaining skills. Such interventions could help the family adjust by decreasing the responsibilities of one person (Audrey) within the family system.

Question: How does the past experience of the family influence their perceptions of the current situation?

Area of intervention: Overall, the family had functioned well together and had had very positive relationships. On the basis of this experience, the practitioner and family were concerned that the transition to residential placement for Elton would involve a degree of sadness for everyone. It was important for the practitioner to consider this information for several reasons. The family had a history of being able to adjust to and handle situations that they had encountered in the past. As they faced the most current challenge, it might prove helpful for the Hamiltons to explore those early years to determine which methods of coping had been successful. Furthermore, the family needed to consider the positive aspects of the shared household as part of the decision making for future plans. What benefits would be lost with Elton's move from the household? Would the loss of his companionship be detrimental, especially for Arthur Sr., who had already experienced a loss in relationships because of his retirement and decreased functioning? In addition, what preparation would reduce the stress associated with a residential transition for the family? Could certain experiences, for example an extended respite or pre-placement visit, assist the parents and Elton with coping with this major change? Because the family members had close ties and a history of positive family functioning, this needed to be part of assessment and intervention planning.

Question: What community resources are available to support the individual with ID and the family?

Area of intervention: The family did participate in established formal service programs. Elton had been a consumer of the ID agency for several years, he participated in a vocational program, and the family occasionally used respite care. The social worker, of course, could explore other potentially beneficial community resources, including those that the aging service network could provide.

Additional information about informal sources of support would also be necessary. The original assessment revealed limited information about the relationships with Audrey and Arthur's other sons, extended family, friends, and neighbors. These would be potential sources of both emotional and tangible assistance and support for the family. The practitioner should explore this information with the family, as well as the relationships of the individual members of the family system: For example, would family functioning be enhanced if Arthur Sr. had a more extensive social support network? For instance, if he had lost relationships because of his health problems, interventions to augment his support system (for example, joining a senior volunteer program or becoming more active in his church) might decrease stress in the family system.

Question: What cultural factors are involved?

Area of intervention: As with all families, cultural factors were involved in shaping the practice situation. The social worker needed to learn whether religious and spiritual dimensions within the family should be considered around caregiving and relocation issues. Spiritual reality is often important to African American families and needs to be considered when conducting culturally competent practice (for a more in-depth discussion of this issue for African American families, see Rogers-Dulan & Blacher, 1995). These factors could influence the relationships between the service providers and family as well as the decisions the family faces.

Question: How can the situation experienced today help prepare the individual with ID and the family for future related issues?

Area of intervention: Individuals and families are dynamic systems—they evolve and continue to change across the life course. In practice, part of the social worker's role is to prepare the consumer for other transitions that he or she might be experiencing by providing an opportunity to identify opportunities and build skills. There were several ways to include a future perspective in the current practice situation with the Hamiltons. The social worker could open a dialogue about the family's concerns or about their future goals. Typically, when a family includes a member with a disability, the practitioner must carefully consider many complexities, including permanency planning of residential issues for the son or daughter, estate and financial planning, and relationships between the son or daughter and other family members (for example, siblings or extended family). Many of these issues involve consultation with a professional—for example, an attorney may need to draft appropriate plans for a property transfer between parents and their adult child with ID. Although such issues are complex within any family, they take on additional dimensions when an adult child has a lifelong disability.

In addition to family system issues, the individuals within the family should also consider their own future and goals. With the Hamiltons, for example, the social worker could help the parents and Elton begin to explore future directions. Particular issues in this discussion might be retirement planning for Audrey, physical and social issues involving Arthur Sr., and Elton's future as an adult with a disability. Again, the goal would be to help reduce the risk of a crisis within the family at a future stage.

Summary

Clearly, practitioners need an understanding of how to apply a risk and resilience perspective to social work assessment and practice with people with ID and their families. Although the number of people with ID who live their entire lives in community settings has increased since deinstitutionalization, few social workers are prepared to practice with this client population. Critical assessment and practice issues were discussed here as they relate to people with ID and their families. Through the use of examples, these concepts were applied to families that included a son or daughter with ID. By using the assessment framework in this chapter, social workers should be able to identify how families have functioned previously, understand the current problems they are experiencing, prepare with them a sensitive and effective services plan, and provide an opportunity to build skills for the future.

Use the CD by Michael Wright to explore the relationship between behavioral challenges and the intensity of care needs among people with disabilities. Prioritize family functioning as a key assessment and the removal of social barriers as an intervention.

You will find a case study on your CD: *Learning about a Consumer Orientation*

References

Adams, M. J., & Hollowell, J. G. (1992). Community-based projects for the prevention of developmental disabilities. *Mental Retardation, 30,* 331–336.

Antonovsky, A. (1979). *Health, stress, and coping.* San Francisco: Jossey-Bass.

Antonovsky, A. (1998). The sense of coherence: An historical and future perspective. In H. I. McCubbin, E. A. Thompson, A. I. Thompson, & J. E. Fromer (Eds.), *Stress, coping and health in families: Sense of coherence and resiliency* (pp. 3–20). Thousand Oaks, CA: Sage.

Antonovsky, A., & Sourani, T. (1988). Family sense of coherence and family adaptation. *Journal of Marriage and Family, 50,* 79–92.

Bigby, C., Ozanne, E., & Gordon, M. (2002). Facilitating transition: Elements of successful case management practice for older parents of adults with intellectual disability. *Journal of Gerontological Social Work, 37*(3–4), 25–43.

Blatt, B., & Kaplan, F. (1966). *Christmas in purgatory: A photographic essay on mental retardation.* Boston: Allyn & Bacon.

Broberg, M., Blacher, J., & Emerson, E. (2009). Editorial for JIDR special issue on resilience and people with intellectual disabilities. *Journal of Intellectual Disability Research, 53,* 955–956.

Clark, E., Olympia, D., Jensen, J., Heathfield, L., & Jenson, W. (2004). Striving for autonomy in a contingency-governed world: Another challenge for individuals with developmental disabilities. *Psychology in the Schools, 41*(1), 143–153.

Costigan, C. L., Floyd, F. J., Harter, K. S. M., & McClintock, J. C. (1997). Family process and adaptation to children with mental retardation: Disruption and resilience in family problem-solving interactions. *Journal of Family Psychology, 11,* 515–529.

Cunningham, C. C. (1996). Families of children with Down syndrome. *Down Syndrome: Research & Practice, 4,* 87–95.

DePoy, E., & Miller, M. (1996). Preparation of social workers for serving individuals with developmental disabilities: A brief report. *Mental Retardation, 34,* 54–57.

DeWeaver, K. L. (1982). Producing social workers trained for practice with the developmentally disabled. *Arete, 7,* 59–62.

DeWeaver, K. L. (1994, May). *Future directions for social work practice and education in developmental disabilities.* Paper presented at the first annual International Conference on Social Work and Disabilities, Young Adult Institute, New York.

DeWeaver, K. L., & Kropf, N. P. (1992). Persons with mental retardation: A forgotten minority in education. *Journal of Social Work Education, 28,* 36–46.

Edgerton, R. B., & Gaston, M. A. (Eds.). (1991). *"I've seen it all": Lives of older persons with mental retardation in the community.* Baltimore: Brookes.

Eyman, R. K., Call, T. I., & White, J. F. (1991). Life expectancy of persons with Down syndrome. *American Journal on Mental Retardation, 95,* 603–612.

Frison, S. L., Wallander, J. L., & Browne, D. (1998). Cultural factors enhancing resilience and protecting against maladjustment in African American adolescents with mild mental retardation. *American Journal on Mental Retardation, 102,* 613–626.

Gardner, J., & Harmon, T. (2002). Exploring resilience from a parent's perspective: A qualitative study of six resilient mothers of children with an intellectual disability. *Australian Social Work, 55,* 60–68.

Glidden, L. M., & Natcher, A. L. (2009). Coping strategy use, personality, and adjustment of parents rearing children with developmental disabilities. *Journal of Intellectual Disability Research, 52*, 955–956.

Greenbaum, C. W., & Auerbach, J. G. (1998). The environment of the child with mental retardation: Risk, vulnerability, and resilience. In J. A. Burack, R. M. Hodapp, & E. Zeigler (Eds.), *Handbook of mental retardation and development* (pp. 583–605). New York: Cambridge University Press.

Greenberg, J. S., Seltzer, M. M., & Greenley, J. R. (1993). Aging parents of adults with disabilities: The gratifications and frustrations of later-life caregiving. *Gerontologist, 33*, 542–550.

Haight, W. L. (1998). "Gathering the spirit" at First Baptist Church: Spirituality as a protective factor in the lives of African American children. *Social Work, 43*, 213–221.

Hanley, B., & Parkinson, C. B. (1994). Position paper on social work values: Practice with individuals who have developmental disabilities. *Mental Retardation, 32*, 426–431.

Hardiman, S., Guerin, S., & Fitzsimons, E. (2008). A comparison of the social competence of children with moderate intellectual disability in inclusive versus segregated school settings. *Research on Developmental Disabilities, 30*, 397–407.

Hill, R. (1949). *Families under stress.* New York: Harper.

Hill, R. (1958). Generic features of families under stress. *Social Casework, 49*, 139–150.

Jacobson, S., & Kropf, N. P. (1993). Facilitating residential transitions of older people with developmental disabilities. *Clinical Gerontologist, 14*, 79–94.

Janicki, M. P., McCallion, P., Grant-Griffin, L., & Kolomer, S. (2000). Grandparent caregivers I: Characteristics of the grandparents and the children with disabilities for whom they care. *Journal of Gerontological Social Work, 33*(3), 35–55.

Jokinen, N. (2006). Family quality of life and older families. *Journal of Policy and Practice in Intellectual Disabilities, 3*(4), 246–252.

Kazak, A. E. (1989). Families of chronically ill children: A systems and social–ecological model of adaptation and challenge. *Journal of Consulting and Clinical Psychology, 57*, 25–30.

Kropf, N. P. (1997). Older parents of adults with developmental disabilities: Practice issues and service needs. *Journal of Family Psychotherapy, 8*, 35–52.

Kropf, N. P., & Greene, R. R. (1993). Life review with older families who care for developmentally disabled members: A model. *Journal of Gerontological Social Work, 21*, 25–40.

Lakin, K. C., Prouty, B., Anderson, L., & Sandlin, J. (1997). Nearly 40 percent of state institutions have been closed. *Mental Retardation, 35*, 65.

Levine, K. A. (2009). Against all odds: Resilience in single mothers of children with disabilities. *Social Work in Health Care, 48*, 402–419.

Llewellyn, G., Gething, L., Kendig, H., & Cant, R. (2004). Older parent caregivers' engagement with the service system. *American Journal on Mental Retardation, 109*, 379–396.

Lutzer, V. D., & Brubaker, T. J. (1988). Differential respite needs of aging parents of individuals with mental retardation. *Mental Retardation, 26*, 13–15.

Mackelprang, R., & Salsgiver, R. O. (1996). People with disabilities and social work: Historical and contemporary issues. *Social Work, 41*, 7–14.

McCallion, P., Janicki, M. P., Grant-Griffin, L., & Kolomer, S. (2000). Grandparent carers II: Service needs and service provision issues. *Journal of Gerontological Social Work, 33*(3), 57–84.

McCallion, P., & Toseland, R. W. (1994). Empowering families of adolescents and adults with developmental disabilities. *Families in Society, 74,* 579–589.

McCubbin, H. I., McCubbin, M. A., Thompson, A. I., & Thompson, E. A. (1998). Resiliency in ethnic families: A conceptual model for predicting family adjustment and adaptation. In H. I. McCubbin, E. A. Thompson, A. I. Thompson, & J. E. Fromer (Eds.), *Resiliency in Native American and immigrant families* (pp. 3–48). Thousand Oaks, CA: Sage.

McCubbin, H. I., & Patterson, J. M. (1983). The family stress process: The double ABCX model of family adjustment and adaptation. *Marriage and Family Review, 6,* 7–37.

McCubbin, H. I., Thompson, E. A., Thompson, A. I., Elver, K. M., & McCubbin, M. A. (1994). Ethnicity, schema, and coherence: Appraisal processes for families in crisis. In H. McCubbin, E. A. Thompson, A. I. Thompson, & J. E. Fromer (Eds.), *Stress, coping and health in families: Sense of coherence and resiliency* (pp. 41–70). Madison: University of Wisconsin Press.

McDonald, T. P., Couchonnal, G., & Early, T. (1996). The impact of major events on the lives of family caregivers of children with disabilities. *Families in Society, 77,* 502–514.

Miller, A. B., & Keys, C. B. (1996). Awareness, action, and collaboration: How the self-advocacy movement is empowering for persons with developmental disabilities. *Mental Retardation, 34,* 312–319.

Nash, J. K., & Fraser, M. W. (1998). After-school care for children: A resilience-based approach. *Families in Society, 79,* 370–383.

Patterson, J. M. (1988). Families experiencing stress: The family adjustment and adaptation response model. *Family Systems Medicine, 6,* 202–237.

Patterson, J. M., & Garwick, A. W. (1998). Theoretical linkages: Family meanings and sense of coherence. In H. I. McCubbin, E. A. Thompson, A. I. Thompson, & J. E. Fromer (Eds.), *Stress, coping and health in families: Sense of coherence and resiliency* (pp. 71–90). Thousand Oaks, CA: Sage.

Petrowski, N., Edwards, M., Isaacs, B., Baum, N., & Brown, I. (2008). Family quality of life: Preliminary analyses from an on-going project. *Journal on Developmental Disabilities, 14*(2), 111–114.

Reynolds, A. J. (1998). Resilience among black urban youth: Prevalence, intervention effects, and mechanisms of influence. *American Journal of Orthopsychiatry, 68,* 84–100.

Roberto, K. (Ed.). (1993). *The elderly caregivers: Caring for adults with developmental disabilities.* Newbury Park, CA: Sage.

Rogers-Dulan, J., & Blacher, J. (1995). African American families, religion, and disability: A conceptual framework. *Mental Retardation, 33,* 226–238.

Sanders, J. L., & Morgan, S. B. (1997). Family stress and adjustment as perceived by parents of children with autism or Down syndrome: Implications for intervention. *Child & Family Behavior Therapy, 19,* 15–32.

Seltzer, M. M., & Krauss, M. (Eds.). (1987). *Aging and mental retardation: Extending the continuum.* Washington, DC: American Association on Mental Deficiency.

Seltzer, M. M., Krauss, M. W., Choi, S. C., & Hong, J. (1996). Midlife and later-life parenting of adult children with mental retardation. In C. D. Ryff & M. M. Seltzer (Eds.), *The parental experience in midlife* (pp. 459–489). Chicago: University of Chicago Press.

Smith, G. C., & Tobin, S. S. (1993). Practice with older parents of developmentally disabled adults. *Clinical Gerontologist, 14,* 59–78.

Smith, G. C., Tobin, S. S., & Fullmer, E. M. (1995). Elderly mothers caring at home for offspring with mental retardation: A model of permanency planning. *American Journal on Mental Retardation, 99,* 487–499.

Sohler, N., Lubetkin, E., Levy, J., Soghomonian, C., & Rimmerman, A. (2009). Factors associated with obesity and coronary heart disease in people with intellectual disabilities. *Social Work in Health Care, 48,* 76–89.

Toth, K., & King, B. H. (2010). Intellectual disability (mental retardation). In M. Dulcan (Ed.), *Dulcan's handbook of child and adolescent psychiatry* (pp. 151–171), Arlington, VA: American Psychiatric Press.

U.S. Congress. (1990). Developmental Disabilities Assistance and Bill of Rights Act of 1990, Pub. L. No. 101–496, 104 Stat. 1191. Washington, DC: U.S. Government Printing Office.

van Alphen, L., Dijker, A., van den Borne, B., & Curfs, L. (2010). People with intellectual disability as neighbours: Towards understanding the mundane aspects of social integration. *Journal of Community & Applied Social Psychology, 20*(5), 347–362.

Walsh, F. (1998). *Strengthening family resilience.* New York: Guilford Press.

Ward, R., Nichols, A., & Freedman, R. (2010). Uncovering health care inequalities among adults with intellectual and developmental disabilities. *Health & Social Work, 35,* 360–372.

16

Resilience and Social Work Policy

CAROL TULLY

On finishing this chapter, students will be able to further

Engage in policy practice to advance social and economic well-being and to deliver effective social work services (Educational Policy 2.1.8) by

- Analyzing, formulating, and advocating for policies that advance social well-being.
- Collaborating with colleagues and clients for effective policy action (practice behavior).

Respond to contexts that shape practice (Educational Policy 2.1.9) by

- Continuously discovering, appraising, and attending to changing locales, populations, scientific and technological developments, and emerging societal trends to provide relevant services (practice behavior).

Chapter 15 discussed issues of risk and resilience among people with intellectual disability and their families. This chapter links the formation of social policy to resilience. A model is presented to analyze social policy: its conceptualization, implementation, and evaluation. Through an analysis of the legislation and the debate leading up to the passage of the Americans with Disabilities Act of 1990 (P.L. 101-336; ADA), the model explains how social policies can foster resilience. The chapter also provides suggestions for how social work practitioners can use policy practice to facilitate the adoption of social policies that promote resilience. Finally, the chapter concludes with a case example of how the ADA fosters resiliency.

Resilience and Social Policy: Defining the Terms and Identifying the Issues

The concepts of resilience and social policy are rarely paired. This is because resilience has traditionally dealt with human behavior theory involving individuals and their social settings, whereas social policy is generally perceived as the result of laws enacted to remedy specific social problems. Although establishing social policy requires an understanding of human behavior, the use of constructs associated with human behavior theory in the analysis of social policy expands traditional analytic parameters.

When one thinks of the term *resilience,* what comes to mind is managing to cope under adverse circumstances, bouncing back after a setback, putting on a brave face, and/or moving forward when circumstances are grim. Thus, *resilience* has been defined as an ability to recover quickly from change, misfortune, or illness. The word *buoyancy* is often equated with resilience, and the term is commonly associated with an ability to regain an original form that has been altered in some way.

The term *resilience* was not listed in the 1995 *Encyclopedia of Social Work* (Edwards, 1995) but is included in the 2008 edition. *Resilience* was defined as successful adaptation following adverse events. This suggests that social work practitioners need to consider client resilience when processing diagnostic information and formulating treatment plans.

However, social policy as a construct that evolved from the philosophical concept of social welfare focuses on the institutional aspects of social life, with an emphasis on society's concern for the well-being of its members as individuals, families, and communities. All societies have some form of *social welfare,* or systems of interlocking preventive and protective laws and organizations unified by a societal commitment to common goals, values, and operating principles. Their intent is to provide, at a minimum, universal access to the goods and resources of the mainstream of society (Axinn & Levin, 1993; Dye, 1987). So although human behavior is considered in social welfare, the emphasis is more at a societal or macro level, rather than the individual or micro level.

A *social problem* is generally viewed as a collective unmet need, the solution to which is perceived to be the responsibility of a social institution (Gilbert & Specht, 1974). It is customarily thought that a social problem is one that cannot be solved with currently available social resources and that may pose a threat to the functioning of society (Barker, 1995). A social problem may be conceptualized as manifesting a universal human need (macro level) or singular (micro level) in both cause and consequence. It is a condition of institutional dysfunction that presents both challenges and opportunities and that requires some sort of social welfare solution in terms of providing services or intervention (Axinn & Levin, 1993; Dye, 1987). Social problems are usually addressed through the development and implementation of social welfare policies designed to create solutions and/or direct how such solutions can be reached.

Social policy has been defined as a product created by lawmakers (Lindblom, 1968). However, such a simple definition seems to severely limit the construct. Social policy also has to be understood in reference to the political continuum, which is generally conceptualized as ranging from ultraconservative (far right) to ultraliberal (far left), with moderates somewhere in the middle. Where individuals' beliefs fall along this continuum influences their definition of social problems and their reaction to government involvement in social welfare programs. In politics, *conservatism* generally refers to a desire to maintain traditional values and to conserve the existing order. Political conservatism seeks to limit government and government intervention and is opposed to the expansion of the welfare state (*Concise Columbia Encyclopedia,* 1995; see http://www.britannica.com).

At the other end of the political continuum are the liberals. Political *liberalism* refers to a worldview that is not bound by traditional attitudes. It is generally open to new ideas related to individual development and progress (*Concise Columbia Encyclopedia,* 1995; http://www.britannica.com). In addition, liberalism maintains the belief that only government, not the private sector, can ensure an adequate safety net. Therefore, liberals favor government intervention in the form of social welfare programs that they believe can provide the greatest good for the greatest number of people (Karger & Stoesz, 1998).

Linking the more animate concept of resilience with the more inanimate construct of social policy, the term *resilience* refers to the development and implementation of social policy to promote and empower people affected by the policy (at both the macro and micro levels). Does the policy allow the individual or the system to gain or regain access to things necessary for adequate societal functioning? The following section provides a framework for examining this question.

Resiliency and Social Policy: A Conceptual Model

When assessing whether a given policy enhances or inhibits resiliency, it is necessary to first present a conceptual model that can be used to evaluate policy as a philosophical statement, a political process, a product, a practice, and a pathway for action (Tully, 1998). As a *philosophical statement* social policy asks, what is the problem that needs to be addressed and what can be done to ensure that it is addressed adequately? The *political process* of creating social policy asks, is the problem defined realistically and is it possible to actually do what needs to be done? The *product* is the laws, rules, regulations, and procedures that are promulgated or enacted as a direct result of the political process.

Hence, the product defines what needs to be done or implemented. Once the law has been passed and the policies about how to implement the law are promulgated and disseminated, the policies and procedures are effectively put into action. The *practice* of public policy evokes questions about what needs to be done and describes the solution to the social problem in practical terms. The practice of public policy also requires an evaluation of the equity of the policy: Are some in need not covered? Do some groups benefit more than others? Who is eligible? Who is not? In sum, the practice of social policy asks, how is what needs to be done defined and solutions actually implemented?

Finally, social policy is a *pathway for action.* The development of social policy is not static; rather, it tends to mirror changing social structures, albeit more slowly. Policy provides a variety of possible pathways, and when one pathway is selected, other options may be foreclosed. But with ever-evolving social welfare legislation come changes to the existing social structures that are affected by law.

Social Worker and Policy Analysis

Philosophical Statement

Social policies evolve based on perceived societal needs within the historical context of the era. Social problems and the policies for dealing with them that were popular in the 17th century are probably not seen today in the same manner as they were in the 1600s. Although similar social problems may still exist (for example, poverty), the policy solutions for dealing with them have changed over time. Thus, social workers need to be aware that prevailing social values, mores, and philosophical views create a climate for the definition of social problems and the solutions proposed. To assess policy, it is necessary to analyze the historical context in which social problems and their solutions are defined, developed, and implemented.

Political Process

Once there is some agreement on the definition of the social problem and alternative solutions proposed, the political processes of formalizing the definition and possible solutions can begin. Depending on the issue, social workers can be part of starting the process from the top down, as with the sweeping governmental welfare reform of the 1990s, or from the bottom up, as with the demands for gun control that followed the Columbine High School shootings in 1999. The political process includes the introduction of legislation that identifies the social problem and addresses the means for solving the problem and the activities necessary for the passage of legislation (including lobbying and testifying before committees). Social workers are often part of coalitions that carry out these activities.

Product

The product of social policy is the laws, rules, regulations, or procedures that are promulgated as a result of the political process. Written and generally considered within the area of administrative law, these formal documents specifically identify how social problems are defined and how solutions to those problems are to be implemented. Social workers are sometimes engaged in defining the policy's purposes, goals, and structures. The written product also describes how the policy will be implemented, the conditions under which the policy will be implemented, the benefits of the policy, how the policy will be funded, and who is eligible for the services provided under the policy.

Practice

Once the law is passed and procedures for implementation are disseminated, the policies can be put into practice. Social workers involved in the practice of public policy evaluate the purpose, goals, structure, and implementation of the policy in terms of who is being served and how well. The primary question related to the practice of social policy is how well (or poorly) the legally defined problems and solutions are being implemented.

Pathway for Action

The development of social policy is fluid providing guidelines to the best solutions in a given historical era. The definitions of social problems and their solutions are confounded by the times in which they are created and tend to mirror the societal eras in which they are developed and implemented. As such, social policy evolves based on existing human and societal needs, philosophical beliefs, and technological advances. Knowledge of these societal needs helps the social worker identify the pathways for continuing action for the development and implementation of social policy. Once social policies are developed and implemented, social workers should be part of the process of scrutinizing and evaluating them to ensure that problems and their solutions remain current and congruent with existing needs. When clients and societal needs change, there is an opportunity if not demand for policy change. In sum, the constructs of resiliency and social policy are interwoven. The following section explores how an existing social policy may promote or inhibit resiliency.

Applying the Conceptual Model: The ADA

Philosophical Statement

The ADA makes it illegal to discriminate against those with a disability in the provision of state or local government services, transportation, telecommunications, public accommodations, and employment (U.S. Equal Employment Opportunity Commission, 1992). This position evolved from a belief that those with disabilities should not face social or economic discrimination.

A philosophical commitment to the rights of those with disabilities is rooted in a Judeo-Christian value base, but treatment of those with disabilities has a long history of being less than tolerant (Trattner, 1999). Emerging from three decades of social action during which various constituent groups gained federally protected rights, the ADA was passed in 1990 and became effective January 16, 1992 (American Association of State Social Work Boards, 1992). The legislation diverges dramatically from the ways in which those with disabilities have traditionally been treated and presents a philosophically compassionate view of those with disabilities.

Political Process

The social upheavals of the 1960s brought about major changes in the way in which minorities are viewed (incl. minorities of color, sexual orientation, and physical ability). Federal regulations related to accessibility were established in the early 1960s (Hooyman & Kiyak, 1999). Promoted primarily by those with disabilities and their families, other legislation evolved in the form of Section 504 of the Rehabilitation Act of 1973 (P.L. 93-112). Section 504 made operational the concept of disability as a socially defined category, requiring that social adjustments be made for those with disabilities by mandating certain nondiscrimination programs and policies for all programs and facilities receiving federal funding (Karger & Stoesz, 1998).

With the passage of the Rehabilitation Act of 1973, the stage was set for future legislation that would further the rights of people with disabilities. Again, with continued support from those affected by discriminatory practices related to employment, transportation, public accommodations, state and local governments, and telecommunications, the most comprehensive legislation related to those with disabilities was signed into law on July 26, 1990, by President George H. W. Bush. The ADA protects the civil rights of those with disabilities much as the Civil Rights Act of 1964 did for minorities of color (Alexander, 1994–1999).

Product

The ADA itself consists of five titles covering employment (Title I), transportation (Title II), public accommodations (Title III), state and local governments (Title IV), and telecommunications (Title V). Each title provides appropriate definitions, describes issues related to discrimination, states how the law is to be enforced, and discusses various regulations. Briefly, Title I ensures that employers cannot discriminate in the hiring or promotion of an individual with a disability. Furthermore, employers are prohibited from subjecting individuals to screening that would eliminate those with disabilities. Also, employers must make reasonable accommodation for employees with disabilities, including job restructuring or equipment modification.

Title II ensures that public transportation is accessible to those with disabilities, and Title III protects those with disabilities from discrimination in restaurants, hotels, and retail stores. Title IV provides that state and local governments cannot discriminate against those with disabilities, and Title V provides access to telecommunications for those with severe hearing impairments or others who use such electronic devices as telecommunications devices for the deaf or teletypewriters.

Practice

Parts of the ADA have been implemented at various times, and some have yet to be implemented. Title I dealing with employment, which became effective July 26, 1992, is used here as an example of how the policy has been put into practice. Discrimination in employment is prohibited for those who are otherwise qualified but have disabilities, including physical or mental disabilities that substantially limit a major life activity. This population may include, but need not be limited to, those who have hearing, speaking, breathing, walking, seeing, or learning difficulties. Although employers have made changes in the hiring and retention of people with disabilities, implementation of the ADA has resulted in lawsuits and both informal and formal settlement agreements (U.S. Department of Justice, 2000).

Countless lawsuits, court actions, and mediated settlements have been brought forward since the inception of the ADA, demonstrating that litigation surrounding the ADA is ongoing. For example, consider the case of Jack Davoll, a police officer with the City of Denver, Colorado. Officer Davoll sought and was originally denied reassignment following work-related injuries to his neck, back, and shoulder that rendered him unable to perform duties essential to the functions of a police officer. He was refused reassignment to a vacant job function within the police department that he was qualified to perform. In *United States v. City and County of Denver,* the U.S. District Court in Denver found the city and county out of compliance with the ADA and awarded Davoll more than $200,000 (U.S. Department of Justice, 2000).

Perhaps closer to home is the issue related to the American Association of State Social Work Boards and Assessment Systems, Inc. (AASSWB). In 1999, this nationally recognized testing organization refused to allow a blind test taker to use his reader for the social work licensing examination. Instead he was required to use a college student who had never read for a visually impaired person. During the examination the reader stumbled over technical terms and made errors in recording the test taker's answers. The test taker filed a complaint using the ADA as his base and was later awarded $3,000. Furthermore, following the award, the AASSWB agreed to provide proficient readers to work with test takers before the examination. Finally, testing entities may allow visually impaired test takers to use their own readers (U.S. Department of Justice, 2000).

These examples demonstrate that although enormous strides have been made as a result of the ADA, enforcement of this act has required ongoing monitoring. And on a practical note these cases show how the law continues to be shaped and redefined by those it is designed to help. Such examples demonstrate how the ADA and other laws, as evolving documents, create pathways for further action.

Pathways for Action

As noted, social policies are fluid, are thought to be rational, and provide guidelines for solutions to given problems. They also create ongoing pathways for continuing action in the development and implementation of future legislation. In the case of the ADA, numerous litigants have used the policies set forth in the legislation as a basis for legal action. Each case further defines and sharpens the existing policy. The decades since the ADA was passed have made a difference in case law defining how this policy is implemented.

This complex legislation has at its core basic concerns for the rights of those with disabilities, a group that has benefited from the implementation of the ADA. The major protector of the rights outlined in the ADA is the federal government. Even 20 years after the implementation of the ADA, each of its various sections is being enforced, and as a result more and more opportunities exist for those with disabilities (U.S. Department of Justice, 2000). Enforcement is monitored in quarterly reports prepared by the Department of Justice in which litigation, formal settlements, and mediation outcomes are outlined. Each case becomes part of the ADA's continuing evolution and legacy.

In sum, the ADA evolved from a philosophical position, was transformed into a political process, became a legal product that is currently being practiced as a social policy, and has, since its inception, been an ever-changing dynamic law as it follows its pathway to continued action. The ADA provides those with disabilities an ability to bounce back or be resilient. It has provided a more positive goodness of fit between the policy and the individual that enhances resilience. In sum, policy initiatives and the way in which they are ultimately implemented can actually foster or inhibit adaptation or resilience.

Facilitating Interrelationships between Resilience and Social Policy

As noted, social policy is intended to alleviate social problems. And although many social policies, like the ADA, fulfill this mission well, some do not. But whether or not the policy mandate lives up to the requirement of alleviating social ills, there is always a relationship between resilience, human behavior, and social policy. Because social policies evolve from philosophical beliefs about how things ought to be, they are defined through the political process into legal practice that ultimately shapes human behavior.

For example, the "Don't Ask, Don't Tell" policy (P.L. 103-160) was enacted in 1993 an effort to stop lesbian and gay members of the armed forces from being harassed, beaten, or worse. Clear behavioral changes were expected from both nongay members of the military and gay or lesbian members. Nongay military personnel were no longer to question sexual orientation; lesbians and gays serving in the armed forces were not to speak about engaging in same-sex relationships. The repeal was supported by many, and the "Don't Ask, Don't Tell" policy was finally revoked on December 19, 2010.

As a more positive example, the ADA was enacted to ensure equal access and nondiscrimination among those with specifically determined disabilities. The belief was that if public accommodations were made more "user friendly," those with disabilities would have increased access. This policy initiative did produce behavioral changes in the workplace. It has provided those with disabilities a positive means of adapting to their environments, and the lives of those with disabilities have been enhanced because of the legislation. Therefore, it can be said that this policy fostered resilience among people with developmental disabilities and their families.

Policy Practice

Social workers need to keep in mind that there is a constant dynamic interrelationship between the development of public policy (as a response to human need), human behavior (as defined and supported by public policy), and resilience (as a positive coping mechanism related to adapting to ongoing change).

Public policy tends to evolve slowly in response to the perception of need, and the behaviors that accompany the change that may take place evolve even more slowly. Policies designed to eliminate racism are in place, yet racist attitudes persist. What policy practice skills are important for helping the social work practitioner facilitate the interrelationship between social policy and resilience?

The term *policy practice* is relatively new in social work education. It pairs the ability to practice social work (traditionally viewed as personal intervention with individuals, families, groups, communities, or organizations) with the more macro-level construct of policy creation, implementation, and evaluation. This connection begins to view policy in a more personal arena, one in which policy is not divorced from those it seeks to serve. Social workers not only think about people in terms of their biopsychosocial and spiritual dimensions but also consider the policy mandates that may define behavior. The question becomes, what do social workers need to know to apply the constructs of policy practice and resilience effectively?

There are three key steps to the policy-practice process: (1) understanding the constructs, (2) applying theory to practice, (3) and evaluating the outcome. One must understand the constructs before they can be applied in a practice setting. This is particularly important in the arena of policy practice. For example, when grappling with any policy, it is imperative for the practitioner to have a good understanding of the philosophy that caused the policy to be enacted, the general history of the policy (its political process), the policy itself (the policy product), how the policy is actually being implemented (how it is practiced), and what changes need to be made (pathway for action). Armed with this information the practitioner is better able to provide clients with an accurate view of the issues.

Furthermore, because social policy influences human behavior, the practitioner must also have a good understanding of the range of human behaviors that may be associated with the implementation of a given policy. Practitioners need to be aware of both policies that encourage positive behaviors—and in turn resilience—as well as policy initiatives that may inhibit resilience. For example, welfare policies that limit benefits without providing adequate job training or jobs may hinder a single mother's resilience, whereas policies that provide early prenatal intervention for teens may enhance an adolescent's ability to adapt. In sum, policy practice requires that practitioners not only have an understanding of all of the associated constructs related to various social policies that influence people's behavior. They must also understand how policies shape one's ability to cope. This complex task must be mastered prior to applying the theory to practice.

From their first foundation course in social work education, social workers are constantly reminded of the continuing need, and perhaps struggle, to apply theory to practice. It is no different with policy practice and resilience. The theoretical position a practitioner takes generally is congruent with his or her philosophical worldview. Some in social work may find the ecological perspective useful, whereas others may practice from a cognitive perspective or from other various theoretical or conceptual orientations. Generally practitioners use concepts from a variety of social work paradigms. It is similar for the application of views about policy. Irrespective of the paradigm used, the practitioner must have an adequate understanding of the model and how it is to be applied. Policy models abound, and the practitioner needs to become comfortable in the constructs and their application to one or more of these models.

The final step in the application of theory to practice for those involved in policy practice revolves around the practitioner's ability to understand the anticipated and unanticipated consequences of human behavior that will result from the application of the policy. For example, the practitioner must ask the following: What consequences could arise from the implementation of this policy, and will the policy foster or inhibit appropriate adaptive responses, coping mechanisms, and resilience? This question is easier to answer with policies that have been in place for a number of years. Answering this question inevitably leads to the activity needed to ensure adequate policy practice—the ongoing evaluation of the existing policy.

The idea of outcome evaluation in social work has an important role in case management and research, but how often is it viewed as vital to the continuing development of social policy? Because many social workers seem to distance themselves from public policy, they may not have an understanding of the ongoing role that public policy plays in people's lives. Public policy regulates many aspects of life, from when we are issued a Social Security number to whether our cremated remains can be spread in our backyard.

Having accepted the inevitable role of social policy in our lives, the policy practitioner needs to be alert to the ongoing evaluation of policies that affect clients. This evaluation may range from informal (noting in a client record the impact of the policy) to formal (presenting legislative testimony based on research) and can involve any number of people from an individual practitioner to an advocacy or constituency group. The important link is to ensure that the policy is in fact promoting healthy and adaptive responses to the problem it was intended to solve. If it is not, the practitioner must find an alternative means of remedying the situation. The most important step in solving the problem of the adoption of poor policy is to generate data that demonstrate how the policy is not meeting its intended purposes. In sum, it is the responsibility of the practitioner to facilitate relationships between social policy, human behavior, and resilience.

How the ADA Fosters Resilience: A Case Example

This chapter has attempted to provide a conceptual model of policy analysis that includes the construct of resiliency. A better way to actually see how a social policy fosters resiliency may be to provide a case example. This section examines how the ADA, as a public policy, fosters resiliency. It relates primarily to the section of the policy model called "the practice" or specifically how the ADA is implemented by those working in the field. This example addresses client resiliency as it relates to public policy related to higher education:

> Magda was a 40-year-old married woman who became blind because of disease when she was 1 year old. She had no memory of ever having been able to see, and she attended a school for the blind until she completed high school in 1979. When she completed high school, she had no job skills and thought she would continue her education by attending college. She began college in 1981 (the ADA would not become law for another 9 years), but because of her disability she was not able to meet the many challenges facing her as a blind person in the classroom. She quit school after one semester and applied for and was awarded a monthly disability check. She eventually became involved with vocational rehabilitation and took a part-time job as a Mardi Gras bead sorter with a local sheltered workshop in New Orleans.
>
> Magda worked in the sheltered workshop from 1982 until 1988. Although the work provided some incentive for her to interact with others and to get out of the house, it was not intellectually stimulating. However, she did meet her future husband Ned. Magda and Ned were married in 1989, and Magda settled into making a home for herself and her new husband. Ned returned to work on his law degree at Tulane University in Fall 1990 (just after the ADA was passed). It was during his study of law that he became familiar with the ADA.
>
> Recalling Magda's failed attempt at college and knowing of her continued desire to have a college education, Ned encouraged Magda to return to college. Magda applied to and was accepted by Xavier University and began her coursework in Fall 1992. Because of the new federal policies, her second attempt at college was much easier than her first. She worked through the Office of Disabilities at Xavier where she had a counselor assigned to her to address potential problems each step of the way. For example, because Magda's skills with Braille were poor, the counselor found readers for each class. Also, because Magda required help with taking class notes and taking in-class tests, appropriate accommodations

> were made to ensure that the content was being made available in a format that met her needs. Furthermore, when Magda needed assistance getting from one side of campus to the other, a guide was provided until she learned her way across the campus.
>
> Magda went on to earn an undergraduate degree and entered a master's of social work program in the fall of 1999. She graduated in Spring 2001 and took a position with an institution of higher education as a counselor in the office of disabilities where she completed her master's program field placement.

The ADA proved to be a social policy that enabled Magda to become resilient, allowing her to return to school, complete her education, and become a more productive member of society. She has said candidly that without the ADA she would probably "still be sorting beads."

Recall the definition of *resilience* that began this chapter—the ability of an individual to return to previous levels of functioning after encountering a stressful life event that created problems by disrupting the person's equilibrium—and consider that definition in the context of a public policy. In Magda's case, the ADA provided a spark that encouraged her to become more resilient and actually go beyond previous levels of functioning. Her case clearly illustrates that a political initiative can promote the strengths of those with disabilities. Furthermore, legislation like the ADA and the countless policy initiatives that have evolved from it provides opportunities for people with disabilities but also fosters a better goodness of fit between individuals with disabilities and the demands of society.

In sum, as a social policy initiative, the ADA has provided opportunities for thousands of persons with disabilities who might otherwise be ignored by potential employers or discriminated against in terms of housing or public transportation. Such a policy initiative minimizes individual risk and enhances resiliency by ensuring that those with disabilities no longer face the kind of discrimination that existed prior to 1990. When individuals with disabilities are accommodated, resiliency is enhanced.

Use the CD by Michael Wright to compile a list the components of resilience-informed policy analysis. Apply a resilience-informed conceptual model to analyze policy.

You will find a case study on your CD: *Getting to Know "Magda"*

References

Alexander, R. (1994–1999). *The consumer law page brochures: The Americans with Disabilities Act questions and answers* [Brochures]. San Jose, CA: Alexander Law Firm.

American Association of State Social Work Boards. (1992). *Dealing with the ADA: A handbook for state boards on the Americans with Disabilities Act.* Culpepper, VA: Author.

Americans with Disabilities Act of 1990, PL 101–336, 42 U.S.C. §§ 12101 et seq.

Axinn, J., & Levin, H. (1993). *Social welfare* (3rd ed.). New York: Longman.

Barker, R. L. (1995). *Social work dictionary* (3rd ed.). Washington, DC: NASW Press.

Concise Columbia Encyclopedia. (1995). New York: Columbia University Press.

Don't ask, don't tell. (2010, December 13). Retrieved from http://www.msnbc.msn.com/id/40777922/ns/politics-white_house/

Dye, T. R. (1987). *Understanding social policy.* Englewood Cliffs, NJ: Prentice Hall.

Edwards, R. L. (Ed.). (1995). *Encyclopedia of social work* (19th ed., Vols. 1–3). Washington, DC: NASW Press.

Gilbert, N., & Specht, H. (1974). *Dimensions of social welfare policy.* Englewood Cliffs, NJ: Prentice Hall.

Hooyman, N., & Kiyak, H. A. (1999). *Social gerontology: A multidiscipline perspective* (5th ed.). Boston, MA: Allyn & Bacon.

Karger, H. J., & Stoesz, D. (1998). *American social policy* (3rd ed.). New York: Longman.

Lindblom, C. (1968). *The policy making process.* Englewood Cliffs, NJ: Prentice Hall.

Rehabilitation Act of 1973, PL 93–112, 29 U.S.C. §§ 701 et seq.

Trattner, W. I. (1999). *From poor law to welfare state* (6th ed.). New York: Free Press.

Tully, C. T. (1998). Culturally sensitive policy. In R. R. Greene & M. Watkins (Eds.), *Serving diverse constituencies: Applying the ecological perspective* (pp. 305–323). New York: Aldine de Gruyter.

U.S. Department of Justice. (2000). *Enforcing the ADA: Looking back on a decade of progress.* Retrieved from http://www.usdoj.gov/crt/ada/pubs/10thrpt.htm

U.S. Equal Employment Opportunity Commission. (1992). *The Americans with Disabilities Act: Your responsibilities as an employer.* Washington, DC: U.S. Government Printing Office.

Index

In this index, *f* denotes *figure* and *t* denotes *table*.

A

AA. *See* Alcoholics Anonymous (AA)
AASSWB. *See* American Association of State Social Work Boards (AASSWB)
ABCX model, 364
absenteeism, 272, 274
academic achievement
  family background and involvement and, 99, 204, 250, 265
  poverty level of schools and, 262
  protective factors and quality of, 101
  risk factors and quality of, 96
  school characteristics affecting, 249, 264–276, 271*t*
  status mobility system and, 215
  See also teachers
Academic Performance Index, 272, 274, 275
academic press, 274, 275
  See also academic achievement
ADA. *See* Americans with Disabilities Act of 1990 (ADA)
adaptation, 50–52, 55
  See also resilience
adaptive resilience, defined, 39
Add Health study, 98–99
additive model, 34
adolescents
  Add Health study and, 98–99
  coping skills in, 175–176
  cyberbullying and, 164
  disadvantaged teens, 36
  peers as support systems for, 153–154
  risk and resilience in, 166–169, 289–302, 363–364
  supportive behaviors for, 74
  violence and suicide among, 166–167
  vulnerabilities and gender differences in, 291
  See also children; youths
adults, 7–9, 100, 103–4, 172–173
  See also older adults; parents; *specific groups*
affiliation, 343, 345, 346–347
Affleck, G., 124–125
Affordable Care Act (2010), 120
African American communities
  church burnings and, 189–190, 217–218
  kin network and, 219, 296
  sense of agency in, 49
  successful coping within, 52
  support systems and, 75, 219
African American families
  biculturalism and, 209, 210
  concept of "we" in, 223
  sense of self within, 223, 225
  socialization within, 221, 222
  spirituality and, 376
  See also Hamilton family
African Americans
  biculturalism and, 205, 207
  educational resilience and academic achievement in, 53, 204, 275, 276, 363–364
  homicide and violence among, 166–167, 215–216
  odds of high school dropouts among, 262, 272, 273, 274
  older adult, 342, 346–347

African Americans (*continued*)
R. Bridges, 152
resilience insights of, 104, 225
segregation and resilience among, 228–230
slavery and, 214
socialization strategies of, 204, 210, 219–222
socioeconomic stressors in, 80
See also African American communities; African American families
After the War Zone (Slone and Friedman), 327
Agbayani-Stewart, P., 52
ageism, 340
aggression, physical, 164
aging population. *See* older adults
Alcoholics Anonymous (AA), 346–347
Alfred P. Murrah Federal Building bombing. *See* Oklahoma City bombing
Alice, 292–293
Allen-Meares, P., 2
allostatic load, defined, 315
altruism, 345, 347–348
American Association of State Social Work Boards (AASSWB), 390
American Holistic Health Association, 117–118
American Psychological Association, 145, 316
Americans with Disabilities Act of 1990 (ADA), 383, 388–391, 394–395
Aneshensel, C., 17
Angell, G., 48
anger management, 46
Anglocentric perspective, 223
anomic survival, defined, 39
Anthony, E., 149, 248
Antonovsky, A., 309, 339
apartheid, 171
Armenta, K., 82–83
Armour, M., 38
Army Master Resilience Training, 326
Arunkumar, R., 263
Aseltine, R., 153
Asian and Pacific Islanders, 167
Asociacion Madres de Plaza de Mayo, 195, 197
Asp, E., 77
assessments
of bicultural incongruence, 206, 206*f*
of effects of oppression, 226
of ethnicity and minority, 209, 210
of hope, 130*t*–32*t*
with the ID population, 371–372, 373–377
of inequality, 213
of older adults, 338, 339
of posttraumatic growth, 309, 310–313, 325
Assessment Systems, Inc., 390
assimilation, 209–210
at-risk mindset, 249
attachment, 14, 45–46
See also caregivers; protective factors
Aud, S., 262
Austin, G., 272
autism, 360–361
autonomy, 43, 338

B

baby boomers, 120, 336
Bachay, J., 52–53
Bandura, A., 14, 47
Barker, R., 345, 346, 347
Barnes, M., 69, 72*f*
Bartelt, D., 252–253
Battle Mind, 327, 328*t*
"bearing witness", 171, 176
Beckett, J., 52, 223
belief systems, 68, 70*t*
See also hope; placebo effects; spirituality
Bell, J., 54
Benard, B.
on communities as support systems, 79
on connectedness and resiliency, 300–301
on educational resilience, 250, 262, 263, 266–267, 270, 277, 279
on recovery from adverse events, 83
on schools as support systems, 77
on strengths perspective, 16
on turnaround mentors, 248
benefit finding, 124–126
See also reframing
Benson, P., 106
Bergin, A., 150, 151
Berkeley Guidance Study, 102–103
Best, K., 150
betrayal, 162
Bettelheim, B., 13
Bickel, R., 264–265
biculturalism, 205, 206–208, 206*f*, 209, 210
biofeedback, 162
biological reactions, to trauma, 316–318
biopsychosocial phenomenon, 43–47, 49–50, 266–267, 340–341
See also holistic health; support systems; youth development model
birth weight, 45
blacks. *See* African Americans
Blieszner, R., 48–49
Bohart, A., 150, 151
Bolton, R., 140–141
de Bonafini, H., 197
Bonanno, G., 323

bonding, 46
Borden, W., 9, 54, 83
Borman, G., 272
Boroto, D., 69, 72*f*
boundaries, work, 163
Bouvard, G., 189, 192
Bowen, G., 12
Bowlby, J., 31, 46
Boykin, A., 205, 221, 223
boys, 164, 167, 291
See also adolescents; children; youths
Boys and Girls Clubs, 296
the brain, 316–317
Brehm, K., 77
Brent, A., 172
Bride, B., 163
Bridges, R., 152
Brodsky, A., 218
Brofenbrenner, U., 18, 43, 152
Brookings, J., 67
Brooks, J., 272–276
Brown, E., 111
Brown, P., 76–77
Buckley, W., 64
buffer, defined, 34
bullying, 164
buoyancy, 384
Burgoa, C., 279
Burkam, D., 272
Burman, S., 2
burnout, 163
Bush, G. H. W., 388
Bush, J., 212*f*
Bush, R., 175
Butler, K., 53
Butler, S., 321

C

Cahill, M., 106–107
Calhoun, L., 311, 322
California Healthy Kids Survey, 272, 274, 275, 278
California School Climate Survey, 278
California School Parent Survey, 278
California Standardized Test, 275
Cambodian refugees, 6, 79
Camp, W., 276
cancer, 126, 128
Canda, E., 48
Cannon, W., 316
Cantrell, B., 328
capacity building, 84, 190
Cappella, E., 273
caregivers, 43, 44, 46, 47, 129, 133
See also families; parents
Carlson, B., 17
Carranza, M., 222
Carter, B., 56, 65, 66*f*, 73
Carter, C., 2, 217
case-control studies, 98, 104
Caspi, A., 102
Center for Disease Control and Prevention (CDC), 314
Chadiha, L., 80
challenge model, 8–9
See also strengths perspective
change-inducing system, 196
character. *See* the self
Charles, 357, 371
Chess, W., 154
Chestang, L., 205, 225
child abuse, 33, 46, 67, 291
children
adaptability of, 8, 148–149, 150, 241, 248
at-risk mindset with, 249
biculturalism and, 205, 207, 210
competence (Erikson) in, 13–14
concept of death in, 172
defended neighborhoods and, 216
educational resilience issues and, 53, 264–276
gender differences in vulnerabilities in, 291
grief work in, 49, 171–172
hostile and oppressive environments and, 5–7, 164, 203–233
in marginalized groups, 219
protective factors as attributes of, 35*t*–36*t*, 41*t*, 44*t*, 149, 252, 254
protective factors for violence and, 6–7, 164, 218
protective factors in environments supportive of, 35*t*, 41*t*, 44*t*, 226, 244, 252, 254
self-righting tendencies and, 247–248
socialization of, 49, 218, 221, 222
See also adolescents; vulnerable populations; youths
Chisholm Elementary School, Oklahoma City, 194
chronic illnesses, 125, 128
church burnings, 49, 189–90, 217–218
churches, 220, 363
See also religion
Cicero, 143–144
Cindy, 293, 295, 297
Cingel, P., 52–53
cities. *See* communities; environments
Civil Rights movement, 84
civil wars, 51, 171
Clark, M., 220
class size, 265
client, as self-healer, 147, 150–151

clinical skills. *See* social work practice
Coatsworth, J., 6, 46, 47, 51, 84, 254
cognitive–behavioral therapy (CBT), 162
coherence, sense of, 309, 339, 365
Cohler, B., 149
cohort studies, defined, 98
Coie, J., 105, 248
Colbert, R., 276
Coleman, J., 263–64
Coles, R., 6, 46, 152
college culture, 280
colleges. *See* schools
Colten, M., 153
Columbine High School shootings, 40, 187
Comas-Díaz, L., 11
combat operational stress (COS), 312
combat stress. *See* posttraumatic stress disorder (PTSD)
combat stress control, 320
combat units, 315
Committee on Prevention Research (National Institute of Mental Health), 254
communities
- affiliation and, 346–347
- capacity building within, 190
- definitions of, 191–192
- deinstitutionalization and, 355, 363
- fostering of social competence by, 49
- ID and risk and resilience factors in, 356–357, 362–364
- meanings of catastrophes and, 187
- mobilization of resources within, 190, 191
- as oasis of resources, 190
- organization within, 186, 189, 193, 194
- powerlessness and, 213
- reestablishing resilience in, 185–198, 185*t*, 186*f*
- resistance and defiance within, 189–191
- retirement, 341
- as support systems, 78–79
- systemic perspective of resilience in, 64
- youth violence and, 167–168
- *See also* environments; *specific communities*

Communities That Care (CTC), 111
community-based interventions, 167
community resources. *See* support systems
community service, 275–276, 282
- *See also* extracurricular activities

community well-being, 215–218
- *See also* violence, community

compassion fatigue, 163
competence, 338, 339
- *See also* cultural competence; self-efficacy; social competence

competency-building approaches, 84
concentration camps, 8, 79
conflict resolution, 174–175
conservatism, political, 385
consumer orientation, 355, 370–372
Coohey, C., 67
coping
- in adolescents, 167
- affiliation and, 346–47
- benefit finding as, 124–125
- after childhood trauma, 175–176
- definitions of, 51
- as a function of context, 52
- humor as, 168
- predictors of quality in, 100, 101
- resistance as strategy in, 297
- spirituality and, 170
- state-sponsored terrorism and, 188
- stress and patterns of, 323
- sustaining hope and, 127–128
- *See also* resilience

Cornille, T., 69, 72*f*
COS. *See* combat operational stress (COS)
Cowen, W., 150
crack, 216
crime, 166–167, 171, 216
- *See also* violence, community; violence, domestic

crime statistics, 164
crisis debriefing, 54–55
crisis intervention programs, 84
crisis theory, 187
critical consciousness, 43, 50
critical incident stress debriefing, 173–174
- *See also* debriefing models

Crockett, L., 168
Croninger, R., 270, 271
Crosnoe, R., 271–272
Cross, T., 224, 224*f*
Crouter, A., 168
CTC. *See* Communities That Care (CTC)
Cultural Awareness in the Human Services (Green), 208
cultural competence
- adolescent girls and, 300
- biculturalism and, 205, 206–207, 208
- church burnings and, 217
- comfort zone versus, 230
- debriefing treatment and, 323
- diversity and, 52
- ethnosystems and, 212, 212*f*
- family resilience and, 73–74
- older adults and, 336, 342
- oppressive environments and, 225–227, 233
- social workers' need for, 52, 73–74, 87

cultural competence (*continued*)
teachers' need for, 53
traumatic life events and, 87
veterans and, 320, 322, 326–327
violence and, 175–176
culture
among older adults, 342
coping and symbols of, 188
definition of, 208
diagnosis isolated from, 141–142
diversity practice and, 19
family resilience and family appraisal and, 73–74, 367, 369
military, 319–322, 323, 324, 326, 391
orientation toward healing and, 11
protective factors unique to, 204, 208
suicide prevention and violence and, 167
variations in resilience and, 52–53, 55
curriculum. *See* social work education
cyberbullying, 164

D

Daisy, 294, 296, 298
Dalton, B., 274
Daly, A., 52, 223
damage model, 8
Davis, K., 212–213
Davoll, J., 389–390
Dean, C., 328
death, children's concept of, 172
death guilt, defined, 7
debriefing models, 85–86, 173–174
debriefing treatment, 323
Defense Centers of Excellence for Psychological Health and Traumatic Brain Injury Resilience Continuum, 325, 325*t*
defense mechanisms, 13
See also protective factors
defiance, 189–191
See also resistance
deficit model, 240, 243
DeHaan, L., 68
deinstitutionalization, 355, 363
See also residential relocation
Dennis, B., 48
depression, 39, 76, 123, 145
Deschamps, J., 142
developmental disabilities population. *See* intellectually disabled (ID) population
developmental psychopathology, defined, 19–20
developmental theory, 19–20, 142–144, 164–165, 168, 240
Devore, W., 210
diagnosis, as bias, 141–42
Diagnostic and Statistical Manual of Mental Disorders, 153, 161, 243, 313
disabilities. *See* Americans with Disabilities Act of 1990 (ADA); intellectually disabled (ID) population
disasters, natural, 46, 54–55
discrimination, 215, 220, 221, 340, 389–390
See also Americans with Disabilities Act of 1990 (ADA)
disparities, in health care, 120
distal risk factors, 33
distress, 99, 311
See also stress
diversity, 52–53, 142, 144, 342, 362
See also culture
diversity practice, defined, 19
divorce, 46
Doise, W., 142
Doka, K., 187
Doll, B., 31, 44*t*, 250, 254
"Don't Ask, Don't Tell" policy, 391
double ABCX model, 364, 365
Down syndrome, 354, 360
dropouts, high school, 261–262
See also graduation, high school
drug abuse, 33, 67, 216
See also substance use disorder (SUD)
DuBois, W., 205
Dubrow, N., 215
Dumain, L., 48
Dumais, S., 276

E

Eckenrode, J., 103
ecological perspective
mental health and, 147, 152–153
physical health and, 118–19
in practice with ID population, 360–364, 370–371
in practice with older adults, 343–48, 344*t*
resilience-based model and, 17–19, 64–65, 160–161, 253–255, 263
risk factors and, 33
stress and, 188
See also educational resilience; environments; goodness of fit
economic differentials, defined, 214–215
See also socioeconomic status
Edelman, G., 255
Edgerton, R., 355, 363
Edmonds, R., 265
educational achievement. *See* academic achievement
educational resilience, 261–282, 271*t*
effectance, defined, 248

ego competence and ego mastery, 13
  See also protective factors; resilience
Elder, G., 80, 102, 271–272
elders. *See* older adults
Ellison, J., 44–45
Elver, K., 367, 368*f*, 369
emergency personnel, 174
  See also helping professionals
emotional challenge, 74
emotional distress, 99
emotionally focused therapy, 175
emotional support, 74
emotional well-being, 147–151
empathy, 223
  See also compassion fatigue
employment, 261–262, 336–337
employment discrimination, 215, 389–390
empowerment, 6, 197, 251
empowerment practice, 84
Encyclopedia of Social Work (Edwards), 384
environmental pressures, defined, 9
environments
  biopsychosocial phenomenon of resilience and, 43–45, 266–267
  children and oppression within, 203–233
  psychological traits impacting, 47
  resilience-supporting, 35*t*, 40, 329–330
  resilient organizations and, 76
  the self and hostile, 225
  value of interventions to change, 263, 264
  See also communities; ecological perspective
Epstein, J., 252
Epston, D., 151
Equality of Educational Opportunity (Coleman), 263
Erickson, S., 168
Erikson, E., 12, 13, 143, 222
ethnicity, 73, 141–142, 204, 209–210, 219–221
  See also oppressed populations; *specific groups*
ethnic minorities, 209
  See also *specific groups*
ethnosystems, defined, 211, 212, 212*f*
Evans, M., 228–230
exercise and recreation, 163
exosystems, defined, 18
expert companionship, 329
extracurricular activities, 269–270, 275–276, 281–282
eye-movement desensitization and reprocessing, 162

f

FAAR model. *See* family adjustment and adaptation response (FAAR) model
Fairfield, H., 218
Faith, 293–294
faith, defined, 48
  See also religion; spirituality
families
  academic achievement and, 250
  Add Health study and, 98–99
  communication processes of, 68, 71
  cultural and economic changes within, 73–74, 208, 367–368
  ID and risk and resilience factors in, 355, 356–357, 360–362
  identity and meanings in, 365, 367
  organizational patterns of, 68, 70*t*
  PTSD and, 160
  resilience factors in, 35*t*, 55, 204, 226
  returning veterans and, 312
  school-based interventions and, 251
  sense of self within, 225
  socialization strategies of, 204, 210, 219–222
  stress through life cycle of, 65, 66*f*
  suicide prevention and, 167
  See also African American families; caregivers; parents
family adjustment and adaptation response (FAAR) model, 364–365, 366*f*, 367
family coherence, 365
family distress and family outreach model, 69, 71, 72*f*
family resilience
  kin network and, 219
  overview of, 65–74, 66*f*, 69*t*, 70*t*–71*t*, 72*f*, 204
Family Resistance Template, 69*t*
family-school partnerships, 77
family stress theory, 364–365, 366*f*, 367, 368*f*, 369–372
family support, 45, 148
family therapy, 85
fathers, 295
Feld, S., 151
Feldstein, S., 168
Felsman, J., 152
fight or flight responses, 316, 318
Figley, C., 163
Filipino American families, 52
firefighters and first responders, 163, 173, 174
  See also helping professionals
flashbacks. *See* posttraumatic stress disorder (PTSD)
flourishing resilience, defined, 39

Folger, J., 175
Folkman, S., 51, 127
Fonagy, P., 20, *35t–36t*, 85
forgiveness, 170
Frank, A., 176
Frank, J., 11
Frankl, V., 166
Franklin, T., 40
Fraser, M., 10, 16, 34, 37, 249
French, T., 250
Freud, S., 12–13, 145
Friedman, M., 327, *328t*
friendship activities, 297
functional community, defined, 191, 192
Furman, L., 48

G

Gal: A True Life (Bolton), 141
Galinsky, M., 10
gangs, 215
Garbarino, J., 6–7, 36, 77, 215, 218, 226
Garfield, S., 150, 151
Garmezy, N.
on challenging mental health professionals, 2
on ecological perspective, 152
on individual and group resilience, 150
on protective and risk factors, 36
on resilience definitions, 20
on resilience in children, 241
on societal inequities, 80
on vulnerability, 33–34
Garwick, A., *366f*
Gaston, M., 355, 363
gay, bisexual, lesbian, and transgender population, 164, 167
General Adaptation Syndrome, 316–17
generalized other, defined, 223
genetic factors, 33
geographical community, defined, 191
Germain, C., 9, 18
gerontologists, 55
Giffords, G., 163
Gilgun, J., 10, 55, 103–104
Gilligan, C., 19, 289, 290, 292
Gingerich, W., 151
girl-centered youth development approach, 300–302
girls, 167, 289–302
See also children; women
Gitterman, A., 9
Glascock, C., 264–365
Glennie, E., 274
globalization, 159–160, 162
goodness of fit
adaptation and, 50–51
definitions of, 18
family resilience and, 68
ID population issues and, 361, 370, 371–372
social competence and school transition and, 53
Gordon, E., 40, 42, 104
Gordon, J., 187
Gore, S., 103, 153
government. *See* society/government
graduation, high school, 270, 272, 273, 274–275, 276
See also dropouts, high school
Graham, S., 38
grandparents, 362
See also caregivers; older adults
Grant-Griffin, L., 362
Great Depression, 80
Green, J., 206, 208, 209
Greene, R.
on clinical model for trauma recovery, 82–83
Family Resistance Template, 68, *69t*
on Holocaust survivorship, 38, 50
on intellectually disabled population, 356
on oppression, 210–211
Greenwald, R., 264
grief work, 49, 171–173
de Gropper, M., 189
Grotberg, E., 37, 40
group cohesiveness, 192
See also military culture
guided imagery, 163
guns, access to, 99, 215
Guralnick, M., 45–46
Gurin, G., 151
Gutman, M., 187

H

Haggerty, R., 110
Haight, W., 220
Hall, P., 69, *72f*
Hamilton family, 372–377
Hanson, T., 272, 274
Hantman, S., 38
Hanushek, E., 264
Harris, J., 51–52
Harris, L., 291
Harvard Project on the Psychology of Women and the Development of Girls, 292
Harvard University, 44–45
Hawaiian Studies program, 267
See also Native Hawaiian communities

Hawkins, J., 49, 102, 111
Hawley, D., 68
Head Start, 80
health. *See* mental health and mental illness; physical health
health care spending, 119, 120
health insurance coverage, 120
health outcomes, 123–124
heart disease, 123, 124
Hebert, T., 276
Hedges, L., 264
Helman, C., 11
helpers, natural, 226
helping professionals, 163, 166, 173, 176, 226
  See also emergency personnel; social workers
helplessness, 316–317
Henderson, N., 267
Herbener, E., 102
Herth, K., 129*t*
Higgins, G., 37–38, 83, 152
Higgit, A., 35*t*–36*t*, 85
High School and Beyond Study, 273, 276
High School Effectiveness Supplement (National Educational Longitudinal Study), 272
Hill, R., 364
Hiroshima bombing, 7
Hispanics, 167, 207, 262, 272–273, 274, 275–276
historic differentials. *See* economic differentials, defined
Hitler, A., 211
HIV population, 49, 84
Hoge, C., 315
holistic health, 117–118, 119, 129
Holmes, H., 219
homeless population, 46, 73–74, 167
  See also vulnerable populations
homocide rates, 166–167
hooks, b., 211
hope
  coping variables and, 127–128
  as new emphasis in research, 166
  overcoming odds and, 149, 250
  as a protective factor, 45
  slaves and, 213
  spirituality and, 170, 226
  strategies for fostering, 129*t*
Hope Assessment Guide, 130*t*–132*t*
Hope High School case study, 277–282
hopelessness. *See* depression; posttraumatic stress disorder (PTSD)
hostility, 124, 164
  See also violence, community; violence, domestic
Howe, I., 207
Howley, C., 264–265
Hoyt, M., 142
Hulewat, P., 68
human behavior theory
  biopsychosocial phenomenon of resilience, 43–47, 49–50, 266–267, 340–341
  deficit model in, 240, 243
  life-course phenomenon of resilience, 53–56
  mental health perspective and, 141–144
  overview of, 1–20, 12*f*, 16*t*
  policy practice and, 392, 393
  spiritual phenomenon of resilience, 47–49
  structuring practice activities in, 30–31
humor, as a coping strategy, 168
Hunter-Gault, C., 219–220
Hurricane Floyd, 55
husbands, 80
hypervigilance, 315, 316

I

identity. *See* the self
ID population. *See* intellectually disabled (ID) population
illness. *See* pathology
immigrants, 207, 221
improvisational theater, 162
  See also psychodrama
indigenous populations. See *specific groups*
indigenous spiritual practices, 160
Ingels, S., 274
Inhelder, B., 13
intellectually disabled (ID) population, 47, 353–377
  See also vulnerable populations
interactive model, defined, 34
International Resilience Project, 85
Internet, 159–160, 164
interventions
  alternative, 160, 162–163
  challenge model, 8–9
  client, as self-healer, and, 150–151
  cognitive behavioral therapy (CBT), 162
  critical incident stress debriefing, 173–174
  damage model, 8
  debriefing models, 85–87
  empowerment practice, 84
  FAAR model, 367
  family distress and family outreach model, 69, 69*t*, 71, 72*f*
  family resilience, 369–370
  grief work, 171–173

interventions (*continued*)
with the ID population, 370–372, 373–377
markers for, 97, 105, 145, 249
narrative orientation, 85
obstacle reframing, 166
peer supervision, 163
play therapy, 162
REEP, 125–126
resilience practice guidelines, 81–87
resiliency model of family adjustment and adaptation, 367, 368*f*, 369
school-based, 101–102, 251, 253, 255
value issues and design of, 253
for veterans, 325–329, 325*t*, 328*t*
See also prevention programs; social work practice; support systems
invulnerability, defined, 20

J

Jacobson, S., 370
Jahoda. M., 144
James, J., 102
Janicki, M., 362
Jennings, J., 52, 223
Jonathan, B., 323
Jordan, W., 276
journaling, 163
Journal of Intellectual Disability Research, 357
joy, 145

K

Kahana, E., 347
Kahn, S., 195
keystone risks, defined, 249
Kim, Y., 274
Kindertransport, 50
kin network, 219, 296
See also relational worldview model
Kirby, L., 34
Klein, D., 148
Knight, J., 170
Kobasa, S., 17
Koenig, H., 161
Koetze, D., 189
Kolomer, S., 362
Kosterman, R., 102
Kraepelin, E., 145
Kropf, N., 356, 370
Kushner, H., 311–312

L

labeling, 141–142, 144
Laine, R., 264
Lambert, M., 151
Land, H., 207
Latinos/Latinas. *See* Hispanics
Laub, J., 109
Lawson, D., 151
Lazarus, R., 51
Leashore, B., 52, 223
Lee, H., 274
Lee, V., 270–271, 272
Lee, Y., 221
Lee-Bayha, J., 272
Leijenaar, M., 212–213
Lepore, S., 329
lesbian and gay issues, 391
Levine, K., 361–362
Lewis, J., 341
liberalism, political, 385
life course
attachment and, 46
of caregiving in ID population, 361
definitions of, 18–19
longitudinal studies and, 104–105
resilience and, 53–56, 107–110, 165, 254–255, 341–342
social competence and, 47
life events, classification of, 54–55
life events, traumatic, 9, 162
life expectancy, 120, 127
Life Model of Social Work, The (Germain and Gitterman), 9
Lifton, R., 7, 81
limitations, in research, 104–107
Lingfield House, England, 8
listening support, 74
Listening to Students Circles, 279
Lokahi, 73
longevity. *See* life expectancy
Longres, J., 15
Lost Boys (Garbarino), 36
Lukes, C., 207
Lutheran tradition, 48–49
Lyon, M., 31, 44*t*, 250, 254

M

MacArthur Studies of Successful Aging, 127
MacIntosh, R., 204
macroaggressions, defined, 79–80, 216
macrosystems, 18, 33, 64, 79–80, 183–98, 344*t*
Madres de Plaza de Mayo, 186, 187, 189, 191, 192, 193–197
Magda, 394–395
Makes Me Wanna Holler (McCall), 220
malaria, 45
Mangham, C., 37
Man's Search for Meaning (Frankl), 166
Marches of Resistance, 194
marginalized groups, 218–219
See also minorities

markers, 97, 105, 145, 249
Maslow, A., 11, 12, 12*f*
Maslow's Hierarchy of Needs, 12*f*, 326
Massachusetts General Hospital, 122
Masten, A.
on attachment and resilience in children, 46
on Cambodian refugees, 6
on dynamics of resilience, 254
on empowering parents, 251
on future research areas, 112
on individual and group resilience, 150
on ordinariness of resilience, 165
on positive life outcomes, 111
on prevention-intervention design, 84
on protective and risk factors, 34, 252
on resilience definitions, 37, 51, 108
on self-regulation, 47
on social assets, 97
McAdoo, H., 207
McCall, N., 74, 75, 215–216, 220
McCallion, P., 362
McCubbin, H., 364, 367, 368*f*, 369
McCubbin, M., 367, 368*f*, 369
McEvoy, A., 67
McEwen, B., 315
McGoldrick, M., 56, 65, 66*f*, 73
McGrath, J., 110
McMillen, J., 125–126
McNeal, R., 273
Mead, G., 223
meaning, 7, 103, 124–126, 161, 166, 174
See also spirituality
Mechanic, D., 153
media, 220, 221
mediation, victim–offender, 170
medical anthropology, 11
medical personnel, 121, 129, 133
meditation, 160, 162–163
memorials, 194, 195
Menninger, K., 145
mental health and mental illness, 33, 49, 139–155
See also depression; posttraumatic stress disorder (PTSD)
Mental Health Study Act (1955), 144
mental health workers, 8, 46, 69, 151
See also social workers
mentally ill population. *See* vulnerable populations
mentors, 218, 248, 266, 280, 295–296
Merriam Webster's Collegiate Dictionary (10th ed.), 144
mesosystems, 18, 344*t*
Metzenbaum, H., 215
Meyer, G., 142
microaggressions, defined, 216
microsystems, 18, 33, 64, 159–176, 252, 344*t*
Midlarsky, E., 347
migration. *See* resettlement
military culture, 319–22, 323, 324, 326, 391
Military Junta abductions, 183–184, 186, 187, 188
military service, 101
See also veterans
military social workers, 2
Miller, D., 204
Miller, G., 77
Miller, S., 205
Milstein, M., 267
minorities, 73, 209, 210, 214–215
See also marginalized groups; oppressed populations; *specific groups*
Moncher, F., 67
Moran, G., 20
Moreira-Almeida, A., 161
Morse, J., 130*t*–32*t*
Moskovitz, S., 8, 147
Moskowitz, J., 127
Moss, H., 240
mothers, 73, 124–125, 218, 295, 361–362
Mothers' movement. *See* Madres de Plaza de Mayo
motivation, 44
mourning strategies, 40
See also memorials
Mozambique civil war, 51–52
Mullan, J., 17
Murphy, L., 240
Murrah Building Survivors Association, 186

N

NAACP. *See* National Association for the Advancement of Colored People (NAACP)
Nagy, M., 172
narrative orientation, 85
See also symbolic interactionism
Nasello, A., 161
Nash, J., 98
NASW members, 55
National Association for the Advancement of Colored People (NAACP), 219, 220
National Child Development Study, 274
National Coalition for the Homeless, 167
National Educational Longitudinal Study, 271, 272, 273, 274, 276
National Institute of Mental Health, 254
National Longitudinal Study of Adolescent Health, 271–272
National Research Council, 270
Native Americans/Alaska Natives, 167, 207, 224, 226

Native Hawaiian communities, 52, 73, 99–101, 226
Nazi Holocaust
aftereffects of, 184
coping patterns of survivors of, 7, 8, 50, 68, 79, 147, 216, 309
Family Resistance Template, 69*t*
oppression during, 211
negative outlook, 123–124
Negroes. *See* African Americans
neighborhoods, 78–79, 216
See also communities
Neimeyer, R., 83
neurobiology, 160
Neville, B., 45–46
New England Journal of Medicine, 122
New York Times, 45, 76
Nicks, C., 357–360
Nicks, R., 357, 358–360
nightmares. *See* posttraumatic stress disorder (PTSD)
Nobles, W., 223
nocebo effects, 122
nondeterministic view, 17
nonplace communities, defined, 192
nontraditional view, of self, 223
Norlin, J., 154
Norton, D., 206*f*, 212*f*
Nuremburg Race Laws, 211

O

object relations, 14
obstacle reframing, 166
offenders, 170–171
Office of Juvenile Justice and Delinquency Prevention, 167
Ogbu, J., 214–215
Oklahoma City bombing, 86–87, 184, 185–186, 188, 194
older adults
as caregivers, 361, 362
with intellectual disabilities, 354–355, 361, 370
overview of, 335–343, 344*t*, 345–348
See also vulnerable populations
Oldersma, J., 212–213
oppressed populations, 210–211, 262
See also segregation and resilience
oppression, defined, 210–218, 212*f*
oppression, environmental, 203–233
oppression, government, 184
See also Military Junta abductions
optimism, 45, 55, 123–125, 133, 166, 169
See also hope
Oregon State Department of Education, 267
ostracism, group, 164
Oxley, D., 253

P

Pacific Islanders. *See* Asian and Pacific Islanders
Palmer, N., 39
parental abandonment, 150
parental death, 49
parents
academic achievement and involvement of, 250
in Add Health study, 99
educational resilience and expectations of, 275
empowerment of, 6, 251
socialization strategies of, 204, 220, 222
See also caregivers; families; mothers
Paris Island, 319
Parker, G., 150
Parsons, S., 274
Parsons, T., 188
partner violence, 164
pathology, 142–144, 145–146, 147
Patterson, J., 364, 366*f*
Patton, G., 326
Paul, E., 102
Pearlin, L., 17
peers. *See* relationships
peer supervision, 163
Penrod, J., 130*t*–132*t*
Pentagon attack. *See* September 11, 2001 attacks
people of color, 209, 214
See also vulnerable populations; *specific groups*
Peres, J., 161
Perlman, H., 13
perseverance, 232
persistence. *See* resilience
personal assistance support, 74
personality evolution, 240
See also Erikson, E.
person-centered practice approach, 11, 12
Peters, M., 221, 222
physical health, 117–133, 129*t*, 130*t*–132*t*
physical resistance strategies, 299–300
Piaget, J., 13
Pinderhughes, E., 209, 210, 213
Pittman, K., 106–107
placebo effects, 121–123
place communities, defined, 192
play therapy, 162
Plaza de Mayo, Buenos Aires, 186, 189
police officers, 163, 389–390
See also helping professionals

policy analysis, 385–388
policy practice, 391–393
political continuum, 385
political resistance, 298, 299
positive coping. *See* resilience
posttraumatic growth, 309, 310–313, 322–330, 325*t*
posttraumatic stress (PS), 312
posttraumatic stress disorder (PTSD), 6, 161–163, 173–174, 313–318, 323–324, 326
 See also military culture; posttraumatic growth
post-Vietnam syndrome, 313
Poulson, B., 171
poverty, 33, 51, 78, 80, 96, 214–215
 See also socioeconomic status
power differentials, 211, 212–214
 See also oppression, government
powerlessness, 79, 187, 188, 213, 215, 225
 See also power differentials
power of one person, 266
pregnancy, adolescent, 99, 103, 291
prenatal care, poor, 45
prevention programs
 conflict resolution as pathway to, 174–175
 overview of, 15, 16, 84–85
 for reducing risks for ID, 370
 school-based, 77–78
 for soldiers, 326
 for suicides, 167
 for violence, 84
preventive science, 85
Pritchard, R., 147–148
problem-solving skills, 43, 50, 167
Prochaska, J., 151
Proctor, S., 214
Program for International Assessment (2003), 274
Prospects Study, 272
protean self, defined, 7
protective factors
 in children and adolescents, 6–7, 8, 149, 244, 252, 294–300
 in communities, 188–189, 191
 as a concept, 97
 culturally unique, 204, 208
 definitions of, 5, 20, 34, 36
 as facilitating intervention, 248
 in ID population, 361–362, 363
 in Madres de Plaza de Mayo, 191
 in older adults, 341, 342, 345–348
 psychological traits as, 45–46, 47
 in schools, 266–276
 in terrorist attacks, 188, 189
 theoretical components as, 13–14
 See also support systems
proximal risk factors, 33
PS. *See* posttraumatic stress (PS)
psychic numbing, defined, 7
psychodrama, 51–52
 See also improvisational theater
psychodynamic theories, 12–14
psychological resistance, 297–298
psychology, 145
PTSD. *See* posttraumatic stress disorder (PTSD)
public policy. *See* social policy
purpose, sense of, 43, 161, 174
 See also reframing; spirituality

Q

qualitative research methodologies, 103–104
quantitative research methodologies, 98–103

R

race, defined, 208–209
Race Matters (West), 227
Rachuba, L., 272
racial socialization, 204, 210, 216
racism, 73, 164, 210
 See also segregation and resilience; slaves and slavery
Ramsey, J., 48–49
Randolph, K., 98
rape, 67
reality confirmation support, 74
Reed, M., 67
REEP, 125–126
reframing, 166
 See also benefit finding; purpose, sense of
regenerative resilience, defined, 39
Rehabilitation Act of 1973, 388
Reid, G., 37
reintegration, after prison, 104
Reis, S., 276
relatedness, defined, 18
relational worldview model, 223, 224, 224*f*
relationships
 between adolescent girls and other adults, 295–296
 centrality of, 294–295
 older adults and, 341
 parent-child, 164, 295
 peer, 47, 49, 74, 75, 153–154, 297
 physical health and, 126–127
 PTSD and, 318
 within schools, 266–268, 270, 271–273, 271*t*, 279–280
 See also caregivers; families; therapeutic relationship

religion
definitions of, 48, 169
as a protective factor, 101
slaves and, 213
socialization among ethnic minorities and, 220
social workers' attitudes about, 47–48
suicide prevention and, 167
See also spirituality
Rennie, D., 151
research methodology, 95–112
resettlement, 68–69
residential relocation, 370
See also deinstitutionalization
resilience
characteristics of, 41*t*, 44*t*, 111
correlates of, 35*t*–36*t*
definitions, as common themes, 36–40
definitions, in terms of risk and protective factors, 31–34, 291–292
as ordinary, 165
as a process, 96–97, 150, 153, 309, 323
as a U.S. concept, 106
variations in, 52–53
See also family resilience; resilience theory; strengths perspective
resilience-based model
context of societal norms in, 252–253
ecological perspective and, 253–255
overview of, 240–241
school-family microsystem in, 250–252
self-righting tendencies and, 149, 151, 190, 247–248
strengths perspective and, 248–250
values versus actions in, 232–233
See also resilience theory; Uncle Edgar
resilience continuum, U.S. military, 39–40, 325, 325*t*, 326
Resilience Module (California Healthy Kids Survey), 272, 274, 275
resilience schemas, 185*t*, 186*f*
resilience theory, 4–10, 11, 12–14, 12*f*, 266–267
See also resilience-based model
resiliencies, seven, 55–56
resiliency model of family adjustment and adaptation, 367, 368*f*, 369
resistance, 189–191, 197, 297
See also physical resistance strategies
resonating trauma, 187
restorative justice, 170–171
retirement communities, 341
Revenson, T., 329
Rice, J., 265
Richman, J., 12
Rigsby, L., 40, 105, 106, 253, 254, 263
risk, as pejorative term, 31–32
risk chains, defined, 33
risk factors, 5, 19–20, 32–33, 96–97, 249, 290
See also vulnerabilities
Rivers, J., 265
Rogers, C., 11–12
Rogers, J., 277–282
role models, 46, 218
See also mentors; Uncle Edgar
Rosenbaum, R., 151
Rosenzweig, S., 147–148
Ross, M., 194
Rothchild, M., 217
ruggedness, 148, 153
runaways, 167
Rutter, M.
on academic achievement and school characteristics, 264
on future research areas, 112
on home environments of resilient children, 67
on protective and risk factors, 34, 36, 39
on psychological characteristics, 45
on resilience in children, 241
Rwandan atrocities, 80
Ryff, C., 340, 341

S

Sacker, A., 274
safety, 189–190, 215, 216, 343, 345–346
Saleebey, D.
on curriculum content, 10
on individual, group, and community resilience, 148, 190
on life course, 19
on social workers' lip service, 147
on strengths perspective, 3, 16*t*
Salthouse, T., 337
salutogenic model of health, 309, 339, 365
Sameroff, A., 106
SAMHSA. *See* Substance Abuse and Mental Health Services Administration (SAMHSA)
Sampson, R., 109
Sanders, C., 212*f*
Sanders, W., 265
Schlesinger, E., 210
school administrators, 273, 275
school–community collaboration, 78
school integration, 152
schools
academic achievement and poverty level of, 262
Add Health study and, 98–99
as facilitating resilience, 250–252
fostering of social competence by, 47
girls and risk factors in, 291

schools (*continued*)
ID population and, 363–364
social competence and transition to, 53
as support systems, 76–78
violence in, 163
See also academic achievement; educational resilience; teachers
school social work practice, 248–255, 277, 279–280, 282
Schoon, I., 274
Schorr, D., 80, 226
Schorr, L., 80, 226
Schriver, J., 19, 50
Schwarz, R., 327
Scientific American, 318
Seattle Social Development Project (SSDP), 101–102, 111
secondary analysis of data, 102
secondary traumatic stress (STS), 163
Section 504 (Rehabilitation Act of 1973), 388
segregation and resilience, 228–230
Seifer, R., 106
the self, 222–225
self-actualization theory, 11, 12, 12*f*
self-advocacy, 357
self-assessments, 125–126
self-determination, defined, 357
self-efficacy
in adolescents, 167, 168, 294
African American communities and, 218
definitions of, 14, 338–339
as a protective factor, 45, 47
See also protective factors
self-esteem
in adolescents, 168, 169, 294, 299
as a protective factor, 45, 167
skin color and, 220
self-regulation, 47
self-righting tendencies, 149, 151, 190, 247–248
self-understanding, 45, 47
Seligman, M., 145
Selye, H., 316
seniors. *See* older adults
Sense of Coherence Scale, 309, 339
sense of community, in schools, 267–268
September 11, 2001 attacks
aftereffects of, 184
critical incident stress debriefing after, 174
mourning strategies, 40
protective factors in, 188–189
PTSD and, 162
recovery efforts after, 87
STS and, 163
serious psychological distress (SPD), 317
service delivery, for the ID population, 355–356
sexual debut, 99
sexual identity and orientation issues, 167, 391
sexual minorities, 207–208
Shapiro, D., 145, 151
Sharabi, A., 38
Shatika, 293
de Shazer, S., 151
shell-shock, 313
Shepard, B., 313
Sherrod, L., 110
Shin, J., 274
Shouse, R., 274, 275
sickle-cell disease, 45
Sierra Leone atrocities, 80
Simon, W., 323
situational awareness, defined, 315
skin color, 209, 215, 220
slaves and slavery, 205, 213, 221
Slone, L., 327, 328*t*
Smith, C., 17
Smith, R.
on adaptability of children, 150
on development of resiliency, 165
on ecological perspective, 152
on prospective study of risk factors, 100–101, 106
on self-righting tendencies, 32, 149, 247, 248–249
smoking, 45
Smyth, E., 272, 274
social assets, 97, 106–107
See also protective factors
social capital, 324
social change model, 196–197
social competence, 43, 47, 49, 146–147
See also cultural competence
social constructionist approach, 190
social injustice, defined, 225
socialization
of children, 49
dual perspective and, 205, 206–208, 206*f*
in ethnic cultures, 204, 219–221
of the ID population, 363
marginalized groups and, 218–219
overcoming adversity and, 225
proactive, 221–222
racial, 204, 210, 216, 221
See also military culture
social justice, 175
See also macrosystems; oppression, environmental; oppression, government
social learning theory, 14
social network composition, 74, 75*f*

social policy, 385–386
See also policy analysis
social problems, 384–385, 387
social skills training, 84
social systems, 65
social welfare, defined, 384
social work education
conflict resolution training in, 174
curriculum content implications in, 10, 151–154, 268, 270, 273–274, 353–354
resilience model and, 232–233
traditional approaches in, 142–143, 144
social workers
assumptions and attitudes of, 47–49, 141–147, 176
compassion fatigue and, 163
placebo effects and, 123
policy analysis and, 385–388
professional development needs of, 120–121
reframing and, 166
strengths perspective and, 141, 148, 154–155
values versus actions in, 232–233, 240
See also cultural competence; social work practice; therapeutic relationship
social work policy, 383–395
social work practice
adaptation as goal in, 51
challenges in, 2–3
community building as part of, 79
conflict resolution training in, 174
cultural orientations towards healing and, 11
ethical responsibilities in, 198
with girls, 290, 300–302
with the ID population, 356–357, 372–377
with older adults, 339, 343, 344*t*, 345–348
with oppressed populations, 160, 175–176, 225–227
physical health issues, 119, 128–133, 129*t*, 130*t*–132*t*
policy practice and, 391–393
in schools, 248–255, 277, 279–280, 282
segregation and implications for, 228–230
social network composition and, 74, 75*f*
spirituality as a dimension of, 169
value of research in, 110–111
with veterans, 325
See also assessments; interventions
social work students, 280
societal inconsistency, defined, 225
society/government, as support systems, 79–80
sociocentric orientation, of healing, 11
socioeconomic status, 78, 80, 100, 164, 261–262, 317
See also poverty
Sokolovsky, J., 342
soldiers, 160
See also veterans
Solomon, B., 211–212, 212*f*, 215, 216
Song, L., 40, 42, 104
Sorokin, P., 196
SPD. See serious psychological distress (SPD)
Special Supplemental Nutrition Program for Women, Infants, and Children, 80
Speece, M., 172
Spiegel, H., 122
spirituality
African American families and, 376
definitions of, 48, 169
fostering hope through, 170, 226
interventions using, 160, 163
older adults and, 341, 347
resilience and, 49, 169–171
socialization among ethnic minorities and, 220
suicide prevention and, 167
See also religion
spiritual phenomenon, 47–49
spiritual practices, 160, 163
Spitz, R., 31
sports participation, 275, 276
See also extracurricular activities
SSDP. See Seattle Social Development Project (SSDP)
Stanford Achievement Test, 272, 274, 275
status mobility system, 214–215
Steele, H., 20, 85
Steele, M., 20, 35*t*–36*t*, 85
Stewart, A., 83
Stewart, M., 37
stigma, 313, 323–324, 326, 356
St. Louis Risk Research Center, 3
strengths perspective
challenge model and, 8–9
diagnosis, as bias, in, 141–142
emotional well-being and, 147–151
as historical perspective, 3
with the ID population, 354
as new emphasis in research, 166
resilience-based model and, 232–233, 248–250
resistance and defiance and, 190
ruggedness as, 148

stress
- adolescents and, 153–154
- allostatic load and, 315
- biological reactions to, 316–318
- critical incident stress debriefing, 173–174
- definitions of, 17–18
- in the family life cycle, 65, 66*f*
- macroaggressions as, 80
- versus risk, 17, 33
- social competence by encouraging, 146–147
- soldier control of, 320
- *See also* distress; traumatic exposure

STS. *See* secondary traumatic stress (STS)
students. *See* schools; teachers
Substance Abuse and Mental Health Services Administration (SAMHSA), 317
substances, access to, 99
substance use disorder (SUD), 317, 322
sugar pill, 121
suicides, 164, 167
Sullivan, H., 146
Sunny, 293, 295, 296–297, 299
support systems
- adolescents and, 169
- affiliation and, 346–347
- in communities, 188, 193, 219
- ecological perspective and, 161
- for ID population, 363–364
- military culture as, 320, 321, 324
- overview of, 74, 75–81, 75*f*
- physical health and, 126–127
- professional caregivers as, 129, 133
- social capital and, 324
- for veterans, 324, 329–330
- *See also* ecological perspective; relationships; schools

support troops, 315
surrogate figures, 46
survivorship, 7–9, 124, 308–310
- *See also* Nazi Holocaust

survivorship model, 38
Susman, E., 240
suspicious of counterfeit nurturance, defined, 7
Suzanna, R., 323
Swanson, C., 262
symbolic interactionism, 109
systemic perspective, 64
systems change, 196

T

Tallman, K., 150, 151
tangible assistance support, 74
Target, M., 20, 35*t*–36*t*, 85
task appreciation support, 74
task challenge support, 74
Taylor, A., 53
Taylor, J., 292
Taylor, N., 231–233
TBI. *See* traumatic brain injury (TBI)
teachers
- adolescent girls and, 296, 299
- caring relationships and, 266–268, 270, 271–273, 271*t*, 279–280
- cultural competence of, 53
- educational resilience and, 264, 265, 268–269, 273–274
- family distress and family outreach model and, 69
- as support systems, 77
- as surrogate figures in attachment, 46
- *See also* schools

technology, 159–160, 162, 164, 220, 221
Tedeschi, R., 311, 322, 329
teens. *See* adolescents; youths
television, 159–60
- *See also* technology

temperament, 43–44
the Temple, Atlanta, 217
Tennen, H., 124–125
terrorist attacks and state-sponsored terrorism, 184, 188, 189
- *See also* Oklahoma City bombing; September 11, 2001 attacks

therapeutic relationship
- mental health issues and, 151, 152–153, 154, 155
- older adults and, 345–346
- oppressed populations and, 225–226
- physical health issues and, 133
- REEP and, 125–126
- strengths perspective in, 83, 142
- *See also* cultural competence

Thomlison, B., 84
Thompson, A., 367, 368*f*, 369
Thompson, E., 367, 368*f*, 369
Thorton, M., 210
threats, 164
- *See also* traumatic exposure

Toms, F., 205, 221, 223
Tracy, E., 75*f*
transaction, defined, 18
transactional phenomenon, 39, 266, 301, 340–341
Trask, H., 52
traumatic brain injury (TBI), 317
traumatic exposure, 314–316
- *See also* military culture

traumatic life events, 9, 162

NANTUCKET 2000

the NANTUCKET *holiday* TABLE

FOR JACKIE,
I WISH YOU MANY HAPPY &
DELICIOUS HOLIDAYS!

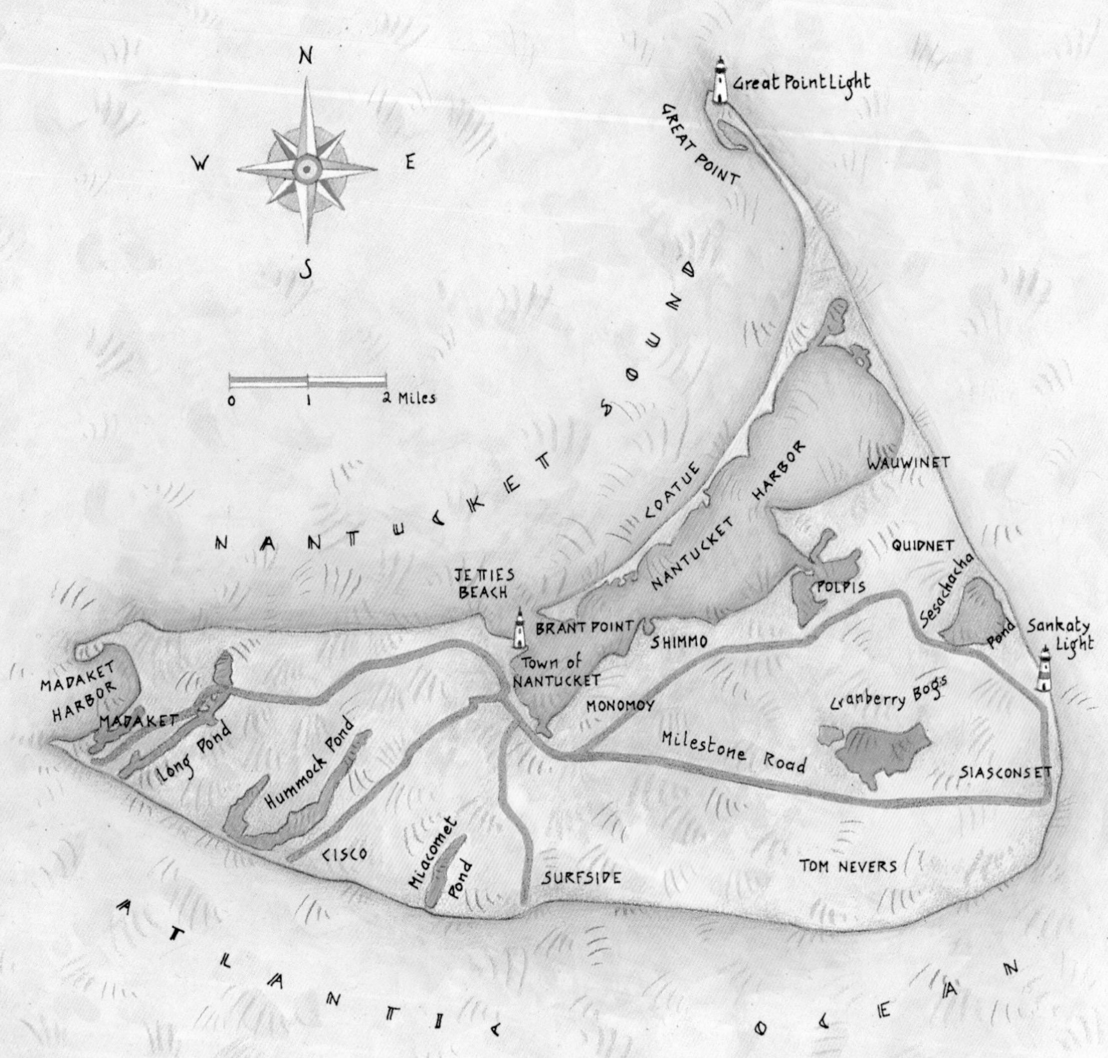
NANTUCKET ISLAND
N
W
E
S
0 1 2 Miles
Great Point Light
GREAT POINT
NANTUCKET SOUND
COATUE
NANTUCKET HARBOR
WAUWINET
QUIDNET
JETTIES BEACH
BRANT POINT
POLPIS
Sesachacha Pond
Sankaty Light
SHIMMO
Town of NANTUCKET
MADAKET HARBOR
MADAKET
Long Pond
Hummock Pond
MONOMOY
Cranberry Bogs
Milestone Road
SIASCONSET
CISCO
Miacomet Pond
SURFSIDE
TOM NEVERS
ATLANTIC OCEAN